THE SOUTH-WEST BOOK A Tasmanian Wilderness

THE SOUTH WEST BOOK

A Tasmanian Wilderness

EDITED BY
Helen Gee and Janet Fenton

COMPILED BY
Helen Gee, Janet Fenton and Greg Hodge

ART DIRECTED BY
Chris Cowles

Collins
Australian Conservation Foundation

First published 1978
Reprinted with corrections 1979
Third Impression 1983

Copyright © AUSTRALIAN CONSERVATION FOUNDATION 1978, 1979, 1983

The views expressed in this book are not necessarily those of the
Australian Conservation Foundation

Published jointly by William Collins Pty Ltd, Sydney and
the Australian Conservation Foundation, Melbourne
Book design and artwork by Chris Cowles, Hobart
Phototypeset by Specialty Press Pty Ltd, Hobart
Printed and bound in Australia at Griffin Press Limited, Adelaide

Text set in Souvenir 9/10 point
with Megaron Condensed 7/8 point captions

National Library of Australia
Cataloguing-in-Publication data

The Southwest book.

New ed.
Previous ed.: Hawthorn, Vic.
Australian Conservation Foundation, 1978.
Bibliography.
Includes index.
ISBN 0 00 217305 0.

1. Conservation of natural resources — Addresses, essays,
lectures. 2. Wilderness areas — Tasmania — Addresses,
essays, lectures. I. Gee, Helen. II. Fenton, Janet.

333.78'2'09946

Cover: *The Gordon River*, oil on board 470 x 620 mm. Painted by Captain Haughton Forrest (1825 – 1925) from the collection of the Queen Victoria Museum and Art Gallery, Launceston, Tasmania. Forrest came from a well-to-do English family with a distinguished military background. He settled in Tasmania with his wife and children in 1876, where he continued to paint until his death in 1925. He was a self-taught and prolific artist, painting mainly seascapes and landscapes in oils. *Photographed by J Barry Laurence Studio*

Frontispiece: The Gordon River below its confluence with the Serpentine River. *Fritz Balkau*

Foreword

This remarkable book presents a compendium of information about Tasmania's South-West, the people who once inhabited it, its geology and geography, its trees and marshes, its rivers, the animals and birds which abound there, and the threats of destruction by forestry, hydro-electric development, mining and tourism. The whole makes a well-told and fascinating story, which is bound to win support for those who recognise the need to keep it undeveloped, whatever the cost.

Geologically, the South-West is ancient, but in terms of human presence it is recent. While the Aboriginal inhabitants of Tasmania lived there for 20,000 years or more, they penetrated to the South-West perhaps less than 3,000 years ago. These decent, peaceful people lived in villages of huts, cremated their dead, and fired the bush and forest to drive out animals for food, changing greatly the original ecology of the region. Once plentiful, and able to eke out a reasonable subsistence in that infertile region, they were wiped out by the white government, which herded them together in settlements where they could become Christians and die of the white man's diseases.

Pursuit of the Huon pine, fine-grained and easily worked, brought Europeans to the South-West early in the 1800's. Later, the loggers came back in earnest, and the stands of ancient Huon pine would have been wiped out but for the efforts of a few enthusiasts, like Truchanas, who persuaded the Government to reserve a small area.

Towards the end of last century, some keen bushwalkers discovered the South-West, the challenge of its arduous tracks through wonderful scenery and true wilderness. Chapters in this book describe all these things with understanding and sensitivity. More technical sections on the natural environment of the region, its geology, climate and climatic changes, its fauna and flora, its fishes and insects, will interest both naturalists and laymen. But it is the final chapters on man's use of the South-West which aroused my keenest interest, for therein lies the key to its preservation.

The case against extension of forestry is put forcibly by experts. The area has considerable further hydro-electric potential, but it is shown that this is fatal to wilderness. Mining and quarrying could result in similar damage. But one of the greatest dangers is tourism. It is possible for preservation of great beauty to exist with highly developed public access, as in Yosemite National Park in California. However, roadways for cars and buses, motels, ski-lodges, and ski-lifts, and large-scale organized bushwalking, are not compatible with biological wilderness.

It is clear that no action should be taken which would prejudice the wilderness character of South-West Tasmania. This means that strong and courageous political decisions are needed **now** to establish the wilderness areas, and to ensure that there is no flouting of the law. The State would have to forego the economic returns which could result from development, but the region is a national, rather than a purely State, responsibility, so that all Australians should contribute, through the Federal Government, to the expenses associated with every aspect of its preservation.

I am confident that this book will help greatly to promote that understanding of our heritage which will result in the conservation measures necessary for the South-West to remain an area of wilderness.

Sir Mark Oliphant,
Past President,
Australian Conservation Foundation

Contents

continued on the following page

Recreation
continued from the previous page

Industry

Conservation & the 1970s

Acknowledgements

The South-West Book results from the voluntary and creative labour of a large number of people. The active co-operation and goodwill of individuals and organisations was much appreciated during the book's compilation. Firstly we thank the individuals whose names appear in the list of contents. Their research and knowledge made this book possible.

We have received assistance and advice from staff and members of the following government and community agencies:

South-West Committee
Tasmanian Conservation Trust Inc.
Tasmanian Environment Centre Inc.
Tasmanian Wilderness Society

Allport Library and Museum of Fine Arts
W E L H Crowther Collection
Royal Society of Tasmania Library
State Library of Tasmania
Tasmanian State Archives

Forestry Commission
Lands Department
Mines Department
National Parks and Wildlife Service
Nomenclature Board of Tasmania
South-West Tasmania Resources Survey

Queen Victoria Museum and Art Gallery
Queenstown Museum
Tasmanian Museum and Art Gallery

University of Tasmania, Departments of
Botany, Geography, Geology and Zoology

We were presented with such a number of photographs and drawings — historical, scenic and topical — that it has been impossible to include them all. We are indebted to all who lent photographs. The photographers and artists whose work we have been able to include are acknowledged individually with each illustration.

The following individuals, newspapers, government and community bodies have loaned photographs or provided prints from their collections:

Helen Chapman
Denis King
Ida McAulay
V C Smith
David Tasker
Eric Thomas

The Australian
The Mercury
The Sun
The Sunday Examiner Express

Allport Library and Museum of Fine Arts
Mitchell Library, Sydney
W E L H Crowther Collection, Hobart
Queen Victoria Museum and Art Gallery
Queenstown Museum
Tasmanian Museum and Art Gallery
West Coast Pioneer Memorial Museum
Forestry Commission
Hydro-Electric Commission
National Parks and Wildlife Service
Tasmanian Environment Centre Inc.
Zoology Department, University of Tasmania

There are a number of individuals to whom we extend our sincere thanks. They have given their time and skill unstintingly:

Milo Dunphy for inspiration and advice at the outset; Susan Vanderwal who tackled the raw manuscript; Fred Koolhof for photographic printing and copy work; Ruth Jennings and John Best who designed and drew most of the black and white maps and graphs; Geoffrey Stilwell and Barbara Valentine of the Allport Library and Carolyn Wesley and Dora Heard of the Tasmanian Collection for their help with historical material; Madeline Hempel of the State Library who assisted so patiently with the bibliography; Alan Gray who proof read the manuscript and galleys with us; Chris Meech, cartographer, who prepared the large colour map using base maps provided by the Lands Department; Penny Tyson who helped with maps and index; Rona Gardner who retouched the photographs and assisted with the index; Sylvia Cowles for endless practical assistance and hospitality; the staff of the Tasmanian Environment Centre Inc.; and the following editorial consultants:

Bob Anderson, Peter Bosworth, Bob Brown, Kath Davies, Bruce Davis, Hilary Edwards, Tom Errey, Peter Faircloth, Geoff Fenton, Bob Graham, Malcolm Grant, Chris Harries, Chris Harwood, Prof W D Jackson, Rhys Jones, Greg Middleton, Peter Murray, Andrew Skinner, Margie Tassell, Jack Thwaites and Peter Waterman.

We would like to thank the typists Karen Alexander, Karen Dedenczuk, Rona Gardner, Ros Gee, Les Gower, Karen Hughes, Yvonne Light, Ann Mainsbridge, Jenny McMahon, Jayne Price, Marie Turner and Pam Wilson.

There are many people we have not mentioned who have helped in one way or another with advice, criticism or practical tasks. These people we also thank.

Those numerous persons who contributed financially are acknowledged and thanked for their faith and positive encouragement at the early stage of compilation. Major contributions (loans and donations) came from G and J Baker, I J Brown, A Crouch, R J Downie, T Errey, C Hale, T A Jordan, M Maxwell, G Middleton, G Richardson, I D Travers, P Wessing, the Canberra Bushwalking Club, the Hobart Walking Club, the North-West Walking Club and the Society for Growing Australian Plants.

We received a grant of $1,000 from the Tasmanian Arts Advisory Board. This grant assisted the design and artwork of the book and we wish to express our gratitude for this encouragement. Paul Stutter assisted with the art work. Our Thanks go to the management of Specialty Press for their tolerance, to Scott Smyth for setting the type and Griffin Press for their co-operation.

Finally, as editors and organisers of *The South-West Book*, we thank the Australian Conservation Foundation, specifically its Director, Dr J G Mosley, for belief in our project and their commitment as publishers.

Helen Gee, Janet Fenton,
Greg Hodge and Chris Cowles

Preface to the First Impression

The need for a resource book on the South-West of Tasmania has arisen from widespread fascination for this unique part of the Earth coupled with a concern for its future — a future threatened by the advance of technology.

With the seventies came wide public debate on the future of the region. Changes came swiftly in the wake of ill informed decisions and general ignorance. This book was conceived as a response to the need for education, and for information to aid rational decision making. It generated interest and evolved to become a community response with the direct involvement of well over one hundred people.

It was a revelation to us just how much material existed — scattered in the dusty corners of museum and library, held in the minds of bushman and academic. As demonstrated in the bibliography, sources are often scattered and obscure. Much of the information stems from fresh research. We have attempted to include the most interesting and important material, bearing in mind that several publications have already dealt with certain aspects of the South-West in detail — notably those books that tell the Lake Pedder story.

Several general photographic books exquisitely describe the area's beauty and changing moods. This book is an attempt to draw together knowledge of all aspects of the area into a reference source. The different styles reflect the diversity of attitudes and levels of interest in the South-West, and we make no apology for the mosaic of ideas presented. No single author could hope to specialize in so wide a range of subjects.

One of the ironies of the continuing controversy over the South-West is that whilst the matter has been an issue for over a decade, few are equipped to argue about it authoritatively. A reason for this has been the lack of a single, comprehensive treatment of the issue. To the public at large the South-West is still a mysterious, empty quarter of Tasmania about which politicians, administrators, commercial interests and a number of voluntary organizations have been arguing for years.

The future of the South-West will depend upon the outcome of a conflict that very few people have resolved, even within themselves — a conflict between the drive towards an ever higher level of material consumption and the feeling that beautiful natural areas should be protected and cherished.

The Editors, 10 October, 1978

Preface to the Third Impression

The South-West Book is going to press for the third time, following two successful print runs of 8,750 and 10,000 copies. The book remains, to date, the single most informative work on the South-West, and its popularity as a reference source has rewarded the efforts of all contributors.

From the proceeds of the book, the Australian Conservation Foundation funded a Tasmanian project officer in Tasmania for a period of three years. Peter Thompson worked on the Foundation's South-West campaign and in particular on the efforts to protect the Franklin and Lower Gordon Rivers.

The South-West has received increasing publicity, both nationally and internationally, since this book first went to press, primarily as a result of the intensifying controversy over the Franklin — Lower Gordon hydro-electric scheme. Construction work commenced in late 1982, polarising the Tasmanian community but arousing widespread indignation beyond our shores. A major archaeological find on the banks of the Franklin River focused further international attention on the threatened river systems, and the 'dams issue' played a significant part in the Labor victory at the Federal election of March 1983.

Over the past five years, there has been further forestry work and mineral exploration in the South-West, as well as a surge of small tourist ventures. Recent ecological and biological studies also need a mention to bring the reader up to date and provide a context for what remains, essentially, a document of the 1970s.

1978–1983

The Gordon-Franklin River Caves

The single most important event concerning the South West since 1978 must be the discovery of deposits from glacial age man in the Gordon and Franklin River limestone area. Caves there were discovered and described by speleologists from 1974 onwards, and a small archaeological expedition to the Lower Gordon River was organised in January 1981. This expedition's chance find of a deposit containing stone tools and charcoal was the first evidence of any prehistoric Aboriginal occupation in the inland South-Western rivers region.

This proof of prehistoric occupation prompted geomorphologist Kevin Kiernan to revisit Fraser Cave (now Kutikina Cave), which he had discovered with Greg Middleton in 1977. The cave contained a large bone deposit, and on his visit in February 1981, Kiernan found stone artefacts on the cave floor.

The find was announced to the press and in view of its importance a second archaeological expedition (Rhys Jones from the Australian National University and staff of the Tasmanian National Parks and Wildlife Service) visited the site in March 1981. First inspection showed hundreds of flakes on the cave floor, and a small trial excavation revealed dense hearths and a multitude of stone tools and animal bones. The site was clearly of major importance.

Kutikina (Fraser) Cave is situated near the banks of the lower Franklin River in a low limestone cliff some 10 metres above the present water level. The archaeological evidence was found in a wide chamber near the entrance, while the cave itself extends a further 150 metres into the cliff.

A test excavation was carried out on a part of the deposit which was covered by a thin layer of soft stalagmite. Immediately under the stalagmite were interleaved hearths, broken animal bones and stone tools and flakes at a density of more than 100,000 pieces per cubic metre. Under these hearths came a layer of limestone rubble, which on geological grounds seemed to be derived from the roof of the cave, under different climatic conditions from the present. Beneath this again was a layer of clays which in turn rested on bedrock. Both the limestone rubble and the underlying clay deposits were also packed with stone tools and animal bones. The total depth of deposit was about 1 metre.

From carbon samples the very top layer could be dated to around 15,000 years ago, and the middle rubble to 18,000 years ago, correlating with the height of the last ice age.

The site was first occupied about 20,000 years ago just as the world started to enter the coldest phase of the last ice age. Glaciers formed in the high mountain valleys of South-West Tasmania and the vegetation of the plains and uplands became open with alpine-type herbfields and grasses. The closed rainforests were probably reduced to their primary heartlands, the river valleys, in particular the gorges of the Franklin and Gordon Rivers. A large population of animals, particularly wallabies, dwelt on the open surrounding plains. The inhabitants of the caves by the Franklin River hunted there and brought back their quarry to their base camps. They had a detailed knowledge of the mineralogy of the area, using excellent fine-grained rocks from which to flake their stone tools. In particular they had discovered the glass-like rock called 'Darwin glass' from a crater some 40–60 km to the north-west of the site, where a large meteorite had plunged into the Earth's surface and formed a crater, melting the surface rocks into glass upon impact. This extremely interesting geological phenomenon has been rediscovered only in the past 20–30 years by modern geologists.

Then, about 15,000 years ago, the world's climate started to warm up, the glaciers melted and the rainforest re-emerged out of its heartland and invaded the slopes above. This eventually blotted out suitable habitats for humans and the cave was abandoned. From then on the dense forests of this valley remained a vast wilderness devoid of people, and the hearths upon which they lived in the cave became covered with thin stalagmite.

These brief archaeological reconnaissances have discovered prehistoric sites which document two phases of prehistoric use of the changing Franklin-Gordon landscapes — firstly an initial dense occupation during Pleistocene times, and later, at least in the Gordon River valley, perhaps a fleeting seasonal penetration of the region.

Kutikina Cave, Franklin River, is

unique in Australia in that there is a large limestone cave of easy access with a level floor in a primary state of deposition. The deposit is immensely rich in stone tools and animal bones and dense hearths show that it was used as a major camp site. The geomorphology and preserved pollen can give primary information as to past climatic conditions in a region of immense geographical significance.

Kutikina Cave has already yielded more than one hundred times the entire stone artefacts recovered from all other Tasmanian ice age sites combined. Its rich animal bone component gives an almost unique picture in Australia of the hunting strategies of inland Aboriginal hunters during the ice age. All the bones so far studied are of modern species, which leads to the important question of when and how did the giant marsupials of Tasmania become extinct, and what was the human role in this process? With so little of the site investigated, there is the possibility of fossil human remains eventually being found.

In South-West Tasmania the inhabitants of such sites as Kutikina Cave were then the most southerly human beings on Earth. They alone of our species were as close to the Antarctic ice-sheet, then only a thousand kilometres to the south, as the Upper Palaeolithic hunters of France, living in tundra conditions, were to the northern ice-sheet. It would take another 10,000 years for equivalent areas of South America to be occupied by humans. It is within this context that Kutikina Cave assumes international importance in our global view of the geographical expansion of modern humans.

Further discoveries have since been made, notably of three major caves near the junction of the Franklin and Jane Rivers. These caves, found in March 1983 by a joint National Parks and Wildlife Service (NPWS) and Australian National University (ANU) expedition, contain extraordinary cave formations and one contains archaeological deposit. The caves are extensive, one extending to 666 metres and others opening into large caverns. Further archaeological exploration is planned. A survey by the Hydro-Electric Commission (HEC) has also discovered numerous cave systems and some archaeological evidence, but details of these finds have not yet been released.

Mention should be made concerning the nomenclature of the cave systems along the Lower Gordon and Franklin Rivers. Although threatened caves were initially named after prominent State and Federal politicians, these names were never officially gazetted. The name Kutikina Cave was given to Fraser Cave on 16 June 1982, the name meaning

'spirit' in current Tasmanian Aboriginal usage. Biglandulosum Cave became Deenareena Cave, meaning 'tears' or 'weeping', also in modern Aboriginal usage.

Other caves were officially given Aboriginal names from Plomley's *Dictionary of Aboriginal Dialects:*

Bingham Arch became Pengana, meaning 'waterfall';

Neilson Cave became Routuli, meaning 'long';

Lowe Cave became Proina, meaning 'large' or 'extensive'; and

Hayden Cave became Payaleena, meaning 'glow worm'.

The Lower Gordon River valley has also been the site of a wide scientific survey organised by the Hydro-Electric Commission to provide an environmental statement about proposed power developments in the area. Field study teams from the University of Tasmania and NPWS have been involved.

Many additions to the list of higher plants for the South-West have been made as a result of these and other studies, and numerous taxonomic revisions have taken place since this book was first published.

Changes and Additions to the Flora

Several completely new species, some of which are confined to the South-West, have been found, but only one has yet been published — *Epacris navicularis,* a small shrub species of alpine heath found on the Arthur, Denison, Hamilton and King William Ranges. Other new species from South-Western Tasmania have been found in the genera *Oreomyrrhis* (Apiaceae), *Persoonia* (Proteaceae), *Centrolepis* (two species) and *Gaimardia* (Centrolepidaceae), *Carpha* (two species), *Isolepis, Oreobolus* and *Uncinia* (Cyperaceae) as well as several new species in the families Restionaceae (cord rushes), Juncaceae (rushes) and Poaceae (grasses).

New records of species not previously recorded in the area include the sedges *Schoenus biglumis* and *Schoenus carsei* and a species of finger-fern previously known only in New Zealand, *Grammitis magellanica.* The genus of eye-brights, *Euphrasia,* has been revised and the following subspecies of *Euphrasia gibbsiae* are confined largely to the South-West: ssp. *comberi,* ssp. *discolor,* ssp. *kingii* and ssp. *microdonta.*

Taxonomic revisions in other groups have resulted in a number of species in the South-West now being considered as Tasmanian endemics. These include the skeleton filmy-fern *Apteropteris applanata* which is largely confined to the

West and South-West, and the widespread species *Plantago daltonii* and *Monotoca submutica.* A taxonomic change of particular significance concerns Huon pine which has suffered a scientific name change from *Dacrydium franklinii* to *Lagarostrobos franklinii.*

There has been a considerable upsurge of interest in the lower plants, especially in the mosses, lichens and fungi. However, the taxonomy and distributions of members of these groups are comparatively less well known, and as yet, little of the work has been published.

Cinnamon Fungus

The factors which determine transition from one vegetation type to another are numerous, fire being the most dramatic. Another agent which has received recent attention and concern in the South-West is the introduced cinnamon fungus *Phytophthora cinnamomi* which now has a widespread but scattered distribution in the South-West. The fungus causes 'die-back' or 'root rot' in susceptible plant species. There has been no record of its occurrence in inland areas of the South-West, or at elevations above 200 metres. A joint field study by Frank Podger (CSIRO) and Mick Brown (NPWS), carried out at a 2 km² area at Bathurst Harbour, found that the fungus is causing a dramatic reduction in cover of many species in sedgeland and heath communities. The sedges generally are little affected but many species of Proteaceae, Epacridaceae, Myrtaceae, Rutaceae and Dilleniaceae are highly susceptible.

P. cinnamomi was not found in any closed-scrub, forest or rainforest communities, although several species e.g. of *Nothofagus, Phyllocladus, Agastachys* and *Cenarrhenes* from these communities were found to be susceptible to the fungus in glasshouse tests. The temperature regime in the soil of these communities is thought to be unfavourable for the fungus, and this factor probably also explains gradients in vulnerability with altitude.

As the researchers have found no evidence of important pathogenic variation in more than 30 Tasmanian isolates of this fungus, all occurrences of *P. cinnamomi* might be regarded as identical.

The fungus appears to be a recent introduction to the South-West, perhaps through introduced plantings, and its distribution is increasing by natural dispersal aided by man (both machines and bushwalkers' boots) and, speculatively, by a variety of animal vectors. The potential threat of *P. cinnamomi* will be influenced by the extent of sedgeland-heath communities. This in turn will be determined by the extent to which fire may increase the area of these communities.

Recent local alterations of the pattern of fire occurrence and frequency and the introduction of *P. cinnamomi* have drastically altered the equilibria in the vegetation. The vegetation of the area at large is in transition and its status will be determined largely by man's use of fire and the effects of *Phytophthora*, as well as other less volatile factors of the environment. If we are to have any success in predicting the likely effects of such changes we need much more information on the vital attributes of individual species and particularly of their relationships to fire.

Fire

The debate over fire and its influence on the composition, structure and distribution of the major vegetation types continues to gain intensity, with Jackson, Bowman and Kirkpatrick putting forward the ecological drift argument (outlined on pages 98 to 101) and Mount arguing for more stable vegetation type boundaries determined by aspect, drainage and soil type.

Fire has continued to be a dramatic and significant natural force in the South-West. A succession of dry winters meant that normally wet vegetation had the opportunity to dry out, allowing fires to penetrate. This was particularly relevant in rainforest areas where it is usual to have at least 300 years between major fires.

The 1980–81 and 1981–82 summers were particularly bad for fires on the West Coast, and resulted in over 123,000 hectares being burnt, including large tracts of rainforest. The incidence of lightning strikes during these summers was high and fires originating from these burnt over 1,600 hectares.

However *people* caused the fires which burnt the remainder of the affected areas, and these fires accounted for about 90% of the fire suppression costs for the West Coast.

These two fire seasons have helped confirm a number of points in regard to fires in remote areas. Some of these are:

1 that most lightning strike fires are extinguished by rain associated with the accompanying storms. However, after particularly dry winters these fires can not only destroy layers of peat but also lie dormant until the next occurrence of hot, windy weather. In March 1981, a fire resulting from a lightning strike burnt approximately 650 hectares on the Hamilton Range adjacent to the Truchanas Huon Pine Reserve;

2 that bushwalkers are becoming increasingly responsible for fires. A fire thought to be lit by a rafter on Butler Island burnt a small but scenically important area, whilst over 12,500 hectares were burnt in a fire originating at the Lake Vera hut in the Wild Rivers National Park;

3 that fires lit by people are responsible for the greatest suppression costs and the greatest financial and social losses;

4 that accessibility can be equated with the incidence of fire. Most of the fires in these two seasons were associated with roads, vehicle tracks or frequently used walking tracks;

5 that educating those using remote areas of the risks and effects of fires can significantly reduce the incidence of fire. In the few years that have elapsed since the opening of the Scotts Peak and Strathgordon roads, very few fires have originated from those areas as a result of bushwalkers, fishermen or other visitors.

A further area of concern is that potential for differences between authorities such as the Forestry Commission, the National Parks and Wildlife Service and the Hydro-Electric Commission in regard to the use of fire as a management tool is likely to be heightened in the current political climate where there is division within the community over the future of the South-West.

These differences in attitude were illustrated by the fact that one authority spent over $100,000 in suppressing a fire which originated from a lightning strike, while many other fires in the same area at the same time originating from the same storm were assessed as likely to burn themselves out naturally, and consequently were merely kept under observation.

An Endangered Species — the Orange-Bellied Parrot

Fire regimes and changing vegetation patterns also affect the fauna. Under recent study is the endangered Orange-bellied parrot (*Neophema chrysogaster*), probably the rarest bird in Australia today. An intensive survey by the Tasmanian NPWS funded by a World Wildlife (Australia) grant estimates a maximum population of 170 birds.

The parrot breeds in coastal South-Western Tasmania during summer, migrating north through the islands of western Bass Strait to southern Victoria and south-eastern South Australia for the winter, and is endemic to these regions.

A proposed petrochemical complex located in one of the Orange-bellied parrot's wintering habitats of coastal Victoria stimulated interest in the species in 1978. Since then, annual summer and winter counts have been carried out in Tasmania, Victoria and South Australia. The first winter sighting of the parrot in its summer breeding range in the South-West was made at Port Davey during the winter of 1982.

Past records show that the species has experienced a dramatic population decline this century. The use of fire in the bird's breeding range has also altered since the removal of local Aboriginal tribes in the 1830s. Substantial stretches north of Port Davey and around Bathurst Harbour have remained unburnt for up to 30 years while others may be burnt at a frequency of 2 to 3 years. Consequently, while some areas have reverted to dense heath and scrubland, others have little soil and a struggling vegetation cover.

Orange-bellied parrots are seed eaters, feeding on various sedgeland and heathland species from October to March and nesting in eucalypts in nearby forest. The survey has found that the food plants used by the birds at different times during summer fit into a mosaic of ages since last burnt. When the Orange-bellied parrots first arrive in breeding areas, the favoured habitat is 7 to 10 years old, followed by a preference for 3 to 5 year old habitat in December, and older creek-side vegetation until February when young birds leave the nest. On very few occasions have birds been observed feeding in vegetation more than 15 years old. Nest trees are from 14 to 50 metres tall in forest patches from 1 hectare to large tracts of temperate rainforest and mixed forest.

Birds

A plan of fire management for the bird's coastal buttongrass habitat is suggested by the survey. NPWS officers Peter Brown and Roland Wilson are currently working on guidelines for such a plan, allowing for a balance between sedgeland, heathland, scrub and rainforest communities.

Another recent survey of birds in part of the South-West was carried out by Randolph Rose from the University of Tasmania as part of the HEC's environmental survey of the Lower Gordon region. During the survey 49 bird species were seen, of which 18 were considered to be common or very common and seven rare.

As a bird habitat, South-West Tasmania is poor compared with the drier eastern parts of the State. However several species are more common here than in the drier regions, including the Grey Goshawk, Ground Parrot,

Warners Landing, Lower Gordon River. Site of HEC road construction work, 1983.

Kingfisher, Southern Emu Wren, Tasmanian Thornbill, Scrub Tit, White-browed Scrub Wren, Pink Robin, Olive Whistler, Crescent Honeyeater and White's Thrush. All but the Ground Parrot, Azure Kingfisher and Southern Emu Wren are fairly well distributed throughout the State where suitable habitats exist.

The status of two species should be of concern: the Ground Parrot and the Azure Kingfisher. The Kingfisher, a subspecies of the mainland form, is uncommon in Tasmania, and appears to be restricted almost entirely to the west of the State. Its preferred habitat is forested streams and waterways rather than open water, hence its status is unlikely to be enhanced by hydro-electric development.

The Ground Parrot is extremely rare in other parts of Australia and is considered an 'endangered species'.

The scientific significance of the survey results is primarily one of extending the known range of the species recorded into areas not previously reported upon. Quantitative data on abundance and correlations with vegetation provide a preliminary insight into habitat preferences, while the lack of exotic species points to the region being a wilderness area. Importantly, the

mammal survey (commissioned by the Hydro-Electric Commission) also failed to locate exotic species of mammals with the exception of one feral cat.

The effects of flooding part of this region may be assessed when it is realised that the habitats most under environmental pressure are the low-lying valleys of heath/sedgeland and the steep banks of the river covered with temperate rainforest. These habitats are best developed in this area of the State and are poorly represented on the mainland of Australia.

Freshwater Fauna

The Hydro-Electric Commission's environmental survey of the Lower Gordon region has included a study of the freshwater invertebrate fauna, carried out by a team from the University of Tasmania. This study aimed to establish the inventory and distribution of freshwater invertebrates in the Gordon River basin, to correlate these distributions with habitat factors and to supply material to taxonomists for identification and description.

Freshwater habitats from pools in crayfish (yabby) burrows to the riffle zones in the main rivers were sampled. Thirteen new species were recognized

from the study, and species previously unrecorded in the area were collected. The fauna collected is of scientific interest for a number of reasons apart from its taxonomic significance.

Many of the animal groups present in the study area are of considerable importance to the interpretations of animal distributions, both past and present. In some cases, the interest is in a local context (Tasmanian and Australasian); for example, the gastropods (snails). In other cases, the interest is centred around distribution patterns in a global context, particularly with regard to circumpolar distribution from Gondwanaland origins. Most are members of very ancient groups, such as the dragonfly *Archipetalia auriculata* and the three genera of crayfish or yabby, *Parastacoides*, *Engaeus* and *Astacopsis*, among others.

A great deal of the fauna collected is endemic to Tasmania, and much of it is endemic to at least Western Tasmania, if not the South-West. Many groups are also of interest by virtue of their rarity.

Numerous species present in the area pose interesting ecological questions. For example, seventeen species of stonefly were collected in the survey (a little over half of the known total) and many of these appear to utilize very similar habitats. Questions are raised as to how these species interact to share physical and biotic resources. Individual species are also of interest for their life histories. There is enough information already to suggest ways in which certain species have devised solutions to accommodate the rather harsh climate characteristic of the South-West.

To the physiologist, the fauna raises fascinating questions concerning environmental adaptations developed by different groups. Investigation has begun on the numerous adaptations required by the freshwater crayfish for life in burrows.

Some of the animal groups found in the study area are of significance in that they have a precise requirement for clean, uncontaminated, well-oxygenated flowing water and their presence/absence provides a very simple and unambiguous indication of the water quality at any point of a river where suitable habitat occurs. A particular study of the Gordon River downstream of the Gordon Dam tailrace during the construction phase revealed that the fauna is markedly reduced in diversity due to pollution, siltation and reduced river flow. Downstream five kilometres to the Albert River junction most species were eliminated, while the fauna remains affected to a lesser extent as far as the Denison River junction (14 km downstream). Below this junction the fauna seems relatively unaffected.

An important finding of the survey is that the freshwater fauna of the region as a whole, particularly in the larger rivers, is very much richer than had previously been thought, the Gordon River itself being comparable with rivers elsewhere in Australia and overseas.

Brief moratorium on developments

In its Report of August 1978 the South West Advisory (Cartland) Committee recommended that ... 'no action that adversely affects a place that is in South-West Tasmania should be taken or permitted unless there is no feasible and prudent alternative, and all measures that can reasonably be taken to minimise the adverse effect of any such action should be taken.' (See pages 256 and 257.)

The Tasmanian Government imposed a moratorium on developments in South-West Tasmania on 19 September 1978 whilst full and open consideration was given to the Committee's recommendations.

In March 1979 the Government decided —

1 to extend the Conservation Area

to include all of South-West Tasmania;
2 to amend the Forestry Act and National Parks and Wildlife Act to require Forest Management Plans to be prepared for those areas in the South-West which were subject to forestry activities;
3 to establish an independent South-West Tasmania Committee to advise Cabinet on matters referred to it by Cabinet; and
4 to continue the moratorium on developments until relevant legislation was amended and the Conservation Area proclaimed.

In July 1980 the Conservation Area was extended and in December 1980 the Forestry Act and the National Parks and Wildlife Act were amended to provide for Forest Management Plans but no plans were actually prepared. In the meantime the HEC (October 1979) proposed a major development in the South-West and mineral exploration guidelines for the Conservation Area were being prepared by the NPWS and the Mines Department.

Consequently, the Government then decided in July 1981 to extend the moratorium on all new developments in the South West Conservation Area until —
1 both the NPWS and the Forestry Commission had completed their respective management plans for land use within that area;
2 the guidelines and procedures appropriate for exploration and mining acceptable to the NPWS and the Mines Department were drafted;
3 the (then) current power development legislation was finalized.

In May 1982 a Liberal Government was elected. The power development legislation and the guidelines for mineral exploration licences were finalized but the respective NPWS and Forestry Management Plans have not been completed. The Forestry Commission has prepared one Forest Management Plan for the southern forests subject to the Australian Paper Mills (APM) concession but this may well be redundant now that APM has closed.

Five further Forest Mangement Plans are required to cover the South-West. The NPWS managment plans have not progressed because of lack of staff.

Mining

In March 1983 the Tasmanian Government decided to drop the moratorium on mining in the South West Conservation Area and invited mining companies to apply for exploration licences.

At the present time, Exploration Licence applications within the South-West are —
Stannous Investments — Cox Bight
White Industries — Picton/Weld area
BHP — Upper Weld/Mt Mueller
Amoco — extensive area from Eldon River to Lower Davey River
Placer Exploration — extensive area between Sloop Pt and Low Rocky Pt on the West Coast.

Other mineral Exploration Licences and Mining Leases are basically the same as published in 1978 although there is currently no licence or application covering Macquarie Harbour.

BHP's application for an Exploration Licence covering 236 square kilometres in the upper Weld/Mt Mueller region has caused some public concern as this area includes some of the finest undisturbed remaining rainforest in the South-West. Inevitable consequences of mining or serious exploration would be roadways and construction sites, and introduction of exotic flora as well as the fungus *Phytophthora cinnamomi.*

The region is within the National Estate area but no management plan has yet been prepared. The biological and archaeological data base for the area is very scant, no comprehensive studies having been undertaken.

The Australian Conservation Foundation's rainforest campaign, which is called 'Rescue the Rainforests (Tasmania)', commenced in 1982 to work towards reservation of rainforests with the dual role of drawing up reserve proposals and secondly publicity. There are two areas in the South-West for which proposals are being prepared: the Mt Bobs area and the Weld and upper Huon River — Scotts Peak vicinity.

Forestry

Public attention to forestry activity in the South-West has been eclipsed by the debate over the Franklin-Lower Gordon power scheme. Since 1977 there have been no major changes in concession or State Forest boundaries in the South-West. Timber leases on Crown Land in the Alma and upper Franklin valleys have been incorporated in the Wild Rivers National Park as has the narrow strip of State Forest bordering the Lyell Highway Scenic Reserves.

Although the concession boundaries have not changed, the forest industries have progressively pushed nearer to their western boundaries. For example, Australian Newsprint Mills have now started operations on the western slopes of the Tiger Range visible from the Vale of Rasselas and the Denison Range.

The major significant extension of development has been along the upper Huon Valley where roads now almost penetrate to Blakes Opening on either side of the stream. There has been continued clearfelling and regeneration burning in the Picton, Weld and Huon valleys which are now heavily roaded, and in the forests on the dry land between the Gordon and Serpentine — Huon impoundments. Since 1977 a bitter debate has raged between a group of scientists who believe that the slash and burn method of silviculture applied to the South-West forests may result in progressive nutrient depletion, and those who reject this prospect. There has also been some cogent criticism made against the practice of broadcast burning of buttongrass plains.

The South-West wilderness is still threatened by forestry development. Almost one third of the South-West wilderness resource present in 1979 would be lost if all areas now legally devoted to forestry were developed. Most of this loss would occur in the southern forests, which are mainly within the Australian Paper Mills' concession based on Geeveston. These wilderness losses could be avoided at little or no cost through substituting plantation wood for wilderness wood. In 1982 APM ceased their pulpwood operation at Geeveston and in June 1983 the Government revoked their operating licence. However, cutting for sawlog still continues in the southern forests of the South-West and the Tasmanian Government is searching for alternative outlets for pulpwood without considering the wilderness alternative.

Tourism

During the past few years there has been an explosion in the number of commercial operators offering 'adventure trips' into the South-West. By the summer of 1982 five operators were offering bushwalking-style trips on a regular basis to many areas of the South-West.

By 1981/82 five commercial operators were offering rafting excursions down the Franklin River, and a total of 220 clients participated in their trips. In 1982/83 another operator was permitted also to use the River, and over 500 clients were shepherded down the River by the six firms. Additionally there has been a dramatic increase in the number of private individuals rafting down the Franklin. Prior to 1979 less than 100 recreationists had rafted or canoed down the River each summer. In the summer of 1979–80 that figure reached 350, and in the following summer, 400. Then, in reflection of the growing concern for the future of the River, over 1,000 people floated down the River in the summer of 1981–82. The size of the population on the River in summer can be gauged by the fact that one party who liloed the Jane River to join the Franklin, simply 'hitch-hiked' with other rafters once they reached the Franklin.

Tourist operators based in Strahan have also flourished. Associated with the publicity surrounding the campaign to save the River has been a flood of tourists eager to journey up the River from Strahan. In the summer of 1981–82 over 50,000 customers experienced the 'Gordon River cruises' and in anticipation of continued demand Morrison's

Clearfelling in the southern forests.

TASMANIAN WILDERNESS SOCIETY.

Tourist Services invested $100,000 in February 1982 in a new twenty-one metre twin-hulled launch designed to augment the present cruises.

The Franklin–Lower Gordon Rivers Issue

The hydro-electric power scheme planned for the Lower-Gordon River region has caused great public outcry, divided the Tasmanian community and significantly influenced major political events over the past four years. Conservation groups, in particular the Tasmanian Wilderness Society, and also the Australian Conservation Foundation, have carried out massive campaigns to halt the flooding of the rivers.

The history of the debate is long and involved. On 16 October 1979, the HEC report on its Gordon River Power Development, Stage Two, was tabled in Parliament. It recommended an immediate start on its 'integrated' scheme involving three dams on the Lower Gordon, Franklin and King Rivers at a cost of $1,364 million. Four months earlier an opinion poll taken by Tasmanian Opinion Polls showed that 53.3% of Tasmanians favoured saving the Franklin.

The reality facing the 2,000 people who assembled at a rally in Hobart organized by the Tasmanian Wilderness Society (TWS) in October to protest the HEC recommendations, was that no HEC recommended scheme had ever been altered, let alone rejected. The HEC had the support of every sector of the Tasmanian establishment, including business, both major political parties, the unions and perhaps most importantly, all three Tasmanian daily newspapers.

Between October 1979 and July 1980, the HEC proposals suffered an almost continuous barrage of criticism from conservation groups and, for the first time, from other Government departments and bodies.

In November 1979 NPWS recommended that the entire Franklin, Lower Gordon and Davey River catchments be made a national park. It followed this recommendation with a report, in March 1979, which was highly critical of the HEC's environmental report on the Lower Gordon dam proposals.

The NPWS doubts were echoed by the Mines Department which, in a leaked report, accused the HEC of 'fixing' figures which argued against a thermal (coal fired) power station.

Crucially, however, the Premier, Doug Lowe, and a substantial section of the ALP Government caucus no longer totally supported the HEC position as had always been the case in the past.

By the period between May and July 1980 when it was faced with making a decision on the HEC's recommendations the ALP, and Lowe in particular, were caught between two irreconcilable forces of the HEC and its allies on one side and the conservation movement and public opinion on the other.

The options facing the Government were to support the first stage of the HEC's integrated scheme, the Gordon-below-Franklin (GBF) dam, thus flooding the lower 35 kilometres of the Franklin River; to opt for the Gordon-above-Olga (GAO) dam and a thermal power station as recommended by the Energy Advisory Unit (Evers); or to build no scheme on the Gordon/Franklin Rivers at all.

The GAO proposal would still flood most of the Lower Gordon River but would save the Franklin.

Faced with this dilemma, the Government switched back and forth three times between the GBF and GAO.

On 10 May 1980 a TOP poll showed that 54% of Tasmanians favoured saving the Franklin. Three weeks later 10,000 people marched in Hobart to oppose the flooding of the Franklin, the largest Hobart rally ever.

By 9 July 80,000 letters had been received at Parliament House, in Hobart, calling on the Government to save the Franklin.

On 10 July the Government announced that it would proceed with the GAO scheme, against the wishes of the HEC. It was, however, a compromise which ultimately would satisfy neither the conservation lobby, who wanted no dams, or the hydro lobby who wanted the GBF scheme.

On 21 November 1980 the House of Assembly passed the GAO Bill. On 17 December the Legislative Council, backed by the interim report of its own Select Committee which recommended an immediate start on the GBF scheme, rejected the GAO scheme and substituted the GBF scheme.

The deadlock between the two houses of Parliament over the choice of power schemes was to last until the referendum of December 1981 resolved it. Those twelve months were crucial in allowing time for the development of the 'No Dams' campaign and for the occurrence of a number of superficially insignificant events which were to play a major part in the later part of the campaign.

The two most important events, which passed almost un-noticed, were the nominations by the Tasmanian Government of the South-West and the Wild Rivers National Parks for World Heritage Listing on 22 December and 31 March respectively. Few people foresaw

the significance of those nominations.

On 19 March came the announcement that Kutikina Cave was of major archaeological significance. Kutikina Cave was below the proposed flood level and its significance, in common with later cave finds, allowed the area to be nominated for World Heritage status for cultural as well as natural value.

While the cave finds were drawing international scientific attention to South-West Tasmania, within Tasmania and on the mainland the issue was increasingly becoming a complex political struggle over Tasmania's economic future, particularly its hydro-industrialisation policy.

The HEC and the major industrial consumers realized that if no dam was built on the Lower Gordon River it was the beginning of the end of the hydro-industrialisation policy on which they depended.

For the Government, the issue was simply one of survival. That position was cogently put by the Energy Minister, Julian Amos, when he wrote in a confidential paper to the Parliamentary Labor Party that a resolution to the power deadlock was more important for political reasons than either the economic or environmental arguments.

Despite the desire for a political solution it was becoming impossible for the Government to achieve, caught as it was between the increasingly entrenched positions of the pro-hydro lobby and the conservation lobby whose 'No Dams' position was gaining popular support as fast as the Government's GAO option was losing it.

In July 1981 the State ALP Council rejected the Government's favoured GAO option and called for a referendum. Throughout August and September the pressure on the Government increased, with the Legislative Council Select Committee bringing down the final report recommending the GBF scheme and on 2 September Hobart's third major rally was attended by 6,000 anti-dammers.

On 17 September the Government announced a referendum, stating that it would also include a 'no dams' option. However, six days later the Premier withdrew the 'no dams' option saying that it was 'unacceptable to this Government even if that were the will of the majority'.

Two months after the announcement of the referendum, the Government lost its majority. Eight weeks had seen the sacking of the National Parks Minister, Andrew Lohrey, for supporting thermal power and the resignation of Premier Lowe after twelve of his colleagues had signed a motion of no confidence. His resignation was followed by that of his strongest supporter, Mary Willey, the

Government Whip.

The political climate had now changed markedly against the conservation cause after the decision to oppose the GAO scheme. On 3 December the new premier, Harry Holgate, announced that a dam would be built regardless of the size of a 'no dams' informal vote that the TWS had been campaigning for. 44.9% of voters responded by refusing to cast a valid vote for either of the two dam options. Only 8% of the vote went to the Government's favoured GAO option. Holgate responded by proroguing Parliament until 26 March 1982.

That decision gave much needed time for the conservation lobby to marshall itself for further campaigns during what amounted to an amnesty on political activity in Tasmania.

Following the 'write in' in the Tasmanian referendum, the technique was transferred to the mainland to demonstrate the strength of feeling against the dam. At the Lowe by-election in NSW on 15 March, 12% of voters wrote 'no dams' on their papers.

By the time the ACT House of Assembly elections were held on 5 June, the lessons of the Lowe by-election had been assimilated and a 40.7% write-in was achieved.

Attention transferred back to Tasmania temporarily with the resumption of Parliament on 26 March. The new session lasted only a few hours before the Holgate Government, which had reversed its policy to support the GBF scheme following the referendum, was defeated in a motion of no confidence moved by Democrat Norm Sanders.

The State election which followed the defeat of the Holgate Government was an unmitigated disaster for the environment movement. The election was fought primarily on the twin issues of stability in government and the popularity of Holgate. The ALP received huge votes of no confidence from the electorate in its worst ever defeat, and a Liberal Government led by Robin Gray was returned with 19 of the 35 seats. Only two 'independents' were returned, former Premier, Doug Lowe, and Democrat, Norm Sanders.

One month after the election the bill authorising the construction of the GBF scheme passed the House of Assembly 29—2. The ALP voted with the Liberals.

The only apparent obstacle now in the way of the GBF scheme was the availability of Federal funding. Despite an apparent commitment to conservation the Prime Minister, Malcolm Fraser, had repeatedly insisted that the dam remained a State responsibility and that the Federal Government could not withhold funding.

In an effort to stop funds for the GBF dam, the Wilderness Society, in collaboration with two tour operators, Morrison Tours and Wildtrek, issued writs against the Federal Government alleging that the provision of funding through the Loan Council would be against the Australian Heritage Commission Act.

On 18 June, Justice Mason rejected the argument on the grounds that the Loan Council was not an authority of the Commonwealth and therefore neither it nor the Federal Ministers on it were subject to the Heritage Act.

The mainland campaign by conservation groups was now causing increasing disquiet within the Federal Liberal Party and throwing up huge majorities against the dam, particularly in Melbourne and Adelaide. In October a Saulwick poll showed that 49% of Australians favoured Federal action over the dam.

The discontent over Federal inaction was reflected in the barrage of 700 letters a week being received by the Prime Minister's office.

In the face of the rising tide of public opinion the Federal Government sought legal opinion about its powers and obligations under the World Heritage convention under which the Franklin-Gordon Rivers area had been nominated for World Heritage status by Prime Minister Fraser in January 1982. The opinion given by the Attorney-General's Department stated that the Federal Government had a duty to use its powers to prevent construction of the dam. It said that only political reasons could prevent that intervention.

Throughout November and December as public pressure built up, expectations of early Federal intervention were high. On 8 November the Federal ALP outlined its package of alternatives to the dam and on 14 November, 15,000 people marched to the Myer Music Bowl in Melbourne to protest against the dam, where they heard Bob Brown announce that the TWS would blockade dam construction work, which had commenced in August, if the Federal Government did not intervene by mid-December.

On 24 November the Senate Select Committee on South-West Tasmania, which had been receiving submissions since 23 September 1981, recommended a three-year delay on starting a major new power scheme, with a subsequent start on a thermal power station plus a smaller hydro scheme.

Throughout this period the Tasmanian Premier, Robin Gray, refused to negotiate or discuss any alternatives or compromises and the Tasmanian Government undertook a major

advertising campaign in mainland papers to support its case for the dam. Gray rejected the Senate report as being shoddy, biased and worthless.

Federal Cabinet met to consider its position on 8 December against the background of a 40.5% 'no dams' write-in in the Flinders by-election and with the knowledge that a decision to intervene to stop the dam would be greeted with widespread opposition from large sectors of the Liberal Party in all States and particularly in Tasmania.

The Federal Government decided not to intervene. Six days later the TWS started its South-West blockade.

The blockade was to last for two months and three weeks. In terms of its effect in actually hindering or stopping work at the time, it was an almost total failure and was greeted as such by the hydro lobby and Tasmanian Government. However the blockade was tremendous public relations success for the wilderness movement. At the same time its financial and organizational cost was large, involving a $2,000 a day cost and thousands of hours of voluntary labour.

The effect of the blockade was indisputable. With over 3,000 people taking part, of whom 1,400 were arrested, it thrust the destruction of the rivers area, and non-violent opposition to that destruction, into the forefront of the national media for weeks.

The majority of the 1,400 were arrested under special trespass laws introduced by the Gray Government. After the arrests started Democrat Norm Sanders resigned his seat in Parliament in protest against what he saw as 'police state' tactics. A few weeks later in January Bob Brown was elected to Parliament on a count-back just a day after his release from jail following his arrest on the Gordon River.

Conversely the blockade also had the negative effect of dividing the Tasmanian community. Blockaders were portrayed by the hydro lobby as interfering mainland 'dole bludgers' and 'communists'. For the first time, on two occasions in December and in January, the pro-hydro 'Organization for Tasmanian Development' (OTD) was able to organize rallies of 2,000 to 3,000 people in Queenstown, Hobart and Burnie.

On 14 December, almost unnoticed by the community at large, amid the publicity surrounding the first day of the blockade, the South-West and Wild Rivers National Parks were accepted onto the World Heritage List. The World Heritage status of the area was eventually to form the basis for Federal action to preserve the area.

On 7 January 1983, three days after the blockade resumed following a Christmas moratorium, a deputation of 20 Federal Liberal backbenchers approached the acting Prime Minister, Doug Anthony, seeking Federal action. The unease of the backbenches, caused by rumours of an imminent Federal election, was reinforced by a Spectrum Opinion Poll on 12 January which showed that Liberals in marginal seats were at risk over the dams issue.

In an attempt to defuse the South-West as an election issue, on 19 January Prime Minister Fraser offered Tasmania $500 million for a coal fired power station, as an alternative to the dam. Gray immediately rejected the offer.

On 1 February, a poll in the *Bulletin* showed that 46% of the population opposed the dam, and 25% supported it. Two days later the Federal Government announced that an election was to be held. The following day 20,000 people marched in the streets of Hobart in a rally opposing the dam.

Later in February the National South-West Coalition, comprising ACF, TWS and 42 other conservation organizations agreed to support ALP candidates in the House of Representatives, and the Australian Democrats in the Senate.

Conservation groups opened campaign offices in 13 marginal seats held by Liberals and held a series of public meetings and rallies as well as doorknocking key sections of 17 electorates and distributing 600,000 pamphlets.

On 5 March all seventeen seats in which conservation groups had campaigned fell to the Labor Party.

An hour after the ALP victory was confirmed, the Prime Minister elect, Bob Hawke, in his first interview, confirmed that the dam would be stopped. Tasmania, however, saw all five seats retained by the Liberals, in a swing against the national trend.

Throughout March, April and May the Federal Government moved to effect its promises by introducing regulations prohibiting further work and subsequently filing a writ in the High Court for breach of the regulations by the Tasmanian Government and HEC.

On 20 May the Federal Government, by passing the World Heritage Properties Conservation Bill, strengthened its position for the High Court action which started on 31 May. The High Court hearing lasted for eight days, with Mr Bob Ellicot QC presenting Tasmania's case and the Solicitor General, Sir Maurice Byers QC, arguing for the Federal Government.

On 1 July 1983, the full bench of seven judges of the High Court of Australia ruled four to three in favour of the Federal Government. Their decision was not based on the value of wilderness to the community, nor on power supply and demand, but strictly on the legal questions surrounding the dam and whether the Federal Government could overrule the State Government on the management of the World Heritage area which involved an international treaty.

As a result of the High Court ruling, the HEC has stopped development work on the Gordon Dam project. Construction crews are expected to be redeployed to other construction projects on the west coast and elsewhere in the State.

The decision has stimulated debate on future directions for Tasmania, particularly with regard to power alternatives, and also debate concerning the balance of power between the Commonwealth and the States.

Public reaction to the decision has so far ranged from nationwide jubilation to disappointment and aggression, expressed mainly in Tasmania. The ruling is a milestone and a victory for conservation in Australia. In his statement to the High Court, Mr Justice Murphy said '... the preservation of the world's cultural and natural environment is dependent upon international co-operation and international concern. The area is the heritage of Australians, as part of humanity.'

Human attitudes of pioneering and exploitation are being replaced by a realization that the world and its resources are finite. The High Court hearing is a reflection of this increasing awareness.

Helen, Janet and Greg, July 1983

(This up-date was written from information supplied by Rod Blakers, Peter Bosworth, Mick Brown, Peter Brown, Bob Burton, Fred Duncan, Chris Harris, Rhys Jones, Jamie Kirkpatrick, National Parks and Wildlife Service, The Nomenclature Board, Frank Podger, Don Ranson, Randolph Rose, Roy Swain and Bob Tyson. Our thanks also to Alan Gray and the Tasmanian Wilderness Society.)

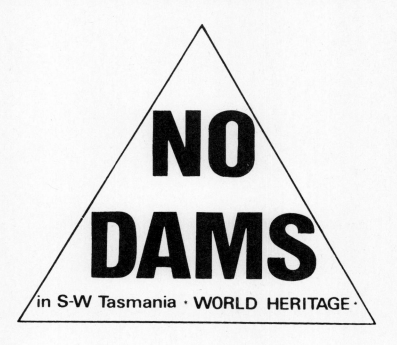

NO DAMS in S-W Tasmania · WORLD HERITAGE ·

Professor W D Jackson

Introduction

This book brings together information about South-West Tasmania from a diversity of sources. Chapters have been written by people familiar with particular aspects. Each has presented a facet or a viewpoint which is not only a personalised account but is often individualistic. However, the wide range of views presented prevents the book being cast with any particular slant. It is not a conservation book striving to deliver a message; rather it is an effort to portray the many attributes, tangible and intangible, the fact, the myth and the legend which draw us to this land.

'Like a flood on the moon', is one of the impressions I remember from a fellow walker on our first view over the Sentinels. The landscapes of the South-West are so different that the viewer gropes for expression. He has no comparisons: so flat, so vast the valleys, so steep and jagged the ranges, so smoothed the hills, so contorted the rocks, so soft the mists, so still, so barren.

This distinction from other Australian landscapes is due to the great geological age of the area, its resistant quartzitic rocks with their refolded and sheared structures, the extensive glaciation in the recent geological past, and its very low fertility. In the South-West the ranges sweep like bent saws around the landscape, rising without foothills from the smooth, brown plains. The white glistening rock, the bare, barren slopes and the jagged strata forming the peaks, make the scene totally unlike that in the dolerite mountains to the south-east. The landscapes of the South-West are formed in Precambrian sediments laid down more than 700 million years ago. The sediments have been modified by heat and pressure into quartzites and schists and episodes of mountain building have thrown these strata into great folds. The present mountains are formed of the resistant strata left after erosion by water, and ice has removed the softer phyllites. The erosion of the intensely folded sediments leaves sweeping valleys and rugged mountain chains broken and sheared so that the strata stand on edge to rake the sky. The area has been glaciated to low altitudes in the recent phases of the Pleistocene, accounting for the jagged profiles of the mountains and the smoothed landforms in the valleys where extensive sheets of outwash gravels have been deposited. During the glaciation small snowfields carved out dozens of cirques. Many of these now carry rock basin lakes hidden between the peaks of the ranges.

One is apt to get the impression from visits to the South-West that the fury of the sea is only equalled by the roughness of the coast. While this impression is certainly an overgeneralization, it must be admitted that the usual sea is impressive, and that most of the coastline is wild by accepted standards. A 'Southerly Buster' is an emotional experience of the first magnitude. There are some fine sandy beaches, but much of the coastline is a succession of rocky headlands and deep gulches, punctuated at intervals with extensive inlets or promontories with sea cliffs. These landforms are those generated by the submersion of a rough terrain. During the glaciation the coastline was 20 to 50 km further out to sea. At the close of the glaciation the sea level gradually rose, drowning the landscape till the sea reached the present relatively stable level some 8,000 years ago. The drowning of river valleys accounts for the two major rias, Port Davey — Bathurst Harbour and Macquarie Harbour, as well as inlets such as Recherche and New River Lagoon. The many islands off the coast, such as the Maatsuyker group, are the tops of hills of the former landscape.

Tasmania lies on the edge of that zone of prevailing winds known as the Roaring Forties. This zonal wind sweeping the southern ocean brings a cool wet climate of misty rain and frequent storms. South-West Tasmania shares this climate with the southern island of New Zealand and Chile, together forming a mere 6% of the earth's surface at this southern latitude. The uniform climate dominated by the marine influence favours the development of evergreen temperate rainforest. The parallelism in the forests of these lands is remarkable. The dominant antarctic beeches of the genus *Nothofagus* are closely related as are many of the subordinate trees and shrubs. The parallelism extends down to the insects, ferns and lower plants such as the epiphytic mosses, liverworts and fungi.

Only in the summer months of January and February does the South-West escape appreciably from the grip of the rainbearing winds which bring an annual rainfall of up to three metres to the mountain areas.

The high rainfall and cool temperature, as well as favouring rainforests and other dense plant growth where there is suitable nutrition, favours the development of peat-forming communities in infertile regions. Much of the South-West is low in plant nutrients and the vegetation tends to non-forest, acid communities such as sedgeland and heath. These communities engender the formation of peaty soils, with acid ground water. The tea-brown water of the creeks, rivers and lakes is typical of the South-West.

Because the rocks of the Precambrian strata were hard, highly siliceous and contained few minerals which break down to form clay, the soils which have been formed since the glaciation are very thin and infertile. This infertility limits vegetation to those species which can recover quickly after being burnt. In the high rainfall the steep slopes lose most of the plant nutrients following fire. Hence the steep northerly slopes of the ranges carry denuded sedgelands of button-grass (*Gymnoschoenus sphaerocephalus*) and low heathy plant communities. In contrast, the southern and eastern slopes, which are seldom burnt, carry pockets of dense thicket rainforest dominated by myrtle beech (*Nothofagus cunninghamii*), leather-wood (*Eucryphia lucida*) and celery - top pine (*Phyllocladus aspleniifolius*). In regions of intermediate fire frequency dense wet scrubs of horizontal (*Anodopetalum biglandulosum*), bauera (*Bauera rubioides*) and tea-tree (*Leptospermum* spp.) form a closed cover.

The heathy button-grass sedgelands make the South-West ideal walking country. In the summer the sedgeland is bright with flowers and the peaty soil is springy underfoot. The wet scrub on the margins of the forests and in dissection gullies is the most difficult travelling. Here visibility is restricted by the dense poles of tea-tree, *Melaleuca,* and *Agastachys,* the endemic white waratah. The lower scrub on margins of the button-grass is dominated by the notorious *Bauera.* This plant, with its attractive rose-like flowers, can provide even more difficulty for the bushwalker than its cousin, the horizontal. It forms a wiry mass of decumbent, intertwined stems scrambling through the erect shrubs. It is usually wise to avoid the strenuous exercise known as 'bauera bashing', trusting to the old adage about the longer way round. There are patches in Western Tasmania where a couple of kilometres may be counted as good travelling in one day.

The inhospitable climate and rugged terrain discouraged human settlement. The climate is unsuitable for agricultural crops and the sedgelands are too sclerotic and deficient in nutrients for grazing exploitations. The settlements established for the extraction of Huon pine and whaling did not form the nucleus for continued land settlement. In 1821 Macquarie Harbour was chosen as an outpost detention centre for the most difficult convicts. The men were employed cutting Huon pine and boat building. Supply from Hobart Town was slow and unreliable, causing the settlement to frequently run short of food. The windy, wet climate affected the minds of the convicts. Murder among the prisoners was a common event and many attempted to escape. Those that did not return to face the lash mostly died in the dense rainforest. The settlement was closed in 1834.

Around 1850 whaling was established along the South-West Coast and at Port Davey, following the decline of whale numbers along the East Coast. By the 1870's Port Davey had a sizable, if scattered, population. Whaling was declining and most were 'piners' with declared stakes over sections of the swamp forests on the banks of the rivers.

The close of the century, from 1870 on, saw the migration of men to the mineral fields north of Macquarie Harbour with the successive discoveries of gold, silver, lead, tin and copper. The South-West soon became empty and forgotten in the furore of the mining boom. The bauera, cutting grass, tea-tree and horizontal gradually closed in over the tracks making access slow and difficult. With the passage of time most of the evidence of human endeavour disappeared.

For a considerable period the South-West was visited only by a few fishermen and trappers. Tin mining in the Cox Bight area eventually brought Charles King as a permanent resident. A summer influx of hardy bushwalkers, prepared to tackle the week's walk from Kallista and carry sufficient food for the return, made the Kings' homestead at Melaleuca their goal. Most of the southern quarter of inland Tasmania appeared on the maps of the time as a large blank space with the printed invitation 'unexplored country'. Three dotted lines suggested the routes of the tracks from Kallista, Judbury and Cockle Creek. Tracks were also marked down the Weld and the Denison Plains but no longer existed.

Interest in the South-West increased gradually after the war as the fishing industry moved to these stormy waters. Forestry roads in the Arve and the Florentine reduced the overland distance, and light planes with longer range than the old Tiger Moths started to ferry passengers to Lake Pedder and Cox Bight. The South-West was becoming accessible to more than the experienced bushmen.

Professor Jackson (right) with a group of his students on a Field Botany excursion in the Florentine Valley.

Julian Gardner

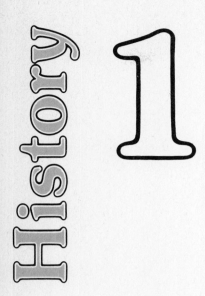

H M Gee

History 1

The Aborigines roamed freely the coastal fringe of the South-West for thousands of years. Then the whiteman came and termed it uninhabitable; a Transylvania in the Southern Ocean; today it is 'a wilderness'. The Tasmanian Aborigines were not able to withstand the aggressive habits of the European settlers and the disease which marked their arrival. The exploitative attitude that now threatens this wild land has its historical echo.

Contrasting with today's technological advances, the bushmen of the past carried on their backs enough to sustain them as they explored and worked in isolation. Their many tracks, cut with such effort, were soon overgrown and their settlements reverted to forest, creating the illusion that here was an untrodden land.

Opposite page
Symbol of the determination to save Lake Pedder, a bust of Truganini, last of the Tasmanian Aborigines, was set into the sands of Pedder close to Maria Creek in March 1972. The effigy looked west over the lake and drowned with the beach later that year. *Geoff Parr*

The inscription read:

Truganini 1803 – 1876
'When we reflect on the beauty and dignity of Truganini we must deplore the destruction of her people. Let us then reflect on the beauty of this lake, dedicate it to the memory of Truganini and her people, and resolve to keep it unspoiled for the benefit of mankind.'

George Augustus Robinson, the first whiteman to walk the south and west coasts on his mission to the Port Davey and Macquarie Harbour tribes in 1830 and 1832 respectively. It is his journals which provide the most information on the Aborigines who inhabited the South-West. *Tasmanian Museum & Art Gallery*

Aboriginal Man

H M Gee

Helen Gee graduated in Arts from the University of Tasmania in 1971. Her wide-ranging interests and activities have taken her to the remoter regions of Tasmania and to several other countries. In 1975 she assisted Dr R Vanderwal in his archaeological investigation at Louisa Bay before working as a site recorder for the Australian Institute of Aboriginal Studies, with the National Parks and Wildlife Service of Tasmania. Convinced of the need for this book Helen concentrated her efforts in 1976 and 1977 on its compilation and production. She is Chairman of the Tasmanian Wilderness Society.

Man inhabited the South-West wilderness one hundred and fifty years ago in what were the last days of an era which extended back perhaps 20,000 years. Some 20,000 years ago the sea level was more than 100 metres below the present, so that a continuous wide corridor of land was exposed on the Bassian floor — the corridor more than 60 kms wide. Around 13,000 years ago the end of the Ice Age caused the sea level to rise. The Aborigines marooned in Tasmania were wholly isolated for a longer period than any other human society.

The tribes whose territory lay within the South-West were largely independent and in 1815 James Kelly described them as 'a much finer race of men than those to the eastward and northward'. The Aborigines were confined mostly to the exposed sea coast, and the skill with which they travelled through their rugged habitat suggests great powers of observation. Indeed, their adaptation to their harsh environment demonstrates intelligent behaviour not often acknowledged by Europeans.

The sources of information about the south-western tribes are few. The records of the explorers, notably the Frenchmen Peron and Labillardière, contain references to sightings of Aborigines and their fires along the coast and on the islands. Furneaux, in command of Cook's ship *Adventure*, made the first British visit to Tasmania. The second lieutenant, James Burney, led the first visit ashore at a point on the south coast which appears from his journal to be Rocky Boat Harbour, east of Prion Bay. In his journal entry for 11th March 1773, Burney records:

'The first thing we saw when we climbed up was a heap of wood ashes, the remains of a fire which had been kindled there and a great number of Pearl Scallop shells. We saw no inhabitants, there was a very good path leading into the woods which would probably have led us to some of their huts, but we could not stay to walk up, the wind coming too fresh...'.

In 1789 J H Cox went ashore in a bay which has since been named Cox Bight. He and his party noted the crude huts and deposits of oyster and scallop shells situated near an abundance of fresh water. The natives remained out of sight on that occasion also, but twenty five years later James Kelly was received in a friendly manner by a large number of natives when he went ashore at Louisa Bay. Five miles south of Low Rocky Point, Kelly met with two Aborigines who were alarmed at seeing him...

'They were above six feet high, their stomachs very large, legs and arms very thin and seemed as if they were nearly starved'.

George Augustus Robinson spent nearly six years in the bush among the Aborigines. His expedition to the south-western tribes was undertaken in 1830 and a second, to the Macquarie Harbour region, in the summer of 1832—1833. *Friendly Mission: The Tasmanian Journals and Papers of George Augustus Robinson; 1829—1834,* contains ethnographic material fundamental to the study of the prehistory of the South-West.

Of the Port Davey natives, Robinson wrote:

'They were fine looking men, about five feet nine inches in height and several of them six feet, well proportioned, broad shouldered, their features resembling that of the European, intelligent countenances and the beard like that of the Poland Jew, growing long and to a point— moustaches gave them a truly majestic appearance'.

Some of the early surveyors penetrating the South-West encountered signs of Aboriginal occupation. In 1832 W S Sharland saw signs of a recent burn on the Loddon Plains. J E Calder found some recently occupied huts near Frenchmans Cap in 1840. But the opportunity to learn of these people directly was soon to be lost.

Today a number of sites are known to exist along the southern and western coastlines. There are middens, caves and rock art sites of much intrigue to the bushwalker, the fisherman, the miner and the archaeologist.

Food resources

Much of the South-West is inimical to the hunter-gatherer. Behind the narrow coastal platform the land rises rapidly to rugged mountain ranges in excess of 1,300m. Robinson was assured that no natives went inland beyond the Arthur Ranges. The vegetation of the coast consists of sedgeland with patches of rainforest in protected areas. The Aborigines successfully coped with an annual rainfall of over 2500mm and the westerly gales and swells along the exposed and rocky coast. Here their major food resources were available: shellfish, crayfish, fur and elephant seal, mutton birds and their eggs, and penguins. On the coastal plains there were wallabies, marsupial carnivores and wombats, birds and their eggs as well as freshwater crustacea, goannas and lizards. Snakes and eels may have been eaten though there is no record of this. In 1815 Kelly observed the natives at Louisa Bay *'puling Vermin by handfulls from their Heads and Beards and Eating them which they seemed to Enjoy.'* At Port Davey Robinson remarked that *'the natives often kill the native cat when in the act of eating its prey'.* There is no ethnographic observation of an Aborigine cooking or eating scale fish.

Vegetable foods are less abundant than elsewhere in the island, but fern roots, seaweeds, berries and fruits are among the edible native plants. Robinson learnt about various berries that were eaten:

'Among them were the native currant, of white colour and pleasant flavour... as well as a small red berry called BORE.RAR by the southern natives... and a native plum called LAY.LUE BER.RY'.

In 1834 James Backhouse produced a list of edible and indigenous vegetables of Tasmania, including descriptions of those the Aborigines ate as well as the way they prepared and cooked them. In 1910 F Noetling attempted an analysis of the diet using secondary sources (mainly Ling Roth), concluding that it was a diet *'in excess of protein and greatly deficient in carbohydrates'.* Noetling saw their existence as a permanent struggle to satisfy the craving of the body for carbohydrates. In a study published in 1967 Betty Hiatt found no major differences between the diet content in the eastern and western areas of Tasmania though there were probably

7

Hanging Lake and Federation Peak

differences in the quantities each item contributed to the total diet. Hiatt compiled the following table from information on record.

SOUTH-WEST COAST DIET

Food Categories	No. of Observations	Percentage of Total Observations
Macropods	5	19
Wombats	7	27
Seals	1	4
Marine Crustacea	3	12
Freshwater Crustacea	1	4
Marine Mollusca	4	15
Vegetables	5	19
Total	**26**	**100**

'The south-west coast in this table is that area south of (and including) Macquarie Harbour down to (and including) Prion Bay on the south coast. There is no problem about how far inland the area goes as there are no observations between the coastal and estuarine regions on the south-west coast and the Derwent River in the east'.

Robinson frequently noted that the men engaged in hunting and the women in fishing. Labillardière related that the men remained near the fire feasting on the best parts of the meal, often while the women were still gathering. The women carried spears and game, all chattels and children; and in an unexpected storm they were observed to build huts over the men where they sat down!

When the Aborigines were hunting wallaby much shouting and noise ensued. At the head of Macquarie Harbour Robinson observed the manoeuvring of kangaroo into a river or lagoon where natives waited to spear them or pull them down to drown them. Frequently, stakes two feet in length were placed in the ground for the purpose of impaling wallaby. Another method of procuring game was to tie tussocks together causing the animal to stumble, impeding its escape from the pursuers.

The women foraged in the water around the rocks for abalone, crayfish, turbo, limpets and bivalves. Robinson observed them standing on the rocks in rather an erotic position and chanting a song before diving in to gather shellfish. They usually carried woven baskets. As protection against the cold they greased their bodies with the fat of seal, whale, mutton bird, or macropod. Fat, when mixed with powdered charcoal and ochre certainly satisfied a love of ornamentation, but more importantly it enabled them to resist the rigours of climate and the chill southern ocean. The natives dived for ochre at Point Hibbs and Robinson also learned that they went to Cox Bight for red ochre. The location of this quarry is uncertain but there is excellent ochre at nearby Louisa Bay.

Seals were greatly prized both for their fat and the feast they provided. Robinson's journals contain several accounts of seal hunts. This one refers to the natives of Louisa Bay:

'Woorady said that the Needwonne subsisted in a great measure on the seal of which they were very fond. Said that the blacks was frequently attacked by the seal ... bitten on the arm, leg, thigh and dragged into the water'.

The seals, cut into strips, were dragged along to the fires where the natives grilled them for eating.

Mobility

Woorady was a valued companion, guide and informant to Robinson. He came from the Bruny tribe and related the exploits of his 'nation' and those of neighbouring nations such as the Needwonne. These nations made trips to Eddystone Rock, adjacent to Pedra Branca, which is fifteen miles off the coast. It is certain that the Aborigines visited Maatsuyker and De Witt Islands, seven and four miles respectively off the south coast. Matthew Flinders noted that the scrub had been burnt and other explorers saw smoke there. Today middens on Maatsuyker testify to their visits. On some of these trips of great enterprise many natives were lost. According to Woorady:

'Their catamarans was large, the size of a whaleboat, carrying seven or eight people, their dogs and spears. The men sit in front and the women behind'.

Robinson thought these canoes to be ingeniously constructed:

'....when properly made they are perfectly safe and able to brave a rough sea. They cannot sink from the buoyancy of the material and the way in which they are constructed prevents them from upsetting'.

Labillardière described native rafts made of thick bundles of bark fastened together by fibrous grasses. The soft, buoyant bark of the tea-tree was used. Long sticks or spears, or bark paddles, propelled the canoe or catamaran but on some occasions females were seen swimming on either side. Robinson was transported across many of the west coast rivers like this. Such craft were used extensively on the south and west coasts of Tasmania.

Technology

With minimum labour aboriginal man adapted natural forms for functional purposes. Large shells served as drinking vessels; implements of stone, wood and bone had their specific uses. Stone tools such as scrapers, cutters, chisels, borers and grinders were used in

The Conciliation, a painting by Benjamin Duterrau, 1836. Robinson depicted with the Tasmanian Aborigines on his 'Friendly Mission'.
Tasmanian Museum & Art Gallery

the preparation of food, the skinning of animals, the manufacture of weapons and the shaving of hair and beards. Ground-edge implements were not known in Tasmania, nor did the implements have wooden handles. Large water-worn pebbles were employed as ochre mills and pounders for shellfish. Baskets, usually of woven native grasses, were frequently mentioned by Robinson:

'In a basket was the claws of some animal, which had been made into beads, and some yellow ochre'.

Thin tea-tree stems were sharpened and hardened by fire for use as lance-like spears. Though simple, this basic material culture supplied the necessities of life.

Along the west coast, between Macquarie Harbour and Port Davey, Robinson saw numerous traps made by the natives for catching crows and ducks:

'The natives erect a kind of hut with grass under which they lay concealed. In front on a rock they place some fish, fastened by stone, and when the crows come to feed they do nothing more than put out their hand and pull them in. They adopt the same plan for catching ducks except that they bait with worms'.

Robinson also mentions what appears to have been a cage trap. The birds entered a 'hut' from which they could not escape. These crow traps of the south-western tribes are the only ones known to have been made by Tasmanian Aborigines.

But their most powerful tool was fire. Contrary to former belief that aboriginal man made little impact on the environment, recent work by anthropologists and botanists suggests that the aboriginal technology had enormous ecological effects. Hunting and gathering made less impact than did fire. Several explorers noted the smoke of bushfires. Kelly, on his voyage from Port Davey to Macquarie Harbour in 1815, noted that the whole coast was on fire; yet the Aborigines appeared to have had no artificial means of producing fire. If their own fire was extinguished it had to be obtained from other natives, if need be from another tribe. It was usual for a lighted fire-brand to be carried, and as the band travelled they would set fire here and there. Tasmanian botanists (Gilbert 1959, Davies 1964, Jackson 1965) have explained the relationship between the vegetation pattern and the fire-lighting activities of the Aborigines as a very close one. A long history of firing has reduced much of the *Nothofagus* dominated rainforest, through a mixed eucalypt-rainforest phase to scrub, and eventually to heath and sedgeland. Prehistorian Rhys Jones regards the coastal sedgeland of western Tasmania as a human artefact formed over thousands of years of constant firing. Burning of the bush was fun, particularly

PLATE 2(A)

Robinson's sketches showing structure of catamaran (see journal, 15 February 1830).

(Mitchell Library.)

This is the craft that carried Robinson across Hannants Inlet, Port Davey, on 15 February, 1830. *Mitchell Library*

in a cold climate and smoke from the fires of other groups communicated their whereabouts, facilitating contact— peaceful or warlike. Removal of scrub made travelling easier; the speed with which Robinson travelled north from Port Davey is evidence of extensive clearing for a native track maintained by regular firing. Hunting was often carried out in conjunction with fire, a sure trap. Regrowth of grasses, young ferns, shoots and leaves in a burnt area attracted animals. Through firing, the Aborigine was increasing his food supply and, particularly in South-West Tasmania, extending his natural habitat by removing the difficult rainforest and replacing it by sedgeland relatively rich in both animal and plant food. Jones refers to this firing activity, whether deliberate or accidental, as 'fire-stick farming'.

Shelter

The Aborigines of the South-West had more substantial shelters than those of the milder east, which is not surprising considering the severe climatic conditions with which they had to contend.

The major food resources of these Aborigines were coastal, and shellfish were readily available. The warrener, or turbo shells (above) and the abalone shells (below) are predominant in midden remains. *Sketches by Janet Fenton*

Tasmanian fur seal, drawn by Jane Burrell. A lively account of a seal hunt was recorded by James Kelly in his journal for January 1816: 'The women lying down on the rocks with their clubs went throught the same motions as the seal, holding up their left elbow and scratching themselves with their left hand... imitating every movement as nearly as possible. After they had lain upon the rocks for nearly an hour... all of a sudden the women rose up in their seats, and, their clubs lifted up at arms length, each struck the seals on the nose and killed him.' From *Captain James Kelly of Hobart Town*, by K M Bowden, 1964, p. 41.

Robinson saw 'upwards of one hundred huts' along the south coast, and frequently passed villages on the west coast. One hut like many that he saw was ten feet by ten feet at the base and seven feet in height. It was:

'in the form of a circular dome and stuck full of cockatoo feathers. The door or entrance was a small hole about a foot wide by two feet high'.

Sometimes huts were lined with tea-tree bark, sometimes with bird feathers, or lined with grass and covered with bark outside. The circular frame was constructed by placing sticks in the ground and bending them over to the ground again. The sticks intersected above the centre of the hut and long grass was placed over this framework. Members of a tribal band lived in a small village consisting of several of these huts situated near fresh water and a good foraging area. Shelter from the brunt of the westerly storms, and proximity to fuel supplies were also important considerations. Robinson often observed the native fig growing close to these huts, and indeed it is logical that the seeds of edible fruits would regenerate where they were discarded and fertilised.

Circular depressions on and near the rocky foreshore of the west coast have been recorded. Their size and proximity to fresh water suggests that they may be hut sites as described by Robinson. One site includes a dozen or more circular depressions situated beside a creek flowing into a sheltered cove that abounds with abalone and crayfish.

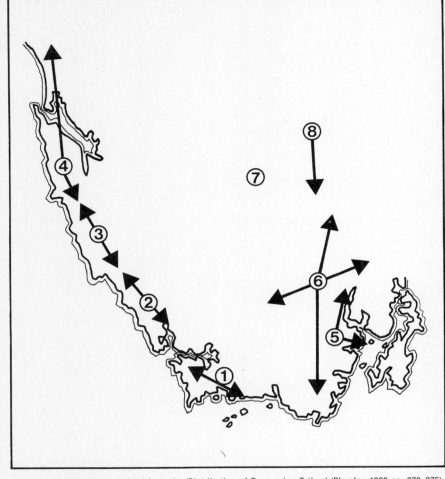

A regional construction derived from the 'Distribution of Tasmanian Tribes' (Plomley 1966 pp. 970–975).

Towterer, the native chief of the Port Davey tribe, at time of contact. From a pencil and wash portrait by William Buelow Gould. *Mitchell Library*

A range of Aboriginal stone implements photographed at Birthday Bay on the west coast. Some of this stone was locally quarried while some of the implements were acquired from extensive forrays as far afield as Cape Grim. The ruler shows measurement in inches. *Peter C Sims*

Midden deposits of bones, shells and stone occur in association with these sites.

Tribal Groups

Robinson intended to draw a map of the island based on Aboriginal principles showing sub-divisions into districts and containing many 'nations'. Unfortunately he never did so, but throughout his journals he made mention of tribal localities. The regional map indicates distribution of tribes in South-West Tasmania as listed by Plomley.

MAP NO.	TRIBAL NAME	TRIBAL COUNTRY
1.	NEED.WON.EE	Cox Bight
2.	NINE.NE	North-west of Port Davey
3.	LOW.REEN.NE) LOW.REEN.NER) LOWREN)	Low Rocky Point
4. a.	MIME.GIN	Macquarie Harbour Heads
. b.	LOW.REN.TOM.MER.NING	MEEBERLEE (Macquarie Harbour)
5.	LY.LUE.QUON.NY	Port d'Entrecasteaux — Huon River
6. a.	Many tribes assigned	Southern Tasmania, South Coast
. b.	to same general area	West Huon River, Head of Huon River, West Ouse River, Northern Arthur Mts
7. c.	BRAYL.WUN.YER	Peak of Teneriffe (Wylds Craig)
8. d.	LAR.MAIR.RE.ME.NER	Northern Arthur Mts

Aboriginal hut as constructed on the south and west coasts of Tasmania.   *Peter Murray*

Tasmanian bark canoe. Sketch by D Colbron Pearse from a model. Such craft, made from bundles of soft, buoyant tea-tree bark were used only on the south and west coasts. *Tasmanian Museum & Art Gallery*

Seasonal Movements

The seasonal movements of these tribes and their political relationships have been dealt with by Rhys Jones in his doctoral thesis, *Rocky Cape and the Problem of the Tasmanians*, which analyses Tasmanian social units, defining the tribe, the band and the family: 'The tribe consisted of a number of bands whose territories were contiguous.' Jones regarded the band as being the basic social unit, owning territory, the core of which was often a prominent geographical location and foraging zone. Boundaries coincided with well marked geographical features such as rivers and lagoons. These band territories became the 'country' of the band it belonged to. The leader, or chief of a band was a mature or old man, a great fighter with considerable powers. In the territory extending along the south-west coast from Macquarie Harbour to South Cape there were at least four bands and Jones estimates that they were comprised of between 200 and 350 Aborigines.

'Movement was mostly parallel to the coast along well defined foot paths, and huts were numerous along these. Rivers and harbours were crossed by means of bark catamarans. Young females towed Robinson across the Giblin. Two routes afforded short-cuts away from the coast. One led from the head of Elliott Bay near Low Rocky Point in a northerly direction inland to Birches Inlet in the south-eastern corner of Macquarie Harbour. This ran in a funnel between two areas of rain forest, and it is likely that Aboriginal fire pressure helped to form or at least enlarge and maintain this disclimax. The other was from Cox Bight across a neck of land to Bathurst Harbour, an inner part of Port Davey, thus avoiding the necessity of going around the exposed south-western corner of Tasmania.

Access away from the region was either to the north across Macquarie Heads or to the east hugging the coast past South East Cape to Recherche Bay. There were no routes leading inland across the mountains to central and eastern Tasmania and Robinson was told the Aborigines did not go there.

Outside their tribal territory the bands of the South-West had close relationships with their neighbours to the north, particularly with the people living between Macquarie Harbour and the Arthur River. They crossed Macquarie Harbour Heads by catamaran, and travelled regularly as far north as Mt Cameron West and possibly Cape Grim. Between March 1830 and July 1832, the Port Davey Nine.ne had made this journey several times, visiting and exchanging gossip with all the bands along the route. Some people probably also visited parts of the north coast, the Low Rocky Point people having a name for Table Cape. At the beginning of September 1832, some Port Davey people were at the Arthur River together with Pieman River and Sandy Cape Aborigines; and it is likely that these journeys were not made during the coldest parts of the year.

To the south-east they travelled along the south coast to Cox Bight where they obtained ochre. At least since the advent of Pax Britannica, some Port Davey people visited Port Esperance to the south-west of the Huon Estuary, and even Bruny Island, though the extent of such journeys in pre-contact times is not known. During the summer months, they crossed over in their catamarans to the Maatsuyker and De Witt Islands to hunt seals.

During the course of a year the Port Davey band, or at least a substantial segment of it, would travel from Recherche Bay or the Maatsuyker Islands in the south, to Mt Cameron West or Cape Grim in the north. Taking a line along the coast these points are some 250 miles apart from each other, and give an idea of the scale of seasonal movements of the south-western bands.

During their sealing voyages to the Maatsuyker Islands they sometimes met Bruny Islanders and other south eastern bands. Although there were some seasonal contacts between the two groups, some people who were able to converse with each other, and some cultural traits in common, there were also major differences in material culture, speech, economy and political relationships. The rugged country of the extreme south coast between Cox Bight and Recherche Bay was an important cultural boundary. Looking further east, there was no contact between the south-western people and those from the southern midlands or Oyster Bay. Mannalargenna from the central east coast could neither speak nor understand the Port Davey language, neither could "Black Richard", probably Drue.rer.-tat.te.nan.ne from Ben Lomond.

The South-West was a natural barrier for the Big River Tribe. This barrier extended along the western side of the Derwent Valley, the Florentine Valley and Lake King William. Robinson gives little information for this locality. The vegetation pattern in the Florentine and other valleys to the south-west of the Derwent suggests that at least periodic excursions were made into these densely wooded valleys though the mountain ranges here marked the limit of their occupation'.

Mythology

The Bruny natives who accompanied Robinson communicated quite fluently with the Toogee of the South-West which is consistent with the account of seasonal movement along the south coast. They shared the same customs in the burning of their dead and the possession of relics of the dead. Ashes of the cremated were often carried in a kangaroo skin laced with sinew. The Bruny natives told mythical stories of the exploits of the Toogee Low (Port Davey tribe) and of spirits who were reputed to live in their land. Woorady gave what Robinson believed to be the traditional account of how and where the first 'black man' came from, and other legends believed by the natives along the south and west coasts. Robinson noted the profound attention the other natives paid to Woorady, and the assent they gave him.

Woorady told of a spirit called Moinee (sometimes written 'Moihernee') who, like Milton's Lucifer, was hurled down from heaven after a fight with Dromerdeem (Dromenerdeene). Moinee dwelt on the land at Louisa Bay. His wife followed him and dwelt in the sea. The subsequent children of Moinee 'came down in the rain and went into the wife's womb and afterwards they had plenty of children.' Woorady related how 'Moinee cut the ground and made the rivers, cut the land and made the islands.' Moinee also fought with devils, and when he died he turned into stone which, it was alleged, is standing at Cox Bight 'in his own country'.

Robinson also recorded the story of the creation of man:

'Woorady said that Moihernee (Moinee) made natives, that the devils stopped in the ground and that Moihernee took him out of the ground and made Parlevar (man); that when he was first made he had a tail and no joints in his legs, that he could not sit down and always stood erect, that Dromerdeem saw him and cut off his tail, rubbed grease over the wound and cured it and made joints to his knees and told Parlevar to sit down on the ground, that Parlevar sat down and said, it was nyerrae good, very good'.

One of the devils, an evil spirit of the Toogee, and perhaps the most frightening, was Wraggeowrapper. They said he was:

'like a black man only very big and ugly ... he travels like the wind, he comes and watches the natives all night and before daylight comes he goes away like swift wind'.

Woorady saw the first ships come to Van Diemen's Land and the natives, much afeared, associated them with this devil, Wraggeowrapper. When Frenchmen landed at Recherche and carved on a tree there, the Aborigines called the strange markings 'Wraggeowrapper', presumably seeing them as his work. According to Robinson the natives had a traditional belief that Wraggeowrapper caused the 'loathsome distemper' or skin infection that they suffered.

After European contact new beliefs were incorporated into the old framework. The Bruny natives said that the sun, the moon, and seals too, came from England — England being a very distant place across the sea. In explanation of the disappearance of the Needwonne natives, they believed these people had made large catamarans and sailed to England. En route:

'Parlevar sleep plenty of night at sea, lost plenty of days, there was big wind and big sea, they see plenty of seal'.

These were some of the intriguing tales told to Robinson as he lay, covered in vermin, sharing food and fire with the Aborigines. He noted their great conviviality on occasions, and their singing and dancing were apparently quite boisterous. Of the Port Davey natives Robinson said: 'they are certainly the best dancers of any aborigines I have yet seen.' He described their agility in bounding from one position to another: 'The whole body was in motion, eyes acting their part also.' They sang during the dance to regulate their motions. Many more details of the customs of these bands, of their marriages and alliances, are contained in Robinson's work, especially the journals of his second and sixth expeditions.

Extinction

The west coast tribes were the last to feel the effects of European occupation. Robinson's journal tells us of his unique contact with the South-West and its inhabitants in their natural state. When he set out on his expedition to conciliate the Port Davey natives he sincerely believed that what he was doing was for their own good, yet his efforts hastened their extinction, for by 1834 he had all but a few west coast Aborigines placed in government settlements. In a letter to the Colonial Secretary on 31 May, 1833, Robinson, after reporting the capture of twelve Aborigines of the Port Davey tribe, wrote:

'These Aborigines being removed, there now remains of this tribe only six adults. I shall proceed forthwith in quest of those individuals, after which my operations will be directed towards two other tribes in the vicinity of Macquarie Harbour Heads, which are the only Aborigines now at large, and I earnestly trust that a short period may suffice for the accomplishment of this much desired purpose'.

In June 1833 the whole of the Port Davey tribe was removed and Robinson completed his work in the South-West on his expedition to Macquarie Harbour in August 1834. *'It cannot hereafter be said,'* wrote Robinson, *'that those people were harshly treated ... that they were forced from their country'.* He believed he had removed them from danger to a suitable asylum for their moral and religious benefit. Constant and strenuous exertion had made these people hardy and healthy. Confined and regularly fed they lost motivation and vigour. Elsewhere in Tasmania conflict followed the territorial aggression involved in colonial settlement. However when Governor Arthur placed the Aborigines of Tasmania under Martial Law he excluded those of the western and south-western part of the island, an area he considered to be bounded by the Huon River and the Peak of Teneriffe (Wylds Craig), and the extreme Western Bluff (Frenchmans Cap). Robinson claimed to have effected an 'amicable understanding' with these Aborigines, but the understanding was all his own. White man was a force beyond their control and beyond their powers of rationality. So quite naturally they linked this threat with their fear of the darkness which held Wraggeowrapper. Both restrained their liberty.

Rhys Jones states the four major causes of extinction as being ecological dislocation, the raids for women practised freely by sealers and other white men, the spread of infectious diseases and the low fertility rate of the Aborigines.

The ecological base of the Aboriginal economy was not disrupted within the South-West, though in the settled areas change was severe. That infection spread along the south coast is almost certain and the Needwonne band may have succumbed in this manner. The modern diagnosis is of viral respiratory infection followed by complication of a bacterial nature. Robinson describes two epidemics in detail. Out of sixteen healthy members of the Point Hibbs and Macquarie Harbour band five were dead within a few days, simply due to a lack of resistance to European infection. By the early eighteen thirties it was only among the west coast bands that there were babies and pregnant women. Many deaths had occurred among the Port Davey natives in 1829, yet the number of huts Robinson noted on the south coast, as well as Woorady's testament, indicates that a relatively large population was there prior to European settlement in Tasmania.

Truganini, close companion of Robinson on his visits to the South-Western tribes, died in 1876. She is reputed to have been the last full-blooded Tasmanian Aborigine.
Tasmanian Museum & Art Gallery

Brian Hamilton

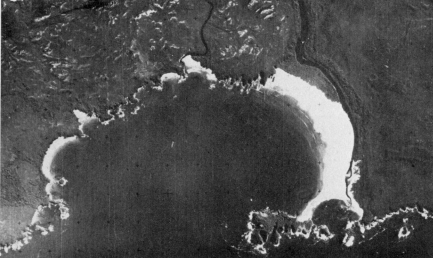

Above.

Little systematic study has been carried out within the South-West. Numerous observations of middens, caves with occupational debris, and circular depressions (probably hut sites), and some rock art have been made by visitors to the area in recent years. Once these sites have been disturbed they lose their potential for scientific investigation. Few foreshore middens have escaped the severe erosion caused by strong winds and high seas, illustrated by this eroded midden at Birthday Bay on the west coast. One Tasmanian who has located and recorded sites, particularly along the west coast, is Peter Sims. He has led five expeditions to the South-West. More recently the Australian Institute of Aboriginal Studies has recorded coastal sites with a view to their protection. *Peter C Sims*

Rhys Jones, referring to archaeological work in Tasmania, says that:

'It is one of the main aims to take the ethnographically documented tribal geography back into the past and thus analyse the course and causes of its history'.

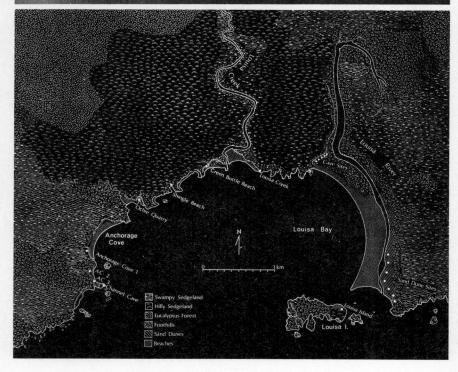

Pre-History and the Archaeology of Louisa Bay

R L Vanderwal

Ron Vanderwal arrived in Australia from the West Indies in 1969. He received his Ph.D. (1973) from the Australian National University for his work on the prehistory of Central Coastal Papua New Guinea. While archaeologist at the Tasmanian Museum (1973–1976) he carried out a research programme of excavation at Louisa Bay, obtaining the material upon which this chapter is based. Dr Vanderwal joined the Prehistory Department at La Trobe University in 1976.

This is a first statement on the Louisa Bay research programme. The Tasmanian Museum and Art Gallery provided the funds for the field work, and the results of the preliminary faunal analysis are by courtesy of Dr David Horton, Australian Institute of Aboriginal Studies.

The Tasmanian Aborigines had a simple material culture consisting of wooden spears tip-hardened by fire, clubs, simple cloaks made from the skins of wallaby or kangaroo, a small variety of flaked stone implements and crude mortars and pestles for grinding seeds and ochres. Their digging stick may have doubled as a chisel for prizing abalone shells from their rock anchors. String made from vegetable fibre was woven into rope and baskets, and canoes or catamarans were fashioned of bark. Shelter reached its greatest complexity on the west and south coasts.

Subsistence depended on fauna, vegetable resources and on certain produce of the sea excluding all manner of scale fish. Archaeological evidence indicates that this picture has not always been the same. Rhys Jones recorded 8,000 years of prehistory at Rocky Cape in north-west Tasmania where he found that scale fish were abandoned from the diet over 3,000 years ago. Jones also discovered that only slightly earlier, highly distinctive bone points, often made from wallaby fibulae, seem to disappear from the occupational debris.

Sandra Bowdler, working at Hunter Island, has extended the archaeological record for Tasmania backwards 23,000 years to late Pleistocene times when Hunter Island was a hill on the Bassian Plain (inundated by ice-melt to form Bass Strait 8,000 – 10,000 years ago). Bone points exactly similar to those from Rocky Cape were recovered by Bowdler from early Cave Bay Cave levels, dated around 18,000 years ago. And in south-east Tasmania, where some 5,000 – 6,000 years of prehistory have been established, Harry Lourandos also found no remains of scale fish later than 3,000 – 4,000 years ago.

This loss of bone tools and the elimination of scale fish from the diet mid-way through Jones' Rocky Cape sequence led him to the conclusion that the Tasmanian Aborigines were undergoing a process of cultural impoverishment, a function of the isolation imposed by the inundation of the Bassian Plain at the end of the Pleistocene. Jones also suggests that 3 to 4 millennia ago the Aborigines had established, or were fast approaching, homeostasis with their environment; that the population was static or may actually have been decreasing.

However, the results of recent archaeological research in South-West Tasmania suggest an alternative interpretation. In the following pages I present data supporting the hypothesis of a late population increase made possible by a more efficient means of exploiting the environment. This adaptation was almost certainly a cultural one, and I suggest it may have consisted of the recent invention of the distinctively Tasmanian bark canoe. Such an innovation, I argue, would have allowed the habitual exploitation of an area like South-West Tasmania which otherwise might have provided only a very marginal or intermittent subsistence.

Louisa Bay is at the eastern edge of an area circumscribed on the west by the Port Davey-Bathurst Harbour waterway, and on the east by the Ironbound Range. The Bay is 7 km wide and 2.5 km long, bounded at the eastern end by Louisa Island. Louisa River and Louisa Creek are formed by massive drainages off the quartzite hills of the hinterland, while smaller rivulets flow into the Bay at several places. The Louisa Plain is composed mainly of swamp and sedgelands. Stands of trees and shrubs are common in the valleys and similar vegetation forms a barrier between the plains and the coast. Lying off Louisa Bay to the south are De Witt and Maatsuyker Islands, 6.5 and 17 km, respectively, offshore.

The map shows the distribution of archaeological sites at Louisa Bay. Test excavations have been made at sand dune sites at the mouth of the Louisa River, the Louisa River caves (2 localities), Louisa Creek, Anchorage Cove and Maatsuyker Island.

The sand dune sites at the river mouth are in the most archaeologically and visibly spectacular area of Louisa Bay. The dune face is retreating under the attack of south-west winds so that today

Right
Modern reconstruction of an Aboriginal catamaran.   *R L Vanderwal*

OPPOSITE PAGE

Top
Louisa Bay, with its river and offshore islands, was the foraging ground and territory of the Needwone people.   *Jim England*

Middle
Aerial view of Louisa Bay.   *Lands Dept.*

Bottom
Archaeological sites at Louisa Bay.

the dune is in places only a few metres wide. The erosional process has exposed a complete section of the dune nearly one km long, laying bare the depositional history of the site. Archaeological deposits ranging from a few to 40 cm in depth are seen at various places along the section, though at no point is the complete range of depositional history clearly evident. What are revealed instead are localized stable periods followed by epochs of sand redeposition. Occupational deposits are found on some of these former stable surfaces.

Bisecting the dune is a single widespread epoch of a stable ground surface and periods of localized occupation are seen both above and below this major stable period.

Excavation area LR1 is below this stability and LR3 is above. Both are characterized by multiple shell lenses, each only a few centimetres deep. Site LR2 is a shell midden of some 40 cms depth. Though predominantly shell, all the deposits contain artefacts and faunal remains.

The time depth of the sand dunes is not yet known though the presence in LR1 of a wallaby fibula bone point, very similar to those recovered from Rocky Cape and Hunter Island, suggests a minimum date of around 3,500 years before the present. At Rocky Cape scale fish remains are abundantly associated with the bone points, but such remains are not present at any of the Louisa Bay sites. It is of course possible that as a food item scale fish were abandoned in the South-West at a time earlier than in the north-west. On the other hand, the Louisa Bay bone point may be a relict from a more remote past, or perhaps the Rocky Cape chronology does not accurately date the disappearance of this artefact class. As observed earlier, scale fish are seen to disappear in the south-east at a time equivalent to their extinction in the Rocky Cape record, so this date is firm. We can therefore suggest with some confidence that Louisa Bay was settled perhaps 3,000 years ago or less.

The lensing at sites LR1 and LR3 may well represent rather ephemeral occupation, perhaps for the seasonal or occasional exploitation of specific resources such as muttonbirds. The faunal record does include mutton birds: other kinds, probably petrels, are present too. Land fauna consists mainly of pademelon, wallaby and wombat, indicating heavy exploitation of open habitats like those known on the eastern side of the Louisa River. Several species of shellfish are represented, but abalone and warrener predominate.

There are some small caves at Louisa Bay, all containing varying quantities of occupational debris, the greatest depth being about 30 cm. As with the sand dune sites, recovered land faunal remains reveal numbers of pademelon and wallaby, but about half the remains are of ring-tail possums, a closed-habitat animal. People living in the caves would have had equal access to the two environments. Compared with remains from the sand dune sites, there is a lower percentage of mutton bird remains, but this might be expected insofar as the mutton bird habitat of Louisa Island is farther away. Abalone and warrener also occur less frequently in the cave deposits. Consistent with this interpretation is the extremely heavy reliance

Seal vertebra recovered from a Louisa Bay site. *A Moscal*

The wallaby fibula bone point present in the sand dune deposit at Louisa Bay. It is similar to others recovered from Rocky Cape and Hunter Island and is 14–18 cms in length. *A Moscal*

on mussels, probably collected from the brackish waters of Louisa River, only a short distance (several metres) to the east. However, no fewer than 68 shellfish species were recovered from the caves, which suggests that there might have been lean times, and that the caves were occupied during periods of very bad weather. So this dependence on shellfish species not normally eaten may simply reflect extended storm conditions—frequent circumstances in the South-West. The Louisa River Cave 2 deposit has been radiocarbon dated to about 870 years before present.

The Louisa Creek site is similar to the sand dune site. Not only is it being rapidly eroded by wind and storm, but shallow lensing of artefact bearing soils suggests short term occupation—perhaps for the seasonal collection of mussels which formed the major part of the deposit. Land fauna is sparsely represented but the presence of some wallaby bones suggests exploitation of the open habitat of the hinterland. A carbon sample collected from a hearth midway through the deposit was dated at approximately 1,250 years BP.

The Anchorage Cove site, like LR2, is a true midden deposit. It is unstratified and consists of 100 cm of closely packed abalone and warrener shells and, also, seal and land fauna bones. The land species recorded indicate a slightly greater exploitation of closed habitats, as represented by ring-tail possum, bandicoot and tiger cat, although almost equal quantities of pademelon, wallaby and wombat remains were also recovered. There are extensive tracts of both habitats near the Anchorage Cove site. Birds are not represented at all at this site. A carbon sample from the bottom of the deposit was dated about 250 years BP.

We have seen that the Louisa Bay sites for which dates are available were all

The exposed and rapidly eroding dune face at the mouth of the Louisa River showing layers of deposition. *Tasmanian Museum & Art Gallery*

occupied within the past 1,200 to 1,300 years. I have suggested that the sand dune site LR1 might date no earlier than 3,000 years ago: by its stratigraphic position above the major stable zone and therefore above sites LR1, LR3 must derive from a time considerably more recent.

Recalling the physical attributes of the three oldest sites in Louisa Bay—the sand dune localities LR1, LR3 and Louisa Creek—it will be recalled that they are all characterized by multiple shallow-lensed deposits. This depositional pattern can be interpreted as short term occupation for exploiting specific, perhaps seasonally available, resources such as mutton birds on Louisa Island. Other and later sites at Louisa Bay have special characteristics which mark them as being more than seasonally occupied. It has been suggested that the caves were sometimes occupied by refugees from the storm tossed coast, that the shelter of the caves would be especially sought during the more severe winter storms whose effects are felt for days, and that during such periods the smaller shellfish species would be utilized. At Anchorage Cove we have evidence for intensive occupation and the development of a true midden structure. A similar midden at the Louisa River site is seen at LR2. Sites LR1 and LR3 are at present some distance from the sea. It is probable that at the time of their formation the sea was closer. In fact, the extensive deflation and erosion apparent on these dunes up river may well have released the sand which forms the fill for the wide beach of today. I would estimate LR2 to date between 500 and 1,000 years old, the most recent of the Louisa River sand dune occupations, giving credibility to the argument for late intensive occupation.

Aboriginal visits to Maatsuyker Island can be interpreted as a sign of intensive exploitation, surely a summer activity and one which required an intimate knowledge of wind and sea currents. Even so, once on the island the birders and sealers would be committed to an indefinite stay governed by prevailing conditions. In historic times, Maatsuyker was only visited when the sea was calm by a people who were noted for their seafaring ability. Rhys Jones suggests that De Witt Island, north-east of Maatsuyker, was a staging landfall. I suggest it was not; in the first place the sea currents are predominantly westerly or easterly and the winds are mostly westerly, so that even with optimum conditions it would be difficult to navigate a bark canoe from De Witt to Maatsuyker. Secondly, I have examined the most likely occupation localities on De Witt—the south central portion which is fed by a creek—and found nothing. Thirdly, seals which probably accounted for visits to Maatsuyker Island, are not found on De Witt.

Given the wind and current directions, the most likely embarkation point would be to the west of Louisa Bay, so that the total distance must have been of the order of 20 km. On the basis of experiment and a thorough search of the literature, Jones suggests that this distance is in the extreme upper range of the capabilities of the Tasmanian bark canoe. Judging by the deposits at Maatsuyker, though, such trips were more commonplace than extraordinary.

So at Louisa Bay we have a sequence of events that began perhaps 3,000 years ago and consisted, at first, of the occasional visit. Such visits are recorded by the shallow lenses of occupational debris in the sand dune sites. Some time later, perhaps between one and two millennia ago, Louisa Bay was occupied more heavily, probably continuously rather than seasonally. The interpretation is that the Tasmanian population was expanding. Finally, by 600 or so years ago, Maatsuyker Island was being visited regularly.

The evidence at Louisa Bay suggests that the South-West coast of Tasmania was inhabited by Aboriginal man only in relatively recent times. It is not known from which direction he arrived: by way of the west coast, perhaps ultimately from the north-west, or from an easterly direction; maybe from localities near the Huon or Derwent estuaries. It could have been from either, for 8,000 years or so of continuous occupation has been recorded in the north-west and the Hobart environs probably had about the same time range.

So why was it that South-West Tasmania was not occupied about the same time as the rest of the island? My guess, and I admit it is only informed speculation, is that a certain limited and highly seasonal exploitation did take place, but perhaps only incidentally and by family groups who left little evidence of their presence. Certainly, at the time of European contact, Aborigines ranged widely, especially in the summer months when the South-West would offer few obstacles. It is inconceivable that Tasmania's Aborigines were unaware of the South-West; it is more likely that they had neither the need nor the ability to fully exploit it until more recent times. Certainly the Louisa Bay data supports the interpretation that within the past 1,000 – 3,000 years Aboriginal man was more intensively exploiting traditional resource zones in South-West Tasmania, but the reason is obscure. Perhaps such additional resources were being sought as a result of dwindling supplies. However, simply in terms of the seasonal pattern of hunter-gatherer economy, seasonal resources are self replenishing and are seldom exhausted even during hard times. Under normal conditions hunter-gatherer man and his environment are in equilibrium.

An alternative hypothesis is a population increase. Such an increase might be generated as a result of natural factors or it might be allowed by a new element within the cultural system. With regard to natural factors it is becoming more and more evident that primitive human as well as animal populations attain a homeostatic relationship with the environment. This balance is maintained considerably below the maximum carrying capacities.

The most obvious environmental alteration which could lead to the development of new resources on which population increase might be built would be climatic variation. But the major climatic change in the South-West occurred thousands of years before the

Entrance to one of the Louisa Bay caves which sheltered the Aborigines in times of storm.
Tasmanian Museum & Art Gallery

DISTRIBUTION OF RESOURCES REPRESENTED IN LOUISA BAY DEPOSITS

	Louisa River				Louisa Creek	Anchorage Cove	Maatsuyker Island
	Site 1	Site 2	Site 3	Caves			
Date (BP)	3000 ?	1000 ?	3000 ?	800	1200	200	500
Lenses	X	–	X	–	X	–	–
Middens	–	X	–	X	–	X	X
Pademelon	P	O	O	M	–	S	–
Wallaby	M	O	O	S	X	S	–
Wombat	S	O	O	F	–	F	–
Ringtail	F	O	O	P	–	M	–
Bandicoot	–	O	O	–	–	S	–
Tiger Cat	–	O	O	F	–	F	–
Seal	X	X	X	X	–	M	P
Warrener	M	M	M	S	S	M	–
Abalone	M	M	M	S	F	M	X
Mussels	S	S	S	P	P	–	–
Others	F	F	F	M	F	F	–
Mutton birds	M	M	M	S	–	–	P
Petrels	M	M	M	P	–	–	F

Legend

O NO DATA
X PRESENT
- ABSENT
F FEW (1—10%)
S SOME (11—24%)
M MANY (25—39%)
P PREDOMINANT (40% OR MORE)

The Archaeologist at Work

THE ARCHAEOLOGIST AT WORK. Midden deposit is preserved in layers and or 'lenses' which are exposed centimetre by centimetre in excavations such as these at Louisa Bay. The material is removed painstakingly with a trowel (far right), sieved (bottom right) and sorted for later examination and dating in the laboratory.

Trench excavation, 1975. *A Moscal*

With a trowel, the archaeologist carefully removes midden deposit from the trench. *Tasmanian Museum & Art Gallery*

Louisa River excavation site. *Tasmanian Museum and Art Gallery*

The archaelolgist examining material from a cave deposit. The sieved material consists mainly of shell, bone, charcoal and stone, which testify to the presence of man in the cave at a time determined by pre-carbon dating process. *Tasmanian Museum & Art Gallery*

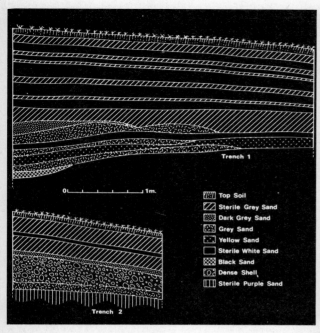

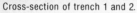

Top Soil
Sterile Grey Sand
Dark Grey Sand
Grey Sand
Yellow Sand
Sterile White Sand
Black Sand
Dense Shell
Sterile Purple Sand

Cross-section of trench 1 and 2.

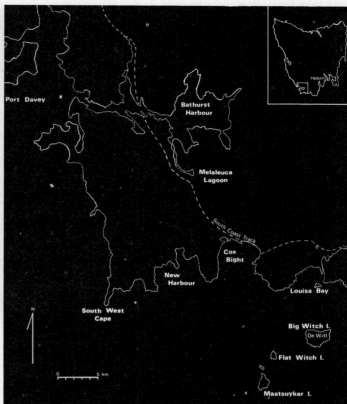

The country between Port Davey and the Ironbounds.   *R L Vanderwal*

period we are considering. It would seem, then, that we must seek an answer from within the culture itself.

Recent research at Hunter Island has provided the first glimmerings of a possible solution. Sandra Bowdler argues that a land link to Hunter Island was severed about 4,000 years ago, and that the island was not visited again for another 2 millennia or so. Yet Rhys Jones' evidence from Rocky Cape and West Point attests to an aboriginal population in the area. So why was this island, only 5 km from the mainland, not visited for so long? Was it that the island was undesirable or was it perhaps that the journey was impossible? In answer, it is extremely tempting to speculate that the distinctive Tasmanian water craft is a relatively recent addition to the sparse cultural inventory, and that its invention allowed the exploitation of such near off-shore islands perhaps only within the last 3 millennia. The development of such a craft might have been the means by which Aboriginal man exploited the South-West, at first hesitantly, as might be indicated by some of the early shallow-lensed dune deposits, then more intensely, finally utilizing the resources of the previously unattainable Maatsuyker Island. Thus, we might be recording a development which allowed movement into areas only marginally productive without water transport, areas such as the South-West with its multiplicity of near off-shore islands, craggy headlands and massive waterways. Of course the expansion seen at Louisa Bay, whether

allowed by the invention of water craft, or by some other technological innovation, is in the end a product of the underlying resources which were then in abundance.

Apart from Hunter Island, the only other large island to have received archaeological attention is Bruny Island, 50 km long and forming the seaward breakwater of the D'Entrecasteaux Channel. This channel is in places only 2 km wide. Two dates of 5,000 and 6,000 years BP were obtained on charcoal from deposits at the northern tip of North Bruny, one of which was in the order of 2 m deep and the other 1 m. The available evidence suggests that the sites are true middens with densely packed shells; shell was contributed at relatively regular intervals. The only other dated Bruny Island site is 2,000 years old. It was inhabited irregularly; layers of sand separate the layers of shell, bone and wood charcoal. At the time of their occupation, the two earlier sites may have been reached across a tombolo connecting Bruny with the mainland—such as the 5 km sand spit currently joining North and South Bruny—or the island might possibly have been capable of supporting for a short time a small population trapped by transgressing waters at the end of the Pleistocene. Whatever the situation, the carbon-14 record suggests a hiatus in the occupation of Bruny Island, and some 4,000 years later we see a site whose attributes suggest sporadic occupation, as if people were canoeing from the

mainland to exploit a particular resource.

I have carefully avoided the question of why a maritime people did not have water craft and how the Rocky Cape people caught their seals, but Tasmanian pre-history is still so full of anomalies that this one may well join the ranks of the scale fish and bone point embargoes. However, it has long been merely assumed that the Tasmanians had water craft from the day his antecedents first set foot on what was to become Tasmania; certainly the dry land link which existed before the end of the Pleistocene would have precluded the need for water craft.

At the time of European contact it was observed that the north-eastern people did not use the canoe. In explanation it has been suggested that as the result of a catastrophic event a cultural prohibition was placed on its use. But is it not equally likely that far fewer islands and a more even-featured coastal terrain would have made water craft redundant?

The interpretations derived from the data used in this paper are challenging, and hopefully they will stimulate discussion. Of course, much more work will be required before the Tasmanian water craft hypothesis can be fully evaluated.

The most important point, I think, is that within the terms of the data, of the interpretation and of the hypothesis, it can be strongly suggested that Tasmanian man was losing neither his fecundity nor his adaptability.

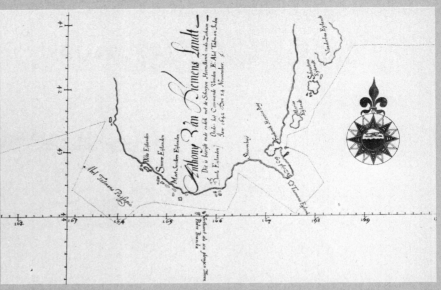

Tasman's ships, the *Heemskirk* and the *Zeehan*, from a facsimile copy of J E Heeres *Abel Janszoon Tasman's Journal.*
Allport Library and Museum of Fine Arts

Anthony Van Diemen's Landt. A chart from a facsimile copy of J E Heeres *Abel Janszoon Tasman's Journal*, published in Amsterdam in 1898.
Allport Library and Museum of Fine Arts

'From the chart of Van Diemen's Land from the best authorities and from actual surveys and measurements by Thomas Scott, Assistant Surveyor General of Lands in the Island... engraved by Charles Thomson (Cross) Edinburgh from the original survey brought home by Captain Dixon of the ship Skelton of Whitby 1824.'
(Published in Edinburgh by Thomson)
Allport Library and Museum of Fine Arts

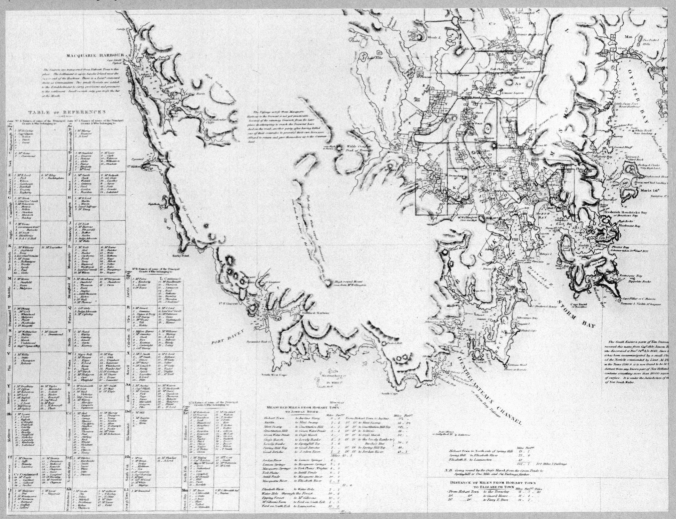

They called it Transylvania

J S Luckman & K Davies

Jessie Luckman has spent many years walking and exploring with her husband Leo, in the remoter parts of Tasmania. An honorary life member of the Hobart Walking Club, which she joined in 1936, she became familiar with the South-West when the area was roadless and relatively inaccessible. Since then, she has contributed much time and effort towards the conservation of the South-West, being a foundation member of the Tasmanian Conservation Trust Inc. and the South-West Committee. Her extensive knowledge of Tasmanian history is well respected. Kath Davies, who shares her interest in bushwalking and history greatly assisted with research for this chapter.

From the early years of last century until near its close, the South-West of Tasmania contributed quite substantially to the economy of the young colony of Van Diemen's Land, particularly in the production of high-quality timber, both hardwood and Huon pine, and in whale, seal and fishery products. Explorations and surveys led to the cutting of tracks, making access by land easier, and small settlements were established as far afield as Port Davey.

But as the stands of Huon pine were cut out and whales became scarcer and less economic to catch, activity in the area declined and finally ceased. Tracks became overgrown through lack of use; bridges collapsed in floods or were burnt by bushfires; surveyors' and prospectors' reports were filed away in official pigeon-holes; and the South-West became something of a forgotten land. In due course press and radio reports on any events in or near the area were usually preceded by adjectives such as 'rugged', 'unexplored' or 'uninhabited', — even by all three! A romantic myth seems to have captured the public fancy and it persists even today.

In the early 1920's there was an upsurge of interest in bushwalking and mountaineering, and outdoor enthusiasts began looking to the South-West for challenge and adventure. Their rewarding experiences, the magnificent grandeur and the isolation convinced them that here was an area which, at some future date, could become another reserve such as those which had lately been declared around Russell Falls, Cradle Mountain, and Lake St Clair. But the concept of conservation of wilderness and natural scenery was still the dream of the few, although the declaration in 1919 of the reserve around the limestone caves and thermal springs at Hastings may, perhaps, be regarded as the first step towards the reservation of the whole South-West as a recreation and wilderness area.

Early explorers by sea

For thousands of years the only inhabitants of Tasmania were the black tribes which had come south from the mainland of Australia. Then in 1642 a new era opened, when that most capable and experienced navigator, Abel Janszoon Tasman, first sighted the mountains and forests of the west coast. On 24th November he wrote in his journal:

'This is the furthest land in the South Sea we met with, and as it has not yet been known to any European we call it Anthony Van Diemen's Land in honour of the Governor General, our master, who sent us out to make discoveries'.

Tasman rounded South West Cape, naming De Witt, Maatsuyker and other islands before sailing south of Bruny Island. His landfall was probably north of Point Hibbs, near Macquarie Harbour, and the mountains he sighted were later identified and named Heemskirk and Zeehan, after Tasman's ships, by Matthew Flinders when he and George Bass sailed around Tasmania in 1798.

With Tasman's discovery the recorded history of South-West Tasmania began. But it was 130 years before the next European encounter, when a French expedition under Marion du Fresne explored the coast in 1772 and made the first contact with the Aborigines. Over the next twenty years the western and southern coasts received visits from both French and English expeditions.

In 1789 Capt J H Cox, in the brig *Mercury*, sailed round the south of Tasmania; Cox Bight is named after him. Two French expeditions commanded by Admiral Bruny D'Entrecasteaux in 1792 and Admiral Baudin in 1802, spent some time exploring the general area of the D'Entrecasteaux Channel, naming many features and collecting biological specimens.

By now, in Sydney, Governor King was taking an interest in Van Diemen's Land and in 1803 he sent Lieut Bowen to establish the first white settlement at Risdon Cove on the east bank of the Derwent River. This was later moved by Lieut Col David Collins to Sullivans Cove on the west bank. Exploration of the surrounding countryside soon began in the hope of finding suitable pastoral areas.

The early settlers were impressed by the great number of whales which appeared during the winter months in the Derwent and nearby waters. Soon whalers and sealers were visiting the southern waters to reap this rich harvest. The port of Hobart also became known for its good anchorage and for the stout wooden ships built there and at nearby bays. Local timber, particularly blue-gum, soon proved itself the equal of teak or English oak, being superior in the lengths obtainable for such parts as keels, keelsons and stringers. Boat builders also soon became aware of the worm-resistant qualities of certain kinds of native pine and of the Acacia known as 'blackwood'.

In 1815 Dr Thomas William Birch, an English surgeon who had settled in Hobart Town, commissioned Capt. James Kelly to explore the south and west coasts of Van Diemen's Land with a view to securing timber, especially locating the source of the Huon pine logs which had occasionally been picked up along the shores. Birch provided the schooner *Henrietta Packet* for the voyage. After discovering and naming Port Davey, Kelly and four crew-men went on in the ship's whale-boat *Elizabeth* to discover Macquarie Harbour, thence up the coast and around to Port Dalrymple and down the east coast back to Hobart. For his contribution to this exploration Dr Birch was granted a year's concession to cut Huon pine at Port Davey and Macquarie Harbour. Birch claimed to have been on the voyage but he is not mentioned in Kelly's journals which were apparently written some time afterwards. Actually there is some doubt as to who discovered Port Davey and Macquarie Harbour as accounts written by Kelly and Birch conflict. Another interesting possibility, that ex-convict Dennis McCarty reached Port Davey a few weeks earlier, is reported in the *Sydney Gazette* and *The Hobart Town Gazette*. McCarty set off to explore the south west coast in his vessel, the *Geordy*, which was wrecked on the voyage. McCarty returned to Hobart and the wreck of the *Geordy* was later reported to be in Port Davey. No doubt he had little time for exploration in the crisis! After this episode he bought another boat in which he continued his west coast exploration. In *The Hobart Town*

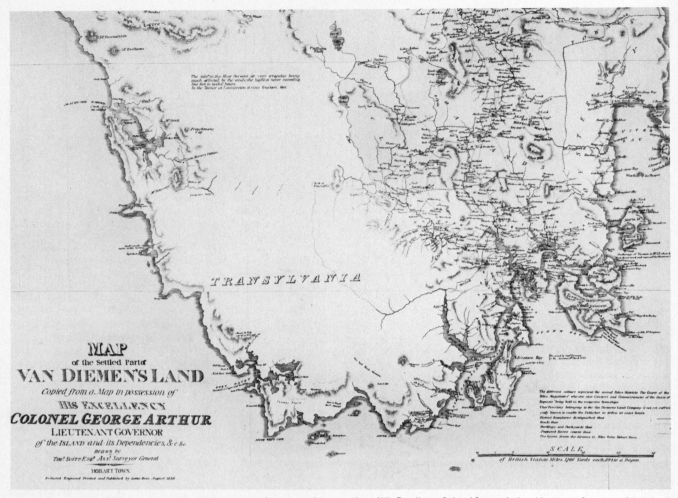

From the *'map of the settled part of Van Diemen's Land copied from a map in possession of His Excellency Colonel George Arthur, Lieutenant Governor of the Island and its Dependencies... Drawn by Thomas Scott... Published (in Hobart Town) by James Ross, August 1830.'* *Allport Library and Museum of Fine Arts*

A surveyor taking bearings. *Forestry Commission*

'This Map of Van Diemen's Land is dedicated to the land-holders of the colony by their faithful servant George Frankland, Surveyor General and sole commissioner of crown lands.' Published in London by J Cross, 1839. (Section south of the 42nd parallel and west of Ralphs Bay.) *Allport Library and Museum of Fine Arts*

Gazette of 8th June 1816 it is recorded:
> 'On Thursday last arrived the brig Sophia, Capt.C Feen, from Gordon's River, with a valuable cargo of Pine, whereat a very fine Coal-mine has been discovered by her owner, Mr Dennis M'Carty'.

In the next *Gazette* McCarty gives an interesting account of his exploration of Macquarie Harbour and his discovery of the coal seams. The issue of 31st January 1818 carries an advertisement for the sale of 62 logs of Huon pine at Mr Jemott's premises in Macquarie Street. One wonders what price they brought— and what they would be worth now!

Because of the buoyant trade in timber Governor Sorell sent Surveyor Florance to Port Davey and Macquarie Harbour in 1818 to assess the forest resources and also to find a site suitable for a maximum-security convict station. In 1820, following Florance's report, Surveyor-General Oxley spent four days in Port Davey which he described as *'a sterile land with a capacious harbour'*, and recommended Macquarie Harbour for the penal station. This was established in 1821 and, on the grounds of security, further activity at Port Davey was discouraged, although some surveying and prospecting along the southern coast was undertaken by boat.

Timber industry

Ship-loads of Huon pine, myrtle and other timbers continued to be taken out of the Gordon River area and the building of useful little trading boats and sea-going craft became a well-established industry there. The 35 ton schooner *Governor Sorell* was launched in 1823 and many fine vessels were built under the supervision of David Hoy who was appointed as shipwright to the penal station in 1827.

There was an increasing interest in finding more sources of timber and in 1829 Surveyor George Frankland investigated the south bank of the Huon River for about six miles beyond its junction with the Arve. In the same year Capt Heniker in the *Mermaid* explored the Huon by boat and reported splendid timber. He built a hut above One Tree Point which may have been the first house in the Huon district. Heniker is said to have:
> 'cut 77 logs of light-wood, 25 of sheoak, 30 of gum as well as 20 stringybark anchor stocks, 40 gum shipknees, 40 sheoak knees, 66 oak planks, 250 stringybark tree-nails and collected 100 tons of mimosa bark'.

The 'mimosa' bark was wattle bark, used for tanning hides.

On the map of Van Diemen's Land drawn by Asst Surveyor Thomas Scott and printed by James Ross in August 1830, the South-West is labelled 'Transylvania' and up to that time exploration of the area had been

Gordon River No 7, Marble Cliffs c. 1895 oil on board 308 x 470 mm. Painted by Captain Haughton Forrest.

confined to access by sea. However, in 1830, in an humanitarian attempt to contact the Tasmanian Aborigines, George Augustus Robinson became the first white man to negotiate the forests inland of the south coast. Friends in Hobart Town told him that this area was *'impenetrable'* but he persisted in his journey and in February 1830 was led by a party of Aborigines along their regular route from Recherche Bay to Port Davey. From the north side of Bathurst Harbour he went towards the Norolds, then north to Mount Hayes which he climbed on 12th March, naming the Arthur Range after the Governor. Turning west along the Crossing River he followed the Davey River down to Bond Bay. He then continued on up the west coast—truly an epic pioneering feat.

In 1831, in an attempt to find the Huon pine forests suspected to be north of Port Davey, Surveyor James Calder went up the west bank of the Huon as far as the Picton River but was prevented by bad weather from proceeding further. In 1832 an expedition led by W S Sharland set out from the northern side, starting from Bothwell. The party was harassed by continuous bad weather and got no further south than Frenchmans Cap which Sharland climbed to within a short distance of the summit.

In 1834, when the penal settlement at Macquarie Harbour was closed and the Survey Department was free to explore the country north of Port Davey, a bridle track was cut from the Huon River to the plains beyond the Arthur Range. In the following year Surveyors Calder and Wedge led a party south from the Vale of

Moraine, Arthur Range. A lantern slide (A N Lewis).

Tasmanian Museum & Art Gallery

Rasselas, discovered and named Lakes Pedder and Maria, continued on down the Huon Plains, crossed the Cracroft River and finally kept their rendezvous with a boat on the Huon River. In his report Calder expressed doubts as to whether sheep could be grazed on the country they had passed through and tendered samples of button-grass as evidence of the harsh type of vegetation. Later, Surveyor Frankland led a party from Lake St Clair to the Serpentine and Lake Pedder, naming Mt Anne on the way to the Huon.

Pining at Port Davey

In 1836 a team of 12 convicts under Alexander McKay slashed a track from Victoria (the early name for Huonville) along the south bank of the Huon River, crossing the Arve, Picton and Cracroft Rivers and heading towards the Arthur Range. Although at first this route was very rough (Calder declared it was *like walking along an almost endless line of upright bayonets*), it was later improved so that travellers on foot could reach the plains east of Port Davey without much difficulty. Access was now open to the

Huon pine forests near the Arthur Range and other stands of timber were found at the headwaters of the Spring and Davey rivers.

Pine cutters quickly moved in. Although the piners were required to be licensed there were many cutting without authority and there was little control over the quantity of trees felled. McKay's track was patrolled by a policeman living at the Picton who went to see the piners every month to collect their licence fees. Some piners took their families around by boat and soon there was quite a village at Settlement Point in Port Davey where over 50 people lived at one time. Although whales were often tried-out ashore, there was little permanent residence in the Port, leaving the pining industry to establish the only real township at Port Davey. The wood was of good quality and commanded high prices, especially in England. However, the piners earned every penny of it, their living and working conditions being harsh in the extreme.

A member of Parliament, the Hon. James Reid Scott MLC, has left an eye-witness account of the arduous and often

dangerous methods used to extract the timber and float it down to the port. He visited the area twice, first by McKay's track in 1871, when he was accompanied by the artist W C Piguenit, and by boat in 1875 when he was taken by some piners up the Davey River to the cutting area at Dohertys Ground. Scott noted that each piner had his own recognised area for cutting, hence the names like 'Dohertys Ground' and 'Longleys Ground' which still appear on maps. The dwellings of the piners up the river were A-frame structures called 'badger-boxes' and those built on the flats where the pine trees were felled usually had one end open, with a bunk raised high at the other, the boat being moored to the bed-post. When the boat floated in over the door-step the owner knew that the river was in flood!

The men often worked up to their waists in water and risked their lives when clearing the channels so that logs would float free to their 'pens' near the mouth of the river. Traces of these pens (stakes standing upright in the water) may still be seen today. When the weather was too bad for felling, time was

A lantern slide of Frenchmans Cap and Lake Gwendolen taken by Fred Smithies on an early bushwalk to the area.
Tasmanian Museum & Art Gallery

Top left.
Panorama from Mt Rugby, Port Davey. Lantern slide.
Tasmanian Museum & Art Gallery

Mt Misery and Bramble Cove, Port Davey. Lantern slide.
Tasmanian Museum & Art Gallery

spent at the settlement in building boats, hunting and fishing. Owing to frequent heavy gales the settlement was often on the verge of starvation and compelled to live on local game such as swan, kangaroo and wombat. Education facilities were non-existent, and medical attention depended on what the piners or their wives could provide. Pining continued at Port Davey on a diminishing scale until the late 1870's when most of the accessible stands had been virtually cut out and the settlement was abandoned.

There seems to have been little appreciation of the length of time it took a Huon pine to grow to commercial size, nor were there adequate controls on felling. Reid Scott expressed anxiety at the rate of cutting and suggested limiting it to trees above a certain size. In 1879 a Parliamentary Select Committee was appointed:

'to enquire into and report upon the necessary steps to be taken for the Preservation from utter destruction of the valuable indigenous Forest Trees known as the Huon Pine and Blackwood'.

After taking evidence from piners and shippers it recommended that:

'the felling of Huon Pine trees be prohibited, save under regulations to be made by the Governor-in-Council'.

Cutting continued under stricter control in the Gordon and other areas, and indeed is still carried on. The story of the piners, their early explorations of the Franklin and the Gordon, how they warped or winched their stoutly built dinghies over rapids and waterfalls, is a saga in itself. Where canoeists go today for adventure and sport, these pioneers went to earn a living. Their stamps, or identification brands, can still be seen on the stumps of pines at the foot of Deception Ridge beside the Franklin Gorge.

Above.
Route to Lake Fenton before the track was cut.
Lantern slide. *Tasmanian Museum & Art Gallery*

Top right.
Resting on a bush track.   *D Pinkard col.*

Middle right.
On the Hartz Track. Packhorses were often used to carry supplies.   *D Pinkard col.*

Bottom right.
Old camp, Arve plains.   *D Pinkard col.*

Below.
Hut on the Franklin River.
Tasmanian Museum & Art Gallery

BAY WHALING

Leases granted by the Crown between 1840 and 1859 for the purposes of bay whaling stations:

Southport	(3)
Recherche	(7)
De Witt	(1)
Louisa Bay	(2)
Cox Bight	(1)
New Harbour	(4)
Port Davey	(2)
Rocky Point	(1)

Most of these were granted by the Lands Office in 1840 and 1841. The terms for such leases were not severe, i.e., 3 acres, a frontage on the sea of 3 chains, and for this a yearly rental of 5 shillings. Sir William Crowther wrote of Bay Whaling and Sperm Whaling in the Royal Society Papers of 1919:

'In Van Diemen's Land it was the practise for a station to be established at a selected bay and for the Oil taken to be shipped by tender to Hobart Town and thence to England. One or more boats' crews were stationed at the establishment, and a lookout posted on a favourable position. On a whale being sighted the crew pulled away, and, if possible, made themselves fast to the whale, killed it, and often after a very long and laborious tow, brought their catch to the shore. There, there was fitted a rough tripod scaffolding, to the base of which the whale was secured, and by the aid of which the blubber was stripped from the whale and taken on shore to be boiled down.'

The Black Whale practically ceased to visit the coast after 1841 and attention was transferred to the more valuable Sperm Whale, which passed the South-Western coast from time to time. By 1850 Sperm whaling was in great prosperity; there was no lack of money to fit out the ships, or of men to man and sail them. The whale was found particularly in the neighbourhood of South West Cape as it passed east and west in its pursuit of the squid. The smaller ships from Hobart Town cruised off the Cape and towed their whales into Port Davey or Recherche to 'try' them out at the stations there. The larger ships passed by way of the Cape to the various whaling grounds.

The Sperm Whale was approached very quietly from behind. One or more lances were 'darted' into him by the boat's steerer who endeavoured to avoid hitting a rib by securing him well forward. If not secured in a vital spot, the whale either sounded or ran, and was lost. Bombs from guns were used as well as lances, in order to kill the whales.

The Right Whale was approached head to head by the boat's crew who waited for the ship to run down to them and make fast to the dead whale. The 'cutting-in' involved removal of the whale's head which, in the Sperm Whale, contained one third of the quantity of oil; this was bailed into barrels. The blubber was then removed from the body. Long strips, 5 or 6 feet long were cut off and hove into the blubber room and there divided into smaller pieces to be boiled down at the 'Try Works'.

Reference:

W Lodewyk Crowther, 'Notes on Tasmanian Whaling', *Papers and Proceedings. Royal Society of Tasmania* (1919), pp.130 – 151.

Whaling, Lady's Bay 1859, by William Duke.   *Queen Victoria Museum*

Whaling

The whaling industry began with the first settlement on the Derwent for it was soon realised that the river itself, as well as the bays and inlets along the south coast, were regular breeding grounds of the Black Right Whale. 'Bay whaling', as the method was called, became a thriving business. This involved selecting a bay or beach where boats could be launched quickly, setting up huts for the crews, sheds and slip-ways for the boats, and try-pots for melting the blubber to extract the oil. Harry O'May, in his book, *Wooden Hookers of Hobart Town*, quotes one sea-captain as saying:

'when black whales were plentiful there was not a sheltered beach from Georges Bay (on the east coast) to the South West Cape, that a boat could haul upon, that was not occupied by one or two stations'.

A small settlement of huts existed for a time at Bramble Cove in Port Davey and quite a lot of trying out or rendering down of whale blubber was done in the Port. Seals were also a profitable haul from the islands around the coast. In addition to bay whaling there was also very extensive hunting in the open sea particularly for Sperm whales by boats from England, America and France. Catching was uncontrolled and indiscriminate, cows with calves being taken as well as bulls. Because of this wholesale slaughter it is small wonder that the remaining harassed animals went elsewhere to find breeding grounds. Whaling returns gradually diminished and by the end of the century the industry had all but collapsed.

An interesting anecdote concerns the last but one of the Hobart whalers, the *Waterwitch*. In 1891 her crew caught a Sperm whale and took it into Port Davey to try it out. After the blubber had been stripped, two observant fishermen asked for and were given the carcase. They set to work and recovered a lump of ambergris weighing over 180 lbs and worth several thousand pounds sterling on the London market!

Fishing

It may safely be assumed that the early settlers were also quick to realise the abundance and variety of edible fish in the estuary of the Derwent, down the D'Entrecasteaux Channel and along the south coast. The many large mounds of oyster, abalone, mussel and other shells at Aboriginal camp-sites also made them aware of other marine food sources. In the near-famine of 1805, when government rations had to be cut by two thirds, fish would have been a welcome addition to the new colonists' diet of wallaby and wombat.

By 1816 commercial fishing as an occupation was apparently worthwhile, as *The Hobart Town Gazette* for 7th

September announces that:

'G Clarke, Collins Street, informs the Inhabitants of Hobart Town, that he has purchased a capital Fishing Seine, for the purpose of regularly supplying all Persons with Fish, after the 1st of October next, being the commencement of the Fishing Season. He also acquaints the Inhabitants that Fresh Oysters may always be had opened or unopened'.

When the Hon J Reid Scott went to Port Davey in 1875 for the second time, the main object of his visit was to have some hunting and fishing, particularly *'trumpeter fishing (for which one has to go outside the Heads)'*. He remarked also that:

'the greatest treat, now as formerly, was the plentiful supply of oysters, Kelly's Basin containing the largest and most easily obtained rock-oysters I have ever seen, and they were in prime condition'.

Fishing on the south and west coasts has always been a hazardous occupation and fishermen have to be very skilful with their craft as well as very 'weatherwise', since the waters are recognized as amongst the roughest in the world. Hidden rocks and reefs abound, and a good knowledge of their whereabouts is essential to safety.

Although there is a wide variety of fish, those most commonly caught nowadays for the commercial market are shark, barracouta and salmon, crayfish, scallops and abalone. While early boats relied on sail only, the present-day craft are powered by diesel engines. Most boats have wells or tanks through which sea-water flows, keeping the catch alive until it reaches port. Many of the larger boats have some type of refrigeration.

Catching crayfish entails working close in to rocky shores and cliffs where the baited cray pots (traps made from woven sticks) are 'shot' either from the boat or from a dinghy—an operation which requires considerable skill and practice in manoeuvring the boat to keep clear of jagged rocks and beds of kelp,

The Rounding, a drawing on stone by William Duke, published in Hobart Town in September 1848. *W L Crowther Library*

particularly when there is a big swell running.

There was some diving for abalone in the nineteenth century, but it was not until 1964 that it became established as a commercial venture on a large scale. Since then it has grown into an important industry, divers operating not only in D'Entrecasteaux Channel and around Bruny Island but also up the stormy west coast.

Agriculture

In their search for more agricultural land the early settlers soon found their way southwards from Hobart Town, first by boat and later by rough foot or horse tracks. No doubt the establishment of the many shore whaling stations encouraged the clearing of land, initially for the timber and then, having opened up the area, for the planting of crops and pastures.

In the early 1840's Lady Franklin, the wife of the Governor, purchased land on the Huon River to sell on instalments to free settlers who were prepared to clear it and establish themselves as farmers; the area became known as Franklin. Further up the river the township of Victoria (later Huonville) was settled, and a ferry and foot-track connected it with Hobart Town.

A whalebone engraving bearing the following inscription: *'The Pacific Whaling Ship. Capt'n Rob Gardiner of Hobart Town, homeward bound, 900 Barrells Sperm Oil, 10 months out, 1840'.* *W L Crowther Library*

In May 1849 a party of pastoralists headed north and crossed the upper Derwent. They put sheep to graze on the country near the Gordon River, being of the opinion that acceptable pasture resulted after the native grasses had been burnt. A month later 31 farmers applied to rent 624,000 acres between Frenchmans Cap and Port Davey. However the area had not been surveyed and the applications were refused.

Governor Denison envisaged the opening up of the southern and western lands by two roads—one from the Huon via Lake Pedder to Port Davey, the other from Dunrobin Bridge on the Derwent via the Gordon River to Port Davey. The latter, known as Dawsons Road after the Superintendent of Works, was begun in 1850 and extended for about 38 miles to the Gordon Bend. However, owing to the increasing costs, the construction teams were withdrawn in 1856 and the scheme abandoned.

Pastoral settlements penetrated south to the estuary of the Huon River and Recherche Bay, all being serviced by boats, since the track to Hobart Town was suitable only for foot or slow horse traffic. Despite the reports of early surveyors on the poor agricultural potential of the lands beyond the Huon, many people were still of the opinion that there were vast areas in the South-West suitable for pastoral use, and exploration and survey parties continued to map and assess the country. As recently as 1949 two Huon farmers took about 40 sheep up the Huon and across the Picton bridge with the idea of grazing them on the button-grass of the Arthur Plains. However, they got no further than Blakes Opening where the unfortunate animals finally died of starvation—as predicted by the Agriculture Department.

Waterwitch, gun brig and whaler, 237 tons, berthed outside Lenna, Hobart, about 1890. Her total catch between 1886 and 1895:

669 tons of sperm oil
7 tons of black oil } valued at
5 tons of whalebone } £23,750
167¼ozs. ambergris

On her last voyage she took 59 tons of sperm oil in 8 months near South West Cape valued at £45 per ton. *W L Crowther Library*

THE ROUNDING.

Surveyors and trackmakers

The pioneers in the South-West were the surveyors, the track-makers and the prospectors of last century. Early sketch maps show quite a criss-cross of routes and staked tracks, now mostly overgrown and obliterated, and the reports of their painstaking authors are buried in old volumes of Parliamentary Papers. One of the earliest to be marked on a map is the *'Route of James Goodwin, May 1828'*. He was a convict who, with a companion named Connolly, escaped from the Macquarie Harbour prison by making a pine canoe. They rowed up the Gordon and the Franklin, and then walked west via Vale of Rasselas and Wylds Craig to the Derwent. He had been in the employ of a surveyor, could use a compass and was used to the bush.

was salt pork, damper, oatmeal, tea, and sugar (or golden syrup, known as 'cocky's joy'). Added to the load were the surveying instruments, measuring chains, axes, picks, shovels, or whatever tools were considered necessary for the expedition. One can sympathise with District Surveyor George Innes who got special exemption from Surveyor Calder to use a compass instead of a theodolite *'because of the nature of the district'*, South Huon! Their field notes and official reports often include remarks like *'returned to camp wet to the skin'*; *'after a long day of cutting through dense scrub, found we had covered less than a mile'*; *'owing to rapid rise in the level of the river we were forced to go on half rations until we could get back to the depot'*, and, *'hail and sleet slowed our progress'*. Present-day bushwalkers in

south of Frenchmans Cap, across the Franklin River to Eagle Creek on the Gordon River. In 1842 Sir John Franklin, the Governor, Lady Franklin and a large party followed this route. A member of this expedition, David Burn, has left a lively account of their experience and an imaginative description of the wild scenery, the appalling weather they encountered—and the food, to which he refers as *'a choice refection of salt pork, tea, and damper'*. As part of Tasmania's sesquicentenary celebrations in 1954 this famous journey was re-enacted (with modern bushwalking gear and food) by two women and four men from the Hobart Walking Club. They even got a medal for it!

While Surveyor James Sprent was making his trigonometrical survey of the State between 1845 and 1855 he covered much of the South-West, erecting cairns—one of which he put on the Arthur Range—and measuring the heights of prominent mountains. His reports contain the first official mention of Federation Peak, a crag which has become a symbol of the South-West to bushwalkers today. He refers to it as *'the Obelisk'*.

The discovery of gold in Victoria inspired prospectors to try their luck in Tasmania and a few found their way into the South-West. In 1859 the Government commissioned Charles Gould and Gordon Burgess to make a geological survey of the western part of the State, during which they found a little gold on the western side of Frenchmans Cap. Gould later staked a route from the Gordon River, near Butler Island, south-east through rugged country to a gap in the Frankland Range, then north-east to The Thumbs and on to Hamilton. In his book *Western Tasmania : - a land of riches and beauty*, Charles Whitham outlines this achievement:

> *'Burgess made a track up the Franklin until he came to Sir John Franklin's crossing at Eleanor Ferry. This old track was then re-opened to the Jane and the Acheron. Gould went up Smith's old track and appears to have reached Mt Fincham. He then returned to a depot they had established on the Franklin, and managed to ascend that river in a boat until they got right under the Frenchman. It is almost incredible that they did so; it was a most difficult and dangerous undertaking, passing about seventy falls and rapids'.*

In 1874 a party including the geologist R M Johnston and the painter W C Piguenit walked along the Huon track to the Cracroft, up the Arthur Plains to Lake Pedder where, as Piguenit recorded, they camped for two days:

> *'experiencing the most tempestuous weather.'* They went on northwards with the idea of *'striking the Gordon*

West Coast pioneering home.   *Eric Thomas, col.*

They had to be tough and very fit, those early bushmen. The surveyors often had to slash through dense scrub in order to get a 'sight' on a known prominent point or climb a peak to set up a cairn as a base for further triangulation. Their gear was heavy and cumbersome and their food was confined to the bare essentials supplemented by what they could snare as they went along. They were frequently out for months at a time, making supply dumps along the way and back-tracking to bring forward more supplies when necessary, so that the party often did many times the actual mileage covered.

Shelter consisted of weighty canvas or 'blanket' tents, made heavier when soaked by rain; utensils were iron; diet

the South-West will agree that at least the climate has not changed much. Clothing was often a problem. When Sharland and his party went to Frenchmans Cap in 1832 they were out nearly four weeks and struck not only very bad weather but also dense scrub. Their clothing was so badly torn that Sharland recommended leather trousers as being more suitable for that kind of trip, having had to mend his own with wallaby skins. Kangaroo and wallaby skins were often used to make knapsacks.

The arduous surveys by Frankland, Calder and Wedge in the Gordon-Huon area have been mentioned previously. In 1840 Calder staked a route from Lake St Clair via Lachlan (or Lightning) Plains

near the Great Bend and of following the Florentine down to its junction with the Derwent beyond Dunrobin Bridge"'.

In his *Geology of Tasmania* Johnston gives a vivid description of their slow progress through the dense scrub which in those days had not been burnt out. They got no further than five miles beyond Lake Pedder, were reduced to one day's supply of food, and had to make a forced march back to the Picton which they reached *'faint with exhaustion'*, having been two days without food. Even in those conditions they could still raise a laugh when two of them disappeared through a dense patch of horizontal scrub and were found hanging by their knapsacks.

Because of the exposure of the west coast to severe storms, the trading

track, to be subsequently converted into a road, between Macquarie Harbour and the Craycroft River'.

Jones and party left the Gordon near Butler Island on July 15th and arrived back in Hobart on October 19th, having experienced almost continual rain, snow, gales and swollen rivers. Although he estimated the distance from the Gordon to the Cracroft to be about 72 miles he reported:

'The distance walked by us cannot be estimated, as some of the ground, while bringing our things forward in the first instance, was travelled 10 times over by all hands'.

Seeking a cross-country route to the coast in 1894 Cullen and Edwin Cawthorne marked a track from near Tim Shea to the Serpentine, through the gap in the Franklands and so on west to

still on a tree on the South Gordon Track in 1939 but the Weld track had disappeared under regrowth. Also, in 1890, Philip Schnell cut a track on the north side of the Huon River to Mt Anne and the Weld River. Schnells Ridge, south of Mt Anne, is named after him. In 1898, still with the plight of ship-wrecked seamen in mind, the Government commissioned Edward Alexander Marsden to cut a track from Port Davey to link up with the South Gordon track near McPartlans Pass. On the official sketch map of 1938 there is a side track from this route marked *'Easy route to Lake Pedder'*. Obviously Lake Pedder was not as 'inaccessible' as sometimes suggested! Marsden's track was, in fact, the one used by walkers until the construction of the Scotts Peak Road, and the southern section is still the route

T B Moore's wife, formerly Miss Solly, crossing the King River in the 1890's. *Eric Thomas col.*

An early photograph of Lake Emily, Hartz Mts, taken by J W Beattie. *Queen Victoria Museum*

vessels, the majority still under sail, were in constant danger of ship-wreck and survivors often found themselves separated from any habitation by miles of rugged, trackless country. To make access easier, surveys and exploration continued throughout the century, particularly with the object of finding feasible routes from Macquarie Harbour to Port Davey and from the coast to the Derwent.

In 1879 Thomas Bather Moore marked a track from Birch Inlet, at the southern end of Macquarie Harbour, to Settlement Point in Port Davey. In 1881 Surveyor David Jones was instructed by the Government to find:

'a line of country suitable for a horse-

the coast. They then returned, 'chaining' the distance—about 50 miles, on the way. Two years later Surveyor Edward George Innes followed Cawthorne's track as far as Rookery Plains, then went north-west towards the Gordon, naming the Olga River which he crossed on the birthday of his youngest daughter. On their return journey, the geologist H M Nicholls took what were probably the first photographs of Lake Pedder.

Other exploratory expeditions were made too, many for the purpose of opening up the area for prospecting. In 1890 Surveyor Thomas Frodsham went from the Russell Falls River (now the Tyenna), around High Rocky (Mueller Range) and down the Weld River to the Huon. The notice *'Huon via Weld'* was

to Port Davey.

In 1901 T B Moore cut a track to Port Davey from the Lune River via the Old River, giving the name Federation Peak to Sprent's Obelisk in honour of the Federation of Australian States.

Numerous geological surveys were made both on the west coast and inland. A track was cut in 1912 by Hartwell Conder between Double Cove on Macquarie Harbour and the Spero River, partly for prospectors and also to give seamen access to the lighthouse at Cape Sorell. In 1915 it was extended down the coast to Port Davey. During World War I a party was sent dashing down Marsden's track to Port Davey to check on a rumour that enemy ships were sheltering there!

'At Fitzgerald in the Upper Derwent, farmers were losing sheep. Early one morning in 1912 Mr Albert Quarrell was yoking his bullock team when he saw the tiger walking up the road. He raised the alarm and with the aid of his boy he managed to get hold of the tiger — but it bit his foot and he had to release it. Neighbours joined in the hunt and the tiger was finally brought to bay in a patch of scrub and killed. Mr Charles Brown, who was given the skin, took this picture.'
(Jeremy Griffith's notes)   *Tasmanian Museum & Art Gallery*

Bushwalking

From the writings left by early settlers it is evident that despite hard living conditions, there were many who were keenly appreciative of the wild scenery and who enjoyed walking and camping in the bush, as well as hunting and fishing excursions. In *The Dark Lantern* Henry Judd gave an interesting account of his family's pioneering life as early settlers on the Huon. His father was one of Lady Franklin's *'respectable free agricult-urists'* to whom she sold land on easy terms at Franklin in 1843, and a brother later cleared and settled land upstream from Huonville at the place now known as Judbury. Henry wrote enthusiastically of his journeys up the Weld River to Mt Anne and across to the Arthur Ranges. He named Lake Judd in 1880 and declared *'the beauty here cannot be exaggerated'*. Describing a visit to Lake Pedder in 1871 he wrote :

> *'this lake had a few swans on it, also a few Cape pigeons diving into the water after fish, but what sort of fish I could not find out'.*

After a description of the view from the top of the northern end of the Arthur Range he wrote:

> *'an easy track could be made to join this district on to the Hartz Mountain track, making the whole a very interesting tourist journey'.*

He also noted *'a splendid cave of a large size filled with stalactites of all forms and size'* on a south-east tributary of the Cracroft River. Apparently there were quite a number of people enjoying bushwalking in the latter part of last century. Surveyor Jones, in a report of track-cutting to Mt La Perouse in 1881 remarked that a well-graded track to this area should prove very popular with tourists, and again, in 1895, he noted that:

> *'the track from Geeveston to the Hartz Range is, in the season, doing good work by attracting numbers of visitors to Geeveston'.*

After World War I there was quite an upsurge in bushwalking throughout the

State and many parties found their way into remote areas, some for delight in rugged scenery, some to collect more data for geological maps. In 1920, 1921 and 1922 parties led by L F Giblin and including geologist A N Lewis made attempts to reach the summit of Mt Anne. In 1924 Giblin led a party via Judd's route up the Weld Valley in an effort to reach Anne from the east. On all these trips the parties met with frustrating difficulties — overgrown tracks, heavy rain and flooded creeks— and, although they climbed to within about 30 feet of the top on the only fine day of the 1922 trip, possibly the actual summit was not gained until bushwalkers Walter Crookall and Geoff Chapman found a route past the final obstructing cliff face on Christmas day, 1929—nearly a century after the mountain was first named. In 1930, V C Smith, G T F Chapman and party explored the lakes and peaks in the vicinity of Anne and Schnells Ridge, and continued down the Weld Valley to the Huon, thus making the first 'round trip' of the mountain.

In 1924 the Southwestern Expeditionary Club was formed by surveyor Len Livingston and friends:

> 'for the purpose of making that little-known portion of the State between Hobart and Port Davey better known to the public of Tasmania'.

On their first trip they carried fourteen days' supplies and took one blanket and one waterproof sheet each, in addition to an 8 ft by 10 ft tent fly. They left the rail terminus at Fitzgerald and got a pack-horse to take their 65 lb swags as far as Mayne's Selection, where they set off on the South Gordon Track, turning onto Marsden's track at the junction. The Huon River was crossed by straddling a log, and after encountering much bad weather, overgrown or lost track and dense bauera scrub, they reached Port Davey where they climbed Mt Berry. Leaving Port Davey on New Year's Day they were back in Fitzgerald on 5th January, having done the 74 miles in 96 hours (43 hours actual walking time).

At the Gordon River, 1921.
(Four glass photographic plates).
Queen Victoria Museum and Art Gallery

Bottom left.
Geoff Chapman & Doug Anderson, Lonely Tarn under Mt Sarah Jane, 1930.   *V C Smith*
Bottom right.
Queenstown; 1932. The first passenger car from Hobart has arrived!   *Eric Thomas col.*
OPPOSITE PAGE.
Centre.
First ascent of Four Peaks, Eastern Arthurs. Cairn building, 1952.   *Max Cutcliffe*
Bottom left.
At Damper Inn on the Port Davey Track, one day out from Fitzgerald on the first recorded ascent of Mt Anne, Dec 1929. Left to right: V C Smith, M Turner, W A Crookall, G T F Chapman.   *G T F Chapman*
Bottom right.
Lots Wife, near Mt Anne, c.1930.   *V C Smith*

In Reminiscence of Recherche

Today few signs remain of the settlements that thrived at Recherche earlier this century. Where productive gardens once surrounded spacious weatherboard homes, the blackberries grow wild and with ferns and tea-tree, hide what fire has not destroyed. For decades timber mills came and went and coal mining, on a lesser scale, followed the same spasmodic pattern. Around the main mills at Leprena, Catamaran and Cockle Creek, settlements flourished in the twenties and thirties. Largely dependent on their own resources, the people of Recherche had excellent vegetable gardens and went fishing and hunting, the men travelling as far as New River on occasions. Blackmans Lagoon, now Southport Lagoon, was a favourite spot for shooting.

Sawmills are traditionally destroyed by fire and the mill at Leprena was burnt down in the thirties but not before it cut its worth in timber. In the twenties 48,000 to 50,000 super feet was cut most weeks. The logs came in almost constantly from the country behind Recherche, transported on trollies that ran on wooden rails over hill and swamp. All the logs were cleared out of a specific location or radius before the tram lines were extended to a new area. Before these were built, the levels were studied carefully; gradient was as important a consideration as a good supply of water for the steam engine which hauled the logs.

The area accessible from a chosen haulage point was referred to as a 'bush'. Felling was a delicate operation demanding precise judgement. Two axemen would first cut the front or 'scarf' and then with a cross-cut saw, two others would cut the back and wedge the cut to drop the tree where they wanted it. Standing as they were, 15 to 20 feet above the ground the men had to be very agile when the creaking signalled that the tree was ready to fall. The trees, varying from 3 to 8 feet in diameter, were cut into lengths of not less than 20 feet for handling. The logs were hauled in on a cable, a metal 'shoe' in front acting as a skid. The 'corner boy' stood in sight of the driver of the steam engine and hopefully in earshot of the 'shoemen', to ensure that the winch stopped as the log reached the 'snatch' block at each change of angle in the haulage line, and then started again when the

'Two axemen would first cut the curve, or scarf, and then, with a cross-cut saw, two others would wedge at the back to drop the tree where they wanted it.' When J W Beattie photographed this eucalypt there were plenty of its size.
Queen Victoria Museum

'The timber came in almost constantly (to the sawmills) from the country in behind Recherche, transported on trolleys that ran on wooden rails over hill and swamp.'   *D Pinkard col.*

shoemen had cleared the block. In this way the logs reached the trolleys on which they freely rolled to the mill. Sometimes though, the horses were used if there was an up gradient on the way.

These fine bushmen, dressed in the old Tasmanian 'bluey' coats and trousers, worked all winter, almost regardless of the weather. For when a man stood to lose a day's pay he had the incentive to carry on. (Wages varied from £2 to £4 a week in the thirties).

The bushmen were responsible to cut enough saw logs to keep the mill going so there was a required number of waggon loads per day from each gang. There was time, none the less, to take a sip of sweet black tea from the kerosine tin billy.

When the logs reached the mill they were rolled off the trolleys, trimmed and barked. One single cylinder steam engine drove everything; its boiler was fed by the waste wood from the docking saw.

A benchman, wearing a tough 'badger skin' apron, sorted and cut the logs according to quality, using a vertical frame saw to produce flitches for final cutting to commercial size on a circular saw. Poor quality timber went to the paling saw for jam case material and the two men on saws often raced each other to see who could cut the most in a day.

Saws ran at high speeds so bearings were quite an important consideration. If trouble was encountered, the men had to level up the shaft, clean and oil it, then pour the molten bearing metal round it on the spot — and operations began again within hours. To have sent the bearings to Hobart would have meant closing down for 2 or 3 weeks! The lubricant used on the saws, the leather guides and the timber chutes was mutton bird oil; readily available by the barrel, and cheap. The combination of wood smoke, mutton bird oil and green timber must be, for the old millers, a memorable smell.

From the Leprena mill the timber was lightered out to Bennetts Point where it was loaded onto the steamer, a round-the-clock operation in the twenties. This mill was subsequently burnt and all the eye can discern now of its heyday is that the area is remarkably clear of tall timbers.   Stuart Dunbar

Hut near Catamaran.   *Howard P Simco*

Loading timber at Port Esperance c. 1900.   *W L Crowther Library*

Soon others were testing their bushmanship and stamina in the South-West, finding the magnificent scenery and rugged wilderness ample reward for the discomforts of heavy packs and aching muscles. Some followed Marsden's track to Port Davey or turned east to the Huon. Others went by fishing boat to Cox Bight and walked back by the south coast track to Cockle Creek. Some visited Port Davey the easy way in 1933 when the passenger ship *Zealandia* took a large party of tourists there.

Because of the increasing interest in bushwalking the Hobart Walking Club was formed in 1929, the inaugural meeting being convened by E T Emmett, then Director of the Government Tourist Bureau. Several members were already familiar with the South-West and it was not long before Club trips were programmed for the area. By 1939 walking in the South-West was becoming quite popular, not only with local folk but also with visitors from the mainland States. In that year there were no less than 43 bushwalkers somewhere along Marsden's track over the Christmas—New Year period. There was even a 'letter box' in a forked stick at the Huon Crossing.

After World War II the increasing efficiency and popularity of light aircraft played a significant role in opening up the South-West, not only to bushwalkers but also to those who were content to 'just look' or to capture its many moods with brush and canvas, or camera. Lloyd Jones of the Aero Club of Southern Tasmania proved the feasibility of landing small planes on coastal beaches and on the magnificent beach at Lake Pedder. The Aero Club also demonstrated the practicability of dropping suitably packed containers of non-perishable foods at agreed sites, thus allowing walkers to stay longer in the area without being limited by their capacity for carrying. The first air drop was made by parachute in December 1947 and, although unsuccessful in that it was never recovered, it paved the way for countless drops.

Because of his skill in aerial photography, Lloyd Jones was the first to gain world-wide publicity for the South-West, through his booklets of excellent colour shots which found a ready sale throughout Australia and beyond. In particular, his daring and dramatic close-up shots of Federation Peak highlighted the attractions of the Arthur Ranges for mountaineers and photographers alike.

Federation Peak

With their sharply jagged skyline culminating in the gaunt quartzite tower of Federation Peak, the Arthur Ranges caught the eyes of early travellers. As mentioned earlier, G A Robinson made the first recorded ascent of Mt Hayes

Passenger ship *Zealandia* which visited Port Davey in 1933. *D Pinkard*

Left and below.
The Norwegian Barque *Svenor*, 1,266 tons, was wrecked in 1914 when on her way to Fremantle in ballast. Three hundred miles off the Tasmanian Coast the ballast shifted, causing the barque to heel over. As she had lost steerage, the crew abandoned ship when they came in sight of land. They were picked up by a passing steamer. Eventually the vessel beached north of Port Davey where she lies rusting on the sand. *Max Cutcliffe*

and named the range, but doubtless, during the survey expeditions in subsequent years, ascents were made of other nearby mountains, if only to gain a clearer view of possible routes ahead.

In *The Dark Lantern*, Henry Judd, describing one of his trips around 1870, wrote:

'From Lake Pedder you can easily travel to the Arthur Ranges, and when on the top of the northern end you have a beautiful view of Port Davey, which is about 15 or 20 miles off, also over the wide extending plains. It is no easy matter to describe this view with all the beauties that surround the lake scenery, rivers rounding through the distant lowlands at the foot of rocky mountains, the winding avenue of trees on each side of the rivers, and the bare open plains at the back'.

In 1898 Osborne Geeves cut a track from the Hartz Mt hut to the Cracroft. Some years later his son, Richard Geeves, followed the same route but continued west, across the South Cracroft and up the button-grass plains in the Cracroft Valley to the east side of Federation Peak. He then turned south-west over a low saddle to Lake Geeves under the south cliff of Federation and went on to connect with Moore's track in the Old River.

To the surveyors these peaks offered useful sites for trig points; to bushwalkers there was the challenging climb with, hopefully, a rewarding view at the top. But the grey cliffs of Federation

Peak proved to be the greatest challenge of all. There seem to have been no serious attempts on the Peak itself until the 1930's. One of the first was a reconnoitre from the New River Lagoon side by Geoff Chapman and Mac Urquhart. Hampered by bad weather they had to spend a day and a night up a large tree when a flash flood roared down the river, separating them from the boat in which they had rowed up the lagoon.

After World War II many parties tried to establish a practical route both from Lake Pedder and from the Huon side. A track was cut through dense scrub up the side of Mt Picton from Blakes Opening. Subsequent parties pushed further and further out, often delayed and thwarted by dense scrub and flooded rivers. In 1946 one party reached a point about 2½ miles north-west of the Peak, gaining a breath-taking view of the whole massif and noting at least two possible routes.

In April 1947 a flight was made to assess the possibility of a western approach. In December, food and climbing ropes were dropped by parachute—the first air drop—and later that month a party of Hobart Walking Club members—Nancy Shaw, Leo Luckman and Bill Jackson—set out via Blakes Opening and Picton. Crossing the Cracroft River, they worked their way up the valley to the steep and thickly forested ridge which they named Moss Ridge for the only water available where they camped on the narrow ridge, was that which they squeezed from the moss.

It was too thick to make tea, so they made porridge—dark purple brown! Working their way to a small saddle directly under the Peak, several climbing routes were tried, but unfortunately curtailed as the air-drop containing ropes had not been recovered. Luckman and Jackson ascended the final south-east rock chimney above Lake Geeves to a point very close to the pinnacle, until fog and torrential rain forced their descent.

Several more parties tried other routes without success, all being dogged by heavy rain, fog and flooded streams. Finally, in January 1949 some members of the Geelong College Exploration Society, led by John Béchervaise, established camp on the plateau. With the assistance of ropes and blessed with two perfect days for the actual climb, they went up the south-east 'chimney' to the summit giving full credit to Luckman and Jackson who had pioneered this route. Since then other successful approach routes have been explored, one of the most scenically spectacular being that via Hanging Lake.

Over the years, both local and mainland visitors found their way into remote corners of the South-West. All were impressed with the beauty of Lake Pedder and the Frankland Range and the feeling grew that something should be done to protect it from exploitation. In February 1954 a proposal was submitted by the Hobart Walking Club to the Scenery Preservation Board that an area around Lake Pedder be proclaimed a national park. The boundaries were finally gazetted in March 1955—a step which showed a changing public attitude, a wider appreciation of the South-West as an area no longer to be exploited for short-term monetary gain but rather to be cherished and managed for its wilderness values, for the benefit of future generations.

Federation Peak; a photograph taken in 1952.

Max Cutcliffe

'There is still adventure to be found in the South-West, and hazards too, for the weather can be as unkind and unpredictable as ever. Everyone who ventures there for the first time is, in a sense, an explorer, for no two people see it with the same appreciation and each will discover his own pleasures. And this, I think, is why we, the lucky ones, who knew the South-West before the great changes of the past decade, are so concerned that as much as possible of the region should be set aside as a national park and wilderness area, so that others, in the years ahead can capture something of the wonder, adventure and joy of discovery that was granted to us.'
From 'We the Lucky Ones',
The Tasmanian Tramp (1968) J.S.L.

Previous page
'The Corridor', Mt Humboldt.   *A Moscal*

Left
Fern and fungus.   *Chris Bell*

Moss capsules.   *Bob Graham*

Fungi.   *Bob Graham*

Fungi.   *Bob Graham*

This unusual flower, *Isophysis tasmanica* (Hewardia) is only found in the South-West of Tasmania.
                                           Chris Bell

Waratah.   *Chris Bell*

Richea dracophylla, Picton River.   *Bob Graham*

PLATE 2

Governor Franklin's Journey, 1842

H M Gee

David Burn was a journalist and settler of Van Diemen's Land. He was present on the Franklin expedition by virtue of his lively interest in it and his friendship with the Governor, Sir John Franklin. His colourful, if somewhat verbose, account contains the details of what was a remarkable pioneering feat. A considerable portion of Van Diemen's Land had not even been superficially surveyed by the early 1840's. Sir John Franklin the Lieutenant-Governor, accompanied by Lady Franklin and some friends, resolved to make a tour which would take them through part of Transylvania, this unknown western land. The party included Lieutenant Bagot ADC; Joseph Milligan, surgeon; James Calder, surveyor; 'the writer O'Boyle'; an orderly and Lady Franklin's attendant. Besides the official party there were the men who volunteered to be bearers of Lady Franklin's palanquin; twenty convicts were included as carriers and some constables were with them. David Burn's narrative commences with a capitulation of the progress of this historic expedition:

'The largest and most laborious portion of the journey was achieved on foot, over watery marshes, nearly impracticable swamps, through tangled forests, across precipitous mountains, boisterous torrents and flooded rivers, which rose in angry turbulence to bar his (Sir John Franklin's) passage, whilst rain, hail, sleet, and snow, descended upon his head. There was no savoury meats, no luxurious viands, no racy wines ... Salt Mess-pork, flour cakes baked in a frying-pan, with a panakin of tea sweetened with brown sugar, this was the sumptuous fare which served his Excellency for breakfast, dinner and supper ...*

Her Ladyship was borne part of the route in a rude sort of palanquin, but in the roughest and most inaccessible parts she was compelled to wade through miry sludge, or scramble the mountain passes, encamping upon the damp cold ground, the green fern leaves her bedding, blankets her seat, and earth her table. Repeatedly were the tents soaked through and through by the deluging rain. Upon one occasion, the

'Her Ladyship was bourne part of the route in a rude sort of palanquin' — from a sketch by D Colbron Pearce. *Tasmanian Museum & Art Gallery*

overflowing creeks reached within a few feet of the entrance.

The strife of elements, the flooding of rivers, and exhaustion of supplies, caused six or seven days' journey to occupy two and twenty, and when the schooner that was to convey his Excellency and suite by sea to Hobart Town was at length reached, a long prevalence of adverse winds precluded the passage of the dangerous bar which shuts in Macquarie Harbour, and that too, at a time when an impoverished commissariat rendered the getting to sea not merely a matter of deep anxiety, but an almost life and death affair'.

Ten convicts under the supervision of Surveyor Calder cut a track through the country to be traversed; it was Surveyor Calder who did so much of the initial exploration in the country and whose efforts made the Governor's trip possible. The official expedition left Hobart Town belatedly on 24th March, 1842.

The route to Lake St Clair passed through New Norfolk and the Ouse district. Leaving the source of the Derwent, Lake St Clair, and its 'stupendous mountains', the party travelled south-west naming 'King William's Mount' and King William Plains after the reigning monarch of the day.

From the first provision depot, eight or nine miles from Lake St Clair, the party travelled through marshlands which were named the 'Burnian Plains'. A

'naked soaring peak' appeared in the SSW. The third bare hill climbed that day may well have been Mt Arrowsmith, but to Calder it was 'Fatigue Hill'. Feeling incompetent to describe the scene from this point, David Burn relates none-the-less, that 'its magnificent grandeur—its pictorial wildness ... astound and delight'. To the south they saw three strongly defined peaks—'The Southern Needles' (The Spires Range), and westward Frenchmans Cap enveloped in cloud.

Descending 'Fatigue Hill' 'put the elastic quality' of their muscles to 'a severe ordeal'. More than once they 'embraced our mother earth; but as the Scotch song says, "When we fell we aye got up again"'.

They were not far from the second provision depot at Wombat Glen. Their discovery of fragments of 'felon' clothing 'bore plain and fearful testimony to the relentless character of the death dealing region'. Burn described the dense scrub and in it read 'the secret history of the runaway's doom'. Governor Arthur had discouraged the investigation of this territory to prevent escapes from the penal settlement operating at Macquarie Harbour from 1822 to 1834.

There was snow on Mt Gell when the party left Wombat Glen and advanced through dense rainforest to the Surprise River. Upon entering the scrub they became 'engulphed, clasped in a living tomb, yawning to devour them' ... The rainforest was found to be 'heaped, *jumbled and inwoven in tortuous complicated folds'.* After crossing the Surprise River, and the Franklin which they mistook for the King River, they passed over the Loddon Plains, distinguishing the lofty peaks of the Frenchman whose *'crags of stupendous height and terrific grandeur'* enchanted them. There were ruthless squalls with *'wind, howling like the sullen spirit of baffled revenge, and the rain streaming in torrents of insatiate wrath'.* Faced with swollen streams and rivers and limited supplies, Calder and a party of men were detached to bring up supplies from Lake St Clair. In 58 hours he returned with a load of nearly 80 pounds having at the same time cut a partly new track and secured the bridges in the rear. O'Boyle and some convicts went forward to detain the schooner, *Breeze,* which awaited the party on the Gordon River. Calder and Burn, *'half wading through bog, brake, mountain torrent and miry sludge,'* reached the noble Franklin near *'Calder Ferry'.*

Calder had made a pine raft on his previous trip. Huon pine flanked the river banks and Burn envisaged *'a certain and lucrative employment'* for lumberers who might one day raft the timber to a port in Macquarie Harbour. Eight miles south of their bivouac on the Franklin River they came across a powerful tributary named by Calder the Jane, in honour of *'the amiable and admirable partner of our worthy Governor.'* Some miles south of this junction the Franklin was found to merge with the Gordon. Pondering the myrtle forests, *'the bog and sludge',* Burn asked: *'How will Lady Franklin ever accomplish so sorry, so harassing an undertaking? —Spirit and indomitable perseverance achieve wonders'.* Calder's labours were incessant: once the official party reached

the Franklin he returned with nine packmen to Lake St Clair. The *Breeze* was low in supplies by this time, so orders were despatched to Hobart Town commanding the immediate departure of another vessel.

One of the party, a shipwright by trade, shaped and hollowed two pine logs, *'treenailed'* them together, and applied side keels. The *Eleanor Isabella,* named in compliment to the Governor's daughter, was launched. Two of the men descended some rapids. Then on the first fine day for eighteen days, the Franklin subsided. The tents were struck after an eight day camp and the party moved to *'Eleanor Ferry'* where they were carried to the farther shore. Calder, who had been away five days and covered 100 odd miles, returned once more with food. Two of his men had *'knocked up',* and one lost an eye:

> *'poor Mumford, Mr Calder's right hand man had his foot upon the end of a sapling, which, as his hatchet divided it in the middle, flew back, hitting him violently on the right eye'...* on the eve of attaining his ticket of leave!

As the Franklin party neared the Gordon River they found the forest much more varied and picturesque. They reached the *Breeze* on 22nd April. It lay in Expectation Reach, one of the bends of the Lower Gordon—*'a perfectly lovely land locked basin'*; it is not hard to imagine their joy as they *'quaffed'* a glass of sherry aboard the schooner.

There was time now to reflect upon the recent settlement in this *'hell upon earth',* Macquarie Harbour. Burn felt its disrepute had veiled the importance and the beauty of the locality. Retrospective thoughts on the route so recently traversed demonstrated the hopelessness of escape from the penal

settlement—the Gordon and the Franklin to negotiate and thirty miles of untrodden forests! Burn had encountered neither animal nor vegetable capable of sustaining life:

> *'The sole living creatures were a few black and white cockatoos, a few straggling parrots, magpies and ravens'.*

On an excursion up the Gordon in a four oared whaleboat, the party landed at Limekiln Wharf, a point near a limestone quarry worked by convicts in the previous decade. From Butler Island, *'a small, rocky, copsy islet',* called after the commandant at Macquarie Harbour, they continued to the junction of the Franklin and the Gordon, through the *'fathomless'* gorge, entranced with the scenery and the solitude. They rode beneath *'high beetling crags of bluish limestone'* and marvelled at the D'Aguillar Range in the cloudless sky.

As the schooner left the *'aqueous avenue'* of the Gordon, the waters expanded into *'a superb and spacious inland ocean, begirt with towering amphitheatrical hills.'* The party disembarked at the jetty on Sarah Island and visited the ruins of the settlement abandoned in 1834. Already the buildings were sadly weatherworn and the gardens in *'rank profusion'.* Native and foreign trees and shrubs were *'interlaced in one inextricable tangle...'.* Burn commented that *'instead of a barren, accursed spot, Sarah Island is remarkable both for its beauty and its fertility'.* He recalled that Governor Arthur's administration had realised considerable sums by the ready and profitable sale of pine logs, boats and vessels built in Macquarie Harbour.

One of the reasons for the abandonment of the settlement had been the difficult and unreliable transit to and from Hobart Town. The west coast is strewn

Sarah Island.
West Coast Pioneers Memorial Museum

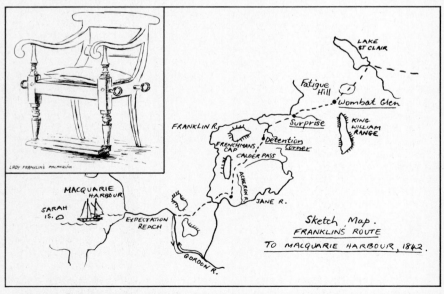

Sketch map by Helen Gee showing Franklin's route to Macquarie Harbour, 1842. The inset shows Lady Franklin's carrying chair sketched from the original in the Tasmanian Museum by Molly Maxwell.

Lady Jane Franklin.   *Tasmanian Museum*

Sir John Franklin.   *Tasmanian Museum*

with remnants of wreckage testifying to the hazardous sailing passage. The Franklin expedition now contended with a frustrating delay of two weeks in the face of strong westerly gales and heavy seas. Burn was fascinated, if perturbed, by the successive squalls and the intervening tranquillity. Even with the supply of vegetables plundered from Sarah Island, rationing was severe at this stage: fishing and hunting expeditions were in earnest. Gulls were cut up and boiled for soup—*'a mess whereat (their) nostrils regaled in anticipation'*. Excursions ashore helped allay discomfort. Visiting the pilot's station and Signal Hill, the party found the cottages to be in a similar condition to those on Sarah Island.

As prospects of the arrival of the relief ship from Hobart Town vanished, Burn tells us he *'felt the pangs of hope deferred'*. So concerned was our writer he took out a bottle in which to place his journal if the need arose. Faced with such constant foul weather Burn saw the ship's company as *'denizens of the region of instability and storm'*. Sir John Franklin read a sermon *'on the dry bones of Ezekiel, Chapter 37 and 9th verse:*

'Thus saith the Lord God; Come from the four winds, O breath, and breathe upon these slain that they may live'.

It is interesting that the party deliberated on an alternative course of action:

'The distance overland to Port Davey, and thence to the settled territory at Recherche Bay, was not great, but it was difficult, and there were waters flowing between us and Recherche, that could not be crossed but by boat. Runaways have, heretofore, made the idle attempt—three at one time were found dead...'.

On May 15th the long awaited easterly change animated all and they weighed

anchor after reading of the trials faced by the Children of Israel:

'They wandered in the wilderness in a solitary way; they found no city to dwell in. Hungry and thirsty their soul fainted in them. Then they cried unto the Lord in their trouble, and he delivered them out of their distress'.
Psalm CVII, verses 4–6.

On an ebb tide the *Breeze* swept through Hell's Gates and onto *'a sad tumbling sea'*. The following day the relief schooner *Eliza* was sighted north of Point Hibbs. As she was carrying abundant supplies it was decided that the Franklins might *'fearlessly venture to look into Port Davey'*. They transferred to the *Eliza*, and the *Breeze* proceeded direct to Hobart Town.

Port Davey was welcomed as a romantic haven with islands of the most picturesque beauty; *'their summits shaded with peculiarly ornamental and umbrageous foliage'*. A trip was made up the Spring River and Burn describes what appear to be the Celery Top Islands of Bathurst Harbour and the succession of bays and *'towering grassy mountains'*. The return to Hobart Town was uneventful, Burn extolling the native grandeur of the south coast.

Burn ends his colourful narrative with the tale of the terrible journey made by the party sent overland to the aid of the overdue Governor. Owing to Calder's lameness, a man named Bastian led the party of twenty men to the banks of the Franklin by mid May. The river was very high, but was crossed after two days. Bastian, with five men, proceeded to push through the scrub along the banks of the Gordon. The effort was fruitless and so a double canoe, twelve feet in length, much like the *Eleanor Isabella* was *'fashioned and launched.'* There was room for only four at a time, so a tedious shuttle conveyed the party of six to the mouth of the Gordon where they made immense fires in the hope of attracting the attention of the *Breeze*, little realising that the schooner had left the harbour.

Proceeding to the pilot's station, by way of Sarah Island and Liberty Point, Bastian and his five comrades saw, written on the walls of the cottage there, that the *Vansittart* had looked in to the harbour after the Governor's party had left. Bastian resolved to *'attempt the coast'* and if possible regain the settled districts via Port Davey. They were miserably equipped for such an expedition, having neither firearms, ammunition, nor dogs. *'They saw great numbers of kangaroos, tracks of wombats, and very large tigers and tiger-cats'*, we are told. They found the coast thickly strewn with wrecks. Little wonder that they began to entertain the possibility of the loss of the *Breeze*. Two large rivers were crossed (the Spero and the Wanderer?) but a third rapid stream

barred their progress. They were eleven days beating down the coast:

'To go on was impossible; to return, almost as hopeless, for their provisions were completely exhausted, and they had no means of capturing any of the wild animals around. Their shoes were worn to pieces'.

Among the debris they found a dead bullock, and with some of its hide they protected their torn and bleeding feet. The remnant of a half decomposed whale and a few mushrooms also furnished food. Bastian, who ate sparingly, alone escaped illness from this *'nauseous putrescency.'* A few limpets, a small parrot-fish, bull kelp and pig-face made possible their return to the canoe.

Four of the men rowed down to Sarah Island, two walked along the coast to the point of land nearest the Barracks. On the island cabbages and potatoes were procured. Bastian resolved to make the best of his way to Marlborough, *'or perish in the attempt.'* Three comrades accompanied him; two were unable to go on. On retracing their steps to the Franklin, Bastian and his mates crossed safely but could continue on for only a couple of miles:

'Their means of lighting a fire was gone—their clothes were torn to rags, and they screened themselves from the piercing cold with the fragments of their tattered blankets. Food they had none. Fifty miles separated them from Lake St Clair'.

Delirium had set in, their powers of endurance over, when on 1st July a party sent to their relief approached. Bastian and his companions had experienced five fine days between May 8th and July 1st. If the Franklin expedition is remembered, then Bastian's remarkable journey deserves the telling.

Among the Western Highlands of Tasmania

W C Piguenit

'The great obstacle that has always presented itself to the examination of this interesting country has been its extreme difficulty of access. Lofty and rugged mountain ranges, deep ravines, great valleys, more or less precipitous, and covered for the greater part with dense forests and almost impenetrable scrubs, and rapid rivers liable to frequent and sudden floods, are among the chief difficulties which beset the explorer in his researches, requiring him to possess not only stoutness of heart and limb, but also those other necessary qualifications which go to make up what is technically known as a "good bushman".

. . . My first acquaintance with the south-western country was made in 1871, when accompanying Mr Scott and a party of three men on an exploring excursion from Victoria (now Huonville) to Port Davey via the Valley of the Huon. Our route was along an old track, which, passing close to that river, ended at the Craycroft.

The water (of the streams in this area) is of a dark brown colour, owing to the peaty nature of the country through which they flow. Singularly enough, they appear to contain but few fish, and those we caught were the small native trout, none of which exceeded six inches in length. In this respect the southern rivers compare unfavourably with those of the northern side of the island, in which the blackfish often reach as much as four or five pounds in weight.

Resuming our journey, we reached Port Davey, where we camped for five days, experiencing during the whole of our stay very rough westerly weather. We nevertheless managed, with the aid of a boat obtained from a resident, to visit many parts of the port on its weather shore, and among others the grandest bit of scenery I believe to be found in the neighbourhood—that known as "Hell's Gates" on the Davey River. The "Gates" are a tremendous chasm between two hills, whose perpendicular sides reach an altitude of from 250 to 300 feet. The river, at the time of our visit, was comparatively low and running at a moderate rate, but in flood time it rushes through the chasm with tremendous velocity. I had much difficulty in making the sketch from which the accompanying illustration has been taken, owing to the furious westerly wind that was blowing through the "Gates", accompanied with driving showers of sleet'.

Hells Gates, Davey River by Piguenit.
Tasmanian Museum & Art Gallery

Piguenit — A Tasmanian Painter

J Fenton

Janet Fenton spent her childhood at Port Davey. Returning frequently to her home there, she has painted numerous landscapes with her father Denis King and sister Mary. An Arts graduate from the University of Tasmania, Janet is now a school librarian with wide creative interests and is a co-editor of this book.

William Charles Piguenit is said to be the first Australian born professional painter. He was born in Hobart in 1836 and from the age of 13 worked as a draughtsman in the Tasmanian Survey Department. In 1871 he joined James Reid Scott's expedition to Port Davey, visiting the pining settlement at the Davey River where he painted 'Hell's Gates'. Inspired by this journey into the South-West, Piguenit left the Survey Department to become a professional painter devoting much time to painting wild landscapes.

He made further expeditions into the western country, including a journey to Lake Pedder with the geologist R M Johnston in 1874 and to the west coast with surveyor Sprent in 1887. After the latter expedition he delivered a public lecture in Hobart and the monochrome paintings illustrating this were purchased by the government. In 1892 he spoke at the Fourth meeting of the Australian Association for the Advancement of Science, from which the extract opposite is taken. This lecture was accompanied by 8 monochrome paintings and sketches of the mountainous country which inspired him.

Piguenit is also admired for his delicate lithographic work and colour paintings. After several visits to Europe, Piguenit settled in Sydney, where he died in 1914.

King William Range, painted by Piguenit.
Tasmanian Museum & Art Gallery

'I should strongly recommend the tourist who does not object to a little mountain climbing, when in the neighbourhood of the King William Range, to ascend the first peak of that range... Upon gaining the summit a magnificent view will reward him for his labour — for he stands in the midst of a vast panorama embracing almost the whole of the Western Highlands...

Looking over this grand landscape he will see an apparently endless succession of deep valleys and ravines, ... clothed with the densest growth of myrtle forest I have ever seen, imparting a soft velvety green to the landscape.' *(Piguenit)*

Top.
The Eastern Arthurs painted by Piguenit from the South Picton Range. A mountain in this vicinity was named after the artist.
Tasmanian Museum & Art Gallery

Frenchmans Cap painted by Piguenit in 1887.
Tasmanian Museum & Art Gallery

Sarah Island in 1830. Considerable profits were realised by the ready sale of pine logs, boats and large vessels.

Eric Thomas col.

SACRED
TO THE
MEMORY
OF
MATTHEW HENDRY
KILLED ON BOARD THE
MAID OF ERIN
FELL FROM THE MASTHEAD
ON THE 29 DAY OF JANUARY 1863
AGED 32 YEARS

Port Davey Cemetery. 22 March 1875.

This inscription was carved on a Huon pine 'headstone'. Huon pine was commonly used to mark the grave both in Port Davey and Macquarie Harbour. *Royal Society of Tasmania*

Relaxing on Balmoral Beach. Mt Rugby in the background. A lantern slide by J W Beattie. *Tasmanian Museum & Art Gallery*

A clay pipe found at Schooner Cove, Port Davey. A similar pipe was found at the site of the early pining settlement at the Spring River. *Jack Thwaites*

Strahan, 1899. This little port in Macquarie Harbour flourished with the developing pining industry. Rafts of Huon pine logs were towed from the mouth of the Gordon to the Strahan mills.
Eric Thomas col.

The Huon Pine Saga

H M Gee

In the 1820's, gangs of chained prisoners from the penal settlement on Sarah Island in Macquarie Harbour cut the Huon pines on the banks of the Gordon River. Some of these pine logs were sent to Hobart and some were used in their own shipyard. Following the closing of the penal settlement many hardy individuals settled on other western rivers, continuing the saga of the pine-getters, or 'piners' as they were known.

Something of the life of a piner last century is told by James Reid Scott who visited Port Davey in 1871 and 1875. His story was published in *The Mercury*, and the following is an extract from that account:

'PORT DAVEY IN 1875...

At the present time Port Davey supplies Hobart Town with the great bulk of the timber known as "Huon Pine" (Dacrydium franklinii), and has done so for several years back. That port may indeed be said to be the chief seat of the pine-getting industry in Tasmania, Macquarie Harbour being deserted, and the Pieman, Picton, and Craycroft, worked to a very limited extent... From the nature of the Port Davey district, the beds of timber are necessarily of limited extent; and although occasional supplies have been obtained for more than 50 years, and a steady industry has been continuously prosecuted there for the last 25 years, still circumstances (such as a rise in prices, and consequent influx of piners) might extinguish the trade for a time, until young trees grow up to a size fit for market...

The pine trees grow in the densely timbered alluvial flat in the valley of the river, subject to frequent innundations, and varying in width from about 100 to 1,200 yards, intersected by a network of creeks and channels formed by the flood waters, and filled in the winter months. These channels have to be cleared of obstructions, fallen timber etc., so that the pine logs may be floated down to the main river. Tracks have also to be cut through the scrub, about 18ft in width, and sets of "skids" laid down so that the logs may be rolled into these channels or into the river. Hence the forests are traversed by numerous skid roads winding in all directions, to suit the trees successively cut down. In some places the floods occasionally rise high enough to enable boats to be used and the logs to be floated out over the ferns and undergrowth.

After the logs are cut to their proper length and stripped of their bark, they are branded at the ends with the initials or mark of the owner,—letters generally an inch in height,—punched into the wood with a smart blow of a hammer...

After the logs are in the river commences the work of "clearing down" whenever there is a flood. The logs on their passage down get jammed at eddies, stranded on low banks, or otherwise detained. Two men go in a dinghy, one to pull, the other with an iron-pointed prodder to release the logs and push them into the current. The dinghies are of the shape commonly used about the Huon,—square stem and stern, and without keel, so that they are quickly turned round and easily guided by experienced hands. From the narrowness of the river in many places, this is the best sort of boat for coming down the rapids. This work is attended with considerable danger, and requires skill and presence of mind.

The men are generally employed in pine getting and rolling into the river during February, March and April and May, with occasional visits home for rations etc. After that they are on a constant watch for floods, and go up the river to clear down whenever there is a chance. When the logs reach tidal water they are caught and put into pens which are enclosures in some eddy or still water, formed of stakes interlaced with brushwood, and a log chained across the entrance as a gate. When a vessel comes for a load, from 10 to 18 logs are fastened together into a raft, and towed down below the bar alongside the vessel at the usual anchorage...

As regards distribution of ground, there is an understood code of honour among them not to interfere with each other within a certain distance, so well observed that I heard no complaint of anyone having taken an undue advantage. A creek or flood channel is usually the centre line of a property and is followed up on both banks. Any new comer wishing to go higher up the same creek must go ahead at least a quarter of a mile...

A diary ("Longley's")for the years, 1863, 1864, 1865, and 1866 will give a fair sample of a piner's employment. He had three others as partners; and I find that his time was occupied on an average of these four years as follows—100 days each year up the river felling timber and clearing down; 135 days at work at home, catching logs, squaring or sawing them, rafting and loading vessels, repairing boats, vessels, huts, pens, etc., gardening and building vessels; 55 days hunting, fishing, and getting Mutton birds; 55 days visiting Hobart Town including voyage and detentions; and 20 days being unemployed, being Sundays, holidays, or bad weather. They built two vessels during these years...

In the season ending June 1864, they got pine logs to the extent of 58,336 feet, the quantities varying each week owing to track or creek clearing and other causes... Logs 10 or 11 feet in girth were counted large; this would represent trees over 4 feet in diameter at the butt. The average seems to be 6 or 7 feet in girth. It is a matter for consideration whether the supply of timber should be preserved, and the destruction of the beds prevented, by prohibiting the cutting of any trees under a certain size.

The dwellings occupied by the piners when up river are of the style known as "Badger-boxes", in distinction from huts, which have perpendicular walls, while the Badger-box is like an inverted V in section. They are covered with bark, with a thatch of grass along the ridge, and are on an average about 14 x 10 feet at the ground, and 9 or 10 feet high. The sleeping bunk, raised about three feet, occupies the whole of one end, and can accommodate six people easily. The other end is enclosed by the fire place, if on high ground; but those in the flats among the pine are left open in front, with the floor slabbed, and provisions made for mooring the boat to the bedpost...'.

The stands of Huon pine on the Gordon and its tributaries were also logged extensively last century. The 1900's found the rugged and resourceful piners venturing further and further upstream to the remotest reaches of these rivers. Men like Charles Abel, J Hadman Sticht and John Patrick Doherty hauled their punts up rapids to explore for fresh stands and cut tracks along the Gordon, Franklin, Denison and Jane Rivers.

Gordon Abel reminisces on the days when, as a lad of thirteen, he accompanied his father Charles into such remote regions as the Jane, hauling logs down into the river and hunting out fresh stands. An incident on the Franklin that illustrates the strength and independence of this passing generation of men is recorded in a letter he wrote in 1976:

'I will give you the details of one incident that happened to me during my years "pining in the River".

It was in 1947—1948 or thereabouts that my father Charles (Barnes) Abel and Harold McClear with myself were cutting a raft of Huon Pine logs just above the Flat Island in the Franklin River. We had been there about one month and were just about ready to return to Strahan for a spell and fresh supplies. We camped at Flat Island and worked with a small log hauler driven by a 5 hp kerosine engine through a system of V Belts and cog drive. One afternoon about 4.30, light rain falling, I was about to grease the cogs of the winch with some grease on a stick when I fell, and the index finger of my right hand went through the cog drive. I could see when I looked at it that there was no hope of saving the finger so I called to Harold to come. I then laid my finger on a log and he finished cutting it off for me with his axe. He was, by the way, about 15 years old at the time.

Harold then went and collected my father and together we returned to camp where we considered the situation, after cleaning my hand and bandaging it. We decided that as it was now dark we would wait until daylight before starting the long row back to Strahan.

Our boat was 18 ft, Carvel built, Huon Pine planked, 6'6" beam and powered by two sets of oars. The distance to be covered was approximately 16 miles down the Franklin, 24 miles of the Gordon River and a further 21 miles up Macquarie Harbour, 61 miles all told.

We started as planned after a fairly miserable night, my father rowing bow to steer, (he was at this time about 60–70 years of age), Harold stern, and myself pretty useless just lying down on the stern sheets with some blankets to keep me warm and a canvas cover for waterproof as it was still raining. We had a fairly hard day down the river as the two men had to launch the boat over two sets of waterfalls. It was later in the afternoon when we reached the old tourist hut on the Gordon River. After a short spell Dad and Harold started off again both still fairly fit and well as they had at this time only done an ordinary day's work. But by the time we reached the mouth of the Gordon at approximately 9.10 pm they were getting tired, especially Harold as he was so young.

We stopped there for an hour or so and made a cup of tea; no bread as there had been no time to cook. Off again, very light north wind on the harbour caused small waves to sit inches high and making the rowing very hard now, also my arm and hand were now starting to ache pretty badly; each time they pulled the oar it felt as though my finger was coming off again. For me the night seemed as though it would never end. But for young Harold and my father it was an exhausting time; for my father in particular, as he had had the exacting task of steering all the way. As you know, with two sets of oars working, the bow man steers by pulling harder on one oar than the other, and after so many hours of continuous effort Harold's naturally stronger right arm was forcing the boat to starboard causing father to use his left arm much more than normally he would.

I tell you the above hoping it will point out (to you) the strength and endurance of the old time river men and the inspiration an old man can give a boy, as that was and probably still is the only time Harold McClear ever rowed more or less nonstop, for 24 hours, and I am sure it was Dad's great example that helped him.

I might add that due to their fine effort I had no complications with my hand'.

Reg Morrison of Strahan has his

Hauling the punt upstream; the Franklin River, 1926. *Forestry Commission*

Doherty's Badger Box, Port Davey, c. 1875. Lithograph by James Reid Scott. *Allport Library*

memories of the closing era also. In an A.B.C. TV programme 'A Big Country' (22.3.76) he reminisced on the days of the thirties, when forty to fifty 'rivermen' forming about six gangs, rowed upstream:

'We worked as far as fifty miles upstream on the navigable parts of the Gordon and put tracks through to the Denison gorge and the Little Wilmot Range... We were six weeks getting up to the Denison one time. We wouldn't have been any tougher only it is difficult country to work in. Young fellers wouldn't do it today; there's too much work that's easier... You worked as hard as you could for three months, then you'd go back and have a holiday. Up the river you had a day off to bake bread, get some wood in for fires, and do your washing. We made a good wallaby stew and pudding of a Sunday. There was no communications then—that is unless you took some carrier pigeons'.

And what of the areas now flooded by the new dams? There was a vast extent of Huon pine there. How many trees were drowned by the waters that flooded Pedder in 1973–1974 and the plains of the upper Gordon in 1974–1975? Efforts to cut timber were concentrated in those areas visible from roads to reduce risk of public outcry at the waste of such resources. It must be remembered that there was no justifiable need for the hasty flooding. (Refer 5.2) However men working fast with chain saws on what they regarded as the last commercial stand of Huon pine secured an enormous quantity, temporarily flooding the market. Some of these men were interviewed on the same A.B.C. TV programme and they said:

'The Gordon's the biggest quantity we ever came across. We were blessed with a million trees and we cut them down, trees a thousand years old... Well, I like to cut it. It's very precious timber and there's not much of it left... It's nice to see it getting out before it's flooded'.

There is another philosophy that has inspired those who would safeguard the future of the Tasmanian Huon pine. It is best illustrated by the story of The Truchanas Huon Pine Scenic Reserve. Olegas Truchanas, who had canoed the Denison River, was the first to suggest the preservation of what was conceded to be the State's only remaining forest of mature Huon pine. The area needed protection against possible resumption of logging activities.

The following is an extract from a report by Truchanas on a 'Survey of Huon Pines in the Denison Valley', February 1970:

'It is generally recognised that Huon Pines are not in any danger of becoming extinct; thousands of small trees are growing on the banks of the Western rivers. However, stands of large, thousand year old Huon Pines growing in groves of their own are now virtually non-existent, all western rivers having been thoroughly logged even before the turn of the century. Yet it has been known for many years that in the upper reaches of the Denison River beyond the inaccessible cliffs of the gorge between the Hamilton and Prince of Wales Ranges some of Tasmania's best stands of Huon Pines existed completely untouched till about four years ago when the advent of the

Gordon River Road and helicopter transport enabled logging operations to begin. Within the three summer periods of 1966, 1967 and 1968 thousands of pine logs were put into the river by a handful of men using chain saws and motor driven winches'.

The Truchanas Huon Pine Reserve of 400 hectares was proclaimed in 1970. It is a tribute to the enthusiasm and perseverance of its instigator who explored and promoted so much of the South-West, until his untimely death in 1972.

Huon pine *(Dacrydium franklinii)* grows predominantly on the banks of the western rivers. The last remaining stands are vulnerable, in view of hydro-electric developments.
Zoology Dept. Uni. of Tas.

A Huon pine, 2,500 – 3,000 years old salvaged from the rising waters of Lake Gordon in 1975.
Forestry Commission

Lake Gordon during flooding.   *Jim England*

Left to right, Harry Kelly, Alan Giblin, V I Chambers and Herman Hutchison, about 1920.   *V C Smith*

Lyndhurst Giblin visits Port Davey in Wartime

H M Gee

In the Spring of 1914 when troopships were about to leave Hobart, reports of objects seen in the sky around Tasmania caused rumours that a German raider with aeroplanes might be lying in wait at Port Davey. There were enemy raiders located in southern waters at the time.

Lyndhurst Giblin and Charles Goddard, a surveyor, were given the job of ascertaining the truth in this rumoured possibility. They set off from Tyenna to walk to the old Port Davey track, built originally for mariners shipwrecked on the south-west coast.

Frank Marriott 'the prince of Tasmanian bushmen' was also a member of the party. He estimated the 70 mile journey would take them 6 days out and 3 back. They took 14 days food and a packhorse as far as the Huon Crossing. They also carried four homing pigeons which were in Giblin's care. In the book 'Giblin; The Scholar and the Man', edited by George Copland, Giblin's own account of this mission is given, and the following extracts are from that source:-

'We took the kind of food you take when you have to hump it—no tins, of course; flour and ships biscuits to use when a couple of loaves ran out. I had brought a half-axe but Frank, with a grin, added two full ones. There would be heavy cutting on the steep sides of High Rocky Mountain over the shoulder of which the track ran; on across Mt Bowes to the button-grass and the Huon Crossing. We took a substantial tent which would just hold four, but I added my favourite shelter, a 12 ft by 10 ft light fly, to be put up as a lean-to, which would shelter four men and gear, and give the comfort of a log fire in front of it for warmth and the drying out of clothes. The others were suspicious of this contrivance but later became reconciled.

Mr Bert Romney came with his

pack-horse as far as it could be got — a clever mare that knew all the tricks with logs across the track on a steep side-hill...

On one side of the Huon or the other, and generally on both, is a broad flood channel, covered with the most luxuriant bauera with a tangle of rope-like branches perhaps 15ft long, trailing lengthwise along the ground or climbing over logs and stumps and making a carpet three or four feet thick. Get a boot well in and it is hard work to pull it out. While it is bad, as it was frequently later as well as here, the best course is to roll on it. The first man goes without swag, rolls head over heels in the right direction, gets up and repeats the performance. The second man, high stepping, can just get his foot on top of the tangle. The third, with less effort, further treads it down and the fourth can move in fair comfort, carrying the leader's swag. In this way slow progress can be made...

So, from the Huon Crossing we pulled out with light swags down the button-grass plains which lead most of the way to the old hut (now burnt down) which stood at the end of the Arthur Range. There the old Craycroft track, then entirely overgrown, joins the Port Davey track on which we were travelling...

The track had, of course, originally been staked, but the stakes had nearly all rotted and disappeared. In making the track, however, every few yards a stunted button-grass right on the line had been mattocked and cast aside. These cut off tussocks did not rot and still kept signs of the cut edge which distinguished them from tussocks which had died naturally. The difference was hardly noticeable even when pointed out but the eye quickly learned to appreciate it.

Once in the Spring River Valley, the track ran along the scantily timbered quartzite hillside. It showed up glaring and unmistakable at several miles distance.

This circumstance gave us some anxiety the next day. If the enemy was in Port Davey they might well have caught sight of this track and set

a watch on it. So we proceeded in two parties at some distance apart, with the tell-tale pigeons in the rear party, and planned our tactics if the first party was bailed up...

Next morning we left the fly standing and skirmished towards the harbour taking cover with care and avoiding the skyline.

At last we got to a point on a heathy moor where we could see Bathurst Harbour and a good deal of Port Davey proper. There was nothing in sight and it was very unlikely that any ship lay in the parts concealed. So we wrote a progress report in duplicate and sent it off on two pigeons.

The birds had, of course, never been within 50 miles of this country. Towards Hobart there was a line of hills and mountains, 10 to 20 miles distant, with one half-gap which by compass observations we reckoned to be in the straight line for Hobart. We had expected, on hearsay, to see the birds soaring in circles to a great height before they decided which way home lay. Our experience was very different. The first bird went up a little way and came to earth again. We wondered whether the long, tough journey had put them out of action. Tearing through the scrub, tripping and falling, you cannot fail to knock about the pigeons you are carrying. We caught the bird again, found it apparently undamaged and launched it again. This time after going up about a hundred feet, it made a bee-line for the gap which was in the straight line for Hobart. The second pigeon without any more to-do, took the same bearing. It seemed a miracle.

Then followed a long and weary day over barren heath and steep, jagged quartzite hills, in parts half covered with stunted gums, until we had examined every part of Port Davey. The other two pigeons were sent off with a final report that no enemy was lying in Port Davey. We found afterwards that three of the pigeons made home in good time. The fourth, which did not arrive, was probably the prey of a hawk'.

Lantern slide of the tin workings at Cox Bight. *Tasmanian Museum & Art Gallery*

A forgotten prospect dish in the old tin workings, Cox Bight. *A Moscal*

Abandoned gravel pump and Lister engine at Cox Bight. *A Moscal*

Reminders of a busy past. Abandoned tin workings, Cox Bight. *A Moscal*

Small Mining Settlements

C D King & J Fenton

Denis King first visited the Port Davey area on a gold prospecting trip in 1931. With his father, Charles King, he worked tin at Cox Bight and after World War 2 settled at Melaleuca where he has operated a tin mine ever since. His daughter, Janet Fenton, has spent much of her life at Melaleuca. She shares her father's interest in the region's history, and both have an artistic appreciation of its landscape which they express in painting and drawing.

Despite today's modern equipment and relative ease of access, there was more mining activity in the South-West at the beginning of the century than there is now. Enthusiastic prospectors explored remote areas in the South-West in search of elusive mineral wealth. Several deposits worth mining were discovered but nothing was found to equal the wealth of the famous west coast mines. Most mining was done by individuals with simple equipment rather than by capital-backed companies and the miners worked hard, often under tough conditions. Transport was a constant difficulty—often the men had to carry stores, equipment and ore on their backs over long distances. Some were lucky and some were not.

Tin was first discovered near Point Eric at Cox Bight on the south coast by Lark Macquarie in 1891. In 1892 the government granted reward claims to Robert Glover and W H Foley in order to stimulate development. Mining continued fitfully until recent years but it is difficult to say how many men worked on the field as Cox Bight was the scene of spasmodic comings and goings of so many individuals and syndicates which formed, dissolved and reformed. According to the government geologist William Hope Twelvetrees, 120 tons of tin ore were recovered from the field by 1906. Mining alluvial tin did not require elaborate equipment, and the transport difficulties precluded the use of heavy machinery. Picks and shovels were the tools of trade and the miners generally sluiced the wash in wooden sluice-boxes using hoses or nozzles. Long catchment races were laboriously dug to supply the large quantities of water required for sluicing. With government aid a water race was dug around the foothills of Mt Counsel to divert water from the headwaters of Cox Creek along a race above the main tin-bearing grounds. Although two miles of race was dug, the project was never completed so the water of Cox Creek never added its pressure to the miners' nozzles. However, the race provided a good catchment for run-off water after rain, and pipes were laid from it down to the claims. Many smaller races were dug by hopeful individuals who coaxed water to flow from its natural course to a chosen

site. Here the layer of peaty top soil had to be stripped off, either with shovels or with a strong water jet, in order to expose the tin-bearing gravels and sands. With picks and plenty of 'elbow-grease' these gravels were broken up, though the harder-packed beds were loosened with explosives. The gravel and mud was then sluiced with running water to separate sand, mud and gravel from the heavy tin ore which settled in the bottom of the race or sluice-box. During the washing or sluicing process miners forked out the larger stones which built up high heaps beside the race. Where gravel beds exceeded five feet in depth, walls of large stones were built to prevent the stone and gravel heaps falling back into the trench being mined. Blocks of peat or tough turf were often used for the same purpose.

Local fishermen shipped the tin to Hobart and also brought mail and supplies to the miners. However Cox Bight with its surf beach open to the

Southern Ocean is a bad anchorage, so these visits were largely determined by weather conditions. Often the fishermen would 'work the boat' in the vicinity while waiting for calm weather. Then the boat would anchor off the point so the crew could bring a dinghy through the surf to the landing site. 'Boat day' was considered something of a gala day by the miners. The first men to sight the approaching boat would light smoke signals and on seeing these the rest of the men would rush to get their supply orders and mail ready.

Heavy bags of tin had to be humped to the landing site from mines sometimes a mile away. Everyone gathered at the landing to hear the Skipper pass on the latest news of the outside world while mail and stores were unloaded. Several dinghy trips were often needed to load the tin ore onto the waiting boat. Skill and seamanship were needed for this hazardous operation—indeed two men were drowned at Point Eric while rowing

This lantern slide of the tin workings at Cox Bight shows the deep trenches (excavated by hand or with a nozzled jet of water), and the quantity of gravel and large stones which had to be pitched out by hand. The man squatting (bottom centre) is washing a sample in a prospect dish. *Tasmanian Museum*

Prospector Mark Phillips with a tiger cat at the Mainwaring River on the West Coast, where he was prospecting for gold in the 1930's. Mark also mined tin at Melaleuca during the 'thirties. *Woolnizer*

Above right.
The prospector goes to town. *Woolnizer*

Adamsfield today. *Howard P Simco*

Streaming tin at Melaleuca in the 'forties. *King col.*

Middle right.
Charles King at the Melaleuca mine in the 1940's. *Brown & Dureau*

Bottom right.
Often topsoil was removed and gravel exposed using a nozzle. Melaleuca tin mine. *Brown & Dureau*

Denis King washing a prospect sample. *Brown & Dureau*

a dinghy load of tin to the boat anchored out beyond the surf.

The miners lived in huts or tents and their diet was typical of that of the early bushmen—damper, bacon, tea, sugar, rolled oats, beans and bully-beef. Nearly everyone had a camp oven in which to bake bread or roast a snared wallaby. The camp oven was hung over a fire of good hot coals and a shovelful of these was placed on the lid. Sometimes fresh vegetables were grown but gardening was a battle against wind and weather. Tinned fruit was an occasional luxury. But whatever they did without, the older, wiser miners, expert in the art of rationing, seldom ran out of tobacco!

Yet despite the hard work, the place itself appealed to many of these men. One man who worked there through his 70's said that Cox Bight was a good place to work even if you weren't getting any tin! During the depression years a number of men sought a living at Cox Bight; in 1934 about 15 men were working the field.

However, little serious exploration was done to ascertain the potential of the area. A systematic scheme of boring and shafting was started by the Port Davey Tin Mines Company in 1913–1914 but it was not completed. Tin Options Ltd contracted to explore the alluvial flats by drilling, but their equipment proved

unsuitable and it did not test the full depth of the ground. Hopes were often high and in the 1920's a survey was made for a tramway to link Cox Bight with Port Davey eight miles away, at an estimated cost of £700 per mile! Evidently this was not considered worthwhile.

In his report in 1928, A McIntosh Reid, Director of Mines, pointed out the main disadvantages of mining in the area—its isolation, severe climatic conditions during winter and the high cost of transport with consequent higher production costs. Indeed these conditions still apply.

Many features in the area bear the names of those early prospectors—Freney Lagoon, Foleys Pimple, Meldon Creek, Pender Creek and Glover Creek. Weber Creek recalls a miner who, heedless of warnings, set out from Recherche Bay bound for Cox Bight in his little boat during very rough weather. He was never seen again.

Cox Bight is now a camping place for bushwalkers and the wide beach has been used as a landing strip for light aircraft. Tea-tree and button-grass silently hide a maze of old, deep races, prospect holes and gravel heaps on the tin field which was once a patchwork of busy claims.

Two extensions of the Cox Bight tin field were found between the Bight and Bathurst Harbour. Jack Lowe discovered tin at the Ray River in 1926, and several prospectors lived there in tents working the area until 1936. A hut was built near the mouth of the river about six kilometres downstream from the mine as a meeting place and a depot for the bags of tin which were carried from the mine.

Another deposit had been found at Melaleuca. In 1935 The New Harbour Tin Company was floated and 19 men were employed at the new mine in 1936. The mine's proximity to navigable water allowed transport of heavy equipment. Six huts were built as well as a storehouse, and domestic equipment even included a stove. The company used two Dorman Rickardo engines, pumps, heavy nozzles and a small generator for lighting, all of which was removed by barge when the company was disbanded in 1937. The lease was then sold to Eric Brock, who employed about 5 men to work the mine over the next two years. Brock's machinery, brought in by barge, included a large Gardner engine driving a pressure pump and a Lister engine driving a gravel pump.

In 1941 Charles King, who had been working on the Cox Bight field for eight years, took over the lease at Melaleuca. His son, Denis, joined him in 1945 and has worked the lease ever since. Several other leases in the Melaleuca area were worked from time to time mostly on a small scale. One company, Quintex Ltd (formerly Ludbrooks Ltd) prospected spasmodically in the Cox Bight-

Melaleuca, taken from the air about 1948. King's house and the New Harbour Company huts can be seen in the centre, with the mine workings in the background to the right. *Brown & Dureau*

Denis King dozing 'paydirt' in the open-cut tin mine, Melaleuca. *Jack Thwaites*

An article in *The Mercury* newspaper for December 1938 demonstrates the labour, as well as the anticipation associated with establishing a settlement on the Jane River gold fields. *The Mercury*

Melaleuca area from 1966 for a decade. Exploration work was done and a pilot plant was set up at Melaleuca in 1974 but the company never started any serious mining. Small scale mining on a regular basis has been carried on for several years by Peter Willson, who recently settled in the area. Melaleuca, with its airstrip, is regarded as a base for visitors to the far South-West.

At the Jane River, a larger, though less permanent settlement sprang up near the west coast shortly after Robert Warne's discovery of payable gold in 1934. Soon afterwards 29 ozs were recovered in a fortnight's work. In 1935, 33 men were working on the field. Access to the area was difficult as the foot track frequently crossed flood-prone rivers and prospectors could be delayed for weeks waiting for the waters to recede. Cinnabar (a form of mercuric

sulphide) was also found there by V Kingston, but it was the gold which attracted most attention.

Until the 1970's some small scale prospecting continued but in 1975 Bennetto gained an exploration and special prospecting licence to operate near Warnes Lookout. The old Jane River pack track (aprox. 25 km) was bulldozed for vehicular access to facilitate the new mining venture.

Adamsfield, near the Florentine Valley, was by far the biggest mining settlement in the South-West. The first record of osmiridium near the Adams River was made by W H Twelvetrees in 1909. Osmiridium, a naturally occurring alloy of the platinum group of metals, has industrial use in the electrical, chemical, jewellery and dental trades, and is also used in the manufacture of fountain pen nibs. In 1925 and 1926 it was a great

Top and middle.
Pack ponies, Adamsfield-bound   *I McAulay*

Bottom
McDermott in the sluice box, Adamsfield.
I McAulay

Mt Procyon and Mt Hesperus seen from
the summit of Mt Orion in the craggy
Western Arthur Range.   *A Moscal*

Centre right
Pause below the lower falls, Sprent
River.   *Bob Graham*

Bottom right
Lake Rhona in the Denison Range is one
of many beautiful, dark mountain tarns
in the South-West.   *Martin Hawes*

Previous page
Big Caroline Rock from Forbes Point,
Port Davey.   *A Moscal*

View of the Central Corridor of the First
Split, Gordon River.   *Bob Graham*

PLATE 4

prize, fetching between £25 and £32 per ounce—about five times the price of gold. After prospecting the area, Boden, Wright and the Stacey brothers were granted reward claims, beginning the mining boom which gave birth to the town of Adamsfield in 1925. The population reached 2,000 in the town's first year. However, by late 1926 the richest and most accessible deposits had been worked, the price of osmiridium declined and wet and uncomfortable conditions disillusioned many miners and their families. By 1927 only 100 men remained. Mining continued, however, and the town lingered on until the Second World War. Adamsfield boasted a hospital, school, police station, post-office, bakery and hall as well as various butcheries and general stores. Like other mining settlements in the South-West, Adamsfield had its transport problems. It was connected by a 22 mile foot track to its nearest neighbour, Fitzgerald, a small town 56 miles by rail from Hobart. Weather conditions and continual use churned the foot track to a bog but some hardy men found their livelihood 'packing' stores to the town. It was not until late in 1926, when the government re-routed and upgraded the track, that pack-horses could be taken all the way in to Adamsfield.

As osmiridium was found in alluvial deposits it could be worked by a simple sluicing method. Except for one short-lived company which tried its luck there in 1928, claims were usually worked on a small scale by one or two men. The peak of production was reached in December 1925 when 2,258 ozs of osmiridium, worth £68,757 were produced. The bush has reclaimed Adamsfield since then, for the signs of civilization quickly disappear beneath moss, bracken and tea-tree in this climate.

At Adamsfield, the Jane River and in the far South-West nearly all mining has been done on single or two man claims. Perhaps this style of mining, in such contrast to mechanised techniques, belongs to yesterday. The pick and shovel can no longer compete with the bulldozer, trommel and jig. Nevertheless, access and weather still pose problems in the South-West so that a mineral deposit would have to be rich indeed to be worthy of large-scale exploitation.

Marshall, Quarrell & Leverton at Marshall's Claim. Water gravell Runs B.

Crisp's Hut on the Gordon Track, 1930. The riders are on their way to the osmiridium field at Adamsfield.   *I McAulay*

Left.
Mining osmiridium at Adamsfield. The gravel pump (seen at the top of the photo) pumped water, gravel and mud up to a streaming box where the osmiridium was extracted.   *I McAulay*

Top and bottom right.
Peter Willson's tin mine at Melaleuca and boring a test hole on his lease.   *Rona Gardner*

'Our camp on the fields.'   *I McAulay*

Ernie Bond with his guests on the verandah of his home.   *D Pinkard*

Top left.
A visitor to Gordonvale with Ernie Bond, about 1950.   *D Pinkard*

Left.
Gordonvale homestead about 1950.   *D Pinkard*

Bottom left.
Gordonvale in the 'seventies.   *Michael Higgins*

Bonds Craig and Reeds Peak on the distant Denison Range overlook the Vale of Rasselas, where Ernie Bond made his home. In the foreground is Lake Curly.   *Maurice D Clark*

Rasselas

There Ernie, ponderous as stone
Stared the long valley down:
In Rasselas
The wedge of time splits shingles from his roof
The lichens steal his cherries and his doors
The quiet bush becomes his garden
And his epitaph.

That was our country
We would know
The bugling of the currawongs in snow
The silence, blue with distance
And the smokes of long ago.

Bill Mollison

Gordonvale 1972.   *Helen Gee*

Ernie Bond of Rasselas

H M Gee

Ernie Bond, the genial hermit of Rasselas, was one of the last of the great hosts of the bush. For 17 years he lived in this valley of the Gordon in the home he called Gordonvale. In 1927 Ernie bought a lease at Adamsfield where he fossicked for osmiridium with some success. After seven years at 'the fields' he had selected some land in the Vale of Rasselas and here he was to build. Ernie's comfortable homestead nestled in a clump of tall trees four miles north of the Gordon Bend. In his early years at 'Gordonvale' he had several men working for him and gardens flourished. During the depression years men were engaged to clear the land, fence, build and farm. Ernie had a tremendous capacity for hard work. In 1937 he began to bake large quantities of bread and to preserve the surplus fruit. He began to carry jars of fruit over The Thumbs range to Adamsfield where they were sold in the shops. In 1940 he purchased a horse and 'Ginger' was regularly loaded down with vegetables and preserves. Ernie's efforts at sheep grazing were less successful. Firing the plains to encourage new growth worried him, and sheep were often lost in the bush. But cows provided a steady supply of milk, cream and butter, and bees were highly successful.

After 1940 Ernie spent more and more time alone. Yet prospectors, surveyors, bushwalkers and search parties enjoyed his hospitality, helping where they could. The 28 mile walk to Gordonvale from Fitzgerald was shortened in 1941 when to Ernie's horror the Australian Newsprint Mills began logging in the Florentine Valley.

After the war Ernie's way of life was modified. He allowed himself the leisure time to observe and record the habits of the wildlife and he collected specimens for the Tasmanian Museum. He was concerned with the depletion of game due to the upsurge in snaring. Though Gordonvale deteriorated in his semi-retirement, Ernie enjoyed deep contentment there. However, in 1950 the bridge at Gordon Bend was destroyed by fire, curtailing his livelihood. The now aging bushman, this 'Prince of Rasselas', was persuaded to leave Gordonvale and for a time he conducted a fruit stall at Austins Ferry near Hobart.

The Gordonvale visitors' book and an extract; photographed in 1974.   *Michael Higgins*

Crossing the river at Gordon Bend on the flying fox which replaced the bridge after it was burnt in 1950.

At Gordonvale: Chris Binks, Max Barnard and David Pinkard arrived in rags from the Jane River.

Bushwalkers pause at the post and rail fence at the entrance to Gordonvale in the 'fifties.   *D Pinkard*

For Ernie exile was hard to accept. Dreams of a return ended when he died in 1962.

As the buildings mellow, Gordonvale is reverting to forest. And those who reminisce on the ingenuity and romance of its seclusion feel sadness only for the modern life that rarely fosters such a spirit as Ernie Bond's. Bill Mollison is one of those who reminisce:

'We were frequent and welcome guests at Gordonvale in the late forties and early fifties, packing in tea, sugar, salt, dripping, and brandy. And Ernie added meat, vegetables, fruit, mead and all the warmth of a bush host.

Gordonvale was a complex of buildings including bakehouse, butchery, office and honeymoon shack around the main house. They were split and adzed from a single giant tree. Even the bath, fireplace, and plumbing were of timber and the salted-meat barrel was an adzed-out log. The fireplace, where we pegged our winter skins on the slab sides, was in scale with its owner. His regal 6' 4", massive frame, and deep, beautiful voice set the mood as we

rolled snares, philosophized, and ate too much camp-oven food at night. Men such as Ernie, and Charlie King of Port Davey, shaped our attitudes to the bush, and inspired hundreds of young people for decades to come. A marvellous raconteur, a reader and thinker, Ernie lives on for all his friends. As a man, he never gave up a man's strengths and weaknesses: he was solitary, passionate, flawed, loving, and magnificently paternal and providing.

There were secret hidey-holes for his out-of-season skins, and hints of unworked pockets of osmiridium. There were tales of old times, bush skills on view daily, grand wassails, and in fact all the trappings of the romantic life. We set out on rescues at night, nursed mountain sickness, hunted in hard winters, packed great loads, walked marathon miles, went thirsty and drank too much. It was a romantic life and in memory remains so. Romances blossomed under the cherry trees, jealousies raged, and the mead mellowed us. We were a company of friends. Ernie Bond can no more die than can Rasselas, as long as we live'.

Charles King at the Melaleuca tin mine. *Smeaton*

Charles King at Melaleuca with his son Denis and daughter Winsome, during the 'forties. *Smeaton*

The King family in 1960. *Jack Thwaites*

n January 1974 Mary King was married to Ian McKendrick at Melaleuca. Over 30 guests arrived by plane, yacht and on foot. *Jim England*

King of the South-West

J B Thwaites

This article appeared in *The Tasmanian Tramp* no. 19, (1970), pp. 72 - 78. Permission was granted for its reproduction and the author made several appropriate changes to the text.

Round the camp fires where Tasmanian bushwalkers gather at the end of the day, talk is soon of the South-West, then, inevitably, follow Port Davey—and 'the Kings'. It could not be otherwise, as for the past 35 years there has been a King at Davey. First there was Charles G King, farmer, tin-miner and veteran of the Boer War (he was a member of the First Tasmanian Imperial Bushmen), and then his son Charles Denison King—'Denny' to his friends. They have always extended the hand of friendship and good hospitality to all comers. Parties of bushwalkers from every state in Australia and many from overseas come to share with us the adventure and rich experience of a trip into South-West Tasmania. Most have experienced the added pleasure of meeting the Kings at some stage of their trip.

Denny's first introduction to Port Davey was in 1930 when he and his father made two trips to Mt Mackenzie to investigate gold deposits there. His father returned in 1933 with a prospecting syndicate when the cruise ship *Zealandia* called there, giving many people, including the writer, a rare opportunity to enjoy the scenic grandeur of Port Davey and Bathurst Harbour.

Although Charles King prospected and spent some of his time mining, he was at that time primarily a farmer. People in the Huon and Uxbridge areas still talk of the terrible bush fires which devastated farms and orchards throughout those districts in the summer of 1934. 'Sunset Ranch', the King's farm back of Judbury, between the Weld and Little Denison Rivers, was one of those burnt out. The homestead, outbuildings and fences went up in flames, wiping out the results of 12 years of arduous toil. During those pioneering days at 'Sunset' Denis got his schooling by correspondence.

The tin mining syndicate having fallen through, Charles King then took up a claim of his own at Cox Bight and worked it for a period of 6 years, during two of which Denis and his father worked the claim together.

To the late Bill Adams of Catamaran goes the credit of discovering tin at Moth Creek, while on a prospecting trip in the *Navaho*. Bill took his dish ashore and found tin on the terrace, about 200 yards west of the present air strip. The New

King of the South-West. *Jack Thwaites*

Harbour Tin Development Company worked the area for about 2 years from 1935. When operations ceased, Denis and his father came across periodically from Cox Bight to check the equipment on behalf of the Company. Eric Brock worked the tin deposits until Charles King took over his mining lease in 1941. Brock's nephew, on a visit about that time, planted a Californian Redwood which is now 20 feet in height.

After war service in New Guinea and Palestine, Denis began mining operations in 1945 and started building his house on the bank of Moth Creek, continuing the work as materials became available. He named his house 'Melaleuca'. From early 1946 he compiled daily weather reports, sending them to the Meteorological Bureau in Hobart as and when an opportunity came to forward letters. With the introduction of the outpost radio service in the early 'fifties, he was able to send his reports daily, weather permitting, and, more importantly, to make immediate contact with the outside world in cases of emergency. To a man often working alone and in such an isolated spot, the ability to summon medical aid is vital. The radio has saved the day on a number of occasions, either by making Flying Doctor calls or relaying messages for fishing boats in distress.

In 1949, Denis married Margaret Cadell, a qualified social worker from New South Wales, and they made Melaleuca their home. In typical fashion, Denis made the wedding ring from gold that he had panned on his mining lease.

From 1956, all Denny's energies over a period of three summers were put into the building of an air-strip on the buttongrass plains adjacent to the house. It was a big job for one man working alone with the little bulldozer he had purchased. This machine had been brought down on the fishing boat *Toora* and was landed some miles away, where the Mines Department's geological camp now stands. Completion of the air-strip brought Melaleuca within an hour's flight of Hobart—weather permitting—for there are many occasions when bad weather prevents flying in the South-West.

Denny goes to Hobart periodically in his 40-foot auxiliary sloop *Melaleuca* to market his tin and obtain stores. At times he is single-handed when his two daughters, Mary and Janet, a capable crew, are away in Hobart. His solo trips of some 140 miles are epics at times should heavy weather set in while rounding South West Cape, where cross seas and turbulent winds are often encountered.

We were all saddened by Margaret's death in February 1967, which broke one of our friendly links with Melaleuca. Denis continues to live and work at Port Davey. When their holidays come round, Mary and Janet rejoin him to revel in the varied activities which make up the normal day at Melaleuca.

Visitors to the King home, one of the most southerly outposts in Australia, find much to interest them. In the house is an extensive library of travel books, some autographed by their authors. Many botanists, historians, photographers and artists have gone to Melaleuca for authentic information on the Port Davey area, so rich is it in history and interest. The bird and animal life is another feature of this friendly home, for many native birds there are quite tame and show no fear of humans.

The large picture window in the living room overlooks colourful button-grass plains, backed by a series of rugged mountains extending to the distant Arthur Range. Surrounding the house and sloping down to the edge of Moth

Creek are flower beds planted with a variety of exotic and native flowers and shrubs. Beyond the homestead flourish fruit trees and gardens which keep the house supplied with a variety of fresh fruits and vegetables.

Pathways are bordered by hedges of the purple-flowered Melaleuca, after which Denis named his boat and home. He carefully clips these hedges each year after they have flowered, to keep their neat shape. He has a lifelong interest in botany and, as a result, has been able to supply information on a number of rare plants. His discovery of the previously unknown plant *Euphrasia kingii* at Port Davey resulted in the species being appropriately named after him. This interest in Tasmanian flora is also shared by his sister Win Clayton, who with her fisherman husband Clyde, lived in the Port Davey area for 30 years. In a way 1976 saw the end of an era, when Win and Clyde retired to northern Tasmania.

During his mining operations, Denis uncovered ancient river beds containing logs of celery-top pine, Banksia and tea-tree. At a depth of several feet, charcoal and the ends of burnt sticks from ancient bush fires have been found. Banksia cones, ferns and leaves also lie in the deposits. From the appearance of the overlying strata the debris would appear to be thousands of years old. In spite of their great age, the salvaged logs burn readily after drying. It is of interest that no celery-top pines grow within miles of this site today.

Denis has his own programme of fine-weather and wet-weather jobs. In the good weather, general maintenance of machinery and boats, wood gathering and gardening occupy much of the day. Being in an area where fine days are infrequent, much activity has to be crammed into the daylight hours. The firewood has to be cut and loaded into the boat at Bathurst Harbour, as there is little available in the vicinity of Melaleuca. On wet days, if the rain is not too heavy, general mining and sluicing goes on. On exceptionally bad days, when the guy wires of the radio mast are screaming, general housework, bread baking and other cooking occupy most of the day. Evening brings a break from chores, and there is time to relax, enjoy radio

Denis King built his home, Melaleuca, on the banks of Moth Creek in 1947. *Brown & Dureau*

The Flying Doctor made his first visit to Melaleuca in 1961 when he delivered a large medical chest to the King family. *The Mercury*

Middle left and bottom.
Denis King taking temperature readings at Melaleuca. A daily weather report is sent to Hobart by radio. The comfortable hut was built in 1960 for bushwalkers as a memorial to his father. The fireplace was made from river worn stone slabs collected from Bathurst Harbour. *King col.*

Below middle.
Dug-out canoe originally built and used by miners at the Ray River in the 1930's. *N E Poynter*

Mary and Janet King were the first Tasmanians enrolled in 'School of the Air' which was based in Port Augusta in South Australia. *The Mercury*

Above and bottom right
Drawings by 'Denny' King and his daughter Janet Fenton, inspired by the landscape and wildlife of the South-West.

At Melaleuca, power for house lighting etc is generated by a windmill.   *Rona Gardner*

programmes and catch up with reading.

A plane comes in, at times bringing several weeks' accumulation of mail. In the summer months, when charter flights are more frequent, the mail comes almost weekly.

In good weather, Denis, with his family and any visiting friends, may set out for a boat trip to Bond Bay in the outer harbour, a half-hour's run beyond Breaksea Island and 18 miles from Melaleuca. Hannant Inlet or the Davey River may also be visited. In the latter case, the party will disembark from the *Melaleuca* into the motor dinghy and go upstream through the spectacular gorge known as Hells Gates.

Denis generally makes a point of lying at anchor in the shelter of Breaksea Island in the late evening, when mutton birds are returning to their nests after a day's food-gathering at sea. On such occasions, it is an unforgettable sight to see them coming over the island in thousands, like a swarm of bees.

Other outings, on the long summer days, include climbs of the nearby mountains which encircle Melaleuca. Favourites are Mt Counsel, New Harbour Range and parts of the South West Range. A wealth of interest is to be found on these trips, for a profusion of flowering plants and shrubs cover the slopes.

In 1951 the Scenery Preservation Board proclaimed the foreshores of Port Davey a scenic reserve and also, in 1962, all the islands within Port Davey and Bathurst Harbour, with a view to protecting the flora and fauna. From 1951, for a period of 14 years, Denis King acted as honorary fire-warden for the Board. His valued service was augmented by the Board in subsequent years with the appointment of fire-watchers during the summer months. Hobart Walking Club members, university students and other outdoor people manned the fire-watch from a base camp at Schooner Cove, near Port Davey entrance. Denis has been of great assistance to all these people throughout their month-long periods of duty, and the arrangement could not have functioned so successfully without his ready help.

Denis King's personal tribute to his father, who died in 1955, is typical of the man. He laboriously set about erecting a large building close to Melaleuca as a memorial. Purchasing the timber and other materials in Hobart on his infrequent visits, he loaded them aboard his boat and took them to the building site. He built the attractive stone fireplace with colourful stones collected from the Old River. The Charles King Memorial Hut is for use by bushwalkers and other visitors to Melaleuca. The Tasmanian walking clubs and a number of mainland outdoor clubs contributed to the cost of the bunks and other furnishings, having requested permission to do so as their own tribute and in gratitude for the hospitality shown their members visiting Port Davey over a period of years.

At Port Davey the water-ways are used as transport links.   *King col.*

Win and Clyde Clayton on their fishing boat *Stormalong* in 1963.   *N E Poynter*

Jack Thwaites   *Adrian Goodwin*

Jack Thwaites is the author of the previous chapter 'King of the South-West' and the following chapter 'Milford Fletcher — Track Cutter'.

The development of bushwalking as a recreation in Tasmania owes a great deal to his work of over a period of more than fifty years.

In the 1920's he was one of the small number who walked and skied in private groups, acquiring a knowledge of the country both around Hobart as well as deep into the mountainous areas of the State to the west and south. Then, in 1929, he collaborated with E T Emmett in founding the Hobart Walking Club on November 12th of that year and became its first Honorary Secretary, which position he held for nine years. His enthusiasm and ability placed the Club on a sound footing. From 1933 to 1946 he helped to edit the first seven issues of the Club's journal *The Tasmanian Tramp*. Even now, over 43 years later, he is back on the editorial committee for a third period and has been associated with the editing of 16 of the 22 issues. He is a regular walker and leader in each year's programme of walks. To all members of the Hobart Walking Club, Jack is the doyen of Tasmania's bushwalkers.

With Max Moore of the National Fitness Council he laid the foundations of the Youth Hostel Association movement in Tasmania in the 1940's and he has been active in this field ever since.

Since the early 1940's he has been deeply interested in the National Fitness Council and has worked tirelessly to help further the broad aims of outdoor recreation supported by the Council.

He is a photographer of note and his work has been used for illustration in many books and publications on Tasmania. He was the first Administrative Officer of the Government Photographic Laboratory and Film Unit for ten years from 1946.

He has also made a great contribution to the State as Secretary and Superintendent of Scenic Reserves of the Scenery Preservation Board (the forerunner of the present National Parks and Wildlife Service) for six years, which was the position he held when he retired in 1967.

In 1960 he organised a walk into the South-West for Sir Edmund Hillary and was associated, in 1963, with the visit of Tenzing Norgay to Tasmania. In recent years he has organised and led several aerial-safari treks to Lake Pedder, Cox Bight, Port Davey and Maria Island for Ausventure and through these treks he has introduced many overseas visitors to Tasmania's wilderness areas.

As a member of the Tasmanian Historical Research Association, he researches in depth into many aspects of Tasmania's history. He is particularly interested in the people who lived in the places visited by bushwalkers and the significance of their handiwork that can still be seen. Jack, when in reminiscent mood around a campfire, holds his audience enthralled and his quiet dry humour, invariably foretold by a gentle chuckle, adds 'savour' to the stories he tells as he dispenses billy tea.

Mt Anne from the Frankland Range.   *Howard P Simco*

Milford Fletcher — Track Cutter

J B Thwaites

There would be few tracks cut in Tasmania's South-West before the turn of the century and since, that Milford Fletcher of Glen Huon has not trodden or recut, some of them more than once, during his 50 years of almost constant activity in that area. You name it—he's been there—be it as prospector, track-cutter, or in response to that mystic but irresistable call of the wild places that motivates so many of us. Milford modestly likens himself to the 'last of the Mohicans'—reflecting no doubt that today no-one else appears to be particularly interested in track work in remote areas as an occupation, even part-time.

For the past 105 years the Fletcher family has had a continuous and active association with the cutting and maintenance of tracks throughout the South-West, so it was perhaps a logical outcome that Milford Fletcher should follow in the footsteps of grandfather Charles Fletcher who had accompanied Scott, McPartlan and Piguenit to Port Davey in 1870. Up to the turn of the century Milford's father and several of his uncles worked on the tracks for some years, including the Overland Track (the Linda) in the 1880's. Several times they walked through to the Huon from the West Coast and on one occasion, in 1900, from Birch Inlet via Lake Pedder.

Milford Fletcher was doing bush trips even before he started school and since then has spent 50 odd years on and off in the South-West, covering most of the area south of the Lyell Highway. During that time he has worked for the Hydro-Electric Commission, Public Works Department, Forestry Commission, Mines Department, Scenery Preservation Board, Lands Department and the National Parks and Wildlife Service.

In 1935 he worked with a Mines Department party clearing a track from the Picton River via Lake Pedder to the Mainwaring River on the West Coast, but the track was never completed beyond Junction Creek as the party was transferred to the Mainwaring by boat. In June of that year, Milford and his mate Tom McGuire tried to reach Strahan from their Mainwaring base, but as the track hadn't been cleared for 30 years, they were unable to follow it beyond the Wanderer River so had to return. The

Milford Fletcher and 'Jason'.   *Jack Thwaites*

Wanderer, a very deep river, has a sand bar near the mouth, but when they arrived there a huge south-westerly sea was sending big waves up the river. Using an old whaleboat found on the riverbank they crossed in that. After returning to their base camp at the Mainwaring, Milford set out with Neville Pegg for the Huon on one of the wettest and most eventful journeys he ever made. Milford speaks of 'swimming that 110 miles in ten days—well, perhaps we did walk some of the way!' Returning to the Mainwaring later, they worked a gold claim until Christmas when Milford again did this homeward trip in five and a half days. Leaving Neville Pegg at Port Davey, he reached his farm at Glen Huon two days later.

In the period 1936—1938 Milford was assisting the Mines Department at Rocky Boat Harbour and also covered a big area of the Jane River country up to the Maxwell River and Prince of Wales Range. In between these jobs he worked a gold claim at the Jane and 'did pretty well at the game'. He had also taken a lot of gold at the Mainwaring.

In 1942, during the search for Critchley Parker, the track was specially cut from Picton River to the Cracroft by a party comprising Denis King, Police officers Sproule and Wetherspoon, and three Huon men, Ray Brown, Jack Woolley and Milford Fletcher. The work took seventeen days.

In 1946 working on the South Coast Track with Walter Adams, they started at South Cape Bay, where Fenton's party had finished and Freddie Edwardsen joined them when they restarted the track at the New River, where they cut ahead to Deadmans Bay and up the eastern face of the Ironbound Range. Clyde Clayton then picked the party up with his boat at Deadmans and took them to Cox Bight where they worked back to join up the track on Ironbound. Later they returned to do the section from the Bight to Port Davey. While at Cox Bight, Milford was engaged by fishermen to cut a track along the coast to Ketchem Bay and Window Pane Bay past Green Island, for use in cases of shipwreck.

In the early 1960's, Milford staked and re-cleared the track from Cracroft River to Junction Creek. During January and February of 1962, he had a contract to bulldoze a track from Picton River to Cracroft Crossing. Later in the same year he staked and cleared the track from the Cracroft to Junction Creek and continued it on to Sandfly Creek. In 1963, with James McLeod, he staked and cleared the track from Junction Creek to Long Bay, Port Davey and in the following year, cleared the South Coast Track from the top of Ironbound to the Surprise River, finishing the final section to Recherche in 1965.

Another section cut out was from the Strathgordon Road where it cut the old Port Davey Track, over Mt Bowes and down to Sandfly Creek; later he continued pegging the track from Junction Creek to the Huon Crossing and Sandfly Creek. Then followed the section from Junction Creek to Long Bay down the Spring River valley. In 1967 Milford worked on this section again and made a diversion from just above the tidal water in Spring River to The Narrows at Farrell Point, where he built a hut, using myrtle and manuka for the frame with galvanized iron walls and roof. The same year the track was continued from the opposite side of the Narrows (Joan Point) to Melaleuca.

The bushwalking fraternity who frequent the South-West and know the vagaries of its climate and terrain, well appreciate the hardships and arduous work of the pioneer bushmen who had a share in cutting and clearing its miles of tracks.

Maatsuyker Island, Lighthouse. Opening day, 1891.
W L Crowther Library

Looking through the lighthouse lens to the Needles, Maatsuyker Island. *John Cook*

Maatsuyker Island, 1891. Horse powered whim at the top of the haulage way, now replaced by a power windlass. From the anchorage, provisions must be hauled up the steep slope to the top of the island. *W L Crowther Library*

The lighthouse supply ship *Cape Pillar* in Bramble Cove, Port Davey. *A Moscal*

Bottom left.
Cape Sorell Lighthouse, about 1900. *W L Crowther Library*

Train line to Cape Sorell Lighthouse about 1900. *W L Crowther Library*

Maatsuyker Island

J Cook

John Cook has been head lightkeeper on Maatsuyker Island since he and his family moved there from Tasman Island in 1971.

We arrived at the same season that Abel Janszoon Tasman first saw the island 329 years earlier in November 1642 during his voyage of discovery. Then, as now, the white tea-tree blossom must have been in full flower. Maatsuyker, translated, means mate's sugar or measure of sugar; though Tasman may have named the island after the Governor of the Dutch East Indies of the day, Lieut Maatsuyker.

The island is situated 13 kilometres south of the Tasmanian mainland at latitude 43° 40′ S, longitude 146° 19′ E and is the second largest of the Maatsuyker group of five islands. It is roughly triangular in shape, and covers some 200 hectares, its highest point being 300 metres above sea level.

The vegetation closely resembles the coastal scrub of the south-west coast. There are even some west coast peppermints *(Eucalyptus nitida)* growing near the top of the island. However the main covering of flora is a mixture of tea-tree, Melaleuca and Banksia, accompanied by luxuriant growths of shrubs, herbs, grasses and ferns.

There are no snakes on this island, so it is a particularly suitable habitat for marsupial mice *(Antechinus minimus)*. Forming a very important part of the diet for the latter are two types of skinks, *Leiolopisma ocellatum and L. trilineatum,* which are the only reptiles on the island.

Bird life is quite prolific; a wildlife officer from the National Parks and Wildlife Service, who visited the island early in 1975, observed a total of forty species—twelve sea birds and twenty-eight land birds. Several breeding colonies are situated on the island, the largest being that of the short-tailed shearwater or 'mutton bird' *(Puffinus tenuirostris)*. These birds arrive late in September and depart in early April.

On the Needles, a series of large rocks which extend from the island to the south-west, lives a large breeding colony of Tasmanian fur seals *(Actocephalus pusillus doriferus)*. In January 1972 I counted approximately fifty adult seals and several pups. A wildlife officer counted approximately 800 in January 1975 and in January 1976 I counted over a thousand. The seals are now wholly protected and this protection is policed.

The most southerly lighthouse in Australia stands on Maatsuyker Island. The light has been continuously manned since 1890.   *Jim England*

Maatsuyker is inhabited not for the protection of its wildlife, but for the manning of the lighthouse. This is situated on the south-west corner, 118 metres above sea level. The lighthouse, 17 metres in height was erected during 1889 and 1890 by J & R Doff of Hobart, when Maatsuyker must have been a very lonely spot.

It is the southernmost lighthouse in Australia and is the landfall for ships making for Hobart from the west or passing south of Tasmania. It is the only manned station on the southern and western coasts of Tasmania, which are uninhabited for a distance of 240 kilometres. There are only three other lighthouses along this exposed coastline. Just south of the entrance to Macquarie Harbour a tall brick lighthouse stands on Cape Sorell. The tower was built in 1899 and the station was manned by two lightkeepers until 1971. It was made fully automatic with a battery-electric light in January 1971 and in March of that year the lightkeepers left on the ship *Cape Pillar*. Today little remains of the lightkeepers' houses.

On Low Rocky Point stands the only lighthouse between Macquarie Harbour and Port Davey. Being such a low-lying tongue of land the point is difficult to see from a distance, particularly when visibility is poor, or at night. The battery-electric light was installed in 1963, access being by sea as well as via a bombardier track from Birch Inlet, Macquarie Harbour. In 1974 the 18 metre steel tower was replaced by a new fibreglass tower, materials and men reaching the site from the lighthouse ship *Cape Pillar* and by helicopter.

Another unmanned lighthouse stands at Whalers' Point on the northern shore of Port Davey. The steel frame supports two acetylene gas cylinders which are replaced at intervals by fishermen hired by the State. The Marine Board of Hobart controlled all lights in the State until 1901 when most important coastal lights were taken over by the Commonwealth.

The light on Maatsuyker was originally a wick burner, then a mantle lamp burning vaporised kerosene; it will be made electric prior to full automation in the near future. It is a group flashing light of 239,000 candle-power with a range of

40 kilometres. The lens is of the dioptric system of the first order. The lenses revolve once every 180 seconds by the aid of a clockwork mechanism which is wound up every hour by the lightkeeper on duty.

The lightkeeper's first and foremost duty is the exhibition and maintenance of the light under his control. The three resident lightkeepers keep a continuous watch system, similar to that on a ship, throughout the day and night. Apart from maintaining his watch in the tower, the lightkeeper is also required to do station maintenance and a regular three hourly weather report, which is relayed to Cape Bruny by radio. Before the advent of radio in the 1930's, short urgent messages were sent to Hobart by carrier pigeon, released several at a time in the hope that one at least would reach its destination! Direct communication with Hobart was made when the radio telephone was installed on 28th June, 1974. This not only enabled the keepers regular communication with the Tasmanian mainland, but provided various services for the general public. For instance, from Maatsuyker one can see the whole coastline of southern Tasmania from South East Cape to South West Cape, so fires can be reported immediately. In reverse, numerous calls are received every day from fishermen, aviators, yachtsmen, the merchant marine and walkers, all requesting information particularly on the weather conditions. Once a 'surfie' rang up to find out if conditions were suitable for surfing!

Stores and supplies were delivered by boat from either Hobart or Dover— normally an overnight trip. However, old methods have given way to new, and the island is now serviced by a helicopter, reducing the trip from Hobart to about one hour. The Department of Transport's supply vessel, *MV Cape Pillar*, calls two or three times a year to deliver bulk fuel supplies and other large cargo.

Maatsuyker has been continuously manned since 1890, however Europeans were not the first people to walk this island. The Aborigines visited Maatsuyker, but just as they vanished, so too will lightkeepers become people of the past.

Replacing gas cylinders at Whalers Point, Port Davey.   *N E Poynter*

Left, top to bottom.
The author with a young mutton-bird. Maatsuyker Island is a weather recording station. Maximum and minimum thermometers and wet and dry bulb thermometers are kept in a ventilated 'weather box'. The haulage way. *John Cook*. Lastly a Tasmanian fur seal, *Arctocephalus tasmanicus*.   *National Parks & Wildlife Service.*

Lightkeeper's home, Maatsuyker Island.   *John Cook*

M Macphail

The Natural Environment

2

The South-West's natural environment is a legacy of many merging but distinct worlds. In this section are presented aspects of the geologic and climatic forces that have shaped it over aeons of time, and of the plants and animals that give life to the present. The perspective of scientific description is necessary in a world where man is the blundering master of al! 'natural environments' but care must be taken to avoid confusing an acquaintanceship with 'ecosystem models' with actuality, understanding or completeness of vision. But with imaginative sympathy, colour sparkles on the surface of the present, landforms seem newly drawn. The *Climate* of the South-West becomes again memories of lead-grey rain-curtained weeks, split aside by days of high, rain-washed blue. *Geology* and *Geomorphology* are translated back: here upland crags fade into a distant guess — the ragged crests in a sea of peaks, an earth-tide whose ebb is frozen in our span of perception. Cirque lakes reflect long-vanished ice; glaciers nourished by ancient waves of cold. To the discerning eye, *Nothofagus cunninghamii* closed-forest becomes again an other-world forest of shadow and green lights, full of leeches. Here against the run of seasons, the red flush of myrtle leaves in Spring deepens to a late Summer mature green, whilst above, its alpine relative the deciduous 'beech' conceives in foliage of fading yellow the echo of far-off European Autumns. Warmth in the glance of sun on the afternoon 'button-grass' stretches beyond the ecology of *Gymnoschoenus sphaerocephalus*, and hidden by shrubs, the moss marked tread of *Antechinus* leads to its own remote conclusions.

A plume of cloud caused by strong wind and turbulence on Frenchmans Cap.

Brown & Dureau

Climate

M Nunez

Dr Manuel Nunez is a climatologist working in the Geography Department of the University of Tasmania. He received his training in Canada, and is currently undertaking radiation and energy balance studies in Tasmania.

The island of Tasmania, located between latitudes 41 and 43 degrees, is under the influence of the westerly wind regime throughout the year. This airstream, which is particularly strong in the southern hemisphere, extends over the Indian Ocean uninterrupted by land masses for thousands of miles before imparting its maritime character to the island. Along its northern flank, anticyclones move across the Australian continent and bring clear sunny weather and subsidence conditions along its path. The properties of these two synoptic systems and their interaction give the South-West of Tasmania its cool and changeable maritime climate.

Some continental influences are nevertheless felt in the area. The coldest temperatures occur inland during wintertime while coastal regions experience the coolest summers. However yearly averages smooth out these seasonal differences so that little variation occurs in mean yearly temperatures.

Total precipitation is considerable as is expected in a region with a mid-latitude west coast location. Precipitation is further enhanced by the topography of the western ranges which run in a north-west/south-east direction, and reach maximum elevations of over 1,200 m at a considerable distance from the coast (80 km). Maximum orographic rainfall of over 3,000 mm occurs in these highlands but rapidly decreases both westwards towards the coast and eastwards. Thus Cape Sorell and Maatsuyker Island receive 1,300 mm and 1,200 mm respectively and a local maximum of 2,400 mm exists at Port Davey. The inland station of Strathgordon reports 2,700 mm while Hastings, located in the eastern fringes of the western ranges, receives 1,400 mm.

The seasonal variation in temperature, precipitation and other climatic parameters can best be understood by a description of the major synoptic circulation of the area. In winter a 'Stormy Westerlies' regime is frequently established. This is an intense westerly flow usually resulting from one or more cyclonic centres moving to the south of the island. Surface isobars are aligned east-west and gale force winds may occur shifting from north-west to south-

Cloud on Mt Anne.   *Michael Higgins*

west. These winds are caused by a series of cold fronts which pass through the region, bringing also heavy rain, and a drop in temperature. Typically this pattern will last up to five days giving overcast conditions and continuous rainfall. Eventually the system will weaken and the weather will clear as an anticyclone approaches from the north-west.

An anticyclone-trough-anticyclone sequence is also typical of winter. The cold marine air behind the trough may be associated with local rain and perhaps with some snow in the highlands. Milder continental air follows the passage of the anticyclone in what is basically a north to north-easterly flow. The flow will intensify and change in direction to the north-west before its sudden extinction with the passage of a cold front.

The coming of spring is accompanied by a southward shift in the mean path of the anticyclone centres and a significant drop in the number of gale force winds. The frequency of anticyclones passing over the State increases and more settled weather occurs as spring turns into summer. However, the anticyclone-trough sequence is often maintained at about weekly intervals and the weather retains its changeable character.

Rainfall is highest in the winter and coincides with the highest frequency of frontal passages and the greatest

differences in sea and air temperatures. Maximum monthly rainfall is in midwinter (July) at coastal stations such as Cape Sorell (160 mm) and Port Davey (260 mm) but may shift to late winter and early spring (Sept.) further inland, for example at Strathgordon (330 mm). Rainfall intensity is strongest in areas near the mountains where orographic convection occurs, and decreases towards the coast. This effect is clearly shown in the records for Strathgordon and Maatsuyker Island. Both stations have an average of 250 rain days per year but winter precipitation is much higher for Strathgordon.

Wintertime air temperatures show the moderating influence of the oceanic environment, an effect which diminishes gradually both with distance from the coast and with elevation. The coldest month is July with a mean daily maximum temperature of 9.2°C reported at Strathgordon. Milder conditions occur at coastal stations such as Maatsuyker Island and Cape Sorell where the mean daily maximum temperatures for the same month are 10.9°C and 12.0°C respectively. July minimum temperatures are lowest at inland stations such as Strathgordon (2.9°C) and increase towards coastal stations like Maatsuyker Island (6.4°C).

Frost incidences are a complex function of topography, elevation and

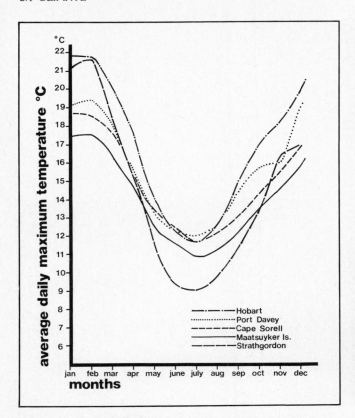

distance from the coast. Nowhere above 300 m is there a frost-free month in Tasmania. However, it is not uncommon to experience frost-free winters along the south-west coast. In contrast, Strath-gordon has an average of 16 days of frost in July. Very often cold air drains downhill during calm clear nights, forming extensive valley and gully frosts in the region.

Total snowfall is highly variable from year to year. Low terrain discourages the build up of permanent snow, although snowdrifts occasionally survive on higher peaks over cool summers. Unstable air masses from the south-west trigger the heaviest snowfalls; these being accompanied by gale force winds and severe drifting of snow under lee slopes. Accumulation of snow is not

OPPOSITE PAGE
Top
Bill Kinnear

Bottom
Winter cloud often fills the valleys in the morning but usually dissipates during the day. Here it surrounds Mt King William I. *Jim England*

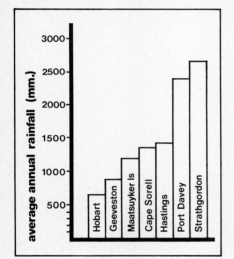

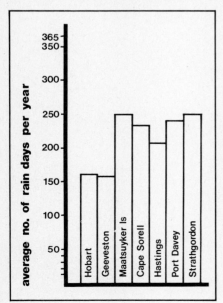

common before June, and then only above 900 m. However snowfalls, blizzards and hail may occur in the highlands at any time of the year and extend occasionally to sea level.

A typical winter day could be one of constant or near constant overcast conditions with the rain occasional along the coast but becoming more continuous inland. Anticyclonic conditions will very often bring low orographic clouds along mountain ridges and morning mists in valleys. These local effects may gradually dissipate with the direct action of the sun, and the weather will turn crisp and sunny with frosts forming in the late evening. In some cases fog will be elevated by low level turbulence and grey stratus clouds will develop. The frequent cloud cover significantly diminishes the sunshine received at the surface so that during the month of June an average of only 1.6 hours of bright sunshine per day is measured at Strathgordon.

As spring progresses into summer, a gradual drop in precipitation and an increase in temperature occurs. Precipitation is at a minimum then although local differences in amount of rainfall still exist in the area. Thus observed values range from a mean January total of 130 mm for Port Davey to 70 mm for Cape Sorell. The effect of continentality is evident in the higher summer temperatures recorded at Strathgordon. Mean January maximum air temperatures there are 20.7°C and are close to the highest measured in the South-West for this month. In contrast, Maatsuyker Island reports a mean maximum temperature of 17.2°C.

The north-west wind which is noted for its moderating influence in winter and spring, can turn very warm and dry during the summer. In some cases a blocking situation is formed with the anticyclone remaining stationary to the east of Tasmania and the northerly wind persisting for several days. A potential fire hazard situation can develop if these north-west winds occur during a particularly dry spell. In some situations lightning from local convective thunderstorms will generate sporadic bushfires.

It is difficult to describe a typical summer day in the South-West since the weather is particularly changeable in this season. Cloud cover can rapidly alternate from near overcast to a few scattered cumulus within one or two hours. Conditions are considerably brighter than in mid-winter and mean January values of 7.2 sunshine hours are obtained at Strathgordon. The hot and dry north-westerly wind often carries dust from the mainland and haze may form along the coast. Many weak fronts pass through the region bringing overcast conditions but little rain. It is not until April that the winter character of the precipitation is re-established, following the northward movement of the frontal systems.

The South-West is a region of dramatic moods characterized especially by intense and rapidly changing weather systems. These help to shape the landscape and are integral with its character and beauty. Climate is thus a vital element and must be studied as an important causal factor in the ecosystem of the region.

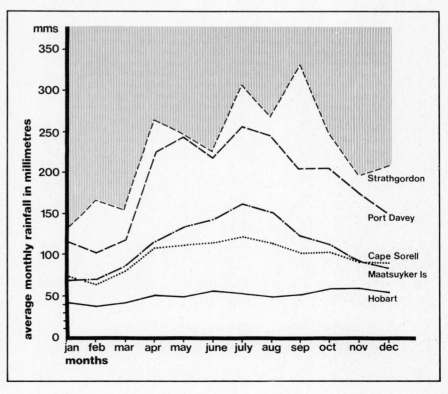

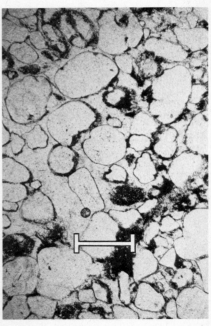

A phyllite with thin quartzite layers which illustrates the complexity of the folding in the metamorphosed Precambrian of the South-West. The end product seen here is the result of several pulses of folding. Though small in scale, such outcrop sized folds reflect the form of structures several kilometres in extent. The ruler measures 150 mm on the top scale.
C Boulter

A photograph of quartzite taken through a microscope. The bar scale is 1 mm long. Fine black lines define the margins of the quartz grains. Their corners have been rounded off by extensive attrition. The deposition is dated at about 1,000 m.y. ago. Murphys Bluff. Frankland Range.
C Boulter

A 100 feet cliff face on Mt Hesperus. Arthur Range. showing the style of folds in well layered quartzites. This now resistant rock folded at considerable depth in the Earth's crust during the 800 m.y. orogeny.
P Robinson

Geology

C Boulter

Clive Boulter graduated with honours from the University of Sheffield in 1970. He then joined the Geology Department of the University of Tasmania where he mapped the geology of the Frankland and Wilmot Ranges and supervised other mapping projects in the South-West. Clive has completed a doctoral thesis and is now working in the Geology Department of the University of Western Australia.

Before the geological history of the South-West can be outlined and even before the geological map is given a cursory glance, a comment must be made on the quality of our knowledge of the region. Large areas have not been mapped in a systematic fashion, much of what is known comes from reconnaissance standard work and quite significant areas are virtually unknown. Each time a detailed mapping project is carried out extensive revision of maps, sheets and ideas is required. Obviously the inadequacy of basic factual information leads to a degree of uncertainty in any discussion of rock distributions and the dating and ordering of events. This should be borne in mind throughout the following discussion where some but not all of the major difficulties will be raised.

South-West Tasmania has had a long and involved history starting approximately 1,000 million years ago. Long periods of deposition of materials in seas, estuaries, lakes and rivers have been interrupted from time to time by relatively short intervals of considerable crustal activity *(orogenies)*. During such disruptions crustal forces tilted and folded sediments that were initially flat-lying layers, even to the extent of turning layers completely upside down. Besides structural effects the active pulses brought about other changes in original rocks through the agency of increased temperature. Minerals that were stable in rivers and seas at the Earth's surface (0-25°C) had to adjust to temperatures (up to 700–800°C) quite different from those they experienced in sedimentation. Collectively known as *metamorphic*, the above processes work in reverse on high temperature minerals that formed from any molten igneous rocks which were also caught up in crustal upheavals.

Through Tasmania's history the intensity of each phase of orogenic activity has decreased with time and on the basis of their effects we can propose a fundamental subdivision into three geological groupings. Rocks formed after 280 million years ago are all very little disturbed from their depositional situation; fracturing, not tilting, is the most obvious sign of crustal forces. Sequences of rocks ranging from the Middle

Limestone cliffs on the lower Franklin River.

Helen Gee

Devonian (370 m.y.) to the late Precambrian (about 750 m.y.) have been well folded but not at very great temperatures so that pre-existing minerals have not always been strongly modified. The oldest rocks, i.e. those older than 800 m.y., are complexly folded with extensively reconstituted minerals so that wet muds are now coarse-grained garnet bearing schists.

The earliest events

In a dynamic system like the Earth's Crust, early events are often obscured by later ones. Detailed work is being carried out in South-West Tasmania to unravel the later effects and to get as much information as possible about the initial condition of our oldest rocks. A high proportion of the South-West is underlain by the metamorphosed Precambrian justifying considerable attention in this article. Virtually all of these rocks were sedimentary prior to folding and heating. Rocks cooling from magmas formed only a tiny amount of the metamorphosed Precambrian areas. Deposition took place approximately

1,000 m.y. ago when conditions at the Earth's surface were possibly quite different from today. Certainly plant and animal life forms were rudimentary and land environments must have been desert-like through a lack of significant vegetation to bind the products of weathering. Such ideas may well explain the formation of sand deposits of extremely highly rounded grains of quartz (SiO_2 mineral) very like the millet seed sands of modern deserts produced by high energy wind abrasion. The evidence from several parts of the metamorphosed Precambrian indicates a great deal of further reworking in a shallow sea where these sediments alternated with clays and clay/lime mixtures. A considerable time span of the order of 200 m.y. is envisaged for the formation of these rock types allowing plenty of time for the quartz grains to be cemented together to form very hard rocks *(quartzites)*. Metamorphic processes acting on these rocks tend to make them even more resistant and they are in fact responsible for many of the prominent mountain ranges in the

South-West including the Western Arthurs, Frankland Range, Prince of Wales Range and the Sentinels. Almost 50% of the metamorphosed Precambrian is the very pure quartzite with extreme SiO_2 values (often nearly 100%). Between the resistant quartzites are the readily erodable phyllites and schists which are the heated and folded forms of the sedimentary muds. Most of the button-grass plains of the South-West are found

overlying these weak materials. The phyllite/schist distinction rests on grain size and generally reflects the varying degree of temperature rise in the outer portion of the Earth. Coarse schists indicate higher temperatures than the finer grained phyllites. Both the Frenchmans Cap region and the West Coast from the Giblin River to Port Davey have particularly fine examples of schists. In the last mentioned case

metamorphic garnets up to 1 cm in diameter, and albite grains in excess of 1 cm, have been found.

Measurements on radioactive materials in the phyllites and schists suggest that these rocks underwent the maximum heating *about* 800 m.y. ago. According to mineral studies the temperatures attained varied throughout the metamorphosed Precambrian with about 550°C being the general

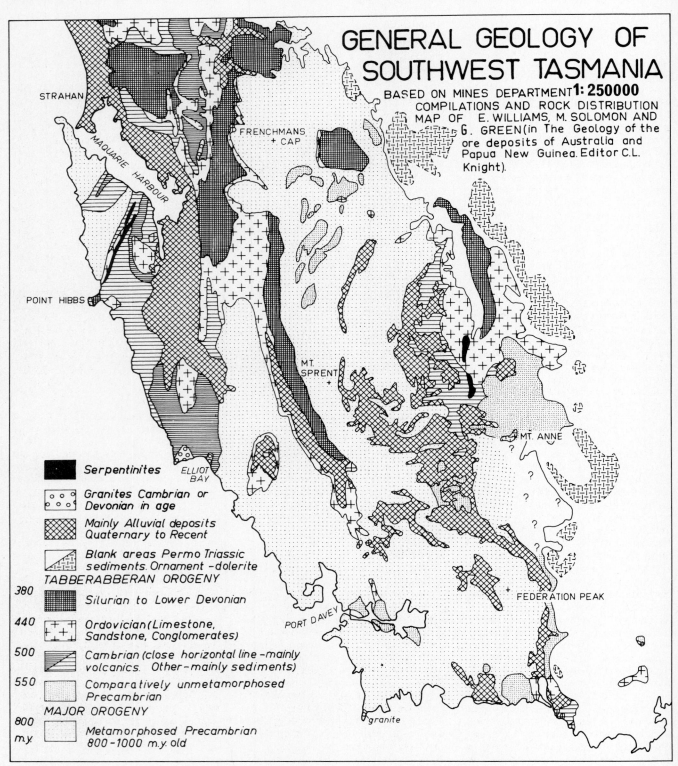

GENERAL GEOLOGY OF SOUTHWEST TASMANIA

BASED ON MINES DEPARTMENT **1:250000** COMPILATIONS AND ROCK DISTRIBUTION MAP OF E. WILLIAMS, M. SOLOMON AND G. GREEN (in The Geology of the ore deposits of Australia and Papua New Guinea. Editor C.L. Knight).

STRAHAN

MACQUARIE HARBOUR

FRENCHMANS + CAP

POINT HIBBS

MT. SPRENT +

MT. ANNE

ELLIOT BAY

Serpentinites

Granites Cambrian or Devonian in age

Mainly Alluvial deposits Quaternary to Recent

Blank areas Permo Triassic sediments. Ornament –dolerite

TABBERABBERAN OROGENY

380 | **Silurian to Lower Devonian**

440 | **Ordovician (Limestone, Sandstone, Conglomerates)**

500 | **Cambrian (close horizontal line –mainly volcanics. Other –mainly sediments)**

550 | **Comparatively unmetamorphosed Precambrian**

MAJOR OROGENY

800 m.y. | **Metamorphosed Precambrian 800–1000 m.y. old**

FEDERATION PEAK

PORT DAVEY

granite

upper limit although temperatures up to 670°C have been claimed for some metamorphic rocks found on the Lyell Highway. Most of the folding of these old rocks occurred at the same time as the metamorphism. Some magnificent examples of folds on all scales are to be seen between Frankland and Terminal Peaks on the Frankland Range, in the Mt Hesperus area of the Western Arthurs and at Harrys Bluff by the Old River.

The metamorphosed Precambrian of the South-West probably was only part of a very large belt of crustal rocks that underwent orogenic activity 800 m.y. ago. On a geological scale the outer layer of the Earth is considered by many to be as active as the scum on a boiling pot of jam. If such activity is real then continental masses could well have been broken up and fitted back together differently several times in an 800 m.y. period. With these ideas in mind people have looked for likely zones of material similar to our older Precambrian and have suggested parts may be in New Zealand and even South America. Needless to say evidence is hard to come by when dealing with such a dynamic system.

The problematic 800 to 550 m.y. period

Certain difficulties arise when applying the first – mentioned criteria for distinguishing between rocks belonging to the main groupings. Perhaps the most important is that the quartzites are so resistant that they often do not obviously display folding. Also their associated much crumpled and contorted phyllites may be so weathered that they are impossible to find in outcrop. For these reasons almost all of the Jubilee Block (from The Needles to Arthur Plains, and from the Weld River to Scotts Peak Road) was considered to be a sequence that had undergone less severe folding and metamorphism than the oldest Tasmanian rocks first discussed. It would now appear that this holds for the northern half of the block but much of the southern portion is of the metamorphosed Precambrian. The rocks in the northern half are unfossiliferous cherts, mudstones, sandstones and dolomites which normally go under the name of the 'comparatively unmetamorphosed Precambrian'. Traditionally these and other rock types in scattered occurrences at Scotts Peak, along Bathurst Channel and at the Ironbound Range are linked with extensive rock sequences in the north-west of Tasmania. Again they are dominantly sedimentary but widely varying types indicate quite dissimilar environments of formation ranging from continental shelf seas to small very unstable basins rocked by frequent earthquakes. It is also possible that these comparatively unmetamorphosed se-

quences were folded at different times, though as yet we have little firm evidence for most of the occurrences. Conglomerates, mudstones and sandstones of the Bathurst Channel and Harbour were folded before 500 m.y. ago and after 800 m.y. The whole sequence is overlain by a Lower Ordovician (approx 500 m.y.) conglomerate and the Bathurst area sequence contains boulders of phylite and schist from the metamorphosed Precambrian. Much more geological mapping is required before facts like these can be obtained from the other problematical Precambrian successions in South-West Tasmania. The future study of microfossils is the greatest hope for our understanding of age relations in the comparatively unmetamorphosed Precambrian.

A further possibility is that the rocks of the northern Jubilee Block are as old as the metamorphosed Precambrian but were not as extensively folded or metamorphosed in the 800 m.y. orogenic event. Careful studies of the contacts between the various rock units are required in this case and even then evidence as to the nature of the boundary may not be forthcoming.

Yet further complexities have recently been brought to light concerning relations between the Precambrian and Cambrian rocks. The events of this 550 to 650 m.y. interval are still being investigated by Mines Department geologists in a region between, on the west, the Junction Range—Pleiades and on the east, the Denison Range—Stepped Hills—Ragged Range. It is an extremely good example of how detailed mapping finds many hitherto unknown events and even whole distinct rock sequences.

The advent of fossils up to the last major earth disturbance in Tasmania (550 m.y. to 380 m.y.)

The story of the Cambrian to Lower Devonian sequences (550 to 380 m.y. ago) is somewhat better documented

than that of the earlier rocks largely due to the more common presence of fossils which allow ordering of rock sequences. A unifying aspect of this group of rocks is that their most important folding event occurred at approximately 380 m.y. ago in the Tabberabberan Orogeny. Conditions in western Tasmania in the earliest of these periods, the Cambrian, have been likened to the recent history of the South American west coast. It is envisaged that a thin line of volcanoes fringed a continental mass (i.e. the stable metamorphosed Precambrian block) with an ocean westwards. Into the ocean volcanic debris and lavas would interfinger with normal sedimentary deposits forming on the ocean floor. Representatives of the Cambrian volcanic association are now found in a belt extending down from Queenstown to Elliott Bay. As they are an extension of the most mineralised belt in Tasmania, they are of considerable economic interest.

Besides fringing areas of Cambrian sediment deposition and volcanic formations, several basins were produced within the continental mass. Such features were strongly controlled by major fracture systems which delineated the size and shape of the internal basins. Perhaps the largest preserved example is the area of Cambrian sediments around Adamsfield where a very major fault—the Lake Edgar Fault—is dominant. The blocks on either side of this fault have moved many times, often in radically opposed directions. The fault seems to have been most active during the Cambrian but has moved intermittently since. Deep faults operating during this period were responsible for the location of serpentinite bodies at Adamsfield and on Cape Sorell. The serpentinites on Cape Sorell have fairly coarse asbestos associated with them whilst at Adamsfield they are a source of osmiridium.

Fracture systems again appear to have exercised tremendous influence on the type of sediments formed in the Lower

An interesting geological feature near Scotts Peak is the Lake Edgar Fault. Some visible movement has occurred along this fault line in the recent past.
A Goede

Ordovician. At this time it appears that the whole of the older Precambrian unit was uplifted with respect to the basins of Cambrian rocks which thus had high scarp faces overlooking them. As a result, coarse boulder material was carried down large alluvial fans spreading out over some of the Cambrian areas. Queenstown has conglomerates which exemplify these times and like the earlier volcanics they in turn are found fringing the continental mass down to Elliott Bay. Similar controls must have operated in the Adamsfield area because on the Stepped Hills, Denison Range and Clear Hill, conglomerates like those at Queenstown occupy almost the same place in the sequence. Gradually the land surface had its irregularities evened out and coarse conglomerate deposits gave way to finer sandstones. Limestone deposits signify the end of this progression to a point where the land surface was very subdued and several regions were invaded from time to time by shallow warm seas. Very little in the way of silica and clay was brought into such areas by rivers or ocean currents. The best modern day analogy is the Persian Gulf, and many structures found within our Ordovician Gordon Limestone can be seen there in recent formations. These limestones occur extensively in the Florentine and Olga valleys though scattered outcrops are found elsewhere. A long belt of country between the New River and the Hartz Mountains extending from the coast to the Weld River is very poorly known geologically but it is in here that several Ordovician limestone outcrops are

found. Little can be said of these because of thick vegetation and widespread cover by younger rock sequences.

The Silurian—Lower Devonian sequence does not form a large part of the area under consideration, being confined to the King River and the region south-west of Queenstown. Rock types range from original quartz sands through silts to muds, implying some reactivation of the source area to supply once again sedimentary detritus after the limestone era. At about 380 m.y. ago an abrupt end to sedimentation was brought about by major forces within the Earth's crust (the Tabberabberan Orogeny), which caused folding of all pre-existing rocks and uplifted them to bring about another cycle of active erosion. Granite intrusion is a related event but its representatives are scarce in the South-West. Probable granites of this period are found on South West Cape and offshoots from a larger body are seen at Cox Bight. Solutions coming from this latter granite carried tin into vein systems; erosion then concentrated tin into small workable deposits in gravels.

Post Tabberabberan events — post 380 m.y.

From the Middle Devonian to the Upper Carboniferous (280 m.y. approx.) there is no geological record but it seems likely that mountain ranges, formed during the Tabberabberan Orogeny, were slowly eroded to extensive flat plains in the east of the state with a good relief being left over the strip of Precambrian rocks. The latter stages of this process must have been under glacial conditions for despite

their antiquity quite a detailed account of ice movement directions can be given. The flat-lying post Tabberabberan deposits fringe our map area running from Precipitous Bluff directly north to Maydena and from there extend NNW to King William and beyond to the Central Reserve. Generally the Permian and later rocks of the South-West are found in difficult country with a lack of access so they have not been the subject of as much study as their correlates in East and South-East Tasmania. The general record of the Permian is of tillite (glacier transported coarse debris) giving way to silts, sands and limestones deposited in a shallow sea influenced by pack ice to varying degrees. From time to time during the Permian the sea level varied, changing the marine conditions to lagoonal or freshwater. Because the South-West was mostly land at this time the Permian deposits found here probably show the effects of such variations more than those further out in the basin. Towards the end of the Permian, climatic conditions had changed sufficiently to allow coal bearing units to form. These were swamp, river and delta deposits which required a lowering of the sea level. Marine influence dropped to zero in the later Triassic sediments which follow the Permian and have the same near flat attitude. Triassic stream and lake sediments are found with features which indicate they developed on broad plains from a system of braided rivers and intervening lakes somewhat similar to the present day channel country of south-west Queensland. Areas underlain

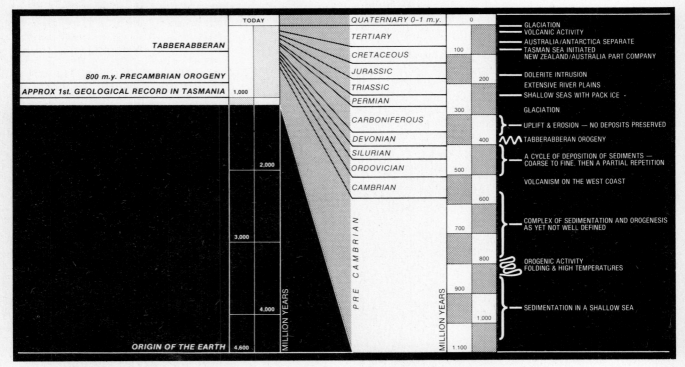

Summary of Tasmania's Geological History.

by Triassic sediments in the South-West are restricted and have not been differentiated from the underlying Permian on the map.

Subsequent Tasmanian geological events generally had minor effect on the South-West. About 165 m.y. ago forces in the Earth's crust produced deep fractures which allowed thousands of cubic miles of molten rock to rise towards the surface. Once this igneous material reached the flat-lying Permian and Triassic rocks it was apparently easier to work its way along bedding planes and displace the overlying sediments upwards, than to break through to the surface. The displacement of such large blocks must have caused great instability in the form of earthquakes and given rise to a rough topography. More recent erosion has

exposed the cooled equivalents of the molten rock, dolerite, and this rock type now forms most of the high peaks that overlook the South-West proper (e.g. Mt Field West, King Williams, Mt Weld, Mt Picton). The dolerite may have been somewhat more extensive, originally, as indicated by the outposts of Mt Wedge and Mt Anne away from the main outcrop.

The Tertiary in Tasmania's geological history (70 m.y. to 1 m.y. ago) was another active period which had some effect on the South-West. Major Earth stresses were again responsible for large faults. A large slab of material was down-dropped along faults running either side of Macquarie Harbour and turning into a north-south direction for some twenty miles. A deep, fault-scarp bounded basin was filled with sediments over millions of

years to become an important structural feature. The Tertiary faulting episode, beside initiating new faults in the younger rock types, would also have caused movement in old established fracture lines in some cases of Precambrian vintage. Remnants of this activity are evidenced by minor earth tremors to this day and some discernible movement on the Lake Edgar Fault in the last 100,000 years. Tertiary fracturing provided a means of escape to the surface for igneous material but again evidence for these varied volcanic events is sparse in the South-West.

The elucidation of the more recent history of the South-West is in the hands of the geomorphologists who are interested in the origin of land forms and the unconsolidated sediments overlying the solid geology.

The Tectonic Evolution of the Australian Region in the past 200 million years

For centuries there have been tantalising suggestions that continents may have once been congregated in a giant land mass. The best evidence was found in the fit of South America and Africa, requiring a pull apart of several thousand kilometres. As studies of geology became more serious so we had the growth of evidence supporting large scale displacements between continents but which stumbled on mechanistic difficulties. Continents are discrete masses which extend to depths of an average 40 km into the Earth. For such a mass to move it would have had to bulldoze its way through the surrounding outer layers of the Earth; a seemingly impossible task. In the 1960's a theory evolved which appeared to overcome many of the difficulties and is variously known

as 'Plate Tectonics' or 'The New Global Tectonics'. It is now postulated that the outer portion of the Earth, roughly down to a depth of 150 km, can be considered as a mosaic of relatively rigid plates. By taking a fixed point somewhere within the Earth's inner shell, say 300 km below the surface, we can envisage motions of the outer thin plates with respect to this point. The essential feature of Plate Tectonics is that the plates are not directly fixed to the inner shell but are separated by a zone which is soft. Such a situation might be likened to two steel sheets separated in sandwich fashion by putty or plasticine. It is possible to maintain cohesion in this system yet push one plate so as to displace it with respect to the other.

Under the Plate Tectonic regime a very dynamic Earth has been displayed where complex variations of plate movements and plate configurations have evolved over the last one or two thousand million years. Much debate is generated by conflicting proposals for continent outlines and positions at any one period in the past but almost all geologists accept the basics of the Plate Tectonic Theory. The younger the events the more general the agreement becomes because a higher proportion of the evidence remains intact. In the Australian region the tectonic scale evolution seems well defined for the past 200 to 300 million years. At the beginning of this period it is fairly certain that Australia, Antarctica, India, South America and Africa all formed one continuous land mass. This grouping is known as Gondwanaland and it is possible that the remaining continents were also physically linked to one another and to Gondwanaland. Such a hypothetical conglomeration has been named Pangea.

The separation of the elements of Gondwanaland has left many geological features which allow timing and rates to be deduced. Australia and Antarctica were together for most of this period of continental drifting. They parted company from India and Africa between 200 and 180 million years ago, though retaining close contact with the toe of South America. About 80 million years ago the Tasman Sea was initiated with the drift of New Zealand away from Australia and at 55 million years ago the Australia/Antarctica couplet finally broke up. During the past 55 million years these two continents have been steadily moving apart and they are now just over 3,000 km apart.

The nature of the relationship between Asia and Australia during the past 200 million years is not as clear as that between our other continental neighbours. A complex and active zone lies between these two continents making reconstructions difficult and uncertain. One interesting prediction under Plate Tectonic theory is that in the next 50 million years Australia will push most of Indonesia and Papua New Guinea against the Asian mainland.

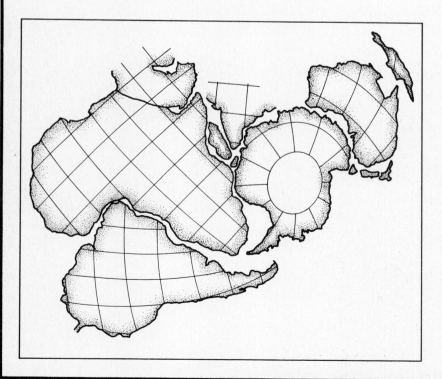

A typical South-West river gorge. The river is not down-cutting as actively as in the past, as shown by the large rocks choking the bed. Note the height of bare rock on the valley sides indicating the usual height of flooding. Middle Franklin River.
R Brown

This characterizes a river between gorges. The shingle bank on the right is probably reworked glacial outwash and is now slowly migrating downstream. Crossing River.
Maurice D Clark

Freezing and thawing of soil water has produced this landscape which was probably just out of reach of glaciation. Sharp frost-shattered tors contrast with the gently rounded and terrace-like forms which are typical of periglaciation.
D Pinkard

A typical glaciated valley at Schnells Ridge. Snow accumulated in the depression now occupied by the farther lake. Avalanches brought down rocks and more snow from the surrounding peaks. Ice formed and flowed out over the rock bar now damming the lake and removed material from behind the bar. It spilled over the valley steps and down the valley (to the bottom edge of the picture). The glacier deposited its rock load on the valley floor and sides forming two lateral moraines. One is the ridge at bottom right and the other is pushed halfway up the side of the ridge on the left. The lower lake is moraine dammed and would have been deeper if meltwater had not carried away rock debris at the glacier snout.
Jim England

A small cirque glacier has pushed up a terminal moraine which dammed this small tarn. On the left the moraine was breached by meltwater which cut a small steep gorge to the plain below. Frog Lake, Schnells Ridge.
Jim England

The Serpentine River, viewed from the air, was inundated in 1972 by the rising waters which flooded Lake Pedder. *'The Serpentine wound its way from the lake over almost dead flat button-grass plains for some miles before descending into the Gordon. It acted as a governor, the water flowed out so slowly and the wind just pushing the water round on Pedder beach levelled it out as though God had a giant trowel, getting it ready for next year. Had it rushed out down a gorge the beach would never have been. The rushing water would have scored the whole thing and carried the sand away with it. But the width of this lake was magnificent sand and the whole thing was a superbly balanced miracle of nature — equilibrium at its finest. Nothing just like this can take place again because the conditions will not apply.'* Max Angus speaking in the Hobart Town Hall (April 1976).
Brian Curtis

Landforms

S H Stephens

Simon Stephens majored in geology and geomorphology at the University of Tasmania gaining his science degree in 1972. Through field work for the Department of Mines and his wide experience in mountaineering he has gained a first hand knowledge of the geomorphology of the South-West. He works as a lapidary in Hobart.

The climate and underlying rocks of South-West Tasmania have led to the evolution of a distinctive landform area which is unique in Australia.

The area is mainly underlain by folded quartzites and phyllites which contrast in resistance to erosion. Thick layers and pockets of quartzite form steep craggy ranges and hills, with softer rocks underlying the alluvial covered plains.

Climatic variations, mainly colder phases, are mostly responsible for the present slopes and detail of the larger features. Glacial and periglacial features

are common-place and much of the river erosion and deposition occurred during these phases.

The elevated regions of the South-West are remnants of an ancient plain which was formed in the Carboniferous period in older rocks prior to the Permian period, 250 million years ago. This plain was formed under conditions of glaciation similar to those which have recently created the surface of Northern Canada. The ice-sheet gave way to swamps and a shallow sea during the Permian period. Sedimentary rocks

were deposited on the old surface during this period and during the following Triassic period. The area emerged from the sea to become a riverine plain in the Triassic (220 million years ago). This marks the last known major stage of deposition in the area, which has been mostly above sea level ever since.

Erosional processes, largely due to the action of river systems, have almost entirely removed the sediments laid down in the Permian and Triassic periods. The rivers have cut deeply into the old (Carboniferous) surface

Lake Judd. a glacial lake below Mt Eliza.

Brown & Dureau

removing the softer phyllites and leaving the more resistant sections of the old surface formed of quartzites and hard schists. These form the level tops of the Gallagher Plateau and other mountains. The fluvial erosion of the Carboniferous surface was further modified in the Pleistocene period by glaciation and periglacial action down to low altitudes.

The exposed surface of pre-Carboniferous rocks display marked fold structures especially in the older Precambrian exposures. Apart from the area just south of Macquarie Harbour there is little evidence of the major faulting which broke the post Carboniferous surface in eastern Tasmania into a series of plateaux and rift valleys in the Tertiary period. One good example of a fault in the fold structure province is the Edgar Fault with a vertical displacement of approximately three metres in the present surface indicating a relatively recent phase of activity.

Rivers and gorges

The rivers of South-West Tasmania are quite spectacular by Australian standards. They are mostly short but carry a large volume of water which is often greater than that of other Australian rivers many times longer. Though the area receives a large amount of rain there is little disruption to human activity by flooding. This is because the rivers run swiftly along beds of relatively steep gradient. The rivers rise and fall abruptly with changing weather conditions but never dry out because of vast amounts of water stored in the surface layers of peat and alluvium.

The sediment load carried by rivers in the South-West appears to be far below their capacity. This is largely due to the dense plant cover and because peak flows are now lower than those during glacial times.

The river profiles from source to mouth are stepped. The steeper portions are usually in the gorges which act as local base levels to plains upstream.

There is a distinct difference in drainage pattern between the fold structure province in the west and the fault structure province east of the Cracroft. In the east the main rivers are relatively straight with three dominant directions:— N W. — S E., N E. — S W. and N.—S. These directions are the dominant ones in Tasmania for rivers running on dolerite country and are due to predominant fault line directions. Tributaries tend to flow along these directions. Main streams often flow straight with segments in any of these directions separated by sharp bends. This is best seen on a map of the Huon and its tributaries. Upstream from the Weld confluence the river bed is in folded rocks but the pattern remains the same, indicating that the drainage pattern has been superimposed.

Only the largest and most vigorous rivers have gorge sections cutting mountain ranges transversely indicating their consequent nature. The subsequent streams have aligned themselves with the folded rocks. It is mostly impossible to ascertain the original pattern for the area but there are many features which with further study could unravel the river history.

Legacy of an icy past

Many of the slope profiles and superficial deposits of sediments in South-West Tasmania owe their existence to past colder climates. During the Pleistocene epoch (2 million to about 10,000 years ago) the snowline periodically descended to about 1,000 metres; present coastal areas were many miles inland and Tasmania was joined to the rest of Australia.[1] These factors combined to put most of South-West Tasmania above the tree line with considerable areas having no vegetation at all.[2]

Below 1,000 metres elevation the dominant agency of erosion was the freezing and thawing of water forcing rocks apart and causing the loose debris to creep down the mountain slopes. This was combined with strong runoff in spring which would wash away much of the weathered rock. This was a major source of sediment in the then more active rivers. This form of erosion resulted in the formation of the familiar tors and crags interspersed with the smoother slopes of the lower mountains. The large quantities of gravel covering the lower slopes of mountains are derived from this agency of erosion.

Above about 1,000 metres elevation there was permanent snow. However, aspect and mountain size modified the thickness of snow deposited and therefore controlled glacier development. The biggest glaciers usually originated on the lee side of mountains. The extent of the most recent glaciers can be seen by steep-walled U-shaped valleys and well developed moraine deposits. Most glaciers in the South-West end at the foot of the mountain where they originated. The main types of glaciers present were cirques and small valley glaciers. There were no extensive ice caps, piedmont or large valley glaciers as in the style of the Central Plateau and the West Coast during the last glaciation.

In general, lateral moraines were better developed than terminal moraines, which were mostly removed by meltwater into large expanses of gravel outwash which is found in many of the lower valleys. Lake Pedder originated as a hollow dammed by glacial outwash from the Frankland Range. Reworking of the outwash sands by waves and wind gave Lake Pedder its shape and formed the dune system behind the beach.[3]

It was unlikely that glaciers reached the present coast of the region. The Narrows at Port Davey were thought at one time to be a fjord; it is, however, a ria or drowned valley.

There have been a number of cold phases resulting in glaciation in the region, with evidence of three such phases separated by warmer phases resembling today's climate. The last phase was responsible for the bulk of glacial features visible today. This lasted from 25,000 to 10,000 years ago. The nature and extent of prior glaciations in the region is not fully known, but the oldest seems to have been much more extensive.[4]

There are some detailed studies of glaciation of particular mountain areas notably those by J Davidson (1970)[5] of the La Perouse area and J Peterson (1966)[6] of the Frenchmans Cap area.

For further detail on particular areas the Glacial Map of Tasmania is useful (Derbyshire, Banks, Davies and Jennings, 1965)[7].

The coast

The coastline is a typical drowned landscape which developed when the sea level was at least 120 m lower during the glacial phases. After the last glacial period the sea inundated the typical South-West topography and has modified it relatively little. The off-shore islands would have been hills on the coastal plain and Bathurst Harbour and Port Davey are typical river valleys now occupied by the sea.

The way the sea has modified the original landscape depended on the nature of slopes. Where slopes were steep there are plunging cliffs and the sea has eroded out many of the lines of weakness to form blowholes and caves. On moderate slopes the sea has eroded out a large amount of the softer patches of rock leaving large expanses of jagged rock stacks and deep gulches. Shore platforms are relatively rare and are mainly limited to areas of horizontally bedded rocks.

Where there is relatively flat land behind the coast there are broad sweeping beaches with dunes and lagoons. Each sandy beach has its own distinctive mineral assemblage indicating little longshore drift from one bay to another. There are few large sand beaches and extensive dune systems. The cause of this may be the lack of large areas of shallow water and, as well, the absence of areas of soft, easily eroded rocks.

Around Port Davey and Bathurst Harbour there are terraces which have been formed by coastal development at slightly higher sea levels than at present.

A small glacier once occupied the site of this lake and fed ice down over the rocks (in the bottom right of the picture) to another glacier below. Hanging Lake.
Jim England

Limestone formation. Point Hibbs.   *Peter C Sims*

Raised marine terraces are present in the Bathurst Harbour area. A raised shore platform can be seen at lower left and a flight of possibly three terraces at middle right. The highest terrace is badly eroded and therefore quite old.
Jim England

Here the sea has etched into what was once a gently sloping hillside, removing the soil and the intricate network of weathered rock. West Coast.
Peter C Sims

Undermining by the sea of a soft layer of rock has caused this confusion of dolerite and sandstone to slump down into the sea at South Cape Bay.
Howard P Simco

Bathurst Harbour, once thought to be part of a fjord, is in fact a drowned valley. The Celery Top Islands are seen in the foreground.   *Brown & Dureau*

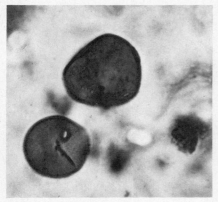

Gramineae; ca .035 mm.

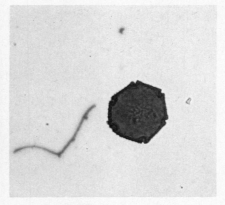

Nothofagus gunnii; ca .033 mm.

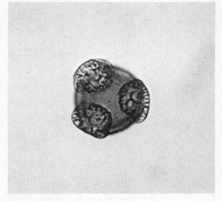

Microcachrys tetragona pollen; ca .033 mm.

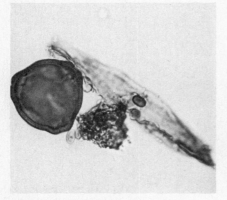

Casuarina sp.; ca .044 mm.

Eucalyptus ovata; ca .037 mm.

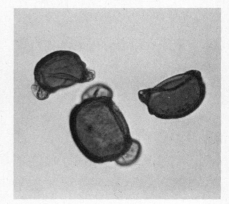

Dacrydium franklinii; ca .045 mm.

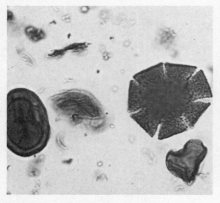

Nothofagus cunninghamii ca .040 mm.

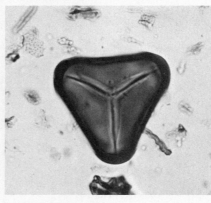

Dicksonia spore: ca .032 mm.

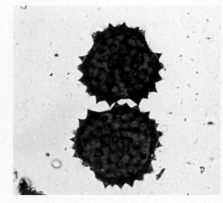

Compositae pollen; ca .028 mm.

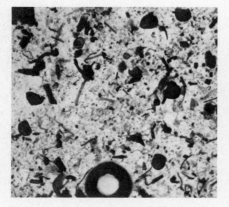

Pollen concentrate from surface sample peat moss. Consists mainly of Restionaceae with single *Microcachrys* (centre).

Epacris (tetrad); ca .089 mm.

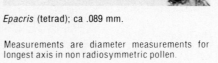

Measurements are diameter measurements for longest axis in non radiosymmetric pollen.

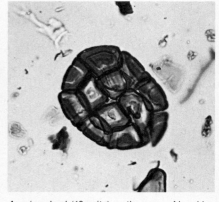

Acacia polyad (16 units) on the verge of breaking up; ca .080 mm.

All photographs M Macphail.

Climatic change in the Evolution of the South-West Wildscape

M Macphail

Dr M Macphail is an honours graduate in Botany from the University of Sydney. In 1969 he introduced Quaternary pollen analysis techniques to the study of Tasmania's past environments. Recently he completed a Ph.D. study at the University of Tasmania. This reconstructs for the first time, the history of vegetation and climatic change during the last 13,000 years over the southern half of Tasmania.

A quality of timelessness appears to be part of the 'essence' of the South-West; a view reinforced by the close similarity between descriptions of the region by the explorers of last century and the present-day wildscape:

'The country is almost destitute of timber, excepting narrow belts of timber along the sides of streams, and the effect from an eminence is that the spectator is looking over a vast extent of well-grassed fertile valleys, bordered by precipitous rocky mountains rising abruptly from the green plains. ... A closer acquaintance with the plains dispels the idea of their fertility, and we found that what appeared undulating or nearly level country, was composed of many steep narrow ridges and broad spurs from the mountains, covered with large tussocks of button-grass—Gymnoschoenus sphaerocephalus—and a jointed rush-like plant — Leptocarpus tenax — with many patches of tea-tree and various plants of the order of Epacridaceae... The plains are well watered by streams of various sizes, each bordered by a belt of thick scrub, chiefly of honeysuckle (Banksia) with a dense growth of bauera and cutting grass from 8 to 10 feet high, closely matted together, so that it is impossible to pass by pressing it aside. It must be either cut through or trampled underfoot... much time is required to cross even the smallest creek'.

Description of the Arthur Plains
J R Scott, 1871.[1]

But the elements that give life and individuality to the South-West are not in themselves static. Because the physical environment inexorably changes over time periods ranging from days (weather), centuries (climatic change) to millennia and beyond (geological processes), and because of the intrinsic variability of living organisms, no part of the landscape is static—even in the absence of man. Like everything else therefore, the South-West has 'evolved'.

In this chapter we will look at the evidence for and the impact of climatic change in the creation of the mosaic of environments we know as the South-West. From this, an aspect of the importance of the South-West as a wilderness is demonstrated. For an understanding of the past is no longer a matter of purely academic interest but essential for a realistic assessment of the present and for prediction for the future. Management plans for even the most natural of ecosystems must take into account the continuous changes that are occurring within and between regions.[2]

That severe changes in climate have occurred in the South-West is evident to anyone who, from the heights of the Arthur Ranges, gazes down onto dense rainforests and scrub anchored on sediments deposited by ice in cirques and U-shaped valleys gouged out of bedrock by ice. Studies of these glacigenic sediments and landforms produced by geomorphic processes no longer operative, have provided evidence of the nature of South-West environments towards the end of the last glacial period. The maximum of this glaciation, the latest in a series of cold episodes ('Ice Ages') to affect Tasmania and the world in general during the past 2 to 3 million years, occurred about 20,000 BP (years before present). Between glacial periods, climates were globally warmer. Fossils implying a riverbank cool temperate rainforest on the Pieman River between 55,000 and 40,000 BP similar to that now present on the Pieman is evidence that the last interglacial period in Tasmania was climatically similar to the present day.[3] So 20,000 BP forms a convenient starting place in considering the evolution of the modern South-West.

The geomorphic evidence of the glacial landforms and ice-deposited sediments suggests that temperatures in Tasmania during the last glacial maximum were markedly colder, possibly 5 to 8°C lower, than present mean temperatures.[3] Overall, western Tasmania appears to have had a cold maritime climate, characterized by snowy, frosty winters with prolonged severe gales from the S W.— N W. quadrant, spring melting of glacial ice and snow and high river flows maintained by melting ice through summer.[3 4 5] The environment of South-Western Tasmania then was one in which short glaciers flowed down valleys on the slopes of mountains such as the Arthurs, Mt Anne and the Franklands. They were fed by snowfields accumulating in the lee of ridges at altitudes above 600 m. Periglacial activity such as frost shattering of rocks and frost heave of soils may have occurred as low as the present day sea level on the plains. Due to the locking up of vast quantities of sea water in the ice sheets covering much of north-western Europe and North America, the sea level on the west coast was probably some 100 m below the present level. Much of the continental shelf off the west coast was then dry land and the present day sea cliffs were well inland of the shoreline. Abandoned sea-cliffs related to a much older, and higher, sea level are a common feature of the west coast, particularly north of the Pieman Heads.

By 14,000 BP, global temperatures began to warm, resulting in the progressive upslope retreat of glaciers into the shade of the cirque headwalls and the progressive raising of sea levels, submerging the continental shelf. For example, on Frenchmans Cap, glaciers had retreated out of the valley now occupied by Lake Vera (560 m altitude) by about 12,000 BP but lingered unmelted in the higher cirques such as that now occupied by Lake Nancy (1,036 m) until about 9,000 BP.[6] The rock basin and moraine dammed lakes and tarns in the mountains, and the rugged coast with its drowned river valleys like Port Davey, etched by rising sea levels, are the product of this period about 14,000 to 10,000 BP. These form the geographic backdrop to the South-West as we know it. What of life at this time?

A rugged topography makes for a diversity of environments. Living populations in Tasmania are therefore well buffered ecologically against climatic change. At the height of the last glaciation, large areas of the State remained ice-free.[7] Plant and animal communities in the highlands were then able to adjust to climatic change by shifts downslope into less severe climates, including habitats on the then exposed continental shelf. This sensitivity of living organisms to environmental change (relative to geomorphic processes) fills out the picture of the development of the modern South-West from the bleak stony landscape of the last glacial age.

The types of palaeo-ecologic evidence used are threefold: there is direct evidence, usually in the form of plant and animal fossils; there is indirect evidence like buried soils and animal burrows; and thirdly, the scientist uses a dating method which allows the construction of a time-scale for the past into which the direct and indirect evidence for former environments may be fitted. For the period from 40,000 BP to the present, radiocarbon dating is used.

No other type of fossil has contributed so much to the reconstruction of environments since the last glacial age (i.e. the post-glacial period, 12,000 to 10,000 BP to the present) as the diminutive pollen grain. Measuring 0.1 to 0.01 mm in diameter and often identifiable down to the genus level of the source plant, pollen and spores are produced and dispersed in astronomical numbers, particularly from wind-pollinated plants such as the grasses, salt-bushes, conifers and trees like the myrtle (Nothofagus cunninghamii) and she-oak (Casuarina). This gives pollen and spores two substantial advantages over plant macrofossils, most of which represent the floras of special environments such as swamps and flood-plains where macrofossils can be preserved. Pollen grains can indicate the floras of uplands; they also lend themselves to quantitative analysis since they are easily identified and counted under a microscope and can be dealt with by statistical methods.

Pollen is part of the reproductive process of the flowering plant and to carry out its function, it must be transferred to other flowers by wind, animals ranging from insects to bats, or water. Inevitably, much pollen is wasted, falling to the ground during dispersal, there to decay rapidly in the oxidizing conditions. However, should the pollen grain or spore fall upon waterlogged peat or into a lake, the outer wall, or exine, can be readily preserved for millions of years under the anaerobic conditions. Pollen and spores so preserved represent assemblages of plants that lived in the near and distant surrounds of the peatbog or lake at the time of deposition. Thus as the peat surface grows upwards and sediments accumulate in the lake basin, the pollen and spore content of the successive layers reflects the history of the vegetation around the bog or lake. By taking a column of sediment (core) from a deposit, and extracting the pollen and spores layer by layer, the pollen analyst can deduce changes in vegetation over the period of time represented by the core. (Since the ecological preferences of many plants analyzed in this way are broadly known it is usually possible to translate the vegetation history into environmental changes like climate, fire pressure and grazing). Animal remains, particularly those of insects, have been successfully used in an analogous fashion in deducing climatic change in north-western Europe. However this approach has not been tried in Tasmania and it is largely by pollen analysis that anything is known about the post-glacial evolution of environments here.[8 9 10]

Two pollen analyses bracket the South-West. The ecological consistency of trends in the vegetation histories of these locations with pollen analyses elsewhere in the southern half of Tasmania, suggest that the results can be broadly extrapolated to the region as a whole, including the South-West. The first pollen analysis is of a core from an infilled cirque lake on Adamsons Peak, inland of Dover on the far south-east coast; the second is from a lake sediment in Lake Vera, Frenchmans Cap. The pollen and spores preserved in these cores are a virtually continuous history of vegetation on the two mountains for the past 12,000 years.

Not surprisingly, the pollen and spore assemblages preserved in the lowest layers of the cores (late glacifluvial clays) indicate a flora that is in close agreement with markedly colder temperatures and probably drier, or more seasonal, climates than at present. The mountain summits were largely devoid of vegetation. The present day alpine fell-field and herb-field plants such as the creeping pine Microcachrys tetragona and species of Compositae grew at altitudes as low as 500 m. Because of the sparsity of vegetation in the immediate surrounds of the lakes, pollen from very distant plant communities was well represented in these clays about 12,000 years old. It is probable that some reflect the vegetation on the Australian continent. Tree species were rare or absent. Pollen evidence strongly suggests that the climatic timberline (the highest altitude reached by timber-sized trees) at the end of the last glacial was as low as present-day sea level on the west coast. Eucalyptus forests may have been established on the exposed continental shelf. Pollen from grasses is the most common type found in the late glacial clays. This was probably derived from alpine grasslands to the north and east of Adamsons Peak and Frenchmans Cap respectively and, it is likely that much of the lowlands of western and south-western Tasmania were covered with floristically diverse assemblages of sedges and heath species. Microstrobos niphophilus and Nothofagus gunnii (deciduous beech) were part of lower altitude shrub associations. Tree species that were to give rise to the major forest types in Tasmania, Nothofagus cunninghamii (myrtle) and Eucalyptus spp., appear to have been rare shrubs in the heathland.

The South-West some 12,000 to 20,000 years ago probably looked like the treeless Arctic tundra of the northern hemisphere. Aboriginal man was present on Hunter Island off the north-west coast before 18,000 BP[11] and in the valley of the Derwent near Hobart at approximately the same time.[12] There is no evidence as yet for late glacial man in the South-West, although the open vegetation conditions would have facilitated his movements inland. It is possible that the evidence lies drowned on the continental shelf although with reference to his presence inland prior to 10,000 BP, ancient lime-encrusted artefacts have been found in cave deposits in the Florentine Valley, central southern Tasmania, so fire may have been introduced into the South-West as early as 18,000 BP.

After about 14,000 BP the ameliorating climate allowed the upslope expansion of the alpine zone; by 11,500 BP, a closed-scrub of Nothofagus gunnii (deciduous beech) and alpine conifers existed around Lake Vera and there was alpine herb-field in the Adamsons Peak cirque. Forests dominated by Eucalyptus expanded across the lowlands. Between 11,500 and 10,000 BP, increasing amounts of Eucalyptus and Pomaderris apetala (dogwood) pollen in the organic sediments overlying the basal clays record the progressive upslope movement of a Eucalyptus climatic timberline and the development of wet sclerophyll communities on the lower slopes. That sclerophyll trees and the dogwood rather than myrtle (which is characteristic of rainforests) expanded in the early phase of the post-glacial strongly implies that rainfall in western Tasmania was less than at present. As temperatures and rainfall levels continued to rise after ca. 10,000 BP, the celery-top pine (Phyllocladus aspleniifolius) then the myrtle (Nothofagus cunninghamii) became common and then dominant in the previously established eucalypt forests. By 9,000 BP, N. cunninghamii forest covered the slopes of Frenchmans Cap and dense scrub of this rainforest species had spread over the Adamsons Peak cirque. By this time it is probable that the climatic timberline reached its present elevation on the mountains of Tasmania.

Since myrtle is a prolific pollen producer, myrtle pollen tends to dominate once rainforest develops around a lake. Accordingly, after about 9,000 BP it is more difficult to trace changes in the vegetation of the South-West from pollen deposits, for instance in the lakes on Adamsons Peak and Frenchmans Cap. For a period of several thousands of years, Nothofagus cunninghamii (cool temperate rainforest) remained the dominant vegetation on both mountains. Evidence from Mt Field National Park suggests that this was a period in which climates were slightly warmer and wetter, or at least more equable than at present: rainforest scrub extended onto the Tarn Shelf and developed into forest around Beatties Tarn, situations where the species is now rare or absent.

We may expect, therefore, that the early to middle post-glacial period saw the maximum spread of rainforest across the South-West. Exactly how much of the South-West was in fact so vegetated remains unknown. The whole region is climatically capable of supporting rainforest on all rock types present — given the long term absence of fire. Further pollen analyses will resolve this point. The history of rainforest on Frenchmans Cap however may give valuable indications as to what was occurring on the lowland plains of the South-West.

Firstly, the manfern *Dicksonia antarctica* appears to have been moderately common on the foothills of the Cap before 5,000 BP. This species requires fairly fertile soils and its presence is evidence for the development of fertile soils on quartzite rocks and the existence of breaks in the canopy of the rainforest. The former is inconsistent with a high frequency of fires in the area whereas the latter is explicable if occasional fires were part of the environment. At about 5,000 to 4,600 BP, dramatic changes occurred in the local vegetation at Lake Vera. Although no charcoal has been found, the botanical changes imply the fire-destruction of rainforest in the cirque. The Huon pines at the southern end of Lake Vera are direct descendants of seedlings that were established 4,600 years ago due to the high light regime established following the disruption of the rainforest.

It seems then that fires lit in the lowlands, possibly on the shores of Macquarie Harbour, had spread inland to reach Frenchmans Cap by 5,000 BP. Aborigines are the most likely source of fire and it is interesting to note the close proximity in time of this event to the age of an aboriginal skull, found near Mt Cameron West on the north-west coast. After the fire, rainforest species compatible with highly acidic and infertile soils, e.g. *Anodopetalum biglandulosum,* (horizontal) became common around Lake Vera whereas *Dicksonia* (manfern) vanished from the mountain. High percentages of *Phyllocladus* (celery-top pine) pollen and constant occurrences of *Eucalyptus* pollen show that broken-canopied rainforest and mixed forest has been present around and on Frenchmans Cap ever since.

The interesting fact is that the floristically simple stands of rainforest developed in the first half of the post-glacial period had, on *all* other mountains for which a pollen analysis is available, begun to deteriorate and become invaded first by *Phyllocladus,* then by *Eucalyptus,* by 4,600 BP. Parallel changes were occurring in New Zealand and Chile and in most cases, either increasing fire pressure or climatic deterioration explains the vegetational changes observed.

A picture emerges then of post-glacial changes in environment leading to the establishment of the present-day South-West wildscape. From about 11,000 to 5,000 BP, climates were probably effective in promoting the establishment of cool temperate rainforest in the South-West. However beginning somewhere about 8,000 BP and ending before 5,000 BP there was an 'optimum' phase in which climates were slightly warmer and wetter than at present, or more equable in terms of the frequency of occurrence of extremes such as severe frosts or drought. Very wet conditions might have contributed to the low soil fertilities in the succeeding phase due to over leaching of soils.

From about 6,000 to 5,000 BP, climates in the South-West, as elsewhere in Tasmania, have become more severe in terms of variability and the frequency of extremes. Climates in this phase promoted the spread of aboriginal fires. This in turn created a vegetation more susceptible to fire and hence a higher frequency of fires again. It is the effect of fire in a feedback relationship with the unequable climates of the past five thousand years which has probably produced the mosaic of rainforest, sclerophyll and sedge species characteristic of the South-West.[13][14][15][16] By inference the vast button-grass plains of the South-West are also a product of this period.

If these are the changes that have created the modern South-West, what is the importance to science of maintaining the South-West as a wilderness? I would like to emphasize the importance of the South-West to continuing studies on climatic change, a phenomenon of considerable relevance to survival on an overpopulated planet.

Conditions necessary for the reconstruction of past environments by pollen analysis are met with in virtually all climatic regions of Tasmania. Thousands of lakes continue to accumulate the pollen record of its natural history. Similarly, climates are sufficiently cool and moist to enable the widespread development of shallow peats. So the South-West is not particularly important with regards to the possession of potential core sites. Apart perhaps from the fact that its inaccessibility favours the protection of such sites, the significance of the South-West emerges more when one seeks to determine the causes rather than the effects of oscillations in climate.

The basic component of climate is temperature. Variation in rainfall is a subsidiary factor related to temperature gradients from equator to pole, between atmosphere and ocean. The same small change in temperature over one big region may increase rainfall in one locality and reduce it in another. Therefore it is only by studying trends in temperature that the scientist can determine whether the change in climate observed is of purely local significance or part of a more significant global trend. The effects of abnormally wet or dry years on Australian vegetation is well known and it is accordingly difficult to distinguish the role of temperature in guiding any observed vegetational changes. Unless, that is, we can find an area in which rainfall is so overwhelmingly high all year round that variations in the amount received will have little or no effect on the vegetation: the South-West is such an area.

The South-West is the cloudiest and wettest region in Australia. Average annual and monthly rainfall everywhere in the South-West exceeds the ecological requirements of the climax forest type of cool temperate rainforest in Tasmania. Rainfall is therefore unlikely to limit the development of this forest type. Temperature however can. Many of the mountains in the South-West rise above the climatic timberline, i.e. the altitude above which temperature and related effects such as exposure, length of snow-lie and the frequency of 'hard' frosts or summer glazing storms, are severe enough to eliminate tree sized species from the mountain vegetation. Conveniently, a considerable number of glacial lake basins and tarns occur in this tension zone where temperature restricts and finally eliminates *Nothofagus cunninghamii* from the highland plant communities.

If the changes of temperature that occur over a number of decades are of sufficient magnitude to cause changes in the elevation of the climatic timberline, then the South-West appears to be the most sensitive area in Australia in which temperature trends may be detected via its vegetation history. And this applies not only to pollen analysis. Variations in the width of successive annual growth rings in the endemic Tasmanian highland conifers give an alternative method of tracing the same trends in temperature.

It is a case of small beginnings where pollen grains are concerned. But the consequences are grand. If, as I have argued, the South-West is a mirror for minor as well as major climatic changes in the middle latitudes of the meteorologically critical Southern Hemisphere, can its images of the past remain unclouded if humans replace climate as the dominant control in its environment?

Huon pine, *Dacrydium franklinii*.   *Neil Davidson*

Button-grass in a sheltered nook on the Frankland Range.   *Reg Williams*

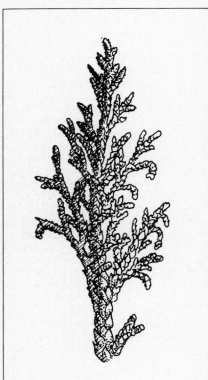
Huon pine branchlet.   *Peter Murray*

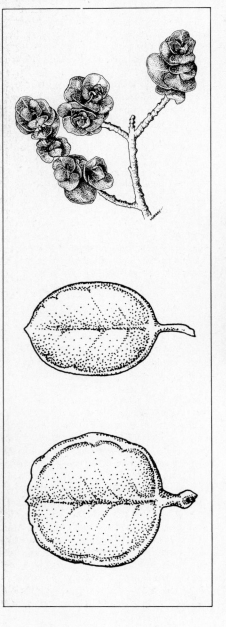

Bauera rubioides, 'dog rose' or 'bauera'. A small twining shrub in many situations but becoming rampant in ideal localities, i.e. wet gullies and river banks.   *Chris Bell*

Button-grass plain in the Valley of Rasselas.
Maurice D Clark

Eucalyptus vernicosa, 'varnished gum'. In its extreme form varnished gum is the smallest of the 450 or so species found in Australia. On the bleak windswept summits and ridges of most of the higher quartzite and conglomerate peaks of the West and South-West, the diminutive varnished gum often grows no more than one foot high, scrambling among the rocks and other small shrubs. From these same peaks may be seen some of the more eastern river valleys wherein grows the largest species of eucalypt, *Eucalyptus regnans*, sometimes attaining heights of 90 metres or more.
Peter Murray

Vegetation

I J Edwards

Dr I J Edwards gained his Ph.D. in the Botany Department of the University of Tasmania from a study of highland vegetation management with respect to water yield on the Central Plateau. He has participated in a number of botanical studies of the South-West and has a keen interest in the ecology and land-use of the area. He is currently researching the cultivation and processing of hops with Australian Hop Marketers Pty. Ltd.

Were it not for bush fires, plant communities in the South-West would consist almost exclusively of rainforest. The only exceptions would be comparatively small areas of high altitude moorland and sedgeland on sites too waterlogged to support tree growth. The existing vegetation however, is complex, due primarily to a probable 15,000 years of burning by Tasmanian Aborigines and occasional lightning strikes. According to Professor W D Jackson,[1] these fires have resulted in interactions between vegetation type, fire frequency and intensity, soil structure and fertility, aspect and parent rock.

The climax rainforest species are difficult to burn, but have no adaptive mechanisms to survive the occasional holocaust that burns vast areas every few hundred years. In the absence of fire, the seedlings grow very slowly in the shade of mature trees, but when the old trees die or are blown over they quickly burst into life to fill the gap in the canopy. In rainforest, growth near the ground is limited by lack of light and the clean forest floor is mainly covered with moss and rotting logs. A severe fire in such an area kills the trees and enables fast growing seedlings to establish in the fertile ash bed. These are usually the eucalypts, which release large quantities of seed from drying capsules a few days after a fire, and grow rapidly. The eucalypts cannot grow in the shade[2], but following a fire soon establish a dense stand of even-aged stems that can reach 5 metres high in 4 to 5 years on fertile sites. The commercially valuable forests of the Arve and Florentine valleys exhibit these conditions, with mature trees over 30 metres high growing in less than 100 years.

With the eucalypts comes an increased risk of fire because eucalypt leaves, rich in volatile oils, are very inflammable. If there are no fires the eucalypts die of old age after about 200 years and the rainforest species, slowly growing in the shade beneath the main eucalypt crown, take over again. Often, though, fire intervenes; if this occurs before the eucalypts reach seed-bearing age, the stand can, depending on the species, regenerate from epicormic buds beneath the bark, from lignotubers

Richea pandanifolia, 'pandani'. This remarkable plant looks more like a tropical palm tree than a member of the heath family *(Epacridaceae)*. It has a slender trunk which often reaches heights of 4 to 8 metres, topped by a crown of leaves nearly a metre long. Pandani is a fairly common plant in shrubberies and forests throughout the West and South-West, and due to its palm-like appearance, pandani seems out of place amongst the cool-temperate vegetation of these latitudes. Many pandanis retain the dead leaves of past seasons, some plants having 'skirts' of leaves draped as much as 5 metres down the trunk. The flowers of the *Richea* genus are of special interest. Instead of the petals opening in the 'usual' fashion, the petals of *Richea* are joined to form a cap which is pushed off by the maturing stamens.
Tasmanian Environment Centre Inc Col

below ground level, or from seeds from adjacent stands. Depending on the frequency and severity of burning therefore, the eucalypt forests may extend or diminish in area.

A secondary consequence of fire is that large quantities of nutrients, normally tied up in organic matter in plant parts, are released. However, significant quantities of the strategic elements phosphorus and potassium can be washed away in rainstorms soon after burning, before the nutrients can be bound to clay molecules. The relatively fertile sites in the South-West, mainly on Permian, Devonian, Ordovician and Cambrian deposits, can maintain productive forests after many fires. On less fertile sites though, especially on soils overlying the extensive Precambrian bedrock which is high in silica and low in basic nutrients, the effects of fire are very marked. In these areas fires every 10 to 20 years produce a predominance of scrub and heath species which are very inflammable and so further increase the possibility of fire. The increase in fire frequency is associated with deterioration in soil structure and fertility, and anaerobic, acidic (pH 3.8–4.5), shallow peat soils develop even on steep slopes.

Gymnoschoenus sphaerocephalus (button-grass) is the climax species on very poorly drained sites where it takes the form of tall tussocks separated by bare boggy depressions. In this form it is almost the sole species, and progress over such an area is quite hazardous, as one must jump from one quaking tussock to the next. The frequent burning of the South-West has considerably extended the area occupied by button-grass, but has also changed its form to that of a small tussock on a comparatively even ground surface. On these sites, occupying over 30% of the South-West, approximately 10 other species occur in co-dominant status with button-grass, and over 100 species may occur in a small area.

This vegetation can readily burn within hours of rain, even in winter. The peculiar situation then arises where the vegetation in the wettest area of Australia is the most readily burnt. There is a marked difference in the inflammability of the various plant associations. Fire boundaries, originally established by aspect or chance variations in wind direction during the occasional big fire, tend to be maintained because of this difference in inflammability between adjacent communities.

The distribution of lowland plant communities is therefore fashioned by factors which influence fire distribution. It follows a pattern in which generally the sheltered river valleys contain rainforest, the windswept plains contain heaths, and the partially sheltered slopes are covered with scrub of varying density and height. The number of species within a given

King Billy pine, *Athrotaxis selaginoides.*
Reg Williams

area increases with increasing fire frequency and decreasing soil fertility.

With increasing altitude, the vegetation changes gradually, until on the exposed moors above 1,000 metres, low heath vegetation predominates. There is no distinct tree line, as in the New South Wales Alps or the mountains of the Northern Hemisphere; instead, the trees become more and more stunted.

The vegetation of South-West Tasmania contains many interesting plants, some of which present ambiguities and difficulties in classification. Eucalypts, normally considered trees, grow in the highlands of the South-West as mature plants less than one metre high. *Eucalyptus vernicosa* (varnished gum) is an example. Other plants, present elsewhere in the State only as small shrubs, may reach tree status in the South-West, for example, *Richea scoparia* and *Agastachys*

odorata. A number of plants exist in clinal form, exhibiting gradual changes in characteristics as altitude changes e.g. *Eucalyptus subcrenulata.* Change in leaf form from large and succulent to small and leathery with increasing altitude is usual.

Some of the more interesting plants include the endemic conifers, the cushion plants, and specific plants commonly known as leatherwood, horizontal, button-grass, Bauera, cutting grass, and deciduous beech. The most interesting and important of the conifers is *Dacrydium franklinii* (Huon pine), now scarce because of demand by boat-builders and furniture manufacturers over the past 150 years. A tree recently floated out of the rising Lake Gordon was aged by the CSIRO at over 2,200 years, making it the oldest tree known from Australia. These trees grow on flood plains and fire-protected river banks and their growth rate is extremely slow.

Anodopetalum biglandulosum, appropriately known as horizontal because of its growth habit, grows on acidic, infertile soils in the South-West. It grows vertically for 5 to 6 metres until the main stem bends under its own weight. New branches arise from the original fallen stem, and these repeat the process until an intertwining mass of limbs results. A forest of *Anodopetalum* can only be crossed by the laborious process of weaving between the stems, an almost impossible task with a backpack, or by climbing over the top of the mat formed 5 to 10 metres above ground level.

Cushion plants (*Abrotanella forsterioides, Pterygopappus lawrencii,*

Rainforest and horizontal scrub. *Howard P Simco*

Stunted myrtle.

Reg Williams

Donatia novae-zelandiae and others) do not exist in mainland Australia, nor in quite the same form anywhere else in the world. Each cushion consists of thousands of tiny branchlets forming a tightly packed mat. The plants are so compact that a man's tread barely leaves an impression. Floristically, a cushion may consist of up to about 6 species, many of which are difficult to identify except when in flower, because of the convergent morphology of plants from different genera and families. The cushions grow slowly into small watercourses which they eventually dam. The water then breaks out elsewhere and a new cycle of growth is initiated. The result is a colourful mat of cushions among small water holes and projecting rocks, rather like a Japanese alpine garden.

There are many other unusual plants in the South-West which add to the uniqueness of the area. Although some of these do grow elsewhere in Tasmania and some in other parts of the world, the concentration and ever changing mosaic in the South-West is unrivalled.

Botanists now usually follow the classification of Australian plant communities devised by R L Specht[3] in 1970 in which the structural life forms are divided into height and crown density categories. Closed-forest (synonymous with rainforest in the South-West) has 70–100% cover, open-forest has 30–70% cover and woodland has less than 30% cover. Trees are woody plants more than 5 metres high, usually with a single stem, and shrubs are woody plants less than 8 metres high. Heaths are composed of

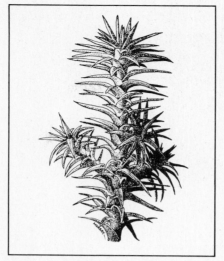

Richea scoparia, 'scoparia'. A bright, prickly, rigid leafed shrub of the sub-montane low-forests. The harsh nature of the plants' leaves may make walking through them painful, especially when wet skin encounters a 'thicket'. The massed spikes of white, yellow, pink or crimson flowers make a grand display in early summer.   *Peter Murray*

shrubs less than 2 metres high. Herbs include grasses, sedges, ferns and moss. The structural formations are subdivided into alliances, named according to the dominant one or more species. In 1974 W D Jackson[4] recorded 140 alliances in South-West Tasmania. The most important structural formations may be briefly considered:

Closed-Forests in the South-West represent an approximation to the climax vegetation which would form in the absence of fire. The lowland closed-forests are dominated by *Nothofagus cunninghamii* (myrtle). On the most

fertile sites *Nothofagus* occurs as the sole tree, or as a co-dominant with *Atherosperma moschatum* (sassafras). *Nothofagus* is able to compete successfully with other species over a wide range of climatic and soil conditions. In adverse conditions it is reduced in size and may take the form of a shrub. On acid sites *Phyllocladus aspleniifolius* (celery top pine) becomes co-dominant with *Nothofagus,* while in protected river flood plains *Dacrydium franklinii* (Huon pine) becomes co-dominant. The alliances found in infertile lowland and intermediate altitude sites include *Anodopetalum biglandulosum* (horizontal), *Eucryphia lucida* (leatherwood), *Leptospermum glaucescens, L. scoparium,* and *Melaleuca squarrosa* (tea-trees) and *Acacia melanoxylon* (blackwood). On fire protected sites, the endemic conifers become more common with increasing altitude. At intermediate altitudes *Athrotaxis selaginoides* (King Billy pine) occasionally forms pure stands, although co-dominant status with *Nothofagus cunninghamii* or *Phyllocladus aspleniifolius* is more common. On exposed highland sites, closed-forest comprises *Nothofagus cunninghamii* (myrtle) and *N. gunnii* (deciduous beech) and the conifers *Diselma archeri, Microstrobus niphophilus, Microcachrys tetragona* and *Athrotaxis selaginoides.*

The Open-Forests are represented mainly by eucalypts. The distribution of different eucalypt species is complex, with small differences in microclimate, soil and aspect accounting for different species occupying superficially similar sites. The broad distribution of eucalypts

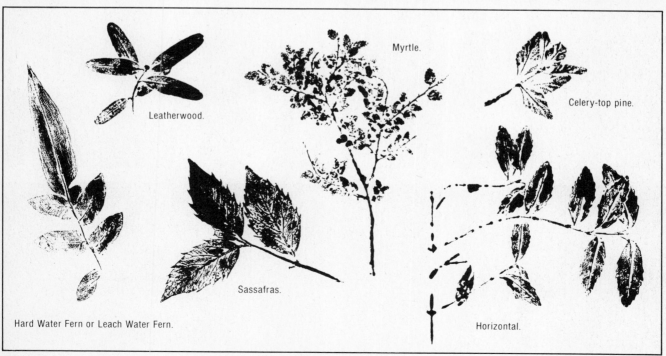

Leatherwood.

Myrtle.

Celery-top pine.

Sassafras.

Hard Water Fern or Leach Water Fern.

Horizontal.

Leaf Prints

Janet Fenton

Top
Dracophyllum milliganii. On many mountain tops and ridges this plant grows to about half a metre, with narrow leaves often spirally coiled and about 200 mm long. In some of the forests of the South-West where rainfall is high and soils fertile, *D. milliganii* may grow to 9 metres, with a trunk and leaves very closely resembling the pandani. The flowers, however, are quite different. They open in the 'usual' fashion and are densely arranged in large, showy, terminal panicles. On the very largest specimens a panicle may be one metre long and half a metre wide with hundreds of little pink, bell-shaped flowers. The only other species of *Dracophyllum* in Tasmania, found on some mountians of the West and South-West, is *D. minimum*. This species is one of the cushion plants, the branches are erect and tightly packed forming hard cushion-like mounds. The small, solitary flowers are borne at the ends of the branchlets and they appear as though set into the undulating mound.   *Alan Gray*

Middle
Lomatia tasmanica — a tall, straggling shrub, known only from dense rainforests on the ranges between Port Davey and the southern coast. It was described in 1967 following its discovery by Denis King. Part of the description reads 'fruit not seen', and although a number of people have searched for a plant bearing fruit nothing has been found — in any season — although the plants flower quite freely. *Lomatia tasmanica* reproduces freely from root suckers and by layering. It may well be that, due to the efficiency of its vegetative reproduction, evolution over the past thousands of years has led to an almost complete loss of reproductive function by means of seeds. Small seeds form following flowering but these soon abort. Bushfires pose a special threat to the survival of this very rare and interesting plant.   *Alan Gray*

Bottom
Asplenium trichomanes (common spleenwort) — a fern from moist sheltered locations.   *Chris Bell*

Opposite, bottom left and right
Lichens are dual organisms formed from symbiotic association of two plants, a fungus and an alga.   *Chris Bell*

Top
Anemone cressifolia — an endemic mountain herb from the West and South-West highlands.   *Jean Jarman*

Middle
Isophysis tasmanica, 'hewardia' was formerly known as *Hewardia tasmanica*. This very attractive small plant is well known to bushwalkers and naturalists. For much of the year the plants go almost unnoticed as they resemble large tufts of coarse grass but in late spring and early summer the West and South-West is renowned among visitors for the displays of large, deep-purple flowers that arise from the tufts of coarse leaves. Each flower, borne on a long slender stalk, may be up to 80 mm from petal tip to petal tip. Although very closely related to the Iris family, it belongs in a family of its own. This delicate flower grows only in the most exposed and infertile mountain soils of the South-West and West.
Rona Gardner

Bottom
Anopterus glandulosus (native laurel). A Tasmanian endemic growing as a shrub or tree in rainforests mainly in the western half of the State.*Chris Bell*

in Tasmania is given by Jackson in *The Atlas of Tasmania*.[5] In general the tallest and most valuable timber species *(E. regnans, E. delegatensis, E. globulus* and *E. viminalis)* occupy fertile sites which are mainly on the periphery of the South-West such as the valleys of the Arve, Picton, Florentine and Styx rivers. The most widespread eucalypt in the South-West is *E. nitida* (formerly *E. simmondsii),* which varies in form from a multi-stemmed mallee-like plant, to a moderate sized tree up to 40 metres high in sheltered locations. This species can tolerate extreme infertility and impeded drainage and rapidly recovers from burning by sprouting from lignotubers below ground level. *E. coccifera* is dominant on highland soils overlying dolerite. *E. subcrenulata* (yellow gum) growing mainly on sandstone, varies from a tall tree up to 60 metres high in

lowland soils, to a stunted form above 1,000 metres in altitude. *E. ovata* (swamp gum) is also a variable species; it can grow up to 50 metres tall but usually much smaller on coastal heaths and poorly drained soils. *E. vernicosa* (varnished gum) in the form of a shrub, dominates on exposed mountain plateaux of Precambrian deposits.

The open-forests, into which the crown permits much light to penetrate, usually have a number of lesser species beneath the main crown. The most common plants indicating soils of moderate to high fertility include *Pomaderris apetala* (dogwood), *Bedfordia salicina, Zieria arborescens* (stinkwood), *Phebalium squameum* (lancewood), *Oxylobium ellipticum* (golden rosemary), *Coprosma hirtella* (coffee berry), *Olearia phlogopappa* and *O. stellulata* (daisy bushes), *Troch-*

arpa spp., Aristotelia peduncularis (heart berry) and *Dicksonia antarctica* (manfern). Species common beneath the eucalypt crown on infertile sites include most of the species forming the heath and scrub alliances where fires are too frequent to permit development of mature eucalypt trees.

The low closed-forests merge into lower vegetation comprising;
Scrub (height 2–8 metres, dense foliage cover) and shrubland (height 2–8 metres, sparse cover). Most of these sites are strongly acid, infertile and frequently burnt. In lowland sites the alliances include *Anodopetalum biglandulosum* (horizontal), *Bauera rubioides, Leptospermum glaucescens, Acacia mucronata, Banksia marginata,* and *Eucalyptus nitida.* At intermediate altitudes the dominant plants include *Telopea truncata* (waratah), *Lomatia*

Coastal plant communities have adapted to survive the strong winds which relentlessly buffet the coast, blowing in salt spray and sand.   *Peter C Sims*

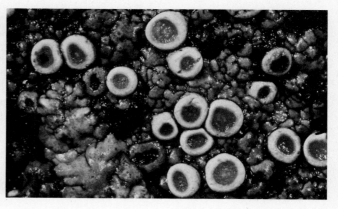

polymorpha, *Nothofagus cunninghamii* (myrtle) and *Richea pandanifolia* (pandani). In highland communities the alliances are *Diselma archeri*, *Microstrobos niphophilus*, *Richea scoparia*, *Orites acicularis*, *O. revoluta*, *Nothofagus gunnii* (deciduous beech), *Eucalyptus vernicosa* (varnished gum) and *Leptospermum rupestre* (tea-tree). As the plant communities become more scrubby, the complexity of the vegetation increases, the number of alliances increases, and the boundaries between alliances become vague and continuous. The complexity is accentuated by the interactions between fire, soil, aspect and vegetation. The scrub communities are essentially transient between heaths which predominate for up to 10 years without fire, and forest which gradually develops after approximately 50 years without fire. **Heaths** occupy over 30% of the South-West and include the so called button-grass plains, in which approximately 10 plants dominate, though they may vary greatly over small distances. These plants are *Gymnoschoenus sphaerocephalus* (button-grass), *Sprengelia incarnata*, *Restio australis*, *Leptospermum glaucescens* and *Melaleuca squarrosa* (tea-trees), *Casuarina monilifera*, *Banksia marginata*, *Bauera rubioides*, *Acacia mucronata* and *Xyris operculata*, although as many as 100 species may occur in a small area.

Along the banks of the many water courses and creeks the vegetation is usually taller and more dense than in adjacent areas, due to better drainage and subsequent soil aeration, and consists of a tangled mat of *Bauera rubioides*, *Calorophus lateriflorus*, *Hypolaena fastigiata* and other scrambling plants, together with the previously mentioned heath species. At intermediate altitudes many of the lower altitude heath plants, such as *Bauera rubioides* and *Sprengelia incarnata*, persist whereas others, for example *Agastachys odorata* and *Baeckea leptocaulis*, are gradually excluded and replaced by plants such as *Baeckea gunniana*, *Boronia citriodora* (lemon-scented boronia), *Richea sprengelioides*, *Cyathodes glauca*, and *Leptospermum rupestre*. In the alpine heath communities, plants unique to Tasmania predominate. These include *Eucalyptus vernicosa* (varnished gum), *Leptospermum rupestre* (tea-tree), *Richea scoparia*, *R. acerosa*, *Epacris gunnii* and the alpine conifers previously mentioned in the closed-forest formation. The cushion plants are also classified with the heaths and are well developed on many of the mountain plateaux.

The herbland communities of the South-West include grasses, sedges, ferns and mosses. The main herbland is sedgeland which is comprised basically of six alliances:- *Gymnoschoenus sphaerocephalus* (button-grass), *Restio australis* — *Hypolaena fastigiata*, *Restio oligocephalus* — *Restio complanatus*, *Restio tetraphyllus*, *Leptocarpus tenax* — *Xyris operculata* and *Lepidosperma filiforme* — *Restio oligocephalus*. All of these plants occupy water-logged sites of extreme infertility. In the highlands, herbland also occurs on water-logged sites where the alliances include:- *Oreobolus pumilio* — *Carpha alpina*, *Rubus gunnianus* — *Euphrasia striata*, *Gentianella diemensis*, and *Milligania densiflora* — *Gleichenia dicarpa*. These communities are relatively restricted in distribution. They occur on flat mountain moors and also on slopes where springs provide constant wetness. A shallow peat layer usually develops beneath all sedgeland.

In coastal communities strong winds blowing sand and salt modify the vegetation. Sand dunes, in varying degrees of stability, commonly extend some distance inland and being freely drained, are covered with species not present in peaty soils further inland. The coastal communities are more frequently burnt than inland areas owing to stronger winds and more frequent visitation by Aborigines in the past and by small boat crews today. Salt tolerant plants which exist near high tide level are the herbs *Salicornia quinqueflora*, *S. blackiana* and *Plantago triantha*. Above the sprayline are the shrubs *Correa backhousiana*, *Rhagodia baccata* and *Cyathodes abietina*. Wind driven sand prunes these shrubs to a uniform height of approximately 1 to 2 metres. Stabilized sand dunes carry heath and scrub vegetation of *Eucalyptus nitida*, (west coast or bassian peppermint), *E. ovata*, *Myoporum insulare* (false boobyalla), *Pteridium esculentum* (bracken fern), *Epacris spp.* and *Acacia spp.* as well as many of the heath plants found further inland such as *Sprengelia incarnata*, *Banksia marginata*, *Casuarina monilifera*, *Melaleuca squarrosa* and *Leptospermum glaucescens*. Coastal herbland alliances include *Stipa teretifolia* above the shoreline and *Lepidosperma gladiatum*, *Arthrocnemum arbuscula*, *Poa poiformis* — *Spinifex hirsutus* — *Scirpus nodosus* around estuaries.

According to Specht the South-West contains approximately 165 endemic species. The number of these that are confined to the South-West is unclear because of a general lack of collections from the inaccessible areas. Plants known only from the South-West include *Milligania johnstonii*, found only recently in the Davey River valley and on the gravelly shores of Lake Pedder prior to flooding, but originally also found on the Huon Plains[6]; *Senecio primulifolius*, from Mt La Perouse and Moonlight Flats; *Senecio papillosus*, known only from Adamsons Peak and Mt La Perouse at approximately 1,000 metres; *Euphrasia kingii* on peaty heaths and mountains, especially near Port Davey; *Lomatia tasmanica*, found in rainforest in lowland sites near Port Davey and the Bathurst Range and *Oreomyrrhis gunnii*, known only from the original collection which was taken from limestone cliffs of the Gordon River. *Prasophyllum buftonianum*, an orchid first collected from Port Davey in 1893, was not recorded again until 1973 when it was found near Bathurst Harbour. An

Moorland on the White Monolith Range.   *Jim England*

isolated pocket of the species was found a few months later on Tasman Peninsula. It is probable that more extensive examinations will reveal the existence of many of these species in other localities as well as those mentioned, and will discover hitherto unknown species, especially of the small and inconspicuous plants.

The conservation areas of the South-West include the main sites in which many of the other endemic plants are preserved. At present the Southwest National Park and Frenchmans Cap National Park are the only large areas of State Reserve in the high-rainfall, low-altitude and intermediate-altitude western part of the State. Approximately 31 endemic plants are known only from the West and South-West, and a further 19 species are known only from the Central Plateau, West and South-West of the State.

Most of the plant species and plant alliances which occur in the South-West are reasonably well conserved in the State Reserve network, since they occur not only in the Southwest National Park, but also in Frenchmans Cap National Park, Mt Field National Park, Hartz Mts National Park and Cradle Mt-Lake St Clair National Park. The main threat to the survival of many of the rare species is the likelihood of change in burning patterns following the incorporation of large areas of the South-West into the State Reserve system. Burning is a natural component of the ecosystems of the South-West and must be continued on a regular basis to maintain naturalness. Since some species are encouraged by fire, whereas others, especially the highland plants, can be totally destroyed in a severe burn, the management policies regarding burning are controversial. The threat to plants from flooding by dams for power generation is restricted to specialised plants of the flood plains and gorges, and even here there is duplication on small streams with no conceivable dam sites. In this respect Lake Pedder was unique.

Endemic plants from the highlands of the Central Plateau, West and South-West are:

Diselma archeri
Microcachrys tetragona
Microstrobos niphophilus
Athrotaxis cupressoides
A. selaginoides
A. laxifolia
Actinotus moorei
Ewartia catipes
Archeria serpyllifolia
Dracophyllum minimum
Richea acerosa
Trochocarpa cunninghamii
T. gunnii
Pernettya lanceolata
Mitrasacme archeri
Plantago gunnii
Cenarrhenes nitida
Pimelea pygmaea
Centrolepis monogyna

The species known only from the West and South-West include:

Dacrydium franklinii,
 (Huon pine)
Aciphylla procumbens
Dichosciadium ranunculaceum,
 var. tasmanicum
Diplaspis cordifolia
Oschatzia saxifraga
Nothopanax gunnii
Anodopetalum biglandulosum,
 (horizontal)
Archeria eriocarpa
Archeria hirtella
Epacris corymbiflora
Epacris mucronulata
Leucopogon milliganii
Prionotes cerinthoides
 (climbing heath)
Sprengelia distichophylla
Eucalyptus vernicosa
 (varnished gum)
Orites milliganii
Anemone crassifolia
Geum talbotianum
Acradenia frankliniae
Phebalium oldfieldii
Euphrasia hookeri
Forstera bellidifolia
Pimelea milliganii
Gaimardia fitzgeraldii
Haemodorum distichophyllum
Blandfordia punicea
Milligania longifolia
Isophysis tasmanica
 (formerly *Hewardia tasmanica*)
Microlaena tasmanica

Caladenia carnea, 'pink fingers'. This dainty little orchid grows in quite large colonies and is very common in the South-West. It tends to prefer drier, stony situations on open plains or the margins of woodlands.   *Chris Bell*

Richea scoparia.   *Reg Williams*

Leptospermum glaucescens. A shrub or small tree mostly found on wet, acidic sites on button-grass plains as well as the margins of forests and on river banks. The small white flowers are attractive and conspicuous.   *Chris Bell*

Left inset
In contrast to fires in alpine areas or on button-grass plains. very little can be done with fires in wet sclerophyll forests, such as this one near Liberty Point in Macquarie Harbour. Although these forests burn in only particularly dry summers, once alight they can remain so, even after heavy rain.   *Greg Hodge*

Background photograph
Mt Anne from the plains near Sandfly Creek.
Howard P Simco

Right inset
Destruction of fire-susceptible pencil pines on the Tarn Shelf in the Mt Field National Park. A regeneration burn in the Florentine Valley caused spot fires to start here.   *Ann Wessing*

Bottom right inset
A fire raging on the side of a mountain with a strong wind, making it very difficult to control. *G Hodge*

Far right inset
In recent years helicopters have enabled small, trained crews of fire fighters, with lightweight equipment, to tackle fires in previously inaccessible alpine areas.   *Bob Tyson*

Fire in the South-West

J B Kirkpatrick
R G Tyson
G Hodge
W D Jackson

Dr J Kirkpatrick is a lecturer in Geography at the University of Tasmania. Native plant communities and their conservation are the subject of most of his current research, although he continues to work on eucalypts. He is author or co-author of several studies on the vegetation of Tasmania, including the Bass Strait Islands, Tasmanian coastal heaths, dry forests near Hobart and the West Coast.

A science graduate from the University of Tasmania, Bob Tyson has a particular interest in the botany of the South-West and knows the area well from walking trips. As Operations Officer with the National Parks and Wildlife Service he is involved with fire control operations in the South-West.

Greg Hodge works with the Rural Fires Board of Tasmania as Fire Control Officer for Special Fire Areas, including the South-West where he has organised many fire control operations. His knowledge of the area stems from active involvement with the Tasmanian University Mountaineering Club, the Climbers Club of Tasmania and the Search and Rescue organisation.

W D Jackson has been Professor of Botany at the University of Tasmania since 1968. He is familiar with the South-West both as a botanist and a bushwalker, having made many trips into the region since the 1940's. Recently his research work has been concentrated on eucalypt ecology, the problem of nutrients and the effect of fire on the distribution of plant communities. He has played an active role in public debate over forestry management practices and the effects of fire in the South-West.

Fire affected the vegetation of Tasmania long before man arrived. Stratigraphic evidence of fire dates back 30 million years. For the past few thousand years the Aborigines burnt the vegetation frequently and used fire deliberately as a tool in their occupation of the land. Then when European man arrived, he was confronted with an alien environment in which the role of fire was not understood. Consequently, since occupation, he has imposed on the environment yet another fire regime, and this change in burning pattern has resulted in repeated burning of areas once free of fire, together with the exclusion of fire from areas which evolved with constant firing.

Major fires have occurred in 1881, 1914, 1927, 1934 and 1967 with an increasing damage to property and cost to society due to the intensification of land use since settlement. However in recent years there has emerged an appreciation of yet another cost as a consequence of fire—the cost of losing diversity in, and balance of, the natural environment. This is occurring particularly in the alpine areas, where endemic species take many centuries to recover. If the incidence of fire in these areas is allowed to increase at the present rate,

then it is only logical to predict the impending extinction of many of the alpine species and plant communities.

Fire and its presence in the South-West has become a contentious issue, reflecting the ethical complexity of fire control and management within a wilderness zone.

A symposium entitled 'The Role of Fire in the Management of National Parks and the South-West' was held in Hobart in September 1976. It reinforced the need for a great deal more thought and research. A panel of four speakers presented papers and discussed the damaging effect of fire on susceptible communities such as alpine areas; the role that fire has played in both plant succession and the distribution of plant communities; fire management overseas and its relevance to Tasmanian National Parks together with the Tasmanian National Parks and Wildlife Service's policy on the management of fire; and finally, the practical aspects of fire control. The following are abridged precis of three of those papers, together with Professor Jackson's subsequent paper in which he outlines his argument against the continued practice of hazard reduction burning. This is based on the paper he presented at the Symposium.

Fire and the Plant Communities in the South-West

J Kirkpatrick

Fire has played a dynamic role in the evolution of the Tasmanian environment for a very long time. Some charcoal deposits date back to 30,000 years BP. Whether man was around then or not, fires were burning the landscape at that time. We know the Aborigines had been here for the past 8,000 years at least and some evidence of their burning habits has been recorded in the journals of early explorers including those of George Augustus Robinson.

We know that Aborigines burnt country for the purposes of hunting, warfare and ease of travel and that they carried with them fire sticks which burnt for a long period and with which they set the country alight (see 1.1). Robinson describes their use of fire as, what we would consider to be, a land management tool. They lit (presumably to attract game to the regrowth) and put out the fires around copses to retain shelter for the game. Fire might also have been used as an encouragement to growth of major food sources such as geophytes and native geraniums.

Although rainforest has advanced into grassland areas (since white settlement) due to reduced fire intensity, on the poorer soils the boundaries have tended to remain more or less stationary. Fire frequency has changed differently for differing vegetation types and within the same vegetation types in different areas.

Tasmania has a range of communities, from those that are completely fire susceptible to those that are extremely fire resistant and fire encouraging. **The communities that can be effectively eliminated through firing are some of the alpine and rainforest communities**, dominated by what we call the native pines—King Billy pine, pencil pine, celery-top pine, Huon pine and alpine pines such as *Diselma archeri* and *Microcachrys tetragona*.

The communities dominated by these species can be completely exterminated by one fire, and the possibility of their reoccupying the site is minimal. Thus these communities have been drastically reduced in area since white settlement. Those who share the blame for the vast areas of stark white trunks of King Billy pine and pencil pine on the West Coast and highlands in particular are the explorers, the prospectors, miners, loggers, foresters, government employees, graziers, pyromaniacs, bushwalkers and fishermen. These are the people who have been utilizing the land that was not utilized by the Aborigines. Frenchmans Cap is such an area. Before the fires of 1966 much of the mountain was covered with fire susceptible rainforest and alpine vegetation. Fire laid

Fire near Precipitous Bluff. 1976. *Jim England*

A fire started by fishermen near Lakes Belton and Belcher and an escaped Australian Newsprint Mills regeneration burn have destroyed much of the alpine vegetation of Mt Field. *Greg Hodge*

the soil bare for accelerated erosion and the loss of hundreds of years of peat and soil nutrients and the limited dispersal ability of the fire susceptible species makes recovery in all but the very long term highly unlikely.

The management of the country surrounding these alpine communities is therefore critical to their survival. Regeneration burns in forest lands on high fire danger days, and/or on days when spotting is likely to occur increases the likelihood of fire in these fragile areas.

Whether a fire deleteriously affects other plant communities, besides the ones that are totally fire susceptible, depends both on the frequency and intensity of fire and on the nature of other environmental variables. However, in my view, not even the most fire resistant and fire encouraging vegetation types can be burnt with impunity. An extreme example is the sedgeland dominated by button-grass, commonly occurring in the South-West. The soils that are formed

under a sedgeland are extremely poor in nutrients. Most of the nutrient capital is concentrated in the peat layer. After a fire the plant species will return and their diversity is usually higher straight after the fire, than 10, 15 or 20 years later. Unfortunately, too frequent firing of these sedgelands has resulted, in some areas, in accelerated soil erosion in the form of slumping, terracettes and gullying. We can assume that this degree of erosion is the result of modern burning practices; if it had been taking place over the past 8,000 years then the present day button-grass hills would be bare rock today.

I think it can be fairly said that there are very few examples in Tasmania of native vegetation that has been improved by firing, and that there are a lot of native ecosystems that have been degraded by firing. Fire as a tool in management should be applied only when its effects are well understood and desirable and then only conservatively.

Fire Management in National Parks

R Tyson

The National Parks and Wildlife Service has the responsibility of formulating a fire management policy for the South-West. The major management aim for all Tasmanian State Reserves is the maintenance of the total habitat and plant and animal associations in as near a natural condition as possible. However, in laying down a policy for fire control in National Parks, several other factors have to be considered in addition to the overall management aims, including the protection of the public and park facilities as well as the practicalities of fire prevention and suppression.

Researchers into the 1972 Nadgee wild fire in N.S.W. stated that:

'Wildfires massively release bound up nutrients. Animal and plant populations explode and species diversity increases. In a way, fire is a renewal of the ecosystem. Fire also removes nutrients — nitrogen vaporises, others are lost by wind and water. With infrequent fires the losses are insignificant. With frequent fires, whether deliberate or wild, there is a progressive decline of nutrients'.[1]

The Australian Conservation Foundation reminds us that in areas which have been successfully protected from fire for an extended period, and which carry a huge burden of dry litter and have a highly flammable shrub understorey, a fire burns with such fury that it leaves a trail of destruction. History has shown time and time again that despite the most diligent efforts, an uncontrollable fire will break out sooner or later in such protected areas. The Foundation suggests the provision of control burnt buffer zones around the edges of parks, in which fire fighters can operate safely. In wilderness areas, it suggests that the fire risk be accepted, but that it should be minimized by the provision of buffer zones and by the restriction of access during periods of high fire danger. No long term policy of reserve management can afford to ignore fire — not merely fire as a destructive intruder that has to be controlled, but fire as a constructive and regenerating agent to be deliberately exploited.[2]

A number of areas which have been control burnt over the past few years have been included within the South-west National Park. The areas are adjacent to the Scotts Peak road and in the Port Davey area. The burns adjacent to the Scotts Peak Road have been designed as a buffer for the Mt Anne area. A wildfire which originated on Mt Wedge in 1972 was largely contained by this buffer area.

Control burns in the Port Davey area in October 1975 were planned to provide

The fire which burnt this ridge on the Lake Shelf near Mt Anne was started by a lightning strike during a dry storm. Using a helicopter, a crew of fire fighters was on the fire edge within two hours and contained the fire with water pumped from numerous small tarns. Ironically, during the night over one foot of snow fell, although it was mid-summer.
Greg Hodge

areas and strips to break the run of wildfires, and to provide fuel reduced strips from which fighters could safely work. No artificial control lines were used. The fires were controlled by the fuel moisture differential between differing vegetation types, by the decreased temperature and increased humidity at night at that time of year and by the barren ridges. The soil was completely saturated, hence no damage to root systems occurred. The last time the Mt Fulton area was burnt was 1934, the Horseshoe Plains area was last burnt in 1956, New Harbour Range in 1947 and the last main fire on the Melaleuca — New Harbour plain was in 1954.

In his introduction to the ACF 'Viewpoint', Bushfire Control and Conservation, Sir Garfield Barwick states:

'It is too easy to advocate extreme caution, and say that we should wait to know the answers before committing ourselves to a programme of control burning. This, in effect, is to demand the launching of a research programme that would be impracticably complex, expensive and long drawn out.'

Every effort should be made at this stage to control fires anywhere within the park system, whether they are natural fires or initiated by man. Depending on the results of research and experience, it may well be that at some future time some fires could be left to burn in some areas including the South-West.

Fire suppression should take account of techniques which cause least damage to park values. Natural fire barriers such as rainforests and rivers must be put to maximum use. Most fire fighting should be undertaken with hand tools and portable pumps. Fire fighters should be transported to the more remote areas by helicopter, by boat or go on foot.

A programme of fire prevention through public education, and enforcement of the Rural Fires Act and Regulations as appropriate in relation to parks, should be undertaken both in local centres and in co-operation with other authorities on a broader scale.

Fire prevention measures are needed to prevent large areas of park being burnt in a single wildfire, in order to preserve the natural and scenic values of the area. To achieve this, some fire breaks should be constructed around huts and along some sections of park boundaries. Either in conjunction with these breaks, or as a separate control measure, hazard reduction burning could be carried out in a strip or mosaic pattern to provide breaks or protective strips. The construction of fire trails, fire breaks, fire towers, helipads, dams and other artificial aids must be kept to an absolute minimum.

Control lines should, wherever possible, be natural barriers. Repetitive burning of the same area must only occur on extremely small areas such as boundaries and around park facilities, and it should be recognised that repetitive burning produces a vegetation which is more fire prone.

Hazard reduction burns might well be used as a basis for research into, firstly, the effect of fire on the landscape, secondly, its effect on plant and animal communities, and thirdly its effect on individual species. Experimental fires may be conducted to research specific management aims.

Detailed basic fire plans will need to be an integral part of the management plan for a reserve but provision is essential for annual review of these plans. Much thought and research is needed to decide how best to protect the alpine and rainforest areas which are largely unique to Tasmania.

The Practical Aspects of Fire Control

G Hodge

Protection of vulnerable areas

If past trends continue, the vulnerable fire susceptible plant communities may well be lost through firing. It is important that those authorities who manage areas within the region agree as to which areas are vulnerable and what signifies a threat to them. On that recognition of vulnerability can hang the decision of whether or not suppressive action is taken.

The protection of these areas from wildfires can be viewed from two aspects. Firstly, we can attempt to suppress fires once they reach such vulnerable areas. This requires efficient, trained teams using lightweight equipment and specialised techniques. Secondly, areas adjacent to vulnerable areas can be burnt to limit the run and intensity of threatening wildfires. Bearing in mind the three basic ingredients of fire — heat, or an ignition source, oxygen and fuel — the only preventative action prior to a wildfire is removal of fuel or vegetation. Hazard reduction can be defined as the application of fire by trained personnel during periods of low fire danger to planned strategic areas in an effort to reduce, in the short term, the quantity of available ground fuel, and by so doing, limiting the size and run of wildfires, leaving little of the vulnerable area (e.g. an alpine plateau) exposed to the path of potential fires. Such strategic burns provide access and retreat for fire fighters. Generally, hazard reduction is not a long term solution since frequent burning must promote more fire prone vegetation; however this has to be balanced against the short term protection gained by 'controlled burns' which should be limited in size and closely maintained.

Irrespective of any precautions or preparations, a time comes when wildfires explode. The combination of weather factors, fire prone vegetation and man precludes a policy of absolute fire suppression. So if the area that is burnt now is decreased, such wildfires will consume larger and larger areas. If we wish to suppress wildfires efficiently, early detection systems are important. As there are no lookout towers in the South-West, aerial surveillance, commercial aircraft, lighthouses and people in the area are relied upon to augment what can be seen from towers near the fringes.

Unlike mainland Australia, lightning strikes rarely cause major fires in the South-West as they are associated with wet rather than dry storms at this latitude. However fire frequency is certainly related to the number of people visiting an area.

'Smokewalkers' training at Rocky Cape National Park. *Greg Hodge*

Bombadiers have proved very useful in transporting fire crews and equipment to remote fires such as this, south of Macquarie Harbour. *Greg Hodge*

The intensity of a fire is directly proportional to the square of the concentration of the vegetation on the ground. On sedgeland plains, fire commonly travels at 4 or 5 km per hour and can easily reach speeds of up to 20 km per hour, depending on topography, vegetation density and moisture content, as well as wind speed and temperature. Hence fires can travel large distances in a short time, making suppressive action difficult.

Control burns or hazard reduction

Since it is undesirable to use bulldozers to create artificial firebreaks, the size of a controlled burn is determined by the natural boundaries of fuel, and the moisture differential between adjacent areas. Thus wet creeks are often used as boundaries, but as summer approaches, their reliability as boundaries decreases until a time is reached when the vegetation dries out and burns with greater intensity than the adjacent plain. Consequently the time of the year is crucial in control burning. In winter and early spring the soil is saturated and the vegetation is dry, whereas in autumn both are dry and deliberately lit fires are more likely to get out of control. If only a

Many lengthy and exhaustive radio exercises have been conducted by the Rural Fires Board, National Parks and Wildlife Service and PMG to determine the most suitable radio sites for each particular area of the South-West. This has enabled fire crews to enjoy both excellent communications at the fire front and to relay information direct to Hobart. *David Allison*

Small, lightweight pumps such as this one have been used on many fires in the South-West. They are particularly effective on the relatively slow moving alpine fires. However, in the height of summer when fires on button-grass plains can easily reach speeds of 20 km/hour, such equipment is ineffective. *Greg Hodge*

small area is burnt, the subsequent new growth can suffer from overbrowsing. Weather conditions must be studied for weeks before hazard reduction burns are carried out. Extremely dry conditions can be masked by brief rain which evaporates within hours.

In 1968 the Rural Fires Board formed a committee which is composed of all the developmental authorities working within the South-West, and provides a unique opportunity for discussion of common suppression problems and conflicting management aims in relation to fire. For example, fire can be used as a clearing agent to facilitate mineral exploration; as a regenerative catalyst for forestry interests, or as a measure for the protection or maintenance of habitats. The implications of such diverse fire practices must be recognized and understood.

Wildfire control

One effective means of fire control is to educate people about the threat that fire poses to susceptible plant communities. However, when a wildfire is raging, there is a need for efficient, trained manpower. In 1975 the formation of the Smokewalkers Brigades comprised of bush-

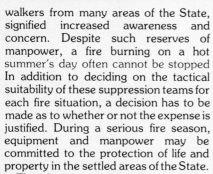

walkers from many areas of the State, signified increased awareness and concern. Despite such reserves of manpower, a fire burning on a hot summer's day often cannot be stopped In addition to deciding on the tactical suitability of these suppression teams for each fire situation, a decision has to be made as to whether or not the expense is justified. During a serious fire season, equipment and manpower may be committed to the protection of life and property in the settled areas of the State.

The ultimate aim must be to care for the area, and that may be the acceptance of nature's timescale and the run of wildfires.

Although there is no simple answer to the question 'What is the role of fire in the South-West?' we are just beginning to understand the **importance** of its role. Research, which is just beginning, into the effects of fire at different times of the year and of repeated burns at a variety of intervals, will take many years to yield results. In the meantime, a balance has to be struck between the beneficial and detrimental effects of fire.

The Forestry Commission, private timber companies, the National Parks and Wildlife Service, the Hydro-Electric Commission and mining companies, all use fire in the South-West as a tool — each with a different aim. Frequently the administrative boundaries between these authorities and interests reflect a legal requirement, and bear no relation to the fire boundaries long since established by nature. Where this occurs, the management aims of each authority in relation to fire are in direct conflict and are likely to remain so.

Co-ordinating and deciding on an appropriate management policy for the South-West presents many problems. One of the major problems in the protection and care of the area is the time scale involved. Any management plan must encompass a number of plant generations and consequently the time involved ranges from approximately 100 years or 3 generations with the most fire prone communities, to many thousands of years for alpine communities.

If species diversity as well as age variation of plant communities is to be maintained, then the implications of fire and its frequency must be recognised, since fire has played, and will continue to play, a fundamental role in the evolution of the natural environment in the South-West.

Top left
Here an officer inspects the seed pods of a *Hakea* after a fire. *Greg Hodge*

Bottom left
Aftermath of a fire in the Cuvier Valley on the slopes of Mt Olympus. Regeneration in such highland forests is slow. *Greg Hodge*

Top right
Each year many fires burn inland from the south and west coasts. This particular fire near Red Point Hills was photographed within an hour of its ignition and shows clearly the two separate ignition points near the waters edge. *Greg Hodge*

Bottom right
This burnt area at Rocky Boat Harbour was photographed after the fire which started on the foreshore in January 1976. A similar fire burnt the same area a year previously. A mosaic can be seen with some islands of vegetation burnt at different frequencies. This latest and hotter fire encroached upon the eucalypt fringe. The wet sclerophyll forest prevented the fire spreading further towards Precipitous Bluff. *Greg Hodge*

'Ecological Drift' An argument against the continued practice of Hazard Reduction Burning

W D Jackson

In Tasmania and South-East Australia the pattern of plant communities is a response to limitations of soil fertility and frequency of bush fires. Climate affects the vegetation more by controlling these interacting factors than by direct influence.[1]

The fire frequency affects the vegetation by selection. Frequent firing encourages more fire prone vegetation which in turn creates an increase in the fire frequency. In addition to this feedback, the loss of nutrients following each fire causes a drop in soil fertility which interacts again with vegetation in another feed-back relationship. Poor fertility is strongly correlated with high fire frequency not only because fires cause a loss of nutrients, but also because poor soils induce open, slow growing, fire prone communities.

Fire has markedly differing effects on different plants and vegetation types.[2] Some vegetation, such as rainforest, is difficult to burn because the closed structure tends to maintain humid conditions. Fire is not only difficult to start, but fuel is reduced because the litter falling from the canopy is destroyed quickly by micro-organisms. As a consequence, rainforest species are poorly adapted to fire and do not regenerate well when they are burnt. They have virtually no vegetative recovery and seed supply often limits regeneration. On the other hand, eucalypts and most dry sclerophyll plants in Australia are strongly adapted to fire.[3] They recover rapidly by vegetative means and by seeding. They are not only fire resistant, but are fire promoters. The open canopy and high water utilization produces dry understorey conditions. The copious litter produced by decorticating bark as well as by leaves, twigs, etc. contains phenolic compounds with bactericidal and fungicidal properties so that decay of the litter is inhibited. The leaves contain highly volatile and combustible aromatic oils and the loose bark and old leaves are effective agents in creating 'spot fires' or further centres of fire in advance of the main fire front.

Plants regenerate, following fires, by recovering vegetative growth or by starting again from seed. Vegetative recovery depends on the adaptations to fire resistance developed by the plants, such as thick bark and protected growing points. Similarly regeneration by seed depends on adaptations protecting the seed in soil or in fire resistant fruit or favouring the wide dispersal of seed by wind or birds.

A few severe fires or a sequence of light fires will rapidly select out sensitive

Mick Brown, Professor Bill Jackson and Bert Shepherd on the Norfolk Ranges, 1975.   *M Macphail*

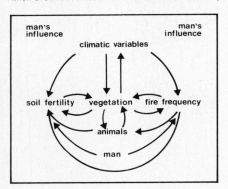

Fig 1 Interactions determining vegetation type.

species with poor vegetative recovery and will result in the spread of species with underground stems, lignotubers or thick resistant bark. Vegetative recovery depends, of course, on the intensity of the fire. This is a function of the weather, fuel type and quantity. In general, fires at frequent intervals tend to be light and infrequent fires tend to be intense because fuel takes time to accumulate. However, this simple relationship is complicated by the natural selection of characters affecting the generation of fuel in those species which already show vegetative resistance. Species such as eucalypts which have strong vegetative regeneration tend to develop characteristics of high fuel production simply because fire is a relative advantage to these species in competition with more fire sensitive plants.

Fire also acts as a selective process causing changes in plant communities regenerating from seed. Species having poor or variable seed reproduction are selected against. Species with poor seed dispersion combined with low seed survival are also adversely affected. Species with advantages are those

producing copious quantities of seed in fire resistant fruits or those with an ability to survive in soil until stimulated by heat to germinate. Poor seed dispersion is an advantage rather than a disadvantage, provided the seed can survive the fire, since the genetic adaptations to the site can bring the plants to a high level of fitness.

The development of pyrogenic communities is associated with a fall in nutrient availability. Each fire causes a loss of about 20% of the nutrients in the forest through vaporisation and particle loss in smoke. This is followed with a loss due to leaching dependent on rainfall. In the densely forested regions of Tasmania this loss is probably of the order of 50%, so that about 70% of the nutrients are lost during and following each fire. Time is required to replenish the source either from the soil or from the rain as cyclic salt. In Tasmania most of the soils in the wetter regions are too poor, and cyclic salt is the major source of nutrient replenishment.[4]

The continued application of fire by the aboriginal inhabitants of Tasmania for the last 10, or more than likely 20, thousand years [5][6][7] has resulted in the establishment of strange disclimax patterns of vegetation. Where fire has been a constant feature of the environment and the soils are poor, the development of forest in the post Pleistocene climate has been prevented. The open communities of sedgeland and grassland with shrub elements which were the prevalent vegetation in the cold dry climate of the immediate post Pleistocene period have continued to survive in an altered form. In the high rainfall regions, ridge tops which dry out more frequently become burnt more often due to spot fires. Such ridges carry mixed forest, wet sclerophyll or scrub and sedgeland reflecting the degree of fire risk and soil fertility (Fig 3).

The type of forest found in the wetter regions of Tasmania is thus dependent upon the frequency of fire. As a consequence climax rainforest is limited in distribution to areas topographically protected from high fire incidence. If fires are too frequent all forest trees are eliminated and button-grass sedgeland or scrubby moorland results. If 25 to 100 years elapse between fires, tall open wet sclerophyll stands of eucalypt forest with dense shrubby understories are found. When 100 to 300 years elapse between fires a mixed forest of eucalypts standing above an understorey of temperate rainforest is formed. If fires are too infrequent eucalypts are eliminated and pure rainforests dominated by *Nothofagus* with *Atherosperma*, *Eucryphia* and *Phyllocladus* form closed stands (Fig 4).

The foregoing evidence suggests that chance processes in the distribution of fires lead to a process of 'Ecological Drift' (Fig 5) in which any given area moves gradually towards climax rainforest or towards sedgeland. The use of 'hazard reduction burning' would greatly accelerate the shift to sedgeland and scrub.

Eucalypt seedlings have a large light requirement, that is, a high compensation point; as a consequence, eucalypt seedlings cannot survive in mixed forests under the rainforest canopy. Hence, there is no continuous regeneration of eucalypts. The eucalypts are not replaced as the old trees die of fungus diseases. As indicated in Figure 4, the mixed forest becomes a pure rainforest following fire free conditions of 350 years. Future fires merely regenerate rainforest since there is no eucalypt seed. Following the conversion to pure rainforest the average interval between fires tends to increase to about 300 years because of the absence of eucalypt litter. Thus, chance long intervals between fires leads to the elimination of eucalypts. This causes a lowering of the fire risk in future generations of forest (top right in Fig 5). At the other end of the sampling range, chance short intervals between successive fires favour the open sclerophyll communities, temporarily eliminating rainforest species. Rainforest species take 40 to 80 years to flower under the intense competitive conditions of regenerating eucalypts. Eucalypts require about 15 to 20 years to produce seed under these conditions. Hence if a second fire occurs before 15 years, both eucalypts and rainforest species will be eliminated. If the second fire occurs between 15 and 80 years the eucalypt is regenerated but the rainforest is eliminated.

A single event of a short interval between fires increases the probability of

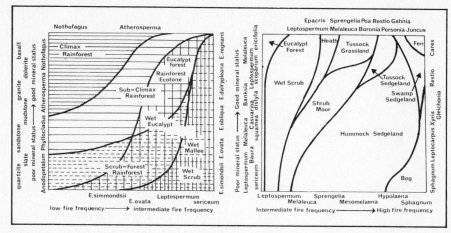

Fig 2 The relationships of community structures in Tasmania as determined by the interaction of fire frequency and soil fertility.

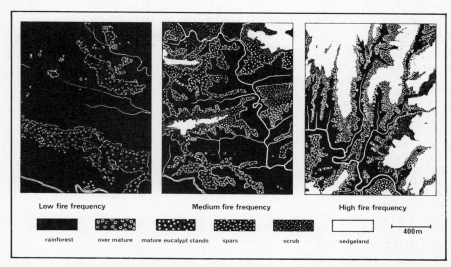

Fig 3 Vegetation patterns associated with various fire frequencies showing the progressive replacement of rainforest on ridge crest by mixed forest, eucalypt forest, scrub heath and sedgeland with increasing fire frequency. Pieman River region. Tasmanian west coast; rainfall 2500mm/annum. For a comparison with aerial photographs see the Occasional paper No 11. *An Overview of Natural Vegetation Research in South-West Tasmania, May 1978, P Faircloth. South West Tasmania Resources Survey.*

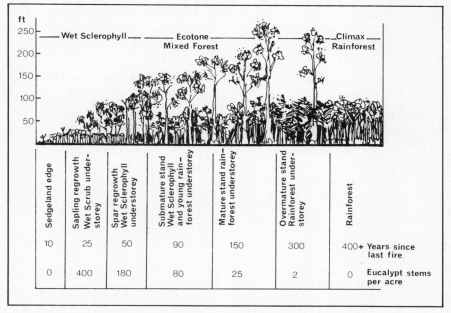

Fig 4 Forest structures in South-West Tasmania as determined by age since the last fire.

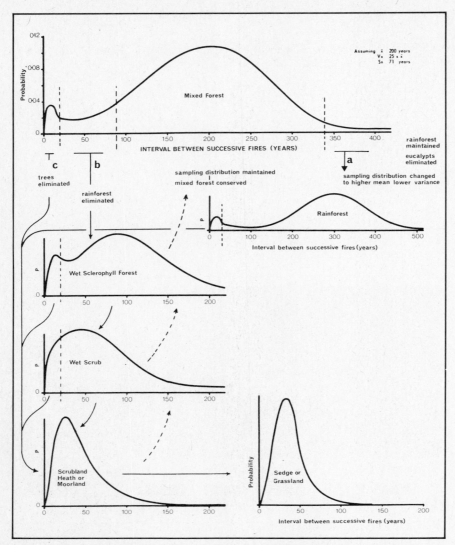

Fig 5 ECOLOGICAL DRIFT. A diagrammatic interpretation of progressive shifts in likelihood of vegetation types and their associated fire frequencies. It is assumed that drift in the sampling distribution occurs through chance occurrences of short or long intervals between two successive destructive fires. Chance long intervals lead to the elimination of eucalypts. This causes a lowering of the fire risk in future generations of forest (a). Chance short intervals lead to the elimination of rainforest (b) or of all forest species (c) with consequent shift to sampling distribution with lower mean intervals between fires. This increases the probability of drift to a degraded open vegetation with high fire frequency, a process which is accelerated on poor soils because of vegetation — fire frequency interactions and increased leaching. The approximate probability functions are estimated from a study of plant age on a large number of parallel sites for each vegetation type.

a drift to a degraded open vegetation with a permanently high fire frequency. This process is more likely on poor soils because of the interactions between the frequency of fires and the structure and floristics of the vegetation, and the slower replenishment of nutrients lost by leaching after each fire.

In Tasmania the resistant products of continued burning, the terminal pyrogenic disclimax communities, are well developed. These communities are apparently highly specialized to various combinations of soil-type and local climatic conditions. The general prevalence of these communities across the ranges of rainfall, altitude and soils, and the degree of specialization, indicate a long association with fire as a selective agent. There is as yet little research to

demonstrate the basis of specialization, although the correlation of certain communities with soil-type and climatic conditions is obvious.

Most of the pyrogenic communities are composed entirely of native plants, a situation in contrast with that in New Zealand, where many of the fire created disclimax communities consist of, or are dominated by, exotic species such as *Ulex europaeus* (gorse) and *Genista monspessulana* (canary broom). In Tasmania there are a number of plant communities dominated by natives with a propensity for vegetative reproduction and which invest much of their productivity in underground parts. Some of these plants actually require fire to stimulate sexual reproduction, e.g. *Xanthorrhoea* (grass tree) species.

Many species require fire to trigger seed release (e.g. *Eucalyptus*, *Hakea*), or to trigger germination (many legumes). Most species require fire in some way as an aid in regeneration, particularly in competition with species not adapted to fire.

In South-Western Tasmania the more important dominants of pyrogenic communities are:

Eucalyptus nitida (syn. *E. simmondsii*), *E. ovata, Melaleuca squarrosa, M. squamea, Leptospermum scoparium, L. glaucescens, L. nitidum, Agastachys odorata, Bauera rubioides, Sprengelia incarnata, Leucopogon collinus, L. ericoides, Gahnia grandis, Gymnoschoenus sphaerocephalus, Lepidosperma filiforme, L. laterale, Restio complanatus, R. oligocephalus, Xyris operculata, Leptocarpus tenax, Hypolaena fastigiata, Calorophus lateriflorus, Pteridium esculentum, Gleichenia dicarpa, G. alpina, Selaginella uliginosa.*[5 8]

Management bodies in Tasmania seem to have adopted control burning without examining their different circumstances. I suggest the following factors as important to a consideration of the unqualified use of control burning in Tasmania:

(1) Fire has a greater impact on plant species in Tasmania than those on the mainland because the mainland species are more adapted to fire. This is partly a consequence of their evolution in a drier, hotter climate where lightning has always maintained a high level of fire incidence, and partly because in the latter part of the Pleistocene the climatic differences were more exaggerated than at present. Whereas the plant communities in New South Wales may not be materially changed by burning at ten yearly intervals, the same cannot be said of Tasmanian communities.

(2) Fuel accumulation in Tasmanian forests is significantly faster than in mainland counterparts. This is due in part to faster cellulose production, a result of greater water availability and longer growing periods, and in part to the slower breakdown of litter in the lower temperatures. The faster fuel accumulation means that control burns have to be made at shorter intervals in Tasmania. The higher fire incidence eliminates those understorey species with slow reproduction and prevents the regeneration of the dominants. Thus Tasmanian forests will be more rapidly affected by control burning.

(3) Since the burning rate will be high and the species ill adapted to this high rate, the change to open communities will be relatively rapid. The high fire incidence, open communities and high rainfalls on the steep Tasmanian topography will induce a faster loss of nutrients than on the mainland. The loss of nutrients will accentuate the

degeneration to pyrogenic open communities.[9]

(4) Finally, people are the only significant cause of fire incidence in Tasmania and therefore it seems logical that control should start with people — not with fuel. Tasmania has a real potential compared with other states to obtain control by public education. Instead, the practice of control burning gives the impression to the public that fire is acceptable and can only be met with fire.

The management objective for national parks and reserves is to conserve the flora and fauna. Policies have to ensure the stability of the plant communities or allow their slow return to a near climax state. Control burning has no part to play in management, since it works directly against the objective by causing a degeneration of climax communities and the development of pyrogenic, high risk disclimax communities. Climax or near climax forest communities will regenerate following hot destructive fires provided they occur at infrequent intervals. However, they are slowly destroyed by constant firing even if these fires are not intense.

Many of our reserves are established to conserve alpine communities. These plant communities carry most of the endemic plants and are particularly valuable scientifically and aesthetically. Production in these communities is extremely low. Diameter increments of 10 mm per 100 years are not exceptional in native conifers (1 inch = 200 to 300 years). Fire has to be completely avoided since these communities are very susceptible, being completely killed and taking an enormous time span to recover. Such areas need special protection during regeneration burning in adjacent forestry areas to prevent spot fires, as have occurred in Mount Field National Park.

This fire near the Sprent River (a tributary of the Gordon) is typical of those fires of which the cause is unknown, and which burn slowly for one or two days before dying naturally in the cool of the night in early or late summer.
Greg Hodge

Hazard reduction burning has proved one way of reducing the chances of fire susceptible areas being burnt by wild fires. However there is continuing debate as to where, when and how often such fires should be lit, if at all. Here a ranger helps to burn out a plain to the north-west of Mt Anne in an attempt to prevent carelessly lit fires from reaching the mountains.
Greg Hodge

Bramble Cove, 1963.
N E Poynter

This photo was taken during the inundation of Lake Pedder in mid 1972. UNESCO described the event as 'the greatest ecological tragedy since European settlement in Tasmania'. During the battle over the fate of Lake Pedder, collections from the lake, especially from the impressive and most unusual beach, revealed at least 18 endemic aquatic species of plants and animals in the lake and its immediate environs. The new water body possesses markedly different characteristics from the original lake and certainly constitutes a totally different biological environment.   *Tasmanian Environment Centre Inc Col*

A gem in rugged terrain. 3750 metres above the lake in late summer 1971 when the water receded to its lowest level revealing the quartzite beach 730 metres wide from dunes to waters edge.
Lands Department

Lake Pedder was renowned for its magnificent, gently sloping beach which harboured a rich and well adapted interstitial fauna (Psammon).
Tasmanian Environment Centre Inc Col

Freshwater Environments and their Fauna

P S Lake, R Swain,
A M Richardson &
D Coleman

Until May 1976 Dr Lake was a senior lecturer in Zoology at the University of Tasmania; he has now joined the Zoology Department at Monash University. Dr Richardson is a lecturer in Zoology, Dr Swain a Senior Lecturer in Zoology and David Coleman is a Graduate Research Assistant in Zoology; all three work at the University of Tasmania. Drs Lake and Swain have published a number of articles and scientific papers on the fauna of South-Western Tasmania. Since 1974, receipt of a grant under the Australian Biological Resources Study has enabled all four authors to collaborate on an extensive survey of the aquatic invertebrates of Western and South-Western Tasmania.

The rugged and often inhospitable nature of Tasmania's South-West has hitherto ensured that much of the region has remained an inaccessible wilderness. Whilst this has certainly helped to reduce exploitation, it has also provided an effective barrier to biological research; consequently biological studies of this very important region have been irregular, infrequent and, at least until recent years, unco-ordinated. Neglect of the region has also resulted from the generally poor support that freshwater biology in Australia has received in the past, while not surprisingly the few workers interested in this field have largely concentrated their efforts on the great number of more readily accessible water bodies in Tasmania.

Work carried out on the freshwater fauna of the South-West in the first half of this century was solely taxonomic, and based on collections made from peripheral localities such as the Hartz Mountains, Mt Field National Park, Lake St Clair and the Queenstown area. Particularly significant collections of freshwater insects together with a number of descriptions, notably of adult stages, were made by R J Tillyard, A L Tonnoir and J W Evans. The interesting crustacean fauna of the region received attention from G Smith, E Clark and G E Nicholls. Other animal groups present were largely neglected.

In the past decade, the freshwater environments of South-West Tasmania and their associated fauna have received considerable attention. The most obvious impetus for this surge in interest was the controversy surrounding the Tasmanian Government's decision to flood Lake Pedder, and the realisation by scientists that a unique and extremely valuable biological asset, about which they knew next to nothing, was to be destroyed for all time. It should be emphasised that whatever desirable attributes the new water body called Lake Pedder (more appropriately called the Serpentine impoundment) may have, it possesses markedly different characteristics from the original lake and certainly constitutes a totally different biological environment. During the battle over the fate of Lake Pedder, collections from the lake, especially from the impressive and most unusual beach, revealed at least 18 endemic aquatic species of plants and animals in the lake and its immediate environs. The four species of endemic plants consisted of 3 semi-aquatic species and one fully aquatic member of the Juncaginaceae. All of the endemic animals were aquatic.

Although collections of animals have been made at a considerable number of widely separated localities, published ecological data is available only for Lake Pedder, Lake Edgar and a button-grass swamp near McPartlan Pass. As yet there is no published work relating to the ecology of the running waters of South-West Tasmania.

Geologically, South-West Tasmania consists predominantly of siliceous Precambrian rocks which are notable for their chemical inertness. Along the Lower Gordon River, and in the Mt Anne and Precipitous Bluff areas, there are outcrops of limestone and dolomite, whilst dolerite outcrops occur in the eastern portion of the region. The soils are generally thin and poorly developed.

Many of the slopes and plains of the region are dominated by button-grass sedgelands, and thick peat deposits are widespread. The inert nature of the Precambrian rocks coupled with the fact that the peat diminishes close contact between the rocks and percolating water, results in very low ion concentrations in the waters draining the Precambrian areas. At the same time, the slow decomposition of sedgeland peat makes available considerable quantities of fine particulate and dissolved organic matter and this gives rise to the deep brown colour, the high acidity and the low bicarbonate content of waters from the peat and button-grass areas. The waters have the same order of ion dominance as sea water, and most of the ions are probably derived from the sea via the region's heavy rainfall. Where outcrops of easily weatherable rocks, e.g. limestone, dolomite and serpentenite occur, the ion dominance changes and reflects the chemical composition of such rocks. Thus the Weld River, which possesses dolomite outcrops in its catchment area, has relatively high levels of calcium, magnesium and bicarbonate ions compared to waters rising in the Precambrian rocks.

While there is relatively little variety in the chemistry of the waters of South-West Tasmania, the high rainfall and rugged nature of the region has produced an impressive range of types of water bodies. Most of the lakes and tarns of South-West Tasmania owe their origin to glacial forces. The region has a considerable number of cirque lakes, many dammed by moraines. Particularly dramatic examples of cirque lakes are found in the Western and Eastern Arthurs, Mt Picton massif, Frankland Range and Mt Anne massif (Lake Judd). Some kettle tarns exist in the Arthurs and in the Frankland Range. The original Lake Pedder was formed by the damming of water behind a glaciofluvial outwash apron descending from the north-eastern flanks of the Frankland Range. It is believed that Lake Edgar (now lost within the Lake Pedder impoundment) was formed as a result of quaternary faulting and provided a fine example of a sag pond. Along the coast there are scattered coastal lagoons formed behind coastal dunes.

Lotic (i.e. running water) environments are abundant, with an immense number of creeks, streams and rivers draining the region. Numerous fast flowing creeks drain the mountain ranges and as they flow through peat swamps and button-grass areas they acquire their characteristic brown hue. Important river systems in the region include the Picton–Huon River system, the New River system, Davey River system, the several short rivers draining the West Coast Range, and the magnificent Gordon–Franklin River system. As they approach the sea, many of these rivers develop extensive estuarine regions. New River Lagoon at the foot of Precipitous Bluff is such a system, whilst a truly superb example of a very gradual longitudinal change from freshwater to seawater is provided by the Lower Gordon River.

As any walker in South-West Tasmania soon comes to realise, mires and swamps are plentiful. In some highland areas protected from fire, swamps may contain sphagnum moss and cushion plant communities, but most of the lowland swamps are dominated by button-grass. Such swamps are riddled with the burrow systems of the so-called 'land crayfish', *Parastacoides tasmanicus*. Strips of melaleuca and teatree swamp are often found alongside the slow-flowing reaches of the rivers.

The freshwater fauna of South-West Tasmania contains many animals of considerable scientific and general interest. A brief account of some of the more interesting groups follows.

PHYLUM PLATYHELMINTHES:

Class Turbellaria: Flatworms or planarians may be found gliding over the surface of small stones in pools, tarns, lakes and streams. They are generally predators but some appear to be omnivorous. Recently, Ball[1] has described a new genus of flatworm from Tasmania called *Romankenkius*. One species, *Romankenkius pedderensis*, was known only from the original Lake Pedder, whilst the other species *R. kenki* is found in Lake Seal in the Mt Field National Park.

Class Temnocephaloidea: These small flatworms are characterised by a series of tentacles at the head end. The class is found mainly in the Southern Hemisphere. The Tasmanian examples live as ectocommensals on parastacid crayfish, using the body of the 'host' as a vantage point from which to collect food. *Temnocephala tasmanica*, *Temnocephala cita* and *Temnocephala fulva* have been found on the crayfish *Parastacoides tasmanicus*.

PHYLUM ANNELIDA:

Class Oligochaeta: These segmented worms are common; typically they are found in the benthic (bottom) regions of lakes and tarns and in the pools of streams. Lake Pedder appears to be the only locality in South-West Tasmania from which oligochaetes have been collected and formally identified or described. Two families, the Tubificidae and the Phreodrilidae, were identified. In the Tubificidae two endemic species, *Telmatodrilus multiprostratus* and *Telmatodrilus pectinatus* were part of the unusual interstitial fauna (psammon) of the famous Lake Pedder beach.

PHYLUM ARTHROPODA:

Class Crustacea:

Subclass Copepoda: These microscopic crustaceans form an important part of the zooplankton community of lentic (standing) freshwaters. Both Lake Pedder and Lake Edgar had a zooplanktonic fauna dominated by the calanoid copepod *Calamoecia expansa*. This species appears to be restricted to acidic waters with a very low ion concentration; it has been recorded only from a few localities in Victoria and Tasmania.

Subclass Branchiura: These animals, often called 'fish-lice', are ectoparasites of freshwater fish. Specimens of a new species, subsequently called *Dolops tasmanianus*, were collected off fish (*Galaxias affinis* = *Galaxias brevipinnis*) caught in Lake Surprise in the Frankland Range. Subsequently the species was obtained from *Galaxias pedderensis* caught in Swampy Creek, the original Lake Pedder, and in creeks running into the Serpentine River. The genus *Dolops* has a most interesting distribution. It is found only in the Southern Hemisphere with at least 9 species in South America, one species in Africa and one species in Tasmania. *Dolops tasmanianus* is one of a number of species of Tasmanian animals, particularly those of the South-West, which may be used to support the hypothesis of 'continental drift'. The close faunal relationships between the Southern Hemisphere land masses is best explained by assuming that the continents were once part of a single land mass (Gondwanaland). Separation is thought to have occurred about 200 million years ago (see 2.11).

Subclass Malacostraca: This subclass contains the shrimps, prawns, crabs, crayfish and lobsters that most people regard as crustaceans.

Superorder Syncarida: Syncarids are, comparatively speaking, primitive and relatively unspecialized malacostracans. They lack a carapace, hence their gills are unprotected, and there is no fusion of the separate segments of the body. Because the group has survived virtually unchanged for some 250 million years or more they are often referred to as 'living fossils'. Tasmania is renowned for its treasure-house of anaspidid syncarids, of which the most celebrated example is *Anaspides tasmaniae* or 'mountain shrimp'. Although this world famous animal was first noted in 1840 (*Hobart Town Courier* and *Van Diemen's Land Gazette*, 1.7.1840) it was overlooked by scientists until 1892 when the New Zealand biologist, G M Thomson collected specimens from pools on the top of Mt Wellington. *Anaspides tasmaniae* is widely distributed throughout South-West Tasmania occurring in lakes and tarns, pools in button-grass swamps, creeks and occasionally in runnels. Despite its common name the species is not a true 'shrimp'. While *A. tasmaniae* appears to be able to co-exist with species of native galaxiid fish, it cannot survive in the presence of the larger and more voracious introduced salmonid fish.

Anaspides tasmaniae is omnivorous, and in small streams and tarns it can be frequently seen eating small liverworts and mosses or browsing on 'aufwuchs' which is the name given to the community of microscopic plants and animals attached to sessile objects or plants. In November 1969, at the height of the Lake Pedder controversy, a new syncarid was collected in crayfish burrows near Pedder. The animal was named *Allanaspides helonomus*. Subsequently a second species, *Allanaspides hickmani*, was found in the McPartlan Pass area. These animals are found in crayfish burrows and in the surface pools often associated with these burrows in button-grass swamps. They seem to be limited to brown, acidic, humified waters with a very low ion concentration. Both species possess a distinctive organ on the cephalothoracic tergite called the 'fenestra dorsalis'. Investigation of the structure of the 'fenestra dorsalis' with the electron microscope has revealed that the organ is almost certainly an active ion uptake organ. The 'fenestra dorsalis' appears to be an adaptation to allow *Allanaspides* to survive in an environment with a low ion concentration and a low ion availability.

The family Koonungidae is represented in South-West Tasmania by the genus *Micraspides*. Specimens of the only described species of this genus (*M. calmani*) are small (13 mm), unpigmented and eyeless. They live a subterranean existence, often dwelling in the burrows of the crayfish of the genera *Parastacoides* and *Engaeus*. *Micraspides calmani* was originally collected in 1928 near Queenstown. Other Koonungids have also been collected within the South-West, from the banks of the Gordon River near its mouth, from the Olga River Valley, Port Davey, Bathurst Harbour and from Crotty. The animals were often found in crayfish burrows, however it is uncertain whether the *Micraspides* collected from these localities are all *Micraspides calmani*, since the family Koonungidae needs thorough revision.

Bathynellids are minute (0.5–4 mm) syncarids found in the interstitial water between grains of sand and pieces of gravel. Representative of two families, the Bathynellidae and the Parabathynellidae, have been collected from the sands and gravels of streams on the fringes of South-West Tasmania such as the Russell River and the Nelson River. They are most likely to occur in the sands and gravels of streams of the South-West. Unfortunately, the collection of bathynellids requires specialized equipment and is both tedious and time consuming. Consequently little work on the group has yet been possible in the South-West.

Order Isopoda:

Sub-order Asellota: These small isopods have been found in numerous lakes, small streams and in 'yabby' pools and burrows in South-West Tasmania. Their taxonomy at this stage is uncertain but it appears that two genera,

Pseudasellus and *Heterias* occur there.

Sub-order Phreatoicidea: This group differs from other isopods in body form, being laterally compressed rather than dorso-ventrally flattened. The sub-order consists of three families, of which two, the Amphisopidae and the Phreatoicidae occur in Tasmania. The third family, the Nichollsidae, is restricted to the Indian sub-continent. The group received considerable taxonomic attention some years ago from Professor G E Nicholls. Recently the group has been investigated taxonomically by B Knott whose findings differ in many respects from those of Nicholls. However until Knott's work is published, the following comments must refer to the taxonomic scheme of Nicholls. Tasmania's only representatives of the family Amphisopidae are to be found in western and south-western Tasmania. The two species concerned are both blind subterranean animals. *Phreatoicoides longicollis* has only been collected once, near Zeehan. *Hypsimetopus intrusor* was originally collected from burrows in the earthen dam of a mine near Zeehan in 1901. It has in recent times been collected from a number of localities in western and south-western Tasmania from near Smithton to the Port Davey area. The

family Phreatoicidae is well represented in Tasmania and specimens of the genus *Colubotelson* have been collected throughout South-West Tasmania, in both standing water (lentic) and flowing water (lotic) environments. An undescribed species of *Colubotelson* was the dominant animal in the most unusual psammon community of the beach of the original Lake Pedder. This species was restricted to the original Lake Pedder and was the only species of phreatoicid recorded in the freshwater psammon. An undescribed species has also been found in yabby burrows in South-West Tasmania. Extensive collecting around the shores of the Serpentine impoundment has failed to reveal any phreatoicids.

Order Amphipoda: These small, shrimp-like crustaceans are laterally compressed. With few exceptions, the taxonomy of fresh-water amphipods in Australia generally and in Tasmania in particular, is not clear. The very widespread and common species, *Austrochiltonia australis,* has been found in both lakes and swamps in the South-West. Two species of the family Eusiridae have been found with *Paracalliope fluviatilis* occurring in the upper freshwater reaches of the

estuaries e.g. Gordon River, Melaleuca Inlet; while a new species of *Paraleptamphopus* has been found at Kelly Basin, in tributaries of the Gordon River and the now flooded Lake Edgar. In many streams and tarns of South-West Tasmania, there is an abundance of large gammarid amphipods. Their taxonomic status is uncertain. Six interesting species of gammarid amphipods have been collected from crayfish burrows. Three of these species are eyeless and unpigmented and may be regarded as leading a subterranean existence.

Order Decapoda: An account of the ecology of the South-West would be incomplete without mentioning the burrowing, land crayfish, of the genera *Engaeus* and *Parastacoides*. All the freshwater crayfish of Australia and Tasmania belong to the large family of Southern Hemisphere crayfish, the Parastacidae. Members of the Parastacidae are to be found on the Australian mainland, in Tasmania, new Zealand, South America and Malagasy (Madagascar).

Parastacoides is an endemic genus whilst *Engaeus* is also found in the south-east corner of the Australian mainland. Six species of *Parastacoides* are currently recognized in the scientific

Colubotelson thomsoni, a phreatoicid found in streams in the eastern part of the South-West. *Zoology Dept Uni of Tas*

Anaspides tasmaniae, a 'living fossil' widely distributed throughout the South-West. Actual size approx 40mm. *Zoology Dept Uni of Tas*

Allanaspides helonomus was discovered in 1969 when specimens were collected from crayfish burrows near Lake Pedder. The unusual organ called the 'fenestra dorsalis' thought to be an active ion uptake organ, can be seen on the cephalothorax. *Zoology Dept Uni of Tas*

Freshwater crayfish *Parastacoides tasmanicus* with its load of temnocephalans. These small flat worms live as ecto-commensals (that is, in close association but without much mutual influence), on parastacid crayfish, using the body of the 'host' only as a vantage point from which to collect food. *Zoology Dept Uni of Tas*

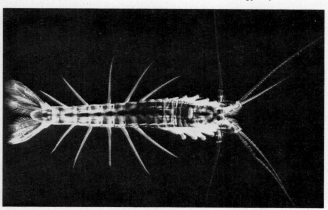

literature. Recent work by C Sumner (in prep.) has shown that there is only one species of *Parastacoides* (*Parastacoides tasmanicus*) with three sub-species. The animal is widespread throughout the button-grass slopes, swamps and plains of South-West Tasmania, being well adapted to the rigours of living in acidic, humified, mostly stagnant water, subject to considerable seasonal fluctuations of temperature and oxygen content. Laboratory studies have shown that the crayfish have a remarkable physiological tolerance of acid pH and of low oxygen concentrations. Recently, specimens of *Parastacoides* were collected from an unusual habitat for this animal: underneath stones in fast flowing creeks near Sir John Falls on the Lower Gordon River.

In the northern part of the South-West, at Kelly Basin and along the banks of the Gordon and Franklin Rivers, there are two species of *Engaeus; Engaeus fossor* and a newly discovered species *Engaeus cisternarius*. Both of these species appear to be confined to lowland forested areas, with *Engaeus fossor* being found close to streams and rivers.

In contrast to the 'land crayfish', parastacid crayfish of the genus *Astacopsis* are found in the streams of South-West Tasmania. There are two species; *Astacopsis tricornis* and *Astacopsis fluviatilis. Astacopsis tricornis* grows to a considerable size (20–30 cm) and appears to be restricted to the slow-flowing lowland stretches of the rivers, while *Astacopsis fluviatilis* (12 cm) is to be found under stones and logs in the fast-flowing streams.

Class Insecta: Our knowledge of the taxonomy and distribution of the aquatic insects of South-West Tasmania is both incomplete and fragmentary. Many of the insects have aquatic nymphal or larval stages and a terrestrial adult stage. In many cases it is virtually impossible to match the form of the larva or nymph with that of the adult without extensive and time-consuming rearing programs in the laboratory.

Comment here will be confined to groups well represented in the South-West or groups of special biological interest.

Order Ephemeroptera: (mayflies). The cooler parts of Tasmania (e.g. South-West Tasmania, Central Plateau) have a rich mayfly fauna. In South-West Tasmania, mayfly nymphs of the family Leptophlebiidae, genus *Atalophlebioides* are often abundant in the stony riffle regions of swift flowing streams. In sandy or gravelly stretches of streams, specimens of the genus *Tasmanophlebia* in the family Baetidae may be collected, whilst in stony areas of tarns and lakes, large nymphs of the genus *Atalophlebia* (Leptophlebiiae) are to be found.

Order Odonata: The Odonata (dragonflies and damselflies) are well

represented throughout the range of aquatic habitats available in South-West Tasmania. The most distinctive of these habitats is probably the pools and runnels in button-grass swamps. This habitat is particularly favoured by dragonflies of the family Synthemidae of which the monospecific genus *Synthemiopsis* (*Synthemiopsis gomphomacromioides*) is endemic to Tasmania. There are two other species in the Synthemidae in Tasmania, *Synthemis eustalacta tasmanica* and *Synthemis macrostigma orientalis.* The nymphs are bottom-dwellers and often cover themselves with mud and pieces of dead vegetation. All three species have been recorded in the South-West. The Synthemidae is an Australian family, the most primitive species being *Synthemiopsis gomphomacromioides*. The restriction of this species to cold temperate regions probably reflects the climatic conditions prevailing when this family first evolved.

In 1917, the eminent entomologist R J Tillyard collected, at Cradle Mountain, a most primitive dragonfly which he named *Archipetalia auriculata*. The species is the most archaic representative of the sub-family Neopetalinae of the family Aeschnidae. The sub-family is represented by five genera, two monospecific genera from Australia and three from South America. Subsequently a nymph believed to be *Archipetalia auriculata* was found in the Tyndall Ranges, and very recently three similar nymphs were collected from a small sandy creek draining from the King Billy Range on the southern side of the Gordon River. The nymphs lurked under rotting sticks and also in recesses in the sticks which had been honeycombed by borers. It appears that the nymphs feed at night on gammarid amphipods.

Order Plecoptera: Tasmania is particularly well-endowed with stoneflies—a consequence, no doubt, of the abundance of cool running waters. The stoneflies, especially the nymphal stages, form a considerable part of the macro-invertebrate fauna of many, if not most, Tasmanian streams. This is particularly true for the fast flowing streams at high altitudes or in the cooler parts of the State such as the South-West.

Recent studies by Illies[2] and Hynes[3] have shown a high degree of endemicity for Tasmanian stoneflies in all of the four families. Out of the 28 species found in Tasmania, only 6 species are also found on the mainland. Undoubtedly the most spectacular adults and nymphs of the Plecoptera to be found in the South-West belong to the Eustheniidae. This family is confined to Australia, New Zealand and southern South America. The genus *Eusthenia* is endemic to Tasmania with two species, *Eusthenia spectabilis* and *Eusthenia costalis* being

currently recognized. Eusthenid nymphs are large (3 cm) and predatory.

The family Austroperlidae is represented in Tasmania by 3 species in two genera, *Crypturoperla* and *Tasmanoperla.* All three species may be expected to occur in the South-West.

The Gripopterygidae is the dominant family of stoneflies of Australia and of Tasmania. Fourteen species in seven genera are found in Tasmania with the monospecific genus *Cardioperla* being endemic. The small to medium-sized nymphs (0.5–1.5 cm) of this family occur in a wide range of habitats and may be found along the stony shores of lakes and both the fast-flowing and slow-flowing stretches of creeks and rivers.

The taxonomy of the Australian representatives of the stonefly family Notonemouridae has recently been revised by Illies.[2] The nymphs of this family are well adapted for climbing on vertical rock surfaces and are to be found in cold springs, creeks and in seepage areas on high mountains or in cool regions such as the South-West, where notonemourids have been recorded at low altitudes. The family is well represented in the South-West with at least 9 species, out of the 16 species recorded in Australia, being found there or in fringe areas such as Hartz Mountains and Mt Field National Park. Of particular interest are the nymphs of the endemic monospecific genus *Tasmanocerca* (*Tasmanocerca bifasciata*) with an unusual investment of stiff bristles on the margins of the thoracic segments.

Order Hemiptera: A number of families of this large well-known order constitute a group termed 'water bugs'. Two families are of interest in this discussion; the Notonectidae (the back-swimmers) and the Corixidae (water boatmen). Notonectids are found throughout the region in lakes and tarns, especially in those with zones of emergent vegetation. Lake Pedder harboured a new, as yet undescribed, species of the genus *Anisops*, an unusual situation considering the high mobility that one expects the winged notonectids to have. The Corixidae are also well represented in the South-West. The three described species of the distinctive genus *Diaprepocoris* are all to be found in Tasmania. *Diaprepocoris personata* was found at Lake Edgar and an endemic species, *Diaprepocoris pedderensis*, was found in the old Lake Pedder.

Order Coleoptera: Many larvae and adult beetles are to be found in a wide variety of aquatic habitats. There is a large number of species in Tasmania and as yet no comprehensive study has been made of their taxonomy, distribution or ecology. The family Psephenidae is of particular interest. The distinctive flattened larvae (referred to in North America as water pennies) cling to stones in fast flowing streams. The species *Sclerocyphon aquaticus* has been collected in the South-West.

Order Mecoptera: The larvae of scorpion-flies are mainly terrestrial, except for the small larvae of the family Nannochoristidae. Three species of adult *Nannochorista* have been found in Tasmania but so far the adults have not been matched with larvae. Larval Nannochoristidae which are small and elongated have been collected in seepages in the Hartz Mountains.

Order Diptera: Although most of the two-winged flies have a fully terrestrial life, a number of families— Chironomidae, Ceratopogonidae, Simulidae and Culicidae for example— have aquatic larval and pupal stages. Simuliid larvae are common, attached to rocks in fast flowing streams in the

South-West. The strange larvae of the family Blephariceridae have also been collected in the region. The larvae have suckers with which they adhere to rock surfaces in fast flowing regions of streams such as waterfalls. The Tasmanian representatives of the Blephariceridae all belong the genus *Edwardsina* which is also to be found in Chile. The sub-family Chaoborinae of the family Culicidae have striking transparent larvae sometimes called 'phantom larvae' or 'glassworms'. Their abundance in a small lake in the Mt Picton massif gave rise to the name of the lake, Glassworm Tarn. In shallow, acidic, humified lakes such as Lake Edgar, Chaoborid larvae were particularly abundant at quite a shallow depth e.g. 1.5 to 2 metres.

Order Trichoptera: The taxonomy

and distribution of larvae and adult caddis flies of Tasmania are currently being investigated by A Neboiss of the National Museum of Victoria, but a few general observations on this order in South-West Tasmania may be made at this stage. Tasmania has a rich trichopteran fauna with many endemic species, the highest degree of endemicity being in the western region and Central Plateau. In the riffle zones of streams, larvae of species of the Hydropsychidae, Rhyacophilidae and Psychomyiidae occur. Backwaters of streams, rich in decaying organic matter, and silty regions of lakes, harbour small larvae of the family Hydroptilidae with their distinctive purse-shaped cases. Trichopteran larvae living in lakes and tarns typically construct cases from sand-grains, detritus, leaves, sticks and

Nymph of the dragonfly *Archipetalia auriculata* collected from a small creek on the King William Ranges. *Zoology Dept Uni of Tas*

Final instar of a stonefly nymph of the genus *Eusthenia*, an endemic species to Tasmania. *Zoology Dept Uni of Tas*

Psephenid larva, *Sclerocyphon aquaticus*, commonly known as a 'water penny'. *Zoology Dept Uni of Tas*

Galaxias parvus, another member of the family Galaxiidae ('native trout') appears to favour small pools and swampy areas. *Zoology Dept Uni of Tas*

Galaxias pedderensis, a 'native trout', is known from the original Lake Pedder and now inundated tributaries of the Serpentine River. *Zoology Dept Uni of Tas*

Saxilaga cleaveri (whitebait) from a pool alongside the Lower Gordon River. *Zoology Dept Uni of Tas*

stems of water plants. By far the most dominant trichopteran family in the lentic (standing water) environments is the Leptoceridae.

From the beach at Lake Pedder, larvae of the family Plectrotarsidae were collected. These larvae were notable for their very well developed tarsal claws.

PHYLUM MOLLUSCA:

Most waters of South-West Tasmania have relatively low calcium concentrations, a condition which is generally unfavourable to aquatic molluscs due to the heavy calcium requirement for shell building. The acid streams appear to be almost devoid of molluscs, but rivers like the Gordon which run through calcareous rocks may contain a rich snail fauna. In some of the lakes and tarns an interesting but not diverse molluscan fauna may be present. In Lake Edgar, a small number of planorbid snails in the sub-family Bulininae were found along with small white bivalves in the family Sphaeriidae. Sphaerids are common in small tarns and pools in button-grass swamps.

At both Lake Edgar and Lake Pedder a new species of snail *Glacidorbis pedderi* was collected. It has been placed in the family Planorbidae. This constitutes only the second species of this genus in Australia and only the third species from the Southern Hemisphere.

VERTEBRATES:

The freshwater fish of South-West Tasmania are of particular interest. In the lower reaches of the coastal rivers, ammocoete larvae of the lamprey species *Geotria australis* and *Mordacia mordax* may be found along with eels (*Auguilla australis*). The very rare species *Prototroctes maraena*, the Australian grayling, has been collected from the Lower Gordon and Arthur Rivers. This species appears to be in very low numbers and to have a rather fragmented distribution in Tasmania. The Lower Gordon River may harbour a biologically significant population of this rare and most interesting fish species. *Pseudaphritis urvilli* (a small fish known as the sandy) also occurs in the lower reaches of the Gordon River.

Fish of the family Galaxiidae are commonly known as 'native trout'. Three species *Galaxias maculatus*, *G. truttaceus* and *G. brevipinnis*— collectively known as 'whitebait'—have been reported in South-West Tasmania. The life history of *G. maculatus*, usually the most abundant species of whitebait, is interesting. Larval *G. maculatus* live in the sea and it is the seasonally migrating juveniles which constitute whitebait. The juveniles migrate to freshwater and thereafter live in lowland streams and rivers. Breeding occurs mostly in early autumn when the sexually mature adults deposit their eggs on grassy flats in the upper estuaries. The eggs are attached among the grasses and hatch when covered by the next spring tides. Land-locked populations of *G. brevipinnis* and *G. truttaceus* also occur in South-Western Tasmania, but no land-locked populations of *G. maculatus* have yet been recorded. The genus *Galaxias* in Tasmania has been recently and soundly revised by A P Andrews of the Tasmanian Museum.

Two recently described species of galaxiid have been collected in the South-West. *Galaxias parvus* has been collected from Lake Pedder, Sandfly Creek near Mt Bowes, Wedge River and now-flooded localities on the tributaries of the Serpentine River. The species appears to favour small pools and swampy areas. *Galaxias pedderensis* is known from Lake Pedder and now inundated localities on tributaries of the Serpentine River. Adult *G. pedderensis* appear to be restricted to fast flowing streams. Both *G. parvus* and *G. pedderensis* appear to be reasonably numerous in the Serpentine impoundment but their future is uncertain in view of the increasing population of introduced brown trout.

In low-lying swampy coastal areas, specimens of *G. cleaveri (Saxilaga)* may be collected in muddy stagnant pools. The species has been collected at Port Davey and in pools alongside the Lower Gordon River. The fish appears to be capable of burrowing in mud, which may assist its survival in periods of low water levels.

AMPHIBIA:

While amphibians are an integral part of the South-West's freshwater environments, they are treated separately by A P Andrews and B McIntosh in the chapter dealing with reptiles and amphibians (see 2.8).

As pointed out earlier, South-West Tasmania possesses a wide range of cold temperate and alpine aquatic habitats, most of which are poorly represented, if at all, in other parts of Australia.

Ecological studies on such systems are only in their infancy, largely as a result of the poor taxonomic basis available for such work until recently. Thus, published ecological data is available only for the lakes Edgar and Pedder, both of which no longer exist. It appeared that most of the energy input into these two lakes was derived, not from phytoplankton production, but as a result of breakdown of organic detritus washed in from the surrounding swamps. Although productivity in the Lake Pedder and Lake Edgar systems was low, there was nevertheless a considerable diversity in faunal species. Lake Pedder was renowned for its magnificent, gently sloping beach, which harboured a rich and well adapted interstitial fauna or psammon.[4] The psammon also contained five species of nematode hitherto unrecorded from Australia. The high acidity, low bicarbonate content and dark colour of the waters of the original Lake Pedder system probably accounted for the lack of any significant phytoplankton crop. A similar situation probably exists in many of the other standing water bodies of the South-West. In water bodies such as the original Lake Pedder, the zooplankton probably used the imported organic matter as a major food source. In the streams of the South-West, as in most streams, the imported organic matter is also the major food source. However, as opposed to the situation in Europe and the United States, we know almost nothing about the food chains involving invertebrates in Australian streams, let alone those of South-West Tasmania.

The possible utilization of organic matter from the button-grass plains by freshwater animals would make a most interesting investigation.

Though little is known of the ecology, taxonomy and distribution of many of the species of freshwater animals in South-West Tasmania, the region clearly has an unusual and diverse freshwater fauna. This may be because of its wide array of water body types, cool-temperate climate and distinctive, highly-coloured, acidic waters of low ion concentration—attributes which differ considerably from those of other Tasmanian regions and almost totally from freshwater environments in mainland Australia.

Compared to terrestrial and marine animals, freshwater animals are not very mobile, although there are of course many exceptions to this generalization such as water bugs and water beetles. Many of the rather immobile groups present in South-West Tasmania such as syncarids, phreatoicid isopods and stoneflies, are geologically old groups with a long evolutionary history. Their distribution may therefore have considerable biogeographical significance. Many of the freshwater animal groups present in the South-West are to be found in cold temperate environments in New Zealand and South America, and a study of their overall distribution patterns may lead to better understanding of the past movement of land masses and the evolution of a distinctive Southern Hemisphere fauna.

South-West Tasmania has many groups of freshwater animals living at low altitudes, which are found elsewhere in south-eastern Australia in alpine environments. Thus, as a region, South-West Tasmania is of immense biogeographical importance. This is particularly so in view of the high degree of endemicity displayed in Tasmania by some of the freshwater animal groups, especially those of the South-West.

A major threat to the intact nature of the freshwater biota and their environments in South-West Tasmania is the introduction of exotic species. The introduction of trout poses the greatest potential danger. In our opinion, no alien species of fish or any other type of animal or of aquatic plant should be introduced in the future into any water-body in the South-West. This is the only region in Tasmania where there is a considerable number of bodies of freshwater not containing alien species of fish or plants. In this regard, the South-West is a region unique in southern Australia and New Zealand. Forestry practices, hydro-electric activities and to a lesser extent, mining, have changed, and further threaten to change the nature of the rivers.

The water bodies of South-West Tasmania are an integral part of a remarkable and challenging wilderness. If it is to survive, the water bodies must be retained in their natural state. The inseparable fusion between land and water is a vital consideration in the management of the South-West.

Anglers on the Serpentine Impoundment catching introduced trout, 1976. *The Mercury*

Opposite page
Serpentine impoundment. *Don Stephens*

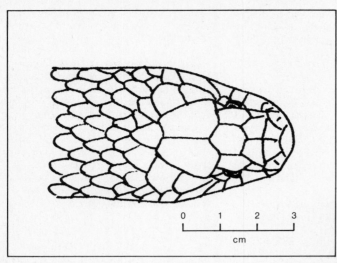

Tiger Snake.
From 'Tasmanian snakes' by Norman Laird.
The Tasmanian Tramp no. 7. 1946.
White-lipped Whip Snake.

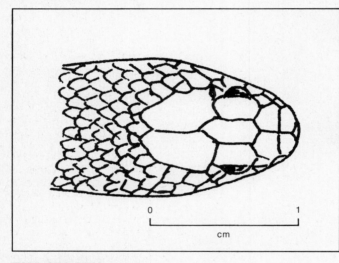

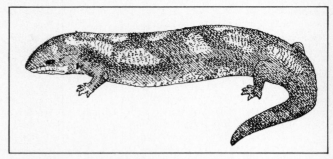

The Bluetongue Lizard, *Tiliqua nigrolutea*, the largest lizard found in Tasmania, sometimes reaching a length of 35 cm.   *Peter Murray*

Ewing's, or Brown Tree Frog *Hyla (Litoria) ewingii.* is common around waterways in the South-West.   *National Parks and Wildlife Service*

The Tasmanian Tiger Snake *(Notechis ater),* is often encountered near the coast. This photograph was taken on Prion Beach. Although the venom of all Tasmanian land snakes is highly toxic, they are as a rule shy, and the fangs, although hollow, are small so the venom is not injected efficiently into the victim. According to the Australian Bureau of Statistics, 15 deaths proven to be from snake-bite have been recorded in Tasmania since 1925.   *Carmel Zappner*

THE SPECIES
Amphibians

Brown Froglet	*Crinia signifera*
Tasmanian Froglet	*Crinia tasmaniensis*
Green and Golden Tree Frog	*Hyla aurea*
Burrow's Tree Frog	*Hyla burrowsi*
Ewing's or Brown Tree Frog	*Hyla ewingi*

Reptiles

Tasmanian Tiger Snake	*Notechis ater*
Whip Snake	*Denisonia coronoides*
Bluetongue Lizard	*Tiliqua nigrolutea*
Slender Bluetongue Lizard	*Tiliqua casuarinae*
Small skinks:—	*Leiolopisma metallicum*
	Leiolopisma entrecasteauxii
	Leiolopisma pretiosum
	Leiolopisma ocellatum

This list is based on the collections in the Tasmanian Museum and on the personal observations of the authors.

Amphibians and Reptiles

B McIntosh & P Andrews

Bruce McIntosh, a Biology teacher at Hobart Matriculation College, is particularly interested in Tasmania's reptiles, while Phil Andrews, Curator of Vertebrate Zoology at the Tasmanian Museum and Art Gallery, is an authority on the State's amphibian fauna. Both have collected and studied fauna in the South-West.

Tasmania's South-West, with its abundant rainfall and numerous rivers and waterways, is an ideal habitat for the water-dependent amphibians but does not appear to be an hospitable area for reptiles. Although both reptiles and amphibians are cold-blooded, the short and often cool summers are not congenial to most reptiles as they require sunshine for basking before they become active. Consequently most reptiles in the South-West hibernate between April and October. They do not inhabit rainforest except in cleared areas and river valleys where the direct sun can penetrate. An example of this distribution is that of the Small Brown Skink *Leiolopisma metallicum*, a common inhabitant of suburban gardens and open woodland, which has colonised the roadsides all the way through the rainforest areas penetrated by the Strathgordon and Scotts Peak roads.

The Tasmanian Tiger Snake is familiar to bushwalkers in the South-West as a beautiful although sometimes frightening reptile. Adults can attain a length of two metres and are usually jet black, a melanic pattern more common in the South-West than in other areas. Like other Tasmanian reptiles, male Tiger Snakes do not breed until late summer, when they mate with females who have just completed a three to four month pregnancy. Sperm cells are stored in the female reproductive tract until the next spring when the female again becomes pregnant. During late summer, females about to give birth and males in mating readiness may adopt an offensive attitude to intruders instead of fleeing as they do at other times of the year. The Whip Snake is widely distributed throughout the South-West area. It never exceeds two-thirds metre and is distinguished by having a white lip extending to behind the eye.

The venom of both these snakes is highly toxic and should always be treated as such. However, the fangs of both species are small; even those of an adult Tiger Snake would be unlikely to penetrate a pair of loose trousers and thick walking socks. The Tiger Snake feeds mainly on other reptiles, small mammals, birds and frogs, whereas the Whip Snake subsists largely on a diet of small lizards and insects.

Both species of Bluetongue Lizard, and the small skink *Leiolopisma entrecasteauxii*, are fairly widely distributed over areas of coastal heath. The other small skinks, however, have fairly definite habitat preferences. *Leiolopisma metallicum* avoids alpine moorland areas which are directly exposed to the prevailing southwesterly weather. Such places are the domain of *Leiolopisma pretiosum* whose darker body colour enables it to absorb the sun's warmth more readily and thus maintain a higher body temperature.

Leiolopisma pretiosum inhabits largely unsheltered areas which are frequently covered with snow for months at a time. Consequently this species hibernates for about seven months each year. *Leiolopisma ocellatum* is a distinctively larger species of skink with a speckled grey-green colour pattern; it is found in boulder fields and open rocky scree areas and is very common in such places as Lake Fenton. If the term 'intelligent' can be applied to reptiles, both these species, unlike the other skinks, display a considerable amount in their ability to avoid capture by playing hide and seek. All the small skinks are mainly insectivores which, in general, limits their active period to the short summer season.

In contrast to the reptiles, the amphibians are ideally suited to the South-West and it is not surprising to find that most Tasmanian species have been recorded there despite the fact that amphibians are usually secretive and rarely attract direct attention. The most abundant species is probably the Brown Froglet (*Crinia signifera*), a species that is widespread throughout the State including the area from the Florentine Valley westwards to the coast. It is a small brownish-grey frog with a pale undersurface marked with dark blotches. Another species, the Tasmanian Froglet (*Crinia tasmaniensis*), which is endemic to Tasmania, is also commonly found in swamps throughout the south and west of the State and has been recorded from Port Davey, Lake Pedder and Strahan. It is small, dark brown in colour with reddish-olive bands along the back. The species breeds in spring and lays its eggs in any small pool, permanent or temporary. The eggs are laid separately on the bottoms of the pools, the tadpoles are bottom dwellers, feeding largely on decaying plant material.

Most conspicuous of the amphibians are the brightly coloured tree frogs; some of these are quite large, growing up to 10 cm in length. The tree frogs were probably so named because of their habit of sitting motionless on wet leaves and foliage during rainy periods. The two most conspicuous species are the Green and Golden Tree Frog (*Hyla aurea*) and the Burrow's Tree Frog (*Hyla burrowsi*). The second species, a Tasmanian endemic, would appear to be the more widespread having been recorded from Cox Bight, Port Davey, Lake Pedder and Strahan, while *Hyla aurea* has been collected from the Florentine Valley. Both species are bright green in colour, *Hyla burrowsi* being distinguished by gold iridescent patches on the back. The adults of the latter species occur in rainforest but are notoriously difficult to catch, even though one may often hear their distinctive ducklike call. The species breeds in spring and lays its eggs attached to vegetation in open pools and tarns. The tadpoles are large active swimmers. The Brown, or Ewing's Tree Frog is also fairly common in the South-West but it is usually found near waterways at ground level. It is fawn to yellowish-grey in colour with a broad dark band along the back and is an excellent swimmer and diver.

Amphibians are almost wholly insectivorous and catch their prey alive. Consequently they are similar to the reptiles in that they are most active during the summer months when insect life is abundant. Unlike the reptiles, however, they are entirely dependent on abundant water for both breeding and survival.

As the South-West is gradually receiving more attention from visitors, it is more than likely that further species of both amphibians and reptiles will be discovered there in years to come.

See the opposite page for a list of species.

Male Pink Robin feeding female who is brooding newly hatched young.
O M G Newman

Bottom right
Lake Rhona nestling beneath Reeds Peak on the Denison Range.
Maurice D Clark

Bottom left
The Tasmanian Thornbill, common in forest and scrub, is easily confused with its relative, the Brown Thornbill, but can be identified on close examination by the white plumage on the sides of the body, flanks and under-tail.
Michael Sharland

Birds of the South-West

R W Rose
C D King

R W Rose BSc. Hons. (N.S.W.) has been a Senior Tutor in Zoology at the University of Tasmania since 1970. He is particularly interested in the birds and mammals of Tasmania.

Denis King has been keenly interested in bird life since his childhood in the Weld Valley. This life-long interest has made him an alert and accurate observer and after living at Port Davey for over 30 years he has become familiar with the birds in the locality. Many birds around his home have become very tame, making it an ideal spot for continued observations.

Diversity and Habitat

R W Rose

The South-West is a large, relatively inaccessible area; because of this, few detailed ornithological observations have been made in the past. As some areas of the South-West are under environmental pressures, it is important that an understanding is gained of the diversity of bird species and their habitat requirements.

Western Tasmania is a high rainfall area so the climatic climax type of vegetation for most of the region is temperate rainforest. However other habitat types reflecting altitude, soil fertility and firing also exist there, often as mosaics.

In their detailed study of Tasmanian birds Ridpath and Moreau[1] classified the island into fourteen different categories of habitat; five of them—temperate rainforest, sub-alpine forest, dwarf mountain forest with shrubberies, wet tussock sedgeland, and high moors—being commonly found in the South-West. They referred to these five habitats as typical of the cold-wet environment and thought that this type of environment represented much of Tasmania as it was during the Pleistocene prior to the flooding of Bass Strait.

It has been realised that the habitat classification of Ridpath and Moreau is an inadequate one in the light of recent botanical knowledge. For the purpose of this article the following habitats are considered present in the South-West: temperate rainforest, mixed forest—comprising both Eucalypts and rainforest species, wet sclerophyll forest, sub-alpine forest containing the snow gum *Eucalyptus coccifera*, sedgeland consisting of button-grass plains surrounded by communities of wet scrub in areas of lower fire danger e.g. creek margins and 'wet mallee' in the less well drained, more frequently burnt areas. Both wet scrub and 'wet mallee' contain the West Coast peppermint *Eucalyptus nitida*. Other habitats are highland moors, aquatic environments (lakes, rivers and creeks) and patchy areas of coastal heath.

In Littler's *Handbook of the Birds of Tasmania*[2] birds were said to be 'absolutely scarce' in the west of the island. Indeed it is recognised that the cold-wet environment provides a poor habitat for birds, probably because food is scarce. Of the 89 common Tasmanian birds only 41 are common in the South-West. This figure was obtained by consulting the distribution maps of the Atlas project of the Bird Observers Association of Tasmania (B.O.A.T.). Ridpath and Moreau stated that there were only 17 common species in the

cold-wet habitats but they did qualify this by stating that bird records for the area were 'very meagre indeed'. However their figure of 17 is also too low because they did not include mixed forest or wet sclerophyll in the cold-wet habitat, nor were they aware of an earlier paper by Wilson[3] which gave fairly comprehensive bird lists for many of the cold-wet habitats.

Ridpath and Moreau list only 6 species—the Black Cockatoo, Pink Robin, Scrub-Wren, Ground Thrush, Tasmanian Thornbill and the Scrub-Tit—as being common in the rainforest. However, there are a number of other birds that also can be considered as common including the Grey Fantail, Green Rosella, Olive Whistler, Silvereye and the Spine-billed Honeyeater. Many of these depend on invertebrates (e.g. insects and spiders) for food. The Tasmanian Thornbill and the Scrub-Tit are birds found only in Tasmania, that is they are endemic species. The Tasmanian Thornbill is very similar in appearance to its relative the Brown Thornbill. Although the Brown Thornbill is generally found in drier areas, both species may be seen in the same region so that great care should be exercised in their identification. The Scrub-Tit is distributed over the State, although tending to be more concentrated in the west and the south. Thomas[4] has suggested that the Scrub-Tit may be found in areas where the rainfall is over 1,000 mm per annum.

Few introduced birds are to be found in the South-West and there is no evidence yet of the Blackbird penetrating South-West rainforest, although there is a record from the rainforests in the Florentine Valley. The Blackbird may be a potential competitor with the Ground Thrush.

Common birds in the rainforest are the Scrub-Wren, a noisy bird usually heard before being seen, the Yellow-tailed Black Cockatoo, another noisy bird which shreds bark to pieces in the search for food, and the very attractive Pink Robin which, although also found on the mainland, is probably most common in Tasmanian rainforests.

At higher altitudes, the sub-alpine forest consists of dwarf trees and as the trees here are not as tall or dense as in the rainforest more light penetrates the canopy allowing shrub growth. Although these mountain habitats have a more extreme climate than the rainforest, both support about the same number of bird species. This is probably due to the extra food provided by the shrubs which occur more frequently in the sub-alpine forest and to the more open nature of the

terrain. Some of the rainforest species—the Tasmanian Thornbill, Scrub-Tit, Scrub-Wren and Pink Robin—are also found at higher altitudes. Over this terrain flies the Wedge-tailed Eagle and possibly the Peregrine Falcon, while nearer the coast the Sea-Eagle occurs. Apart from these three species and the Brown Falcon and Grey Goshawk, birds of prey are uncommon in the South-West. This may be due to a lack of suitable habitat or food supply although there appears to be plenty of food for the not uncommon carnivorous marsupials.

Because of the more open nature of the terrain honeyeaters are more often seen at the higher altitudes; two are common, the endemic Yellow-throated Honeyeater and the Crescent Honeyeater. The Crescent Honeyeater, a noisy inhabitant of the South-West, is an altitudinal migrant, for in the winter it descends to lower ground. Another altitudinal migrant is the Flame Robin, its bright red chest a feature of the higher altitude forests. Two other endemic birds are common here, the Green Rosella with its tell-tale call 'kussick kussick' and the well known Black Currawong often known as the 'Black Jay'. The Grey Thrush is also frequently seen and heard.

Ridpath and Moreau found the high moors (usually above 1,000 metres) to be the most barren environment of the South-West as they believed only two birds were common. These birds, the Peregrine Falcon and the Australian Pipit, are birds with wide distributions throughout Australia and possibly they are better able to exploit the habitat than many other birds. The Pipit is a ground feeding bird, eating insects and seeds. It probably is an altitudinal migrant leaving the higher moors when they are covered with snow in the winter. While there are few recent records of the Peregrine Falcon in the west, more detailed observations over the moors may show that it is still common. Wall has shown that the Black Currawong, Forest Raven, and Flame Robin are also common species on the moors. Wall[5] shows that moorland is characterised by low vegetation and innumerable small lakes and tarns. On the shores of these tarns occasional pencil pines grow and in shallow valleys snow gums with a few shrubs can be found. Some 30 or so birds are found on the moors, confined mainly to the pockets of scrub, whilst others are seen on the water of the tarns.

The mixed forest (composed of eucalypts and rainforest vegetation) contains the largest number of bird species. Common birds include the Crescent Honeyeater, and the Yellow-throated Honeyeater. Others found in this environment include the Green Rosella, Golden Bronze Cuckoo, Pink Robin, Dusky Robin, Olive and Golden Whistler as well as the Grey Thrush and many rainforest species. Flocks of Strong-billed Honeyeaters are often found in the eucalypts.

The sedgeland which extends from sea-level to approximately 900 metres (at high altitudes it may form a type of moorland) contains a few common species including the Ground Parrot (rare on the mainland), Emu-Wren and Striated Field-Wren. As these birds are somewhat restricted in their habitat it was thought that they were uncommon, but in the button-grass plains these birds are quite common. The Ground Parrot, as its name suggests, frequents the ground. Usually the only way to see this parrot is to flush it out by walking through the sedges. On being flushed the bird rises rapidly in the air only to alight nearby, presumably relying on its camouflage to prevent detection. The habit of flying for only a short distance has led to the suggestion (probably incorrect) that Ground Parrots are poor flyers. The Emu-Wren and the Field-Wren are also ground lovers, the Emu-Wren in particular being quite a poor flyer—indeed one of the early observers was able to catch this bird by hand. Both birds are insectivorous but the Emu-Wren differs from the Field-Wren in having a long filamentous tail. These three common sedgeland birds tend to be shy, shunning civilization, although the Ground Parrot has, in the past, been recorded near Hobart. These birds are

particularly vulnerable to environmental disturbances such as the feral cat or flooding for hydro-electric purposes. The wet scrub which surrounds the button-grass contains quite a few species including the common Crescent Honeyeater, and the Dusky Robin as well as the beautiful Firetail Finch and Yellow-tipped Pardalote.

In the coastal heath it is possible that one may find the Tawny Crowned Honeyeater. It has been recorded from two widely separated regions bordering the South-West—Strahan and Southport Lagoon—and surprisingly, from the old Lake Pedder in 1972 when Johnson[6] reported it as being common in the button-grass around the lake. As the Tawny Crowned Honeyeater is restricted to the coastal heath environment in Tasmania this may be a case of mistaken identity. Indeed Sharland[7] has remarked on the similarity between the Tawny Crowned Honeyeater and the female of the very common Crescent Honeyeater, illustrating the point that careful identification is required.

Commonly found in the aquatic environment are a number of Cormorants, the Black Swan, Black Duck and the White-faced Heron ('Blue Crane'). Recently, a Great Crested Grebe (*Podiceps cristatus*) was recorded at the new Lake Pedder. This is interesting as this bird had not been sighted previously in the South-West. It appears that although the flooding of Lake Pedder must have had an adverse effect on the birds in the nearby button-grass plains, species previously unrecorded in the area may possibly visit. Very few

observations have yet been made near the new lake and these will be necessary before any generalisations can be made regarding the future of bird life in the immediate area.

One bird rather uncommon in Tasmania, the Azure Kingfisher, is known to occur in the South-West, being recorded from several rivers including the Gordon and the Davey. The status of this bird in Tasmania is not yet well established but it is known to favour creeks and small rivers associated with rainforest.[8] Although there is a record of this Kingfisher from Macquarie Harbour, these birds are not usually found on large expanses of water, so flooding of river systems is hardly likely to result in increasing numbers of this bird.

Probably the rarest bird in the South-West and one of the rarest parrots in Australia, hence one most worthy of further study and conservation, is the Orange-bellied Parrot. This bird and the related Blue-winged Parrot, from which it is not easily distinguished, have both been sighted in the South-West. The Orange-bellied Parrot has been recorded from such diverse locations as Strahan, Port Davey and, possibly, Maatsuyker Island.[9] In their study of the birds of Port Davey in 1961 Green and Mollison[10] only sighted Blue-winged Parrots. Milledge states that these birds were 'wrongly listed' and that they are obviously Orange-bellied Parrots; he is probably correct although he was unaware at that time that the Blue-winged Parrot occurs in the west of the State and possibly in the South-West.[11] Orange-bellied Parrots are migrants, wintering on the mainland

A Port Davey cove, one of the coastal areas where the rare migrant Orange-bellied Parrot has been seen.   *Jack Thwaites*

in coastal regions of South Australia and Victoria. They arrive in Tasmania in September/October and leave again in February/March. From this information it is logical to assume that they breed in Tasmania, but there are no recent records of this, the last breeding recorded being about 50 years ago near Macquarie Harbour. As this bird is virtually restricted to the west of the State (most records are for the South-West), and as it probably only breeds in Tasmania, a good case can be made of the conservation of areas it is known to inhabit.

With further observations more species of birds may be found to inhabit the South-West. Although observation is often difficult where scrub is dense and light poor, accurate identification is necessary when making a case for conservation or noting a species previously unrecorded for an area. Particular care must be taken when identifying birds like the Orange-bellied Parrot and the Tasmanian Thornbill which closely resemble related species also found in parts of the South-West.

So far marine birds have not been discussed; of course these birds are likely to be seen near the coast or on the nearby off-shore islands e.g. the Maatsuyker group. Without going into too much detail, mention should be made of the following birds that breed in the area. The Mutton-bird breeds on most of the small islands off Port Davey. The Little Penguin breeds in large numbers on the coast as well as on the islands. Fairy Prions breed in the area, probably on Isle du Golfe and Flat Island, while Diving Petrels breed on Maatsuyker Island itself. There is a large colony of Shy Albatross on the Mewstone, a rock 13 km south-east of Maatsuyker Island, and a large breeding colony of Gannets on Pedra Branca, a rock 25 km from the coast. Gannets, although generally uncommon, are frequently seen off the South-West Coast. Other seabirds may occasionally be washed ashore by south-westerly gales e.g. The Cape Petrel (*Daption capense*).

Finally, although there are many more birds in the South-West than was once thought, the actual number of species present is about half that of the drier areas of the State. With the exception of the Orange-bellied Parrot, the avian fauna of the South-West is not unique, being similar to that of the north-west and other areas in the State with cold-wet habitats. However this fact should not lead to complacency in regard to the conservation of the birds in the South-West as the cold-wet habitat is now constantly under environmental pressures from various sources. In Australia, the South-West of Tasmania is the ideal and obvious cold-wet habitat for preservation.

The 41 bird species common in the South-West

(This lists those land birds commonly found breeding over much of the South-West; other birds not included in the list may be locally common.)

Brown Quail	*Synoicus australis*
Brush Bronzewing	*Phaps elegans*
Lewin Water Rail	*Rallus pectoralis*
Grey Goshawk	*Accipiter novaehollandiae*
Wedge-tailed Eagle	*Aquila audax*
Peregrine Falcon	*Falco peregrinus*
Brown Falcon	*Falco berigora*
Boobook Owl	*Ninox novaeseelandiae*
Yellow-tailed Black Cockatoo	*Calyptorhyrchus funereus*
Sulphur Crested Cockatoo	*Cakatoe galerita*
Green Rosella	*Platycercus caledonicus*
Ground Parrot	*Pezoporus wallicus*
Azure Kingfisher	*Alcyone azurea*
Fan-tailed Cuckoo	*Cacomantis pyrrhophanus*
Golden Bronze Cuckoo	*Chrysococcyx plagosus*
Welcome Swallow	*Hirundo neoxena*
Tree Martin	*Petrochelidon nigricans*
Grey Fantail	*Rhipidura fuliginosa*
Flame Robin	*Petroica phoenicea*
Pink Robin	*Petroica rodinogaster*
Dusky Robin	*Petroica vittata*
Golden Whistler	*Pachycephala pectoralis*
Olive Whistler	*Pachycephala olivacea*
Grey Thrush	*Colluricincla harmonica*
Ground Thrush	*Zoothera lunulata*
Tasmanian Thornbill	*Acanthiza ewingi*
Scrub-Tit	*Acanthornis magnus*
White-browed Scrub-Wren	*Sericornis frontalis*
Striated Field-Wren	*Calamanthus fuliginosus*
Southern Emu-Wren	*Stipiturus malachurus*
Superb Blue-Wren	*Malurus cyaneus*
Silvereye	*Zosterops lateralis*
Strong-billed Honeyeater	*Melithreptus validirostris*
Eastern Spinebill	*Acanthorhynchus tenuirostris*
Yellow-throated Honeyeater	*Meliphaga flavicollis*
Crescent Honeyeater	*Phylidonyris pyrrhoptera*
New Holland Honeyeater	*Phylidonyris novaehollandiae*
Pipit	*Anthus australis*
Beautiful Firetail	*Emblema bellus*
Forest Raven	*Corvus tasmanicus*
Black Currawong	*Strepera fuliginosa*

Birds that are less common include:

Brown Goshawk	*Accipiter fasciatus*
Spur-winged Plover	*Vanellus novaehollandiae*
Swift Parrot	*Lathamus discolor*
Blue-winged Parrot	*Neophema chrysostoma*
Black-faced Cuckooshrike	*Coracina novaehollandiae*
Brown Thornbill	*Acanthiza pusilla*
Scarlet Robin	*Petroica multicolor*
Yellow-tipped Pardalot	*Pardolotus striatus*
Orange-bellied Parrot	*Neophema chrysogaster*

Many other species from the drier habitats penetrate parts of the South-West, often becoming well established, particularly in coastal areas. A comprehensive list of the birds around Port Davey and the South Coast of Tasmania was compiled by R H Green and B C Mollison in 1961.

The Striated Field Wren is a ventriloquist and songster of the marshy country and button-grass plains.
Michael Sharland

Top right
The noisy cries of the Black Currawong can be heard on the high moors and among the mountains throughout the year.
O M G Newman

Middle right
The Ground Thrush, or Mountain Thrush. The speckled plumage of this thrush merges well with its surroundings. It is a ground feeder, inhabiting forests and scrub.
Michael Sharland

Bottom right
The attractive Yellow-throated Honeyeater, though confined to Tasmania, is widely distributed throughout the State. This bird is usually seen singly or in pairs, and is quite territorial in habit. It nests quite low to the ground in low bush and bushy trees.
Michael Sharland

The Scrub Tit, a bird confined to Tasmania, is common in dense scrub and rainforest.
Michael Sharland

Notes on the Birds around Port Davey

C D King

Birds are most plentiful in coastal areas where food is reliable and the climate most favourable. Abundant bodies of fresh and brackish waters provide habitats for a number of water birds. Large flocks of Black Swan, Black Duck and Chestnut and Grey Teal are found on rivers, estuaries and small lagoons behind coastal beaches. On such waterways White-faced Herons and Black and Little Pied Cormorants are also common.

Though not as plentiful as in the past, flocks of 60 or more Black Swan flying in formation overhead are still an exhilarating sight at dawn and dusk. In the Port Davey area swan are most plentiful on Hannant Inlet, the Davey and Spring Rivers and on North River Bay. They nest in tidal reed beds and on some estuarine islands where Ravens (crows) prey on their eggs. One nest was found in a cave at water level on a small islet in Joe Page Bay.

From my home I often hear flocks of swan honking, then taking off with a noise like the applause of a large audience. One winter the tides were so consistently high around Melaleuca Inlet that the swans were unable to feed on the mud flats and in the shallows as they normally do, and they moved onto the button-grass plains in search of food, but several were found dead there.

Although Pelicans are not seen in the South-West today, their skeletal remains have been found in aboriginal middens on the coastal dunes.

White-faced Herons are always present individually or in small groups and I have only twice, in 1956 and 1975, seen large flocks of over 50 birds here. White Egrets are regular winter visitors and White Ibises were seen in the South-West during the 1958 Australian drought.

Bitterns are occasionally seen around the shores of lagoons and rivers. Bald Coots (Eastern Swamphens) visit in small groups or individually in the autumn and winter while Lewin Water Rails are rarely seen during the winter months.

Snipe, which breed in Japan, arrive in September and depart in late March. They are often flushed from the plains, though their numbers have decreased over recent years.

Wedge-tailed Eagles are not very plentiful in the area but White-breasted Sea Eagles are to be seen in most places around the coast and harbour. On several occasions in autumn when tides were running very strongly, schools of mackerel and 'whip-tails' entered the fresh waters of Melaleuca Inlet, many fish being stranded on creek banks when the

The White-fronted Chat is a visitor to the Port Davey area.   *Michael Sharland*

tide ebbed. The stench was sometimes quite overpowering to boat travellers on the river. In a few days Wedge-tailed Eagles and White-breasted Sea Eagles arrived for the feast of fish, staying in the vicinity for several months. On the last occasion about 20 eagles were in the area, and when travelling on the rivers by boat one would see at least eight birds in the air at one time—an unusual sight in the South-West. White Goshawks occasionally visit Melaleuca, staying only a few days before moving on. Small flocks of Black or Yellow-tailed Cockatoos are a common sight among the Banksias on which they feed. These birds also eat the seeds of other bushes as well as beetle larvae found in the wood. Large flocks of 40 or more birds are an uncommon sight. White or Sulphur-crested Cockatoos are also seen in small flocks. These birds are fond of acacia seeds as well as berries growing around coastal beaches, and they dig for roots of the Hewardia (*Isophysis tasmanica*), Blandfordia (*Blandfordia punicea*) and the pineapple plant (*Haemodorum distichophyllum*), especially after a fire.

Orange-bellied Parrots are summer visitors arriving in October and remaining in the area until April. Numbers have decreased since the 1950's when flocks of 20 to 30 birds would visit my garden almost daily in late summer. Flocks seen here today number less than 12. Though these parrots nest

in the area, their eggs have only been seen once.

Ground Parrots are distributed widely in the open country and their nests are occasionally encountered on the ground among tussocks and grass. Green Rosellas are plentiful everywhere, congregating in flocks in the autumn, winter and early spring—and they play havoc in the garden! When the eucalypts are in blossom Musk Lorikeets visit the area.

When high tides rise over heath and button-grass river flats it is interesting to watch small birds including White-browed Scrub-Wrens, Blue-Wrens, Pink Robins, Dusky Robins and Ground Thrushes foraging for invertebrates along the edge of the rising water.

Emu-Wrens are more often heard than seen on the plains. These dainty birds move about in small groups, showing themselves only briefly from bush or tussock top. Their plumage is a beautiful golden-brown streaked with black and the males have a bright blue throat. Their fine tail feathers, filamentous like those of an emu, gave the birds their name.

An interesting bird, widely distributed throughout the South-West, is the Olive Whistler. Its call varies a great deal from place to place, for instance the whistler's call at Melaleuca differs from that heard at the Old River 12 km away while calls heard in the Weld Valley are identical. Olive Whistlers live and nest in the bush near my house, and often venture onto the open plains. These birds, as well as Dusky Robins, Grey Thrushes, Ground Thrushes and others spend a lot of time foraging on the plains soon after a fire.

While tramping through the bush on a dull and dismal day, how cheering it is to come upon a flock of Crescent Honeyeaters among the flowering shrubs and heaths, their lively songs making up for the lack of sunshine. These honeyeaters gather in flocks in autumn, many descending from the high mountain slopes for the winter.

Of the five introduced birds found in coastal and fringe areas of the South-West, the Blackbird is the only known resident, being well established along the coast. The Goldfinch is seen particularly during the autumn months, and the Sparrow and occasionally the Green-finch also visit the area while Starlings are seen regularly throughout the year.

Large masses of kelp torn up by huge seas are washed into nooks and bays around the coast. Kelp flies breed in these rotting piles and many different birds come to feed on the larvae, including Oyster Catchers, Ducks, Ravens, Currawongs, Scrub-Wrens and Blue-Wrens.

One should not leave the South-West without a glance at the interesting bird life on the shores and adjacent ocean. On the beaches one is sure to see groups of Hooded Dotterels, small birds which run along the sand in front of you almost as though they are on wheels, often for half a mile or more. They nest on the sand above medium-high tide level. Pied and Sooty Oyster-Catchers also nest on the sand but more often their nests are found on rocky shores and islets. These birds are common and their whistling cries of 'quick-quick-whill' blend well with the sound of wild seas.

Pacific Gulls and the common Silver Gull are seen all around the coast and occasionally further inland, the latter being recorded at Lake Pedder in 1939. When travelling around the South Coast by boat I usually see Gannets, individually or in small flocks. They are a fascinating sight, when they fly at considerable height then fold their wings to plummet like a bomb into the sea, only to reappear in a few seconds with a shake of the head before taking off again. Terns also fish in this manner but are not so noticeable.

Sooty Albatrosses are always to be seen in ones and twos around the coast. Other albatrosses, including the Shy or White-capped Albatross which breeds on the Mewstone rock (22 km off the South Coast), are often seen around the Maatsuyker group of islands. Albatrosses will often follow a small vessel during rough weather. I never tire of watching their flight as they glide over the sea, execute a tight turn, and glide on with wing-tip nearly touching the water.

Water Birds and Sea Birds

King Penguin (occasional visitor)	*Aptenodytes patagonica*
Royal Penguin (occasional visitor)	*Eudyptes schlegeli*
Little Penguin	*Eudyptula minor*
Hoary-headed Grebe	*Podiceps poliocephalus*
Mutton-bird (Short-tailed Shearwater)	*Puffinus tenuirostris*
Sooty Shearwater	*Puffinus griseus*
Fairy Prion	*Pachyptila turtur*
Diving Petrel	*Pelecanoides urinatrix*
Shy (White-capped) Albatross	*Diomedea cauta*
Sooty Albatross	*Phoebetria sp.*
Wandering Albatross	*Diomedea exulans*
Black Cormorant	*Phalacrocorax carbo*
Little Black Cormorant	*Phalacrocorax sulcirostris*
Black-faced Cormorant	*P. fuscescens*
Little Pied Cormorant	*P. melanoleucos*
Gannet	*Morus serrator*
Caspian Tern	*Hydroprogne caspia*
Silver Gull	*Larus novaehollandiae*
Pacific Gull	*Larus pacificus*
Skua (occasional visitor)	*Catharacta sp.*
Pied Oyster-Catcher	*Haematopus ostralegus*
Sooty Oyster-Catcher	*H. fuliginosus*
Hooded Dotterel	*Charadrius cucullatus*
White Egret	*Egretta alba*
White-faced Heron	*Ardea novaehollandiae*
Bittern	*Botaurus poiciloptilus*
Black Swan	*Cygnus atratus*
Black Duck	*Anas superciliosa*
Chestnut Teal	*Anas castanea*
Grey Teal	*Anas gibberifrons*
Musk Duck (occasional visitor)	*Biziura lobata*
Lewin Water Rail	*Rallus pectoralis*
Eastern Swamphen	*Porphyrio porphyrio melanotus*
Coot	*Fulica atra*

The list of water birds and sea birds was compiled from observations by Denis King and with reference to 'Birds of Port Davey and the South Coast of Tasmania' by R H Green and B C Mollison in *The Emu*, December 1961, Vol. 61, Part 3. The list could well be enlarged with future observation as it is suspected that several more species are in the area; their presence needs substantiation for the record.

When a camp is established in the bush White-browed Scrub Wrens are the first birds to become used to human presence. They soon become very tame, entering tent or hut and hopping about one's feet.
Michael Sharland

Echidna. *Peter Murray*

Bottom
The pademelon or scrub wallaby has almost vanished from the mainland of Australia but is still a common marsupial in Tasmania. It prefers scrub and forest habitats where it browses on shrubs at night or at twilight. *J Wapstra*

The brush or Bennett's wallaby is plentiful in areas of eucalypt forest. It is a grazing marsupial and often travels long distances to reach good grazing ground, forming distinct runways from patches of scrub and forest where it hides during the day. *J Wapstra*

The platypus, a shy animal, but quite common in the numerous waterways of the South-West. *Peter Murray*

Brush, or Bennett's wallaby. *Jane Burrell*

The southern potoroo, now rare except in Tasmanian scrub and forests. It went unrecorded in the South-West until recent years, although quite common in the east of the State. *Ann Wessing*

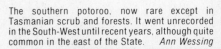

Mammals

G Hocking

Greg Hocking has studied science at Monash University and the University of Tasmania. Under a Forestry Commission scholarship for a Master of Science degree he is presently studying the population ecology of possums and other small mammals in relation to forestry practises, including burning and logging in southern Tasmania.

It is often thought that mammals are scarce in South-Western Tasmania. When compared with other parts of the State both the numbers and species of mammals appear to be low. However, because of the nocturnal and cryptic habits of many mammal species, this paucity of mammals may be more apparent than real.

Despite a lack of scientific work in the area, a total of 21 native species have so far been recorded in the South-West. This figure represents some two-thirds of the 32 species known in Tasmania and includes representatives from most groups of Tasmanian mammals.

The egg-laying monotremes, the platypus (*Ornithorhynchus anatinus*) and the echidna (*Tachyglossus aculeatus*) both occur in the South-West. The platypus has been recorded in freshwater streams and lakes from sub-alpine regions to sea level. It can be readily observed in the quieter backwaters of the larger river systems like the Huon and Gordon, where platypuses are known to feed on small aquatic animals in the early morning and evening. The echidna is one of the most successful and widely distributed mammals in Australia today. In the South-West it is apparently widespread, having been encountered within the dense cover of the temperate rainforest, in the clearer eucalypt forest and on the open heathlands.

The marsupial mammals have evolved in isolation within Australia, free until comparatively recently from competition from the eutherian mammals which characterise the other continents. Thus marsupials have been able to radiate throughout Australia, now displaying a diversity of habits in all habitats, to become characteristic of the continent's mammalian fauna.

Wallabies (*Macropus rufogrisseus*) and pademelons (*Thylogale billardierii*) are both members of the macropod family. Because of their size they are among the most conspicuous of the mammals of the South-West where both are widespread. The smaller of the two species, the pademelon, browses on shrubs in areas of wet sclerophyll forest and rainforest. In mature forest the population density of this species is

The ringtail possum is more common and widespread in the South-West than the brush-tailed possum. It lives among the tree-tops in forested areas, spending little time on the ground. *Peter Murray*

The tiny eastern pigmy possum is a rainforest dweller. It spends the daylight hours in a nest of dry bark or leaves, coming out at night to feed on insects. *J Wapstra*

generally very low. However under favourable conditions when suitable vegetation is abundant, after fire for example, populations may increase. In contrast, it is the more open areas, like the interface between sedgeland and eucalypt forest, where wallabies are most likely to be encountered. Another macropod, the potoroo (*Potorous apicalis*), is commonly known from the forested regions of eastern Tasmania. Until recently it had not been recorded in the South-West, but it has now been observed in forest along the lower reaches of the Gordon River.

The brush-tailed possum (*Trichosurus vulpecula*) is frequently found throughout most of eastern Australia and Tasmania. To Tasmanian bushwalkers it is well known for its nocturnal depredations around popular huts and campsites. However it is not abundant in the South-West, being recorded from peripheral areas such as the Florentine and lower Huon rivers. Here, as distinct from the less heavily wooded parts of the State the black form of the brush-possum is seen more frequently than the grey. Populations of brush-tailed possums, like those of the pademelon, are known to increase in density in the habitat created following a fire. Thus, forestry regeneration practices have produced habitats which facilitate the local build up of possum and pademelon populations to levels atypical of mature forest.

Unlike brush-tailed possums, ring-tailed possums (*Pseudocheirus pereg-*

rinus) are rarely encountered on the ground. Instead, the presence of these arboreal animals is usually apparent from the nests that they construct of twigs and leaves in pockets of dense sclerophyll vegetation. In common with those of many marsupials, the Tasmanian population of the ring-tailed possum undergoes marked fluctuations. Dr Eric Guiler has noted a reduction in possum numbers in the period 1950 to 1953, and attributes it to the effects of an epidemic disease. More recently the population has recovered and the animal is known to be common in the South-West.

Two species of pigmy possum are found in Tasmania and both are known to occur in the South-West. These mouse-sized marsupials are occasionally seen when dislodged in a torpid condition from rotting logs or felled trees. Such periods of dormancy and lowered body temperature occur throughout the year although the intervening bouts of activity are more frequent during the warmer months. The eastern pigmy possum (*Cercartetus nanus*) is found predominantly in rainforest where its diet consists of insects obtained from the litter layer. The smaller of the two species, the little pigmy possum (*C. lepidus*), is mainly found in sclerophyll woodland and heathland within its limited range of Tasmania and Kangaroo Island off South Australia.

The wombat (*Vombatus ursinus*) is a widely ranging species, found through most of south-eastern Australia

including the South-West of Tasmania. Its numerous burrows and systems of tracks are a conspicuous feature on and about the moraines that rise out of the sedge covered plains of the region. Other habitats in which wombats may be seen include eucalypt woodland and the sub-alpine moorlands.

The carnivorous and predatory marsupials of the South-West are contained in the dasyurid family. There, as in the rest of Tasmania, marsupial carnivores are present in large numbers, something which is attributable to the absence of competition from eutherian predators such as the dingo.

Among the smallest of the dasyurids are the antechinuses, or marsupial mice—small nocturnal insectivores. Of the two species known to be present in the South-West, the smaller swamp antechinus (*Antechinus minimus*), is recorded only from the sedgelands. However within this habitat it appears to be both widespread and common. The dusky antechinus (*Antechinus swainsonii*) is similar in appearance to the swamp antechinus, but its distribution is confined to the rainforests and wet sclerophyll forests where it is commonly met. The life history of this species is not without interest: all males in the population die within several days of mating, thus leaving the population devoid of males until the next generation is born several weeks later. Closely allied to the antechinuses is the white-footed dunnart (*Sminthopsis leucopus*), an inhabitant of the more open eucalypt

Tasmanian devil.

Jane Burrell

forests. To date it has only been observed in the South-West at Maydena, on the periphery of the region.

The other dasyurid marsupials, the native cat (*Dasyurus viverrinus*), tiger cat (*D. maculatus*), Tasmanian devil (*Sarcophilus harrisii*), and thylacine (*Thylacinus cynocephalus*) are known from the South-West. The tiger cat and native cat are agile, medium-sized predators. Both can be found at night in a variety of habitats, from the dense rainforests to the open plains. The devil, in contrast to these, is not an active predator but a scavenger. This species is now confined entirely to Tasmania, although fossil evidence indicates a former distribution encompassing a large part of mainland Australia. In Tasmania it has a wide distribution through most dry forest and heathland areas—indeed it sometimes reaches pest proportions. However, devils are only occasionally reported from the South-West, a fact that may be attributed to the comparative paucity of game.

Like the Tasmanian devil, the predatory thylacine is known to have once roamed on the mainland, where it became extinct prior to European settlement. Up to the beginning of this century the thylacine was widespread, though never common, in Tasmania. Now it is believed to be extinct, however the South-West, because of its comparative inaccessibility, is held by many to be one of the last refuges of the thylacine. In 1938, naturalist David Fleay made plaster casts of footprints of a

Wombat with young. *Zoology Dept Uni of Tas*

The wombat is common in sedgeland areas and its runways and burrows are seen everywhere from sea-level to high on the mountain slopes. *Jane Burrell*

The Tasmanian devil is a sturdy scavenger common in most parts of the State, though populations fluctuate markedly. *Zoology Dept Uni of Tas*

thylacine near the Jane River. However Dr Guiler concluded, on the basis of the distribution of bounty payments on thylacine scalps, that they were never plentiful in the South-West.

Bandicoots are notably absent from the South-West. As the short nosed bandicoot (*Isoodon obeselus*) inhabits areas of dense cover elsewhere in the State there is some reason for thinking that it may yet be found there. Evidence derived from archaeological excavations at Louisa Bay, on the south coast, indicates that bandicoots were part of the diet of Aborigines.

In addition to the monotremes and marsupials, a number of eutherian or placental mammals are found in Tasmania. As well as those species introduced by European man, the eutheria are represented here by native rodents and bats. The five species of bat

known from Tasmania are all found in forest areas. Being nocturnal and difficult to study, very little is known of their habits and distribution. Some species may occur in the South-West.

Despite the fact that all of the Australian rodents belong to one family, the murid rodents, they occupy a wide variety of habitats over the entire continent. In Tasmania there are five species of native rodent, four of which are recorded from the South-West. The water rat (*Hydromys chrysogaster*), is the only specialised freshwater mammal apart from the platypus, in the South-West, where it has been seen along the lower reaches of the Gordon River. The velvet-furred rat (*Rattus lutreolus*) is perhaps the most common species, having been recorded in all of the major habitats of the region. In thick vegetation it forms networks of runways and

tunnels which may be frequented by other small mammals. In the South-West the broad-toothed rat (*Mastacomys fuscus*) is often found in association with the velvet-furred rat where it occurs in a sedgeland habitat. The broad-toothed rat is regarded as being a relict species, surviving from a cooler, wetter period. It is now found in isolated colonies only in far south-eastern Australia where the cold and humid conditions that it requires exist. Another species with a relict distribution confined to Tasmania is the long-tailed rat (*Pseudomys higginsi*). Known from fossil deposits in south-eastern Australia this rat is now found only in rainforest and the adjacent sclerophyll forest of the higher rainfall regions of Tasmania including the South-West.

Rainforest and sedgeland have acted as an ecological barrier preventing the

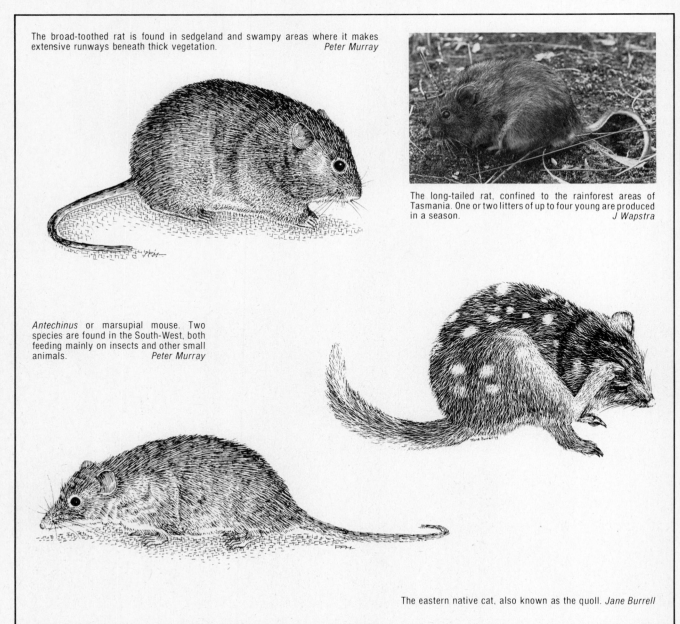

The broad-toothed rat is found in sedgeland and swampy areas where it makes extensive runways beneath thick vegetation.   *Peter Murray*

The long-tailed rat, confined to the rainforest areas of Tasmania. One or two litters of up to four young are produced in a season.   *J Wapstra*

Antechinus or marsupial mouse. Two species are found in the South-West, both feeding mainly on insects and other small animals.   *Peter Murray*

The eastern native cat, also known as the quoll. *Jane Burrell*

spread of the rabbit into the South-West. However other species have become established. Feral cats (*Felis catus*) occur around Strathgordon, and have been located as far down the Gordon River as its junction with the Olga River. Occasionally dogs (*Canis familiaris*) lost in the area have survived, adopting a feral existence.

The mammal fauna of the South-West does not appear to include any endemic species. Nevertheless it has, in common with other parts of Tasmania, a number of species which are either extinct on mainland Australia or otherwise endangered there. For some of these species, like the broad-toothed rat, long-tailed rat, swamp antechinus and pademelon, the South-West must act as a major refuge since rainforest and sedgeland habitats there are rarely disturbed.

The tiger cat is a swift predator and also an agile tree-climber. *Zoology Dept Uni of Tas*

SPECIES		HABITAT TYPE	LOCALITIES
Platypus	*Ornithorhynchus anatinus*	Lakes & river systems	Widespread
Echidna	*Tachyglossus aculeatus*	Sclerophyll forest & moorland	Widespread
Wallaby	*Macropus rufogriseus*	Sclerophyll forest — sedgeland mosaic	Widespread
Pademelon	*Thylogale billardierii*	Forest areas, favouring dense cover	Widespread
Potoroo	*Potorous apicalis*	Sclerophyll forest	Lower Gordon River
Wombat	*Vombatus ursinus*	Open forest, sedgeland & moorland	Widespread
Brush-Tailed Possum	*Trichosurus vulpecula*	Forest areas	Huon & Florentine River Valleys
Ring-Tailed Possum	*Pseudocheirus peregrinus*	Eucalypt forest & woodland	Widespread
Eastern Pigmy Possum	*Cercartetus nanus*	Rainforest	Widespread
Little Pigmy Possum	*Cercartetus lepidus*	Dry sclerophyll forest & heathland	Widespread
Tasmanian Devil	*Sarcophilus harrisii*	Sclerophyll forest & heathland	Widespread
Tiger Cat	*Dasyurus maculatus*	Wet sclerophyll forest & rainforest	Widespread
Native Cat	*Dasyurus viverrinus*	Sclerophyll forest, heathland & rainforest	Widespread
Dusky Antechinus	*Antechinus swainsonii*	Wet sclerophyll forest & rainforest	Lower Gordon River, Mt Anne, Picton River
Swamp Antechinus	*Antechinus minimus*	Sedgeland	Pedder plains, Olga River, Maatsuyker Island
Water Rat	*Hydromys chrysogaster*	Inland waterways	Gordon & Huon Rivers
Broad-Toothed Rat	*Mastacomys fuscus*	Sedgeland	Pedder Plains, Olga River
Long-Tailed Rat	*Pseudomys higginsi*	Rainforest & wet sclerophyll forest	Lower Huon & Gordon Rivers
Velvet-Furred Rat	*Rattus lutreolus*	Sedgeland, sclerophyll & rainforest	Widespread

This table indicates the distribution and usual habitat of the native mammals found in the South-West. Localities from which the native rodents and marsupial mice have so far recorded are also listed.
I Skira and G Hocking

The Thylacine

'So much of Tasmania remains in a state of nature, and so much of its forest land yet uncleared that ... this singular animal ... is secure from the attacks of man; many years must therefore elapse before it can become entirely extinct.' (John Gould. 1863)*

The thylacine was the largest marsupial carnivore, a nocturnal hunter, the 'doe' carrying 3 or 4 young in her pouch. Many thousands were killed by the colonists and 2,184 £1 bounties were paid by the Government between 1888 and 1909.

The last known specimen, a male, was brought to Hobart from the Florentine Valley in 1933, possibly by Elias Churchill. He snared 8 'tigers' in the 1920s and '30s — 4 in the Florentine Valley and one each at the Needles, Mt. Bowes, the Vale of the Rasselas and the top end of the South Gordon Track — and he saw many more in the area.

But now the Florentine Valley is riven by forestry roads and nearly half a century has passed without any irrefutable evidence for the thylacine's continuing existence. Perhaps a remnant few still hunt in the South-West. But the likelihood has faded and it may be time to accept that Gould's familiarity with modern man, if not the thylacine, led him to a sadly exact prophesy.
Bob Brown

*'Mammals of Australia.' Vol I. John Gould.

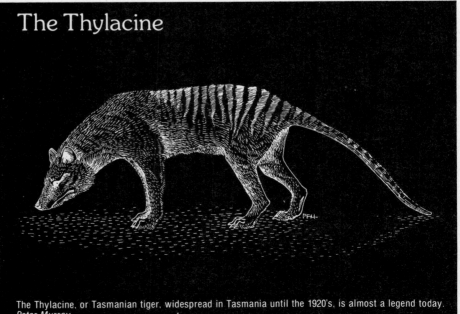

The Thylacine, or Tasmanian tiger, widespread in Tasmania until the 1920's, is almost a legend today.
Peter Murray

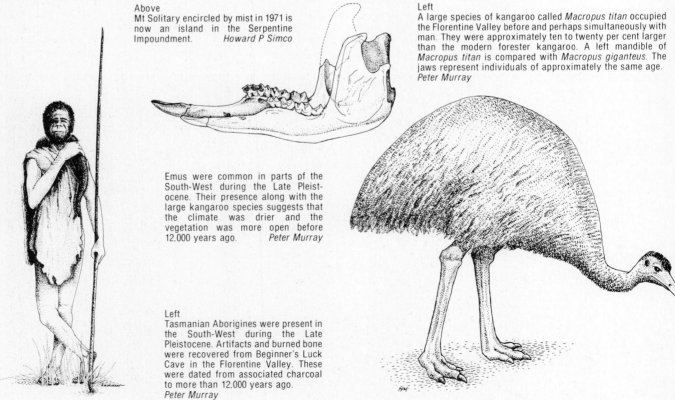

Life During the Late Pleistocene

P Murray

Dr Murray is Curator of Anthropology at the Tasmanian Museum and Honorary Research Associate in the Department of Anatomy, University of Tasmania. He received his Ph.D. in Physical Anthropology from the University of Chicago in 1973. He has done archaeological field work in Oregon, Michigan and Tasmania. His major interests are primate evolution and Pleistocene paleoecology.

Evidence of animal life in Tasmania during the latter part of the Ice Age or Pleistocene has come primarily from caves. Fossil deposits in small caves in the north-western portion of the State indicate that dramatic changes in the climate and associated mammalian communities occurred within the past 20,000 years. In 1975, geomorphologist Albert Goede and I began to investigate recently discovered fossil deposits in the South-West. These localities are within a cave-riddled limestone belt at the foot of Mt Field West, about forty kilometres north-west of the village of Maydena. The area is known as the Florentine Valley. Our investigations revealed that the South-West, as exemplified by the Florentine River Valley, must have gone through an equally if not more pronounced climatic, floral and faunal transformation.

Three agencies are responsible for accumulations of fossil and recent bones in the caves of the Florentine Valley. The vertical shafts that characterize the cave systems of the Florentine Valley are obvious hazards to terrestrial animals. Many kinds of animals, even a platypus, must have accidentally fallen into these natural traps to become faithfully preserved by the carbonate-rich

environment of the cave. Carnivores, scavengers and man also bring bones into caves in the form of food remains. Finally, owls that nest in cave mouths deposit pellets consisting of bones of the small animals that form their diet. In some caves all of these factors may work together producing an exquisite puzzle for the palaeontologist.

We are just beginning to expand on the small amount of information available about the kinds of animals, living and extinct, that inhabited the South-West during the terminal Pleistocene, 10,000 to 20,000 years ago. Unfortunately, each fossil deposit appears to represent a comparatively short interval of time. An individual site is a narrow, slit-like window into the past. Through several of these 'windows' we may see different aspects of life during roughly the same period or we may find that times have changed: that a particular fauna is significantly earlier or later than another. So far, we have dated two deposits that appear to span approximately 2,000 years, from 12,500 to over 14,000 years ago. It is probable that we have slightly older fossils from an unnamed cave. Other fossil sites span a time period from the end of the Pleistocene to the recent past.

The most recent of the carbon-14 dated Pleistocene sites (400 to 12,800 years ago) consists entirely of modern species. These fossils are the food remains of a human occupation site in Beginner's Luck Cave. The lack of extinct species may indicate that they had vanished from the valley by the time man arrived there some 12,000–13,000 years ago. It is also possible that man did not hunt the larger mammals or that we have not obtained an adequate sample of the deposit to account for their presence. It is significant that the most common food remains in the deposit are of the brush wallaby. The tiger cat and wombat are also present. Bird remains include the Tasmanian native hen. Many hundreds of bones of the broad-toothed rat were deposited by owls roosting in the mouth of the cave. Fragments of the extinct, short-faced browsing kangaroo (*Sthenurus occidentalis*) were recovered from a separate deposit within the same cave system. Carbon-14 dates obtained from bone collagen suggest that the *Sthenurus* remains are slightly older than the archaeological horizon. Emus and wallabies were also present at this time.

Another cave deposit contains the remains of a 'giant' kangaroo named *Macropus titan*. The titan kangaroo was very similar to the modern forester kangaroo, but significantly (perhaps 20%) larger. Remains of the ordinary pademelon and the brush wallaby are associated with the large kangaroo species. This site is almost certainly within the late Pleistocene but we do not have a reliable means for fitting it into the sequence. There are two possible clues; a small piece of burned bone was found in the upper part of the deposit. This suggests that man may have been present at the time. The other tantalizing hint is that the titan kangaroo remains are buried within the same kind of deposit associated with the *Sthenurus* and emu remains from Beginner's Luck Cave. The titan kangaroo remains may even be slightly older than the *Sthenurus* fragments. They come from within the deposit whereas the *Sthenurus* fossils appear to lie on top of it.

These then, are the several slightly different assemblages from the Florentine Valley that we have had the opportunity to examine. In brief, (1) there are modern deposits, (2) an archaeological horizon dating to slightly more than 12,000 years ago, (3) a nonarchaeological horizon containing emu and the short-faced browsing kangaroo at slightly more than 14,000 years ago, and (4) a possibly older assemblage containing the titan kangaroo.

Today the Florentine Valley is a moderate to high rainfall area supporting dense stands of wet sclerophyll forest and rainforest. The dominant larger animals include the pademelon and the brush wallaby. The forester kangaroo was never present in this habitat nor did aborigines frequent this type of forest environment.

The titan kangaroo, like its modern counterpart the forester, probably preferred lightly wooded habitats in association with grasslands. The emu also showed a preference for open woodlands. Similarly, the large browsing kangaroo was poorly suited to life in a densely wooded habitat littered with rotting logs and dense undergrowth. So the kinds of animals present about 14,000 years ago suggest that the Florentine Valley might have consisted of rolling grassy hills dotted with shrubs and isolated copses of eucalypt forest.

During the human occupation of the valley, 12,500 years ago, the habitat must have remained relatively open. The brush wallaby appears to have been more common than the pademelon suggesting that dense undergrowth was rare or absent. The abundant broad-toothed rat remains suggest a cold wet sedgeland, its exclusive habitat today. Barred bandicoots are more prevalent in open habitats than brown bandicoots. Significantly, the brown bandicoot is present in recent cave deposits, but not in Pleistocene ones. The Pleistocene

sites in turn contain only specimens of the barred species. Finally, the presence of the Tasmanian native hen in the archaeological horizon also favours the interpretation of an open grass or sedgeland habitat.

Geomorphological evidence substantiates the interpretation of the fauna and adds several dimensions of its own to the reconstruction of the environment of this part of the South-West.

The archaeological horizon occurs within a deposit of small, angular limestone fragments that have become partially cemented together by flow-stone. Albert Goede interprets these as weathering products characteristic of a cold, dry environment. Large amounts of sediment consisting of rounded cobbles and pebbles are found near the sites. These are as yet undated, but some of the deposits are undoubtedly late Pleistocene. This sediment is interpreted by Eric Colhoun and Albert Goede as being the result of seasonal meltwaters pouring off nearby accumulations of snow and ice.

Another kind of deposit consists of fine sediments that have literally flowed into the openings of the caves. These deposits may have occurred during periods when the ground thawed and became highly mobile on the limestone slopes in which the caves are formed.

The remains of the titan kangaroo and the short-faced browsing kangaroo are associated with this type of sediment.

Each of these sediment types could be interpreted as having occurred under different kinds of climatic conditions or they may represent different depositional aspects of the same general kind of climate at different locations. Until these various deposits can be dated accurately, we can only speculate. What they all indicate is an accelerated erosional sequence characteristic of cold conditions where dense vegetation was either restricted and localized or absent.

In conclusion, it is probable that this part of the South-West was once much colder and drier than it is now. The vegetation was comparatively sparse but it may have supported a much more varied population of mammals during the Pleistocene. Both the tiger cat and the native cat appear at times to have occupied the same habitat. The large titan kangaroo and the short-faced browsing kangaroo may have existed in the same general habitats feeding on different kinds of vegetation. The primary change in the mammalian community as the Pleistocene ended was the depletion of the larger elements of the fauna, due perhaps to the encroachment of the grazing areas by forest, wet scrub and sedgeland.

Sthenurus occidentalis was a short-faced kangaroo adapted for browsing. This now extinct genus and species was present in the South-West slightly more than 14,000 years ago. A fragment of upper jaw is figured along with a reconstruction of the skull and a restoration of the appearance of the animal.. *Peter Murray*

Opposite page
Lots Wife: Mt Anne in the background.   *Jim England*

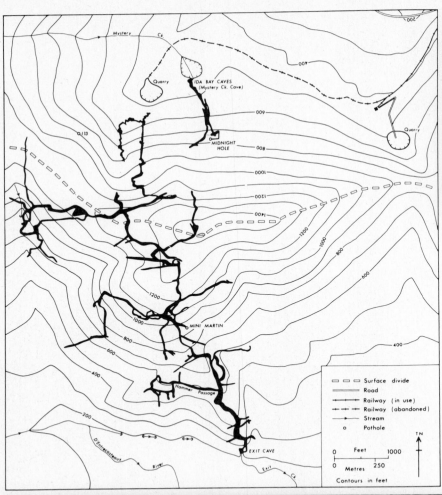

Cave formation near the Colonnades, Exit Cave.
Lloyd Robinson

Fig 1 Plan of Ida Bay and Exit Caves.   *Albert Goede*

Main streamway, Exit Cave.   *Lloyd Robinson*

Caves — A World Below

A Goede

Albert Goede is a lecturer in Geography at the University of Tasmania. His research includes geomorphology, hydrology, karst and stratigraphy. He has a strong interest in scientific speleology and the conservation of Australian caves. He is currently researching the stratigraphy and age of Pleistocene cave deposits in Tasmania.

When considering the moon we picture the side that is always turned towards the earth—few of us think much about the other hidden side. It is much the same with Tasmania's South-West — we think of its mountains, rivers, lakes and forests, but there are also the hidden parts of which few of us are aware.

Scattered throughout this wild and inaccessible region are areas of Ordovician limestone and Precambrian dolomite. Rocks that, given enough time, are soluble in water — particularly water enriched in carbon dioxide derived from the respiration of plants and soil animals, and in organic acids derived from the decay of organic matter.[1] The continuous solvent action of water over long periods of time has created unusual landforms — solution flutes, sinkholes and disappearing streams—typical features of karst, a landscape formed as a result of the solubility of the limestone. Another feature of many karst areas is the absence of running water. Creeks and even rivers disappear underground into stream-sinks and caves soon after reaching the limestone, sometimes to reappear several miles away. The presence of dry valleys indicates that in the past, water did flow on the surface but it has long since disappeared underground, often carving out caves in the process.

Unfortunately these caves are not always easy to find, especially in areas of such dense forest vegetation as we find in parts of the South-West. We have to know something about geology in order to pinpoint likely limestone or dolomite areas. Such areas may or may not have accessible caves and the only way to find out is to walk over the ground. Once a cave is discovered, its exploration may require specialized equipment. Even if it does not, a caverneer has to carry in standard equipment such as a light, helmet and special clothing, which adds to an already heavy load. Under these conditions, it is perhaps not surprising that the exploration of the caves of the South-West has lagged far behind surface exploration.

Speleology—the scientific study of caves—includes aspects of such a diverse range of sciences as geology, hydrology, geomorphology, zoology, palaeontology and archaeology. To the

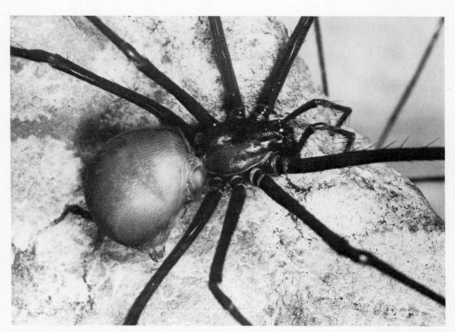

The Tasmanian cave spider. *Hickmania troglotytes.*   *Anthony Healy*

zoologist the caves of the South-West are of interest because, like caves everywhere, they contain animals that have become adapted to living underground and are no longer able to survive on the surface. They are known as troglobites and in Tasmania are usually small invertebrates including beetles, harvestmen, pseudoscorpions, millipedes and several other groups. They are frequently blind and depigmented and some have developed elongated appendages and sensory hairs. The last two adaptations probably assist them in finding their way in the absence of light.[2] Because they can only survive in caves, each limestone area has developed its own fauna and areas which are only a few kilometres apart may contain separate, although frequently closely related species. An eyeless variety of the mountain shrimp *Anaspides* occurs in Wolfhole at Hastings adjacent to an underground occurrence of the usual eyed form in nearby Newdegate cave. Because the South-West contains a number of discrete areas of limestone and dolomite separated by non-cavernous rocks it has considerable potential for a variety of troglobitic species. Although little study

and collecting has been done yet, the more accessible areas like Ida Bay, Hastings and the Florentine Valley are known to have an extensive cave fauna. Preliminary collecting in caves at Precipitous Bluff has turned up several new cave-adapted species. Of the six known troglobitic species of beetle in Australia, five occur in caves of the South-West. Of these five, three belong to the genus *Idacarabus*, a genus known only from caves in South-Western Tasmania.

To the hydrologist, karst areas are of interest because of the unpredictable paths followed by underground water. In limestone terrain such water may pass beneath major surface divides as at Ida Bay where Mystery Creek, a stream rising in the apparent catchment area of the Lune River, flows underground through Marble Hill to become a tributary of the D'Entrecasteaux River (Fig 1).[3] Underground drainage through a surface divide has also been demonstrated recently in the Cracroft area. Because underground water in limestone areas frequently flows through sizeable conduits it is particularly prone to pollution. Polluting substances are transported rapidly over surprisingly

131

long distances and frequently to unknown destinations. Several years ago a cave stream at Ida Bay was badly polluted by waste oil dumped in a nearby sinkhole.

To the geologist and geomorphologist, caves in the South-West are also of considerable interest because they can tell us much about the past climatic history of the area during the Quaternary. This is a geological period which began about 2 million years ago and continues to the present. It is characterized by the repeated occurrence of cold climate conditions known as the Ice Ages or glacial phases. There may have been as many as five or six separated by much milder eras known as interglacial phases. In the South-West there is surface evidence of at least two phases of glaciation, probably the last two, earlier evidence having been destroyed by erosion.

Every time an Ice Age occurred cirque and valley glaciers developed in the mountains. Bare of vegetation, most of the remaining land surface was being actively weathered and eroded by frost. Under these conditions streams carried heavy loads of coarse detritus, and where water flowed into caves they were quickly filled with sediments. Some of the older caves in the South-West—Exit Cave and Judds Cavern for example— show several phases of infilling, each one apparently related to the occurrence of cold climate conditions. Such deposits are much longer and much better preserved in caves than on the surface. Until recently they had received little attention because it was virtually impossible to determine their age. However, the picture has changed dramatically as new methods have been developed to date fossil bone, flowstone and stalactites in caves. Some studies have already begun in the Florentine Valley and investigations will be extended to Exit Cave at Ida Bay in the near future. What makes these studies even more interesting is the discovery that sediments in these two localities contain bones of an extinct giant browsing kangaroo (*Sthenurus occidentalis*).

Until recently no archaeological remains had ever been found in Tasmania's limestone caves. However, in August 1975 an archaeological site was discovered in the Florentine Valley. It appears to be an ancient one and may date back to the last glacial phase. At that time the Florentine Valley would have been open alpine country instead of being covered with dense wet sclerophyll forest. This discovery opens up the exciting possibility that archaeological sites may be found in other limestone caves in the South-West.

Two of the caves in the South-West have particular tourist potential. Exit

Cave at Ida Bay offers excellent prospects for this kind of development, as it would be quite unlike any other tourist cave in Australia. The most outstanding feature is the very impressive glow worm display in the first 400 metres of stream passage. The display consists of concentrations of luminous larvae of the fly *Arachnocampa tasmaniensis* which is closely allied to the New Zealand species responsible for the famous glow worm displays at Waitomo. Although glow worms occur in other caves in the South-West, Exit Cave has the largest concentration. Other features of the cave are the enormous dimensions of the river chambers and the presence of an active underground stream. Unusual and spectacular formations are found in the upper levels not far from the entrance. This includes columns, stalactites and stalagmites as well as formations of 'moonmilk', a spongy variety of calcium carbonate and other minerals probably produced by bacterial action.

In the Cracroft area Judds Cavern has an underground stream emerging from a spectacular entrance. Nearby, Matchlight Cavern is dry and has a wealth of cave formations.

Well decorated caves are extremely vulnerable to damage by man. Even the experienced cave explorer, who is usually an ardent conservationist, will do some damage as he walks across delicate flowstone floors in dirty boots or accidently brushes his muddy clothing against cave formations. Formations sometimes have to be broken to gain access to further extensions of the cave. Most caverneers will keep damage to an absolute minimum and for this purpose where floors are likely to be soiled, as in some decorated parts of Exit Cave, routes are marked out.

Much more damage can be done by the casual adventurer who is not aware of cave ethics. Stalactites may be removed as souvenirs and names and dates scratched or marked on formations. An even greater threat is posed by mineral hunters and rockhounds who may systematically strip caves of decorations to display in their homes or sell for profit. This has already become a problem at Mole Creek in northern Tasmania. The caves of the South-West have so far escaped significant damage by vandals and mineral collectors but with access improving rapidly it is only a matter of time before this becomes a problem. Already King George V Cave at Hastings and Exit Cave at Ida Bay have had entrance gates installed to keep out unwanted visitors. A law to prohibit the sale of cave formations would help to prevent future damage.

A soil cover on limestone plays a very important part in the development and

maintenance of formations in caves. Only a fraction of the total amount of limestone is in solution. Most of the solution activity of water is due to the fact that it contains carbonic acid derived from the carbon dioxide content of the free atmosphere and soils. Soils usually contain much higher concentrations of carbon dioxide than the free atmosphere, hence seepage water percolating through a soil is much more aggressive and dissolves much more limestone.[1] When seepage water emerges through a cave roof it comes into contact with the cave atmosphere which has a lower carbon dioxide content than the soil. Carbon dioxide diffuses out of the seepage water and calcium carbonate is deposited. Limestone caves throughout the world owe their actively forming formations to the presence of a soil cover. Removal of that cover through soil erosion may lead to long term damage and removal of formations through resolution processes. The smooth interface between limestone and soil encourages soil stripping.[4] Numerous examples of the aftermath can be found in Europe. The process has already begun on the steeper slopes in the Junee-Florentine valleys where clear felling is followed by soil erosion.

The cave fauna is entirely dependent on an outside food supply. Such supplies are sometimes carried in by floods as well as being brought in by other animals like cave crickets, rats and possums. Therefore the state and nature of the surface vegetation indirectly controls the available food supply in the cave system. Wholesale removal of vegetation and selective regeneration of species of economic importance will change the surface fauna and so the food supply available to the cave system. Most of these changes are likely to be detrimental and may even cause partial destruction of cave fauna and extinction of some unique cave-adapted species. The scientific, scenic and recreational potential of the South-West is seriously endangered by rapid development of water, mineral and timber resources.

OPPOSITE PAGE

Top
Plan of Judds Cavern.   *Albert Goede*

Middle right
The Colonnades, Exit Cave.   *Albert Goede*

Bottom right
Cave formation near the Colonnades, Exit Cave.
Albert Goede

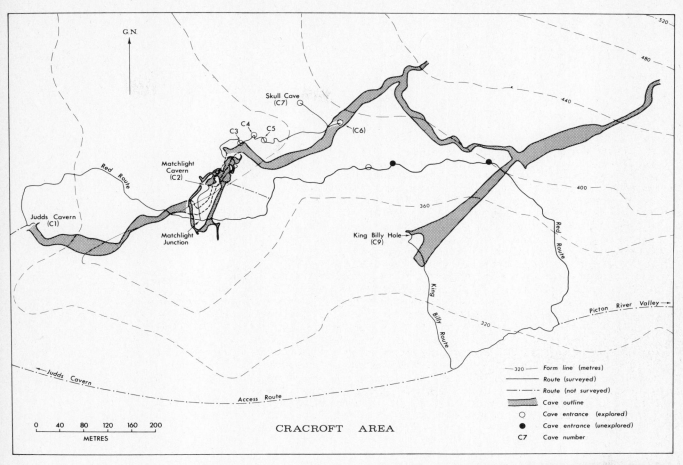

CRACROFT AREA

Legend:
- —320— Form line (metres)
- ——— Route (surveyed)
- —·—·— Route (not surveyed)
- Cave outline
- ○ Cave entrance (explored)
- ● Cave entrance (unexplored)
- C7 Cave number

Scale: 0 40 80 120 160 200 METRES

MATCHLIGHT CAVERN

Surveyed by: Mike Martyn, John Taylor,
Brian Lefoe, Mike Butler,
Bob Woolhouse, Neil Hickson
on 30th January 1975

Plotted by: Mike Martyn

MAGNETIC DEVIATION 13°

Legend:
- ▲ Survey station
- — Floor slope
- ☼ Daylight hole
- ♧ Floor hole
- ⌐2m Roof height
- Flowstone
- ✴ Column
- ⬭ Pool

Scale: 0 10 20 30 40 METRES

7C2. TCC 113

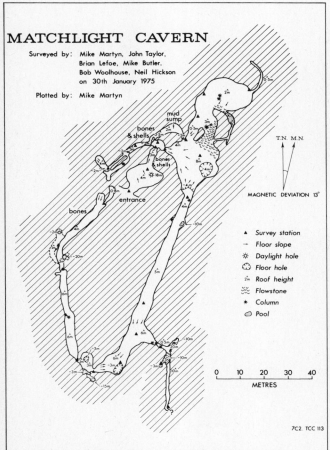

King Billy pine (*Athrotaxis selaginoides*) forest, North-East Ridge, Mount Anne.

Reg Williams

Origins and Affinities of the South-West Biota

B Knott

During his years as a post-graduate student in Zoology at the University of Tasmania, Brenton Knott B.Sc. Ph.D. (Tas.) made many field trips into the South-West. In his detailed taxonomic study of the phreatoicid Isopods in Tasmania for his Ph.D. thesis, Brenton has contributed significantly towards a scientific understanding of the complex and interesting biota of Tasmania's South-West.

The cool wet environment of South-West Tasmania is quite unlike all others in Australia, although similar conditions do prevail elsewhere in the Southern Hemisphere, in parts of New Zealand and southern South America for example. The sea barrier which now separates Tasmania from the mainland formed approximately 65 million years ago[1], but since its formation, it has been dry at least twice, most recently during the Pleistocene period. So we are faced with the intriguing question: is the South-West biota derived from a widespread Australian biota which was able to cross a land bridge into Tasmania and which has since adapted to cool, wet conditions? Alternatively, it may be relevant to consider that Tasmania was, for approximately 240 million years, from the Lower Carboniferous to the Cretaceous era, lodged between Australia and Antarctica. These land masses together with New Zealand, South Africa, South America, India and Madagascar formed the large continent of Gondwanaland. Is the South-West biota a relict from a previously pan-Gondwana biota? In this case closely related forms would probably occur in cool, wet areas of the other Gondwana fragments. Or is the biota of the South-West unique?

Let us begin by looking at the higher plants of which there is no lack, for there are at least 226 genera from 63 families of the higher plants represented in the region's flora. These genera can be grouped into 2 categories—Antarctic or Australian—according to their present world distribution. Since their recognition by Hooker, the 'Antarctic' elements have interested biogeographers because of their widespread but disjunct distribution in the Southern Hemisphere. These elements occur in the cool temperate rainforests of New Zealand and its sub-Antarctic Islands, southern Chile and Tierra del Fuego, the sub-montane areas of eastern Australia, New Caledonia and New Guinea, as well as in Tasmania. The Australian elements comprise genera which have evolved in, and are still predominantly distributed in, the Australian region.

The genera *Nothofagus*, *Dacrydium* and *Podocarpus*, represented locally by the species *Nothofagus cunninghamii* (myrtle), *Nothofagus gunnii* (tanglefoot or deciduous beech), *Dacrydium franklinii* (Huon pine) and the montane shrub *Podocarpus lawrencii* are 3 examples of the Antarctic elements. Fossil pollen studies have revealed that these genera plus *Microcachrys* (which is now confined to Tasmania), were, towards the end of the Mesozoic era, quite widely distributed throughout Gondwanaland.[2] Following the contact of South America with North America, and the near contact of Australia with South East Asia (the northward drift of the southern continents having commenced with the fragmenting of Gondwanaland), several of the Antarctic elements, *Podocarpus* and *Gaultheria* for example, have successfully colonized limited areas of the northern continents. Another noteworthy collection of Antarctic elements consists of the small herbs and monocots belonging to the genera *Abrotanella, Astelia, Donatia, Gaimardia, Nicotiana, Oreobolus, Oreomyrrhis* and *Phyllachne*, which aggregate and form the intriguing highland cushion and bog plant communities.

Many species which make walking in the South-West such a unique experience are derived from an essentially Australian biota. The families Epacridaceae, Myrtaceae, Protaceae and Rutaceae particularly, are prominent not only because of the diversity of their representatives (32 genera in all) but also through the dominance of their members (e.g. *Richea, Eucalyptus, Leptospermum, Melaleuca* and *Banksia*) in the various plant alliances recorded from the South-West. However, nowhere outside South-Western Tasmania can you walk through horizontal scrub (*Anodopetalum biglandulosum*), for the species is endemic to the island. *Bauera, Richea* and *Gymnoschoenus* (button-grass), although not strictly endemic to Tasmania, attain their most vigorous growth there. Mountain rocket (*Bellendena*), climbing heath (*Prionotes*) and white waratah (*Agastachys*) are examples of the many plants which add colour to the Tasmanian bush.

The Antarctic and Australian categories cover most but not all of the plants found in the South-West. Sassafras trees (*Atherosperma moschatum*), which are in many areas co-dominant with myrtles, belong to a family of essentially tropical distribution.[3] Pencil pines (*Athrotaxis cupressoides*) and King Billy pines (*Athrotaxis selaginoides*) add considerable charm to the highland tarns and rainforests. The genus *Athrotaxis* is endemic to Tasmania, but all other representatives of the family in which it is currently placed, the *Taxodiaceae*, are confined to the Northern Hemisphere.

Animals are much more troublesome than plants! Although animals abound in the South-West, and in reasonable diversity, they tend to show retiring habits and are frequently revealed only after diligent searching. Practically all the known fauna belongs to the Australian category. For example, the majority of fish, amphibian, reptile, bird and mammal species are closely related to forms found on the mainland. This is also true of the freshwater crustaceans, the koonungid syncarids; the hypsimetopid, phreatoicid and asellote isopods; the gammarid, austrochiltonid and calliopid (excluding *Paraleptamphopus tasmanicus*) amphipods; and the parastacid (yabby) and palaeomonid (shrimp) decapods.

Few animal genera are strictly endemic to the South-West. The greatest concentration of endemic forms is centered on the plains about the upper reaches of the Huon, Serpentine and Wedge Rivers. The endemic species from these plains include the syncarids *Allanaspides helonomus* and *Allanaspides hickmani*, the isopods *Uramphisous binksi* and *Uramphisopus baylyi*, the snail *Valvata(?) pedderi*, and the fish *Galaxias parvus* and *Galaxias pedderensis*. Of these the only endemic genus is *Allanaspides*. Two groups of crustaceans, now classified into the genera *Micraspides* (syncarids) and *Parastocoides* (yabbies), probably evolved in the South-West, but they are now more widely distributed throughout western Tasmania.

Several faunal groups are disjunctly distributed within the southern continents[4] but few of them can be classed with reasonable certainty as belonging to the category of Antarctic elements; those which are so classed embrace animals which, in the main, inhabit cold freshwaters at some stage of their life cycle. The Antarctic elements include insects which have aquatic immature stages, (especially stoneflies of the families Eustheniidae, Austroperlidae and sub-family Notonemourinae), scorpion flies (of the family Nannochoristidae), chironomids (of the sub-family Podonominae), several families of caddis flies, fish (of the genus *Galaxias*) and the freshwater snail *Valvata* (?). In addition, two terrestrial examples—pelorid bugs and some tribes of carabid beetles have been cited.

Available evidence thus indicates quite emphatically that the South-West biota is derived from a variety of sources, each of which exhibits its own separate evolutionary history. This is not an original or surprising observation, for it follows the pattern typical of continental biotas and, after all, Tasmania is a 'continental' island.

Moreover, it is unrealistic to regard the South-West as a separate biogeographical unit isolated from other montane areas of Tasmania and south-east Australia. These mountains have served as areas enabling the evolution of new plant and animal groups and also as refuges where biotas of ancient origin have survived. Clearly the mountains have played an important role in the evolutionary history of the higher plant genera endemic to Tasmania. The 13 strictly endemic genera plus the 14 genera restricted to Tasmania in the Australian region (but occurring elsewhere), listed by N T Burbidge[5], are widely distributed throughout western Tasmania. Many of the endemic faunal genera—*Anaspides*, *Micraspides* (Syncarida), *Parastacoides* (Decapoda) and *Synthemiopsis*, (citing only those known to occur in the South-West)—are restricted to montane or western locations.

Given that the biota of western Tasmania is formed predominantly from Australian elements, it is still of interest to query the possibility of a closer relationship with the biota of New Zealand or South America. However, it is doubtful whether any meaningful answer can be supplied at present. Certainly, examples of genera common to Tasmania and either New Zealand or South America can be quoted to demonstrate the propinquity of many of the trans-oceanic biogeographical ties: the freshwater *Paraleptamphopus* and plants *Archeria*, *Phebalium* and *Eriostemon* in Tasmania and New Zealand; the plants *Orites* and *Eucryphia* in Tasmania and South America — to name but 6 examples.

The problem still remains that any attempt to compare the biotas of different regions of the world is fraught with difficulties, not least of which is to decide the level of taxonomic ranking (i.e. family, genus, species etc.) at which the comparisons should be made. Any comparison requiring the comprehensive treatment hinted at above is well beyond the scope of the present discussion, and could not even be attempted yet. We still have so much to learn concerning the fauna of South-West Tasmania.

Readers who wish to pursue the subject of Tasmanian biogeography to greater depths are referred to several detailed studies, notably discussions of the flora by Burbidge[5] and Good[3] and zoogeographical aspects in the volume edited by Williams in 1974. Darlington[6], in a very readable account, examines the relationship between the biotas of the southern continents.

Atherosperma moschatum, 'sassafras'. A tall tree, up to 20 m, common in wet forests, especially in gullies. The shining, toothed leaves have a very pleasant aroma when crushed.   *Peter Murray*

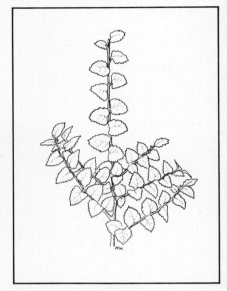

Nothofagus cunninghamii, 'myrtle beech'. A large, spreading tree, 5 – 25 m high, often dominant in rainforests and extending from sea level to sub-montane shrubberies.   *Peter Murray*

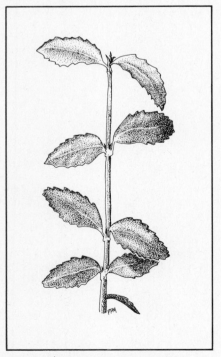

Anodopetalum biglandulosum, 'horizontal'. Restricted to wet gullies in southern and western Tasmania. Commonly called 'horizontal' due to the manner in which the branches bend under their own weight, then intertwine horizontally and often form distinct platforms above the ground. *Peter Murray*

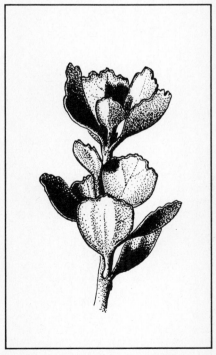

Bellendena montana, 'mountain rocket'. This small shrub, 20 – 80 cm, is a common component of high moorland vegetation. It has white or pink flowers densely packed in short spikes. In autumn the spikes of bright crimson or scarlet fruits are very conspicuous, especially en masse, thus the name 'mountain rocket'.   *Peter Murray*

Australian Conservation Foundation

The Australian Conservation Foundation is a national non-profit organization which has been striving since 1965 to further the code, philosophy and practice of conservation.

The ACF has policies and programmes on all major areas of conservation and environmental concern. It elects 35 councillors nationally every two years to guide its affairs and make policies. There are some 7000 members. The ACF exists to give them a voice, particularly at the national and international levels. Foundation members receive the ACF Newsletter 11 times a year. The ACF also publishes its own colour magazine *Habitat Australia* to provide information and inspiration on the environment.

The Foundation recognised the national and international importance of the South-West early in its life and has been adding its weight to the calls for protection of these values ever since.

To date, a number of compromises have seen some areas of the South-West protected as a part of a general opening-up process associated with hydro-electric power development. The Foundation believes the compromises, including the one which led to the unnecessary destruction of Lake Pedder, have gone too far, and will fight for the retention of the wilderness values of the Lower Gordon and its tributaries against further proposals for power dams.

If you are a conservationist, the kind who wants to see an effective effort at the national level, join us at ACF. Ordinary membership is $12; student or pensioner $6. A *Habitat Australia* subscription is $7 for six issues.

The Foundation believes that South-West Tasmania is one of the great natural areas of the world and is one of the crown jewels of Australia's natural heritage. It is considered one of the last remaining temperate wilderness areas in the world, and possesses outstanding landscape, aesthetic and scientific reference values. It is an asset which, unlike those utilised for the immediate material needs of society, is best maintained by permitting it to exist free of development.

The Foundation has taken a deep and longstanding interest in South-West Tasmania, and has been consistently urging its preservation since 1967, when the present Director of the Foundation, Dr. Mosley, presented evidence to the Select Committee of the Legislative Council Inquiry into the Gordon River Power Development.

The Foundation has been heavily involved in defending the preservation of the South-West by direct submission to public inquiries, such as the Lake Pedder Inquiry, by opposing the issue of mining and prospecting leases through the courts, and by continued negotiation with the Tasmanian and Federal Governments and government departments. It has also been involved in the holding of several symposia on the future of the South-West and in proposing the establishment and extension of the Southwest National Park.

The Foundation believes that the major overall threat to the South-West is constituted by the dependence of Australia on a growth economy which requires increasing amounts of raw materials and energy for its sustenance irrespective of any effects on values not readily quantifiable in economic terms. Such growth cannot be maintained indefinitely due to the finite limits of resources. The Foundation asserts that in the making of land-use decisions, quality of environment must replace growth as the over-riding criterion.

The Foundation believes that the best way of ensuring maintenance of the optimum environmental quality in relatively pristine natural areas is by their management as national parks, a principle that applies at its strongest. for wilderness areas which in many respects epitomise most national park values. As such, the Foundation believes that the significance of the Southwest National Park and its proposed enlargement revolves largely around the wilderness character of the area.

The Foundation believes that the future of the South-West is of critical importance nationally and that decisions affecting options for its future should not be made without full knowledge of their widest ramifications.

Proposed hydro-electric developments pose the greatest threat to the wilderness nature of the South-West. The construction of Strathgordon Road alone did more to reduce the area of wilderness in Tasmania than any other single development, and the flooding of Lake Pedder obliterated South-West Tasmania's foremost natural gem. The proposed damming of the Lower Gordon, Franklin, and King Rivers would completely shatter the South-West and reduce the area of wilderness to a small number of isolated pockets.

In view of the international calibre of the wilderness of South-West Tasmania, and the integral nature of the Lower Gordon and its tributaries in that wilderness, the ACF believes that no further hydro-electric power development should be permitted in the region.

The ACF's 12th Annual General Meeting, held in Hobart on October the 7th, 1978, declared the Franklin — Lower Gordon campaign to be a prime focus of the ACF for the coming year. Consideration was to be given to the appointment of a full-time officer to co-ordinate ACF's campaign from the Tasmanian Environment Centre Inc.

The ACF calls on:

the Australian Government to recommend the South-West for World Heritage status immediately.

the Tasmanian Government to declare the Franklin — Lower Gordon region a wilderness within an enlarged Southwest National Park;

the Tasmanian Government to commission an independent study into the state's short and long term alternative energy sources including the immediate potential of a realistic public and industrial energy conservation programme, and the development of potential solar energy resources which would promote employment in Tasmania.

October, 1978.

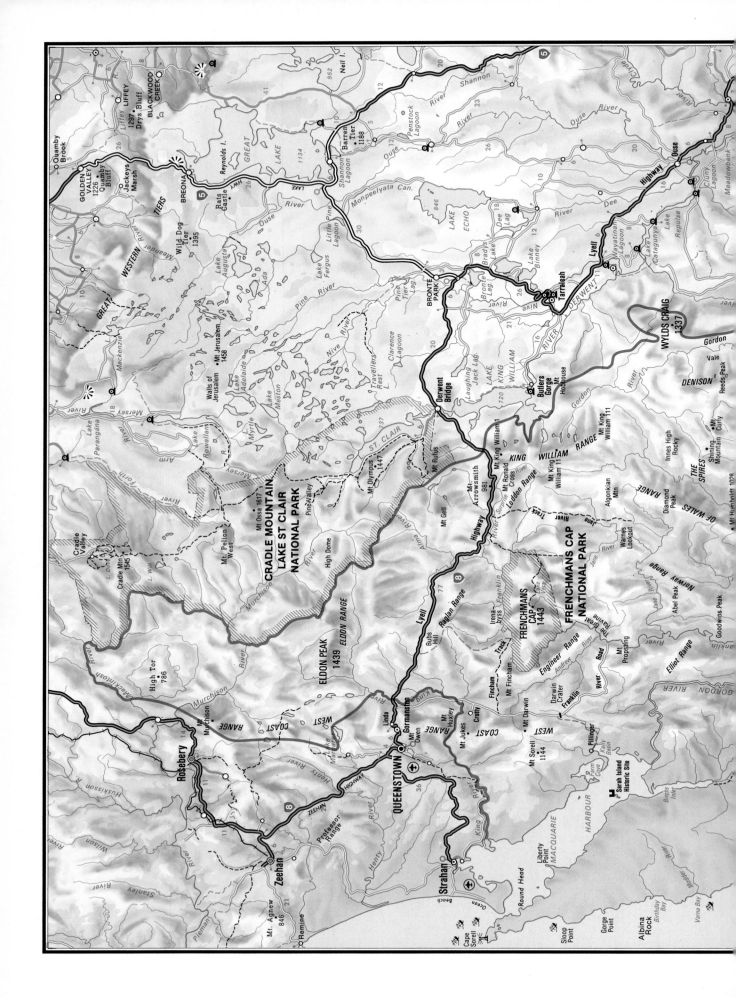

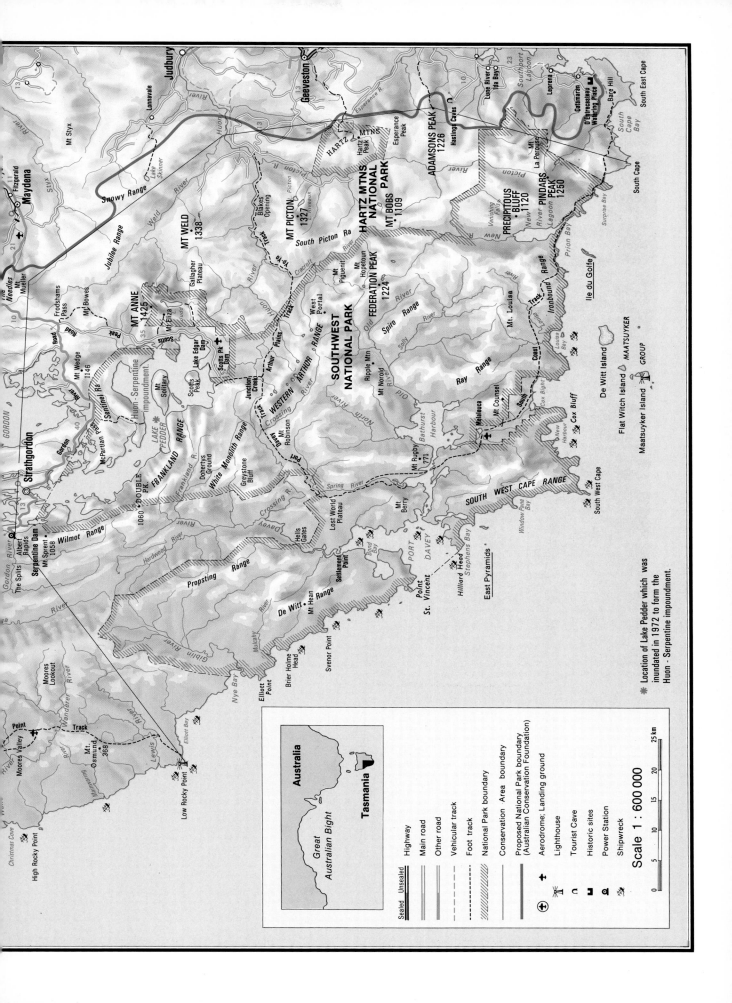

Judbury

Geeveston

HARTZ MTNS

Hartz Peak

Esperance Peak

ADAMSONS PEAK
1226

HARTZ MTNS
NATIONAL PARK

MT BOBS
1109

Hastings Caves

Lune River
Ida Bay

Southport
Lagoon

Leprena

D'Entrecasteaux Watering Place

Catamaran

Bare Hill

South East Cape

South Cape Bay

South Cape

PRECIPITOUS BLUFF
New 1120

PINDARS PEAK
1250

Mt La Perouse

Maydena

Fitzgerald

The Needles

Mt Mueller

Lonnavale

Mt Styx

Lake Skinner

Snowy Range

Weld River

Jubilee Range

MT WELD
1338

Blakes Opening

Gallagher Plateau

MT PICTON
1327

South Picton Ra

Picton River

Yo-Yo

Mt Piguenit

Mt Hopetoun

FEDERATION PEAK
1224

Esperance R.

Huon River

Cracroft River

West Portal

SOUTHWEST
NATIONAL PARK

Vanishing Falls

New River

Prion Bay

Surprise Bay

Ile du Golfe

Strathgordon

GORDON River

Gordon

Albert Rapids

Serpentine Dam

The Splits

Mt Sprent
1058

Wilmot Range

McPartlan Pass

Sentinel Ra

Mt Wedge
1146

Frodshams Pass

Mt Bowes

MT ANNE
1425

Mt Eliza

Scotts Peak

Lake Pedder

Huon-Serpentine impoundment.

Scotts Pk Dam

Lake Edgar Dam

Mt Solitary

Scotts Peak

Junction Creek

Arthur Plains

WESTERN ARTHUR RANGE

Mt Robinson

Old River

Salisbury River

Spiro Range

Ripple Mtn

Mt Norold

Ray Range

Mt Louisa

DOUBLE PK
1060

FRANKLAND RANGE

Frankland R.

Dohertys Ground

Greystone Bluff

White Monolith Range

Port Davey Track

Port Davey

Bathurst Harbour

Mt Rugby
771

Melaleuca

Mt Counsel

South Coast Track

Ironbound Range

Louisa Bay

Louisa River

Cox Bight

De Witt Island

Flat Witch Island

MAATSUYKER GROUP

Maatsuyker Island

Moores Lookout

Christmas Cave

High Rocky Point

Point

Track

Mt. Osmund
368

Low Rocky Point

Moores Valley

Lewis River

Wanderer River

Gibiln River

Mulcahy River

Nye Bay

Elliott Bay

Brier Holme Head

Svenor Point

Elliott Point

Spring River

Lost World Plateau

Crossing R.

Davey River

Hells Gates

Hardwood River

Propsting Range

Mt Hean Range

De Witt

Mt Berry

PORT DAVEY

Settlement Point

Bond Bay

Point St. Vincent

Hilliard Head

Stephens Bay

East Pyramids

SOUTH WEST CAPE RANGE

Mt Rugby

New Harbour

Window Pane Bay

South West Cape

South West Cape

* Location of Lake Pedder which was
inundated in 1972 to form the
Huon - Serpentine impoundment.

Tasmanian Wilderness Society

A Society to foster Tasmanian wilderness, and in pursuance of this aim:

>to promote the concept of wilderness;
>to prevent the destruction of wilderness;
>to secure the future of wilderness;
>and to promote the rights of wilderness.

The Tasmanian Wilderness Society is one of the focal points of a new attitude — an intelligent humility towards man's place in nature. It is philosophically a disclaimer of the biotic arrogance of *homo tasmanicus*.

The Society is an amalgam of individuals who feel that the entire nation and they themselves are losing something of value when a road is built in a wilderness, when a wild river is dammed, when a primaeval forest is logged, when aeroplanes bring the noise of urban life into a wilderness and destroy the charm of remoteness, or when mechanical civilization encroaches in any way on the last remnants of wilderness.

This group, formed to defend Tasmanian wilderness, has branches and affiliated organizations in four Tasmanian centres and all mainland state capitals.

The Society was launched in August 1976 through the amalgamation of a number of existing action committees and individual activists concerned with the protection of Tasmanian wild lands, principally the South-West, the Western lakes district of the Central Plateau and the Norfolk Range. Lake Pedder was a catalyst. The spirit to defend the environment, and to challenge government on its behalf, was strengthened in that national campaign.

Members are most active in their efforts to protect the South-West as Australia's outstanding temperate natural area. The Society is outspoken against continuing logging of the Southern forests and plans afoot to dam the western rivers. Over the past decade the chain saw and the bulldozer have effectively reduced the area of true wilderness by half.

The same pressures which are threatening wilderness in this State are destroying wild areas all over the world. Not only does this make the Tasmanian wilderness even more valuable, it also places an additional burden on the Society.

Wilderness protection groups, like everything else on our earth, are interdependent, and the Society assists other organizations when it can. In recognition of its wide wilderness interests, the Society has recently been accepted as the first Tasmanian full member of the International Union for the Conservation of Nature and Natural Resources, the conservation wing of UNESCO and the world's premier conservation body, based in Morges, Switzerland. It is also in touch with the United Nations Environment Programme in New York and the Environmental Liaison Centre in Nairobi. The Tasmanian Wilderness Society has already acted in support of campaigns outside Tasmania to protect wilderness in tropical rainforests, has protested against the Canadian harp seal decimation, and is maintaining a close watch on the gathering Antarctic situation.

All this costs money. Those who would destroy the wilderness have the advantage here. They can throw vast sums into the battle because they reap the profits from the sale of the resource. There are no monetary gains to be made in saving the wilderness and environmental groups must substitute enthusiastic volunteers for hired help. But enthusiasm can only go so far and some money is essential.

The Society would welcome your support. We do not receive any government funds and rely heavily on our membership for revenue. At the moment, our enthusiasm and resources are stretched to the limit — and the problems keep multiplying: Woodchips, Dams, Roads, Urban Encroachment. We'd like to upgrade and increase circulation of the Journal to keep environmentalists up to date with developments here and overseas, but the funds are lacking.

In 1978 the Society launched a major campaign to save the King, Franklin and Lower Gordon Rivers from the imminent threat of damming. Organizations and individuals everywhere are asked to join the campaign. Please send your donations to the Tasmanian Wilderness Society, 102 Bathurst Street, Hobart 7000 (Phone [002] 34 5543). Booklets, posters, cards, car stickers and pamphlets are available.

You are invited to lend your strength to our fight by joining us.

Membership is $10 and this includes subscription to the Journal which is published several times a year. Newsletters keep the lines of communication flowing while regular meetings enable members to co-ordinate their activities and discuss projects and political events. Organizations are invited to join the Society for a fee of $20.

'There is just one hope of repulsing the tyrannical ambition of civilization to conquer every niche on the whole earth. That hope is the organization of spirited people who will fight for the freedom of the wilderness.'

Robert Marshall

STOP PRESS: 20 March 1979

The Tasmanian Government today decided on the South West Advisory Committee Report. The Wilderness Society regards its decision as a compromise on a compromise. Although it decided to extend the Conservation Area to include all the area recommended by the ACF as national park (see map on previous page) and that the NPWS should draw up management plans for this area, it also decided that the Forestry Commission would maintain power over all lands now under its control and that all existing exploitation rights would be upheld.

The government refused to establish an inquiry into forestry, regarded as being 'a matter of urgency' by the Advisory Committee, and refused to set up an independent Authority to determine land-use in the region. Instead, a much weaker South West Tasmania Committee would be established to advise Cabinet when requested.

No definite alterations regarding land-use appear to have been made.

H M Gee

Recreation

3

Bushwalking for sheer enjoyment, independent of any formal objective, brought about a changed attitude toward the South-West. Increase in leisure time, income and education have contributed to the massive upsurge of interest and activity over the past three decades. As material well-being estranges man from the natural environment the wilderness becomes fascinating.

Physical challenge is no longer a condition of life; one must actively seek it. Reliance on one's own strength and skill to climb a mountain, cross a wilderness or an ice field, negotiate an ocean or a river, becomes a rich and intensely personal experience.

Diamond Peak is a rugged quartzite outcrop on the northern end of the Prince of Wales Range. Before the seventies, few had visited this remote area. The range was first traversed in 1966.
Maurice D Clark

Vanishing Falls.   *Jim England*

Reeds Peak and Lake Rhona, Denison Range.
Brown & Dureau

What is Wilderness to Man?

P E Smith

Paul Smith, a forester trained at the Australian National University, has spent much time in the Tasmanian bush and mountains in the course of both work and recreation. His love for the South-West stems from childhood years in Queenstown. Having worked in Papua New Guinea for a year, he is currently working on management planning for the Forestry Commission, Tasmania.

'A wilderness, in contrast with those areas where man and his works dominate the landscape, is an area where the earth and its community of life are untrammelled by man, where man himself is a visitor who does not remain.'

This is the introduction to the definition of wilderness given in the United States Wilderness Act of 1964. This definition provides a useful foundation for an appraisal of the value of wilderness in today's world. However, it lacks a critical specificity on the minimum size of wilderness. With this in mind and quoting from this Act, wilderness is defined here as having the following characteristics:

1. Ideally, it is undeveloped land *'retaining its primeval character and influence, without permanent improvements or human habitation'*. To include wilderness of lower quality in these respects, this statement may be qualified by saying that wilderness is land which: *'generally appears to have been affected primarily by the forces of nature, with the imprint of man's work substantially unnoticeable'*.

This is especially relevant to the work of

modern man. Imprints of natural appearance, such as grasslands developed by the burning practices of extinct aborigines, would be considered 'substantially unnoticeable'.

2. It 'has outstanding opportunities for solitude or a primitive and unconfined type of recreation'. By this is meant that a tract of land does not have the quality of 'wilderness' unless it is a considerable distance, at least half a day's journey, from a road or other commonly used access route such as a navigable river.

3. It is of sufficient size as to make practicable its preservation and use in an unimpaired condition'. This condition includes ecological processes native to the area, such as wildfire and cyclones.

4. It 'may also contain ecological, geological or other features of scientific, educational, scenic or historical value'.[1]

Having described what is meant by wilderness, an attempt must be made to summarize its main benefits—the scientific benefits, aspects of importance to the community as a whole, and benefits to the individual.

The Australian Conservation Foundation stresses the major value of wilderness as a provision for biological conservation. The following is a statement from the A C F 's submission to the Government Inquiry into the South-West in 1976:

'Wilderness areas can be regarded as vast storehouses of genetic materials, such as new strains of crop plants, that may be found to be essential to man's survival in the future. Wilderness constitutes an essential yardstick against which the continued and drastic changes to land in settled areas can be measured, and provides a buffer or safety valve against the long-term disturbance by man of the global eco-system'.[2]

A reverence for nature and a better understanding of ecology are community attributes of growing importance in a world increasingly subject to massive transformation by human activity. The wilderness visitor may gain a new perspective on man and his environment and the relationship between them. The collective insight acquired might well stimulate a more harmonious future relationship with the environment and avoid an over-reliance on technology.

The diversity of our environment is the basis of much human interest and satisfaction. As worldwide communications, trade and industrial growth tend to mix and homogenize the different races, cultures and environments, the retention of many wilderness areas would contribute a fascinating dimension of variety to our total environment.

The intensity of the experience of wilderness can be gauged to some extent by the strong feelings expressed by a growing number of individuals. The knowledge that such wild places exist is of psychological importance to the majority whose enjoyment is vicarious, or whose experience is of the edge of wilderness. Exploration of a truly remote region demands skill and self reliance. There are many uncertainties and surprises—the terrain, the vegetation, the weather, encounters with wildlife, observations of botanical and geological features. Thus the experience is a vital contrast to that of the completely man-made urban environment which increasingly dominates our lives. Escape from all this tends to give an emotional catharsis, revitalizing the individual for a return to the pressures of his daily life.

An essential quality of wilderness for most visitors is solitude, the awe of being alone and small in an environment which is vast and indifferent to one's safety and comfort. The knowledge that one is really on one's own is a powerful tonic and the negative impact of motorboat, off-road vehicle, or aircraft is particularly severe in a wilderness environment. To travel with few aids — on foot, on skis, or in a canoe—moving slowly with little or no sound, allows for intimate sensual contact with the environment. Solitude heightens the appreciation of beauty, harshness, mystery, menace and other subjective interpretations. This facilitation of perception includes a strong awareness of the passage of vast stretches of time—one is surrounded by such evidence as rock formations, fossils, glacial landforms and ancient forests. The sweep and spaciousness of a wilderness in this way inspires a fresh perspective on mankind.

What then is wilderness? A dimension of mystery, wonder, aspiration and delight; a safeguard of life on earth, and a rapidly diminishing resource.

Pack Ponies on the way to the Fields.

Starting out to go up the Valley Rasselas & to the Denison Range

Looking into the Florentine Valley from the Gordon Track near the top of the Divide

Our swags on Board

Four photographs taken along the Gordon Track in the late twenties. The bottom centre photograph shows the timber trolleys that ran from Fitzgerald to Holmes' mill where the walkers, after their ride, rejoined the Gordon Track to the Rasselas. *Ida McAulay*

Right
Geoff Chapman, Doug Anderson and V C Smith. 1930.   *Cecil Murray*

Bottom left
Ida McAulay, in a graphic description of this trip for *Walkabout*, wrote: 'With his shovel, during that trip, Denis washed for gold in every creek we came across, and invariably found either black or ruby tin'. *Ida McAulay*

Bushwalking for sheer enjoyment independent of any formal objective brought about a changed attitude toward the South-West. This is reflected in the quite poetic descriptions written by those who had the time for such subjective experiences and reflections. In the twenties and thirties a strong bond developed between a small group of adventurous Tasmanians. Ida McAulay recorded some of their early trips: for instance she wrote of the time in March 1938 when she and her friends were passengers on board the crayboat *Ronina* to Port Davey, from where they walked some way north along the West Coast.

Below
'Winter and summer the men who owned the ketch catch crayfish and trumpeter round the coast, pitting their caution and skill against the fickleness of the sea and the impersonal cruelty of Nature. They sail one of the most dangerous coasts in the world, and they have a due respect for it.' Herb Mackay, the skipper, bagging crays. 1938.   *Ida McAulay*

On the summit of the peak

Bagging up crays in the Channel.

Bushwalking — Three Viewpoints

I A McAulay
K Lancaster
R Saunders

These three views give some impression of the changing attitude to the South-West over the past half century. During that time the South-West has become increasingly accessible, inviting greater numbers with a new range of equipment. Ida McAulay records a trip in the 1930's, while Keith Lancaster knew the area in the 1940s and 1950s and writes of that era. Bob Saunders was first introduced to the South-West in the 1970s.

Wylds Craig
I McAulay

Wylds Craig attracts the eye because it stands alone, under a triangular peak with deep blue shadows under its cliffs. In 1935 Mac Urquhart, Geoff Chapman, Donnee Travers and I resolved to go to its summit.

The Craig had beckoned us for many years and we had talked of it among our Tasmanian friends at Cambridge. Surveyor Frankland in 1835 was the first white man to see the view from the top:

'With knapsacks weighing eighty pounds', he said, *'we started for the mountain vulgarly called the peak of Teneriffe but originally named Wyld's Craig. From the summit of that lofty eminence I anticipated an extensive view of the country through which the Huon was supposed to run'.*

Whereas Frankland had started from Marlborough, we started near Mt King William the First, on the West Coast road. Having plunged off the shoulder of King William through bauera and pandani we came to the shores of Lake George in the north end of the Valley of the Rasselas. King William with his great crown of cliffs loomed above us blackly and wetly through mists. The Gordon was crossed near its source and we climbed out of the scrubby tea-tree flats up an easy rise. The sun was setting on a wild riotous jumble of delicately blue mountains—tossed and jagged—floating in haze. We saw the Spires with their glistening turrets, the Prince of Wales Range and the peaks of the Denisons. And there was Mt Curly where we knew there was a beautiful lake, with a white beach. We talked of camping there some day. There were hundreds of mountains, so alluring in the evening shadows.

We crossed the Gell, a most dramatic river flowing darkly under the trees, and between their twisted roots and branches. After we had made our camp on the second evening, the clouds ahead quite suddenly rolled apart and there stood the Craig, a delicate rose turned violet, dark blue and then slaty black. The following day the Gordon was crossed again and we made our camp beside two little lakes in a hollow under Wylds Craig. Frankland had bivouacked at the same spot, and similarly waited for

A rest on the Florentine bridge. 1930's.
Cecil Murray

On the Gordon Track. which ran from Fitzgerald to the Florentine River and thence on to Gordonvale.
Ida McAulay

the mists to clear about a hundred years before us.

In less than an hour we were on the pinnacle. 'One step, and the whole country lies stretched at your feet', wrote Frankland as he gazed at the Florentine and a sharp ridge of hills (the Tiger Range) sloping down

'to an extremely clear plain watered by a river, running south-west, and which we afterwards discovered to be the Gordon. This beautiful plain I named the Valley of Rasselas'.

Frankland noted the lofty and rugged nature of the country to the west 'apparently opposing no object to the traveller.'

For our party in 1935 the base of the great cliffs on the southern side of the Craig were hidden in swirling mists; occasionally we saw an isolated peak afloat in a sea of cloud.

On our return we waded the Florentine using strong green poles for support. Mt Misery separated us from Dawsons Road, which had been built in 1830 by convict labour with the idea of connecting up the settlement at Macquarie Harbour with the eastern settled areas. It was never finished. But here Dawsons Road was a well marked sandy cart track sprinkled with native lilac. To us it was a broad highway to Dunrobin Bridge eighteen miles away.

The Call of our Great South-West

K Lancaster

Our great South-West holds a ceaseless appeal to nearly all those who have become familiar with its mystic charm. Each is motivated by some specific attraction which asserts an intrinsic fascination upon him.

When I first visited the South-West in 1946, I am sure that the governing influence was the spirit of adventure. It meant the penetration of what seemed a Terra Incognita where few had gone before. At that stage the nearest road contacts were at Kallista, from which the Port Davey Track started, and just above Upper Huon, from which the Huon Track commenced. The only map of the area for reference was the Mines Department's *South-West Sketch* and it certainly was sketchy, with numerous inaccuracies. There existed also an Army map which splashed the following grim words across the area:

> 'Rugged Uninhabited Country. Valleys and Low Lying Areas Covered with Impenetrable Bauera and Horizontal Scrub, Interspersed with Open Button-Grass'.

However, local mountaineering was just becoming established and the thrill of being the first to scale some unclimbed peak became an irresistible impetus to quite a few. To fulfill these missions, one often had to leave the indistinct lifelines of the Port Davey or Marsdens Track far behind and depend upon one's own ability to keep a full written record of directions, times and altitudes in order to ensure a safe return.

A grievance I have against many bushwalkers of today is that they are out to secure the fullest information concerning the whole proposed route of their trip, preparing a similar record to that provided by a rock-climbers' guide. It may ensure greater safety and perhaps easier planning, but to me it appears to take away much of the aspect of adventure from the undertaking. If you diminish the challenge and your journey becomes just an exercise in accurately following a documented description, it surely is a duller affair and thus places the entire responsibility upon the ultimate goal to provide an outstanding reward.

Here is a region where future generations may still enjoy the same absorbing adventures as those of my generation if wisdom prevails. The unclimbed peaks may no longer be there, or so very few in number, but there still remains much to challenge the keenest. With adventure fields steadily diminishing in other parts of the world, let us not squander the opportunity to preserve a big slice of this area in its natural state for the youth of tomorrow.

Looking towards Shining Mountain from The Spires. *D Pinkard*

Top. left and opposite page Bushwalking in the 1950s. *D Pinkard*

DAY BY DAY

SCENIC ASSETS
Unexplored Territory In Tasmania

EVEN if there were a good track, the route from Port Davey to Fitzgerald would be an adventure for a lone pedestrian—and in many places the former track has disappeared. This route, where a man recently is believed to have perished, passes through some of Tasmania's most rugged and beautiful scenery. Always there will be people who will attempt such a journey; in fact, but for the exploration urge possessed by the British race most of us would not be here at all. Tasmania is unique among lands of the temperate zone in still having unexplored territory to offer the more rugged type of tourist. After the war there is no reason why tracks should not be developed through some of our more inaccessible areas, and advertised as a world-wide attraction, to compare with the remote scenic charms of Norway and the American Rockies. Most walkers nowadays carry tents and sleeping bags, therefore large expenditure on huts would be unnecessary, although no doubt some would be useful. Motor touring roads should be kept away from the walkers' areas; they could be made a separate developmental scheme of their own.

The Mercury, 10 June 1942

THEY TOOK FIVE DAYS TO WALK 20 MILES

CROSSING the Western Arthur Range in the far South-West is considered by many experienced mountaineers to be one of the most difficult climbs in Australia.

Since the first crossing in 1960, seven parties have covered the 20-mile climb over rugged country and dense undergrowth.

Last week, a party of three made the crossing climbing to altitudes over 3,000ft.

It consisted of Mr. Ron Brown, a member of the Legislative Council, his 19-year-old son Chris, and Mr. Geoff Bannitcha, of Hobart.

They spent 11 days in the area and needed five to make the 20-mile crossing. Their travels and the type of country they had to cross are illustrated here.

RON BROWN and his son Chris negotiate "Tilted Chasm" as the party passes through the most difficult part of the route — an area of sheer cliffs, precipitous gullies, and dense vegetation.

LOOKING back to the previous night's camp site, showing the route down a precipitous creek gully from the saddle between Peak H (left) and Conaghan Castle. In the foreground is Lake Arthur, the largest lake on the range, and one of the few named.

RON BROWN (left) and Geoff Bannitcha at an exposed camp site on High Moor. Bad weather kept the party in their tents on this site for some 16 hours. While they were there, High Moor was studded with air-drops for two incoming parties—the Melbourne University Mountaineering Club and the 10th Malvern Rovers. Mr. Bannitcha, one of Tasmania's most experienced mountaineers, has had extensive climbing experience abroad, particularly in the Andes.

A LEAP and Ron Brown gets over a 5ft. wide chasm at the end of "Beggary."

AN unnamed glacial lake set high in the range. Such lakes made good camp sites for the party. Small quartzite beaches added to the appeal, but the cold water did not encourage swimming.

THE spectacular view looking across to the summit of Mt. Hayes. There are more than 30 peaks in the Arthur Range, and 32 lakes, most of which are unnamed.

Bushwalking Today
R E Saunders

Today, bushwalking is the most popular activity in the South-West, with 400 or more people travelling through the area on extended trips each year. Although a reasonable degree of fitness and self-reliance are required for lengthy trips, the ease of access to Melaleuca (30 minutes by light aircraft from Hobart) and Junction Creek (8 kilometres from the Scotts Peak Road) facilitates shorter visits to the area. Since the bulldozing of the 'Yo-Yo' Track, access to the Eastern Arthurs and Federation Peak has been improved (a term despised by many bushwalkers) to such an extent that a walker was able to complete the round trip from the Picton River bridge to Federation Peak and back in 22 hours, in 1973. It is sobering to consider that when first ascended, Moss Ridge, Federation Peak, required three weeks of hard cutting through dense scrub.

On the basis of Bardwell's Pilot Study into wilderness use in the South-West, several bushwalking zones can be determined.[1] The areas most frequently visited are those with tracks or well marked routes: the South Coast, Scotts Peak to Melaleuca in Bathurst Harbour, the Mt Anne circuit, the South Picton Range, the Southern Ranges to Precipitous Bluff, the Western and Eastern Arthurs traverses and French-mans Cap. Prior to its flooding, Lake Pedder was regarded as the heart of the South-West, being both a base camp and meeting ground of immense significance.

Bardwell found that for most bushwalkers, the days and weeks of hard walking, combined with the element of remoteness, provided the challenge. The question of 'development' of the wilderness for recreation, with sealed tourist roads and unsealed access roads received a resounding veto.

In reaction to the growing popularity of bushwalking, many more parties are visiting more remote areas where there are no tracks: South West Cape, The Thumbs—Stepped Hills—Denison Range—Wylds Craig region, the Davey River—West Coast region, the Wilmot—Frankland Range, the King William Range, the Prince of Wales Range and the Mt Curly—Conical Mountain—Spires region. Although there are often recognized routes, the approaches and diversions are individually plotted.

On the mainland of Australia, Kosciusko is the pre-eminent park for recreation, with 54% of its area zoned for wilderness.[2] Very little of this area, however, is significantly remote from a road, a common definition of Wilderness. Much of South-West Tasmania, by contrast, is still roadless, and with the exception of the desert areas of continental Australia, is the most remote area of land remaining. The national significance of the South-West is further exemplified by the usage of Federation Peak. Of the 154 parties visiting the peak in the years 1964 to 1973, 48 were from Victoria, 46 from Tasmania, 40 from New South Wales, 12 from Queensland, 7 from South Australia, and 1 from the Australian Capital Territory. The predominance of Victorian and New South Welsh (as well as Tasmanian) visitors in these figures possibly reflects the accessibility of the South-West (Hobart is one hour by plane from Melbourne), as well as its size and wilderness character.

Launceston Walking Club bus at Catamaran. *Michael Higgins*

Awaiting the plane at Melaleuca Airstrip. *Michael Higgins*

South Cape. *A Moscal*

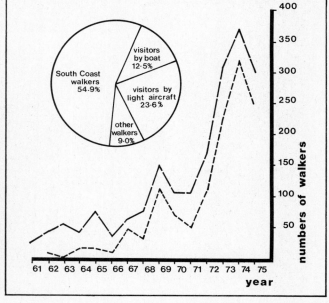

Visitors to Melaleuca. (Graph: Top line: total. Bottom line: via South Coast)

Michael Higgins

Top left
Capricorn, Western Arthurs.   *Michael Higgins*

Top
One of the many lakes and tarns that punctuate a
summer traverse of the Western Arthurs.
Maurice D Clark

Left
The Mercury, 17 December 1971

The South-West kitchen.   *Michael Higgins*

SOUTH WEST GLORY

Traversing the Prince of Wales Range the 'yabbie hole' is often the only source of water. A bushwalker has a drink using his 'yabbie tube', an indispensible item on such a trip.   *Maurice D Clark*

In the hut below Adamsons Peak.   *Bob Graham*

The hut at the Florentine Crossing.   *Michael Higgins*

Pindars Peak seen from the summit of Mt La Perouse.   *Maurice D Clark*

Above
Federation Peak and the surrounding ranges.
Brown & Dureau

Left
A climber on the North-West Face of Federation Peak.
Chris Baxter

Below
Federation Peak from Thwaites Plateau.
Brown & Dureau

Climbing

M S Tillema

Mendelt Tillema graduated in Engineering from the University of Tasmania in 1968. A past president of the Climbers Club of Tasmania, he is a keen rock climber and bushwalker with experience from the European alps, England and Nepal. He has climbed extensively in Tasmania, notably in the South-West at Federation Peak, Frenchmans Cap and in the Western Arthurs.

The reflections of one climber
Federation Peak

'This is the perfect site for a rock climbing centre of the future, where the standard of crag equals many of the finest examples abroad... truly this is edge-of-the-world territory and its ruggedness and beauty, its fierce storms and primordial scrubs and forests are part-and-parcel of the thought.'

These are the words of John Béchervaise who made the first ascent of Federation Peak in 1949. The initial route to the mountain lay over the Picton and South Picton ranges and the ascent of Federation was for a long time regarded as the mark of a hardy bushman, although access has become easier. John Béchervaise was right:— the area has been a focal point of Australian rock climbing since the years of its first ascent.

I first came to Federation Peak with a party from the Climbers Club of Tasmania. At Christmas 1970 we spent a week in tents waiting for the continuous rain to stop. The atmosphere was lyrically described by Reg Williams in an article he later wrote:

'A world of sinuous tree trunks. Contorted alpine myrtle and scoparia writing in the mist and rain of the far South-West. Tiny tents tucked like "Hobbit Holes" amid "Goblin Woods" lifted it seems out of a Tolkein fantasy. However, the spectral beings grouped around that fire in the hollow are not wizards and witches, but scruffy climbers. They huddle beneath a flapping fly-sheet inhaling pine smoke through nostrils and eyeballs. The cauldron they are tending is an airdrop tin; the potion, a two-gallon stew containing among other things a goodly quantity of ash, leaves and similar local fallout. Were this group possessed of unearthly powers, Hughie the Rain God would be there too, turning on a spit, his hide nailed to a convenient tree'.

The weather finally abated and we went off to climb. Mike Douglas and I teamed up and climbed a small section of the standard routes. Then we launched ourselves on the North-West Face. We could see the start of the blade ridge 2,000 feet below, in the valley,

On Wurlitz's Spire near the normal route up the 400 metre face of Federation Peak.   *Reg Williams*

Rain sheathed the rock where once I climbed,
In swirling mist, route undefined.
Scoparia glistened, dewy wet,
As rough my labours upwards yet.
At my feet dark chasms yawned,
Sombre forests, yet undawned,
Here no place for mortal feet,
Grey cold crags and stark defeat!

Bruce Davis

culminating in the massive expanse of the North-West Face, the sharpest face on Federation Peak, the most striking piece of rock architecture in Australia.

'That line on the right, Mike! Can't you see it? It must go!'

The first pitch—delicate face climbing to the large ledge. Mike leads on—up a chimney—stops when it runs out at an overhang.

My lead—I lead diagonally up to the right, the holds getting thinner as I go on. I hang delicately—very delicately, fingernails on quartz crystals. The whole world narrows down to myself and the few immediate and very intimate feet of rock I cling to.

Suddenly the shrill laughter of a girl far below breaks my concentration—I almost lose my balance and have to regain confidence. On I go to the one and only small ledge I can see on this vast area of cliff. I look across to the southern traverse and see that my situation has created great mirth amongst other members of our group who have a great gallery view of the proceedings.

Mike's turn to come across.

I sit and enjoy the second part of climbing—the contemplation in solitude. I quietly absorb the atmosphere while I belay, occasionally humming quietly just for the joy of being there. Looking down is quite an eerie experience as the whole face undercuts below me.

Mike finally joins me and are we in trouble! It's late and the ledge could not be called comfortable by any stretch of the imagination. I can't make the few feet off the ledge and it's too difficult to reverse the last pitch.

Retreat . . . .

Tie the two ropes together. Knock in a few pegs. Throw down the double rope—it should reach.

Down I go. I abseil and find myself swinging free from the face. *Bloody Hell—the rope won't reach the ledge.* I pendulum into the face and perch by my toes on a three inch by three inch ledge.

Mike sends down some cord to lengthen the rope. I tie it on, adjust the abseil and down I go.

I reach a good ledge and let go of the ropes. They disappear. Mike comes down carefully.

'Don't forget to hang on to one end!', I warn.

We both haul on the end praying the rope's tight and not jammed.

Mike cheerfully relays the fears he had when he saw the pitons move as I abseiled down the rope. Sudden leaden feelings in my stomach. One more abseil—straightforward, thank the Lord—and a grateful tramp back to the campsite.

A few days later four of us made camp on a saddle above Béchervaise Plateau. Our intention was to climb the established route up the North-West

Face. Next morning we rose before the sun at an hour before even the birds made their presence heard. There was a gentle tinkling of gear as we prepared some breakfast and sorted our climbing equipment. We stood around and watched with awe the mountains around us rising as islands in a great sea of mist. We watched the sun rise, wine red, and to the south the great walls on Precipitous Bluff glowed red and purple.

The day was born and we scrambled down the gully to the foot of the face. We climbed pitch upon pitch of really enjoyable rock to Bus Stop Ledge. Above this the route goes through a steep overhang via a bottomless diagonal chimney. There is an awkward stance at the base and one has to struggle to stay in the chimney, let alone to gain any height in it. The legend of the first ascent of this route is a tale of incredible hardship. The party was benighted and spent the entire night jammed in the chimney. Next morning the smallest climber stripped off his clothes and chimneyed through a small hole in the back, throwing the rope over the top when he got a good stance. I spent an hour looking at this hole while I was belaying and it's my opinion that passing a camel through the eye of a needle would be simpler than that feat.

The rock on Federation Peak is technically quartzite, but it has an unusually abrasive texture. It is firm and interlaced with pockets of harder quartz. For the climber this means a gift of many routes though they often involve delicate fingernail holds. I have found a great attraction in the size and sharpness of feature of Federation Peak. One can stand on this peak high above the South-West and realise that it is one of the few left in the wilderness from where one can see no sign of man's interference anywhere in the immediate or distant surroundings.

To the north Frenchmans Cap holds an equally revered place in Australian rock climbing and far more routes have been climbed here than on Federation Peak. Mt Anne is well known for its winter climbing in snow and ice conditions. Some climbing has been done on the Western Arthurs, the Needles, the Spires and the Sentinels, but there is vast scope for pioneer rock-climbing on such mountains as the Western Arthurs and Coronation Peak. Last but not least is Precipitous Bluff with a vast area of cliff on which little serious rock climbing has been done. The challenge is immense and the rewards magnificent.

On the North-East corner of Béchervaise Face; a climber 30 feet above his belayer. *Reg Williams*

Bottom right
Climbing The Spires. *D Pinkard*

Opposite page
Frenchmans Cap. *Reg Williams*

SKIING IN THE 1920s and 1930s MOUNT FIELD

Above
'The feet of the skier are cunningly bound
To slide with celerity over the ground
To perform Christianas, to stem and to learn
To execute neatly the Telemark Turn.'
(A L McAulay, 1927) *Ida McAulay*

Above
On Twilight Tarn. *Ida McAulay*

Below left
The title page of a book which was typed, illustrated and hand-bound by keen skiers of the twenties.

Building the Tasmanian Ski Club Hut at Twilight Tarn. 1920's *Ida McAulay*

> The Westerlies batter the trees and roar
> And lash the snow across Kangaroo Moor
> And Windy Moor and Wombat Moor,
> While Newdegate Snowfields mutter and growl
> As gusts sweep over the Tarn and howl
> That Winter is out and upon the prowl;
> And our ghosts awake and return to seek
> The mountains we knew above Bunyip Creek.
>
> from What Happened at the Hut of the Gurgling Hearth.
> A L McAulay, (unpub. McAulay family MS., Tasmania, 1927).

Fun and games with the sledge. *Ida McAulay*

Inside the hut at Twilight Tarn, on the left, and on the right the 'Hut of the Gurgling Hearth', (the Tasmanian Ski Club Hut) having early morning tea on 4th September, 1927, are E Ward, Professor Pitman and A L McAulay. *G T F Chapman*

Skiing

W Hamilton

W J Hamilton, a farmer on Tasman Peninsula, formerly from Ouse, is a skier with a preference for the remoter ski fields. Over a period of forty years he has observed many changes in Tasmanian skiing.

In the Australian Ski Year Book of 1931, Miss Ida McAulay wrote of skiing as it was then in Southern Tasmania:

'The Ski Club of Tasmania knows two kinds of skiing—the day on Mt Wellington and the long weekend or longer trip to the skiing grounds at National Park. The Park gates are forty-eight miles from Hobart, and the journey thither can be made by car or train. There are two distinct skiing centres at National Park. The first is the group of government huts at Lake Fenton. . . . A second centre is the Ski Club hut at Twilight Tarn, about four miles further out. This accommodation hut is very conveniently placed for all the best ski running in the Park. The trip to the Club Hut takes the best part of a day from Hobart, but the return journey can easily be made in half a day . . . . It is usual to take horses from the Park gates to the Fenton Huts, so that the long pull up the six and a half miles of track can be made very easily. From Fenton onwards skiing conditions should prevail. The Ski Hut looks rather like a cottage in one of Grimm's fairy stories. Compact and homelike, and smoothly roofed with white, it shelters under the lee of a wooded hill. The first comers see it at twilight across an unspoilt stretch of snow. The tired stragglers are greeted with a comforting orange glow from the windows. The midnight travellers find it quietly asleep under the moonlight. The members of the Ski Club are greatly attached to their Hut. It is picturesque, convenient, comfortable, and home-like. It is also situated well from the all-important view of skiing. Practically at the door good nursery slopes run into the tarns which, when frozen over and covered with snow, makes an excellent run out for practices. Half a mile away, on the track to the Newdegate Ranges, there are good sheltered slopes with a cleared run where Telemarks can often be practiced when the higher slopes can only offer hard packed snow. These slopes can also be used when blizzard conditions make the higher regions more or less impossible. A rise of a thousand feet takes one to the top of the Newdegate Pass. From

Party near the top of Mt Mawson, 1928.

Tasmanian Museum & Art Gallery

here there are good runs over into Valhalla Valley, or in the other direction to what is known as the Tarn Shelf— a sort of terrace strung with tarns which are often frozen and snow-covered. Day expeditions with good long runs can be made to the top of Mt Field West, Florentine Peak, or down into the Hayes Valley. Considerable variation in snow conditions can be found in a single day.

The scenery for the most part is on a grand scale. There are magnificent views westward from Mt Field West, the top of the Newdegate Pass, and from another mountain known to the Ski Club as the Watcher, whence range upon range of snow-tipped mountains can be seen extending ever westwards towards the coast. The country has been carved by glacial action into large, sudden and unexpected shapes. Such scenery adds to the joy of skiing.

The best time is perhaps in the evening, when from somewhere out on the mountains the homing run is begun. It is practically all downhill. The skis by this time seem to have come alive. They make a skittering noise over the frozen snow. A few glorious sweeps interspersed with gentler slopes, and easy switchback

runs, a little track running, and then out on to the top of the nursery slope, and the Hut seen at twilight across the tarn.

In a normal winter, such is the skiing enjoyed by the members of the Ski Club of Tasmania in their long weekends and the August vacation'.

Forty-five winters later ... the hut at Twilight Tarn is still there; more rustic and with far more character than could possibly be built into any modern ski-lodge. It is visited occasionally by small groups who stay a night or two to relive the past. The slopes are still there; Valhalla Valley, Newdegate Pass, Cider Gum Hill, the superb sweeping descent from the top of the Watcher ... down through the Enchanted Forest towards Lake Hayes, and the great variety of slopes both on the eastern and western sides of the Rodway Range. Many of the slopes remain unmarked winter after winter, although the skiing population is increasing rapidly every year.

Modern downhill skiing equipment demands that the skier be transported uphill. Ski queues are as much a part of skiing as the packed-down slopes that make techniques so much easier to master. Leg muscles once accustomed to long hours of climbing no longer have to tolerate this work load just for a few thrilling runs. Technique and style have improved, but ski-lifts are fixtures and skiers have become centralized on the mountain.

Driven away from these crowded slopes, an ever increasing band of cross-country skiers discovers the beauty of the mountains under winter conditions. Lightweight langlauf skis permit the skier to travel long distances on a good winter's day. If the season is a good one, vast areas of snow country beckon.

Early ski pioneers of the thirties and forties sampled the magnificence of many snow covered ranges. These included the Hartz Mountains, the Snowy Range, Mt King William, Cradle Mountain to Lake St Clair, the circuit of Mt Rufus from the Lyell Highway along the Hugels down to Lake St Clair, and latterly, trips into the Du Cane Range and the Labyrinth, north of Lake St Clair.

Hardy skiers who have carried their skis from Condominium Creek up the climbing ridge to Mt Eliza and skied the plateau towards Mt Anne claim that this area is enjoyable both for its terrain and the expanse of touring country. The Memorial Hut, built in 1973 as a tribute to Agnete Damgaard, Olegas Truchanas and John Plaister, provides a high altitude base.

Anyone skiing in these remote mountains must be experienced, perfectly equipped, and familiar with the area from summer walks. The mountains are not always kind in the summer; in winter they can test the hardiest mountaineer. With this knowledge an increasing number of keen Tasmanians are heading to the mountains on combined ski and snow-climbing expeditions often inspired by experiences in the New Zealand Alps. Snowfalls vary from year to year and it is true to say that there are relatively few weeks when Tasmania experiences ideal skiing conditions, and fewer when gullies are icy enough for crampons. None-the-less, enthusiasm prevails.

'Big fire camp' in the Styx Valley, August, 1928.
G T F Chapman

Lake Newdegate in mist, Tarn Shelf, 1976.
Helen Gee

Hut at Twilight Tarn 'forty-five winters later'.
Helen Gee

Two Worlds

By IDA McAULAY

Ski-ing, as I first knew it, seemed to me an Olympian pastime with a spirit all its own. It took me into a world of mists and mountains, of great endeavour and beauty, a world of snow stained unimaginable hues by the setting of the sun, or flashing with crystals in the unearthly light of the moon—a world of blizzard-driven snow and terrifying wind, of wonder and fear, of struggle with the elements, painful climbs and rare, swooping runs—a world inhabited by heroes and heroines who were my friends.

Then something made me take to racing and I entered another world—a world bounded by flags, where time and space were measured, not by hunger and fatigue and the rising and setting of the sun and moon, but cut into intervals by stop watches and aneroids—a world regulated by committees and meetings and speeches, where the spirit of competition supplanted the spirit of ski-ing. The Gods were no longer the Gods of Valhalla, but those of skill and technique. It was a world of waxes, bindings and steel edges, of team badges and coloured shirts, where the noble fears had vanished in favour of the more petty ones of disgracing one's side or making a fool of one's self. The people who inhabited this world were more clever and more skilful in their ski-ing, more industrious on their practice slopes, more beery and cheery and sportsmanlike than the romantics of the mists, but there was less among them, so it seemed to me, of real mountaincraft and friendship. The gaze of the racer never lifted from his course. He had lost the gifts of discovery and joy.

It was like coming from the Home of the Gods to play hop-scotch at a school.

From the Tasmanian Section of the Australian & New Zealand Ski Year Book, 1938.

High Camp Memorial Hut.   *Bob Graham*

The commemorative plaque.   *Michael Higgins*

DOWN HILL SKIING AT MOUNT FIELD IN THE 1960s and 1970s

All of these photographs are by Fred Koolhoff

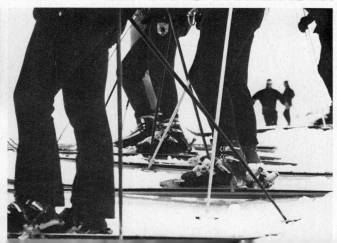

Glow-worm threads in a cave on the Lower Gordon.
G Middleton

Top left
Stalagmites and stalactites in Fraser Cave.   *Kevin Kiernan*

Top right
Rimstone or gours formation in Fraser Cave on the lower Franklin River. This cave was named in 1977 after the Australian Prime Minister.   *Kevin Kiernan*

Left
Cave formation near the Colonnades, Exit Cave.
Lloyd Robinson

Opposite page.
Main streamway, Exit Cave.

A dry streamway, Entrance Cave.   *Greg Hodge*

Caving

K Kiernan

Kevin Kiernan has been an active member of the Southern Caving Society for many years. He is a speleologist and conservationist of considerable repute and author of many articles on caves and their conservation. Kevin has a special interest in the caves of the South-West, notably those of the Franklin and lower Gordon. He was founding Director of the Tasmanian Wilderness Society.

In 1821 what was probably the first limestone quarry in Australia was opened. From the Sarah Island penal station in Macquarie Harbour, convict labour travelled daily several miles up the Gordon River to procure the dark, hard stone for the production of agricultural lime, elsewhere derived from the burning of shells. Their impact on the landscape was small, their quarry site now indistinguishable. Today the deposit they quarried, part of the extensive tracts of limestone in South-West Tasmania, is of great interest to speleologists throughout Australia.

It was on the periphery of the South-West that Tasmania's first discoveries of limestone caves were made. In remote areas, early explorers and timber cutters located imposing cave entrances but it was usually beyond their limited means to explore them to any extent. In 1881 a party of four, including Henry Judd, discovered a cave in the Cracroft Valley and reported enthusiastically of the 400 yards of passage explored. By the 1890's forestry workers in the Ida Bay area had explored a cave associated with Mystery Creek's disappearance underground. The stream reappears on the southern side of Marble Hill over a kilometre away. Deep water at the entrance appears to have prevented these first explorers from realising the massive size of Exit Cave. Near Fitzgerald, the Junee Cave, source of the Junee River, possibly the largest underground stream in Australia, was discovered around the same time; while a major stream-sink in the Florentine Valley, known today as Growling Swallet, was also discovered quite early. In the early 1900's forestry workers in the Hastings area discovered Newdegate Cave, which was developed for tourism in the 1930's and today attracts over 22,000 visitors each year.

When Australia's first cave investigation group was formed in Hobart in the mid 1940's deeper probing of caves in the South-West was undertaken. A large rockfall blockage halted penetration of Exit Cave after 800 metres of wide passage. By the late 1950's Growling Swallet had been descended to a depth of 150 metres, making it the deepest known cave in Australia, and in 1959 it was bottomed at 170 metres. The mid

1960's saw a great increase in activity with the location of a route through the Exit rockfall. Soon the known length of passage in this cave had extended to 6 km, and a few months later to 8 km. Today Exit Cave with its spectacular glow-worm display is easily the longest known cave in Australia with over 19 km of known passage and probably more awaiting discovery. Furthermore, the location of Mini-Martin, a second entrance higher on Marble Hill, gave the system a total vertical range of 219 metres, an Australian depth record. This was to stand from 1967 until the bottoming of 243 metres deep Tassy Pot in the Florentine Valley in 1970. In the early 1970's interest in the source of the Junee River led to the exploration of a number

of very deep caves. The exciting streamways and cascades of one of these, Khazad-Dûm, were explored first to a depth of 255 metres, and later 295 metres during an horrendous 21 hour epic descent which ended with a half-drowned caver being hauled to safety after an abortive attempt to descend the fierce final waterfall. Khazad-Dûm was apparently bottomed at 320 metres some months later and via a dry bypass of the lower waterfalls. Today eight of the nine deepest known caves in Australia are in these two areas, the odd one out being Kellar Cellar at Mt Anne with its stupendous 128 metre entrance pitch, the longest single natural shaft in Australia.

However, knowledge of the caves in more remote areas is scant, for interest

in exploration as a form of recreation is a comparatively recent phenomenon. The early 1960's saw a few epic pioneering jaunts: by tiger moth floatplane to Precipitous Bluff and by small boat to the caves of the Gordon and Franklin Rivers. But these were of such a preliminary nature that they served only to extend our appreciation of the potential of these areas. So today the South-West is seen by speleologists from throughout Australia as offering an opportunity for real cave exploration, something no longer available on the mainland.

The most extensive caves are developed within the Gordon Limestone which includes those at Tyenna—Florentine and at Ida Bay. In 1972 a major expedition of speleologists from all over Australia and from New Zealand visited Precipitous Bluff. The party explored and mapped two caves for over a kilometre without reaching the end of one of them, and discovered several others and undertook some studies of cave fauna, collecting invertebrate species new to science.

Shortly afterwards speleologists first penetrated to Vanishing Falls, north-east of Precipitous Bluff where the Salisbury River disappears underground from a deep pool at the foot of a 60 metre waterfall, to re-emerge two kilometres away. No caves have yet been discovered in this end of the limestone outcrop although the potential is there.

To the north the Cracroft Valley has seen some investigation. Following the re-discovery of Judds Cavern some years ago exploration penetrated over 2 kilometres of passage in this cave and it was established that the cave stream originates near the head of Farmhouse Creek in the Picton Valley.

Numerous outcrops of limestone occur in the basin of the Gordon River from which the formation derives its name. North of Adamsfield limestone occurs in parts of the Vale of Rasselas and, while the local relief of the limestone is probably insufficient to offer much potential for major caves, the reported presence of natural arches and other karst features offers some promise. Further downstream limestone has been reported near the northern shoreline of Lake Gordon although its potential is not known. Limestone occurs in the valley of the Orange River near the Gordon Splits, and, downstream, caves adjacent to the Nicholls Range include at least one with over 500 metres of passageways.

A massive belt of limestone extends through part of the Gordon—Franklin river systems and as far as the Davey River to the south. During the mid 1970's parties from Sydney and Tasmania undertook some investigation of this area using jetboats, canoes and rubber boats. Caves were discovered and the area is thought to have great potential. Caves also exist in the Butler Island

The entrance to Judds Cavern.
Chris Rathbone

Opposite page
Bingham Arch on the lower Franklin River. Named in 1976 after the Leader of the Opposition in the Tasmanian House of Assembly. *John Best*

Entrance to an unnamed cave on the Franklin River. *Kevin Kiernan* area and along the section of river known as Limekiln Reach. Small caves are also known in limestone deposits at the Nelson River, in the Jukes—Darwin area and at Bubs Hill. In the Forest Hills south of Federation Peak a number of streams disappear into a huge and seemingly inaccessible sinkhole, but no caves have yet been explored in this locality. Less significant outcrops of Gordon Limestone occur in other parts of the South-West but the low relief the limestone attains above the local water table holds little promise of significant caves.

The Precambrian dolomite deposits of the South-West have not yet revealed caves of the magnitude of those occuring in the Gordon Limestone, as this rock appears generally more siliceous and resistant to erosion. Undoubtedly the best known dolomite caves are at Hastings. These have been developed for tourists, but other major caves are known at Mt Ronald Cross and Mt Anne. The Mt Anne outcrop probably represents the greatest local relief of any karstic rock attained anywhere in Australia (and therefore theoretically at least the greatest potential for deep caves). Snow probably rests at the bottom of the deepest shafts for much of the year. The highest shafts on the mountain, however, have been infilled with rock debris as a result of frost wedging and splitting apart rock at the entrances. The Mt Ronald Cross area is also regarded as having great promise. Other dolomite caves occur in the Weld River Valley, at Tim Shea, Scotts Peak, the Jane River and the Cheyne Range.

South-West Tasmania is truly a cavers paradise. Potential for further discoveries has been largely exhausted on the mainland where even the legendary Nullarbor Plain has given up many of its secrets. The South-West offers caving in a wilderness setting, with the challenge of real exploration both in the bush and underground, and it is this which encourages speleologists from far and wide to visit the area in increasing numbers each summer.

The Wild Rivers

H M Gee

'From the foot of the bluff, great forests stretched away almost unbroken to the shiny waters of the west coast, covering a large area of virtually uncharted country, including the lower course of the Gordon, the region of the Deception and D'Aguilar Ranges, the valleys of the Maxwell and Franklin rivers and northward towards Frenchmans Cap. Isolated plains stood out close behind the western slope of the Prince of Wales and across towards Mt Elliot and the Jane River. To the south, between the Prince of Wales and the Hamilton, the Denison passes through a deep gorge as it swings away to join the Gordon many miles west....'
(Chris Binks, "The North Gordon Country", *Skyline* No. 5, October, 1954.)

The largest river system in Tasmania is the Gordon River with its major tributaries, the Franklin, the Denison, the Jane and their tributaries in turn. The stumps of Huon pine along their banks record the extent of the journeys made upstream by those hardy explorers, the piners. In more recent years extended river expeditions (whether by canoe, raft, rubber-dinghy or lilo) have been motivated differently. Such recreation is a response to the character of the spectacular gorges, the fast flowing waters, the rapids and eddies and the surrounding wild country through which these rivers flow. Increased leisure time has brought about this new perspective. With the availability of a new range of equipment, including contour maps and aerial photographs, a new generation emerged with a philosophy of its own.

In 1958 John Hawkins and John Dean canoed the Franklin River, and in the same year Olegas Truchanas canoed the Gordon from Lake Pedder to Strahan. These pioneers were inspired by the character of the wild rivers, returning with tales of the splendour of deep, furious gorges. The following accounts of their journeys reflect the strongly individual approach of each.

Opposite page
The exit from Glen Calder, the lowest gorge on the Franklin River.   *Bob Brown*

Right
Entrance to the Second Split. Gordon River.
Mike Emery

The Franklin saga (1951–1958)

Hawkins and Dean first attempted to canoe the Franklin in 1951, and recalling their 500 pounds of food and equipment, Dean said:

> 'We were pioneering ... great big heavy canoes like that... Future canoeists will no doubt smile at our heavy handed attempts, but perhaps they will never experience the exhilaration of conquering dangerous and largely unknown rivers'.

John Dean, John Hawkins, Jeff Weston and Joe Scarlett knew there was no habitation along the 125 mile route to Strahan from the Lyell Highway. On exploration flights they had glimpsed plunging waterfalls and rapids deep in terrific gorges to which they would be committed.

A dramatic account of their canoe saga that entailed three separate expeditions was published in *Australian Outdoors* in July 1959. John Hawkins outlined the logistics of their pioneer 1951 venture:

> 'Our two army disposal collapsible kayaks were the type of craft used in wartime to land agents from boats or subs .... Each could take up to 500 pounds of food and gear;.... We took a .303, two .22's and one shotgun to shoot for the pot, about 200 yards of rope for climbing, three extra paddles and an inflatable Mae West life jacket each...
>
> The river was in semi-flood, with a churned current raging and whirling. The canoes raced swiftly down-river through the rapids...
>
> We were confronted by the terrific sight of a gorge whose rocky walls rose hundreds of feet into the sky.... The tremendous force of the current swept the canoe down-river between the rocky walls of the gorge. Suddenly we saw we were heading straight for a jutting rock in midstream! ...We hit it; the bows lifted six feet vertically and the canoe sank by the stern'.

Hawkins and Dean were swept down-river away from their two companions and through the gorge—the canoe was torn from them and the nightmare that ensued may well be imagined:

> 'I could just see things going past me ... the walls of the gorge, jutting rocks, boulders... I was going straight for a rock... I was going to hit it...then I was past it and another rock loomed up... for a split second I clung to it like a spider, then I was swept downstream again... I must have lost consciousness'.

Meanwhile Dean had been hurled against the foot of a cliff:

> 'I was forced to climb 1,000 feet up a cliff and over a quartz peak. It was then that I was able to see how big and fierce the gorge really was.... In response to frenzied calls, I heard a faint reply... Hawkins had recovered in time to make a feeble effort to haul himself onto a rock just above water level'.

With the canoe plastered against the cliff face there was no hope of continuing and the foursome walked for eighteen hours back to the Lyell Highway.

> 'Six years passed.... In the back of our minds there was always the Franklin trip... We knew we'd have to give it another go.'

In January 1958 Hawkins and Dean were back in the Collingwood river, a tributary of the Franklin. This time their companions were Henry Crocker and Trevor Newland. The two canoes were fibreglass and each was equipped for the entire party. But disaster struck again...

> 'We jammed one canoe under a 15ft waterfall and there the craft was broken in halves. It took us two days to rescue it and the gear, and for our second expedition to be abandoned'.

December 1958

After months of elaborate preparations, Hawkins and Dean, Crocker and Newland were off for a third attempt and they now had three canoes loaded with such items as a portable radio transceiver, smoke bombs, markers to stain the water, gelignite, and specially made boots with rope soles. They also took 100 yards of rope, machetes, an automatic rifle, a primus and a movie camera. Hawkins and Dean started the trip in one canoe and were to meet Crocker and Newland at the H E C hut some days' journey downstream. They tackled the river cautiously. It was in semi-flood and they nearly lost the canoe in a log jam at the very start. A two feet square section was painstakingly repaired with plywood and fibreglass.

> 'Then we were off; and around the next corner... we were right in the gorge. Rocky walls rose high above us. The river was a roaring torrent, a boiling cauldron of savage rapids.

The banks became so steep and difficult at one particular point it took us over one hour to portage canoe and gear over a distance of 75 yards... Weary, cold and wet we camped in a stand of Huon pines as darkness fell.'

The following day was perhaps the climax of the drama for Hawkins and Dean—they went through the Franklin Upper Gorge *backwards!* The force of the current swept them from the slippery rocks and all they could do was to keep the bows pointing upstream. They were terrifyingly powerless:

'... we raced over waterfalls in sickening swagers, burrowing stern first at the foot of each fall. I was in the cockpit and remember seeing Dean rise several feet before me as we lunged over each fall in turn. Then the canoe stood almost vertical and I was engulfed in icy waves of water... we must have been travelling about 20 mph'.

"A water filled canoe is as hard to balance as a log," Dean remarked, *"but we did make the bank".*

'It felt incredible to be still alive and we were hysterical with joy as we lit a fire to thaw out and have a meal by'.

Hawkins recalls the trip down to the HEC hut that same day:

'We travelled in an eerie half light in the narrow winding gorges, with mists billowing in the gusts of rain, the rocky sides streaked with cascading streams, and the river itself dark and swollen, swinging our faithful canoe from side to side in its coiling whirlpool surface...'.

At the hut they met Newland and Crocker and after repairing the radio and packing air drop supplies the foursome were off once again. The Franklin drops sharply through dense rainforest-clad gorges toward Deception Gorge. The party regarded this as the main obstacle of the trip, advancing perhaps four miles a day and spending hours lining and portaging. Once Dean was jammed upside down in a narrow gap; once the canoe sank and was swept away leaving him clinging to a partly submerged rock!

'Deception Gorge... It's no longer than six miles, but it took us all of six days and the loss of one canoe to get through it. In places sheer cliffs rose 2,000 feet on each side of a wild dangerous river... like a giant stairway; the waterfalls and rapids dropping 300 feet through the depths of the gorge.'

Once below Deception Gorge, the rest of the trip was relatively easy and they eventually reached the Lower Gordon and met with the launch which carries tourists from Strahan:

'The tourists stared at us incredulously, as bearded and ragged we paddled alongside the launch.... With our battered canoes in tow we crossed Macquarie Harbour to Strahan. Behind us lay a wild river, five weeks of rough canoeing, three

HE GORDON RIVER
Exploration of "The Splits"
The Show Place of Tasmania'
ent Falls Alone Worth the Trip

("Mercury" Special.)

With the return of Messrs. J. Hadmar Sticht and G. W. rrison, who some five weeks ago left on a prospecting tour the Gordon River, has come reliable information regarding t section of the river formerly known as "The Gorge," but ich has now been appropriately named "The Splits."

The portion of the waterway referred to is that which for ny years was believed to flow through a huge tunnel in the untain. The rocky slopes rise precipitously on either side hundreds of feet, and viewed from down stream present appearance of the river flowing through an underground ssage.

This conception was disproved some years ago, when ssrs. C. Abel and C. Doherty, who were able to get within hort distance of the spot, discovered that such was not the e.

rs. Sticht and Harrison, accompa by Mr. C. Abel, owing to excep favourable conditions, succeed- heir arduous and extremely haz- task of making a complete exam- of this remarkable section of the They have been where no other as been. They found the water river lower than it has ever been to be, due to the abnormally long y summer, and this facilitated progress.

er to accomplish their task they scale cliffs, crawl round narrow wade through swirling water, ver rock faces of every conceiv- pe and polished as smooth as risk the possibility of the river preventing their return. But adventurous trio "the gains were m worth the pains," and they delighted with the result of their pedition. Fortunately, except bruises and scratches they re- ne the worse for their strenuous taking. They were most for- having fine weather, and after the last hut in the Gordon, slept ound each night. A tiny clear- the forest, a camp fire, a bundle for a pillow, ferns or leaves the ground, with the foliage pine, myrtle, or man fern, con- their nightly shelter.

ers. Sticht and Harrison, who out on the big cattle stations nacoyne River country, this was ntly, neither was it to their mpanion, Abel, although the of the two countries is as wide- ed as the poles. The one, flat clothed with salt bush and peppermint, the other wild and covered with dense vege-

nected by three chambers, and is most striking, being overhung by the cliff. The water is very deep. The second is covered with huge rocks and whirlpools. It is not possible to get into either of these basins except by means of ropes. These splits resemble the Swiss Kamms. In time to come they will be visited by thousands of people annually."

ABEL GORGE

The Abel Gorge is another split. Mr. Sticht said. The cliffs are about 350ft. high, but are not so overhanging. It is about 1½ miles above the first split. The river bed rises about 50ft. in that distance. To get to this a track had to be cut over the Wilmot Range, through a dense forest of horizontal and baura. The eastern side of the mountain is terraced with small cliffs from 10 to 20ft. high. The baura was so thick and tall that they were negotiated by sliding down on the branches. The horizontal was literally matted together. "We had to either walk over the top," he remarked, "and this we did in some places for good distance, or crawl along on the ground. Horizontal and baura were bad both in the gullies and on the top of the range."

"Looking north-east from the top of the Wilmot Range, near the Gordon River, towards Mount Robert, the view was wonderfully striking. There are dense forests down to the water's side, the river winds through like a silver ribbon, and the foliage is typical of the West Coast, with the exception of some huge stringy barks growing on some of the slopes, and Mount Robert 3,000ft. high towering overhead. It is a wonderful show place. The grandeur of it derful show place. The grandeur of it derful surpassing that of the lower

Canoeist's Epic Voyage Through Wild South-West

THE first man to paddle down the Serpentine and Gordon rivers from Lake Pedder to Strahan returned to Hobart last night — tired, but safe.

He is Olegas Truchanas, a new Australian who has been in Australia seven years.

Three weeks ago he set out from Lake Pedder alone, with a collapsible canoe and an iron determination.

Three years ago he lost a similar canoe and all his equipment in his first attempt at the trip through some of the wildest country in Australia.

But this trip, through rocky gorges with portages across mountains, was almost incident-free.

The worst part of the trip was one of two capsizes in the Gordon.

Mr. Truchanas said last night: "When the canoe overturned everything was wet, even my matches.

"I walked around for half the night, over the rocks and through the bush, then climbed into my wet sleeping bag."

Mr. Truchanas shot at least 100 rapids and waterfalls on the Gordon, and he had to lower the canoe down 30 or 40 of them on a rope.

"The others I just simply shot through," he said.

At 1 p.m. on Saturday he sailed into Strahan Harbour

before the wind with a groundsheet rigged on sticks. His wife was there to meet him in a car.

Thick Jungle

Mr. Truchanas told a story of fast white water, and overhanging jungle.

During his three weeks alone on the lonely rivers he passed through impenetrable forest and overhanging jungle that hides the rivers from the air.

His canoe wound through button grass plains, and raced down foaming rapids.

Four times he took the canoe to pieces, folded the aluminium struts and canvas into his pack — an hour's work — and carted his gear over mountains and up jagged rocks.

The overall weight of his craft, including an aluminium paddle, was 50lb.

Inflated rubber mats and pillows were placed in the canoe to give it buoyancy.

At the junction of the two rivers he carried the canoe past a gorge with walls 3,000ft. high.

Several times he by-passed cracks where the river

flowed through rock — "Gordon Splits."

"They're not gorges," Mr. Truchanas said. "The river didn't wear through the rock; the rock has cracked apart."

He said the splits were sometimes only 15ft. wide and the vertical walls were hundreds of feet high.

Flood level was often 100ft. overhead.

After 20 days on and near the river Mr Truchanas stopped at an H.E.C. camp near the mouth of the Gordon and radioed to his wife: "All safe."

While traversing the Wilmot Range, Mr. Truchanas recovered the 14-day food supply he had previously dropped by plane high up on the range, near the junction of the two rivers.

He said last night that the seven men at the Hydro-Electric Commission camp shook their heads when they saw him and said they wouldn't try it.

Mr. Truchanas' frail looking canoe is only 11ft. long, and looks like a Kayak. But it is very strong and can be dropped many feet without damage.

It was not holed on the trip.

The Mercury, 10 February 1958

Left
This report, published in *The Mercury,* 12 April 1928 inspired Truchanas, who journeyed down the Gordon to Strahan in 1958.   *The Mercury*

OPPOSITE PAGE

Top
Negotiating the last rapid in Deception Gorge (Great Ravine) are Trevor Newland and Henry Crocker on the third and successful trip down the Franklin in 1958.
John Dean

Bottom
Shooting the rapids below Fincham Hut.   *John Dean*

expeditions and almost ten years of planning. But all the toil, the hardship and the narrow escapes were forgotten in that exquisite feeling of accomplishment'.

Extracts from: 'Canoe Saga', *Australian Outdoors* (July, August 1959). by Dr John Hawkins as told to Harry Frauca.

Lake Pedder to Strahan 1958

An extract from the diaries and notes of Olegas Truchanas.

'The first attempt to canoe Lake Pedder to Strahan route was made in December 1956.

The specially designed and built dismantlable Kayak (11 ft long aluminium and canvas) was flown to Lake Pedder....

Three days later, following torrential rain during the night, in an attempt to reach the Gordon ahead of a major flood, the Kayak and much equipment was lost on the top of a large waterfall in the Serpentine River, some 300 yards before the junction. The capsized Kayak was wrapped around a large rock in midstream, on top of a 20 foot fall making it impossible to reach or free it.

A pack containing the sleeping bag, tent, camera, films, a book (The Worst Journey in the World by Cherry - Garrard) were saved. Amongst the items lost—trousers. Henceforth it has been possible to use the parka, pushing legs through the sleeves and tying around the waist with a piece of string. It is very necessary to take care of one's legs in these parts....

The way back to Pedder was taken along a ridge of the Detached Peak, avoiding the low scrubby country....

By some coincidence a plane piloted by Mr Lloyd Jones visited the beach and a quick flight to Hobart put an end to the tragi-comic situation.'

Truchanas' second and this time successful attempt to reach Strahan from Pedder commenced December 1958:

'Again heavy rain set in, making the passage through the main Serpentine gorge extremely difficult. Kayak had to be dismantled for the major portage and assembled again close to the junction of the two rivers.

Its design and construction was much improved following the 1956 experience and it has remained the same since, for subsequent journeys.

The journey down the Gordon proceeded without mishaps although several capsizes occurred when large rapids were attempted in midstream to avoid portaging.

Large rapids and 3 waterfalls immediately downstream from the junction presented no difficulties,

EPIC CANOE JOURNEY | **Talks**

A HOBART canoeist yesterday completed a rugged three-week journey down the Huon River from near Lake Pedder to Huonville.

He is Lithuanian born Mr. Olegas Truchanas (38), who is believed to be the first to make this journey down the Huon.

Two years ago he made a canoe journey from Lake Pedder to Strahan.

Mr. Truchanas and the canoe he designed were flown to Lake Pedder by Mr. Peter Tanner, of the Aero Club of Southern Tasmania.

They followed the course of the Huon, dropping two thirds of the food supply by the Arthur Ranges.

At Scotts Peak, the nearest point on the river to Lake Pedder, he dropped the canvas covering the canoe, more food and ropes. Mr. Truchanas carried the framework of the canoe to the Huon River.

About five miles after the start the river dropped 300ft. in a little over a mile.

Falls of rapids up to 20ft high were encountered.

In places the river was only three feet wide, with steep cliffs on each side.

Some of the rapids were negotiated by letting the canoe down on a long rope, but at other points the canoe and gear had to be carried around the falls.

On the twelfth day of the trip the canoe was swept away by swirling water, hit a log and capsized.

In the fairly deep water Mr. Truchanas righted the craft with difficulty.

All his gear was saturated.

When he reached Huonville Bridge yesterday, he was greeted by his wife, who is a keen bushwalker, and his infant daughter.

● Mr. Truchanas is pictured at the end of his adventure.

*The Mercury
1 January 1961*

although one of them required a more laborious portage over huge boulders and a passage through a large tunnel-like hole under the rocks.

Comfortable camp was established and much scrambling with the camera on the surrounding cliffs done. An airdrop, this time on the top of a high hill overlooking the junction on the left side of both rivers, was collected and brought down into the

gorge. On the way a spectacular vertical waterfall was visited.

Further downstream, below the main gorge and some more open country yet another small rocky gorge was negotiated just up from the Albert River junction where Gordon makes a prominent loop. It appeared reasonable to regard it as a Third Split, additional to the other two splits further down—already known and explored.

The rocky summits of the scrubby hills on the left bank of the Gordon were climbed to photograph the split from above, to see if there was enough clear ground to use these in future for airdrops and to test the theory that Messrs Harrison, Sticht and Abel must have climbed these hills in 1928 mistaking them for the Wilmot Range. Did they mistake Albert River for the Serpentine? Could one possibly see Lake Pedder from these summits as they claimed? The answer: They could not.

There is a long stretch of relatively calm, deep water to be traversed until the Second (upper) Split is reached. Due to abnormally high water the Kayak had to be dismantled once again to portage it around the major obstacles—steep blade-like buttresses of polished rock forming narrow channels containing

TODAY'S WEATHER
STATE: Showers about the North Coast. Hobart: Fine, warm. Max, 78 deg. Sunrise, 5.49 am. Sunset, 8.50 pm. Map — Page 19.

22 pages.   5 cents.   117th Year. No 31,200   HOBART: THURSDAY, JANUARY

Adventure in the wilds

Epic hike, raft trip

By Chris Lewis

TWO parties of young men came out of the wilds of Tasmania's rugged South-West yesterday at the end of history-making journeys.

Four Hobart men cheated death on their two 18ft rafts, and completed a hair-raising 90 - mile trip down the Franklin and Gordon Rivers.

And three young men, their shirts hanging off their backs, finally made it to Catamaran on the South Coast, after walking around the South - West Coast from Cape Sorell at Macquarie Harbour.

Ate snakes

On the 19-day raft trip down the Franklin River, David Hansen (25), Tim Downie (24), Fred Koolhof (22), and John Morley (22), all of Hobart, wrecked their rafts on waterfalls, were swept down rapids, and ate snakes when their food ran out.

When the pleasure cruiser Denison Star picked them up in the Gordon River on Tuesday afternoon it was a dream come true.

On Christmas Day they left the Collingwood River bridge at the Lyell Highway, 20 miles west of Derwent Bridge, to raft down the Collingwood River, into the Franklin, and to the end of the trip in the Gordon River.

One of the three rafts crashed on the third day of the trip, and the other two were later wrecked on the big waterfalls, including one 70ft drop in the Franklin River, which runs for miles on end between 2,000ft sheer cliffs,.

Boiling rapids

Downie and Koolhof once survived being swept off their rafts in boiling rapids, and in another incident one raft was swept away at night in a flash flood.

The four men took 25 tractor tubes to support the rafts on the trip, and when they reached the Gordon River, they had four battered tubes left.

"A couple of times we thought it was the end — but we managed to keep going — how I don't know," Hansen said.

"Imagine going over a 70ft waterfall with the crew hanging on for grim death.

"But that was the Franklin River—a once-in-a-lifetime experience."

The walkers who made it to Catamaran were Bill Kinnear (20), of Gowrie Park, Dick Ashby (24), of Latrobe, and Ian Cameron (20), of Launceston.

25-day trek

They covered 500 miles in their 25-day trek along the edge of the Indian Ocean.

In a straight line the distance is not quite 150 miles, but their round-about route took them up gorges, across rivers and through bays.

Consume PRICE FOOL

● TOP: The raft trip down the rugged Franklin River over, David "Doc" Hansen (left), Tim Downie, and John Morley (front), joke about shooting rapids, and skating down waterfalls. The remaining tractor tubes, one paddle and the clothes and lifejackets they stood up in was all that survived.

● BOTTOM: Those never - say - die walkers, Bill Kinnear (left) and Dick Ashby, relive on a map their trek from Cape Sorell to Catamaran.

They climbed rock faces, and even had to swim across open sea in difficult sections.

waterfalls. Several days were spent exploring the two Splits and the surrounding country: evidence of the piners activity was found for the first time just downstream from the Second (upper) Split and signs of a long abandoned route on the right bank high along the top of a ridge flanking the First Split were observed.

Once downstream of the First Split it was possible to enter it in the Kayak by working upstream and to inspect and photograph this incredible place better than it has been possible from above.

Further downstream the progress was more rapid; Sprent River was reached and explored for a couple of miles upstream. Immediately upstream of the Sprent River junction, high up on the left bank of the Gordon, the remnants of the stables and huts built by the piners before the end of the century were visited. These appeared to have been wrecked by a flood of unusual magnitude. It must have been the same flood which carried away most of the Pyramid Island, transforming an island carrying large trees growing in much loose rock and soil into a flat slab of bare bedrock only a few feet above the water. A mile downstream from the Sprent junction a comfortable night was spent in an HEC construction camp. A new hut and cage for the future river gauging was being built. The following day Franklin River was traversed for about 1 mile up from its junction, Limestone Cliffs were scrambled up and down and Sir John Falls visited and photographed.

Having entered Macquarie Harbour a night was spent on the Sarah Island amidst the ruins of the penal settlement to test the theory of ghosts at this cruel and lonely place.

The remaining journey to Strahan was accomplished by sailing the Kayak with a sail made of a ground sheet tied to a system of sticks. Within sight of the town, at Sophia Point, a short time was spent on shore to repair the clothing, to tidy up one's appearance and eat the remaining food. An hour later, and 24 days after leaving Lake Pedder, the little boat was tied to a pile of the Strahan wharf. A few people, mostly children, gathered to see a craft quite new to Strahan; they didn't know where Lake Pedder was and didn't appear to be impressed.

It may have been the neat and shaven appearance of the stranger that misled them. They didn't know that a very tough and possibly the most interesting of all the journeys to Strahan had just been accomplished'.

The challenge of the wild western rivers

will never be greater than it was for the river pioneers—but it draws more water-borne explorers every year. And the HEC's interest in these rivers adds increasing urgency to the challenge: how little time before none of them run free and that challenge is lost forever?

For the very character of the wild rivers threatens their existence. The rainfall is very high and the narrow gorges make ideal dam sites. With man's transformation of many rivers in the island, these rivers have become a focal point for white water recreation of the most challenging degree.

The challenge is accentuated by the isolation and the uncertainty of the flow. The rivers can rise dramatically in a matter of hours. Access, whether by way of the King William Range, the Spires or the Jane River track, can be difficult. Yet these are no hardships to deter those who know the exhilaration of life out 'there'; the great beauty of the rainforest-clad gorges, the sculptured rock faces and the roaring chasms. Truchanas' journey is part of history now; the Gordon River has lost its wild fury.

With the construction of roads into the heart of yesterday's wilderness and the extension of the network of tracks and huts by the HEC, the isolation has been rapidly diminishing. The following letter gives a vivid impression of the Gordon in 1976. Mike Emery wrote it whilst seated in his canoe at the end of his journey:

TASMANIA'S rugged south-west has some of the most breathtaking and exciting scenery in the world.

The Franklin River, which flows into the Gordon 23 miles south of Macquarie Harbour, is one of the few rugged waterways left untouched by man.

Its grandeur as it winds through gorges hundreds of feet high lured six young men to try to conquer the miles of rapids and waterfalls on three rafts.

Flimsy rafts challenge tempestous Franklin

By Chris Lewis, who accompanied the expedition.

THE 18ft raft slithered over the rocks in midstream, crashed 6ft into a pool of foaming water, and careered sideways into rapids.

The crew of two, Fred Koolhof (22) and Andy Lawrence (19), swung it around trying to beat the current, and momentarily won the struggle with the river before the raft suddenly flipped over on to its back.

The other three members of the Franklin River expedition and I bit our lips as the white water tumbled over the raft. Seconds later we were all smiles as Fred and Andy's white helmets and life-jackets bobbed up, and they climbed on to a rock.

Then the six of us who were trying to float down the tempestuous Franklin River splashed across the rapids to the disabled raft.

With a lot of effort it was pushed clear and party leader David ("Doc") Hansen jumped aboard as it drifted away.

He manoeuvred it into a backwater behind a fallen tree where the other two rafts were already tied up, and the rest of us clambered along the rocky bank to join him.

First rafts

That was December 28, three days after the start of the expedition down the Franklin, and it was the end of the road for Raft No 3.

The aim was to raft from where the Franklin crosses the Lyell Highway west of Derwent Bridge. The route went down the Franklin around French-mans Cap National Park, south to the junction of the Franklin and the Gordon, and then up the Gordon to Macquarie Harbour — 80 miles of meandering waterways.

The river had been conquered before by canoe expeditions over several Summers, but this was the first attempt by rafts, and the time limit was a mere 28 days.

Four men on two rafts completed the trip last Thursday, but Andy Lawrence (19) and I retired when the raft came to grief.

After the pile-up, the crews were hastily reorganised, with "Doc" Hansen (25), Tim Downie (23), John Morley (22), and Fred Koolhof (22), all of Hobart, crewing the other two rafts.

The remains of the damaged raft were salvaged from the rapids, the other rafts strengthened, and the depleted expedition soon went out of sight as the river descended down half a mile of white water.

Long climb

Back on the beautifully rugged Franklin river bank, Andy Lawrence and I sorted out our gear.

Andy was limping — his left knee was heavily bandaged because of a snow skiing accident six months ago.

That was late afternoon. The following morning we were up before dawn, discarded damaged gear, and began the long climb out.

● To Page 11

Fred Koolhof has a trial run at the top of the Franklin before the expedition began. Once underway, everyone wore roll-collar life-jackets obtained in Hobart, and plastic crash helmets. Hiking boots and thick socks to withstand the bumps of jumping into rapids also were standard equipment. No pictures were taken after this — everyone was too busy and too wet to think about cameras.

● From Page 10

Not caring about the pouring rain, we reached the road by mid-afternoon, and, in luck again, had a ride back to Hobart.

It took nearly six hours to reach the top of the 2,000ft high gorge through which the Franklin winds.

Portunately luck was on our side.

After stumbling, slipping, and dragging our way through the thick scrub in which it was impossible to see each other 20ft apart, we found an easy route to the Lyell Highway from the top of the gorge.

The other four battled on, smashing their raft to pieces on the foaming waterfalls, including one 70ft drop, on fhich

Morley and Koolhof lost all their gear.

They cheated death in dozens of hair-raising incidents.

Endless rapids dropping about 6ft, rocky outcrops in midstream, submerged trees, and the rugged country provided a thrill a minute as the 18ft rafts snaked their way downstream.

The continuous gorges on either side of the river, dark overhanging bush down to the water's edge, jagged rocks, and swirling white water formed an unmatched setting for adventure.

Clad in shorts, hiking boots, bright life-jackets, and crash helmets, the team was a crazy sight poling along on the unsightly rafts.

But it was well worth it — and an exciting way to spend Christmas.

Top picture: Hours were spent in a sheltered back-water lashing additional thick spars to strengthen the rafts for the trip down the Franklin. The 18ft rafts, each supported by four big tractor tubes, needed more strength to stop them twisting unnecessarily when shooting rapids.

Above: These are the crews who made it Fred Koolhof and John Morley (left) and David Hansen and Tim Downie. Right: Working their way against the current, Tim Downie and Fred Koolhof salvage the remains of the first pile-up of the expedition. The raft frame, on which four packs, climbing rope, and other gear was lashed, is under water.

'Dear Alie and Tony,

I've just fulfilled an old ambition—I've paddled down the Gordon. It's the biggest river we've got, and the one whose mention excites the most interest. It has a long history commencing with the convict settlement near its mouth and the Huon piners who took convict gangs up the lower reaches to saw logs, and later, the unsuccessful search for gold.

Both ends of the river have always been readily accessible yet most of its length lies in a little explored region of our South-West. As late as the 1920's, people looked at its route from a distance and shook their heads; and the rumour was spread that somewhere in those mountains the river flowed through a huge natural tunnel. I've often walked along its upper reaches in the Rasselas Valley; wide, silent, black, a large body of water moving gently but purposefully with just a hint of another character in the driftwood and debris caught in the trees above one's head. I've sailed up the Gordon from Macquarie Harbour where it is rough when the sea is rough and mirror flat when the sea is calm. On the banks thick forests hide the remains of old pine-cutters' jetties and old bits of iron from saw-millers' horse-drawn railways.

So what does lie in between? Until the Hydro-Electric Commission started using helicopters to bring in whole camps of surveyors and geologists a few years ago, there were probably only four people who had seen the gorges which cut those mountains — Abel, Sticht and Harrison who discovered them in 1928 in an epic trip up the river using a small punt (helped by an exceptionally dry summer), and who named them "The Splits"—and Olegas Truchanas who first canoed solo from Lake Pedder to Strahan in 1958. Since then, there have been only two other groups that I know of who have canoed the river, plus a handful of people who have reached The Splits from above or below using methods which ranged from swimming with wet-suit and flippers to sitting on lilos and paddling with webbed gloves.

So four of us set off to negotiate the river, beginning at the H E C 's dam near Strathgordon. Since the dam was still filling we anticipated little water for some miles below the dam and needed equipment that was easily carried: two of us took tiny inflatable canoes, about 8 feet long and 2½ feet wide, the others took portability to the extreme and went with lilos in their packs.

Initially we walked along the near-dry river bed, or waded through still pools between steep, heavily forested hillsides. Here the only water is leakage from the dam works and the rocks are coated with sediment washed down during construction. At times we were knee-deep in sludge. Then, cliffs on either side falling straight into the water, we inflated our crafts. A long succession of pools are separated by rock outcrops or gravel banks. Although the flow increased rapidly as we passed successive tributaries, the liloists had a decided advantage, for a canoe portage entails more effort.

Since we were travelling down-stream, the Third Split was the first that we came to. It is also known as the Abel Gorge. It's an impressive place: two rock walls 15 or 20 yards apart, and between them a mass of enormous boulders; some jagged and sharp edged, some smooth and rounded, many sculpted, with spherical holes that must have carried magnificent eddies before the river flow was cut off. Some of these

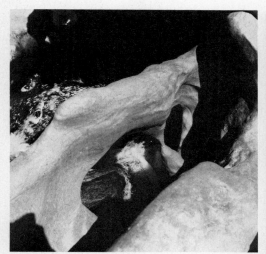

Rock formations in the Second Split: 'Some of these holes are 8 feet in diameter.... In semi-darkness you sit in the heart of the rock, pounded by the reverberating din of the water flowing out of sight beneath'.   Mike Emery

Rubber dinghies in The Splits.   Helen Gee

holes are 8 feet in diameter and merge into other holes at other levels inside the same boulder until you are left with a maze down through which you climb. In semi-darkness you sit in the heart of the rock, pounded by the reverberating din of the water flowing out of sight beneath. Echoes raise the sound level until it is out of all proportion to the meagre bit of water in the river. You climb out again, pick up your pack and canoe, jump to the next boulder, scramble over a jammed driftwood log, and below you is another system of spherical cavities; so you drop everything and explore that. This time you get right down to the rushing water and stand in it, shin deep, looking up through one round hole at the sky above and through two others at different views of the gorge.

An hour or two later you are paddling from gravel bank to gravel bank no gorges, no cliffs; just thick forest on both sides.

The Second Split is more dramatic still—two sheer walls about ten yards apart, one of them overhanging a deep pool which blocks the entrance. You float across, scramble up onto the first of the boulders, deflate, and

start picking your way through; passing packs to one another, balancing on edges, holding onto boulder faces with finger nails, wading through pools. What a wild place this must have been when the river was free! On both sides the cliffs are vertical; it would be impracticable to cut a foot track in the gorge. You scramble on with the sound of rushing water filtering up gently through the boulders. You find one rock perhaps twenty feet in diameter with three intersecting spherical holes, which leave between them a sliver of stone an inch thick, three inches wide and nearly two feet long; gently curved, with rounded edges and polished like a piece of exhibition woodwork.

The gorge ends; it opens into a forested valley with wide shelves of rock and sand on one bank. There you find a pile of old fuel drums, then two helicopter pads and an HEC hut. The hut is deserted but in good condition. On one wall is a large engineering plan of a dam to block the Second Split. It is complete in every detail: access roads, construction roads, spillways, diversion tunnels—the lot.

Then the First Split; a series of narrow vertical cracks separated by small basins, through which the whole of the Gordon flows. One slit is so narrow you have to hold your paddle parallel to the canoe. Then a small, still pool, a bit of juggling to pass between two boulders just a canoe's width apart, and you slide down a small rapid, spin round and paddle out of the current as the water disappears under the boulder bed of another basin, cliffs on all sides. Behind is the crack through which you've come; ahead is the most impressive crack of all. You clamber over the boulders to a ledge on one of the basin sides, passing canoes and packs to each other, and slowly make your way round. You stop on the last boulder and look straight down the Split. Two dark, vertical, sculpted walls rising to between 100 and 200 feet; shiny, scalloped, patterned. Between them the water is quite still, black and deep. You throw your canoe into the water, and lower yourself into it. Floating motionless between those walls you look up at the crack of sky and your ears are filled with the din of water cascading through the boulders in the

previous basin only yards away; yet here there is no movement. Beside you on one of the walls is another of the spherical chambers. You float backwards into it until only the nose of the boat projects and , looking up through a hole in the ceiling at the crack above, you slide your fingers over the polished rocks. And all the time you have this eerie sixth sense of something being wrong; that where there is noise there is turbulent water, which means rapids and movement and being on your guard; and here you're in a black space and everything is so still.

You drift out again and paddle gently for 30 yards along the crack examining the markings on the rock—the lines, the curves, the concavities, all highly polished; and all the time the roar of rushing water. Then there ahead is another basin, again with high cliffs almost all around but this time filled with deep motionless water. And as you drift into it, quite suddenly, all sound stops. Ahead, through a much wider gap, is a sunlit hill. All is calm and silent, with the sound of water entirely confined to echoes within the gap.

In the stillness you lie back in the canoe and look at the trees, at the tops of the cliffs and the bit of sunlight playing up there; there is no sun in the basin. Then you look below the trees at the cliff face and find a cave... a big cave with a long sloping floor going back far into the cliff. The ceiling is flat and perhaps 80 feet above water level. Jammed into a crack in the ceiling are two enormous driftwood logs.

We spent three days exploring The Splits, climbing around them, paddling into odd corners, just floating and contemplating. How can a river the size of the Gordon fit through a 10 foot crack? If those logs were 80 feet up in the basin, how far up the crack do the flood waters go? We looked for evidence of driftwood high up, but our search was inconclusive. By climbing up through the forest well to one side of the cliffs, we found an excellent look-out point on a high rock knoll, already occupied by a large and discerning snake. He did move for us, but looked decidedly irritated.

That was two days ago. Soon after leaving The Splits, we came to the Denison River, which was a joy since

it meant at last we had ample water to shoot all the rapids. The Denison is narrower than the Gordon and lacks any formations as dramatic as The Splits, but it is an even more beautiful river. The forests on its banks are much taller than the river is wide, giving the impression of a deep canyon. In January many of the leatherwood trees are covered in large white flowers whose petals drift down to float around you on the dark water. The Denison had in its motion a feeling of silent power. Where we were the Gordon is so wide that you get no feeling of motion at all.

We came across other signs of HEC activity: a footbridge across the river at Sunshine Gorge and a substantial cableway climbing up the hill; huts, helipads, pontoons and many signs of drilling in the few miles above Butler Island.

Now I'm floating in the middle of a large basin just above Butlers Island, waiting for the Denison Star's daily trip. She should be along soon; I've been floating here a couple of hours already and my writing hand is getting cold.... Here he comes!
Regards,
Mike'.

In Sunshine Falls Gorge on the Gordon.   *Bob Graham*

Opposite page, below and right
ASPECTS OF THE FIRST SPLIT, GORDON RIVER: The upper entrance. Travelling through the Split. Shiny, scalloped and patterned walls rise between 30 and 60 metres high. The lower corridor. Leaving the Split. Camping below the Split.
Mike Emery

The Jane country

'South-west of the Frenchmans Range, beyond the Calder Pass, lies a tract of country ... rugged mountains, impetuous rivers rushing through precipitous gorges ... amber creeks bubbling and singing through colonnades of pine and beech, then breaking into white laceries of foam against the walls of black ravines. Here are the formidable Algonkian Mountains, precipitous and covered with almost impenetrable growth, the Prince of Wales Range, whose gleaming white quartzite peaks scintillate in the sun ... the wonderful, mysterious Jane River, along whose banks are the most extensive forests of Huon pine in the island.'

(Balfour Johnston, 1935)

The Jane River rises about 12 kilometres south of Frenchmans Cap in the Glow Worm Forest below Lake Whitham. It flows east across the Lightning Plains to its junction with the Erebus River at the base of Warnes Lookout. In the 30 kilometres between 'Warnes' and the Franklin River, the Jane falls a total of 250 metres, flowing through three

magnificent gorges. Bare rock faces tower impressively above a dense tangle of rainforest. In the river bed, gigantic boulders are moss-encrusted and bedecked with dwarf foliage. Between the gorges there are tranquil pools where platypus play. In summer the white petals of the leatherwood drift on the black water.

Limestone is extensive in the 'Jane Country'; mysterious grottos and overhangs conceal the dark river entrances of unexplored caves. Though piners hauled their punts a good way up the Jane and prospectors fossicked in the upper reaches, it remains remote and inaccessible.

The Jane, like all south-western rivers, can rise swiftly to dramatic heights. Huge logs jammed high in notches on cliff faces illustrate its potential fury. Early in 1976, five people (John Davies, Neil Davidson, Mark Errey, Stuart Graham and Helen Gee) found the river to be a feasible pathway down to the Franklin. The lilo, or air mattress, proved to be the appropriate transport, easily portaged down the boulder-choked sections. When afloat, the effortless stance allowed a full appreciation of the scene drifting by ... the insect world, the bird life and the swirling patterns in a back eddy.

Not the least motivation for the increasing number of 'river trips' has been the sharp awareness that these beautiful wild rivers enjoy a precarious freedom. Whether paddling down the Gordon, the Franklin, the Jane or the Denison, the signs of Hydro-Electric Commission investigations confront and disturb one at journey's end in the Lower Gordon—the pontoons, drilling rigs and oil drums, the gouges in the side of the gorge, the rubble, the oil slick, the floating aluminium can. Many other rivers in the country have been dammed ... this one is already dammed near its source, leaving the Franklin as one of the last major wild rivers in temperate Australia; perhaps the most magnificent.

The Denison

Mark Errey was a member of a party who travelled down the Denison River in 1975. To their knowledge only one man had been that way before them and again it was Olegas Truchanas in the mid 1960's. To the very few who know this wild river from its source to its junction with the Gordon, it means a great deal. Mark Errey describes its features:

'Rising in rugged country west of the King William Range, the Denison River flows through varied terrain— from the flat plains of the upper reaches to the 'Splits' near its confluence with the Gordon. It passes through different vegetation zones including one of the last significant stands of Huon pine left in Tasmania. These marked changes in the character of the river can best be described in sequence.

Once beyond the foothills of the King William Range the river flows south along a broad plain flanked by the rugged quartzite crags of The Spires and Prince of Wales Range. Hence the river is placid, meandering between myrtle clad banks and tumbling over gravelly rapids, and its negotiation by canoe or inflatable craft is very easy. But towards the southern end of the plain, the river steepens to become much narrower and faster moving, and its banks are steeper and very rocky. The myrtle forest gradually gives way to Huon pine until at the Truchanas Huon Pine Reserve, the pines comprise the dominant species. Inland for hundreds of yards large stands of Huon pine are found and along the river old gnarled pines droop their needles into the water. One can appreciate Truchanas' enchantment with this area, and his enthusiasm for its preservation.

Immediately after leaving the Pine Reserve, the river enters the Denison Gorge. So deep and narrow is this

gorge, that even up till a decade ago maps did not reveal its existence. It was assumed the Denison continued southward to meet the Gordon above the present dam site. Early piners could not penetrate the gorge because of its precipitous walls—more than 250 metres in places—and a series of steep cascades.

Beyond the gorge, the river widens out again entering a different vegetation zone. Recent fires have destroyed old rainforest replacing it with Eucalyptus species but few Huon pines remain. Before one reaches the plains of the lower Denison, there is a "split" to negotiate. The river has sliced its way through a small, sharp ridge leaving a passage of no more than 6 metres. Its width 30 metres up would be no more than 15 metres, hence giving it a split-like appearance. The river widens again after this feature, becoming easy going for a canoe. Several miles after the Maxwell River joins the Denison, another gorge is entered, this time via a break through the Nicholls Range. Several splits are found here including one comprising two knife-edge ridges dropping vertically into the river. Before entering the Gordon, the Denison drops very steeply over a mile or so, disappearing under huge boulders, some the size of small houses. In flood conditions, this steep section could be a sight to behold with surging water and mighty pressure waves'.

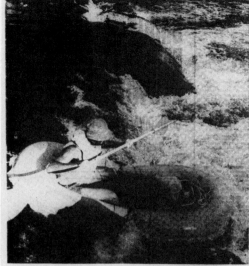

The Franklin: Our greatest challenge

By JAN HASWELL

You needn't be an expert to canoe down the powerful rivers of Tasmania's West Coast — just pick your time carefully and get fit first.

That's the message brought back by Launceston men Bob Brown and Paul Smith, who recently covered 110 km of the Franklin River in 15 days.

Paul had previously made one canoe trip from Evandale to Longford, but Bob had no experience at all.

The river they tackled — the fiery Franklin — is considered the greatest natural challenge a canoeist can find in Tasmania.

"Bouncing down rapids and shooting small waterfalls was exhilarating sport," Paul said this week.

"And it's the only way to see the superb scenery that lines the river."

Rather than canoes, the men used inflatable rubber dinghies bought in Launceston for $70.

"Dinghies are easier to handle because they travel forwards, backwards or sideways with equal ease," Paul said.

"Instead of coming to grief against rocks you bounce off."

Altogether we went through about 300 rapids — about 20 a day and usually only 50 to 100 metres long.

No spills

"I was lucky enough to have no spills, but Bob went under twice. All he lost was his hat."

Paul said fitness was essential because there was so much furious work with a paddle trying to steer a reasonable course.

"And there were plenty of times when we had to carry our gear on foot around cascades or log jams.

"Sometimes it took several trips so that a 200 metre hike became a two-hour exercise over rough country."

Bob and Paul chose March as a month when the water would be fairly tame.

They advise anyone considering a rush trip that April might be a different story.

And they recommend advance research. They sought advice from well-known hiker and canoeist Dr John Hawkins, who had made one of only three known expeditions along the river.

"If heavy rain had raised the river and made things too dangerous, we'd have pulled out," Paul said.

"It would probably have meant a walk of 30 km over the mountains to a hydro road."

But the weather held back.

Fifteen days after launching their dinghies at the Collingwood Bridge, 40 km east of Queenstown on the Lyell Highway, they reached their planned conclusion.

Just 10 km past the junction of the Franklin and Gordon rivers they climbed on to Butlers Island.

There they simply hitched a ride on the launch Denison Star as it passed on a tourist cruise.

"Looking back it was exciting, but quite comfortably done," Paul said.

"We kept fairly civilised hours, never starting before 10 a.m. or finishing after 5 p.m.

"It's the sort of holiday that should be taken by Tasmania politicians before the H.E.C. has transformed the region with power schemes."

ABOVE: Paul Smith takes his dinghy over small rapids. "Bouncing over rapids and small waterfalls was exhilarating sport," he says. PICTURES BY BOB BROWN.

BELOW: The Pig Trough — where the Franklin River emerges from the mountains and enters the flatter country close to the Gordon. "If the H.E.C. has its way these cliffs will be submerged in the cause of a power scheme," says Paul Smith.

Sunday Examiner Express, 31 March 1976

Opposite page, left to right
THE JANE: Lunchtime on a gravel bank. Swirling patterns in a back eddy. Travelling by inflatable air mattress down the river during 1976.   *Helen Gee*

Below
THE FRANKLIN: Man's basic attraction to water could well involve deeper evolutionary ties leading back to the very first forms of life. Wild rivers epitomize the spirit of wilderness in a visually and aurally dynamic form. They provide a physically arduous challenge that is ecologically sound; the canoeist leaves only the ashes of his fire, and they are swept away in the next flood.
Top left, bottom left, top right and bottom right
Descending the rapids; Glen Calder.   *Bob Brown*
Canoeing on the river.   *Don Hutton*
Bob Brown near the Loddon Junction.   *Paul Smith*
Paul Smith in 'rubber duckie'.   *Bob Brown*

Old Bob Muff yarning to Rex Wells on the Strahan wharf, 1937. *Eric Thomas*

At sea on a calm day. *Ann Wessing*

Tasmanian fur seal. *A Moscal*

Top
Coastal seagulls. *Ann Wessing*

Rock platform, South Cape Bay. *Howard P Simco*

Wrecked fishing boat on Deadmans Beach, 1953. *Max Cutcliffe*

Young fur seal, South Cape Bay. *A Moscal*

Howard P Simco

The South Coast from the Sea

A Wessing

Ann Wessing became familiar with the South-West from bushwalking trips and in 1976 worked as a deck hand on a crayboat working off the South Coast.

The South Coast seen from the walking track has a magnificence that is all its own. Discovering it from the sea adds another dimension to the experience. Changes of mood in the weather there are so much more apparent from the now wildly—now gently rocking deck of a fishing boat. The winds each add their characteristic touch to the slop and swell. Clouds, sky and birds combine to give the mood of the coast by their abundance, colour and movement. The hard isolated life on a fishing boat gives a detached yet strangely close feeling of identity with the wild and infinitely varying coastline.

I found a summer as a deckhand on a fishing boat along these shores exciting in the rediscovery of a well-loved place. Fishing itself has changed little along the coast in Tasmania's settled history except in the greater number of fishing vessels, and in the use of radio and echo-sounder, radar and autopilot. Cray-fishing still involves the early rise before dawn to pick up the 'night shot' that begins a day's work. There are stifled yawns heard over the drumming of the engine and the struggle into gumboots and waterproofs against the roll of the boat. Reaching the marker buoys, wet rope and seaweed come up on the hauler and then the cray-pot itself, with crayfish, crabs and eels, or the hated 'ocky' (octopus) that kills the crays. Then the sorting, the measuring of crayfish, re-baiting and stacking of pots on deck, and finally they are reset on another part of the coast for the first of the day shots. The sun is already a dazzling glare on the water.

The fisherman's day is a succession of these shots, marked between 'scheds' on the radio. Talk and jokes crackle back and forth between boats; the character of each man is vividly recognizable. Meals come in the lulls between pulling shots, and there is also time for the odd jobs around the boat—getting out more frozen bait or washing down the sides of the boat. Time for me to sit on deck up in the bow; gaze slit-eyed out to the islands off the South Coast.

Coming around from Recherche Bay past Whale Head and South Cape the coast is gradually revealed: South Cape Range juts out ahead—a solid uncomp-

Off 'the Big Witch', Precipitous Bluff on the horizon.   *Ann Wessing*

romising ridge, while to the south, on the edge of vision, one can see two solitary pinnacles: Pedra Branca and Eddystone Rock. To landward, first Pindars Peak and La Perouse appear and then Precipitous Bluff towering over Prion Beach with a tiny blue tooth to its north-west—Federation Peak! Heading out to sea over the long flat swell, the Maatsuyker group of islands opens out: first the Big Witch (De Witt), large and forested, her forbidding cliffs and low north shore, then the two Sisters, one of which has a hole through which you can see the horizon. Beyond Flat Witch and Walkers Island lies Maatsuyker itself, with its haulage way up to the lighthouse—the lighthouse that guards the line of evil rocks and reefs—The Needles—running out to its south-west. Then South West Cape can be seen to the west of the islands at the end of a string of headlands and deep bays.

To a person new to the ways of the sea, the abundance of life there is a constant source of amazement and delight. Seals live on the inner Needles, and any boat that goes there to observe them will surprise these creatures where they love to lie on the rocks in the sunshine—groaning, basking, slumping into the water. Yet once swimming they are transformed into graceful creatures

of the sea. Penguins are shy and avoid boats and humans, appearing only as small dark heads peering out of the water before diving. And there are dolphins—travelling with the boat along the coast; curving up and out side by side; blowing for air with a little whistle before diving down again and rolling sideways, to smile up at you.

The birds of the sea give the coastal world character and life: the albatross, large and rather ponderous, heavy and cumbersome in take off, yet, like the seals, transformed in his element; a gannet—a white diving rocket in the distance; terns, small and light, flickering along through the wave hollows; mutton-birds, neat and unafraid, diving beside the boat to catch the sea lice that fall off the craypots; and the ever-present, squabbling seagulls wheeling and dipping, screaming in the wind behind the boat.

These creatures blend with the wild seascape in a rich, lively mosaic that is the south-west coast. The discipline and isolation of fishing provide a fitting framework for the contemplation of the moods of this elemental region: the meeting of mountains and oceans; the mixing of storm clouds and Antarctic winds; the dancing of shadow and light. It has a timelessness.

Breaksea Island from the sea.   N E Poynter

'Breaksea Island, which, as its name implies, lies across the entrance to the harbour, giving it shelter, is the home of many thousands of mutton-birds which have their burrows in the soft earth above sheer white cliffs that drop into the sea. Though Port Davey has been partly charted by the Australian Navy, its entrance is dangerous because the approach is strewn with hidden reefs and rocks awash at low tide, as well as being studded with conical points of rock that stand high above the fringes of continually breaking water!'
(Ida McAulay, 1938)

Breaksea Island from the air.   Jim England

Fishing boats often shelter in the coves of Bathurst Channel, Port Davey.
Jack Thwaites

Above and right
Some aspects of the Needles, a jagged cluster of rocks off Maatsuyker Island.
Charles Wessing

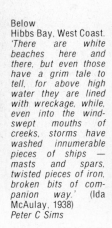

Below
Hibbs Bay, West Coast. 'There are white beaches here and there, but even those have a grim tale to tell, for above high water they are lined with wreckage, while, even into the windswept mouths of creeks, storms have washed innumerable pieces of ships — masts and spars, twisted pieces of iron, broken bits of companion way.' (Ida McAulay, 1938)
Peter C Sims

174

Aboard an Abalone Boat

C Wessing

Over a period of four years, Charles Wessing has worked along the south and west coasts as a deck hand on both abalone and cray boats.

The chill silent beauty of New Harbour at dawn is something that is never forgotten. The dark hills are steep and close around. A white blur of a beach whispers across the still distance. Out to sea a row of jagged teeth guard the entrance of this anchorage on the South Coast.

In the darkness of the fo'c's'le the 6 am radio report sounds loud against the slap of waves on the hull. While dressing you listen to the language of the sea....

'Maatsuyker Island; northerly 1, smooth sea and a low, long sou'westerly swell; Tasman Island... Cape Bruny... Neptune Island...'.
There are upwards of one hundred people waking to life and work along one of the roughest stretches of coast in the southern hemisphere.

The skipper vanishes down the engine-room hatch to check the oil levels, then with a puff of white smoke the diesel settles down to a low rumble. The harsh clatter of chain coming aboard echoes across the harbour. Lash the anchor, stow the rope, take the wheel; the skipper is making a cup of tea. As the sun touches the tip of the western hills the little boat is heading out. Past the outer rocks she bursts into sunlight and a still blue sea. The swell deepens and the feet shift to meet the lift and plunge, fingertips lightly shifting on the wheel, and its good to be alive.

The first word of the day seems almost a pity. Its the skipper passing a cup of tea: 'West?'

And a nod is all the answer as the bow swings slowly round to brush the tip of South West Cape; three granite peaks pointing a white tipped finger to Antarctica. The rest of the crew come on deck. For a busy hour breakfast is prepared, the dinghies are fuelled and diving gear is checked for the days work. By the time all is settled the boat is rounding South West Cape with the East Pyramid and Hilliard Head showing grey in the northern distance. The radio echoes the chatter of others coming out of the precious few anchorages; West Louisa, Spain Bay, South-East Bight. Those who lie elsewhere stake their knowledge and prediction of the weather against the possibility of a rising gale and having to 'feel' their way to a safer anchorage.

'It is beautiful in its own savagely relentless way.' (Ida McAulay, 1938). South West Cape. *Jim England*

Aboard our boat the abalone divers suit up, the anchor goes down and the dinghies swing out. Compressors are put down into the pitching dinghies; they roar off towards the shore. The day's work is demanding for the divers and also for the dinghy boy. A hundred metres from the shore, on the edge of the white water, he has one eye on the diver and one eye on the breakers further out. He balances the dinghy against the drift of wind and tide. Meanwhile, on the sea bed and at the end of a line, the diver fills his net, cutting the abalone off the rocks with a knife. He is mindful of his oxygen supply and any signals sent down by the line. The compressor is not capable of supporting a diver at a depth of more than 95 feet (16 fathoms), and for safety reasons most divers are reluctant to go below 50 feet (8 fathoms). Fine judgement and experience are required by all who 'work' this coastline.

In the late afternoon the 'ab' boat 'up anchors' and noses out to open sea. The fish are emptied into the tank where they are kept alive, and the gear is stowed and lashed.

The boat rolls around the Cape and runs with her stern to the setting sun. There's time to relax a bit, to talk about the weather, or just stand quietly at the wheel and watch the colours change and fade on cliffs and islands off the coast. Later when the 'pick' (anchor) has gone out again and the engine is quiet there's a certain satisfaction in sitting on deck in the twilight, smoking a last pipe and listening to the rumble of the surf or the call of a late sea-bird; the satisfaction of having earned, and enjoyed earning, the day's reward.

De Witt Island lies in the path of the Roaring Forties off Tasmania's South coast. The island's vegetation is severely wind-pruned and the foreshore is rocky and rugged with spectacular cliffs on the southern side. The South-West coast is notorious for its rough seas and few anchorages, so the lee of the island provides a welcome shelter for small fishing boats.
Tony Moscal

Opposite page
Surprise Bay with South Coast islands, including Maatsuyker, De Witt and Isle du Golfe, on the horizon.
Jim England

de witt island

de witt island is a friend of mine,
and i choose to call her, as do her other friends, the fishermen and the bushwalkers of the s.w. coast, by the more familiar and affectionate name the big witch.
she is a big and rugged island, standing with her back hunched against the south wind, somewhat awesome looking with her cliffs and hills usually covered by a blanket of black clouds and violent sea spray;
yet,
she, being essentially female, is gentle and loving to those who live with her, as i did, alone, for a little time;
her forests hold delicate enchantments, myriad ferns and mosses carpet, with countless greens her feet,
tall trees of gum and blackwoods reach into the skies and sing and moan with the wind and the singing and moaning
of those happy folk the fairy penguins,
mutton birds in season circle low over the bracken ferns, landing with a crash and a thud their favourite 3 pointed way,
her love too embraces wallabies and they, having no reason to fear man, are tame, almost to the point of being bossy,
for well i remember how they used to come and stand, impatiently chatting their teeth for any food we had for them,
and there are lessons to be learnt from them, their care for each other and their care never to taint the laughing burgundy coloured creeks that run, winding through dark cool shadows into the sunlight and into the sea;
her softest and gentlest parts are these,
where the white quartz and the black leech together lie;
yet, being a woman she changes, drastically and rapidly, her nor-west is barren, with coarse tussock grass and tangled horizontal tea-trees,
it is here, where her cliffs drop straight down 1,2,3 hundred feet into the kelp deep ice water,
where not a blade of grass can find a safe foothold, where nothing, except millions of savage black ants run free,
but, the sunsets are nicer from here, eternity is before you,
and it is good, in the failing light to feel humbled before this,
Gods' beauty, to know, that with the blood red sky a day of calm tomorrow will come, that the wind shall cease to sing awhile
and that the sea shall be a smooth mirror to the sun;
and turning your head to the east, you see, beyond the great white rock blaze, the moon rise silver
then, silently for a moment, you wonder, is this, is this but a dream?

Earth Flute (Jane Cooper).

De Witt Island

G White

In 1975 Gary White, a Victorian, fulfilled a wish to visit De Witt Island. On subsequent visits he observed the interactions of the wild-life and the effect of fire. His book, *De Witt Island Experiences*, was published in 1976.

The largest island off the South-West coast is 518 hectares in area and lies 6 kilometres south of Louisa Point, its nearest point to the Tasmanian mainland. The island is hilly with a peak of 354 metres above sea-level. On the southern side this summit drops sheer to the sea forming a spectacular cliff face. A prominent quartzite peak, appropriately named Baldy Point, dominates the north-eastern corner of the island.

Eucalypt and some myrtle clothe much of the northern flank of the island. Unlike many of the south-western forests this one is easily penetrable though there is a small patch of the notorious horizontal scrub. Stunted, wind-pruned coastal tea-tree scrub clings to the more exposed slopes, while bracken grows tall and dense near the sheltered northern shore—a mark of recent firings. On this side two inlets are suitable for landing, though strong winds, particularly from the north-west can prevent landing for days on end, even in summer.

In a sheltered spot near one of three permanent streams on the island are some remains of a hut and its basic furniture. Jane Cooper camped here for several months in 1971. She was then 17 years old. People don't often visit the island and even fishermen seldom land. It is the domain of 5,000 penguins and 15,000 mutton-birds in the breeding season. The red-bellied wallaby or pademelon is another inhabitant. The eastern swamp-rat occurs in thousands at the peak of breeding. Normally herbivorous, it has taken to eating the available chicks and eggs. The rat is prepared to tackle live mutton-bird chicks much larger than itself, and in February and March 1976 I often saw packs of 200 or more rats gathered around a chick, fighting among themselves as they consumed it. The number of parent birds landing at dusk declined during March, till only the odd one was to be seen at the beginning of April—a sure sign that most of the chicks had been taken, as this was still some time before they were due to migrate north. It is not known whether or not this is an annual occurrence though several years ago mutton-birders left the island without a catch. Further observations of rat and mutton-bird populations would certainly be of interest.

Fire may be another threat to the island's bird life. In December 1975 a fisherman's fire burnt 6 hectares of the main bird rookeries, destroying many penguins with their chicks, as well as mutton-birds.

De Witt Island with its outstanding wild features is very much an inherent part of the South-West, deserving our protection.

Flying in the Past

Above
Plane on Pedder Beach
in the 1950's.
Max Cutcliffe

Below
Auntie, a de Havilland
Dragon on Cox Bight
Beach.
Brown & Dureau

Above
At Lake Pedder in the
1950's.   *D Pinkard*

Left
Auntie at Pedder.
Brown & Dureau

Below
Auster on Cox Bight
Beach. 1954.   *D King*

During the 1940's the photographers Brown & Dureau were engaged in aerial photography for the Department of Lands and Surveys. Two light aircraft were used, a deHavilland Dragonfly for high flying and a deHavilland Dragon for oblique and low shots. These were twin-engine planes capable of carrying 7 to 8 passengers, and were constructed from wood and fabric.

Their work took the pilots over the South-West and the two planes often landed on Cox Bight Beach. In 1947 the Dragon, affectionately known as *Auntie*, was landed on the buttongrass at Melaleuca but proved unequal to the rough landing. Both propellors were broken, as well as some of the perspex around the front of the plane. A corduroy strip of poles and gravel was constructed to get the plane airborne again.

However this was not the first plane to land at Melaleuca. In 1935 a Fox Moth was flown there with a surveyor for the New Harbour Company which was mining tin there at the time. The Company's lease had not been surveyed and a surveyor was needed rather urgently since suspicions were rumoured that someone was about to jump the claim!

The pilot of the Fox Moth, thinking the ground was flat, touched down too late and ran over the edge of a bank into a bog, breaking the propellor. Replacement parts were flown to Cox Bight Beach and carried the 8 miles to the plane stranded at Melaleuca.

Above and far left
Auntie at Melaleuca.
1947.
D King

Opposite page
Cessna, 'Tango Oscar'
over Bathurst Harbour,
piloted by Max Price.
Jim England

Right
Melaleuca 'airport',
1951. This strip was
built in 1947 to enable
a plane which had
landed on the rough
button-grass to take off
again.
Lloyd Jones

Bottom
Austers at Bond Bay.
1954.
D King

A Pilot's View

J W England

Jim England has piloted light aircraft in Tasmania for many years. Also a highly skilled aerial photographer, his magnificent prints have gained much publicity for the South-West in exhibitions and publications around Australia. He has conveyed his deep concern for the protection of the area and his appreciation of its beauty, to the many local and interstate visitors who have been privileged to fly with him over the South-West.

One of my favourite spots in the South-West is at the side of the creek which drains Freney Lagoon on the western beach at Cox Bight. The clear tea-coloured water runs quickly over white quartzite stones into the ocean. The colours here are magnificent—white sand, blue sky; green scrub and the golden button-grass. The still, warm air is heavily laden with the scents of native flowers and there is the constant roar of surf. Beyond the silhouetted New Harbour Range, the light at Maatsuyker Island has commenced its nightly flashing.

I have flown from Cambridge Airport to spend the night at this spot. In the morning I will check the aircraft and take off along the beach, bound for my office job in Hobart. Reflecting on 17 years of walking and charter flying in the South-West I recall the many people I have met—their wide range of interests and character. To me the South-West has become a familiar three dimensional map that can be flown around in a four hour flight, although many flights are required to see the area in detail.

The first light aircraft landing was made on the Lake Pedder beach about 1936. The number of flights over the South-West has steadily increased since then, until today it is not uncommon for several light aircraft to be in the area at the same time. Bushwalkers have been flown in to Lake Pedder, Cox Bight and Bond Bay beaches, and to the Melaleuca airstrip since its completion in 1956. Light aircraft have provided a reliable service to walkers on extended trips; extra food has been dropped for them at prearranged 'drop sites' and many airborne tourists have been able to view the magnificent scenery of the South-West. I have flown over 2,000 people into the area, all of them appreciative of the untouched wilderness. *'Don't let them spoil it,'* they say.

On a walking trip one adapts to the natural environment and the senses are tuned up. In the air the experience is essentially visual in a domain you share with the wedgetailed eagle, the cockatoos and the seabirds.

A rough trip

On most occasions, scenic tourist flights are flown on clear days but sometimes light aircraft go into the South-West in quite rough conditions. This is a brief account of such a trip to Melaleuca airstrip at Bathurst Harbour, Port Davey.

Today is Christmas Eve and December has been extremely windy and rough. Normally the windy weather occurs during October. I start to do a few odd jobs about the home. At 3 pm the phone rings:

"Can you come and do a flight down to Davey? There's a party there that wants to get home for Christmas. There's four adults and five kids plus packs".

Having already looked at the foul weather I reluctantly say:

"I'll be over in about an hour at Cambridge to do the flight".

On the drive to the aerodrome I picture the weather map in the paper showing cold fronts coming up from the Antarctic like spokes on a giant cartwheel. Between the fronts are strong westerly winds; take your

pick.... *Mt Wellington is covered with white curtains—rain showers.*

After I arrive at the aerodrome I get the 3 pm forecast and prepare the aircraft. I note that the windsock is nearly horizontal, it only gets like that in strong winds. The forecast reads: "Wind 250 degrees, 30 knots at 2,000 feet, 40 at 4,000, 45 at 6,000, cloudbase 1,000 on the south coast, freezing level 3,500, moderate to severe turbulence, visibility 5 miles reducing to ¼ mile in rainshowers." This all means a rough trip ahead, and it definitely means a coastal flight path as the mountains are obviously covered with cloud and the turbulence over them would be hell. As I complete the flight plan I decide to phone Maatsuyker light station and get their actual and up-to-date wind strength reading. One of the lightkeepers answers the phone:

"G'day Tony, How are you?"

"Oh not bad. Say, you're not coming down today are you?"

"Yes, what's the wind like down there? Got a couple of trips down to get some bods out for Christmas".

"Just hang on, I'll have a look", In a couple of minutes Tony is back:

"The wind is getting up to 40 knots and the coast is hidden by low cloud, raining at the moment but seems to improve every so often".

"Well, it's not too good but I'll give it a go. By the way how are Robyn and the kids?"

"Pretty well Jim, but looking forward to coming off for the holidays in February, there's been nothing but wind here for four weeks now".

"Thanks Tony, must be off now". I submit the flight plan to the briefing office and then check the aircraft. I'll have to take the big Cessna 206 to get them all out in two flights from the airstrip at Melaleuca. There'll be a strong, gusty cross-wind to contend with, both landing and taking off. The telegram from Melaleuca said 4 adults and 5 kids; they could be any size since they walked the South Coast track. I climb into the left hand pilot's seat and close the door. Even in the shelter of the hangars the wind is rocking the '206, making the perspex windscreen squeak as it

Cox Bight, South Coast.

Jim England

flexes slightly. A brief burst of sun floods the cockpit and I start to perspire as I have a heavy woollen shirt on for the cold winds at Davey. Seat belts secure, doors locked, seats secure, master switch on, fuel on, cowl flaps open, mixture rich, pitch fine, throttle set, fuel booster pumps on, pumps off, engage starter. The big three-bladed prop growls evenly into life. Must have primed it right. Instruments indicate everything is functioning normally as I call:

"Hobart Tower, this is Papa Kilo Mike (registration letters of the aircraft PKM), taxiing Cambridge for Bathurst Harbour, using runway 27, requesting clearance."

The Tower replies: "Papa Kilo Mike this is Hobart Tower, wind 250 degrees, 20 gusting to 30 (knots), Q.N.H. 997 (millibars), time approaching 32 (32 minutes past the hour), clearance; proceed coastal to Bathurst Harbour, not above 3,000, report on course."

I reply "Papa Kilo Mike, not above 3,000" and taxi out to the end of runway 27 holding the controls

correctly to minimise the effects of the wind on the aircraft as much as possible. I line up at the end of the runway after completing all the other necessary checks in the aircraft, in particular checking for any loose articles that could be thrown about inside the cabin. A friend of mine was hit in the back of the head by a can of pears one day as the aircraft hit some bad turbulence off Cox Bight.

All checks complete. I open the throttle, the big prop bites at the air as the revs build up. The acceleration increases and with the strong headwind down the runway the aircraft becomes airborne quickly. The moment we are up the turbulence starts. Power settings back to climbing power, flaps up.

"Papa Kilo Mike on course at 37".
The Tower: "At Snug call Launceston Control on 122.1".
"Papa Kilo Mike", I reply.

Climbing over the hills of Mt Rumney on Hobart's Eastern Shore the turbulence makes me thankful that I'm not in a lighter Cessna 172. On days like this, it pays to anticipate

where the worst turbulence will occur; today it will be worst off Snug, Dover, and South Cape. At 2,000 feet over the Derwent River I can see black squall patches on the water spreading out like fans. We approach Snug.

"Launceston, this is Papa Kilo Mike, departed Cambridge at time 37 for Bathurst Harbour via the South Coast, estimating South Cape at time 0507".

"Papa Kilo Mike, this is Launceston; at South Cape if no contact on this frequency, call Melbourne on 6575 or 8938".

As I reach down to replace the microphone in its clip, bang, the aircraft drops. I drop the mic. and immediately throttle back as I don't like bashing aircraft through turbulence. Bang, and my posterior catches up with the seat, compressing my back. The left wing drops; I pick it up with the ailerons and rudder; nasty words go through my mind. The first of the rain showers is ahead near Dover and soon severe turbulence is encountered. Should

Mt Rugby reflected in Bathurst Harbour.

Jim England

have stayed out a bit more over the Channel, may have been a bit smoother there.

Looking south I can see huge creamy white towering clouds, obviously the start of some cumulonimbus; steer well clear of those, they drop the lot from their violent interior. Approaching Catamaran I have to reduce height from 3,000 feet down to 2,000 feet as the cloudbase is lowering near the coast at South Cape Bay. The water is streaked with spray and those big clouds must be the beginning of a cold front. They didn't forecast that so soon. The weather deteriorates rapidly and I'm forced to take the aircraft down to 600 feet. As I do so I manage to get Melbourne Control on the high frequency radio and establish contact with them. At South Cape the cloud is down, right down with little tufts actually touching the water. I reduce power, lower the flaps and proceed cautiously around South Cape—very low and close to the cliffs. Around the Cape the position is actually worse with

rainshowers and squalls. Just as well I know where those cliffs are on my right! After a couple of minutes the rain eases and Isle du Golfe appears dramatically with beautiful rays of light falling symetrically along its entire length. It only lasts for a few seconds; just long enough for me to snap a quick photo. When flying the scenery changes rapidly and therefore the camera must be loaded and ready for instant use or a good shot is missed. The brief burst of sun causes the water droplets streaming back off the wingstruts to sparkle before being blown off with the slipstream. The scene is gone and the cliffs on the end of the Ironbound Range appear mist shrouded and grey. I pass them at 150 feet above the water. The wind is coming from the south-west at the moment and the turbulence has eased. Can't see the Maatsuyker Island group. Next, Louisa Bay's sandy beach, Louisa Island and the pretty little bays and coves of the Bay slide past. Around Red Point and into Cox Bight, still hugging the coast. It's a couple more minutes before the

beach and Point Eric come into view. I must stick to the windward side of the hills going up to the airstrip, now only about five very bumpy minutes away. I manage to get back to about 300 feet past Half Woody Hill.

Arriving in circuit area of the Melaleuca airstrip I try to raise Melbourne Control on the high frequency radio but I'm too low and the weather conditions are too bad for reception. The strip materialises out of the rain and mist. Air-speed back to 90 knots, flaps at 20 degrees. Its raining so solidly I can hardly see the windsock. It is sticking almost straight out and waving about, indicating at least 20 knots, with some crosswind as well. A check on the water on Melaleuca Lagoon confirms the wind conditions. On the downwind section of the circuit, the stall-warning horn is blipping on and off due to the variations of airspeed caused by the gusty wind conditions.

Turning onto the final approach I lower 30 degrees of flap and reduce airspeed to 70 knots. Then 40 degrees of flap is lowered and the dragging

Flying over Louisa Bay on a late winter's afternoon.

Jim England

effect on the aircraft can be felt. My hands are continually working to keep the aircraft on line with the strip. The driving head-on rain makes it difficult to see the end of the strip and there's bound to be a downdraught right at the last second before touchdown. A brief burst of throttle and back pressure on the controls and the wheels firmly crunch onto the white quartzite gravel of the strip. Controls forward, brakes on and I stop about 100 feet past the parking bay. As I turn back towards it the wind pressure on the tail surfaces forces the use of a lot of power to turn around and this sends up small white stones, some hitting the propeller. This is undesirable as it causes small nicks and abrasions in the leading edges of the propeller blades. I taxi into the parking bay and shut down all the aircraft systems. Reaching for my waterproof parka I climb out onto the ground. I notice a group of people coming down the track from the Charles King Memorial hut, some dressed in yellow parkas, others in black. The rain is coming down, or

rather in, at about 60 degrees to the horizontal as the passengers arrive dripping, their faces wet and smiling.

"Thought you weren't coming today".

"Well you are lucky I'm here", I reply. "I'm in a hurry so who's coming out on the first trip back?"

I supervise the loading of three adults, one ten year old girl and three packs. I strip off my parka and climb into the pilot's seat again. I'm just about to close the door when Denny King arrives handing me a small bundle of letters to take back and post for him. After a few words of greeting I begin start-up procedures again and taxi to the eastern end of the strip to turn the aircraft into the wind. There is a final check on fuel, oil pressure and flaps. On some occasions I have had to ask people to physically hold onto the wing struts to help hold the wings down especially with the lighter aircraft. With the wings rocking in the wind I open the throttle fully and immediately sheets of spray stream from the aircraft as it gathers speed. I lift off about two

thirds of the way down the strip (the headwind gives quite a lot of extra lift over the wings giving a shorter take-off run). Sometimes after a lot of continuous rain, the strip becomes very soggy and even the 300 horsepower of the '206 is tested to the limit to get it airborne. There have been a few occasions when I've used every foot to get airborne off this strip.

As we head for Cox Bight again, I notice the sideways drift of the aircraft over the ground; must have 30 knots of wind out there.

"Sorry I can't give you much of a commentary of the trip" (to the passengers) "got my hands full for a while".

We reach Cox Bight in record time with the strong tailwind, caused by the wind shear around the hills, arriving in time to see the sea mist down to 220 feet again. At 150 feet above the water we follow the coastline around Red Point into Louisa Bay. Those rocky inlets look beautiful even in dirty weather. Now there's cloud on Louisa Island and

Flying over Bathurst Harbour.

Don Stephens

that is just over 100 feet above sea level. I fly cautiously along at 50 feet, the lowest I've ever had to fly to get home. Just off the end of Louisa Island a flock of startled seagulls rise up, right in front of us. A bit of rudder and aileron and I dodge them; never a dull moment. The cloud-base begins to get higher and by the time we pass Havelock Bluff we are at the more respectable height of 700 feet; at least that's legal. At South Cape the rain has almost stopped and I manage to establish radio contact with Melbourne and advise them that I will be contacting Launceston at Catamaran. The remainder of the trip back is uneventful except for one or two bad pockets of turbulence.

On the ground at Cambridge I submit another flight plan for the second trip. By now the front has nearly passed and the trip is much better than the first; only a bit of low mist at Catamaran. The vegetation looks fresh and green in the failing light. It is now 8 pm. Flying at 3000 feet along the coast I can see a faint colouration on the undersides of the clouds and even see some rays of sunlight falling on the Mewstone Rock 16 miles off the South Coast. Maatsuyker is clear and I wish I had the time to circle over the island. I change films in both cameras to colour as it looks like one of those magnificent sunsets is on the way. I pick up the remainder of the passengers at Melaleuca and head for home. The trip back is quite leisurely with cameras clicking, recording the best sunset I've ever seen in 17 years of flying.'

Thoughts go through my mind when I think back to the time last year, when the barometer at Maatsuyker fell 11 millibars in 3 hours to a record low reading, and how immediately after that the winds reached over 90 knots with 100 foot waves lashing the coast and the scrub on the islands. What hope would a light aircraft have in that?

Supply dropping

The airdropping of supplies to bushwalkers in Tasmania reputedly began in 1947, but no doubt odd packages were dropped before that date by enterprising low flyers. The first supply drop to bushwalkers in the South-West was arranged by Leo Luckman for his party of three, at Federation Peak, but was never recovered. A few weeks later two drops to a Hobart Walking Club party exploring the approaches to Federation Peak was the first successful air support of bushwalkers in Tasmania. Non-perishable food was packed in a sealed tin and Brian Simmonds, piloting a Tiger Moth, made the drop near Cracroft Crossing. Since 1947 the amount of supplies dropped each summer season increased to about five

tonnes in 1974–1975, but is declining with the recent ban on airdropping in national parks.

When supply dropping, the pilot's main concern is the weather conditions at the drop zones, and between the drop zones and the aerodrome. Light easterly winds from a strong high pressure system usually provide the still, clear, 'blue air' conditions ideal for dropping in the South-West. It is often supposed that as long as the sky is blue a pilot can drop bags in any situation. There are many less obvious factors involved, however. In the middle of a hot summer's day the sun warms the ground and causes hot air to rise in a thermal. It is preferable to drop supplies in the early morning or evening when turbulence from these thermals is at a minimum. The terrain at

the drop zone is of great importance. It is extremely dangerous to attempt an air drop in windy weather over rugged terrain. At high altitude mountain zones a 10 knot wind can cause turbulence which makes a drop run very dangerous, whereas at a coastal beach zone, with wind blowing from the sea, airflow is usually smooth and laminar with little turbulence. In such conditions a drop may be made in a 20 knot wind.

Visibility is also a major problem. If a drop zone is in cloud a pilot must simply turn back with his load of supplies, so he needs to forecast the weather as accurately as possible. This only comes with experience. During seven seasons of dropping I have only had to return with one full load. I use a very simple set of rules to determine the weather conditions at the drop zones:

1. Look at the daily weather map to determine the approximate position of the high and low pressure systems and their likely influence, including wind velocities and cold fronts.
2. Look at the type of clouds, if any, and note their direction of travel.
3. Check a barometer to ascertain whether it is rising or falling.
4. Check with the local aerodrome meteorological office for an official forecast.
5. Check that 1, 2, 3 and 4 correlate.
6. If there is any doubt ring Maatsuyker Light Station. (I am indebted to them for their help in recent years.)

If a decision is made to undertake the flight, the task of preparing the aircraft begins and, indeed, deciding which aircraft type to use. The door is removed along with all passenger seats. The supply bags are weighed, checked and loaded in the correct order for dropping. They must be loaded so that if one zone is unfavourable then the bags can be reorganized in the aircraft's confined cabin, ready for the other zones. The aircraft's balance must be considered whilst loading, and care taken not to weigh down the aft end of the plane.

The pilot takes as crew a dispatcher who is trained in the technique of dropping. He must have a good stomach to stand the tight turns on the drop runs! Incidentally the bags are always dropped by the free drop method, ie. no parachute or drags attached. The flight plan, worked out to give an economical round trip, has to be filed.

On arrival at a zone, a preliminary low-level circuit is made to determine the suitability of the air conditions before commencing the actual drop runs. Now the pilot has to quickly consider many factors such as the approaches to and from the zone, the weight and performance of the aircraft, the particular zone and its features and the presence of any people on the ground. (Some even stand right on the drop site itself, which makes accurate dropping rather a problem!)

Above all else there should be a workable escape route should anything go wrong. If engine failure occurs at a high level zone there should be plenty of height for the pilot to restart or work out a successful forced landing, but at low level zones such as Cracroft Crossing, engine failure means almost instantaneous contact with the ground. Cracroft Crossing is a particularly hazardous zone, as any wind from any direction means downdraughts on the climb out after every run with the often heavily loaded aircraft. After experiencing these conditions myself I feel that the safety of pilots should be considered more in the choice of airdrop zones!

The shape and weight of the bags, as well as the speed and height of the aircraft, determine when the bags have to be released. Round, heavy bags roll further than light, loosely packed bags. Providing all factors are suitable, the bags arrive on the required zones with all the contents intact. A walker's main consideration is that the bags are delivered on time and in one piece; and the loss rate is now very low.

With air dropping comes the problem of litter and its disposal. Rusty tins still mar some high altitude sites where burying is not feasible. Several methods to overcome this problem have been tried recently. For example food can be placed in cardboard boxes inside strong plastic ex-fertilizer bags.

I feel that though air dropping will still be required in the future, particularly for extended trips, dropping could be restricted to two sites only; Pass Creek and Prion Beach. These sites could be cleared up at intervals by rangers or volunteers. Walkers should be aware that air dropping should not be relied upon or regarded as a luxury service for dropping tinned 'goodies' or 'grog'. Indeed, there has been much discussion concerning the compatibility of such an aid with wilderness travel.

When weather conditions are unfavourable for weeks on end, trying to forecast the weather with the hope of a break long enough to fly the bags in can be most frustrating, as well as disrupting to one's personal time and commitments. However, in good weather I find supply dropping most enjoyable.

Retrieving airdrops at Prion Beach. *David Tasker*

Opposite, top
Landing airdrop bags at Lake Pedder Beach, 1961.
Brian Curtis

Opposite, bottom
Showers at sunset — Melaleuca airstrip, February, 1963.
N E Poynter

Retrieving and opening airdrops generates interest at Junction Creek. *Maurice D Clark*

In all rescues radios play a critical role in the co-ordination of field parties. However, most volunteers need to maintain proficiency by participation in regular exercises. Such exercises introduce both the bushwalker and the police to the Search and Rescue system and to each other. Wise planning by the P.M.G Department, and recently Telecom, has created a co-ordinated radio network between the Police Department, The National Parks and Wildlife Service, the Rural Fires Board, the Forestry Commission and other government instrumentalities.   *Steve Wilson*

Winter conditions add a more difficult dimension to search and rescue operations. Searches frequently take place in bad weather, so ground parties must be very experienced and suitably equipped for such conditions. Since snow on the high ridges is not uncommon even in January, walkers can be caught unawares and may suffer from exposure at any time of the year if not properly equipped. Mt Weld.   *Brown & Dureau*

Search and Rescue

C Hocking & G Hodge

Col Hocking and Greg Hodge have worked closely with the Search and Rescue organisation which has developed a significant role in the 1970's.

As bushwalking and mountaineering gain in popularity it is inevitable that persons are reported lost or injured from time to time. Extensions of roads into the South-West have resulted in easy access to rugged mountainous country that challenges even those familiar with the basics of survival in harsh conditions. For the newcomer to the Tasmanian wilderness, experience must be gained slowly and surely. Whilst some have simply lost their way through lack of both familiarity and map reading skills, others have suffered exposure because they were ill equipped for sudden changes in weather. Some have simply over-estimated their physical and mental capabilities.

In recognition of the positive need for a Search and Rescue team to be 'on the ready' for such occurrences, a small but efficient organization has developed in Tasmania. 'Search and Rescue' operates as the close liaison between the Police Search and Rescue Squad, members of more than 10 walking and mountaineering clubs, and a number of other organizations: the National Parks and Wildlife Service, Rural Fires Board, the Ambulance Board, the St John Ambulance Brigade and State Emergency Services. Each organization has expertise, man-power and specialized equipment that can be called on as required. A major search would involve everyone available working closely as a team. In this way the resources of the State can be utilized quickly and in the most appropriate way with the Police as the overall co-ordinators.

The Search and Rescue organization goes into action as soon as possible after a party or individual is reported overdue or injured. The Police usually receive the message direct from the concerned friends or relatives and immediately telephone the contact officers of the clubs and organizations of Search and Rescue. Each club has three contact officers who hold lists of their members able and willing to be called on at any hour.

Depending on the scale of the operation, and the course of action warranted, the volunteers assemble at Police Headquarters within an hour or two. Transport, equipment and food

Cliff rescue on a search and rescue exercise in 1975.

Alex Sklenica

rations have by then been organized and departure is usually immediate.

In most search operations a base is established at the end of the road. The volunteers are briefed on the nature of the operation by the Police who then rely heavily on the local knowledge and bushmanship of the volunteers—the bushwalkers. With the circumstances of the emergency in mind, including the ages, abilities and equipment of those

who are lost (or in need of help), the bushwalker plans specific tactics in the field. He works with his mates as one of a team using skills of map reading, radio operation and sound common sense.

Those police remaining at base relay feedback to all search groups including aircraft involved in the operation. Radio communication ensures that all possibilities are deduced, that clues are followed immediately and that when appropriate, search groups can be directed to saturate a specific area for a concentrated search. A spirit of friendly co-operation and mutual respect has developed over the years through the experience of a great number of searches and exercises. This respect for the special abilities each person has to contribute has cemented the organization. Experience has increased its efficiency so that the response to the call for help can be immediate.

A very good example of a successfully planned and executed search was one that took place at Mt Field in the winter of 1975. A visiting professor was reported overdue on a day walk by his friends in Hobart late on Sunday night. It was known that he was not properly equipped for the prevailing snow conditions and although he carried a map he had no knowledge of the area.

In the early hours of the morning a search was planned, and in the face of deteriorating weather, volunteers and members of the National Parks and Wildlife Service were driven to Lake Dobson where four search parties were quickly formed and despatched. Each was to cover a separate area checking tracks, routes and huts, for it was not known which direction the man had taken. Movement was difficult in the soft snow and visibility was extremely low. The Police maintained radio contact from their Lake Dobson base and so all parties were informed when the man was found, shortly before nightfall. Having lost his sandshoes, he was suffering exposure and severe frostbite to face, hands and feet. He was immediately placed in a sleeping bag in a tent, fed and carefully observed until daybreak. Weather conditions prevented the use of a helicopter which had been in readiness. A rubber dinghy was used to transport the man along Lake Seal to a track along which he was then carried on a stretcher to the awaiting ambulance. The co-operative efforts of the searchers, their speed and knowledge, had brought them to the snow tracks of the lost man only just in time.

In the past few years there have been Search and Rescue operations on the south and west coasts, at Mt Picton, Mt Lot, Mt Anne, Mt Field, Scotts Peak, Federation Peak and Frenchmans Cap. Although the majority of lost or injured persons are found or rescued in time, there have been gruelling searches abandoned only after many days. Such searches entail the expenditure of considerable public funds and test the energies of large numbers of volunteers and police.

Several deaths testify to the harsh and changeable nature of the weather and the terrain. This fickleness of the South-West can be grossly underestimated on a clear summer's day. It must be impressed upon all who venture forth

on extended trips the need to leave, with a responsible person, accurate details of route plans and the expected date of return. An essential requirement for such trips is self-dependency. This entails a certain preparedness for emergencies that could arise at any time. For those who are equipped, the knowledge of being alone and utterly dependent on personal strengths is a powerful and enriching experience.

Regular Search and Rescue training ensures that expertise is maintained in constant readiness and that necessary skills are acquired. Mt Wellington has provided a convenient location for both specific training sessions and full scale mock searches. For instance, officers of the Ambulance Board have been trained in rock climbing techniques to ensure that a reserve of trained and competent personnel are available for such an emergency as a cliff rescue of an injured person.

Search exercises ensure that the channels of communication are operative and that volunteers are sufficiently familiar with Search and Rescue procedures. They present the opportunity for a trial of equipment and manpower alike; a chance to learn what can go wrong and a test for the system. Weaknesses can be subsequently eliminated. Such exercises, along with quarterly meetings between bushwalking representatives and the Search and Rescue Squad, reaffirm resources and readiness.

Today most Search and Rescue operations involve aircraft to some degree. Pilot Jim England discusses their often vital role.

'Light fixed-wing aircraft have been used extensively for aerial searches in the past. Recently the helicopter has added greatly to the versatility of search methods, providing quick access to remote areas. Its ability to hover over rough terrain and to land without a strip for the recovery of an injured person circumvents days of arduous effort by ground parties which may be too late to save a life.

However, as the operating costs are about six times greater than those of light aircraft, the latter still play an important role in searches, especially in the early phase when walking tracks or possible routes can be checked quickly. At 60 knots, the slowest speed of flight, a lot of detail can be observed and any signs of the lost persons can be relayed to the ground parties immediately.

Messages, contained in an aluminium can to which a bright orange streamer is attached, are sometimes dropped from the air. Advice or instructions include hand or arm signals with which the ground party can communicate with the aircraft. Emergency ration packs and medical supplies can then be dropped as required to sustain the party. Sometimes in thick scrubby country, pre-printed leaflets have been dropped in an effort to saturate an area and ensure that at least one reaches the ground party.

Search and Rescue flights are quite exacting for the pilot, requiring intense concentration and a personal knowledge of the terrain and the possible weather changes.'

A group of NP&WS Rangers struggle with a stretcher in the winter snows on the Labyrinth during a search and rescue exercise in October of 1974. Such exercises, held at regular intervals, aim to develop proficiency in professionals and volunteers alike.
National Parks and Wildlife Service.

B W Davis

Industry

4

In recent years, throughout the world, considerable attention has been focussed on environmental issues. Significant advances have been achieved in our knowledge of ecosystems and the economics of resource utilization. But technology and information alone do not provide the foundation upon which effective resource management rests. The essential prerequisites must include acceptance of diverse community values, plus appropriate legislation, policies and administration within government.

Australia is perhaps unfortunate, in that much of the nations' natural resources legislation is based on exploitative values and orientated towards serving private interests. The Australian states are in active competition for development and do not hesitate to sacrifice environmental quality in order to attract investment. Within government, narrowly specialised agencies and hydra-headed planning inhibit rational resource management. No wonder the idealistic conservationist often feels oppressed, squeezed between an apparently insensitive bureaucracy and a relatively apathetic community which seemingly condones the nibbling attrition of its natural heritage!

These fundamental weaknesses in Australian resource management are exacerbated by the influence of certain professional and technical groups on government decision-making and the penchant for secrecy which pervades both public and private sectors. The average citizen often feels powerless in the face of entrenched elites who interpret 'the public interest' in terms of their own value orientations.

These factors have significant implications for the future of South-West Tasmania, since they illustrate the barriers which need to be overcome if one of the few remaining large scale wilderness areas of the Southern Hemisphere is to be preserved. If the Tasmanian people are to be persuaded to conserve their South-West inheritance, then certain long-standing myths must be dispelled. It is time to stop looking at the resources of the South-West merely from the short-term viewpoint of quick economic gains and to put resource management in a proper long term perspective.

The stump of a Huon pine tree felled at Kelly Basin about 70 years ago. This tree grew from a seed germinating on other Huon logs lying in the forest. Foresters estimate the larger log started growing about 700 A D. *Forestry Commission*

Top left
Robert Hay, a forester in the 1920s. *Forestry Commission*

Top right
Cutting a pack track.
Forestry Commission

Middle left and right
Early days of the timber industry. *D Pinkard*

Bottom, this & opposite page
Forestry Commission

DEPT. AGRICULTURE TASMANIA. Nº10.

Log Train Geeveston Forest

190

Forestry

F P Frampton
J B Kirkpatrick
B W Davis
P T Unwin
C Harwood

Fred Frampton, B.Sc., B.For., Dip. For. (Canb.), M.I.F.A. is the Forestry Information Officer for Tasmania, a position he has held since 1971. He has 34 years experience as a field forester working primarily in the Southern and Central regions of the State.

Dr J Kirkpatrick (see biographic details on page 93)

Bruce Davis is a senior lecturer in Administration at the University of Tasmania. His acquaintance with the South-West began in 1954 and he has walked extensively in the area. His academic interests include research in conservation issues and resource management. He has studied national park management in the United Kingdom, the USA and Canada. Author of numerous submissions and papers, he has influenced the level of decision making in the management of Tasmania's natural resources.

Paul Unwin, Chief Commissioner, Forestry Commission of Tasmania.

Dr Chris Harwood studied at the University of Tasmania before carrying out doctoral studies in Environmental Biology at the Australian National University. Author of *Forestry and Wilderness in South West Tasmania,* he is currently working on a survey of Tasmania's wetlands. Both projects have been funded by the Tasmanian Conservation Trust.

On the track to the Florentine.
Forestry Commission

— Log Hauler, Steam driven —

191

Forestry and the South-West

F Frampton, Forestry Commission

One of the few activities for which the far South-West holds little interest is the wood using industry. Effectively, a line drawn north from De Witt Island could reach the northern boundary of the South-West Conservation Area without excluding any native forest area to the west capable of permanent economic timber production. Indeed, with the exception of the Mt Wedge, Mt Hobhouse and lower Gordon zones, the same would largely be the case if that line were extended as far north as the Derwent River.

So much for the 'true' South-West. Parts of the south-east however, so often lumped into the broad 'South-West' area are a different consideration altogether. This area has been, is and will continue to be one of the most bountiful wood producing areas in the whole State and must figure prominently in any historical outline of Tasmania's forest development.

FOREST HISTORY The pine story

Despite what has already been said, it would be a major omission not to draw attention to the colourful saga of timber production from the western rivers. That such production is now largely historical and can sustain no major economic future is to be deplored, but it is a fact of life that the slow growth rates of the magnificent west coast softwoods, Huon pine and King William pine, rule out investment in their regeneration and management as a commercial crop. (In 100 years diameter growth would be about 120mm).

Both are timbers of outstanding quality, they are both endemic to this State and unlike most other native Tasmanian trees, they will float in water while still green. This property was the very basis of timber harvesting by the hardy 'piners' who since early colonial days braved the wet and miserable climate of the west and its rugged inhospitable terrain for weeks on end, while rowing, wading and humping their boats up the wild rivers to seek out these trees which grew not only on the river banks and flats but often extended up the nearby steep slopes. The trees were felled and the logs manhandled to the stream-side, there to wait until flood waters raged by, sweeping them miles downstream to be retrieved at log booms across the river. Needless to say, breakages, loss and theft were all too frequent and were accepted as a hazard of the operation.

Huon pine is a mellow, easily worked timber with a very fine grain and is highly resistant to damage by rot and other organisms. Favoured for boat building

Logging road, Catamaran, 1976
Tasmanian Environment Centre Inc Col

and joinery the wood was also used as a source of essential oil by distillation. Today the more readily accessible stands of mature Huon pine have been harvested and current supplies of its timber are most readily available from salvage operations in the area flooded by Lake Gordon. This salvage project felled some 10,000 or more trees ahead of the rising waters which in due course floated the logs and enabled them to be salvaged by a jet propelled tug boat.

Natural regeneration of the species can be found on riverside reserves, but two 'museum' type reserves of mature Huon pine have been set aside—the 400 ha Truchanas Huon Pine Reserve on the Denison River, and the 20 ha Gilbert Leitch Memorial Forest Reserve which ultimately will be accessible both by the waters of Lake Gordon and by a disused logging road.

The hardwood harvest and its industries

The history of the southern and south-eastern forests in fact parallels and is a major part of the forest history of the State as a whole.

Production of timber in the Huon by pitsawing is recorded as early as 1822 followed by the introduction of several sawmills powered by waterwheels. Such mills were perforce located on or near streams of fresh water and frequently were close to deep water anchorages for transport of the sawn timber by ship. (An experimental shipment of 200 tons of timber was dispatched from Southport

to London in 1829). The first use of steam to power a sawmill was reported as being at Geeveston in 1874. The period from that time until the 1920's represented the heyday of sawmills working in the Derwent-Huon area. Some mills undertook the distillation of eucalypt oil as a secondary product.

The forests cut over by these mills were the scenes of repeated and holocaustic wildfires, notably in 1881, 1898, 1914 and 1934, which in turn were responsible for re-establishment of the magnificent even-aged stands of trees now being harvested again. Evidence of this can be seen in the old stumps still remaining amongst the lofty trees along the Forestry Commission's new road south from Lune township. These reconstituted forests demonstrate the dependence of the eucalypt on fire as an essential ingredient of its ecology. Research by Tasmanian foresters Gilbert and Cunningham has confirmed this inter-relationship and in so doing established the basic techniques of assisted regeneration of the eucalypts now being practised in many parts of Australia.

By about the 1920's the stands of mature timber more easily accessible to the logging tramways had been cut out and the major milling enterprises declined. At about the same time, the flourishing apple industry created a demand for wooden cases and a large number of small 'box mills' arose to meet the demand, mainly cutting regrowth timber from private property.

As supplies of mature timber became scarce in the Huon area the focus shifted to highland country both north and south of the upper Derwent River, using a species (*Eucalyptus delegatensis*) previously very poorly regarded due to the problems with seasoning of its timber. However improved techniques of kiln drying and reconditioning of timber overcame these difficulties and lumber from the species took its place in sales under the name of 'Tasmanian Oak' along with the two prime lowland species *Eucalyptus obliqua* and *E. regnans*.

It is interesting to note the early opinions of some experts in regard to other uses for the timber of the eucalypts. H E Surface, a consulting engineer in forest products, reported in 1915 that the eucalypts were 'all unsuitable for paper making', while others suggested that the bark of some species may be suitable for this purpose. Both were wrong—it turned out that in all commercial paper making processes to date, the bark of the tree is discarded as unsuitable, while eucalypt wood has now become established as an excellent source of fibre for a wide range of paper making.

Intensive research at Geeveston by L R Benjamin and others resulted first in the establishment of a paper factory at Burnie in 1937, followed in 1941 by production of newsprint at Boyer by Australian Newsprint Mills Ltd. This company now markets some 200,000 tonnes of newsprint each year from the forest resources of southern Tasmania. Twenty one years later a mill at Port Huon commenced production of woodpulp for shipping to the mainland paper mills of Australian Paper Manufacturers Ltd—again dependent on the resources of southern forests.

This was a major step forward towards improving the efficiency of forest utilisation. Whereas previously the sawmill industry had been entirely

Integrated logging of sawmill logs and pulpwood during salvage from Southport forests killed in the 1967 wildfires.
Forestry Commission

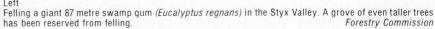

Above and below
Modern equipment for loading and carting logs. *Forestry Commission*

Top left
Family forest use. The Forestry Commission's Tahune Forest Park on the Huon River is a popular picnic spot. *Forestry Commission*

Left
Felling a giant 87 metre swamp gum *(Eucalyptus regnans)* in the Styx Valley. A grove of even taller trees has been reserved from felling. *Forestry Commission*

selective as to the trees it felled and took only the better quality stems, it was now possible to fell any tree with commercial wood in it, using the better sections of the log for sawmilling, with the poorer quality sections being sold as pulpwood for fibre production. Quite apart from greater economic returns, two other massive benefits to the forest estate followed the introduction of pulpwood harvesting—a more efficient utilisation of the timber resource, and for the first time, a dependable technique for full regeneration of cut-over forests.

Social benefits quickly occurred in the country towns of New Norfolk and Geeveston which became decentralised population centres for the wood-using industries—improved housing, education and health services, water and sewage reticulation and associated commercial facilities.

Forest administration

Any attempt at legislative control over the public forests was restricted to the early Waste Lands Act of the colony which authorised the issuing of licences for the felling of timber—without any royalty being payable.

It was not until the Waste Lands Act of 1881 that any provision was made to reserve land for 'the preservation and growth of timber'. The State Forests Act of 1885 authorised the appointment of a Conservator of Forests within the Lands Department and also introduced the concept of timber royalty payment—one penny per super foot for pine from the West Coast 'Pine District' if felled for export and a halfpenny for Tasmanian use. However the rates were considered too high and about 1890 were reduced to one halfpenny and no charge respectively.

The exercise of any control over bush operations was left to police officers acting as Crown Land bailiffs. Illegal timber getting was rife and the general position was described as 'chaotic'.

Previous legislation was repealed by the Crown Lands Act of 1890 and when this was in turn amended in 1898 its regulations confirmed the principles of granting exclusive rights to sawmillers on their cutting leases and of royalty payments on all timber cut.

In 1920 the Forestry Act was passed setting up a separate Forestry Department with a conservator as its head and with its own forest staff.

The reservation of some 21,270 hectares of Timber Reserve had occurred in the late 1880's and under the 1920 Act much of the present day State Forest in southern Tasmania was dedicated in 1926, 1928 and 1933. These State Forests have not only formed the long term resource for forest based industries but have in fact secured the forest estate in perpetuity. Without

wood-using industries the long term reservation of forested land would have been neither motivated nor possible.

Forests and their management today

In the true South-West where forest does occur it is essentially rainforest, but unlike the sub-tropical rainforests of mainland Australia with their immense complexity of species, it is simple in make-up. Typically, the climax temperate rainforest of Tasmania consists of an overstorey of myrtle (*Nothofagus*) and sassafras (*Atherosperma*) trees. Other species such as the native conifers occur locally. Also typically the ground cover is open with a very limited range of species. Shrub density increases at or near the margins of rainforest areas.

Moving further eastwards, the forest climate improves and so does the quality and height of the resultant forests. These pass through the unstable 'eucalypt over rainforest' complex which will revert to pure rainforest unless regeneration of the eucalypt component has been made possible either by periodic uncontrolled wildfires as in the past, or more recently by logging activity.

Still further eastwards the highly productive wet sclerophyll forests flourish under almost ideal conditions with the eucalypt trees growing in stands of an essentially even-aged nature which demonstrates their common origin stimulated by a particular wildfire.

Mature forests of the south-east range in age from 200–400 years, with proportionate onset of degeneration and over-age symptoms. The stands of spar-like younger eucalypts, also even-aged, resulted from early logging and fire and are magnificent in their vigour.

In developing systematic management of these forests, the most significant aid to the forester was the post-war boom in aerial photography. Aircraft flew along parallel flight lines at predetermined heights while fixed cameras automatically took vertical photographs at regular intervals.

Using overlapping pairs of photographs, trained interpreters used the resultant stereoscopic effect to mark out the boundaries of differing forest vegetation types, separating them into classes according to height and major species changes. These data were then correlated by ground surveys so that forest type and topographic maps could be prepared.

Armed with this information on the whereabouts and distribution of forest types, field parties were then able to carry out sampling and assessment of forest volumes and growth rates. This information in turn enabled forest planners to prescribe harvesting regimes tailored to the growth potential of the forest. Such prescriptions form the basis of systematic forest management to

ensure conservative use of the forest resource in perpetuity and are implemented by working plans for each major harvesting licence area.

Felling of the crop after the necessary roads have been built, is perforce a one-lick operation due to the even-aged nature of the wet sclerophyll forest. It is a forest type which does not lend itself to a system of selective felling because of the intolerance of the eucalypt to shading and suppression by its neighbours during seed germination and early seedling growth.

Harvesting therefore is now an integrated operation in which all commercial wood is utilised at the same time. On State-owned lands, this is carried out under close supervision by forest officers to ensure both the non-wastage of wood and the correct classification of timber as sawlog or as pulpwood.

When the timber has been harvested, the area is prepared for the next crop. To do this remnant scrub is felled, the total debris is allowed to dry out and then is burned intensively under selected conditions during the autumn months. This produces conditions akin to those following the historical wildfires and the resultant ash-bed provides an ideal environment for germination of the eucalypt seeds which are sown from aircraft as soon as possible after the burn.

When the new crop has been established it must be protected from damage by browsing animals during the first two years and by wildfire for most of its growing life. In southern Tasmania, fire protection is variously the responsibility of the Forestry Commission, the Rural Fires Board, wood using industrial companies and private individuals. Fire lookout towers, aerial surveillance, sophisticated communication, heavy equipment and simple hand tools all play their part in the early detection and prompt suppression of potentially damaging fire.

Major industries with high capital outlay have been established over the years relying on the southern forests as a resource base. Government has recognised this dependence and has accepted responsibilities for continued supply, not only in the enabling legislation but over the decades in the progressive permanent dedication of State Forests.

Such dedication in perpetuity guarantees a forest estate not only as a raw material supply for a wide range of commodities based on wood fibre, but as an ecological and environmental complex to ensure maintenance of wildlife habitat, water quality, scenic values and soil protection along with a venue for man's recreational, scientific and educational needs.

Accepting these constraints on the management of public forests State-wide, the Forestry Commission has adopted the following guidelines of policy—

Commission policy seeks to systematically manage the Crown forest estate and its renewable resources in perpetuity, with the aims of ensuring stability in the wood-based industries, whilst maintaining acceptable standards of forest environmental values.

It seeks to implement this by:—

(i) The dedication to permanent forest use as State Forests of all productive forest lands not held under tenure as private property or as National Parks or other reserves. A minimum target area of 1,618,000 ha (four million acres) has been accepted.

(ii) The continued protection of the forest estate from damage by wildfire, insects and disease.

(iii) Extending the integration of use of forest products to reduce wastage, to provide an improved harvest of sawlogs, to service the expanding market for hardwood pulpwood and to enable efficient programmes of forest regeneration to be undertaken.

(iv) Rapid escalation of regeneration programmes to cope with reforesting the increased area of forest harvested by integrated logging.

(v) A steady annual programme of softwood plantation establishment located in selected areas where large units of softwood forest can be aggregated.

(vi) Increased research activity to progressively improve forest health and growth and the techniques of forest regeneration and fire protection.

(vii) Inculcating standards of forest management and harvesting so as to satisfactorily protect and maintain environmental forest values like air and water quality, wildlife habitat, aesthetics, recreation etc.

(viii) Intensification of management of State Forests for recreation activities and wildlife conservation.

In applying these principles to forests in the south of the State the Commission accepts that although the concept of multiple use is realisable in most forests, production forestry is not compatible with wilderness maintenance. However, the South-West wilderness is not threatened by forest activity; indeed, a dedicated State Forest can be and is a handmaiden to wilderness by acting as a buffer zone between it and the more intensive forms of land use.

Recognising this, the Commission in no way wishes to extend dedication of State Forests to the virgin areas of the true South-West but instead seeks to maintain the production of wood products and non-wood values from those forests of the south-east long since dedicated for their multi-purpose potential.

The Picton Valley with Hartz Mountains on the skyline, east of the roading and logging activities of the mid-seventies. *Helen Gee*

A clear-felled area in the Florentine Valley. *Alan Gray*

The South-West and Forestry

J Kirkpatrick

The area of potential commercial forest within the South-West wilderness forms only a small proportion of the area of both the South-West and the actual and potential commercial forests of the State. However, this area is large enough not to be readily forsaken by the wood-based industries or by the Forestry Commission whose prime perceived purpose is ensuring the stability of the wood-based industries through sustained production from the maximum possible area of forest land. (see 4.1).

During the past few years forestry roads have been rapidly extending in the Huon, Picton and Cockle Creek valleys, thus, inevitably, diminishing the wilderness area. The impact of this intrusion on wilderness values may be gross, even in places far removed from the actual forestry operations. The scars resulting from clear-fell harvesting and the regeneration process may heal but, with rotational use, will always be visible. The scars of roads, quarries and pits will persist. Given only the development of forests already dedicated to the wood-based industries, such scars will be visible from a large proportion of the mountains of the South-West, including many of those, such as Federation Peak, included within the inadequate national park of 1978.

The case against further intrusion of development into the wilderness forests is strong simply based on the maintenance of wilderness values (see 5.1), but is reinforced when the need for reserves typifying the commercially valuable tall open-forests dominated by *Eucalyptus regnans* (swamp gum) and *E. obliqua* (messmate, stringybark) is balanced against their present reservation and the nature of their lifecycle. Reserves such as national parks serve the community in many ways. However, there are three functions of reserves that are most severely affected by forestry activities, the first of which has been mentioned in the previous paragraph. The second function is that of a benchmark. The effects of forestry activity in tall open-forests can only be adequately assessed in the long-term if untouched ecosystems of the same type survive. The Forestry Commission may need a large area of untouched eucalypt forest of various ages to be able to adequately research such problems as the dieback evident for some time in the regeneration forests serving the Geeveston Mill.[1]

The benchmark function of national parks is strongly linked to the third function considered here; the conservation of variety. If a reserve is large

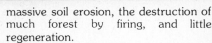
Eucalyptus obliqua.
David Tasker

enough, species, communities of species and structural types will be able to survive the developmental present to perhaps give joy to the inhabitants of a non-developmental future. Most species and communities found in the tall forests may survive forestry activity, although information is lacking on much of the fauna. However, the full range of structural types cannot survive exploitation. We cannot look for survival of the mature and overmature stages of the tall forests within areas developed for wood production. Similarly we cannot expect that all stages in the lifecycle of the tall forests will survive within the present 1,460 ha reserved in Mt Field National Park, the 2,400 ha threatened by boundary changes in the Hartz Mountains National Park or the other small fragments found in reserves in the north of the State.[2] Research by foresters has convincingly shown that natural regeneration of the tall forests is dependent on periodic severe wildfires which devastate large areas.[3][4][5] Thus, the presently reserved tall forests may be of inadequate area to fulfil either the benchmark or the variety preserver function.

Of course, the tall forests dominated by *E. regnans* and *E. obliqua* are far from the only types of potential commercial forest found in the South-West. There are also reasonably large areas of open-forest dominated by eucalypts and closed-forest (temperate rainforest) dominated by one or several of *Nothofagus cunninghamii* (myrtle), *Atherosperma moschatum* (sassafras), *Phyllocladus aspleniifolius* (celery-top pine), *Athrotaxis selaginoides* (King Billy pine) and *Dacrydium franklinii* (Huon pine). Little is known of the ecology of the closed-forest. Yet, lack of knowledge has not prevented exploitation of these forests in accessible areas, and in most cases such exploitation has lead to

massive soil erosion, the destruction of much forest by firing, and little regeneration.

The forestry claim on the South-West forests is ultimately based on two major arguments. The first of these is the projected demand for wood products. The demand projections made at the FORWOOD conference rely on spurious population projections, and reflect more the optimistic desires of the wood-based industries than the real needs of the Australian people. A considerable proportion of the effective demand for wood products is created, and in turn creates a considerable part of our rubbish disposal problems, while enhancing only the welfare of the wood-based industries. The extreme example is the mass of unnecessary packaging found enveloping and obscuring consumer goods. If our society avoided creating such rubbish we would not need to exploit as much forest. Also, as the Australian Conservation Foundation points out, our forests are valuable for other uses apart from those easily quantifiable, and the extent of our commercial use of forest may be necessarily limited to below the material optimum in order that the total well-being of Australians be optimized.[6]

The second argument is based on the employment provided by forestry operations and the wood-based industries. This argument assumes that employment in rural areas is linked to the area of forest exploited. Yet, employment could easily be provided by governmental definition, and much of this employment could be in forestry without expanding the exploited acreage. For example, the development of plantations of *E. regnans* on marginal farmland in the Esperance municipality would both create employment and reduce the pressure on the wilderness forests.

The Tyenna-Florentine area is being clear-felled by Australian Newsprint Mills Ltd. Revocation of part of the Mt Field National Park for forestry development left many important caves unprotected. Severe soil erosion from the limestone surface has resulted in thick sediment accumulation in stream caves. Spot fires burnt out much of the alpine vegetation around Mt Field West and Florentine Peak in 1965.   *Kevin Kiernan*

Window Pane Creek, south-west coast.   *A Moscal*

Previous page
First Falls, Serpentine Gorge.   *A Moscal*

'*Cushions of Donatia novae-zelandiae on Pandani Shelf, Mt Anne, with Lots Wife in the background. The branches of these unusual small shrubs are erect and tightly packed together and rarely more than 300 mm long. A number of plants from different families may grow together and coalesce, forming an extensive undulating mosaic. The cushion plants are of considerable importance to the drainage patterns at the headwaters of many streams and rivers. Slowly, a group of plants may dam and eventually divert many of the smaller streams and drainage channels.*' (Alan Gray) If burnt, the fragile plant communities of Mount Anne would take hundreds of years to recover. Fires associated with forestry activities threaten this alpine vegetation increasingly as logging roads extend up the Huon and Weld River valleys.   *Chris Harwood*

PLATE 6

I had a desire
to pray
to a wooden God;
to ask it
to confound
the man who sold my bush
for ten pieces
of silver.

I had a desire
to be left alone
awhile;
to walk slowly
where manferns grow;
to see the bronze-tipped myrtles
and to know
I was alone.

I had a desire
to move into the bush;
to see the scrub wrens
poised on shadowed branches,
watching;
to touch cool trunks
with my hands;
to be alone.

Today I saw two men
with yellow hats
and two red chain-saws;
and saw a bulldozer
crashing,   slashing
thrashing through the manferns
that had taken
Christ knows how long to grow.

I have a desire
now
to give my secret
to the button-grass
to keep;
to watch it,
silently,   softly
weep.

From the poem
'WHERE MANFERNS GROW'
by Barney Roberts

The impact of operations on the Picton Valley.
Tasmanian Environment Centre Inc Col

Myth and Reality in Forestry Management

B W Davis

One of the more disturbing aspects of resource management disputes is the tendency for impartiality and reason to decline, as conflict escalates. Conservationists, government agencies and private interests clamour for the public's attention and try to persuade politicians towards particular courses of action. Statistics are quoted out of context, insults are traded and the community gradually becomes confused as claims and counterclaims are made. If the future of South-West Tasmania is to be rationally determined, then reason will have to replace rhetoric. This will not be an easy task, as people often cling to beliefs even when contrary evidence is available. The situation becomes even more difficult when 'facts' turn out to be judgements made by particular individuals. This especially applies in forestry management, where crucial decisions often rest less on silvicultural factors than on estimates made about yields, demand and pricing. We should be extremely sceptical about some of the claims made for forestry potential in the South-West region, as many of the statements made do not stand the test of evidence or evaluation.

The first notion that needs to be dispelled, is any belief that South-West Tasmania will provide a limitless store of forest wealth, guaranteeing the pros-perity of certain municipalities. Not only are large areas of the South-West devoid of forest cover, but the timber stock has already been reduced by the creation of the Hydro-Electric Commission's Gordon impoundment. This is not the place to repeat the history of the Lake Pedder debacle, but it is interesting to note that in carrying out project evaluation for the Middle Gordon Power Scheme, the value of timber assets was entirely neglected. Moreover it can be seriously questioned whether South-West forestry operations could ever guarantee the financial prosperity of municipalities such as Huon and Esperance. As the current economic recession has demonstrated, forest products are as vulnerable to shifts in world pricing and demand as other basic commodities. Transferring people from sawmilling activities to woodchip production does not necessarily enhance employment prospects and the general economic problems faced by some municipalities are essentially long-term structural difficulties which no individual strategy will solve. Forestry activities **are** important and should be continued, but they are not the panacea that some developers and politicians claim.

The next question to be posed is why the forest resources of South-West Tasmania should need to be exploited. After all, nearly forty per cent of the State's total area is wholly or partially forested and approximately two-thirds of Tasmania's surface is already allocated to forestry interests as production or reserve concession zones. The answer is simple. The forest resources of the State are overcommitted and current regeneration rates fall far behind regeneration needs and estimates. Pressure is mounting on the South-West as developers are forced to penetrate further westwards to exploit hitherto virgin areas, such as the Weld and upper Picton valleys. This process cannot continue indefinitely, for there is a limit to new areas, but in the interim there is a grave risk of options being foreclosed and serious damage caused to the South-West environment.

Presumably no-one considers undertaking forestry investment unless there is an assured market. But how realistic are the national and state estimates upon which Tasmanian forestry programs are based? In the short term, perhaps market demand is an accurate indicator, but even here the massive subsidies provided for timber and paper interests are masked from the general public. Even if one accepts some of the initial optimistic estimates made about possible demand for paper products in

Forests inundated by the Gordon Hydro-Electric Scheme, Stage One. Gordon flood plains, 1977.   *David Tasker*

Top left, right and below
Forestry Commission signs. Arve Road. *Alan Gray*

Clear felled cutting area of wet sclerophyll State
Forest in the Dover district being aerially sown with
pelleted eucalypt seed after intensive controlled
burning. *Forestry Commission*

the year 2000 (see the FORWOOD Conference Reports 1974), these projections have since been invalidated by revised population estimates (see the Borrie Report, *National Population Inquiry* 1975).

Another aspect warranting attention is project evaluation methodology. The traditional tool of forestry economics is cost-benefit analysis, a technique notoriously weak in handling time scales of the kind inherent in forestry production and also highly vulnerable to assumptions about yield, demand, pricing, discount rates and inflation. The woodchip legislation of the early 1970's was passed without any detailed economic or social evaluation of prospective costs and benefits to the Tasmanian community. This essential analysis has still not been completed, hence the future of South-West Tasmania is likely to be decided more by current expediency than by rational evaluation of options.

Some development interests have claimed an inalienable right to exploit the resources of the South-West. In some instances these putative 'rights' were obtained via private agreements between developers and government agencies without any opportunity for public comment. In other instances 'rights' are claimed to exist under State

legislation, but such Acts in fact permit the Tasmanian Government to withdraw permission, without compensation, when areas are required for conservation purposes. The Second Schedule of the Forestry Act, which includes these provisions, has already been used on a number of occasions (see *Tasmanian Government Gazette* 9th July and 10th December 1975, also 5th May 1976). It is therefore incorrect to assert that development interests have any exclusive or inalienable right to exploit the resources of the South-West region.

Given the above pressures and issues, is there any prospect that we can both conserve and develop the South-West? The answer is 'yes', provided prompt and effective action is taken. Scenic areas devoid of mineral, forestry or hydro-electric potential should be granted immediate national park status. The need to preserve a wide scale and diversity of ecosystems, including rainforest, should be recognised. Production forestry should be encouraged on the eastern fringes of the South-West region, such as the Arve and Hastings valleys, with some zones of virgin forest retained in their natural state. Financial assistance should be provided to persuade farmers in the Huon and Esperance municipalities to convert marginal land into forestry production.

Pressure on South-West forest resources should be relieved by more effective regeneration programmes elsewhere in the State. The Tasmanian Government should carry out a detailed economic survey of forest industries to discover the true costs and benefits to the community and focus more attention on mixed development strategies for municipalities with sustained employment difficulties. The tourist potential of these municipalities should also be examined.

There is a grave risk that if these planning provisions are delayed, irreparable encroachments will be made upon the South-West wilderness. If government agencies are left free to pursue purely parochial interests, then co-ordinated planning will be absent and piecemeal destruction of the South-West will increase. The Tasmanian Government has primary responsibility for ensuring that the South-West is saved for current and future generations; it can only achieve this aim through clear policy directives and sanctions against those who transgress basic environmental safeguards. The Australian Government should provide sufficient funding to ensure that South-West Tasmania is retained as a World Heritage Area. The real question is whether the nation can find the statesmen needed to achieve these desirable aims.

The Value of a Forest

Wood Based Industries in the Southern Forests

P T Unwin, Chief Commissioner,
Forestry Commission

Significant industries have developed based on the southern forests. Using sawlogs and pulpwood they exercise a major influence on the economy of the Esperance and Huon Municipalities. Continuity of supplies of sawlogs and pulpwood from the forests in question is essential, in the view of the Commission, to maintain these industries and the benefits that flow from them for the welfare of the community.

Forest resource assessments undertaken during the late 1940's and early 1950's led to the passing by Parliament of the Forestry Act 1954 with a view to attracting a pulp and paper industry in the Huon. After attempts were made, world wide, to establish an industry, Australian Paper Manufacturers Ltd reached agreement with the Commission to do so and further legislation was passed by Parliament in the form of the Huon Valley Pulp and Paper Industry Act 1959.

Harvesting of sawlogs for the sawmilling industry and pulpwood for APM is carried out from the Pulpwood and Reserve Areas which are shown on p. 252. Management of the forests is regulated under a working plan. Cutting is carefully planned by the Commission and necessary road construction carried out in advance. These activities are agreed upon at annual conferences between the Commission, APM and the Sawmilling Industry. At the completion of cutting the Commission undertakes re-establishment of the forest and ample evidence of this can be seen on areas that have been logged since 1962 when APM commenced operations.

At the present time there are some 25 sawmills ranging from medium size to very small, dependent upon Crown land logs from the southern forests. In addition a further 26 or so small mills rely on logs from private land within the same area. Sawlogs comprise overmature logs from forests which have not been cut in the past and logs from regrowth resulting from early milling operations.

Likewise pulpwood is obtained from overmature forests. Regrowth of the latter is in strong demand because of superior fibre quality.

The total resources of sawlogs and pulpwood on the Pulpwood and Reserve Areas under sale to APM and are needed, in the Commission's view, to maintain existing sales committments to both these important industries.

As production forestry is incompatible with wilderness, conflict was the inevitable result of the acceleration in the 1970's of road construction and logging operations by the Australian Pulp Mills in the southern forests.

Conservationists regarded the virgin forests of the Weld, the upper Huon, the Picton and the Catamaran river valleys as belonging to the South-West wilderness. The topography of these outer zones had guarded the heart of the region into the 1970's.

To the Forestry Commission such arguments were emotional, selfish and ill-founded. The forests represented an economic resource to be exploited seemingly at all environmental cost. APM was operating within concession boundaries granted by Act of Parliament in 1954. This was, they argued, a binding commitment to harvest forests. When the Governments' South-West Advisory Committee recommended in 1976 a review of such boundaries, the Forestry Commission refused to concede that concessions were available for review. However, part of APM's concession was in fact incorporated in the Precipitous Bluff region of the Southwest National Park. Simultaneously part of the Hartz National Park was conditionally revoked for forestry purposes. The history of such revocations by the Tasmanian Government has demonstrated that legal agreements can be broken but unfortunately rarely is this in the best long term interests of the island.

PRECIS OF FOREST OPERATIONS IN THE SOUTHERN FORESTS 1976/77

1. Timber cut from Crown Forests

Sawlog	79 149 m³
Pulpwood	157 100 m³
Total	236 249 m³

2. Employment by Forestry Commission and Forest Industries in Municipalities of Esperance, Huon, Cygnet, and Bruny.

Forestry Commission	88
Industry	393
Total	481

3. Forest Regeneration

Forest seed extracted	951.9 kg.
Area burnt for regeneration	722.5 ha.
Area sown	630.2 ha.
Area planted	32.5 ha.

4. Construction of logging roads on State Forest. Measured in Kilometres

Financial Year	1973/74	1974/75	1975/76	1976/77
By Forestry Commission	11.27	10.10	13.60	15.50
By Forest Industries	6.76	1.90	7.70	9.30
Total for Year	18.03	12.00	21.30	24.80
Grand Total to date	518.91	530.91	552.51	577.01

The soil surface is disturbed over a large area in the Picton Valley where clear felling has been practised. There has been great wastage of wood, and erosion may become severe in this region of high rainfall. *Helen Gee*

Cartage of 'old man' stringybark sawlogs.
Forestry Commission

Precipitous Bluff overlooks New River Lagoon.

Jim England

In the Picton Valley; logs stacked ready for transport to the mills.

Helen Gee

The Precipitous Bluff — Hartz Swap

C Harwood

Prior to its inclusion in the Southwest National Park in 1976, the Precipitous Bluff area lay within the Australian Paper Manufacturers' (APM's) pulpwood concession, which is regulated by the 1954 Forestry Act. This act has the provision that timber rights can be withdrawn (without compensation) from land which is required for public purposes, as was clearly the case for the Precipitous Bluff area.

However, the Forestry Commission and the Tasmanian Parliament took the view that APM should be compensated for the exclusion of the Precipitous Bluff forests from their concession. Justification for this view has been given in terms of maintaining employment, and the resource base of the company, so that it and other industry is not alienated from Tasmania.[1] Compensation took the form of an Act of Parliament, passed in November 1976, that will revoke 2,150 hectares of forest from the Hartz Mountains National Park for timber production in January 1979, unless an alternative is found.

If the proposed swap is to go ahead, issues additional to the obvious one of alienation of a national park are raised. In its 1975 submission to the South West Advisory Committee, APM was prepared to accept the swap on the basis of the current Forestry Commission estimate that there were 209,000 tonnes of pulpwood at Precipitous Bluff and 224,000 tonnes at Hartz (sawlog volumes were not stated). However, a later Forestry Commission estimate revised the volumes upwards, to 121,000 m³ of sawlogs and 487,000 tonnes of pulpwood at Precipitous Bluff, the corresponding figures for Hartz being 120,000 and 310,000. The 1976 Act was written with reference to these later estimates. More accurate figures, based on ground survey data, have not yet been released, but it appears that much of the pulpwood at Precipitous Bluff is too badly fire damaged to be usable. For the first harvest, the Hartz forests appear to be a much superior commercial proposition, as the quantity of sawlog is the same, and oldgrowth pulpwood is in oversupply in the concession — it is sawlog and regrowth pulpwood that are in limiting quantities. The Hartz site is much closer to the mills, greatly reducing roadbuilding, maintenance and transport costs. These factors would appear to give a commercial advantage of over $1,000,000 to the Hartz site.[2]

It is probably true that the greater area of eucalypt forest at Precipitous Bluff (3,450 ha, compared with 1,800 ha at Hartz) would provide a greater yield of regrowth pulpwood, but this would not be harvested for at least 45 years after the oldgrowth cut, which at Precipitous Bluff would not have occurred for at least 10 years, if ever.

Although the possibility is not mentioned in the 1976 Act, it now seems probable that part of the upper Weld Valley, rather than the Hartz forests, will be offered to APM as compensation. But even if the principle of compensation is fully accepted, it is fallacious to assume that this must involve destruction of forest wilderness in the Hartz National Park or the Weld Valley. Sawlogs can be supplied by diverting from Australian Newsprint Mills' Florentine Valley concession a very small proportion of the fine sawlog material that is presently converted to newsprint at Boyer. Furthermore, a small area of intensively managed eucalypt plantation, much closer in to the APM's Geeveston pulpmill, would provide an alternative source of regrowth pulpwood, and its establishment would provide much-needed extra employment.

Alarming Rate Of Denudation Threatens Industry

By a Special Correspondent.

REFERENCES are made frequently to the rapidly diminishing supply of timber in Southern Tasmanian forests and an immediate re-afforestation scheme on a large scale is urged. The general opinion among bushmen and sawmillers is that the supply could be stabilised by assisting regrowth of native timbers. Attempts to introduce imported softwoods as a substitute are regarded as waste of time and money.

ENORMOUS quantities of timber have been exported from Tasmania since early in the 19th century. The first Huon settlers engaged in splitting shingles and palings were paid 4/ per 100ft., but when the discovery of gold in Victoria called for large quantities of props for stopes in the mines, the price rose to 25/ and even 30/ per 100 super feet.

Trees of enormous size made an almost impenetrable forest along the banks of the Huon River and throughout the coastal area of Esperance. One tree at Franklin provided 50,000 shingles, another 7,000 28in. fruit cases. The beams in the first Huonville bridge came from a tree at North Franklin, and were 90ft. x 18in. x 12in. Blue gums at Geeveston were found 180 to 200ft. clear of limb and with straight boles. These huge trees were at first dealt with by pit saws, but in 1849 a power mill, driven by water wheel, was erected by Richard Hill at Geeveston, followed by another mill erected by the Rev. Andrewarthur, at Flights Bay. In 1852 Charles Oates built a mill at Mountain River, and the next year Thos. and William Walton a steam sawmill at Huonville. This was bought by John Geeves and re-erected at Geeveston in 1870. John Hay brought out a steam mill from Scotland, and erected it at Franklin in 1853. This was re-erected at Hastings 14 years afterwards.

In the Huon and Esperance districts more than 50 mills were operating in the '80's, and the rising output of timber required a fleet of schooners and steamers to transport it to the Mainland and overseas. The biggest sawmill at the beginning of the present century was at Port Huon, operated by the Huon Timber Co., whose leases comprised 21,000 acres.

THE reputation of Tasmanian hardwood was well established before the close of the last century, and in 1893 Phillip Schnell received a commission from the South African Government to supply 25lb. of blue gum seeds. The seeds were planted near Cape Town and in Southern Rhodesia, and the trees are now of commercial size for milling. Mr. Schnell stated that, as far back as 1896, Mr. W. H. T. Brown, forest officer, put up a scheme to re-afforest some of the land that had been cut, but he could get no official support. The improvement of milling machinery and haulage appliances has hastened the denudation. Some idea of the consumption of these mills can be gained from the fact that during the past five years the quantity of timber sawn in Tasmania totalled 909,237,402 super feet, about 25 per cent of which was for fruit cases. Obviously this enormous destruction cannot go on indefinitely without bringing about a famine in sawn timber, unless steps are taken to refurnish the areas.

If intelligent and continuous assistance had been employed to encourage the growth of these trees during the past 50 years, Tasmania would have been in a far better position today to meet the ever-increasing demand for sawn timber.

Millers, especially those cutting fruit cases, are greatly concerned at the prospect of not being able to keep plants operating in the near future, owing to the difficulty of getting logs within an economic distance of mills and markets. One box miller in the Huon states he is transporting logs on an average of 23 miles from bush to mill. Others are in much the same position.

Practically nothing has been done to make good the denudation of forests, except what Nature has supplied by regrowth. The planting of imported pines is described as a waste of time and money. Even if they grew as well as in the country of their origin they would be nothing like as valuable as stringy bark, swamp, and blue gum.

ADVERSE criticism has been levelled against the Forestry Department by bushmen in all parts of Southern Tasmania for its waste of money in making so-called fire-breaks. The general opinion is that, in the event of a serious outbreak, they would be of no value as the fire would race across the narrow clearing or leap from tree-top to tree-top if a strong north-westerly were fanning the fire. Similarly the portable pumps obtained for spraying a bush fire would, bushmen maintain, be useless against a line of flame a mile or so wide. Bush fires travel at such a speed that, before one could be reached, it would be exceedingly dangerous to attack from the front, and ineffective if approached with the wind in the rear.

Millmen and bushmen agree that, if the money thus spent had been used for clearing scrub and sags where regrowth timber was re-establishing itself, a real benefit would have been conferred on the timber industry. One millman stated: "If the Government allotted a square mile of forest per man, in cut-out country, to keep down spindly growths and sags, the young timber would re-establish itself, and in 30 years the crop of trees would pay handsomely for the outlay."

Improvement of milling machinery and haulage appliances has hastened the denudation of the forests. Here a log hauler is shown at work.

The Mercury, 25 August, 1942

The Environment, Growth Projections and Hydro-Electricity in Tasmania's South-West

P D Wilde

Dr Peter Wilde is a lecturer in Geography at the University of Tasmania. His teaching and research are concerned with the location of economic activity and job opportunities and with regional development and planning. He has written articles on various aspects of planning in Tasmania including one on 'The problem of planning Tasmania's electricity supply', published in Geography, November 1975.

Introduction

The South-West of Tasmania has considerable attractions for hydro-electric development. The relief is rugged and variable and major river valleys are deep, producing many potential dam sites and good heads of water for power stations. Total rainfall is sufficiently great and reliable, despite seasonal fluctuations, to prevent water storages falling to critically low levels except in occasional drought years.[1] In addition, human activity in the South-West is very limited so that there is little conflict between hydro-electric schemes and existing settlements, roads or economic activities. On the other hand the remoteness and inaccessibility of the area has always presented a barrier to hydro-electric investigations and development, and although some installations have been built on the region's more accessible fringes, the South-West itself has been avoided while more easily developed hydro-electric potential elsewhere remains unutilised. However, with the completion of the Mersey-Forth scheme in 1973 over 40 per cent of all Tasmania's water power potential, estimated to total between 14 and 15 million megawatt-hours per annum, was harnessed. Virtually all of the remaining potential was located in the South-West,[2] which inevitably has become the focus of the Hydro-Electric Commission's planning for future power supplies.

But while the hydro-electric development of Tasmania's South-West may be economically and technically feasible, the view is increasingly being expressed that environmental values must also be considered in assessing the worth of any project or the future of the area. From this viewpoint any development is considered undesirable. This is because the South-West is a major wilderness area which has hitherto been largely untouched by man's activities and the incursion of hydro-electric schemes into the area is incompatible with its maintenance in this state. The environmental issues involved will be discussed after the proposed hydro-electric schemes have been outlined and the problem of planning Tasmania's electricity supply considered.

Opposite page
BEFORE (The Franklin)

Bob Brown

Above
AFTER (The Gordon)

David Tasker

205

Hydro-electric developments

The first hydro-electric scheme to be commenced in the South-West was the Gordon River project. The first two of five generators planned for the Middle Gordon Scheme have been installed and electricity was first produced in November 1977. Meanwhile, construction work was begun in 1973 on the Mackintosh and Murchison dams in the upper Pieman River and detailed investigations and planning is continuing for dams and power stations on the lower Pieman and Gordon Rivers. Closely linked with the Lower Gordon power scheme is the investigation of the Franklin River—a major tributary of the Gordon—and the independent King River system. Current investigations by the Hydro-Electric Commission suggest that the power potential of these rivers could be harnessed in a number of ways.[3]

Integrated development could occur with water from the upper King River being diverted by the Tofft Dam near Crotty into the Andrew River and so to a power station below the Franklin Dam about one kilometre downstream of the confluence of the Andrew and Franklin Rivers. A 76 metre dam and associated power station on the Lower Gordon, a short distance downstream of the Franklin River junction, could then use this water again and also the flow of the Gordon itself to generate more power. A small dam and power station at Albert Rapids, downstream of the confluence of the Serpentine and Gordon Rivers could harness the 24 metre difference in elevation between the Middle and Lower Gordon River schemes and maximise the use made of water in the Gordon River (Fig 1).

Alternatively part of the flow of the Franklin River could be diverted to a power station on the King River with an independent scheme developed on the Lower Gordon. In this arrangement there would be virtually no change in the position or size of the Franklin and Tofft dams but the flow would be reversed and the Franklin River catchment would be discharged into Macquarie Harbour via the King River. On its way it would pass through a second dam and power station at Sailor Jack, which would also use the water of the Queen River. On the Gordon River the Lower Gordon dam would probably be dispensed with and a dam built above the Olga River confluence. A less likely alternative is for the Gordon to be diverted into the Denison River by the Splits dam and the water then returned to the Gordon through a power station at the Denison dam (Fig 2). Table 1 indicates the yield of the alternative schemes. The Integrated Development is capable of generating more electricity but the Separate Development has the virtue of enabling one scheme to proceed without the other.

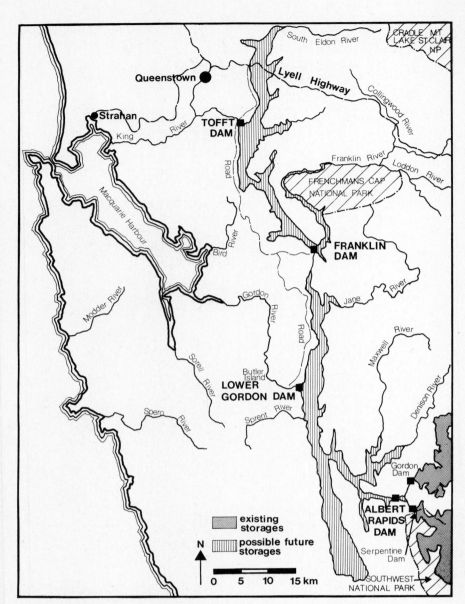

Fig 1 INTEGRATED DEVELOPMENT: King diverted into Franklin: power station at Franklin Dam. Lower Gordon Dam to back up combined water of the Gordon and Franklin. *Source: HEC publications.*

An important aspect of any Lower Gordon development is that the considerable water storages, already completed in the Middle Gordon Scheme, would increase considerably in value since their water would be used again on its flow to the sea. As a corollary, the actual size of the lower storages is relatively insignificant, though of course, the height of the fall to the turbines is important. A considerable amount of investigation remains to be done on these schemes and it is expected to be some time before sufficient information is available for meaningful economic evaluation of the alternatives.

The Hydro-Electric Commission is also considering the potential of the Davey River for power production. This river could be used in the integrated scheme outlined above by diverting it into the Lower Gordon via the Olga-Hardwood saddle adding a further 236 million kilowatt hours to the average annual output of the Lower Gordon power station. Alternatively, an independent water storage and power station could be built on the lower Davey River.[3] There is also the potential for relatively small hydro-electric schemes on the Huon and Arthur Rivers. Although these projects are both technically feasible, they are economically unattractive at present and it is likely to be a long time before they are considered further.[4]

Electricity demand and generating capacity

These plans to develop more hydro-electric power are open to criticism at a fundamental level in that they are bound up in the modern economy's preoccupation with growth without any consideration of the consequences of

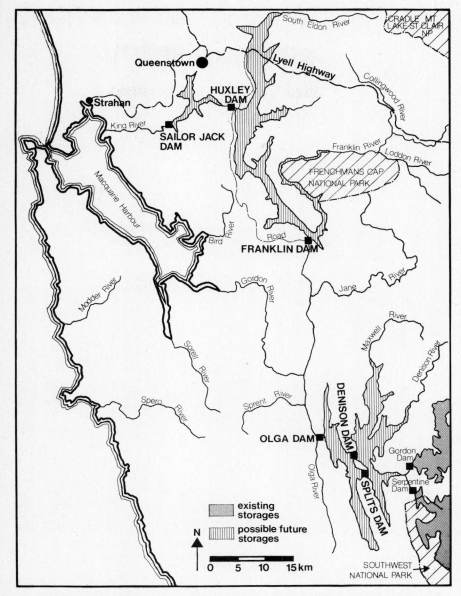

Fig 2 SEPARATE DEVELOPMENT: Franklin diverted into King; generation of power on the King River. Gordon dammed upstream of the Olga River. *Source: HEC publications.*

last few years. To meet growth of 6 to 9 percent, capacity needed to be doubled every 8 to 12 years and even to meet a steady annual growth rate of 3.6 per cent (the average for the period 1972 to 1977) capacity would need to be doubled every twenty years. If the generating system were to continue to expand at this rate there would be strong arguments for more and bigger hydro-electric installations which would inevitably have an even greater physical and environmental impact, since over the next 10 to 20 years as much new capacity could be used as has been added to the system over the past 60 years. Even with average annual growth rates of only 2 to 3 per cent, which many of those involved see as likely in the immediate future, the remaining hydro-electric potential in the state begins to look not only finite but almost insignificant in amount.

The growth in total generating capacity has broadly paralleled the growth of demand but for a number of reasons it is misleading to expect a very close correspondence between installed capacity and annual consumption. Firstly, as well as supplying the total power demanded in a year the generating system must also be able to meet the peak load required—a peak which usually occurs late on a winter's afternoon when many industries are still operating and when households are also making heavy demands for cooking, lighting and heating. Table 2 and Figure 3 consequently show the growth of peak as well as total loads.

Secondly, the generating system must have some spare capacity to allow for breakdowns and the servicing of equipment. Calculations are based on the largest machine in use and in accordance with prudent international practice almost 20 per cent of installed capacity is currently held in reserve for this reason.

A third reason for installed capacity not necessarily keeping in step with demand is that some equipment is designed to be used heavily but seldom. For example, 'run of the river' schemes, such as Mersey-Forth and Pieman, are able to store only a few weeks' supply of

and limits to growth in a world of finite resources.[5] Within the limited framework of current economic attitudes the plans must be examined in relation to the growth of consumption of electricity in the State. Since 1940 the

total demand for electricity has grown at varying rates. In some years figures as high as 15 or 20 per cent have been recorded, but 6 to 9 per cent each year were more common growth rates before the marked slowing of growth over the

TABLE 1

CAPACITY OF ALTERNATIVE HYDRO-ELECTRIC SCHEMES IN TASMANIA'S SOUTH-WEST
Millions of kilowatt hours per annum

Integrated Development	A	Separate Development	B	C
GORDON RIVER		FRANKLIN & KING RIVERS		
Franklin	1170	Tofft and Sailor Jack	1740	1740
Lower Gordon	1800	GORDON RIVER		
Albert Rapids	245	Olga	1070	
Davey Diversion	236	Splits/Denison		895
Total	**3451**	**Total**	**2810**	**2635**

Source: Hydro-Electric Commission *Power scheme investigations* (March 1976)

Quarry for road building and dam construction at Scotts Peak. *Jim England*

Scotts Peak rockfill dam under construction. *Hydro-Electric Commission*

Strathgordon construction village was established in 1969, and at peak the population reached 2,000. Though construction work on the power scheme has finished, part of the village will be retained for the use of maintenance staff and visitors. *Hydro-Electric Commission*

The Serpentine Impoundment: Lake Pedder flooded. The South-West, with its characteristic dark waters, is renowned for magnificent reflections. *Hydro-Electric Commission*
'wherever there is a body of water there will be reflections...' *Max Angus*

The Middle Gordon Scheme

The Dams:

Dam	Type	Height (metres)	Crest Length (metres)
Serpentine	Rockfill	38	131
Scotts Peak	Rockfill	43	1067
Edgar	Rockfill	17	460
Gordon	Concrete	140	190

The Storages:

Volume — 14,700 million cubic metres
Area — 520 square kilometres

The Power:

Installed capacity — 288,000 kw.
Annual average output — 1,333 million kwh.

Source: Hydro-Electric Commission publications

Radial gate on McPartlan Pass Canal under construction. The canal from Lake Pedder to Lake Gordon was opened in July 1974. On rare occasions flood flows may be discharged in the reverse direction as there is no normal spillway at the Gordon Dam. The flow is controlled by a single radial gate. *Hydro-Electric Commission*

The double curvature arch dam on the Gordon River, situated in a narrow, deep gorge of intensively folded quartzite. The concrete dam, 140 metres in height, impounds about 12,000 million tonnes of water, of which 10,400 million cubic metres is usable storage. The average natural flow in the Gordon River at the damsite is 59 cumecs. The dam was completed in November 1974.

Hydro-Electric Commission

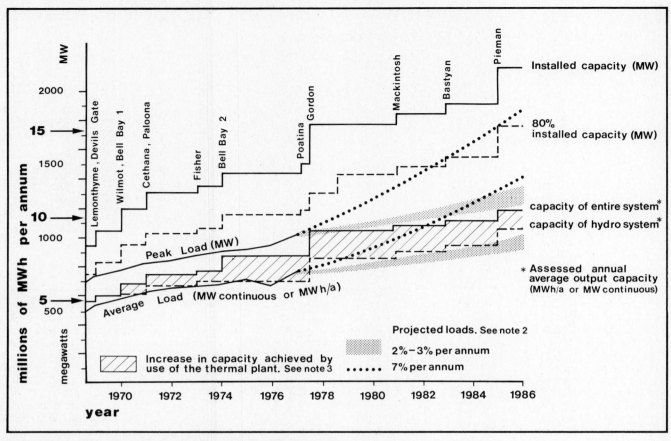

Fig 3 GROWTH OF TASMANIA'S ELECTRICITY TOTAL ENERGY DEMAND 1965-1975
Notes
1) For reasons outlined in the text all installed capacity cannot be continuously operated and the figure for installed capacity can thus be misleading. 80% of installed capacity is shown to allow for some of these circumstances. It can be regarded as approximating the effective peak capacity of the system.
2) Growth in the demand for electricity is difficult to project but on present evidence seems likely to fall in the 2–3% band over the next decade. However the 7% rate is included to indicate the situation typical before 1967.
3) The assessed annual average output capacity for the hydro system takes into account the average rainfall and storage capacity (to tide the system over periods of drought). and is the best guide to the hydro system's capability to produce energy. At certain stages of the system's development water storage capacity is less than ideal. notably before the extensive Gordon water storage was available, and progressively with the development of the Pieman scheme with its relatively small storages. Consequently some of the thermal capacity is earmarked by the HEC as reserve to tide the hydro-system over possible periods of drought. Hence the assessed contribution of the thermal station to the entire system varies with the system's development as indicated.
Source: HEC Annual Reports and unpublished HEC estimates of annual average output capacity.

water and so have some generators installed to make maximum use of periods of high rainfall and river flow. Conversely the schemes with large storages, notably the Middle Gordon and Great Lake, have some installed capacity which is only used in periods of drought when some storages are almost dry. The installation of a sixth generator at Poatina, for example, has this use in mind. With these various components the operation of the entire system requires careful and intricate balancing of the levels of various storages.

Another characteristic of any generating system is that the commissioning of power schemes is inevitably 'lumpy', with large blocks of power becoming available at one time. This extra power is usually surplus to current requirements since almost always the pre-existing capacity is sufficient to meet the demands on the system. Thus it is a number of years before supply and demand are again in balance.

As well as these essentially technical

reasons why the capacity of the generating system may be out of step with the demands made on it, there are the problems of projecting and meeting the future demand for electricity, both of which are extraordinarily difficult tasks.

The very long period of time required for the investigation, planning and construction of an installation inevitably means that power schemes are planned long before the demand for electricity can be known with any certainty. In the case of the Middle Gordon Scheme, for example, water gauging began in the early 1950's, detailed surveys of the area have been made in every summer since 1956, the scheme was approved by Parliament in 1967 and the first power was produced in 1977. Thus over 20 years elapsed from the initial investigations to the eventual production of power. In the even more remote areas now being investigated the exploratory stage is likely to be longer and it will be years before these current investigations give rise to power producing schemes.

It is clearly difficult to judge demand

over such long periods and in this situation it is extremely useful for the Hydro-Electric Commission to have a well-advanced scheme on which work can be accelerated or slowed down as circumstances warrant. Currently the Pieman scheme is fulfilling this useful but expensive role. When the scheme was approved in 1971 it was intended that power would first be produced in 1978 and the scheme completed in 1980.[6] But the demand for electricity since then has grown more slowly than expected and so the first power station is not now planned to be completed until 1981 and the scheme will not be fully operational until at least 1985.[7] In the late 1960's, in a very different situation, the time taken to construct hydro-electric schemes also created problems. Then, a decision was made to commence building an oil-fired power station at Bell Bay. The reason for this, in part, was that the Mersey-Forth hydro-electric scheme, then under construction in the north-west of the State, could not be completed in time to meet an expected sudden upsurge in

TABLE 2

GROWTH OF TASMANIA'S ELECTRICITY SYSTEM, 1950-1977

Year (a)	1950	1955	1960	1965	1970	1975	1977
Total consumption (b)							
000 MWh	865	1324	2173	3381	4566	5413	6150
% increase over previous decade	71	99	151	155	110	60	69
Peak load							
MW	188	282	413	587	779	917	1030
% increase over previous decade	124	135	120	108	89	56	66
Installed capacity							
MW	185	372	541	857	1032	1442	1443(c)
% increase over previous decade	46	110	192	130	91	68	70
Number of power stations	4	7	9	11	17	22	22

Notes: (a) Figures refer to years ending 30th June.
(b) Units sold, including King and Flinders Islands.
(c) The first Gordon generator added 144 MW to the system in late 1977 and the second Gordon generator added 144 MW in mid 1978.

Source: Hydro-Electric Commission. *Annual Reports.*

demand. On the other hand, a thermal station could be planned and built much more rapidly and so avoid any shortfall in the electricity supply.[8]

The problems created by the long time lag between the planning of a power scheme and its eventual production of electricity are exacerbated by the difficulties of accurately predicting demand even over quite short periods. These problems arise with regard both to the few big bulk users of electricity and, to a lesser extent, to the 170,000 or so households and commercial customers.

Increased power consumption by the larger group of general customers will result both from population growth and from the increased use of electricity by existing customers, particularly for household equipment. The establishment or growth of commercial firms, especially manufacturing enterprises, will also give rise to increased power consumption. In the 20 years to 1975 the consumption of electricity per general customer doubled from 5,400 units to 10,800 units, an average annual growth rate of 3.5 per cent, and the number of customers increased by just over 60 per cent from 101,500 to 163,500.[9] Total consumption by these general customers consequently increased 3¼ times—an average annual growth rate of 6.2 per cent. But growth rates were quite erratic from year to year, with the mean increase in consumption per customer ranging from 1 or 2 per cent to 6 per cent and even higher and with the overall growth in some years below 4 per cent and in others over 8 per cent. Clearly it is not satisfactory to take long term growth figures from the past and expect them to apply in the future since circumstances are constantly changing. For example, by the late 1950's, most of the growth in customer numbers derived from extending the electricity grid to outlying areas had been experienced,[10] the 1960's saw the growing use of electricity for

cooking and water heating, but with about 90 per cent of Tasmanian homes now using electricity for these purposes[11] further growth from this source will be small. As well as short term fluctuations there are thus structural changes occurring in the general demand for electricity, and these make projection very difficult.

The future demand for electricity from the bulk users is even harder to project. A mere 15 to 20 enterprises engaged in mining, metal refining, heavy chemicals or pulp and paper production take about 70 per cent of the power generated in Tasmania each year, and since 1970 have usually consumed about half of the peak load.[12] The production levels of these firms are likely to fluctuate markedly from year to year as supplies, the international marketing situation or internal conditions change. In the longer term major expansion projects or the establishment of completely new power intensive firms in the State cannot be foreseen with any certainty. Conversely the scaling down of output levels can also be rapid and unpredictable.

In the mid-1960's one aspect of this problem was apparent when 8 major undertakings made decisions to expand which together added over 127,000 kilowatts to the load at a time when little new power was immediately available.[13] In combination with a long and severe drought it produced a severe shortage of power which in 1967 necessitated rationing and the acquisition of an emergency generating ship. In the early 1970's the reverse situation occurred: a worldwide recession reduced output levels and power requirements for many of the major firms, resulting in a slowing growth rate and in 1975 an actual reduction in the electricity consumed. In this situation expansion plans are few and the continuing existence of at least one plant, the calcium carbide works at Electrona, was for a time in considerable

doubt.[14] Clearly the future power demands of these major users of electricity can only be estimated with any certainty on a short term and individual basis.

When considering the large bulk users, it is particularly dangerous to assume that trends of the past will be continued in the future for conditions are changing quite markedly. One important change is that hydro-electric power has gradually been losing its cost advantage over other forms of power. This is because on the one hand the costs of hydro-electric schemes are increasing while on the other some other generating systems have become relatively cheaper.

In general the cost of building hydro-electric installations increases as the more easily developed potential is exploited and schemes are begun in more remote areas or on less easily dammed rivers. In the South-West of Tasmania it seems likely that both the investigations and the actual construction are becoming more difficult and costly than previously, though a number of earlier schemes have also been in relatively remote areas. Few basic facts are known about the area and so there is more likelihood of striking unexpected and perhaps insoluble problems. Access is difficult, and is often limited to helicopters in the early stages, while major roads, such as the 90 km Gordon River Road and large construction villages, such as Strathgordon whose population reached 2,000, often have to be built before dam construction can commence. In fact five million dollars of the cost of the Gordon River Road was met by a non-repayable Federal Government grant which need not enter into the Hydro-Electric Commission's costs. But the community as a whole is still paying for a road which, despite the varied use made of it, had virtually no justification except in terms of the power scheme. Because of these problems, and because technically less desirable schemes are considered as more and more potential becomes utilised, costs of hydro-electric developments tend to increase, even though higher costs may be offset to some extent by larger scale projects and more efficient designs. It is almost certain, for example, that power from the Middle Gordon Scheme is significantly more expensive than that from the earlier installations. In addition, the interest payments on money borrowed are an important cost in such capital-intensive projects and the increases in rates of interest which have occured over recent years have had a major impact on the economic evaluation of schemes.

For some types of thermal power stations, on the other hand, costs have become relatively cheaper. In particular, improved coal mining techniques and innovations in the design of steam generators have considerably increased the attractiveness of coal as a power source. Linge in 1968 suggested that the

cost of bulk power in Tasmania had increased eightfold over the previous 50 years while the cost of coal in eastern Australia had risen only four times over the same period.[15] And in 1967 the Hydro-Electric Commission admitted that the unit cost of base load thermal generation was, in some circumstances, approaching the cost of new base load hydro generation.[16]

More recently the Callaghan Report has presented evidence that for many industrial users electricity costs are probably very little different from those applying on the mainland.[17]

Although hydro-electricity still possesses considerable technical and economic advantages for meeting peak loads, these relative cost changes mean that Tasmania has increasingly been losing its advantages for bulk users of power who everywhere tend to be offered rates related to the cost of generating base rather than peak loads. Appendix 1 gives an indication of the different costs involved in supplying the major industrial and the retail users.

Some of Tasmania's major users of electricity, notably the electro-chemical processors, are extremely sensitive to power costs and these plants were initially established in Tasmania because of the availability of large amounts of cheap electricity. When to the declining advantage of relatively cheap power is added the remoteness of the State from large markets and often from raw material sources as well, and the weaker bargaining power of the Tasmanian government, it is not surprising that Tasmania no longer seems to attract much of this type of industry. The establishment of new electro-chemical and similar power intensive enterprises in the future seems to be very unlikely, while even the consumption of electricity from existing enterprises which are sensitive to power costs may be expected at most to remain virtually static and may even decline as production becomes more concentrated in better placed locations, which have, for example, easy access to plentiful coal. In this situation the growth of the overall generating system would be quite low since it would come entirely from the general customers who currently consume only 30 per cent of the total power generated.

Comalco, the State's largest user of electricity, for example, has a 50 per cent share in a hydro-powered aluminium smelter at Bluff, New Zealand, which began operating in 1971, and another smelter, jointly owned by Comalco and other international aluminium producers, is being planned for Gladstone in Queensland. The Gladstone plant, which will use electricity generated from Queensland's low cost coal, emphasises that cost differentials between electricity from hydro and coal-powered installations are now very slight, allowing other factors, such as transport costs to enter into locational decisions. Moreover, for Comalco, which is already capable of consuming about one third of Tasmania's annual electricity output, it is also clearly undesirable to be too dependent on a single supplier of power. In fact the economic situation over the past five years has delayed Comalco's start on the huge $280 million Gladstone plant. One result, ironically, has been a much more limited extension to the Bell Bay smelter, costing a total of about $20 million and increasing output capacity there by about 20 per cent.

While a number of Tasmania's power-intensive enterprises were initially attracted by cheap power, some other major users of electricity are established in the State primarily to exploit natural resources, such as forests or minerals, and their growth prospects are relatively unaffected by power costs. However, there is a worldwide trend for a minimum of processing to be carried out at raw material sources. For example, in the

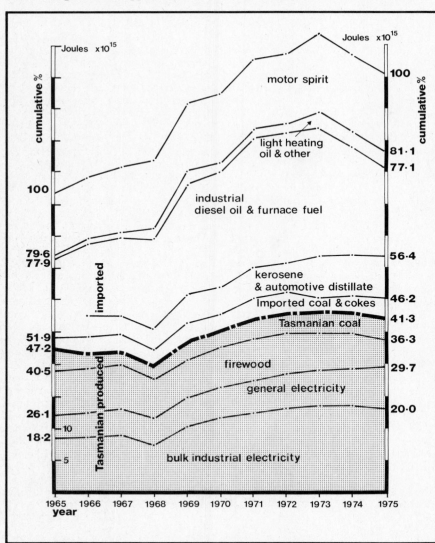

Fig 4 COMPONENTS OF TASMANIA'S TOTAL ENERGY DEMAND 1965-1975

Mt Anne and the Lake Shelf from the air.
Jim England

Bottom
Eldon Bluff and Lake Ewart.   *Chris Bell*

Centre right
Tea Trees in mist.   *Martin Hawes*

Mt Anne and Sarah Jane from Junction
Creek.   *Rhona Gardner*

The Gordon Dam site seen from the Hamilton Range, 1978. Exposed quartzite surfaces like these provide almost no plant nutrients and heavy rains cause severe erosion.

A Moscal

The Pig Trough, Franklin River — threatened by a potential hydro-electric scheme.

A Moscal

past it was usual to establish complete pulp and paper mills near their major raw material, as seen in Tasmania at APPM's Burnie plant and the Boyer newsprint mill. But currently there is often little more than basic woodchipping plants built close to the forest resources. The semi-processed product is then exported. A similar trend has been seen in the smelting of mineral ores. In Tasmania the recent investigations by Renison into the establishment of a smelter[18] went against the trend but the decision not to proceed with the project was in keeping with experience elsewhere. In general, it may, be concluded, the demand for electricity in Tasmania from new resource based users is also liable to grow more slowly than it has in the past.

All this evidence suggests a much slower growth rate for electricity production and consumption in the immediate future, but possible reasons for further structural changes and a renewed growth in the demand for electricity need to be considered. One possible cause of structural change is a rise in the cost of alternative power sources, particularly oil. Thus domestic space heating for example may in the future rely less on oil, which currently supplies 36 per cent of needs, and turn more to electricity at present used to heat the main living rooms in only 12% of homes.[11] Industrial heating and steam raising may also find electricity an economic alternative to oil, and even major industrial users of electricity could conceivably be attracted to Tasmania again when faced by a worldwide energy shortage. However, such scenarios of rapid growth presuppose that the electricity is obtained from relatively cheap hydro-sources. If on the other hand hydro-carbon fuels are used as an energy source it is far more efficient, and hence considerably cheaper, to burn the fuel directly for home heating or industrial steam raising rather than to involve electricity generation as an intermediate stage. Thus, depending on the precise timing and size of the changing relativities in cost and availability of the various power sources, and on the long term view taken by the HEC, industry and householders, the substitution of electricity for other sources of power may not be widespread, while major industrial users of electricity are likely to continue to prefer locations close to major and easily mined coal supplies.

But it is sobering to realise that Tasmania, far from being an all electric island, in fact derives well over half and probably as much as 70 per cent of its input of energy from hydro-carbon sources (Fig. 4).[19] Thus there is not sufficient hydro-electric potential to meet even the present total energy demand of the State, assuming

substitution between sources was technically feasible. It is timely therefore to consider more carefully how to optimise the use of high grade electrical energy and for more emphasis to be put on the development of available low grade energy sources (such as coal, wood or solar energy) to be used directly (and hence in general more efficiently) to meet low grade energy needs, especially heating purposes.

The supply side also needs careful consideration. Not only is Tasmania's hydro-electric potential finite, it is also very expensive to develop. Capital funds, especially from government and semi-government sources now and most probably in the future are not as easy to obtain as they have been in the past. Consequently the commissioning of schemes even after they have been approved by Parliament may well be delayed as a result of capital shortages. Thus shortages of power or the need to make extensive use of the expensive Bell Bay oil fired power station are possibilities even in the relatively near future while hydro-electric development is actively taking place. (Indeed the use of the Bell Bay station was averted prior to the commissioning of the Gordon scheme in 1977 only by operating the hydro-electric system at higher level than rainfall would permit on any extended basis).

If the high and inflation-prone capital requirements of hydro-electric development are set against the possibility of long term capital shortages and the unpredictable but generally high interest costs, then the question is raised of whether a coal fired plant may not become an attractive economic alternative to further hydro-electric development even before potential is exhausted. Such a plant would have lower and more certain capital costs, it would commit that capital expenditure over a shorter time period and so be less susceptible to problems of uncertain capital availability, and with a shorter lead time a coal fired plant could be built to come on stream more precisely when required. Against this, of course, running costs would be based on fuel prices which would be relatively high and to a degree unpredictable. Moreover, the Lower Gordon Scheme has the specific attraction of being operationally linked to the major storage of Lake Gordon and Lake Pedder and so could play an important role in the entire hydro system, especially in times of drought.

Whether thermal or hydro-power is considered, it seems certain that the marginal costs of generating extra power in the future will be considerably higher than the average for the system now. It seems proper that, as in New Zealand, the major industrial users of electricity should be required to pay these high rates in circumstances where their

demand necessitates the use of these expensive facilities. There is evidence that the HEC is considering such opportunity cost pricing in any future negotiation for bulk contracts. Of course, these supply and pricing considerations reinforce the demand aspects discussed earlier and make much growth in bulk electricity sales unlikely.

Thus the projection of electricity requirements is made very difficult by changing short term circumstances and unpredictable long term trends in both the bulk and general markets for electricity. Reliable forecasting techniques simply do not exist and yet, somehow, the Hydro-Electric Commission must attempt to plan its future building programme. Excess capacity is costly—the Hydro-Electric Commission had a gross interest bill of over $44 million in 1977—and it is wasteful of scarce capital resources which could be put to more valuable uses. On the other hand there is a natural tendency to err on the side of security and overprovision in an agency which, in the present social climate, would be severely censured if it was unable to meet the demand for electricity from either domestic customers or employment-creating industry. This tendency is reinforced by the memory of years such as 1967 to 1968, when shortages did occur due to unforeseen increases in demand or exceptionally dry weather.

Given the problems of forecasting demand, and the generally ready acceptance by Parliament of proposals for hydro-electric development there has been a tendency for very little detail of the methods of projection used by the Hydro-Electric Commission to be made public, and justification or criticism tend mainly to be by hindsight. In fact it appears from the proposals put to Parliament that projections are based on detailed forecasts for major Tasmanian industries, when available, and a broad estimate of general demand, but that weight is also given to the very general trends in electricity consumption in countries around the world. Thus in proposing the Middle Gordon Scheme it was emphasised that the doubling of demand every ten years was an accepted and normal rate of growth, while in 1971 a generalised projection was used to modify the recommendation based on the Commission's detailed forecasts.[20]

The use of international and historic bases in projection may be questioned, since the State does not have a broadly based industrial structure but depends on a few specialised industries for growth. Nor is experience overseas necessarily an appropriate basis for projections in a small sub-national unit in which the growth of population and employment has been slow and outmigration high over a long period. But it is difficult to suggest more reliable

TABLE 3

ACTUAL AND FORECAST LOADS, 1960–1977
Millions of kilowatt-hours per annum

YEAR	ACTUAL LOAD	FORECAST OF TOTAL LOAD *(With Report and Year of Forecast)*					
		Catagunya 1956	Great Lake 1957	Lower Derwent 1961	Mersey Forth 1963	Middle Gordon 1967	Pieman 1971
1960	2506	2590	2680				
1961	2602	2715	2830	2698			
1962	2836	2855	3080	2914			
1963	3311	3020	3265	3254	3373		
1964	3563	3190	3455	3446	3454		
1965	3746	3375	3665	3659	3746		
1966	3951	3585	3900	3858	3988		
1967	3902			4117	4117	4250	
1968	3944			4406	4392	4842	
1969	4873			4688	4591	5100	
1970	5166			5000	4811	5510	
1971	5552				5035	6110	5888
1972	5659				5285	6410	6399
1973	5850				5519	6680	6663
1974	5994				5780	6970	7120
1975	5773					7280	7633
1976	6373						8059
1977	6930						8462

Note: Figures refer to calendar years

Source: Hydro-Electric Commission, *Report on the Gordon River power development stage one* (1967); Hydro-electric Commission *Report on the proposed Pieman River power development* (1971); *Unpublished H.E.C. system load statistics* (1976).

projection methods and in fact the Commission's projections have usually given reasonable predictions of demand (Table 3). For the years since 1970, though, projections have been well above the actual load. Clearly the world-wide recession and the consequent poor marketing situation for major Tasmanian firms is largely responsible for this. But perhaps, for reasons suggested earlier, a new long term trend is also being established in which the major users of electricity have permanently lower growth rates.

Essentially, however, it is only because of the recent concern in society to question the proper balance between growth and conservation, and because the Hydro-Electric Commission has come under close scrutiny that so much criticism has been levelled at these particular projections. Rather than concentrating on the current and temporary supply position it would perhaps be more profitable if conservationists, the Government and the Commission alike examined in much more detail the problems that will soon be upon us when hydro-electric developments are unable to meet the demand and other power sources are increasingly expensive. At that time the problems facing the big industrial users

of electricity would seem to have very broad implications: on the one hand the economics of production in the State may be seriously affected if higher prices were charged for power; on the other hand, society may consider their great use of a scarce commodity undesirable, as has already happened, for example, in the USA.[21] These problems call into question the appropriateness of policies which encourage capital and power intensive industry as a means of tackling Tasmania's problems of unemployment and outmigration. Employment in such industries is clearly not a long term solution and even for the present more labour intensive enterprises would be more generally beneficial, as current government policy seems to recognise.[17][22] But the State can obviously only attract industries, whether capital, power or labour intensive, to which it can offer advantages compared with other places. At the present time these advantages appear to be very slight for any activity.

Some action should also be taken immediately in the light of the shortages of power which may eventually affect the State. For example, the investigation and promotion of methods of conserving power and the development and encouragement of alternative sources,

such as solar energy for water heating, should perhaps become a major role of the Hydro-Electric Commission. It also seems urgent, given the probable continuing demand for more electricity, that society and government should consider what institutional machinery is required for conservationist values to be adequately taken into account in future power developments. Ultimately, however, a radical restructuring of the local and world economies to take account of the limitations to growth imposed by the exhaustion of finite resources is inevitable.

Hydro-electricity and environmental conservation

While economic considerations possibly point to the harnessing of all hydro-electric power in Tasmania's South-West within a relatively short space of time, there are strong and increasingly widely accepted arguments against such development based on the values of environmental protection and conservation. The philosophical foundation of the conservationist viewpoint need not be elaborated on here: suffice it to say that it is concerned with the perception of man as but one element in a complex and interdependent natural system and that the continued operation of the entire system is more important—ultimately for man's social and physical survival — than the development and 'conquering' of the environment solely for man's short term economic benefit. From this stems the justification on moral, aesthetic and scientific grounds, for the conscious maintenance of the availability of natural resources and the sustenance of the complexity and variety of all forms of life.[23] The strong claims that conservationist values should be recognised as pre-eminent in Tasmania's South-West and that economic development should be excluded and careful conservation measures implemented are also well treated elsewhere.[24] The major aim here is to examine the points where hydro-electric development in the South-West conflicts with conservationist values.

The broadest argument against hydro-electric development in South-West Tasmania is based on the belief, referred to above, that all economic development should be excluded from the area because of its inherent value on both local and global scales as a wilderness area functioning almost entirely in a natural way. Because it is one of the few remaining temperate wildernesses in the world and since any change in its character would be irreversible, its maintenance is even more crucial.

Incursions of human activity on the scale of hydro-electric development are quite out of keeping with such maintenance, since disturbances to natural systems are inevitable and these have widespread repercussions on the natural functioning of the entire wilderness system.

As well as jeopardising the maintenance of the South-West as a meaningful wilderness, hydro-electric development in the area is also a cause for concern because of its impact on more restricted localities. In particular natural environments are liable to be disturbed, degraded and destroyed and some entire species of plants and animals which are endemic to quite small areas may be lost. The most obvious and permanent disturbance to natural systems associated with hydro-electric development arises from the destruction of existing ecosystems by the flooding of water storage areas. But, in addition river regimes are changed by hydro-electric development and, with the diversion of some rivers, the total volume of flows may also be considerably altered. Siltation and salination are perhaps the most obvious and extreme results of these changes, but many subtle and unnoticed changes also inevitably occur to a wide range of ecosystems. The ecosystems of the Gordon and Huon Rivers have already been affected

in ways which will never be known and if Hydro-Electric Commission plans come to fruition there will be a further impact on the Gordon, Franklin, King and Davey Rivers and their tributaries.

The permanent destruction of fragile plant communities and animal habitats may also be caused by the disturbance associated with access routes and at investigation, dam and quarry sites. Unfortunately, in the South-West such disturbance often appears to be unnecessarily violent and extensive. Moreover both road and river systems can facilitate the spread of exotic species deep into an area. In the hostile environment of the South-West the spread of exotics is relatively slow and undisturbed communities are seldom penetrated, but the visual degradation and invasion of exotics is still all too evident along disturbed roadsides and remote river banks.

As well as these direct environmental consequences of hydro-electric development there are also indirect effects arising especially from the increased accessibility of the area to the public. Already the roads built to service the Gordon power development have opened up to some 50,000 visitors a year a huge area previously scarcely influenced by man and unless access and land use are properly managed, serious

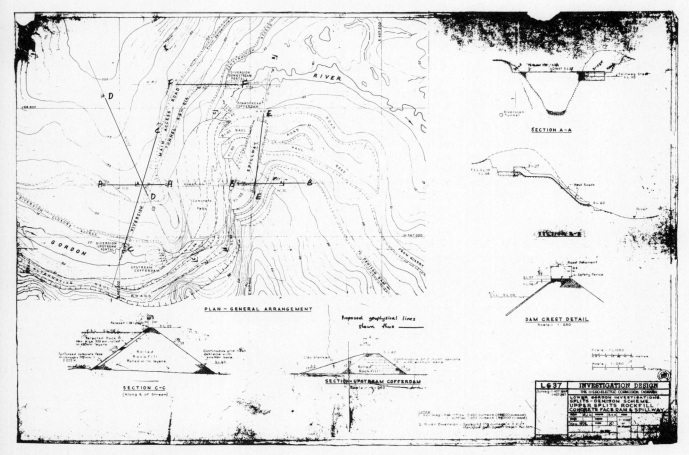

Field plans found near the potential dam site in the Second Split on the lower Gordon River. Designs of individual engineering structures are not finalised until investigations are completed. Such plans are not officially available to the public before the scheme is finalised.

degradation of natural systems is likely. Perhaps the most ironic example of this degradation occurred in the vicinity of Lake Pedder immediately before its inundation when it was visited by hundreds of people. But the Mt Anne area too is suffering extensive damage now that it is accessible and attractive to many for day or weekend excursions. This damage is evident both on the slopes where footpaths are being abandoned and duplicated because constant use is initiating gullying, and on the plateau where the flora, especially the cushion plants, suffer badly under even moderate tramping.[25]

As well as protecting the environment essentially for its own sake, the conservationist case is also in part man-centred and pleads for the retention of areas in their natural state on emotional, spiritual and aesthetic grounds. Important issues include the protection of areas of high scenic quality, the minimisation of aesthetic degradation by, for example, visually unattractive power lines and disturbed roadsides and the conservation of wilderness primarily for man's enjoyment.

Certainly increasing numbers of people are seeking peace and relaxation remote from man-made environments and, even for people who never experience it at first hand, wilderness and scenically attractive areas appear to have considerable emotional and cultural value, as seen for example in the popularity of films and books featuring such areas.

It is often argued, sometimes with justification, that hydro-electric development does not necessarily conflict with these aspects of conservation, and indeed may lead to an overall gain in enjoyment and appreciation. A few who are particularly sensitive to the replacement of natural features by man-made installations or to the presence of other people may feel compelled to seek more remote areas. But many more will benefit from the improved accessibility and the wide range of recreational activities which usually accompany a hydro-electric installation. Thus, in justifying the Middle Gordon Scheme, the Hydro-Electric Commission emphasised that a large scenically attractive area has been made accessible to visitors of all ages and income groups which previously had been known by very few.[26] Similarly in its report on the Pieman scheme, the Commission emphasised that the lakes created should add considerably to the tourist and recreation potential of the area by permitting boating, water sports and the development of new angling areas, by adding to the scenic attractions of the Murchison Highway, and by creating access by boat to areas previously almost inaccessible to the general public.[27]

However in a broader context these indirect effects of hydro-electric development are of considerable concern. The dangers to wilderness areas of increased accessibility indicate the need for careful planning, including the control of accessibility and actual access.[25] Intensive recreational use is compatible with some zones but others must be of very limited access even to the hardened bushwalker. Planning for the activities in a wilderness area is far from easy but it is clearly impossible if the accessibility of particular areas is determined merely as a by-product of hydro-electric or other developments. Thus the impact and desirability of increased accessibility and recreational activity are factors which must be taken into account in assessing whether development should proceed in environmentally important areas: proper environmental management requires that some zones are left exclusively as wilderness and in these any use must inevitably be in conflict. In the Pieman valley careful hydro-electric and recreational development is probably not as serious a concern since an extensive wilderness area is not being threatened. However, the proposed Lower Gordon and Davey River schemes conflict with any serious conservation measures since the water storages and associated roads effectively cut the most satisfactory management area in two and permit relatively easy access to what should be the heart of the wilderness zone.

Against the conservationist case for the limitation of hydro-electric development in the South-West must be weighed the cost in economic and environmental terms of alternative sources of power for Tasmania. Hydro-electricity is of course efficient on both counts in that it does not use non-renewable and increasingly expensive fuels, at least after the investigation and construction phases. It is also more efficient than any widely used alternative sources of power in terms of the balance between the energy obtained and the energy input in both building and operating. Moreover direct and continuous pollution is not caused by the generation of hydro-electricity.

But against these arguments must be placed the loss of scarce and irreplaceable resources both in the particular natural systems which are drowned and in the more extensive wilderness area which is irreversibly modified. If the South-West of Tasmania is to be conserved as a meaningful wilderness area, then conservationist values must be given priority and man's activity within the area managed accordingly. Hydro-electric development, which can jeopardise the maintenance of true wilderness by both its direct and indirect effects, must be

subservient to the requirements of conservation and take place only where it is compatible. This may appear wasteful of hydro-electric resources, but the limited potential remaining in Tasmania means that alternative energy sources will in any case be needed in the relatively near future. It may be very worthwhile to start using these alternatives some five to ten years earlier in order to conserve the resource of the wilderness which otherwise would almost certainly be lost for all time.

Because of these conflicts between resource development and conservation, hydro-electric development in Tasmania's South-West has been for more than a decade a major focus of the growing concern that conservationist values should be expressed in land use planning for wilderness areas. The plans of the Hydro-Electric Commission to drown Lake Pedder as part of the Middle Gordon Scheme gave rise to the first major confrontation between conservationists and the operations of a statutory authority which for a long time had played an unequivocal role in the economic development of the State. In the dispute itself, and even more as a lesson for the future, the reasons why the Commission and Government behaved as they did are probably more important than the detailed arguments for or against the drowning of the lake, important though these were.[28]

The final report of the Inquiry set up by the Federal Government gives a valuable perspective to these particular aspects.[29] Considerable powers have been vested in an authority with a narrow statutory duty, interpreted as providing electricity at as low a cost as possible. Like many similar single-purpose, resource development agencies, the report suggests, the Hydro-Electric Commission has tended to develop a narrow expertise, for example in engineering and the evaluation of projects in terms of cost minimisation, it tends to be biased in favour of large and unusual projects and to over-evaluate schemes compared with independent assessors, and its employees inevitably become committed, at least subconsciously, to the completion of the schemes they have developed. For all these reasons the Commission is likely to pursue narrow objectives with scant regard for, or even understanding of, other values or land uses. In particular it is almost inevitable that a minor place is given to recreational, environmental, aesthetic or scientific values or indeed to any costs or benefits not directly related to power generation. Consequently adequate consideration of these aspects of a scheme is virtually impossible. The Hydro-Electric Commission did in fact commission a biological study of the Lake Pedder area but this was quite inadequate, as shown by subsequent

Above
The Gordon Road between Tim Shea and The Needles.   *Michael Higgins*

Where once the Gordon raged...   *Helen Gee*

Below and right
Working site near the outlet tunnel below the Gordon Dam.   *Helen Gee*

Left
The outlet tunnel for the Gordon dam, under construction in 1977.   *Helen Gee*

Bottom, left and right
Sample of oil collected from an oil slick below the Gordon Dam, 1976.
Tasmanian Environment Centre Inc Col

Left
Mt Anne, several days walk from Maydena in the sixties, now overlooks the Scotts Peak Road.   *Helen Gee*

intensive studies which found some twenty species endemic to the lake and an ecosystem scientifically important both for its simplicity and stability and for its limnological characteristics.[30]

Further problems were created by the secrecy which surrounded the planning stages—the Commission's intentions were not made public until Parliamentary approval was sought in 1967 even though some dam sites had been tentatively fixed and major road building had begun in 1963—and by the practice of the Commission of offering only a single proposal for Parliamentary approval with no indication of alternatives which might serve ends other than cost minimisation. There was disquiet, too, at the ease with which an area, once it became economically attractive, lost national park status.

Given the growing concern about environmental issues it was inevitable that intense political activity and confrontation between conservationist and developer should ensue, once the details were known. In 1967, a Select Committee of the Legislative Council, set up in response to the public outcry, reluctantly concluded that no economically feasible alternative existed, and the scheme was rapidly approved by Parliament. Concern continued to be expressed, especially from 1972 when changes in government at both state and federal levels raised conservationists' hopes that the decision could even then be reversed. In the renewed bitter exchanges, scoring points from opponents seems to have been more important for all parties than attempting to reach a compromise or to understand alternative viewpoints,[31] and both the power of the Hydro-Electric Commission and the widespread and

Denison dam site, Nicholls Range. A dam here would flood the Denison Gorge and water would back-up into the Truchanas Huon Pine Reserve. *Helen Gee*

Lower Denison HEC camp, serviced by helicopter. Exotic weeds (foreground) are introduced accidentally to such sites. They are spreading. *Helen Gee*

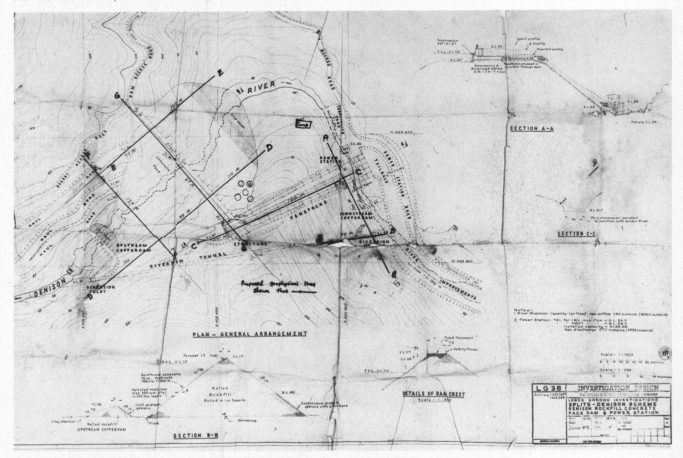

Field Plan for a dam on the Lower Denison, Nicholls Range. Designs of individual engineering structures are not finalised until such time as an investigation is complete. They are not officially available to the public before that date.

deep public concern were clearly seen. The United Tasmania Group, an environmentally conscious political party, was formed; considerable pressure from many sources was applied at both state and federal levels but, despite a proposal by the new Federal Labor Government to provide eight million dollars for a three to five year moratorium on the flooding of Lake Pedder, the scheme continued.

The Federal Committee of Inquiry recommended, among many other things, a series of measures designed to reduce such unbalanced decision making and consequent conflict in the future. Although these recommendations were primarily directed to the Federal Government they clearly have relevance at a state level and could be related directly to hydro-electric development. Most important was the recommendation that adequate provision be made for effective public and parliamentary involvement in the planning process. This requires that information is publicly available right from the initiation of the project and that machinery is created for formal, effective, rational and informed public involvement in the planning process. In addition, Parliamentary approval should be specifically required when projects are initiated and at the preliminary and final investigation stages. Perhaps more importantly, the Committee recommended that the planning of water and land resources should involve all relevant interests and should have a region-wide, multi-objective approach in which a broad range of objectives are evaluated so that balanced and consistent rather than *ad hoc* development can occur. Finally, to overcome the inevitable narrowness of view, any development

HEC pontoon at an investigation site on the Lower Gordon. *David Tasker*

Top left and right
The bridge (left) and the haulage way (right) at the Mt McCall dam site. Franklin River, 1976.
Bob Brown

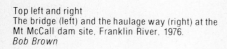

Entrance of an HEC investigation tunnel. Lower Gordon River. 1975. *Greg Middleton*

Lake Pedder as it was in 1972, prior to flooding. Several publications deal with the story of Pedder. Refer to 5.2 and the bibliography. *Brian Curtis*

The rising waters changing the character of the landscape. *Michael Higgins*

Left, right and below
Construction of the Middle Gordon Dam, 1974.
David Tasker

An aerial view of the southern end of the Serpentine Impoundment showing Scotts Peak dam and a section of the road.

Vern Reid

Engineering marvel or environmental disaster?

John Best

The road above Strathgordon along the Twelvetrees Range to the HEC transmitting tower. No attempt was made to minimize the visual and environmental impact of this road. *John Best*

The rising waters of the Serpentine Impoundment, 1973. *Zoology Dept University of Tasmania*

This octagonal tourist shelter and lookout overhangs the Gordon Gorge and commands a magnificent view of the Gordon Dam which has been promoted as a tourist asset. The photograph was taken while the building was under construction in 1977. *John Best*

Power lines extend from Strathgordon to Hobart. *John Best*

proposals from a single-purpose development agency should be subject to external review by an expert and interdisciplinary team.[32]

It is unfortunate that in Tasmania few steps have been taken to implement these recommendations either for hydro-electric developments or for planning in the South-West generally. The mechanism for the review of the Commission's development proposals remains quite inadequate, for without the involvement of outside bodies in the planning stages, the quite proper trading off of economic efficiency against environmental and other values is virtually impossible. Consequently developments are likely to proceed in part because alternative schemes are considered too late to stand a real chance of implementation. Moreover, without an overall multi-objective plan giving guidelines as to permissible developments in different zones, the Hydro-Electric Commission almost inevitably continues to judge schemes from a very narrow viewpoint. Nevertheless, it is disturbing that the Commission seems quite unwilling to take any account of the broader issues or even to consider that a multi-objective approach to land and water management is desirable or necessary.[33] It is strongly opposed, for example, to the Davey or Gordon Rivers being included in the National Park, since it fears that (for the future at least) national park boundaries may be regarded as inviolate for all time, and it could find management plans for the Davey River (part of the South-West Conservation Area) acceptable only if they enabled hydro-electric development to proceed virtually unrestricted.

Inevitably, though, the Hydro-Electric Commission has been influenced by the Lake Pedder conflict and has adapted, even if only slightly and primarily out of self-interest, to the greater public interest in environmental issues. Most

Public sign displayed near the Clear Hill Road on the Gordon Road overlooking the flood plains. *Michael Higgins.*

importantly, the Commission is much more concerned about maintaining good public relations and is much less secretive about its investigations, although there are still criticisms that important information is being suppressed.[34] On the other hand, some still argue that nothing is gained from public discussion of tentative proposals and that it is pointless to consider schemes until firm proposals are put to Parliament. But surely adequate and early public discussion is the only way for a properly informed and reasonable debate to take place about alternative land uses and for alternative proposals to be explored before a point of no return is reached in the development process.

In addition to becoming rather less secretive the Commission has also encouraged much more comprehensive investigation of areas likely to be flooded and teams of scientists have been given assistance, particularly with accommodation and transport, in their studies of these remote areas. There are also some attempts to minimize and repair environmental damage, for both ecological and aesthetic reasons. The main attempts have been to regenerate vegetation along the Scotts Peak Road beyond Condominium Creek where extensive planting has taken place both along the roadside and on quarry faces. However, the best results can only be described as moderately encouraging and much more experience with a variety of techniques is required. Perhaps a slower programme with more emphasis on trial plots using differing techniques would have been more profitable. To date the Hydro-Electric Commission has financed most of the work, although federal unemployment relief funds have also been used and the Department of Lands and the National Parks and Wildlife Service are both increasingly devoting many of their own scarce resources to this end.

The Gordon River Road at Frodshams Pass. The South-West has been divided by this road since 1967. *John Best*

The Lower Gordon is attracting more boating visitors each year.   *Michael Higgins*

But, despite these small changes, the Hydro-Electric Commission, not surprisingly, remains a single-purpose authority with engineering and economic matters dominating its thinking, and it would be unrealistic to expect it to be otherwise. Inevitably therefore, decisions about hydro-electric developments will become increasingly political in nature and the formal mechanism of Parliamentary approval for schemes will become much more important. The recent (1976) resolutions of the Liberal Party State Council to seek an inquiry into the functions, plans and future prospects of the Hydro-Electric Commission and to call for full investigations before further power development occurs in the Lower Gordon are examples of growing political concern.[35]

Conclusion

There is no doubt that conservationist values are gaining increasing acceptance by society and are being given greater weight politically, as seen in Tasmania for example in the growing influence of the National Parks and Wildlife Service, established in 1971, and in many of the clauses of the Planning and Development Bill which seek to ensure that environmental and social values are given due weight alongside economic ones in decisions about future development. Thus it is possible that before long these broader issues may be seriously taken into account in the State's planning. At the same time there is no doubt that eventually the demand for electrical power in Tasmania could justify, from an economic viewpoint, the installation of hydro-electric schemes in the remote South-West.

Consequently, decisions about electrical power (and other) developments will inevitably become increasingly political in nature as an attempt is made to satisfy society's multiple objectives. Comprehensive land use planning provides an effective and orderly framework for such decision making. The continual review of development proposals from the early planning stages both by an official external review body and by the public is also essential to allow the incorporation of values other than purely economic ones into schemes finally implemented. It is to be hoped that such broad approaches can be adopted in time to avoid further *ad hoc* and unbalanced decision making and to maintain Tasmania's South-West as a priceless, multiple-valued natural resource.

POSTSCRIPT

There have been a number of developments in 1978 which need brief comment.

1. The Premier announced in August 1978 that the role of the HEC would be widened to make it responsible for general energy issues in Tasmania. Outside expertise and independent consultants were seen to be playing a role in advising government.

2. Two important papers were tabled in August 1978 concerning the cost escalation of the Pieman scheme and the capacity of the HEC to meet further increases in load. While they leave many questions unanswered they appear to be in agreement with many of the conclusions of this paper and provide supporting facts not previously available:

(a) Little spare capacity exists in the system as a whole and so some use of the Bell Bay thermal station is likely. (The amount of use is critically dependent on the precise actual growth rate in demand, and especially on whether additional industrial load eventuates.)

(b) The suggestion is made that some measure of discouragement should be given to the use of electricity for steam raising and space heating.

(c) A slowing in the growth rate of electricity use is expected, particularly in the demand from major industrial users. Except for growth from current negotiations with Comalco and Temco no further increases are projected for major users in the period to 1991. Overall growth is projected at about 2.7 per cent per annum with an average of about 5.5 per cent growth per annum in the general load. (However given the restraint mentioned in (b) above it is hard to see how this level of growth will come about.)

(d) Some impacts of capital shortages are explored, particularly the likely delay in the completion of the Pieman Scheme to 1986 or 1987.

(e) The impact of cost escalation is noted, and the Pieman Scheme is now estimated to cost over $400

PUBLIC DEBATE

"I know that some think that there is a question of whether we develop the King, Franklin and the Gordon or whether we have wilderness. They say it's a choice of one or the other. I don't believe that. In my view both can go hand in hand. The power schemes in the Gordon, King and Franklin occupy only a very minute area of the countryside there and with proper treatment I think those schemes can contribute to the area."

Russell Ashton, Chief Commissioner of the Hydro-Electric Commission, speaking in a TNT 9 documentary, Voices of the Rivers, *televised in October 1978. The film was produced by Ed Sykes, Phil Lohrey and Phil Shaw.*

The Saturday Evening Mercury, April 1973

Right
The Australian. 24 February, 1976.

The Examiner, 12 July, 1973

'DAM WON'T RUIN RIVER'

THE Hydro-Electric Commissioner (Sir Allan Knight) yesterday denied that a possible dam on the lower Gordon River might harm the river's tourist potential.

"Possible construction of a dam on the lower Gordon River at any of the sites now under investigation would have little or no significant effect upon the popular tourist trips up the river," Sir Allan said.

He said Butler Island was the furthest downstream the proposed dams would be placed, and this was the upstream limit of the present cruises.

It could be argued that a dam at Butler Island would add further interest to the trip, he said.

Dam sites inquiry 'like Lake Pedder'

TASMANIA'S Hydro-Electric Commission is surpressing information about dam sites with a degree of secrecy "reminiscent of the darkest days of Lake Pedder," the Australian Conservation Foundation claimed yesterday.

The director of the ACF, Dr G. Mosley, said the commission was investigating potential dam sites in the southwest of Tasmania but had failed to disclose the effect this would have on the Lower Gordon and Franklin rivers.

He said the commission had an unwritten responsibility to keep the public informed of its investigations and intentions.

"The HEC must shrug off its secrecy syndrome and take the public into its confidence," Dr Mosley said. "Otherwise there could be another bitter campaign like that over Lake Pedder."

He said the commission had over-estimated its gross rate for power during the Lake Pedder inquiry and misled the State Government on the amount of power needed for the future.

It had refused to tell the foundation of its present potential generating capacity and estimates of the cost of hydro-electric schemes.

"The proposed Lower Gordon scheme, if allowed to proceed, would destroy a part of the Franklin River and obliterate the gorges and forests of the Lower Gordon River," Dr Mosley said.

million, compared with the original estimate of \$134 million in 1970. The cost of generating power from the Pieman is currently estimated to be 2.0 cents per kWh, twice the cost of power from the Gordon Scheme (about 1.0 cent per kWh) which is itself about half as much again as the average of 0.67 cents per kWh for all previous schemes. These compare with the figure of 0.81 cents per kWh calculated in Appendix 1, based on July 1977 (pre-Gordon) costs. The figure for the Pieman (2.0 cents per kWh) is rather lower than HEC estimates for local coal fired thermal power (2.2 cents per kWh), imported coal thermal power (2.7 cents per kWh) and the Bell Bay oil fired thermal power (rather over 2.4 cents per kWh). The future movement of fuel costs is of course unknown.

3. Discussion on equitable pricing policies for major industrial users *vis a vis* the general consumer is occurring. Given the higher costs entailed in generating additional power the question arises of whether all would-be users (established and new, domestic and industrial, large and small, labour intensive and capital intensive) should have equal access to the cheaper power already available, or whether some — notably the larger, capital intensive, industrial enterprises desiring additional power — should be expected to pay the higher marginal rates of producing the extra power they require, while other consumers who are not making additional demands, continue to pay the lower rates.

4. Partly arising from these reports there is a more general awareness of the finite nature of hydro resources and an increased public debate on the need for energy conservation and the careful examination of alternative power sources for Tasmania. Coal fired thermal generators, the need to define coal reserves in the state, and the employment-creating potential of such a station is one theme being widely discussed as well as the role of wind and solar power.

Taking all of these together it seems reasonable to suggest that a major reassessment of energy policy is occurring with previously entrenched ideas being thrown open to question. An exciting and critical period for establishing new directions for Tasmania's energy future is upon us.

Grateful acknowledgement is given to the Hydro-Electric Commission and the Tasmanian Conservation Trust Inc for their considerable assistance, and to Dr R J K Chapman, Mr P Faircloth, Dr A J T Finney, Dr J B Kirkpatrick, Mr D Steane and Mr A Were for their helpful suggestions.

APPENDIX I: An example of an approximate method of allocation of costs of supply between major industrial loads and retail loads

1. From Balance Sheet as at 30th June 1977.

CAPITAL EXPENDITURE

	10^6
Power Branch	440.822
Hobart District	22.315
Launceston District	6.993
Country Districts	31.214
King & Flinders Islands	.563
Offices, Stores & Land	8.162
Total	**\$510.069**

2. From Trading Account for year ended 30th June 1977.

	10^6
Interest Charges	29.860
Depreciation	6.296
Total	**\$36.156**

3. Average rate of interest and depreciation

$$= \frac{36.156}{510.069} \times 100 = 7.09\%$$

4. Annual Charges resulting from interest and depreciation on Capital Expenditure may be approximately apportioned on a pro-rata basis as follows:-

		10^6
(a)	Power Branch	31.250
(b)	Hobart District	1.580
(c)	Launceston District	.496
(d)	Country Districts	2.212
(e)	King & Flinders Islands	.040
(f)	Offices, Stores & Land	.578
	Total	**\$36.156**

5. From Trading Account for year ended 30th June 1977 expenditure recorded as follows:-

		10^6
(a)	Power Branch — Operation & Maintenance	9.923
(b)	Distribution Expenses	11.591
(c)	Gauging and Recording	.267
(d)	Administration & General	8.812
(e)	Superannuation	7.572
(f)	Investigations & Surveys	1.220
(g)	Other	.412
	Total	**\$39.797**

6. From the above total annual costs in 4 and 5 amounting to \$75.953 m it is possible to extract the amounts attributable solely either to generation or distribution and also those general charges which must be split between these two.

GENERATION	10^6
Power Branch — Annual charges	31.250
Power Branch — Operation & maintenance	9.923
Gauging & Recording	0.267
Total	**\$41.440**

DISTRIBUTION	
Hobart District — Annual charges	1.580
Launceston District — Annual charges	0.496
Country Districts — Annual charges	2.212
King & Flinders Islands — Annual charges	0.040
Distribution Expenses	11.591
Total	**\$15.919**

GENERAL	
Offices, Stores & Land	0.578
Administration & General	8.812
Superannuation	7.572
Investigation & Surveys	1.220
Other	0.412
Total	**\$18.594**

7. The allocation of the \$18.59 m in General Charges is a complex matter but in general they are charges which are proportional to the number of employees. It is thus approximately correct to allocate them in accordance with non capital related costs of Generation (\$10.190 m) and Distribution (\$11.59 m). Thus the total costs become:

	10^6
Generation	41.440
$+ 18.594 \times \frac{10.19}{21.781} =$	8.699
Total	**\$50.139**
Distribution	15.919
$+ 18.594 \times \frac{11.591}{21.781} =$	9.895
Total	**\$25.814**

8. Total units sold 1976-77 = 6,153.452 $\times 10^6$

Thus average cost per unit for generation, transmission and transformation $= \dfrac{50.139 \times 10^6 \times 10^2}{6153.452 \times 10^6}$ cents = **0.81 cents**

9. The cost of distribution, metering, etc. must be added to the above average generation cost. In the case of major industrial loads these extra costs are in general zero.

In the case of the retail load the total cost of distribution is \$25.814 m from 7 above. This cost must be distributed over the 2,074.438 $\times 10^6$ kWh sold to the retail consumers during 1976-77.

Thus average cost of distribution, etc: $= \dfrac{25.814 \times 10^6 \times 10^2}{2074.438 \times 10^6}$ cents = **1.244 cents**

10. Approximate total average costs per kWh are thus:

	MAJOR INDUSTRIAL	RETAIL
Generation	0.81	0.81
Distribution, etc.	0.0	1.24
	0.81 cents	2.05 cents

In actual practice, due to the very different load factors, the cost of generation to meet the major industrial load is somewhat less than that for the retail load. Furthermore, some major industrial consumers have their own substations, thus lowering the cost of supply to them and the average for the class.
Thus a fully comprehensive analysis will produce a somewhat higher figure for the retail load and somewhat lower figure for the major industrial load. However the above average costs can be taken as indicative of these actually involved. Accuarate calculation of the exact figures is a long and involved process.
It must also be realised that the above costs are only *average* costs for each of the two main categories of load considered. There are differences within each category due to the characteristics of particular loads.

Source: Calculations by Hydro-Electric Commission using the Commission's audited accounts and published information.

Note: These calculations retain the confidentiality of the actual cost of supply to any particular customer but they are intended to give a reasonably accurate indication of the disparity of cost of supply between major industrial and retail loads.

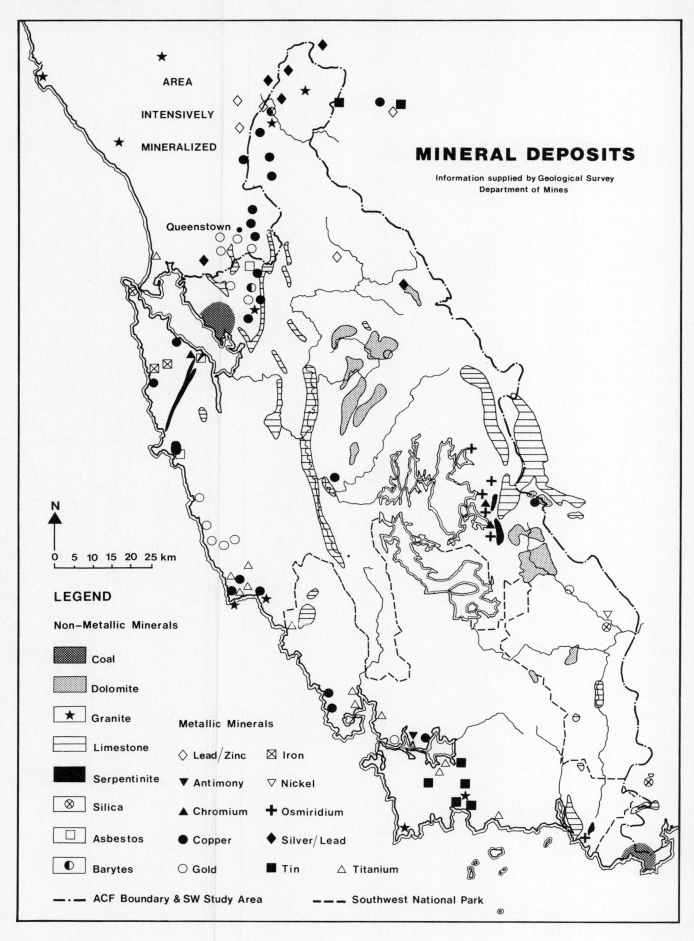

AREA

INTENSIVELY

MINERALIZED

Queenstown

MINERAL DEPOSITS

Information supplied by Geological Survey
Department of Mines

N

0 5 10 15 20 25 km

LEGEND

Non–Metallic Minerals

Coal

Dolomite

★ Granite

Limestone

Serpentinite

⊗ Silica

▢ Asbestos

◑ Barytes

Metallic Minerals

◇ Lead/Zinc   ⊠ Iron

▼ Antimony   ▽ Nickel

▲ Chromium   ✛ Osmiridium

● Copper   ◆ Silver/Lead

○ Gold   ■ Tin   △ Titanium

—·—·— ACF Boundary & SW Study Area   — — — Southwest National Park

Mineral Deposits

D J Jennings

After two years of national service with the R A F, based on Malta, David Jennings graduated in Geology, Zoology and Chemistry in England. He spent eight years working with the Kenya Geological Survey on mapping projects. In 1964 he joined the Tasmanian Geological Survey, where he works within the Economic Section. Though he works state-wide, his special interest in tin mining takes him particularly to the north-east, Bass Strait islands and to the far South-West. His interests include nature conservation, bushwalking, canoeing and skin-diving.

The economic mineral potential of South-West Tasmania remains virtually unknown. This is for two reasons: firstly exploration has been inadequate to establish what is present on the surface, without consideration of deposits at depth: and secondly a product which is unwanted or a deposit which is uneconomic today may assume importance with improving technology and mining skills, developing transport systems or changing world markets. Our current attitudes are based on today's circumstances, today's affluence and today's moral standards; it is presumptuous to pre-judge the future.

The first recognition of economic minerals in Tasmania was by Labillardière who, when searching for La Perouse, recorded coal seams inland of South Cape Bay in 1793. The main influx of mineral prospectors reached Tasmania in the closing years of last century but the South-West of the State yielded fewer rewards than the areas in the west and north-east. Even there the enigmatic nature of ore deposits and the paucity of prospecting clues often resulted in failure to recognise the significance of the finds. They then lay for half a century untested and unexploited, awaiting improved extraction technology and mining techniques.

In the South-West, the rugged quartzite ridges with intervening buttongrass plains and patches of impenetrable scrub hid its treasures well, and scenic grandeur proved no compensation for the trials of hostile terrain and severe climate. Prospectors commonly approached from the sea and pushed inland along the creeks. The distribution of known mineral occurrences, concentrated around the coastline but more sparse inland, reflects the areas of easier access and superior rock exposure (see map). Many successful prospectors were encouraged to exploit their finds by the granting of rent-free 'Reward leases' for mineral deposits located in new areas, (Warne, at Jane River for example) and substantial monetary rewards were paid if townships subsequently developed on the mining fields. The Stacey brothers at Adamsfield were among the miners who benefited from this policy (see Table).

Mine workings on the plains between Bathurst Harbour and Cox Bight. From left to right are the Melaleuca Airstrip, Denis King's tin mine. the area mined by Qintex (ex Ludbrooks) — in the foreground on the bank of Melaleuca Creek — and the New Harbour Tin Development Company workings. Peter Willson's tin mine is adjacent to the latter. *Jim England*

Subsequent mineral exploration in the South-West has been of a preliminary and superficial nature, still hampered by the problems of access and difficult terrain which dogged the original prospectors. It is interesting that in a small area south of Bathurst Harbour a geochemical survey in 1965 revealed anomalously high values of copper, zinc or tin at nineteen different localities, but even the most promising have yet to be investigated in detail.

The major central part of the South-West is composed of a basement of

Vanishing Falls, north of Precipitous Bluff.
Jim England

ancient Precambrian rocks, which have locally formed the 'host' for small deposits of copper, gold, antimony and tin. Confined to east and west are slightly younger rocks of Cambrian age which form the richly mineralised belt extending from Waratah to Queenstown and which can be traced south from Macquarie Harbour to Elliott Bay. Narrow tracts of serpentinite and later intrusions of granite occur, both proven sources of mineralisation; small deposits are common and present exploration is enthusiastic. Serpentinite appears again at Adamsfield and Rocky Boat Harbour, both sources of chromium and osmiridium, and later intrusions of granite are present at South West Cape and also associated with tin mineralization at Cox Bight (see map). Postdating the Cambrian rocks, vast north-south tracts of Ordovician limestones have been preserved within the Precambrian basement, but are only well-exposed where currently traversed by major rivers. Flat-lying sedimentary rocks, younger in age again, are preserved beneath the dolerite caps of mountains such as Precipitous Bluff and Mt Picton, and with them the included coal-measures are confined to the east of the longitude of New River Lagoon (see map). Heavy minerals, concentrated by river action, form the alluvial tin deposits at Cox Bight: local wind and marine action has enriched beach and dune sands in titanium ores.

In the past the vast reserves of dolomite and silica (from the Precambrian) and high grade limestone (from the Ordovician) have never been assessed, but advances in technology, bulk transportation and industrial demand now suggest economic extraction will be feasible in the future. Australia's demand for limestone is increasing, and we currently import some 1.5 million tonnes annually. On the other hand lithographic stone has been superseded and the Reward lease, pegged at Point Vivian in 1892 looks like a non-starter.

The mining and mineral processing industries in Tasmania are major employers and income earners for the State, involving some 10,000 workers and an annual production valued at nearly $300 million. Few Tasmanians stop to reflect on their utter dependence on mineral products, or the chaos and drop in living standards which would follow their withdrawal. Unfortunately ore deposits are finite and non-regenerative, and they turn up capriciously where nature wills, not where we might wish to locate them. An economically viable ore deposit is as unique an item as any other aspect of Tasmania's heritage! The industry is based on a wasting asset, and dependent on exploration (and its own profitability to finance that exploration) to locate new ore bodies, develop them and survive.

Therefore, whilst it is impossible to guess the economic potential in an area of unknown geology, it is not only possible but imperative that we work out a policy which represents a balance between the protection of our environment and the future availability and supply of essential minerals.

RECORD OF LEASES HELD ON MINERAL DEPOSITS IN SOUTH-WEST TASMANIA

Location

Pt Vivian (East of Rocky Boat Harbour)		Reward lease for Lithographic stone	1892–1913
South Cape Bay (North East corner)		Reward lease for Coal	1890–1902
Weld River (East of Mt Anne)		Lease for Gold	1897–1919
Weld River (North junction Barnbuck Creek)		Reward lease for Nickel	1916–1928
Weld River (South junction Barnbuck Creek)		Reward lease for Osmiridium	1926–1936
Weld River	*Scheppein*	Lease for Marble	1970–........
	Forster	Lease for Quartz-Silica	1974–........
	Electrona	Lease for Silica	1977–........
	Picton-Huon Junction. *Duggan*	Lease for Quartz Gravel	1976–........
Warnes Lookout (East of Jane River)		Reward lease for Gold	1935–1953
	Bennetto	Reward lease for Gold	1968–........
Headwaters of Florentine River (North & West of Tim Shea and Mt Mueller)		Lease for Silver-Lead	1891–1892
Mt Mueller Mine (South East of Mt Mueller)		Reward lease for Gold	1889–1910
		Copper & all minerals	........–1936
Humboldt Mine (East of Mt Mueller: South East of Tim Shea)		Lease for Silver-Copper	1918–1919
Adamsfield (South of The Thumbs)		Reward lease for Osmiridium	1925–........
	Bennetto	Reward lease for Osmiridium	1969–........
Cox Bight		Lease for Tin	1892–........
	Alstergren	Lease for Tin	1966–........
Ray River (North Mt Counsel)		Lease for Tin	1928–1929
		Lease for Tin	1933–1934
Melaleuca	*New Harbour Tin Development*	Lease for Tin	1936–........
	Charles King	Lease for Tin	1941–1960
	Denis King	Lease for Tin	1960–........
	Qintex	Lease for Tin	1972–........
	Willson	Lease for Tin	1975–........
Joe Page Bay (West of Mt Rugby)		Reward lease for Antimony	1897–1912
	King and Clayton	Reward lease for Antimony	1970–........
West Coast (South of Wreck Bay: West of Bond Bay)		Reward lease for Copper	1907–1908
Low Rocky Point		Lease for Copper	1907–1924
Birthday Bay (West Macquarie Harbour)		Reward lease for Copper	1900–1903
Asbestos Point (West Shore Macquarie Harbour)		Reward lease for Asbestos	1900–1905
Asbestos Point (West Shore Macquarie Harbour)		Reward lease for Copper & Silver	1897–1905
Cape Sorell	*Comalco*	Lease for Silica	1975–........
Gordon River, Marble Cliffs (West of Elliot Range)		Lease for Limestone	1890–1896
Bubs Hill, Victoria Pass, Lyell Highway		Lease for Silver-Lead	1890–1893
Arrowsmith, Lyell Highway		Reward lease for Silver-Lead	1928–1929
Headwaters Surprise River, (East of Lodden Range)		Reward lease for Silver-Lead	1890–1893

Maps indicating areas currently held under lease or exploration licence are retained for public scrutiny at the Department of Mines in Hobart

THE HARTZ MOUNTAINS

A Fine Tourist Attraction That Awaits Development

By a Special Correspondent

LOOKING to the south-west from Geeveston, and above the timber-clad foothills which rise in ascending ridges up to 2,000ft., one sees a solitary mountain peak— the Hartz. From a more elevated viewpoint the peak is revealed as part of an extensive range, which runs south for some 30 miles at a general elevation of about 3,000ft., rising to 4,300ft. at the Hartz, 4,017ft. at Adamson's Peak, and 3,800ft. at La Perouse. In lavishness of scenic attraction the Hartz makes a particular appeal to tourists, with its extensive and beautiful stretches of plain, its rugged escarpments, and hidden lakes. At present, however, it is accessible only by pack-horse or by foot. It is an area calling loudly for development.

The Mercury, 20 September, 1938.

THE HARTZ MOUNTAINS, about 40 miles south of Hobart, with Lake Laurie in the foreground.

First tourist flight to Port Davey about to take off from Brighton, c. 1931.

Tasmanian Museum and Art Gallery

Tourism

H M Gee

Compiled by Helen Gee, with an introduction by J B G Hulton, Director of Tourism.

To deny the increasing international importance of Tasmania's South-West as one of the great remaining temperate wilderness areas of the world and a place of great incomparable beauty and significance would be sacrilege.

Fortunately the trend has been towards investigating all avenues within modern experience to achieve management and conservation ideals for the area. Draft management plans have been conceived and revised and the State Government has had a special advisory committee present its views on the South-West's future.

Rightly in all this debate, the needs of tourism have been evaluated and allowed for.

Increasing awareness of the South-West as a precious wilderness can only intrigue more visitors, for whom proper facilities must be provided.

The tourist industry, while recognising the inviolability of parts of the South-West, must be allowed to continue to operate on the edges of the wilderness and within some sections of the park itself.

Strathgordon and Scotts Peak are virtually on the doorstep of the remoter lands and rainforests and here adequate accommodation and amenities like lookouts, parking areas, boating ramps and limited walking tracks must be planned.

Scenic flights to such incomparable spots as the cliffs and offshore islands and waterways of Port Davey and Bathurst Harbour must continue to be encouraged. Boat cruises across Macquarie Harbour and up the Gordon River have proven so successful that further similar services could be entertained.

Enterprises such as Tasventure and Wilderness Tours bring the bushwalking visitor on closer terms with nature in the wild.

Within the bounds of flexible planning (including reasonable access) and strict management, the South-West could become one of the great visitor destinations of the world.

Top right
Tourists flocked to Lake Pedder prior to its flooding in 1972. *Tasmanian Environment Centre Inc Col*

Middle right
The *Mascarin*, owned and skippered by John Brettingham-Moore who introduces many tourists to the waterways of Port Davey.
J Brettingham-Moore

The *Denison Star* on the Lower Gordon River.   *David Tasker*

Scenic flights

Sight-seeing flights over the South-West have been popular for the past twenty-five years (see 3.10). Summer is the most reliable season for scenic flying, though flights are made throughout the year depending on local weather conditions. The cliffs and islands of the South Coast, the waterways of Port Davey and the jagged peaks of the Arthur Ranges are spectacular sights from the air. Planes often land tourists and bushwalkers at Cox Bight Beach and Melaleuca airstrip where landings are now around 200 per year. Prior to flooding, Lake Pedder Beach was a popular landing site for thousands of tourists.

Light aircraft, usually four to six-seater Cessnas, are available for charter from various aviation companies in northern and southern Tasmania. The southern charter companies, Tasair and Tasmanian Aviation Services, take frequent flights over the South-West from the airport at Cambridge.

Tasmanian Charters

Since 1973, Tasmanian Charters has operated four-day cruises during summer months in Port Davey. Parties are flown in by light aircraft and board the luxury motor vessel in Bathurst Harbour. Apart from sightseeing, observing wildlife, fishing, swimming, water skiing and picnicking the *Mascarin* caters for those who wish to have 'a quiet and relaxing holiday in luxurious comfort'.

Wilderness Tours

Robert Geeves' 'Wilderness Tours' began in 1975, offering the opportunity of an organized flying/hiking holiday in the South-West during summer months. The tourist/walker is flown to Cox Bight by light aircraft; the beach forms a perfect natural airstrip. From Cox Bight, the guided party walks the South Coast Track to Cockle Creek and then travels by road through the Huon Valley to Hobart. The eight days' walk entails an average distance of ten kilometres a day. Variations of this walk are offered

to those keen for an extended trip. Such an organized venture as 'Wilderness Tours' is no doubt a catalyst — a valuable introduction to the wilderness for those who need some guidance to put them 'on the track'. Such tours can foster initiative and self-dependence, opening up new vistas to all people wishing to experience a wilderness environment.

The Denison Star

Morrison's Tourist Services Pty Ltd of Strahan operates launch cruises on Macquarie Harbour and the Lower Gordon River. The Director-Skipper, Reg Morrison, realised a life-long ambition when his luxury tourist vessel, the *Denison Star* was launched in February 1969. It is named after the river from where much of the construction timber was obtained. The vessel was built on a 90 foot long blue gum keel with blue gum ribs, stringers and deck beams. 12,000 superfeet of Huon pine was used for planking, decking and cabin structure. All the timber for the vessel was felled and cut by Reg Morrison and his brother and sawn at their mill at Strahan. 107 feet in overall length, the *Denison Star* is powered by diesel engines and attains a maximum speed of 14 knots.

Tourists travel 33 kilometres across Macquarie Harbour, then up the Lower Gordon River for about 30 kilometres to the Marble Cliffs and Butler Island. (From this point the *Denison Star* returns to Strahan.) It is the magnificence of the unspoilt shores, the rainforest and the reflections that account for the popularity of the excursion. However tourists are told that immediately upstream of Butler Island commences a string of exploration sites where the Hydro-Electric Commission is investigating possible dam sites. Any further dam on the Gordon would have dire consequences downstream. The *Denison Star* could be impeded by siltation and changed water levels; vegetation could be adversely affected by the salination of the river. Therefore multi-million dollar HEC investigations pose a serious threat to the Gordon River and to this West Coast based tourist industry.

Tasventure

Tasventure—'to explore, study, protect and promote Tasmania's scenic resources'.

Tasventure is a non-profit organization initiated and run by Peter Sims of Devonport. Since 1972 its environmental activities have become widely acknowledged. Peter, who is the Honorary Director, leads walking parties into the South-West, specifically to the coastal regions. People from many parts of the world, including members of the Sierra Club of the USA, have participated in his expeditions. His wilderness philosophy may be illustrated by his own words:

> 'Its not only showing but sharing and feeling—a heightened awareness and respect for the wholeness of the environment that we are seeking. What do we care if the camper fails to remember the name of a wild flower: Does he know where to find it? Does he remember its fragrance? The texture of its leaves? And does he know, not because someone told him he should, but because for him it is a thing of enjoyment and beauty which he has discovered?'

Cave Excursions

Exit Cave Adventure Excursions, led by Roy Skinner, provide the opportunity for tourists to visit Australia's largest cave. Exit Cave is near Ida Bay, south of Huonville and is still in its natural state. The Newdegate Caves and Thermal Springs complex at Hastings have become a popular tourist asset with 24,300 people visiting the caves during 1973.

Bizjets Tours

'Bizjets Special Tasmanian Holidays' offer a two day tour of the Gordon River and the West Coast. This direct flight from Melbourne to Strahan was initiated in 1977. Tourists are firstly taken by four wheel drive along the dunes and surf beach to Hells Gates. Here the *Esperance Star* is boarded for a cruise across Macquarie Harbour, via Sarah Island, to the Gordon River. The night is spent aboard the boat 25 miles upstream, near Sir John Falls. Returning to Strahan, tourists are invited to join a four wheel drive along the track of the old railway line that hugs the King River. The King River Valley and the Mt Lyell Mine are viewed on the departure flight.

Scenic Gordon and Hells Gates Charters

Scenic Gordon and Hells Gates Charters on the *Matthew Brady* commenced operating out of Strahan in the 1977–78 summer season, under the proprietorship of R F & J A Kearney. The 70 foot *Matthew Brady*, originally built for trans Derwent Crossing, now cruises approximately 10 miles up the Gordon River before travelling back across Macquarie Harbour to Hells Gates where the boat stops for an inspection of Ocean Beach.

Lake Pedder Scenic Cruises

Tourist cruises aboard the *M L Bundeena* commenced in December 1977. In fine weather the 3 hour scenic cruise from Strathgordon wharf is popular with tourists. The number of tourists travelling on the Gordon River Road during the 1975–76 financial year was 56,105 according to HEC records. Sightseeing may be assumed to be the predominant activity. Boating and fishing are also popular and the road provides access to bushwalkers.

Top
Crossing the mouth of the New River on a 'Wilderness Tour' along the South Coast.
Bob Geeves

Middle
Peter Sims in camp at the Hibbs River on a Tasventure trip to the west coast.   *Peter C Sims*

Bottom
Earlier this century tourists landed at this spot to visit the Sir John Falls, Lower Gordon River.
Helen Gee

R E Graham

Conservation & the 1970s

5

Many Australians advocate wilderness preservation for their own recreational pursuits; they enjoy the feeling of seeing, feeling and experiencing a wild place. Some do not look beyond these arguments.

But although people need wilderness, and will need it increasingly in the future, wilderness does not need people. It is the growing pressure of people that is destroying the last strongholds of the natural world. Although we may appreciate that world, we still do not understand its complexity, its vitality and its delicacy.

For many thousands of years man lived in comparative harmony with the natural environment, taking what he needed for survival and immediate comfort. In our estrangement from that life of harmony our greed has driven us to modify much of the Earth's surface. Now there are only small isolated areas on Earth retaining their biological life systems in balance. As this natural balance is destroyed, so our chances of survival are lessened.

Let us be aware, too, of the dignity of nature. Compare it with the dignity we accord man: we honour the fine deed of saving a human life. But what of the preservationist striving to save a wilderness and all its life systems — the species that have their right to exist? How can he be complacent who understands that the overturning of a single stone can destroy a world too small for the human eye to perceive or the mind to comprehend? Worlds revolve within worlds. The intricate beauty of a wilderness sustains a web of life far too complex for our understanding. It exists apart from us, yet for us; it is best without us.

Consider the Earth as a tree. We are among the branches of human endeavour. Looking down we see only the ground, unaware of the underlying roots that supplied needs and supported the tree from its creation. In destroying wilderness we are severing those roots. The tree must die.

233

The Spires Range.

Maurice D Clark

The Great Ravine, Franklin River.

Don Hutton

Wilderness Conservation

R E Saunders

R E Saunders, B.Sc.Hons., became interested in South-West Tasmania in 1973 as a keen bushwalker. He prepared a critique of the Draft Management Plan for the South-West National Park in 1975, as part of a Masters degree in Environmental Science at Monash University. His contributions to this section are based on a paper he subsequently presented to Section 21 of the 47th ANZAAS Congress in Hobart, in 1976.

It is perhaps ironic that Australia, with its large area and relatively small, highly urbanized population, should be poorly provided with regions of 'recreation wilderness'. However, most substantially natural areas that are large enough to need little management are too arid and distant from the centres of population to be attractive for recreation. The 'wilderness experience'—the feeling of being close to nature and remote from civilisation—is likely to be stronger where a considerable part of an area is more than a half day's walk from the nearest road, and an overnight stay becomes necessary. In south-eastern Australia, where most of the population is concentrated, the largest such area is South-West Tasmania, which covers more than one million hectares, and is almost as extensive as New Zealand's Fiordland National Park (1.17 million hectares). In a region this size, it is possible to walk for three or four weeks without sight or sound of civilisation. It is the potential for such experiences which makes the South-West unique in Australia, and a highly prized recreation area.

The value of this 'wilderness experience' has been an integral feature of the developing 'wilderness movement' in the United States during the past century, and has been compellingly presented in the past by such people as Aldo Leopold and Robert Marshall, and more recently by Roderick Nash.

'Wilderness visits instil a reverence for nature and a better understanding of ecology—attributes which are of growing value in a world increasingly subject to massive adverse transformation by human activity.' [1]

However, as Sir Frank Fraser Darling points out:

'nature exists in its own right, and our attitude towards it is a measure of our consciousness of the whole situation, of which our own survival is a part, not be-all and end-all'. [2]

Wilderness, nevertheless, is of considerable value to mankind as a source of inspiration and as a retreat from modern urban life.

Extensive natural areas contain floral and faunal communities essential for the maintenance of biological and genetic diversity, and for world ecological stability. Areas such as South-West Tasmania, where physical and ecological barriers have prevented colonisation by imported and alien species, are particularly significant scientific reference sites. Though there is little detailed knowledge of the ecology of this region its importance is well established:

'South-West Tasmania is not just Australia's finest wilderness area, it is undoubtedly a rich source of biological material of world as well as local interest'. [3]

Although the inclusion of a sample of every habitat will not necessarily ensure that all species of wildlife are present in large enough numbers to provide viable populations, [4] South-West Tasmania provides a rare opportunity for the creation of a national park that is large enough to be a self-regulating ecological unit. To this end, it is essential that the natural boundaries of the region are respected in order to maintain its 'in-built capacity for self-preservation'. [5]

The demand for wilderness recreation has grown significantly in recent years, and in many countries it has been found necessary to buy back privately owned land for national parks, in order to off-set

A sign in Nepalese and English, Himalayas.   *Joseph Donnelly*

the damage caused by increased usage. There are already signs of over-use in some areas of South-West Tasmania, and it was inevitable, for example, that airdrops of supplies should be banned in certain areas due to the problem of litter. Unless regulations enforcing self-reliance are instituted, management practices and user facilities will become more apparent, and the wilderness quality of the region will deteriorate. This degradation—the general trend for an area to become increasingly man-altered—may be visualized as a tendency to 'slide-down' the wilderness hierarchy of Table 1. Movements in the reverse direction are considerably more difficult, as it may take many hundreds of years for an altered ecosystem to re-establish the climax community. Since diversity of experience is the source of much of the satisfaction people derive from their environment, it is essential that the increasingly rare 'Recreation Wilderness' and 'True Wilderness' zones are protected, and preserved intact for future generations. (See Table 1)

The case against further development and exploitation in the South-West is based upon the assertion that this area is of more 'real value' to the community left as it is, than in terms of its potential for hydro-electricity, mining, forestry or any other development. It is important to realise that 'the community', in this instance, refers to **the people of Australia**, rather than the people of Tasmania alone, since the area is of international and therefore national significance. Consequently, the responsibility for any financial compensation rests firmly with the Federal Government.

Hydro-electric development poses an immediate threat to the South-West, specifically:

because of the length of time necessary for the construction of major power generation and distribution works, it is necessary to plan activities well ahead of requirements'. [6]

Thus although they are ostensibly 'post-Pieman' (post 1985) schemes, Hydro-Electric Commission 'Investigations' have already begun in the Lower Gordon and Franklin Rivers. Large work sites have been constructed on the Lower Gordon River (upstream of Butler Island), and roads have been pushed through to the Franklin River. These activities are shrouded in secrecy, and continued with an air of inevitability throughout the hearings of the Committee of Inquiry into the South-West in 1976 and 1977.

The South-West is also immediately threatened by forestry interests,

---

PLAN FOR NATION PARK IN S. WEST

This map shows the boundaries of the proposed national park in South-Western Tasmania.

THE declaration of a large area of Tasmania's rugged and spectacular South-West Coast as a national park is the object of a plan prepared by the State Fauna and Flora Conservation Committee.

The president of the committee (Mr. L. Wall) yesterday stressed the need to establish the park before there was any commercial development, and before wildlife was disturbed.

The Fauna and Flora Conservation Committee, which is a permanent organisation consisting of delegates from the Field Naturalists' Club, the Hobart Walking Club, the Youth Hostels Association, and other organisations concerned with the preservation of wildlife, has greeted enthusiastically the recent formation of the South-West Committee.

Mr. Wall said there was no immediate need to spend Government money in the area if the plan was accepted. The South-West already was open to bushwalkers, and private money was being spent to keep the access tracks open.

There were minimum landing facilities for aircraft at Lake Pedder, Cox Bight and Port Davey, the latter being open to boats.

Much of rugged scenery unique

Mr. Wall said that much of the scenery in the South-West was unique.

'Because of its ancient geological structure, it presents a rugged terrain peculiar to this State,' he said. It was eminently suitable for mountaineering and rock-climbing, yet was easily accessible.

Nowhere else in Australia was it possible for the average citizen to fly from a capital city and be landed within an hour on a picturesque beach in the midst of spectacular mountain ranges as was now the case at Lake Pedder.

He stressed that:

● Because of its variety of scenery and terrain, the South-West presented possibilities of development as a tourist asset in many ways.

● Because of its comparative isolation, it was one of the last strongholds of some of the State's interesting fauna and flora in their natural state, and if these were to be preserved it was essential that their environments be protected now.

TO INCLUDE ISLANDS

The committee recommended that the boundaries of the proposed national park should be from Low Rocky Pt. on the West Coast to Mt. Sprent, the north-west corner of the present Lake Pedder National Park; Mt. Anne; the junction of the Huon and Cracroft Rivers; along the Cracroft and New Rivers to the mouth of the New River Lagoon; and the coastline north-west to Low Rocky Pt.

The offshore islands should be included.

Mr. Wall said that as a long-term plan the committee recommended three types of development.

The first was a tourist and recreation area with considerable facilities in Bathurst Harbour, with another non-residential area at Lake Pedder.

Accommodation at Bathurst Harbour should include a chalet providing full board. A suitable site would be near Mt. Beattie, overlooking the harbour and commanding a fine panorama, including Mt. Rugby on the opposite shore and the mountain ranges beyond.

From the chalet, it would be possible to run motor launch trips to the outer harbour, and guide-conducted tours to many lookout points, beaches, and other attractions by easy walking tracks.

A vehicle track to Cox Bight also might be considered, and there could be facilities for swimming, water-skiing, and sailing.

Other accommodation recommended was Government-owned "housekeeping" units with facilities for cooking, on the lines of the present Government huts in the Mt. Field National Park.

Larger dormitory huts, as at Lake St. Clair, could be provided for large parties, with camping areas, toilets, and a laundry.

Accommodation at Lake Pedder should be restricted to camping facilities and a toilet block.

The second type of development suggested was the creation of wilderness areas, in which accommodation should be restricted to huts for bushwalking parties, similar to those in the Lake St. Clair-Cradle Mt. National Park.

Existing tracks should be kept clear, and other routes marked.

The third type should be completely closed, and there should be no access other than by special permission for scientific study.

Mr. Wall said that as far as was known Australia had none of these areas and it was essential that tracts of land be set aside so that native animals and birds, which all too often were fighting a losing battle against the encroachment of man, might thrive undisturbed.

It was recommended that two such areas be reserved—one north of the Ironbound Range and incorporating the headwaters of the Solly and Watts Rivers, and the other west of the Frankland Range and including a more open type of country.

The committee suggested that a road to Bathurst Harbour be built from the end of the existing Forestry Commission road near the junction of the Huon and Picton Rivers.

● Continued on Page 2
● Editorial, Page 4

Huge spirit theft

SYDNEY. — A daring gang of thieves yesterday hi-jacked a truck loaded with six tons of whisky from outside a Sydney suburban hotel.

The whisky was valued at £4,000.

The thieves vanished within the space of a few seconds.

Police said last night the whisky robbery was planned with the precision of a military operation.

In a wave of Christmas thefts in Sydney yesterday and last night:

● Cracksmen stole more than £2,000 from a safe in a Bondi Junction store;

● A man and a woman escaped in a high-powered sports car after a smash grab raid at the suburb of St. Marys.

● The ticket office at Marayong railway station was robbed of £150 after the 16-year-old attendant was knocked unconscious; and

● Two girls were used as decoys by thieves who robbed a Redfern service station.

In the liquor theft — at the Queen's Hotel, Enmore — the truck was driven off within a minute of the driver and his assistant starting to unload.

Police believe the thieves had been watching the driver's movements and drove off as soon as he entered the hotel.

The Bondi Junction robbery was at the store of Household Distributors Pty. Ltd.

The thieves apparently used a duplicate key to open the safe.

The theft was discovered when a cleaner opened the store yesterday morning.

At St. Marys, a night watchman chased a man and a woman in his utility after a smash-grab raid on an electrical store in Queen St., but lost them.

State Country

To be laun by Mr. Mc

By E. J. Balfe

THE Federal Leader of the Countr Ewen) will inaugurate the Country Tasmania towards the end of April

Mr. McEwen will make a special visit to the State to launch the movement at a conference to be held in Launceston.

In the meantime, Mr. W. Carew, Press Liaison Offi-

The Mercury, Front page, 19 December 1962

principally in the Huon Valley—Picton Range area and in the Lower King and Gordon River area.[5] Although about two-thirds of Tasmania is covered by timber concessions already (see 4.1), the Draft Management Plan described the revocation of almost one third of the Hartz Mountains National Park (an area of 2,150 hectares) for forestry purposes as a necessary condition for the inclusion of Precipitous Bluff in the proposed Southwest National Park.[7] This exchange did in fact pass through the House of Assembly in October 1976 causing a public outcry at the continued violation of the principle of permanency inherent in the national park ideal. As zoologist Dr P S Lake et al stated:

'Such a trade-off is iniquitous. It indicates clearly that the Tasmanian Government does not regard National Parks as permanent treasures but rather as negotiable depositories to be opened up and plundered when desired. Such an attitude to National Parks is outrageously out of line with international thinking and reeks of insincerity as regards conservation. What is the point of adding new reserves to the Tasmanian system (often using Commonwealth money) if there is no guarantee that they will remain reserves and not be alienated to meet the pressures of exploitative interests?'.[8]

There is concern, too, for the continued presence of mining companies within the region. Modern mining procedures often scar the landscape, and subsequent erosion can prevent regrowth of vegetation. A number of licence areas exist along the west coast from Macquarie Harbour to Nye Bay, a region integral to the South-West wilderness. 'If development of even one licence area is permitted' warns the Australian Conservation Foundation,

'the domino principle will follow... Thus far, the South-West has survived the quarrying that has demolished mountains, poisoned flora, killed rivers and driven out fauna north of the Lyell Highway'.[5]

This 'nibbling away' of the South-West wilderness must cease. The declaration of a moratorium on developmental activities would ensure for future generations the option to retain this natural treasure.

TABLE OF ZONES	Accommodation & Services	Type of Access	Access	DEFINITIONS	TASMANIAN EXAMPLES
TRUE WILDERNESS	None	Foot access	No Tracks	* reference areas * no or restricted access — access for controlled scientific study (but no vehicles, no quadrats)	THE NEW RIVER BASIN
RECREATION WILDERNESS	Tents for recreation	Foot access	No Tracks	* no permanent construction or sign of man — no defined tracks or huts * camping allowed * unmotorised access	THE FAR SOUTH-WEST CORNER
WILDLANDS I	No huts, Simple huts	Foot access	No Tracks Marked tracks Snow Poles	* mildly developed * unserviced facilities — some simple refuge shelters * access by marked walking tracks, pole lines	FRENCHMANS CAP HARTZ MOUNTAINS
WILDLANDS II	No Tows, cable cars No services No telephones	Management, emergency vehicles	Jeep tracks	* more developed areas * limited access for management purposes (e.g. fire, animal survey rubbish collection) by road * shelters to be sympathetic in design with natural environment * no ski-tows, no services, no telecommunications	CRADLE MOUNTAIN-LAKE ST. CLAIR
MODIFIED NATURAL	Some services Some tele-communications	Four wheel drive Motor vehicles	Unsealed roads	* modified environments, but still predominantly natural * high usage, extensive road, jeep track network * recreational use by 4WD * simple accommodation	MOUNT FIELD
PREDOMINANTLY MAN ALTERED	Private lodges, fully serviced	Motor vehicles	Sealed roads	* predominantly extensive man-made environment	FREYCINET PENINSULA (COLES BAY AREA)

Table 1 Wilderness Management Zones. *Adapted from Hooley et al., 1975.*[9]

Mt Counsel, Moulters Cove, Bathurst Harbour.   *Jim England*

Age is no barrier to travel. Pictured are four young women who joined nearly 2,000 people who hiked or flew to Lake Pedder over the March long weekend in 1972. *Don Stephens*

Dawn at Pedder. *Howard P Simco*

Young visitor to the Arve River. *Ann Wessing*

The Evolving Consciousness

H M Gee

Prior to November 1970, the principal legislation governing nature conservation in Tasmania was the Scenery Preservation Act 1915 and the Animals and Birds Protection Act 1928.

Despite many deficiencies these Acts permitted important areas of the State to be gazetted as scenic reserves and sanctuaries. There was no distinction made between national parks and other types of reservation; indeed the term 'national park', now common usage, was omitted from the legislation. The Animals and Birds Protection Act protected fauna, but not the habitat on which their survival depended.

The prospectors and piners, the whalers and the miners of last century left few signs of their passing interest in the South-West. And then, early this century, the climate and the remoteness of the region deterred and delayed interest. Only the occasional bushwalker and prospector were not to be dissuaded by the lack of detailed maps. But by the mid 1950's the area was gaining greater attention from mainland and local bushwalkers. In 1954 the Hobart Walking Club recommended to the State Government that the Lake Pedder area be gazetted as a scenic reserve. The following year the Lake Pedder National Park of 23,800 hectares was proclaimed. At the same time HEC investigation of water power potential commenced, with field journeys to examine geology and potential damsites.

The penetration of more people into the area, coupled with attendant fire damage, led in 1962 to the formation of the South-West Committee, a voluntary organisation dedicated to preserving the South-West as a major scenic and ecological resource.

In 1963 the Tasmanian Government applied for and received a $5 million Commonwealth grant in order to build a 55 mile (90 km) road deep into the area for the purpose of surveying the hydro-electric potential of the region. Man's major impact on the South-West commenced, although the Tasmanian Government was extremely secretive about intentions. After much lobbying, the South-West Committee managed to persuade the Animals and Birds' Protection Board that a major reserve —

a Faunal District — should be established in the South-West. The area reserved was 646,000 hectares. By the mid 1960's, conflict over the future usage of the South-West was growing. The Government was denying that any major modification of the Lake Pedder National Park would occur, but all HEC activities pointed in that direction.

In August 1964, the Premier, Mr Reece, announced the appointment of an Interdepartmental Committee 'to handle arrangements and recommend reserves to protect the region against undue damage' (*The Mercury* — 31

August, 1964). The proceedings of this Committee and the circumstances are outlined by Dr Richard Jones in this extract from his submission, as Chairman of the United Tasmania Group, to the Committee of Inquiry into Lake Pedder in 1973:

'The Committee was headed by the Chief Commissioner of the Hydro-Electric Commission and consisted of the Surveyor-General and representatives of the Forestry Commission and the Department of Mines. Proposals by the South-West Committee for a South-West

The Mercury 13 April, 1960

239

National Park were then passed by the Government to the Interdepartmental Committee rather than to the Scenery Preservation Board and the Premier refused representation on the Interdepartmental Committee to the South-West Committee. Clearly the Government had no sympathy with the conservationists and it was using every administrative possibility to bring about a chosen, but undisclosed, end. In this way the Interdepartmental Committee, reporting in June 1966 on Hydro-Electric Commission paper, was able to say with confidence that the Scenery Preservation Board was likely to accept its recommendations.

Thus the long history of interest by conservationists in the South-West was being systematically crushed by a refusal, on the part of government, to heed the representations of the South-West Committee and by the government's muzzling of the administrative machinery set up to promote the preservation of the natural scenery of the State. Nor was this all; in place of the Scenery Preservation Board, the Hydro-Electric Commission was emerging as the decisive authority on matters relating to the creation of national parks, the preservation of scenery and the recreational needs of bushwalkers and other members of the public. Not only was the Scenery Preservation Board overshadowed by the Interdepartmental Committee dominated by the Hydro-Electric Commission, but other government departments were effectively brought under the influence of the Hydro-Electric Commission. Thus, the Commission contracted with the Tasmanian Museum for a biological survey of the Lake Pedder area to be made, but the only ensuing information on the results of the survey was released in the Hydro-Electric Commission's Report to Parliament on the Gordon River Power Development Stage One and Thermal Power Station. Thus, all the administrative machinery of government representative of interests likely to conflict with those of the single-purpose Hydro-Electric Commission was rendered ineffective. It would be no exaggeration to say that the community was now denied certain government services because independent reports were no longer forthcoming and that the normal business of government had become subservient to particular interests. In these circumstances, the Save Lake Pedder National Park Committee emerged on 29 March, 1967.

Meanwhile it had become apparent that another technique used by the Hydro-Electric Commission, and encouraged by the government, to achieve the aims of development involved the withholding of all information of a technical nature regarding the scheme in preparation.

The Hydro-Electric Commission claimed that it was obliged to place completed details of its plans before the responsible minister before any public disclosure of information was possible. In this way fears for Lake Pedder could only be based on the Premier's disclosure, on 21 June 1965, that "there would be some modification of the Lake Pedder National Park". In the event, the Report on the Gordon River Power Development Stage One and Thermal Power Station, when made public, preceded only by a few days the introduction of enabling legislation to the Legislative Assembly. No alternative scheme was presented to this House and the Bill was passed without any debate whatsoever on possibilities for saving Lake Pedder. Also the Report by the Interdepartmental Committee had preceded the Hydro-Electric Commission's Report by only a few weeks, and the programme is now seen as a carefully stage-managed series of events leading to the fait accompli of Parliamentary approval. This set the seal on public indignation, resulting in a call by the South-West Committee for a Select Committee of Inquiry'.

In response to the public outcry, the Legislative Council appointed a Select Committee empowered to enquire into the effect of the proposed scheme on the Lake Pedder National Park, and possible modifications to the scheme. Before the results were presented, the Premier

introduced the HEC Bill, 1967, into the House of Assembly, seeking authorisation for an expenditure of $116 million. A second Bill gave the HEC temporary control over the entire South-West Fauna District and $47 million special bridging finance was obtained from the Federal Government.

Only at the last moment did the HEC inadvertently disclose that options existed which could save the Lake. The Select Committee examined these but the Hon. Mr M Hodgman MLC, a member of the Committee, later admitted that insufficient attention had been given to the question of alternative proposals which would have saved Lake Pedder. The Select Committee gave its assent to the proposals involving the flooding of Lake Pedder, and recommended the establishment of a new national park of 363,000 hectares.

The Government immediately halved this area but included the previous Lake Pedder National Park of 23,800 hectares. The west coast region, including the Port Davey area beyond the Foreshore Reserve was still unprotected. The eastern boundary failed to protect Precipitous Bluff and the surrounding wilderness, foreshadowing subsequent problems and stimulating lobbying for reconsideration of the boundaries.

In 1969 there was a State election and the Liberal Party formed a coalition government with the support of the Centre Party. The Lake Pedder issue played a part in Labor's first electoral defeat since the Depression.

The Scenery Preservation Act and the Animals and Birds' Protection Act were replaced by the National Parks and Wildlife Act in 1970. The National Parks and Wildlife Service became the administrative body for the management of national parks in Tasmania.

Meanwhile concern for the fate of Lake Pedder became nationwide. Access provided by the Gordon Road had increased traffic into the Pedder area. The petition presented to Parliament carrying 13,000 signatures signified the increasing numbers eager to see the Lake, either on foot or by landing on the beach in light aircraft. More and more spokesmen for its preservation were won. People now knew that direct action was needed if the decision to flood Pedder were to be reversed. Thus, the Lake Pedder Action Committee came into being in April 1971. The assumption that Pedder could not be saved by means of an alternative scheme was severely questioned and in Parliament, but neither Liberal nor Labor governments presented any hope that Lake Pedder would be saved. So when, early in 1972, the Bethune Government tendered its resignation, the opportunity was seized by conservationists to attempt to grasp the balance of power at the forthcoming election. Dr Jones, in the submission cited above, described the formation of the United Tasmania Group:

'Independent political action was the only avenue open. A public meeting was therefore called for 23 March. By advertising simply for "People who care" to discuss "Lake Pedder, The Quality of Government and use of Resources", the Lake Pedder Action Committee attracted an overflow audience to the Town Hall. A pamphlet distributed before the start of the meeting stated: "the intention of the meeting is to ensure that your vote for conservation at the coming election is not wasted" and people were asked to think of "some effective way that a combined united group can be created who will attract all the available (conservation) votes"...

One of the earliest features of the campaign during the state elections of April 1972 was the announcement by the leaders of both major parties that Lake Pedder was not an election issue. It was quite clear now that there existed a strong political motivation to drown Lake Pedder. It became clear later why the government and the opposition could afford to ignore an issue of which the electorate was very well aware. The Hydro-Electric Commission was soon to emerge as a political force upon which the major parties relied to counter the electoral propaganda of the United Tasmania Group.'

In February 1973 the Federal Minister for the Environment appointed a Committee of Inquiry to study the Lake Pedder case. The urgency for a stop to the flooding of Lake Pedder was regarded as considerable, based on the evidence gained by this Committee. It recom-

Far left
Olegas Truchanas with his daughter Rima at Lake Pedder, 1970. Truchanas knew Pedder intimately in all its moods and communicated the sense of awe and wonder he experienced there. Through his photography he showed the people of Tasmania what they were about to lose. Thousands remember his unique audio-visual presentations in the Hobart Town Hall, his lucid speeches and his breadth of vision, described by his friend, Max Angus, in *The World of Olegas Truchanas*, 1975, a tribute to this remarkable man.
Melva Truchanas

Centre left
'It seemed incredible that this could happen.... As this lake is out of sight it is obvious that the Government, for the sake of the development and to assuage their guilt, have to promote the new lake — "much better than the old; bigger and better."'
(Max Angus, Hobart Town Hall, 14 May, 1976)
Lake Pedder; its last days.   *Don Stephens*

Left
'Showers, Frankland Range', a watercolour painting by Max Angus, an artist who frequented Lake Pedder.   *K Iredale*

THE MEN WITH THE POWER IN THE PEDDER DAYS

Eric Reece, Labor Premier 1958-1969 & 1972-1975, and Leader of the Opposition 1969-1972. *The Mercury*

Angus Bethune, Leader of the Liberal Opposition 1960-1969 and Premier 1969-1972. *The Mercury*

Mervyn Everett, Attorney General, 1972-1974. *The Mercury*

Sir Allan Knight, Chief Commissioner of the Hydro-Electric Commission, 1946-1977. *The Mercury*

mended that a moratorium proposal should be adopted with a view to assessing the feasibility of restoring Lake Pedder (which had in fact been inundated during late 1972). The Committee proposed that the costs be borne by the Australian Government. The Federal Government supported these findings and made an offer of $8 million to the Tasmanian (Labor) Government. However, the Tasmanian Government refused Federal assistance. The Pedder tragedy is recorded more fully in a number of publications (see Bibliography).

The struggle to save Lake Pedder did a great deal towards the awakening of Tasmanians to their natural heritage. Thousands who deeply regretted the destruction regretted also the political

and administrative machinery that permitted it despite such enormous opposition. It was felt that citizens ought to have the right to be heard in court to protect the quality of the State's environment. A second major issue in the seventies is that of Precipitous Bluff. The attempt to safeguard this magnificent jewel of the south coast followed the application for a prospecting licence by Mineral Holdings Australia Pty Ltd in 1971. Since December, 1972—when the application was successfully stopped by objectors—the issue has been from a Mining Warden's Court, to the Supreme Court, and then before the Full Bench of the Tasmanian Supreme Court in a series of appeals. In May 1975 the Full Bench dismissed the conservationists' appeal on the grounds that ordinary

people had no rights of interest in the area. Many Australians claim that they do have a right to use this Crown land for recreation in peace and seclusion.

Believing that it is vital to the well being of Tasmania, and the South-West specifically, to use every legal opportunity to broaden the definition of interest to include long term community interest rather than confine it to economic interest, conservationists lodged a final appeal to the High Court of Australia in 1976. This appeal was dismissed in 1977.

Acts such as the Mining Act 1929 were framed to aid 'development' and exploitation of resources in line with the then current thinking, before there was any general acceptance of either ecological principles and needs or the

Young people were also aware of the issue, 24 July, 1971. *The Mercury*

Lake Pedder book cover, 96 pages. Published July 1972.

BEFORE THE FLOOD

LAKE PEDDER POWER FAR DISTANT

A power scheme is not likely in the foreseeable future for the Lake Pedder area.

This was stated yesterday by the Hydro-Electric Commission when commenting on a letter in "The Mercury" regarding a report dismissing the proposal to flood the Lake Pedder area.

Mr. Knight said the water power potential of South-West Tasmania, including Lake Pedder, was being assessed in common with similar work elsewhere in the State.

No firm proposals had yet been prepared on the topographical, hydrometric and geological information which was being collected.

Mr. Knight said that, so far as could be seen at present, the possibility of power development in this area in the foreseeable future was remote.

Wildlife fund's p... save Lake Pedder

A WORLD-WIDE organisation, of which the Duke of Edinburgh is president, has supported the fight of the Lake Pedder National Park Com—

---

serenity, of aloneness, not loneliness. It is a picture of peace, a picture of a reflection of God's Beauty. It was first made by glaciers about the time man first appeared on earth. It is over such waters that the Spirit of God hovers. God sees it, and sees that it is good.

FUTURE OF LAKE PEDDER QUERIED

THE Hydro-Electric Commissioner (Mr. Knight) states that "a power scheme in the Lake Pedder area is not likely in the foreseeable future." The inference is that such a scheme, with the inevitable flooding of Lake Pedder, is probable at some future date. Why?

Preserving the S.W.

Sentiment appears to be too big a part in the case put up by conservationists opposing the proposed South-West hydro-electric scheme. The arguments do have merit. On past performance the scheme's opponents have good reason to fear that once the Hydro-Electric Commission moves into the area, much of its beauty and attraction will be lost.

It is unrealistic to advocate the development of natural resources be curtailed in order to preserve in its primitive environment a huge area, accessible only to those with the time and inclination for marathon hikes. On the other hand, with tourism potentially our biggest industry, it would be senseless to destroy in time could be our greatest asset.

Both the Government and the H.E.C. have paid lip service to conservation, but if sincerity is measured by deeds, neither has much of which to be proud. Despite present water resources, especially in the Central Highlands, has given the State some of its tourist roads. But too often these roads lead to monuments to ugliness.

Few people would now find beauty in the muddy, dead tree-lined shores of the Great Lake. Lake St. Clair is little better. The Shannon Rise, once famous among trout anglers all over the world, is ruined. Launceston's unique Gorge, once a torrent roaring through a chasm, is now a trickle in a rocky bed.

The Government and the H.E.C. have said Lake Pedder would not be ruined, but raising its level must destroy one of its greatest charms, the sandy beach. They have said the Gordon River would not be destroyed. The same was said about the Shannon Rise and the Gorge.

The Government has repeatedly stated it is doing something to ensure that the State is not raped of its natural beauty by industrial development; it has not said what or how. It must now adopt a firm policy on conservation, tell the public what it is, and see that it is adhered to. And its policy must be based on knowledge of conservation requirements, best obtained by consulting the people who know the area, and not on the opinions of politicians and others who have never seen the South-West.

New H.E.C. grab

IF Tasmanians retain any capacity for amazement they surely will be stunned by the terms of a Hydro-Electric Commission Bill which will be before Parliament this week. The Commission is to be given virtual sovereignty over the whole of the South-West — a tenth of the State's area.

The public was decidedly uneasy when it was disclosed that the Commission proposed to destroy Lake Pedder in the course of building a power scheme on the Middle Gordon. However, it was generally disposed to accept that the price of commercial progress is sometimes high; in this case it involved the rape of a national park proclaimed only a few years ago.

But now it is planned to vest the whole of the South-West in the Commission — 1,600,000 acres of it. The boundary of the Commission's new principality runs from Low Rocky Pt. to the junction of the Gordon and Serpentine Rivers, to Mt. Mueller, to the junction of the Huon and Weld Rivers, to Adamsons Peak, and to South Cape.

This area includes two existing national parks, Lake Pedder and the Hartz Mountains, and the Commission will have complete control over it, including the entry of Tasmanian citizens. Tasmanians will require the equivalent of a visa from the Commission before they can visit the most picturesque parts of their State.

No explanation has yet been given why the Commission needs what amounts to sovereignty over such a vast area. Seeing that its purpose is the exploitation of natural resources for power, the Tasmanian people have every cause to be worried about what is likely to happen to the national parks, and indeed to the South-West generally.

Even if the parks are preserved the people will have no right to visit them except by permission of the H.E.C. It is hoped that Parliament will be ultra cautious before it gives away a tenth of the State as a sacrifice to "progress".

The bill also provides that the Commission "shall be deemed to be the agent for the Government of Tasmania". At least this clears up one point. The impression had been gaining ground that the Government is an agent of the Commission.

STANDARD

IT'S NOT TOO LATE TO SAVE THIS LAKE

Hobart: March 12, 1971 16 Pages: Vol 37. No 1,736. Price

---

review urged

H.E.C. PLAN AND LAKE PEDDER

The Government's statement that it does not know to what extent the character of Lake Pedder would be changed by the Gordon River scheme makes one rather suspicious.

The H.E.C. employs scores of competent and experienced engineers, but if they are incapable of estimating the effects of the scheme, more help should be brought from the Mainland.

One is reminded of the Trevallyn scheme. Before that we started, reassuring statements were made about its possible effect on the Launceston Gorge. The spoliation of the Gorge which followed was supposed to come as a surprise to all the experts.

CYNIC.

Power plan inquiry

WHATEVER the outcome, the Legislative Council's decision to appoint a select committee to inquire into the Gordon River power scheme was sensible in view of the public controversy the proposal had aroused.

The Hydro-Electric Commission presented a powerful case in favour of flooding Lake Pedder to create a new 200 square mile lake, the main point of criticism. It said this would provide about 40 p.c. of the whole scheme's output and gave assurances about avoiding the unsightliness of dead trees and mud flats on the shores of the new lake.

So far there is one indisputable fact: the road giving access to the dam sites would be the most spectacular mountain scenery tour in Australia and equal to most offered anywhere else in the world.

But for many people H.E.C. reports are suspect. The commission's concern is to produce power and there is a feeling, quite strong in some sections of the community, that in producing the technically best scheme it disregards other factors. In this instance, the inter-departmental committee's confirmation of H.E.C. assurances about the area has done nothing to allay any of these feelings; it appeared too much a rubber-stamp approval.

Those who wish to save Lake Pedder will need to produce strong evidence to shake the departmental case. But at least the select committee will provide them with an opportunity to put forward their views fully to a House which is not yet tied to party affiliations.

They may be able to impress the committee with alternatives to the full scheme which will satisfy everyone. The chances may be slim, but they have a right to be heard by people not yet committed definitely one way or the other.

They may be able also to raise the question of national parks in general. At present declaration of an area as a national park means very little. Lake Pedder is condemned for a power scheme; others could go just as easily for other reasons, such as mineral discoveries. A firm statement on Government policy is needed.

Fortnight too short for thorough inquiry into Gordon R. Scheme

I AM astonished to read that the select committee appointed by the Legislative Council investigate the Gordon River-Lake Pedder project hopes to complete its inquiries in two we...

On the 10 March, 1971 many Tasmanians anxiously awaited a decision of Parliament. Mr Shoobridge MLC was addressing the Legislative Council on his motion for a referendum on the 'Save Lake Pedder' issue. He asked 'that the Legislative Council ... recognize the planned flooding of Lake Pedder as the loss of a unique natural feature of high long term value and accordingly, jointly, call upon the Government to hold a referendum on whether this lake should be preserved in its natural state...'. The motion was defeated in a 14 – 3 vote.
(Votes and Proceedings of the Legislative Council, Session of 1971. Third Session of the 35th Parliament No 4, Wed 10 March, 1971.)
The Mercury, 10 March, 1971

Don't drown our Pedder

WHAT a mighty response from readers to the referendum on the "SEM" and future of Lake Pedder!

HEC chief raps 'vocal minority'

Petition on Lake Pedder

HEC blamed for Huon pollution

THE pollution of the Huon River by the Hydro-Electric Commission had gone on for too long, Mr Michael Hodgman (Huon) told Legislative Council.

'Save lake, 500 call

final struggle save Lake Ped— began at a public meeting in Hobart last night when 500 people called on the Tasmanian Government to save the lake at all costs.

MARCHERS IN PEDDER PROTEST

THE SOONER 18-year-olds have the vote better, Launceston conservation, Mr Fleming said after a march... The rally, or...

Plea to make Lake Pedder facts public

The public were ref—

The Saturday Evening Mercury, March 5, 1971—Page 11

11th H... TO PR... LAKE P...

No HEC ala... over tremor...

'H.E.C. PROB... WASTED ON CRACKPOTS'

A COMMITTEE to investigate H.E.C. schemes would never convince "crackpots and ratbags" their views on the H.E.C. were wrong, a Liberal backbencher declared yesterday.

Mr. Breheny (Lib., Braddon)

LAST PILGRIMAGE TO PEDDER

Mass wa... to picni... doomed...

LAKE PEDDER — that tiny blob of water set on a button grass plain in Tasmania's South West — will die in 1972.

When it goes under for some hydro power other ... to Tasmanian

---

D-DAY

der will ... yet on ... is not.
P-DAY
y fin— d the d of ding

No... tho

HEC prays for rain as Pedder protests flood...

Edmund Mercedes S.-West

...ND Hillary has asked the council's select committee

25-11-1971

...ordon filling be delayed for timber

THE filling of Lake Gordon in the Gordon River power scheme may be delayed to allow more time for timber to be salvaged.

A poet fights for our 'wonderlands'

By TESS LAWRENCE

CLIVE SANSOM of Hobart, is normally a gentle soul but at the moment he is busy waging war against the Hydro-Electric Commission.

Above all, he is a poet these areas are good roads,

Tonight at 8.25 Special Report on Lake Pedder

4 corners

ABC-TV The look to look forward to.

"Choice is clear" Premier backs HEC projects

THE cause of conservation and development had to go hand-in-hand for the benefit of Tasmania, the Premier (Mr Bethune) said on Saturday.

GREEN LIGHT ON TAMAR, GORDON

H.E.C. PLANS APPROVED

CONSTRUCTION of the $95 million Gordon River hydro scheme and the $20.75 million Tamar thermal station was recommended to Parliament last night by a Legislative Council select committee.

The select committee said that no practicable or desirable modifications could...

Australia Party joins Pedder dispute

THE Australia Party wants the Common... Government

Conservation symposium

Speakers blas... 'authorised desecration'

THE Tasmanian Government and the HEC have been put on the spot by a hard-hitting public symposium.

Latest... Queen will get petition for Pedder

"Save Lake Pedder" Election move

WHY Doesn't Premier Bethune Want to SAVE LAKE PEDDER?

Federal aid to SAVE

Concern over dam admitted says MLC

It's mainly water that flows in Tasmania's corridors of power
By JOHN HALLOWS

International body pleads THE FLOOD

Why Lake Pedder is being Enlarged

Lawyers...

Bar join the critic Challenge on lake "stifled"

EXTRACT TAKEN FROM INTERNATIONAL BIOLOGICAL PROGRAMME PROJECT AQUA.
Joint venture with UNESCO.

BISHOP SLAMS GOVT

Bethune slated for early flooding for years

Waters doom animals

PEDDER ANIMAL RESCUE

REECE RESPONSIBLE FOR PEDDER, SAYS BARWICK

Questions in Parliament $8,000 bill for HEC's adverts

Hydro ads cost $50,000

EVERETT RES

CABINET

Wr save lodge

"If I am wrong, God will be my judge . . ."

REECE REBUFFS BISHOP

Lake Pedder

SAVE LAKE CANDIDATES

Pedder group forms party
By JOCELYN FOGAC

TWO MISSING IN TIGER MOTH ON PEDDER PROTEST

Duke to see Lake Pedder?

'THREAT' BEFORE PEDDER FLIGHT

Reece to see P.M. over

Pedder legal problem for Cabinet?

DDER BILL ENDMENT FAILS

ERETT IS B

Will

Opposition failed

A public advertising campaign was waged by the Hydro-Electric Commission, at the consumers' expense. The full story of this strategy was published by the Australian Conservation Foundation in *Pedder Papers. Anatomy of a Decision*, 1972, pp. 31–39.

The flooding of Lake Pedder aroused numerous protests throughout Australia.
The Mercury

PEDDER GETS ITS INQUIRY

But it's really an inquest

PM'S PEDDER OFFER "OUT"

Reece sinks to his Pedder guns

POLITICS

CASS TO URGE LAKE

WHITLAM OVER LAKE

NEW LOOK AT FLOODING

Cass stirs ake waves

THE CONTINUING SAGA OF THE PEDDER INQUIRY...

The Saturday Evening Mercury, 5 May, 1973

KNELL FOR PED

REECE WON'T BUDGE

SIR MARK SUPPORTS LAKE PEDDER PLEA

CANBERRA — SA's Governor (Sir Mark Oliphant) urged the Federal Government last night to try to save Lake Pedder in Tasmania.

H.E.C. won't testify at inquiry

Everett, HEC to testify

Crumbledown Island,
Lake Pedder
October 12, 1972

Dear Australians,

    At the end of July, winter was entrenched, the lake was breaking its natural boundaries with the flood; storms were lashing into the dune. I have camped here alone on this island in the lake for five months now. Destruction is imminent and I shall have to leave.

    I will not go into the politics of the case — I am tired of it. The issue is a deep one to me though. It seems we have challenged the H.E.C., the Government and the pretext of economic growth. But the challenge is founded on a deep dissatisfaction of my young dissident age group with the quality of life and the assumptions made on our behalf.

    The H.E.C. is a presence at the opposite end of this valley. I can understand an engineer's satisfaction in designing and building; in harnessing power potential. It is a technological feat.

    But what does the Gordon Dam complex imply for this 'unique wilderness of incomparable significance and value', to quote UNESCO?

    Pressurised by a system which I, and many, many of my contempories find hard to live with, the young have no alternative but the path constricting them either to the old economic system or the decadent slide into the drug-pop-commercial culture.

    There are some who challenge both these paths by seeking the hard way — in the bush, on the land, and with the natural forces. They capture some of the pioneer strength in their lives; its great spirit inspires them. It is vital that we make a space for this vision of reality.

    Living at the lake, our long term struggle has become clear to me. We fight for the South-West to be set aside and saved for the diversity and richness it offers. We challenge not the H.E.C. but the whole mechanism of supply and demand and the mentality that sustains it. We fight to retain the cycles of nature; health of body, openness of mind and eye. Here in the wilderness a great personal deed has room. Men and women of spirit and strength are fostered.

    Pedder is more than most could ever have foreseen and embodies the idealism of youth. How can a young person give up the struggle to further life beyond the old confines?

    It is raining now as I write this; a swell is up on the lake and minor erosion continues. Tomorrow the sun will be evaporating the rain. So you see how precariously balanced is the continued existence of the dune and its ecology? A banksia, submerged, survives many months; and so too the long beach of quartz and the shallow lake basin are merely buried in pent-up winter rains.

    The struggle for survival is far from finished; the species are hardy and will regenerate if the decision is reversed. Some of the strength of this tough native fauna and flora has been imparted to our spirit also.

Chris Tebbutt.

Chris Tebbutt, South African by birth, spent 7 months of his 20th year living alone on a dune at Lake Pedder that eventually became an island. His vigil, a protest at the destruction of the lake, ended in December, 1972. He is seen here at the camp site on the dune — "Crumbledown" — where he wrote this letter to *THE MERCURY* and *THE AUSTRALIAN*. It was never published.

The Sun

United Tasmania Group car sticker.

A cartoon by Jim Nickolls.

This caravan, parked outside the Lake Pedder shop in Elizabeth Street, Hobart, was taken around eastern Australian states to inform people about the issue.
Chris Cowles

Three 140° panoramic views of Lake Pedder at the beginning of 1972. Early morning, midday and evening at Lake Pedder. *Chris Cowles*

Top, left and right
Lake Pedder flooding late in 1972 and the immensity of the beach dwarfs the 70 metre high Wrest Point Casino superimposed on the photograph. *Tasmanian Environment Centre Inc Col*

A number of demonstrations were held on the same day in eastern states of Australia during the early 1970s to stress the national significance of Lake Pedder. This one was in Hobart. *Chris Cowles*

THE CAMPAIGN

The Future of Lake Pedder book cover, 72 pages. The Australian Government's Lake Pedder Enquiry Report was reprinted in 1973 in this format, with photographs, by Lake Pedder Action Committees throughout Australia.

Badges

Lake Pedder National Park

Poster

SOUTH-WEST TASMANIA WORLD HERITAGE
PRODUCED BY THE TASMANIAN WILDERNESS SOCIETY

COME TO TASMANIA

Save Lake Pedder ♥

PEDDER LIVES !

LET THE GORDON RUN FREE

Save Lake Pedder * SAVE COCKLE CREEK ****

HALT WOODCHIPPING!
Save the wood for the trees

LET THE GORDON RUN FREE

Save Lake Pedder

Return the People's Pedder!

BEFORE IT SINKS!

SAVE LAKE PEDDER SAVE TASMANIA *

SAVE NATIVE FORESTS— STOP WOODCHIPPING

The Hydrocrat's mania for building dams does not balk at the destruction of the most beautiful lake in Australia, or at the prospect of ruining our finest remaining wilderness area in the Southwest of the island. Lake Pedder will soon disappear under a desert of water called the Gordon Scheme in the most spectacular act of Government vandalism in many years.

LAKE PEDDER MUST BE SAVED
Phone your Federal Parliamentarian today. Tell him your vote is at stake unless he takes urgent action to save Pedder.

Authorised by Milo Dunphy, 18 Argyle St., Sydney. Hon. Sec., The Colong Committee, a national wilderness society. Donations welcome.

POWER WITHOUT PURPOSE

Above & far left
Car Stickers

Poster

247

LET THE GORDON RUN FREE

(1)
We've all heard of islands that vanish,
That sink without trace in the sea,
But our island won't sink,
It'll fill to the brink, So
LET THE GORDON RUN FREE.

(2)
For the Hydro keeps damming our rivers,
And making one vast inland sea,
And we feel that it's time
They drew the line,
And LET THE GORDON RUN FREE.

(3)
These lakes are promoted for sportsmen,
To fish and catch rainbow for tea,
But the last Huon pines,
Will be snags for their lines, So
LET THE GORDON RUN FREE.

(4)
These Huon are pretty slow growers,
Some living a century or three,
If they drown the lot,
They're all that we've got, So
LET THE GORDON RUN FREE.

(5)
They make an environment study,
To see what their impact will be,
Why do they wanna know,
Cause it's all gonna go,
Unless they LET THE GORDON RUN FREE.

(6)
We've a national park near the Gordon,
With platypus and wallaby,
But a walk in the Park
Will be a swim in the dark, So
LET THE GORDON RUN FREE.

(7)
We asked the wildlife what they thought,
An old platypus said to me,
If we had our way,
All we would say is,
LET THE GORDON RUN FREE.

(8)
We're told that the harbour won't suffer,
They say they will just let it be,
But the *Denison Star,*
Will be aground on a bar,
Unless they LET THE GORDON RUN FREE.

(9)
They say the employment is needed,
And this is important we see,
but we'll get the same line,
In twenty years time, So
LET THE GORDON RUN FREE.

(10)
More power they say we are wanting,
For bringing lots more industry,
But I don't think its so,
they all seem to go, So
LET THE GORDON RUN FREE.

(11)
For Pedder we sacrificed plenty,
The power was needed you see,
But since they spoiled the lot,
We know that it's not,
So, LET THE GORDON RUN FREE.

(12)
For Pedder's not working full power,
They use about one out of three,
But still they go on,
Its the people they con,
So, LET THE GORDON RUN FREE.

(13)
This song tells of H.E.C. power,
They've too much of that you'll agree
Put you name on the line,
You've still got the time,
To LET THE GORDON RUN FREE.

We've all heard of islands that vanish, That sink without trace in the sea, But our island won't sink, It'll fill to the brink, So LET THE GORDON RUN FREE.

Mt Anne Massif. This computer diagram was prepared by Murray Dow, a Mathematician who completed his doctorate at the University of Tasmania in 1977. Using the 1:100,000 Tasmap of the area, about 4,000 spot heights were plotted in a grid of points spaced 250 m apart. The resulting surface was projected mathematically onto a plane at right angles to the observer's line of sight. The observer is assumed to be at infinity. Such computer processed drawings can be programmed from any angle and are not subject to haze, shadows or other natural effects.

right of public interest. Precipitous Bluff has become a testing ground for a law that currently fails to protect our most valuable and diminishing assets.

With the intensification of conflict over land use and management of the South-West, the Tasmanian Government prepared a Draft Management Plan for the area in 1975.

The South-West region was, by this stage, widely interpreted as encompassing the entire area south and west of the Lyell Highway. Furthermore if some area to the north were preserved, a geographic link could be maintained with the Cradle Mountain—Lake St Clair National Park. This large area, proposed by the Australian Conservation Foundation for national park status contains no fewer than 13 existing State Reserves, National Parks and Conservation Areas. Immediate adoption of the Australian Conservation Foundation boundaries would have given the South-West status as a World Natural Heritage area as defined in the UNESCO Convention for the protection of the World Cultural and Natural Heritage. Australia is a signatory to this Convention.

Late in 1975, the Minister for National Parks and Wildlife set up a South-West Advisory Committee of three to examine land use of the South-West and determine the boundaries of an enlarged national park. This committee, subsequently also known as the Cartland Committee, received over 120 submissions and presented a preliminary report to the Minister in June 1976. However, throughout the on-going Inquiry developmental activities continued. In the Catamaran, Picton, upper Huon and Weld valleys in particular, costly roads were forged ahead of schedule by the Forestry Commission. In November 1976 Cabinet approved plans for the construction of a bridge across the Picton River. At an approximate cost of $75,000, this concrete structure facilitates roading westward. Opposition from the State Department of the Environment was overidden and the spirit of the Inquiry ignored. Hydro-Electric Commission Investigations continued in the Lower Gordon and Franklin rivers. The expenditure of taxpayers' money on these projects and on propaganda, aroused public agitation. The Advisory Committee had recommended that the entire South-West region be zoned as national park and reserve for multi-purpose use. However their long awaited final Report was pre-empted by the *fait accompli* of the Forestry and Hydro-Electric Commissions.

Areas of the so called South-West Reserve of little developmental interest were subsequently, in 1976, added to the existing National Park. These included the Port Davey region, the South West Cape area and the Giblin River catchment. But the Davey River basin was still excluded, obviously to avoid yet another revocation in the event of HEC demand for the area.

In August 1976 the Federal Government granted $75,000 for the State to carry out a study of the natural resources of the South-West. This came at a time when many conceded that not enough was known about the area to make irreversible decisions of use and management.

The Precipitous Bluff appeal came before the High Court of Australia in February 1977 and was dismissed in June of the same year. The inclusion of Precipitous Bluff within the Southwest National Park guaranteed some measure of protection for the area, though not without ignominy. For, to effect this worthy addition to the National Park, an area of 2,150 hectares of forested land in the Hartz Mountains National Park was conditionally revoked and made available for forestry purposes. (The Bill passed both Houses in October 1976).

The twin tactics of delay and re-vocation are the political tools that whittle away the wilderness of the seventies.

The long awaited Report of the South West Advisory Committee was tabled in Parliament on September the 19th, 1978. The Report left the status of the South-West unchanged. The Cartland Committee had side-stepped the vital issues, handing the responsibility of the decision making straight back to the Government. (For details on the Recommendations of the Report see 5.4)

There has been a definite upsurge in awareness of the rights of wilderness and its species and in the value of wilderness to man and the biosphere. As this book goes to print the Franklin-Lower Gordon issue is rapidly emerging as a focal issue of the conservation movement in Australia. The Tasmanian Government now faces the crucial challenge to make a decision which future generations will applaud.

The Picton Bridge near Pear Hill. This bridge, completed in August 1977 by the Forestry Commission, opens the way, for bulldozers and log trucks, west along the south bank of the Huon River.   *Chris Harwood*

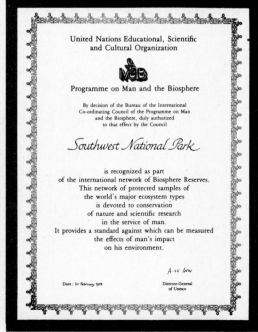

The international significance of the South-West was formally acknowledged by UNESCO in February, 1978.

249

Committee set up to check on South-West

AN organisation to be known as the South-West Committee has been formed in Hobart to inquire into the best means of preserving the scenic attractions of the South-West corner of Tasmania.

The appointment of the committee and the adoption of a draft constitution came about as the result of two meetings of representatives of clubs and organisations vitally interested in the area.

The committee's aim is to promote the right type of protection and development so that from a national scenic point of view the utmost will be done to safeguard the area from fires, destruction of wild life, and general despoilment.

Mr. Brown, M.L.C., who was appointed chairman of the committee, said at Huonville last night that confirmation of appointment of accredited representatives to the committee from organisations which had shown great interest in the South-West over a number of years was awaited.

These organisations were the Launceston, Hobart, and North-West Walking Clubs, the University of Tasmania Mountaineering Club, the Aero Club of Southern Tasmania, Tasmanian field naturalists, Federated Walking Clubs of Mainland States, Canine Defence League and Youth Hostels associations.

Public concern

Mrs. Denis King is to represent residents of the South-West, and Mr. G. Bonnitcha has been appointed secretary.

Mr. Brown said plans for opening up tracks leading to the area had given rise to public concern that without some form of protection the fauna and flora and the scenic attractions could to a large extent be destroyed.

Mr. Brown said the committee had a full programme on research work on the problem confronting the area and in educating public opinion of the tremendous scenic value of the South-West together with the need to protect it adequately.

He said that while members of the committee were pleased to know that the access track from Blake's Opening to the Craycroft was to be opened soon concern was expressed that the work was to be done by a bulldozer.

He said the secretary had been asked to request the Minister for Lands and Works (Mr. Cashion) to ensure that the bulldozing be carried out with the least possible destruction of bush scenery.

The Mercury, November, 1962

"Fauna district" for South-West

AN area of 1,600,000 acres of Tasmania's rugged South-West has been declared a "fauna district".

The Mercury 15 April 1966.

district and regulations for the area would be framed.

The district extends from south of Rocky Cape, near Port Davey, north to Mt. Sprent, east to just north of Maydena, and across to South Cape on the southern tip of Tasmania.

No one will be allowed to take any animal or bird from the area, or enter it with guns, dogs, traps or snares without the written permission of the board.

Dr. Guiler said Tasmania once again had gone to the front in conservation programmes. With the exception of the Northern Territory, it would be the biggest area reserved for wildlife in Australia.

The chairman of the Animals and Birds Protection Board (Dr. E. R. Guiler) said yesterday the "fauna district" was the result of negotiations between the South-West Committee, the Hydro-Electric Commission, and the board.

"Initially, the South-West Committee requested the area be proclaimed a sanctuary," Dr. Guiler said.

However, this was incompatible with the need to develop certain areas of the South-West for H.E.C. or mineral purposes.

The Animals and Birds Protection Board found that all parties would accept the area being proclaimed a

Premier testy over the South-West

CONGRATULATIONS on your recent editorial "Progress in the South-West" recommending a parliamentary inquiry into possible future developments in that area.

I particularly commend your insistence on immediate action before we are presented with a "fait accompli" as has happened in the past.

It is unfortunate that the Premier has displayed such a testy and impatient attitude towards those many people who, remembering past industrial despoliation elsewhere and knowing the South-West at first hand, are sufficiently interested to submit their ideas and recommendations. He says that "the whole of the present planning will be designed to satisfy them." Without disclosing these plans, how does he know they will be satisfied?

The Premier's statement that "some people were protesting about the entry of man into the South-West corner of the State for developmental purposes" surely does not apply to the South-West

Committee's submission, since it not only recommends the setting up of an authority to plan co-ordinated development there but also devotes a whole section of "Tourist and Recreation Potential."

To his remark "there may be some who will protest about progress but there is no one who can stop it," I will reply with the motto of modern conservationists — "Not blind opposition to progress, but opposition to blind progress."

New Town.

CUSEC.

The Mercury 18 October 1966.

Far right
The Mercury 23 September 1966.

South-West preservers

'Grab the Tiger by the tail'

PEOPLE fighting to preserve the South-West as a wilderness reserve were grabbing the Tasmanian tiger by the tail, the Premier (Mr. Reece) said yesterday.

He told the House of Assembly that he could never subscribe to the view that an area that covered 25 p.c. of the State should remain untouched.

Mr. Reece said an inter-department committee was watching all aspects of development in the South West: water potential, forestry resources, mineral resources and "what area in the early future should be dedicated as a reserve."

Mr. Reece said that for some years there had been agitation to have the area made into a reserve.

Some people had suggested the State should not "interfere" in the area at all. They argued "don't give away your natural heritage" —without any thought to the economic potential of the area.

Mr. Reece estimated that only .01 p.c. of Tasmanians had ever been to the South-West. He said he was sure some of the interstate organisations who had contacted him had no experience and little knowledge of the area.

Mr. Reece said that Tasmania had a bigger proportion of reserves already than any other State. Apparently the Lake St. Clair reserve was "becoming too common" for some people.

He said the South-West had "a few badgers, kangaroos and wallabies, and some wild flowers that can be seen anywhere."

An Opposition member interjected: "And the Tasmanian tiger."

Mr. Reece: "We haven't been able to catch up with him yet. These people (preservationists) are grabbing him by the tail when they grab this issue."

Mr. Reece denied that the massive Gordon River hydro-electric project would ruin the area. "The Gordon River and its tributaries will continue to run in their beds," he said.

He said there was a "possibility" that some mineral and forestry resources would be exploited.

There were areas in the South-West that "could reasonably be regarded as areas for retention in the form of a reserve."

He said he thought the Federation Peak area would be a reserve.

But: "We don't want to reserve the area piecemeal," he said.

Mr. Clark (Lib., Franklin) suggested that Federation Peak, the Port Davey, Lake Pedder and Lake Judd areas be made reserves.

Mr. Mather (Lib., Denison) said he hoped the Government would give serious consideration to the submission by the South-West Committee.

He said it was a well-reasoned report which took into account the necessity for economic development.

The South-West Committee

M S Grant

Malcolm Grant, Chairman of the South-West Committee, 1976.

Prior to 1960 South-West Tasmania, at least in political terms, was little more than a non-issue. While a small band of visionaries had long been aware of its potential, it was the events of the late sixties, and in particular, the catalytic effect of the Lake Pedder controversy, which gave meaning and perspective to the totality of the South-West. The political significance of the South-West as an issue of nation-wide concern could no longer be ignored.

Much of the credit for stimulating public opinion and generating an interest in the South-West which extended far beyond the confines of Tasmania is due to the work of voluntary conservation organizations.

Of the many proposals and plans which have been submitted to the Tasmanian Government and its agencies in the past fifteen years by such diverse organizations as the Australian Conservation Foundation, the State Inter-Departmental Committee of 1966, the Sea Fisheries Division of the Department of Agriculture and the Society for Growing Australian Plants, the most comprehensive in terms of recreational usage and of preservation of the wilderness character of the region have come from the South-West Committee.

The South-West Committee was formed in 1962 by representatives of a number of organizations which shared the conviction that Tasmania's South-West was a unique asset which deserved something better than the kind of ad hoc exploitation which had characterised the opening up and development of all other virgin areas in the State. The Committee is therefore one of the oldest conservation groups in Tasmania, and in 1976 comprised representatives of the following organizations:

> Blandfordia Alpine Club
> Climbers Club of Tasmania
> Hobart Walking Club
> Launceston Walking Club
> North-West Walking Club
> Residents of Port Davey
> Tasmanian University
> Mountaineering Club
> Scrub Club

> Society for
> Growing Australian Plants
> Southern Caving Society
> Tasmanian Caverneering Club
> Tasmanian
> Conservation Trust Inc.

Faced with the belief, clearly held by certain government departments, that the South-West region was large enough for unrestricted exploitation of non-renewable resources eg. minerals and native timbers, and aware also that this was the only temperate area in Australia capable of offering the community a wilderness recreation experience of more than a few days duration, the South-West Committee saw the need for a rational but expert land use plan for the area.

Such a plan would integrate and balance the need for wilderness and activities associated with it... mountaineering, bushwalking, caving, rock-climbing, ski-touring and canoeing. It would also provide for areas on the perimeters of wild country which could be developed specifically for the kind of brief wilderness contact which tourists and day visitors can experience.

From the outset the South-West Committee has emphasized and drawn attention to the wide implications of any management decisions made for the South-West and has encouraged the general public to understand the extent and quality of their loss, if apathy and ignorance persist.

Sadly the patterns of the past continue, with short term economic interest still the principal criterion on which decisions are based. Investing interests have considerable resources at their disposal which allow them to press ahead with development while alternative land use values are defended by voluntary groups of concerned and dedicated people and organizations.

In 1966 the South-West Committee submitted to the Government its first report dealing with the conservation and development of the South-West. At that time the Committee defined the South-West as the area south and west of the Lyell Highway. Also in 1967 the South-West Committee gave evidence to the Legislative Council Select Committee of Inquiry into Lake Pedder and South-West Tasmania.

Following the proclamation of the Southwest National Park late in 1968, the Committee forwarded a second submission to the Government recommending extensions to the National Park to include areas and features which in the Committee's view merited particular protection. Five years later, in 1973, the South-West Committee published its proposals for the future controlled development of the South-West in the form of a master plan.

In 1975 the Government released a Draft Management Plan for an enlarged South-West national park. The South-West Committee furnished the Government's Advisory Committee with a submission detailing its boundary and management principles and drawing attention to the shortcomings of the Draft Plan. (This submission was one of 122 presented to the Inquiry.)

The South-West Committee has developed its proposals for the South-West with the aid of surveys, questionnaires, submissions from and discussions with a wide range of interested and dedicated people from Tasmania, interstate and overseas, most of whom know the South-West well and visit it frequently.

During 14 years of changing attitudes and values, it has been apparent that concern for wilderness has increased while conversely, the area of wilderness has diminished in a startling manner. And there is an urgency in the tensions between conflicting land use demands, between one government department and another, between individuals and government departments.

Far from decreasing in value, the role of voluntary conservation groups will become increasingly important as pressures on unalienated land increase. Organizations like the South-West Committee carry a heavy responsibility if there are to be political and administrative safeguards which will conserve Tasmania's wilderness heritage.

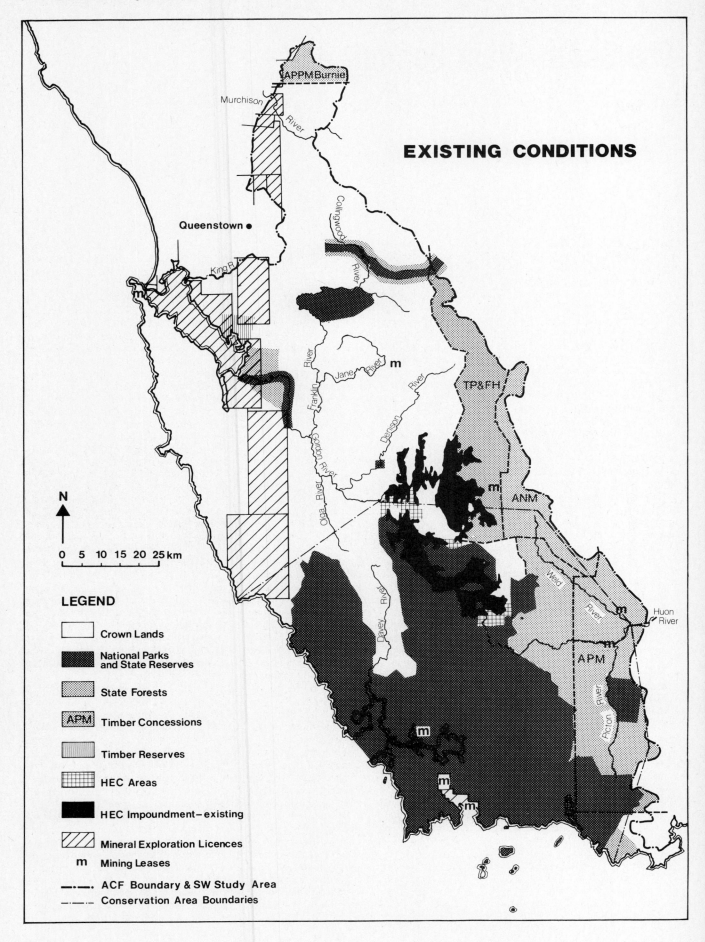

EXISTING CONDITIONS

Murchison River

APPM Burnie

Queenstown ●

King R.

Collingwood River

Franklin River

Jane River

Denison River

Gordon River

Olga River

m

TP&FH

m

ANM

Davey River

Weld River

Huon River

m

APM

Picton River

m

m

m

LEGEND

Crown Lands

National Parks
and State Reserves

State Forests

APM   Timber Concessions

Timber Reserves

HEC Areas

HEC Impoundment—existing

Mineral Exploration Licences

m   Mining Leases

—·—·—   ACF Boundary & SW Study Area

—··—··—   Conservation Area Boundaries

N

0 5 10 15 20 25 km

The Boundary Question

R E Saunders
B W Davis & H M Gee

The Government's South West Advisory Committee — left to right, Sir George Cartland, Albert Ogilvie and Geoff Foot. The photograph was taken at Cox Bight during a visit to the South-West by light aircraft.
Jim England

An Evaluation of the Tasmanian Government's 1975 Draft Management Plan for the Southwest National Park

R E Saunders

The natural boundaries of the South-West derive basically from the physiography and climate of the region. The folded and contorted Precambrian quartzite of the Western ranges forms a back-bone of ridge-like mountain ranges running approximately parallel to the west coast. These cause the prevailing westerly winds, the 'Roaring Forties', to lose their moisture, creating the high rainfall belt of South-West Tasmania. The high level of precipitation in this area (the second highest in Australia), is the major ecological determinant of the South-West, and the extent of the rainforest and sedgeland communities is largely defined by the 200 centimetre isohyet. To some degree, this almost impenetrable vegetation and rugged terrain has restricted the exploitation of the region in the past, and a large proportion remains as it was before European settlement of the island. As a result, the wilderness area of South-West Tasmania bears a close resemblance to the extent of this high-rainfall ecosystem; the major intrusions being the Lyell Highway, the Gordon Road, the Scotts Peak Road and the rapidly extending forestry roads of the eastern catchments.

The Australian Conservation Foundation proposal for a Southwest National Park[1] (p. 252), was based upon these natural barriers, with relatively simple boundaries corresponding in most cases to the edges of complete catchments (in the north and east), and the coastline (in the south and west). This proposal followed closely the definition of 'the general area of South-West Tasmania' given in the Draft Management Plan; however it also included an area to the north of Frenchmans Cap National Park, extending to and abutting the Lake St Clair National Park. This extension provided for the additional protection of the borders of these parks, each to effectively act as a buffer zone for the other.

Unfortunately, the boundaries proposed in the Draft Management Plan of 1975 bore no relation whatsoever to the physical and ecological barriers, the extent of the existing wilderness area, or the major recreational zones. It is evident that all areas of potential interest for forestry, mining and hydro-electric development had been excised from the South-West Conservation Area (p. 252), — and the remainder became the 'proposed Southwest National Park'. The creation of a national park in this manner — almost by default — will cause many management problems which

According to the Department of Tourism Visitors Survey 1978, 31% of visitors to the state went bushwalking or climbing. We leave it to your discretion whether these facilities are appropriate in the South-West. Picnic area. Lake Gordon.   *John Best*

simply would not exist if more rational boundaries were to be defined.

The exclusion of the Davey River basin would completely isolate the catchment of the Giblin River, the largest single addition to the Southwest National Park proposed in the Plan. The apparently arbitrary, straight line boundaries of the corridor along the Davey River would be extremely difficult to police, and would provide little protection for the west coast region. The irrationality of this extension is further exemplified by its southern border, which followed a straight line from Castle Hill to North Inlet, rather than the coastline.

'The non-inclusion of the Davey-Hardwood River catchment and the Olga River catchment are presumably to allow the Hydro-Electric Commission to build dams and accompanying facilities as part of the Gordon Power Scheme Part 2 without having to be answerable to outraged public opinion. It appears that something has been learnt from the Lake Pedder controversy. The non-inclusion signifies that the Tasmanian Government considers exploitative values to have greater merit than conservation values in South-West Tasmania.'[2]

Despite the statement that an extension of the Scotts Peak Road:

'would constitute a harmful influence on the qualities of the environment of the wilderness area south of Scotts Peak',

the Draft Plan went on to state that the

Gordon Road:

'may eventually have to be extended in a westerly (sic) direction to serve further Hydro-Electric Commission developments west of the Park'.

The attitude towards roads into the South-West appeared to be somewhat inconsistent.

But it was not the only inconsistency in the Plan: although the South-West Cape Range and Mt Picton are listed as among the six 'major areas' of the South-West they were excluded from the proposed National Park. The South West Cape region, containing some of the most beautiful and secluded beaches of the south coast, as well as some of the most rugged cliffs, was added to the National Park in August 1976. It is a highly valued walking area. Mount Picton and the South Picton Range (including Burgess Bluff) are part of the classic route to Federation Peak via Moss Ridge, and are consequently of extreme importance recreationally, providing a more challenging alternative to the bulldozed 'Yo-Yo' Track approach. Interest in this area has increased recently with the discovery of Judds Cave system, which was described in the Plan as being:

'of more than ordinary interest because of its underground features, and (it) is likely to be connected with a number of depressions higher up on the slopes of Burgess Bluff'.

These slopes consist of large dolerite blocks, and support no timber.

On the south coast, Precipitous Bluff is undoubtedly an outstanding and worthwhile addition to the Southwest

National Park, both for its recreational value and its scientific significance. However, until the **entire** catchment of the New River is included within the National Park boundaries, the scenic and biological value of this area will not be adequately protected.

The idea that a 'nominal strip of 100 meters wide' along the eastern banks of the Cracroft River, the New River and the Salisbury River would 'secure the protection of the scenic values of these rivers' was a very misguided one. Beyond such a narrow band of vegetation, forestry practices would prevail.

'In such steep country with a high rainfall, it is most likely that forestry practices will lead to a deterioration of the water qualities of these rivers... in spite of these nominal strips.' [2]

It is also easy to foresee management problems associated with the 'coastal strip' from Point Cecil to Fishers Point (south coast) and the similar narrow strip of foreshore reserve around Port Davey and Bathurst Harbour. The concept of a coastal region divorced from the adjacent hinterland and marine formations demonstrated an alarming lack of understanding of ecological principles, especially in a body concerned with national parks and wildlife. Although there are historical precedents in areas of high population density, such as Great Britain,[2] these lengths of foreshore have been found troublesome to protect from, for example, fire. However, as the Plan envisaged access through these areas for forestry, mining and tourism purposes, the coastal regions of Port Davey and South Cape did not appear to be regarded as a permanent part of the National Park.

In contrast, the islands and rocks off the Tasmanian south coast are an excellent addition to the Southwest National Park, as many of these are important breeding grounds for seals as well as for mutton-birds and other migratory species. Many of these islands are visible from the Ironbound and Southern Ranges, and contribute to the spectacular scenery of this coastline.

The proposed new boundaries around Mt Anne went some way towards incorporating this area within the Southwest National Park, from which it was previously isolated by the Scotts Peak Road corridor. However, as the entire Mt Anne massif and the Gallagher Plateau constitute an area of immense scenic, recreational and biological significance, these proposed extensions appeared to be a token gesture. The magnificent alpine and sub-alpine mountain flora of this region, some 50 per cent of which is endemic to Tasmania,[3] is particularly vulnerable to fire and sensitive to trampling. In this environment, especially, it is essential to create viable boundaries in order to

effectively manage its use, and so preserve this unique treasure intact for future generations.

From a management viewpoint, the major problems associated with the national park proposed by the Tasmanian Government in 1975 stemmed directly from the inviolability of its boundaries. The control of access to sensitive areas like the Mt Anne massif, and regions of scientific importance such as the Giblin River catchment, would be impossible in such a park. Degradation of these inadequately protected areas would be inevitable, despite the intentions of the National Parks and Wildlife Service. Even in the central regions of this national park, especially with its complex and somewhat arbitrary boundaries, the control of numbers using the area will soon become necessary, if the wilderness quality is to be preserved. As restrictive management practices are unpopular, it is probable that other 'alternatives' will be attempted, such as the provision of access and services, similar to the Cradle Mountain—Lake St Clair National Park. This possibility has already been alluded to, for example, in the proposed 'coin-in-the-slot barbecues'. Such facilities are entirely out of place in a 'recreation wilderness', as this is exactly what people are attempting to get away from when they visit such an environment.

The introduction of brown and rainbow trout into the lakes, rivers and streams of South-West Tasmania is a similar example of inappropriate compromise. The fresh water biota of the South-West is of considerable scientific importance[2] and many unique

species, already endangered by the flooding of Lake Pedder, could be exterminated by the introduction of these fish.[4]

'Trout are voracious feeders, and unquestionably alter the aquatic environment greatly, not only for the species on which they feed, but for other fish.' [5]

For example, the introduction of trout into Kosciusko mountain streams caused the disappearance of fish of the genus *Galaxia*. Some species of *Galaxia* were known to be endemic to the Lake Pedder area, prior to its inundation.[6] It is totally incomprehensible that one of the last remaining native fresh-water ecosystems in Tasmania should be sacrificed in this manner, especially when one considers the number of lakes and streams of this State already stocked with exotic edible fish.

The true role of the wilderness manager should be the study and protection of these native ecosystems, and the education of park visitors so that they too will appreciate and protect their natural heritage. In South-West Tasmania, there is obviously potential for the creation of one of the world's finest national parks, a potential that would be realised by instituting the proposals of the Australian Conservation Foundation, and managing the area as a 'recreation wilderness' and scientific reference area. The developments of the past decade have been a great step backwards in the conservation of the wilderness quality of the South-West, and unless action is taken now, the next decade may see its complete destruction.

The South West Advisory Committee

B W Davis & H M Gee

The 1975 Draft Management Plan stimulated wide debate and concern. It did not persuade either politicians or the public that the draft proposals were worthy of adoption. In consequence, the Minister for National Parks and Wildlife appointed a South-West Advisory Committee in November 1975 to re-examine the matter. One hundred and twenty-two submissions were received by the Advisory Committee and its Preliminary Report was released in June 1976. The Preliminary Report was an attempt to provide a long-term solution to conflicts about resource utilization, by zoning the South-West into a series of usage categories ranging from national park wilderness to outright exploitation.

The Advisory Committee recommended that a Zoning Committee be established to prepare a new draft zoning plan for an area equivalent to that proposed by the Australian Conservation Foundation for national park status. The Advisory Committee did not

favour immediate preservation, but suggested that the South-West Region should ultimately be zoned into a National Park or Parks plus a South-West Reserve in which some development activities would be permitted.

The NATIONAL PARK (or Parks) would be zoned into:
- wilderness areas;
- natural areas;
- park development areas for tourism and facilities;
- special areas of historical, anthropological or scientific interest.

Short of Parliamentary approval, no development other than park amenities would be permitted in national parks.

The SOUTH-WEST RESERVE would be zoned into:
- utilization areas;
- exploitation areas;
- development prospects;
- special areas.

Subject to the exercise of development

rights, the provisions of the National Parks and Wildlife Act and regulations would apply.

The Preliminary Report suffered from two serious deficiencies. The procedures suggested did not provide any guarantee of protection for areas outside the existing Southwest National Park boundary. And secondly, existing development rights were to continue to be exercised until the completion of the new zoning plan. This permitted considerable damage to be caused to the South-West region in the interim period, and still no administrative decisions have been finalised.

Thus the Preliminary Report of the Advisory Committee ensured a continuation of the process of delay which had characterized all previous moves for the preparation of a Management Plan for the South-West. Such postponement further jeopardised any chances of retaining a wilderness of international standing.

Although the Tasmanian Government's attitude to conservation was placed under direct test in 1976, HEC, forestry and mining activities continued unabated throughout the next phase of the long inquiry.

The final Report of the South West Advisory Committee was tabled in Parliament on September the 19th, 1978. Side-stepping a unique opportunity to make a firm recommendation to protect the South-West, the Cartland Committee, as it was widely known, clearly found the issues too hard to handle.

Though they recognized the need for prior public consideration of any HEC proposals, and the need to curb its wide investigatory powers, they failed to recommend a halt to development within the region.

Throughout the Report there runs a strong thread of contradiction: Although the Committee was 'totally convinced of the importance of South-West Tasmania from the point of view of its natural and aesthetic value', and although they concluded that 'the area is of world heritage status and is a unique national asset', they stated that 'it would be impracticable and unwise to constitute the whole of South-West Tasmania as a National Park forthwith'.

The Committee described the management vacuum that has resulted in the *ad hoc* development of the region. They believed that co-ordinated land-use planning and management must take into account all legitimate interests in the area.

Having received submissions and oral evidence on the Preliminary Report, the Committee decided that it was inappropriate to advise on the general suitability of the original Draft Management Plan. Instead they recommended that the Conservation Area be extended to include the whole South-West region under review. This will represent no change, in reality. Existing developmental rights are preserved in a conservation area, and it is vulnerable to new activities unless and until a management plan is approved by government.

The Cartland Committee proposed that a new independent South West Tasmania Authority be established to recommend to the government what actions should be taken within the Conservation Area. As appointment to the three man Authority will be made by the Government, its impartiality will be suspect.

The recommendations give development interests the continued opportunity to argue each case for future development as it occurs. The final decision has been left to the government of the day. The Tasmanian Government now faces a challenge more critical than ever before.

Mt Anne from the Frankland Range.   *Olegas Truchanas*

Opposite page
The Conclusions and Recommendations of the Report presented to Parliament in September 1978 by the South West Advisory Committee. The area referred to in the Report as South-West Tasmania corresponds to the area proposed by the Australian Conservation Foundation for national park status. (Refer to the colour map.)

PART 5 — Conclusions

35. We have given careful thought to various possible solutions to the problems referred to in paragraphs 22, 23, 24 and 25 above.

    After taking into account all of the evidence and the issues involved, we have reached the firm view that in future decision making processes concerning South West Tasmania, the two broad considerations of conservation and development must both be taken into account and given due weight depending on the specific facts and circumstances in question in each case. We have given special consideration to objections raised to further controls within the area. However, we are persuaded that there is a real need for the protection of the natural environment in South West Tasmania. We believe the procedures we propose will not unduly restrict legitimate commercial activities. We recognise and accept that a balancing of value judgments is involved. There is no escape from this and the procedures we propose in our Recommendations provide for this process. In arriving at our conclusions as to how this might best be achieved, we gave special consideration to the proposals of the Lands' Department but we have formed the clear view that it would be more appropriate to use the existing legislative and administrative structure of the National Parks and Wildlife Service as a basis for our proposals for South West Tasmania rather than recommend the establishment of alternative field staff and administrative procedures in the Lands' Department. Many of the residual interests in need of protection are closer to the concern of the National Parks & Wildlife Service than to the Lands' Department. The National Parks & Wildlife Service has acknowledged expertise in nature conservation and is already charged with the responsibility of managing significant areas of South West Tasmania.

36. In our view, the concept of a conservation area can be well used as part of the solution to the basic problem in South West Tasmania referred to in Part 4.

37. We believe that a practical, effective system of planning, land-use, management and administration in South West Tasmania can be based on the following:-

    (a) The proclamation of the whole of South West Tasmania as a conservation area;

    (b) The creation of a permanent independent authority to examine and advise upon any proposed changes and other matters affecting land in South West Tasmania.

    The extensive range of public and government interests in South West Tasmania persuades us that the establishment of a permanent independent authority is necessary to provide a forum in which competing claims for change can be impartially investigated as a basis for considered advice to Government. We also note that at present, matters of concern relating to South West Tasmania are raised in a variety of ways including statements in the media, approaches to the department or authority concerned and approaches to Ministers and other members of Parliament. The authority we propose will constitute a body to which members of the public may refer these matters.

    A special advisory committee established under the National Parks & Wildlife Act could not fulfil these functions.

38. The result of our proposals will be that the National Parks & Wildlife Service will continue to fulfil the functions assigned to it by the National Parks & Wildlife Act. However, the question of changes in land-use including approval of management plans, will be dealt with by the Authority. Consequently neither the development authorities nor the National Parks & Wildlife Service will be able to significantly alter the present status or use of land whether, for example, to create a National Park, a State Forest, a new hydro-electricity installation, or a new mineral exploration or extraction area without public exposure and consideration of the proposal by the independent body we propose. In addition, all existing rights would be preserved.

39. In accordance with the fourth preliminary recommendation in our Preliminary Report (Appendix A, p11) and the terms of reference set out above, we now make the following recommendations.

PART 6 — Recommendations

40. We recommend that:-

    (1) This Report be published;

    (2) With the consent of authors all submissions received by the Committee subsequent to the publication of the Preliminary Report be made available for perusal and copying by the public in the same manner as was arranged in the case of the Preliminary Report;

    (3) Pending the implementation of the following Recommendations in this Report and subject to existing legislation and rights, no action that adversely affects a place that is in South West Tasmania should be taken or permitted unless there is no feasible and prudent alternative, and all measures that can reasonably be taken to minimise the adverse effect of any such action should be taken;

    (4) The existing conservation area should be extended to include the whole of South West Tasmania as defined in paragraph 8 of this Report;

    (5) The Director of the National Parks & Wildlife Service should prepare National Park and conservation area management plans for the whole of this area as a matter of priority;

    (6) Legislation should be enacted to establish a South West Tasmania Authority and provide a system of land use determination. Our proposals for this legislation are contained in Appendix E;

    (7) The Government should engage an independent expert consultant or groups of consultants to carry out an investigation into the matters relating to forestry referred to in paragraphs 10, 11 and 12 of this Report;

    (8) The Government should submit a case to the Commonwealth Government for substantial annual funding for South West Tasmania on the basis that the area is of world heritage status and is a unique national asset. These funds should be sought for assistance with the establishment and operation of the South West Tasmania Authority, park development and administration and for the continuation and completion of the South West Tasmania Resources Survey.

Signed by the South West Advisory Committee this 29th Day of August 1978
Sir George Barrington Cartland
Geoffrey James Foot
Albert George Ogilvie

The South West Tasmania Resources Survey

P Waterman *et al*

Peter Waterman is a professional environmental resources management consultant with wide experience in Australia. In April 1977 he became the Survey Leader of the South West Tasmania Resources Survey and is responsible for the multidisciplinary team making an inventory of the material, recreational and cultural resources of the region.

'A Federal Liberal Government will provide finance to the Tasmanian Government to enable a significantly enlarged South-West national park to be developed and maintained.'
(Advertisement, *The Mercury* 13th Dec 1975)

This electoral promise was honoured in March 1976, when the late Senator Ivor Greenwood, then Minister for Environment, Housing and Community Development, informed the Tasmanian Government that

'We will assist the Tasmanian Government in establishing a national park of world significance in South-West Tasmania to include a substantial wilderness area'.

Before financial assistance could be forthcoming, it was necessary to amend the States Grants (Nature Conservation) Act, 1974. This amendment made it possible for the Australian Government to allocate funds to the States for land use management programs for nature conservation.

Under the Commonwealth - State Agreement signed in February 1977, an initial $75,000 was made available for the Survey, originally programmed to take about one year to complete. A further $50,000 was allocated in the 1977/78 Commonwealth Budget for work to the end of June 1978. Work will however need to be funded until June 1980 when the project will be completed.

Following the appointment of a Steering Committee, the position of Survey Leader was advertized. Work on the SWTRS formally commenced on the 14th of April, 1977, with the Survey Leader's appointment. A survey team was then assembled to prepare the *Interim Report*. Critical assessment of the draft document and further collation of material resulted in the public release of the *Interim Report* in March 1978.

THE SURVEY

The aim of the survey is to compile an inventory of the natural, recreational and cultural resources of the South-West — in particular those attributes of the area that may require its reservation and management as a national park. The Australian Conservation Foundation's

Tea-trees at Citadel camp, in the Frankland Range.   *Reg Williams*

OPPOSITE PAGE

Mt Solitary and the Frankland Range, 1971.   *Howard P Simco*

Tasmania photographed from a satellite. Note the road to the Gordon River Power Development and route of the transmission lines, bottom centre.   *Tasmanian Environment Centre Inc Col*

proposed boundary has been adopted as the Study Area for the survey.

Information is being collected on the resources of the South-West covered by the following resource categories:-
(i)   Landform and Soils
(ii)   Geology and Minerals
(iii)   Climate and Hydrology
(iv)·   Vegetation and Timber
(v)   Biology and Habitats
(vi)   Landscape and Aesthetics
(vii)   Marine
(viii) Recreation
(ix)   Wilderness
(x)   Historic Sites
(xi)   Anthropology and Archaeology
(xii)   Energy
(xiii) Agriculture
All information is systematically collated under six headings:- land resources, climatic and hydrological resources,

biological resources, marine resources, recreation resources and cultural resources. Where possible information is mapped at 1:250,000 or 1:100,000, using the existing Tas map series as base maps, on a catchment by catchment basis. The Franklin and the Picton River catchments were the first to be mapped.

RATIONALE

Conflict over land use in South-West Tasmania is considered by many observers to constitute a somewhat divisive political situation with ramifications of both state and national significance, involving a wide range of social, philosophical and economic implications. Recent issues in the South-West, such as the Gordon River Power Development Stage 1, proposals for extractive industry around Precipitous

Bluff, and the proposed excision of parts of the Hartz Mountains National Park for logging have engendered periods of bitter controversy within the state and in some cases across the whole country. As future resource developments and nature conservation proposals move close to implementation, similar disputes will continue to occur; the inventory is anticipated to provide concerned parties with an objectively collated body of information, forming a basis for decision-making, or for essential further research requirements to be identified to enable satisfactory resolution of such conflicts.

It is not the concern of the resources survey to evaluate the conflicting land use claims that are already apparent. However, it is clear that the nature, extent and long-term implications of various competing land uses are such that satisfactory conflict resolution is unlikely under existing circumstances. For example, land use issues are currently evaluated individually, often at short notice, and within tightly defined terms of reference set (or at least heavily influenced) by long-standing statutory provisions, which many people, after a decade of philosophical re-evaluation, may no longer accept.

Therefore, although beyond the specific scope of the work with which the SWTRS is concerned, it is necessary for the Survey to be aware of the contentious nature of existing arbitration procedures and to consider how land use conflicts in the South-West may be more appropriately evaluated. This is essential if the resources inventory is to meet the requirements of those responsible for decision-making in future years. That is, how will such objectively gathered facts be used by politicians, administrators and land-use planners in future years?

To this end, the following conceptual stages may be envisaged for the total planning of the Southwest National Park. It is emphasized that this is conceptual but nonetheless is essential for understanding the contribution of the SWTRS to the overall planning process.

(a) Inventory of Resources: This comprises the present phase of work, and will include a series of descriptive reports and, as necessary, maps showing the areal extent of the existing and potential resources of the South-West, accompanied by brief quantitative descriptions of each.

(b) Conflict Identification: An overlay of the various resource maps will reveal all areas of multiple land use potential, and the comparative evaluation of each will reveal potential conflicts.

(c) Research Priorities: The initial list of conflict areas may then be ranked according to priority for investigation by various authorities, including administrative bodies, such as the South West Advisory Committee, statutory bodies, such as the National Parks and Wildlife Service, the State Department of Planning and Development or the Lands Department, or alternatively, by a separate body established to manage the South-West.

(d) Conflict Resolution: Investigations by appropriate research authorities independent of the interests in conflict would then be made. Such authorities would work under broad terms of reference and, as necessary, would make recommendations on all aspects of the land at issue. These would include, for example, recommendations on primary use, secondary uses (if any), zoning, financial adjustment, compensation and resources and general environmental management.

It is again stressed that this outline of procedure is notional and conceptual, and has been formulated in order that a resources inventory is prepared that is as useful as possible in the initial and subsequent stages of conflict resolution.

'Hydro energy is non polluting power.' J R Ashton 1978.   *Kevin Kiernan*

POLLUTION

Pollutant is interpreted under the Tasmanian Environment Protection Act 1973 Part 1.2-(1) to mean 'any substance, whether liquid, solid or gaseous and whether living or not, which directly or indirectly —
  (a) causes pollution of the environment; or
  (b) causes odours or noises that are offensive
      or prejudicial to man.'
It then follows that pollution 'means any direct or indirect contamination or alteration of any part of the environment so as —
  (a) to affect any use adversely; or
  (b) to cause a condition that is detrimental or hazardous or likely to be detrimental or hazardous to —
      (i) human health, safety or welfare;
      (ii) animals, plants, or microbes; or
      (iii) property;
caused by emitting anything'.
Within the terms of these definitions, pollutant sources within the South-West are identified as those associated with:
  (a) past and present mining activities;
  (b) disposal of domestic sewage and sullage;
  (c) structural alterations to major natural features of the environment such as the construction of water impoundments;

  (d) clearing of the landsurface in order to carry out pastoral agricultural or forestry activities in the past and at present;
  (e) provision of human access by road, boat or aircraft;
  (f) uncontrolled human access causing fire, physical destruction of habitats, loss or damage to prehistoric or European settlement sites.'

To date only three systematic attempts have been made to assess the implications of three of the forementioned sources of pollution. First, there is the hydrological, water quality and biological work being carried out downstream from the present Middle-Gordon Dam as part of the HEC Scientific Survey. Second, there is the work on *Heavy Metals and Mine Residues in Macquarie Harbour*, reported by the Department of the Environment in June 1975. The third area of work on sources of pollutants has been the study of fire recovery by native vegetation. This considers the botanical and biogeographic aspects of wildfire rather than the implications of run off from burnt out areas and the subsequent short term high nutrient discharges into nearby water bodies.

Extract from the South West Tasmania Resource Survey Interim Report.

'— behind the Truth of Wilderness.'

The choice was his
to slosh through water
or leap
precariously from clump to clump
of button-grass.
He found no preference.

It was easier on the higher ground.
The rain   streamed
                horizontal
across the mountains;
plucked at the lake's surface;
                spat at the leaves
of the eucalypts.
The smaller bushes bowed
                surrendering
under the weight of the rain.

He walked on

His brow
(from which the water ran)
was frowning.
His analytic brain,
from habit,   seeking
to gauge costs and overheads.
Of what?

On the lake's shore,
lone, leaning melaleuca;
thin, twisted trunk;
sparse crown   reaching;
                weeping
on the sand.

The rain had found a way
through his gear.
Drops of water runnelled
down his chest.
A message there,
Somewhere.

        Short life.
        Quick turn-over.
        High profits.
He leaned
against the storm.

The rain stopped
when the mountain
stood above him.
Only the fat drops
        fell
from the leaves and the branches
of the taller trees.

He pressed
into the harder going;
wrestled with the bauera vines
and profit margins
and bauera vines;
toiled upwards,
on   and upwards.
Once he stopped,
his eyes held by
a giant richea,
        knowing
but unrecognising,
like an old friend
long forgotten.
He didn't wait to speak;
        embarrassed —
concentrated
on a 12% growth figure
and
an upward struggle over logs and rocks.

Trees fell behind him;
their tops at his feet.

In front
and above
the rocks glistened.
He felt the water
dripping from his lip.
The rain had stopped.
The water drops were drops
                of sweat
salt on his tongue.
The pack straps cut
into his shoulders,
that cried out (like his legs)
        to stop,
        to stop.

But it was not time.
The directors demanded
        maximum effort
        and
        maximum profit
        but —
'You have done well,'
they say,
fat-fingering the balance-sheet,
'You have done well.'

Then he was standing
        on the saddle,
and the world of wilderness
lay spread before him;
daring him to enter.
The siren-calls of business,
                comfort,
                luxury
                and profit
faded.

        ;   water-falls
            and rivers;
            sounds of silence;
white mists wreathing
mysteries in the valleys;
clouds touching mountains;
moving shadows
like giant Zeppelins,
sweeping across the trees.

He smiled
and the wind carried
the words, as he spoke them,
from his lips.
'Jesus Christ,' he said and, 'Wilderness.'

He moved on, down,
        easy going,
                down
into a place of wondering
where dragon-flies
flew locked together
over pools;
where scientists
went sometimes
to search for understanding
and were granted
surface compensations.

He went on down
        and down
        and up
        and down through valley mist
and over mountains,
searching for that thing
he knew he'd never find
but would seek for ever;
a truth he could not express
a truth
that lay behind
                the Truth
of Wilderness.

Barney Roberts, April 1977

In the Franklands. *Reg Williams*

Sea of cloud. *Jim England*

Celery Top islands. *Jim England*

Vanishing Falls, 70 metres high. *Maurice D Clark*

'It is not feasible to separate this area from the Southwest National Park. Indeed it is one of the intrinsic gems. Precipitous Bluff is an unrivalled scene in coastal Australia. Within the space of 2 kilometres one looks up to a peak 1200 metres above sea level. The upper 300 metres consists of dolerite cliffs rising sharply out of the forested slopes. The vegetation forms a sample in sequence of the whole western flora in a pristine condition, unfired for 300 – 500 years.'
Dr J G Mosley, Director, Australian Conservation Foundation. Precipitous Bluff overlooks New River Lagoon.   *Jim England*

Each summer hundreds enjoy visiting Precipitous Bluff and its wonderful environs, Prion Beach and New River Lagoon.   *Joseph Donnelly*

The Precipitous Bluff Case

P Wessing

Patricia Wessing B.A. Hons (Tas.) is currently head of Hobart Matriculation College Geography Department. A dynamic force in conservation in Tasmania, she has been involved in numerous campaigns, most recently the Precipitous Bluff case. She is currently a councillor of the Australian Conservation Foundation, State Vice President of the Tasmanian Conservation Trust Inc., President of the Blandfordia Alpine Club and a member of the South-West Committee.

Experience confirms that presently existing political and administrative mechanisms do not suffice to safeguard the Tasmanian South-West wilderness. Politicians are susceptible to the claims of economic pressure groups, for the exploiters pose as public benefactors offering intensive developmental employment in the short term. Those who would preserve the heritage of South-West Tasmania have therefore resorted to legal action, encouraged that such proceedings by conservationists in America have met with success. Through a series of court actions the Tasmanian Conservation Trust Inc. hopes ultimately to gain acceptance of broad principles, such as the right of public interest and specifically a declaration that Precipitous Bluff can be legally protected from mining. At stake is the right of the ordinary person to appeal against the despoliation of Crown land for short-term economic gain; to defend his right to beauty, quietness and solitude, and the right of the land itself.

Precipitous Bluff constitutes the western and southern bastion of a short range of mountains familiarly known as the Southern Ranges, including Mt La Perouse, Pindars Peak and the South Cape Range. Midway along the wild and rugged South Coast, it rises steeply and abruptly to heights of over 1,300 metres. Precipitous Bluff is massive and spectacular, towering above the waters of New River Lagoon and completely dominating the scene for considerable distance along the walking track and out to sea, from the Arthurs and Mt Anne. It is most impressive viewed from light aircraft.

The natural features of the area were recorded by A Gray and J Hemsley who conducted a survey in March 1969.[1] They reported that a broad band of Ordovician limestone occupied the lower slopes of Precipitous Bluff—from near sea level to about 1,000 metres. Cave systems underlie the forested lower slopes, capturing much of the water run-off. But where drainage is less adequate and the soils are deep and fertile, typical climax rainforest conditions have evolved. Coastal mists and cloud effects would contribute to the total rainfall of approximately 2,000 mm per annum.

The vegetation on the western slope of the Bluff, as observed in a traverse from the lagoon at sea level to the upper forest limit, forms a series of altitudinal zones. A great range of species and plant associations, of the wetter forest types, exist in a remarkably compact and undamaged state—there is a complete absence of any intrusion by fire on these slopes for a period of 300–500 years. There are few areas of any primeval vegetation type remaining in Australia, and none with such a complete set of rainforest vegetation zones adapted to different altitudes.

The lagoon is an open stretch of relatively sheltered water, approximately 14 kilometres in length and 3 kilometres wide. It is probably the result of a broad deeper valley having its outlet blocked by a dune building sequence, possibly as the sea levels rose following the last period of glaciation. Subsequent silting has resulted in a shallow lagoon. The water is brackish, and coloured the characteristic black—and burgundy in the sandy shallows—by the organic humic acids from the peat catchments. Platypus are frequently observed in the river and around the lagoon. Black and white cockatoos fly in to feed in the tops of eucalypts; the olive whistler calls strongly from the lower forest zones and the yellow-throated honeyeater is also frequently heard. But scattered along the lagoon in small groups are black swan, black duck and white faced herons. Near the seaward end of the lagoon, the silver gulls feed on berries and strut along the sand of Prion Beach. Sea eagles and wedge-tailed eagles soar in to perch on trees beside the lagoon.

The tiger cat, the native cat and the possums, the pademelon and the Tasmanian devil claim this as their world at night. Their tracks and droppings are frequent on the margins of inlets, and along walking tracks that they, with the wombat, help to maintain.

In 1966 the land was declared to be a Fauna Conservation District under the Animals and Birds Protection Act, 1928. The South Coast walking track was first cut by W H Tyler and W T Harper in 1906 and has been partly maintained by usage and partly by track-cutters at government expense. Of the hundreds of annual visitors, some climb the Bluff,

some enjoy the lagoon and the New River, and others explore the extensive cave systems. Boats were provided by the Public Works Department for walkers to cross New River Lagoon.

Deposits of high grade limestone were reported on the east side of New River Lagoon by Tasmanian Department of Mines geologists Twelvetrees, in 1915[2] and Blake, in 1938.[3] But it was in December 1971 that the threat to Precipitous Bluff first emerged. A Melbourne based prospecting company, Mineral Holdings (Australia) Pty Ltd advertised, as required by the Tasmanian Mines Act, their application for a Special Prospectors Licence in respect of an area of approximately 15 square miles at Milford Creek. The limestone is a hard grey homogenous rock, containing plentiful white calcite.

Although two thirds of Australia's limestone is used in cement manufacture, which tolerates fairly high levels of impurities, the largest possible end use for the reportedly high purity limestone from New River Lagoon area would be iron and steel fluxing.[4] At present good transport economics are practised by the steel industry which has much limestone back loaded from Japan in iron and coal ships.

Mineral Holdings placed their datum peg, defining the prospective licence area just inside the boundary of the Southwest National Park on the western shore of the lagoon. This application was objected to by the Mines Department. Many who objected to the first advertisement (which the Liberal Government allowed the National Parks and Wildlife Service to object to) did not realise the mistake contained in it, were not notified and went to the bush before Christmas. A second datum peg was placed and few saw the second advertisement, but objections were lodged by a number of individuals and bodies including the Tasmanian Conservation Trust, the South-West Committee, the Launceston Field Naturalists' Club, The Society for Growing Australian Plants and Mr R Wyatt.

When the Precipitous Bluff Case was heard in the Devonport Mining Warden's Court, on December 4th 1972, Mineral Holdings claimed that the objectors had no legal interest in the area or an adjoining area. The Director of National Parks, being in control of the adjoining Southwest National Park, had a clear interest, which could not have been disputed, had the new State Government allowed the Director to be a party to the case. The new Labor Premier, who was also Minister for Mines, had refused to allow the National Parks and Wildlife Service to continue.

The objectors' counsel claimed that the maintenance by the Public Works Department of boats to cross New River Lagoon, and the cutting of tracks, gave the public the right of usage of the area, and hence, an interest in it in the legal sense.

Mineral Holdings did not dispute the inherent value of the Precipitous Bluff region but proceeded to outline the following programme:

'A geological survey of the limestone deposits would entail investigating means of access and would include cutting tracks and sampling the limestone faces. It would require further sampling by diamond drilling and possibly trenching. 10 or 20 sites would necessarily be cleared for the drilling. Access tracks would have to be cut between the 10 or 20 holes proposed to be dug and a base camp would necessitate further clearing'.[5]

One Mineral Holdings witness said he expected the base camp to be 'about half an acre'. Initial field parties for exploration were estimated at 10 to 20 men for six months, and it would be anticipated that they would light fires. Regrowth to match the complexity of the climax forests would take thousands of years.

It is not so much a matter of misunderstanding, as of the fact that both sides mean different things by the same words—if the miners and the conservationists spoke different languages an interpreter would be used. Perhaps the real trouble is not so much the unseeing eye of the trained geologist or forester, but the blinkered brain which will not or cannot perceive the contrast between a naturally evolved rainforest ecosystem and a commercially grown crop of one or two species of eucalypt.

The Mining Warden's summing up reveals a breadth of vision and understanding of modern social values all too rare in the Law—

'... I find that the evidence is quite overwhelming that any mining activity, and this includes activity limited only to prospecting and investigation—would have a deleterious effect upon the environment of the locality in question, quite out of proportion to the supposed advantage which might result from a successful sampling of the deposits of limestone thought to be present in the area. In spite of the evidence of Mr

Hughes (the chief geologist)... 'I am quite satisfied... that the risk of fire in the fire free area would be substantially increased by the activities envisaged by the Applicants, with the potential consequent loss of a unique Australian asset.

The hypothetical advantages of discovering quantities of high grade limestone in marketable quantities are, according to the weight of the evidence, not to be compared with the despoliation of the area which would be caused by the scarring of the landscape by channelling the faces, by the clearing of sites for diamond drilling and the construction of a base camp, and by the "Q" operations necessary to keep a number of men and machines in the field... the advantages of retaining the area in its present primeval and

pristine condition far outweigh the nebulous benefits to be derived from the mining activities proposed'.[5]

Conservationists had won an important precedent when the Warden held that bushwalkers using the Precipitous Bluff area had the right to object to its use for mining purposes. It is believed to be the first time in Australia that members of the public have been given some 'status' in Crown land disputes. The Mining Warden held that an individual can object against mining applications on unoccupied Crown land. Government cutting of tracks, provision of boats and declaration of the Conservation Area for public use made it impossible, he felt, to hold that the public had no estate or interest.

However, with the encouragement of the then Minister for Mines, and Premier, Mr E Reece, Mineral Holdings appealed

Saturday Evening Mercury, 2 December 1972 and three car stickers.

The view west over Prion Bay at evening to the islands of the South Coast.   *Maurice D Clark*

to the Supreme Court of Tasmania. In June 1973 Mr Justice Nettlefold handed down a reserved decision in their favour. His 'Reasons for Judgement' were that:

'the objections were incompetent as the objectors did not hold any estate or interest in the area of land within the meaning of S.15C (3) of the Mining Act (1929)'.[6]

Satisfied that none of the objectors had any right to be heard by the Warden, he stated that 'their objections should have been struck out'. Basically conservative, this judgement is a narrow, nineteenth century view of interest: originally the term applied strictly to owners or lessees of land. Any use of the word 'interest' in other than proprietary meaning is termed using it 'in any loose sense'.[6]

However, Professor H W R Wade Q.C. was one of several who interpreted section 15C of the Act differently:

*'The Mining Act gives the right to object to "a person who claims any estate or interest and an objector need only **claim** to have an interest in order to have it determined by the Warden..."* Furthermore: *'It is widely recognized that the narrow basis of private interest is inadequate, and that persons or associations who are genuinely concerned ought to be allowed to represent the public interest'.*[7]

It was declared that the decision as to whether the lease should be issued lay with the Minister—making the final decision political. Nettlefold J also stated that the Warden's decision on the matters within his jurisdiction should be regarded as final, thus disposing of the right of appeal.

These limitations, with the denial of the right of objection, were felt to be so vital that a further appeal was lodged with the Full Bench of the Supreme Court of Tasmania. This appeal, on purely legal points, was heard by three judges—Green C J, Neasey J and Chambers J in May 1975. The Full Bench agreed with the proprietary interpretation of interest:

'In my view, no wider definitions of the words "estate or interest" are reasonably open. To give the phrase any wider meaning by, for example, including amongst those who have an interest in the land persons who are merely concerned about the land, would, I think, be giving the expression a meaning not hitherto known to the law'.[8]

The appeal was dismissed, but the Chief Justice's judgement further limits objections:

'the legislature did not intend to confer upon all the world a right to object but intended to confine the class of objectors to those who might in some way be especially affected by the application because... they have some right connected with the land'.[8]

There are many Australians who claim that they have the right to use this Crown land for recreation, bushwalking, caving and climbing in reasonable peace and seclusion, a right which has been granted by the government's provision of tracks and the boats for crossing New River. This right would be affected in many ways by limestone mining there, from their point of view, but not in the legal sense.

The Chief Justice's judgement, upheld by the High Court of Australia, reveals the inadequacy of the current mining legislation which needs re-drafting as a whole. Environmental rights must be defined and government should be lobbied to this end. The Chief Justice set out six narrow proprietary grounds for legal objection, any of which he felt the Mining Warden could rightly determine. These grounds alone, he said, could disqualify an applicant from holding a special prospector's licence:

(a) 'that the Applicant was under 18 years old;
(b) that the Applicant (other than a Company) already held a prospector's licence;
(c) that the area applied for exceeded 25 square miles;
(d) that the land was not un-occupied land, within the meaning of the Act, or reserve land;
(e) that the Applicant had failed to comply with the requirements of the Act as to marking out;
(f) that there was a previous applicant'.[8]

The Chief Justice concluded this section by stating that 'the right to object to the granting of applications made under the Act is confined to a limited number of cases'. In giving no reason for this, he has interpreted the minds of members of the Tasmanian Parliament in 1929.

Believing that it is vital to the well being of Tasmania to use every legal opportunity to broaden the definition of interest to include community interest rather than confine it to economic interest the conservationists lodged a final appeal to the High Court of Australia. In 1975 the author was present when discussions took place between the Director and Senior Project Officer of the Australian Conservation Foundation (Dr G Mosley and Mr Doug Hill), and the Deputy Director of Mines (Mr P M Johnston) who said: 'Well you haven't had this heard in the High Court, so you cannot really prove that the Mining Act needs amending'.

Because of the principle involved the Federal Government of 1976 has conditionally granted further legal aid. Funds were raised by the public appeal opened in 1975. Legal aid will help the Tasmanian Conservation Trust to meet the overall cost which will include all of Mineral Holdings expenses. Since, at the beginning of the Court action, neither the

Tasmanian Conservation Trust nor the Australian Conservation Foundation was an incorporated body, the appeal had to stand in the names of individuals and the officers of groups and societies who originally lodged objections, but the Trust Inc. guaranteed to meet these costs.

The legal and administrative procedures with regard to mining applications in Tasmania were mostly laid down before there was any general acceptance of either ecological principles or the right of public interest. The regulations were framed to aid 'development' and exploitation of resources, in line with then current thinking. The Planning and Development Bill 1975 would have modernized the process, but was possibly too advanced in concept for the legislature. The Bill was delayed and required re-drafting.

We have seen in Tasmania, in 1976, in the case of the application to quarry granite at Coles Bay—in Freycinet National Park—and also in the case of the Picton bridge, how Tasmanian politicians can and will override responsible environmental decisions by their own department and an environment review committee.

Aesthetic and environmental well-being, like economic well-being, are important ingredients of the quality of life in our society. It is widely recognized in other countries that environmental interests are deserving of legal protection through the judicial process. Indeed, a law that fails to protect our most valuable and diminishing natural asset: wilderness, is failing to meet the dynamic needs of modern society.

Courts in England, and USA in particular, have recently extended their ideas about what constitutes a sufficient interest for challenging the legality of actions of public authorities. Two American decisions were spectacular successes for the preservation of the scenic Hudson Valley. It was asserted in court that:

'The public interest in environmental resources... is a legally protected interest, affording these plaintiffs, as responsible representatives of the public, standing to obtain judicial review of agency action alleged to be in contravention of that public interest'.[9]

Australians must see the reality of the Precipitous Bluff case in the light of such contemporary decisions. Reform of the Mining Act (1929) is obviously essential but must be demonstrated to both political parties, the Mines Department, the media and the public. Wide public education about the value of our natural heritage is essential.

The road ahead is rough for those for whom the South-West wilderness is an entity not to be fragmented.

Still a chance . . .   . . . to make Truchanas' dream come true

In the past year — I've been one of those lucky Australians travelling far and wide in the world.

I'll readily agree with those who say, "there's no place like home."

That old saying is true in so many ways. Tasmania is a place of special beauty, peace and warm people.

Tasmania also has a wonder which is quickly making the island nearly unique in the developed world our — south-west wilderness.

But like the Tasmanian tribal Aborigine and the Tasmanian tiger, it will soon be only a memory, unless we act now.

By Peter Thompson, conservationist and former Launceston radio announcer.

In the next year, the Hydro-Electric Commission will propose to parliament a new power scheme on the Franklin-Lower Gordon Rivers. If it goes ahead, Tasmania's best and last wild river will be destroyed, as will the remaining untamed stretches of the Gordon River.

The dream Olegas Truchanas held when he made his fateful trip down the Gordon River in 1972 will be lost forever. But what does his dream of wilderness mean?

Firstly, wilderness is not just beautiful country. It is beautiful, but it is also lonely, remote — it stands at a distance from man.

If man wants to be nourished by the values it has to offer, he must get far away from the beaten track, from the world we all have access to every day.

In Tasmania, all of us have opportunities to be moved by beauty in visiting great tracts of mountain, lake, farm and seaside scenery. So, we're not really in need of 'new frontiers' of scenery to be viewed from the comfort of our cars.

But we are in need of setting aside areas which provide a unique 'experience' of travel, that is, travel which is challenging, hardy and vigorous.

In this case, it is not the special quality of the beauty which is of primary importance, but the 'nature' of the travel experience.

Until recently, this experience has been available because our daily community life has not seriously impinged upon the remote south-west wilderness.

Our traditional means of economic development have come to the stage where we must decide whether to keep it or destroy it. It is a fact that unless there is a public clamour, it will be destroyed.

It will be destroyed by the same Government departments which met our needs in the 40s and 50s, but which are not sensitive to the need for changing values in the 70s.

It will be destroyed if public apathy allows it.

The HEC will try to convince us that we need more hydro power to keep up our present level of prosperity. That is its logic only!

As power has increased this decade, manufacturing jobs in Tasmania have declined. They dropped by 200 in the years 1970-1974, that's before the textile collapse set in!

With 3 per cent of Australia's population, Tasmania uses 10 per cent of

the nation's power, but traditionally we have always been at or near the top in the dismal story of the percentage unemployed.

Our surplus power has attracted a few capital and energy intensive industries which offer precious few jobs considering the investment ploughed into power schemes.

Our energy strategy is all wrong. It makes sense to use the next $300 million-plus needed for the Franklin-Lower Gordon scheme in other investment priorities.

Trade union and employer groups should be pressuring the State Government for more jobs and more money for the

'one hundred' and one' other areas of economic activity in Tasmania, rather than the traditionally favoured areas of power development and huge energy-using low employment industries such as heavy and light metals.

Tasmania faces this prospect in the near future anyhow, because the

Franklin-Lower Gordon scheme would be the last major hydro development.

If we stop the Franklin-Lower Gordon scheme, our lights will still burn, our cars will go on increasing job opportunities, and we will have a wilderness of world importance.

If it goes ahead, tradition rather than sense will be honoured. Let's be the masters of our own future!

[Statistics gained from *Tasmania Year Book 1977* (loss of jobs) p.330; *Australian Year Book 1975-76* (Power consumption vis-a-vis other states) pp984-

FRANKLIN THE LAST WILD RIVER
PRODUCED BY THE TASMANIAN WILDERNESS SOCIETY

The Examiner 29 June 1978.

The Cauldron;
Great Ravine
Don Hutton

Opposite page
Irenabyss;
the middle Franklin
Don Hutton

Left
This full colour poster was produced by the Tasmanian Wilderness Society in 1978 as was the car sticker above the photograph.

DON'T FLOOD THE FRANKLIN!
YOU MUST SAVE TASMANIA'S LAST WILD RIVER FROM NEEDLESS DESTRUCTION

CONTACT TASMANIAN WILDERNESS SOCIETY ...

Telephone 30 1101
Telegraphic & Cable Address 'Waterpower'
Telex 58091

4-18 ELIZABETH STREET,
HOBART,
TASMANIA

THE HYDRO-ELECTRIC COMMISSION. TASMANIA

OUR REF. 5541
YOUR REF.
IF TELEPHONING OR CALLING
ASK FOR

POSTAL ADDRESS:
G.P.O. Box 355 D 7001

1 MAY 1978

Secretary-Co-ordinator,
Tasmanian Wilderness Society,
102 Bathurst Street,
HOBART, Tas. 7000

Dear Sir,

I acknowledge receipt of your letter dated 12th April, 1978 in which you ask for information relating to expenditure on investigations into the water power resources of the State.

The total cost of investigations to date in the Gordon and King Franklin catchments is approximately as follows :-

Gordon River below Gordon River
Power Development Stage 1 $3,900,000

King, Franklin and Jane Rivers $2,400,000

It has been brought to my attention that your recent advertisement in the Tasmanian Mail states that "The H.E.C. will say that so much public money has been spent on investigations that the scheme must be built".

I have no doubt that you are aware that in 1973 the Commission gave an undertaking to the Legislative Council that the amount of money spent on investigation works would not be used as an argument for the adoption of a power development in the area.

It seems a pity that in your advertisement you should choose to distort the truth in this manner.

Yours faithfully,

(J.R. Ashton)
Commissioner

In the USA, the Wild and Scenic Rivers Act, 1968, provides for the establishment of a National Wild and Scenic River System incorporating and protecting three specific categories of rivers. Their classification overides the previous authorisation for dams or other conflicting structures. The South-West contains a large number of pristine catchment areas and the last truly wild rivers in Australia. They are valuable assets in their own right, apart from their scientific and recreational value.

The Franklin

R Brown

Bob Brown of Liffey is a medical practitioner in Launceston. He is well known for his social and political involvement in the Tasmanian community. In 1976 and again in 1977, he journeyed down the Franklin River with friends. The second trip was a filming expedition and part of a continuing effort by the party to publicize the natural beauty of this river and the plans afoot to dam it. Bob is a member of the Tasmanian Wilderness Society and the United Tasmania Group.

The Franklin River rises high in central Tasmania's Cheyne Range. At first a joining of runlets from ice-rimmed tarns, trickling between snow-clad boulders and cushion plants, it quickly becomes an exuberant stream racing through alpine grasslands nearly 1,400 metres above sea level. Rushing south past snow-capped Hugel and Rufus, it tumbles over icicled falls and slows momentarily in the glacial lakes, Undine and Dixon. Then, pouring down through the gorge beneath Mt Arrowsmith, it meets its first large tributary, the Surprise. Here in the rainforest, explorer-surveyor James Erskine Calder first came upon the 'dangerous' Franklin, and wondered at the flood-logs 30 feet up in the trees.

Now turning west, the upper Franklin twists for nine kilometres through forest clad hills to be joined by its major tributary, the Collingwood, which brings with it the waters of five other mountain rivers — the Alma, Inkerman, Patons, Cardigan and Balaclava. And veering south past the Raglan Range, it picks up the Loddon River where the first Huon pines lean from its banks, and its valley changes character — this is the middle Franklin.

Forty-five kilometres from the river's source the middle Franklin enters the first of the gorges it cuts in its 50 kilometres sweep around the massive block of Frenchmans Cap (1,433m). This is a long, narrow gorge where steep, forested hillsides on the south are looked down upon by the shadow-throwing cliffs of the north. It is punctuated by a series of rock-strewn rapids and ends abruptly between two ninety-degree bends, in a reach some 150 metres long.

This reach — the finale to the gorge — is the Irenabyss, a 100 metre deep chasm over a dark ribbon of slow-moving, silent river, at places only five metres wide. Named for its summertime peace, its cliffs and amazingly deep waters, the Irenabyss is an enchanting place; and from it the Franklin opens out into a wide, sunlit pool where it is joined by the creek from Lake Tahune, high on the shoulder of the nearby Frenchman.

Flowing west and south, the Franklin continues to wend its way through the valley between the Engineer Range and

the foothills of Frenchmans Cap, digging down another 200 metres as it goes. In places the valley is wide and resembles those of many mainland coastal rivers, and in places it is closed and cliffed like a forested version of a Central Australian gorge. But it is never consistent: each bend brings new, unexpected features into view.

In one great bend, the Crankle, the river flows in every compass direction, within two kilometres. On another bend the Blushrock Falls cascade 100 metres to the riverside. Here and there other surging creeks cut through the valley walls, and all the way the Franklin continues to gather flow.

While animal life seems scant in this remarkable steepness, white and black cockatoos wheel, screeching overhead, in contrast with the low, silent sweeps of the fish-seeking cormorants. Migratory martins call and dart from their nests on riverworn cliffs and grey fantails flit, insect-snatching, across the wilderness waters.

Just after the river leaves the western fringe of Frenchmans Cap National Park, its waters steady for their spectacular transit of the Great Ravine, a ten kilometre gorge extending from the Brook of Inveraestra to the Andrew River confluence.

The Great Ravine proper is paved by five long river reaches—Inception, Serenity, Transcendence, the Sanctum and Deliverance—separated by four major rapids—the Churn, Coruscades, Thunderush and Cauldron. In Serenity Sound the Ravine is 1,000 metres wide but its banks tower 400 metres to the west and 550 metres to the east; while from Mt Lyne the drop to the Coruscades is more than 800 metres.

Legends of a '100 foot' whole-river waterfall in the Ravine kept river explorers from moving through it for a century after its discovery in 1840. On Christmas Eve of that year ex-convict Alexander McKay, working for Calder, had looked down into the Great Ravine from Deception Range to the east, but 'at

night had found no place where his track could be carried across' (Calder). Calder himself was in the area, cutting a track for Governor Franklin's expedition, and for two days examined this 'abrupt country' for himself:

'I tried to lead the road across at several points, but was thwarted by the intervention of a tremendous ravine .... This locality presents no other view but that of a sterile wilderness, and scenes of frightful desolation. The great ravine, which bounds Deception Range to the westward, is very deep; I dare say 2,000 feet; is far too steep for travelling, and not to be crossed without excessive fatigue and risk. ... I twice got to the bottom of this hideous defile, but was at last forced to relinquish the idea of a direct course, ... utterly disgusted with the adventure. A large and furious torrent flows through it, which, collecting all the water that falls on a wide extent of mountainous country,

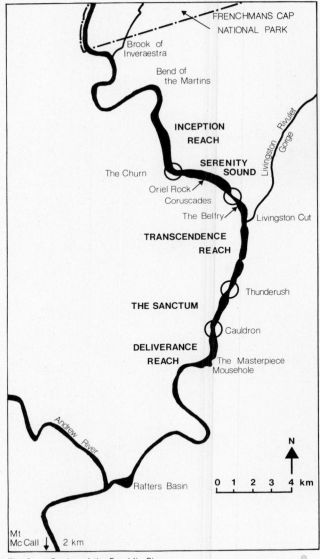

The Great Ravine of the Franklin River.

The Franklin River Road to the site of HEC investigations below Mt McCall (above). This road, constructed in the early seventies, is closed to the public; the devastating scars were unreported. It terminates at a potential dam site, on the Franklin River, where a cableway drops 300 metres into the gorge which is bridged for exploration purposes (below). Expenditure on investigation in the King, Franklin and Gordon River catchments exceeded $6.5 million in mid 1978. This is prior to approval by Parliament for a Franklin-Lower Gordon scheme. Will this expenditure be used again by the HEC as justification for the destruction of our last wild rivers?
Helen Gee

In March 1977 on ABC television, the HEC implied that there had been no bulldozing or major works at Mt McCall for the past 5 years. In February 1977 a river party observed four enormous earth scars in the gorge between the Great Ravine and Mt McCall and a suspension bridge at the McCall dam site. Neither the earth scars nor the bridge were present in February 1976.
Helen Gee

emerges from the glen a large and beautiful river. I called it the Franklin'.

In midsummer the river in the Great Ravine presents great, languid pools and rapids splashing beneath and around the boulders in their bed. But fifteen metres up on the scoured rock walls is the floodline—and in recorded history no one has witnessed the maelstrom that the surging winter river must create in the Ravine.

In the centre of the Ravine the Livingston Rivulet meets the Franklin through a sharp cut, completing the Franklin's drainage of the whole Frenchmans Cap massif. The final reach of the river in the Ravine proper, Deliverance, is a beautiful and diverse place: among its features are the Masterpiece (a bronzed in-stream monolith), the Mousehole (with its cat-like boulder overlooking a waterfall-worn niche in the river's rock wall), two fine tributary falls, a small but singular river-width rapid and two 'exit gates' where rock walls obtrude into the waters.

Emerging from the Great Ravine, the middle Franklin opens into a broad valley to receive the Andrew River from the north-west. A few kilometres above this junction the Andrew is indented by the large meteoritic Darwin Crater. Flowing on, the Franklin enters the Propsting Gorge—a gentler run, with thickly forested banks and the reappearance of the longer, more open rapids like those above the Ravine.

Then the last gorge, Glen Calder: an engaging race between the pool where the Nicholls River comes in from the west, and the Newland Cascades — which are just beyond the tributary falls from the gully the convicts called the Pig Trough.

Suddenly the valley widens and flattens—this is the lower Franklin, 'large and beautiful', with low verdured banks and occasional limestone cliffs lining broadwater after broadwater. Slow, reflective acres of river broken by long, splashing, shingly rapids.

In its last 30 kilometres the Franklin has only five of the steep, noisy rapids that characterise its middle reaches; and the largest of these is the Big Fall where the river closes and thunders two metres down from a step in its bedrock. But first it is joined by its largest tributary, the Jane, a forest-flanked torrent which is smaller, faster and steeper than the Franklin.

Most of the Huon pine forests of the lower Franklin are gone; their only reminder is the myriad of small pines and the few gnarled old 'unsuitable' trees which escaped the piners' axes. Yet the other forest giants remain — the statuesque blackwoods and lofty eucalypts and myrtles, towering over the sweet-smelling leatherwoods and riverbank acacias.

Wallabies and potoroos dart through the undergrowth, while the sea-eagles soar watchfully overhead. In the evenings foraging swifts spiral-dive and hurtle low over the shoals and sandbanks in a race against the setting sun.

Finally the Franklin joins the Gordon above Butler Island, almost at sea-level, but still 45 kilometres east of Macquarie Harbour.

The upper, middle and lower Franklin — three differing parts of the one great river: a river fed by twenty others and a host of fast-flowing creeks. And though it is only 125 kilometres from the Cheyne Range to the Gordon, the Franklin's inordinate volume is testimony to the plentiful rain and snow driven across its basin by the Roaring Forties.

The Franklin is a remarkable wilderness. In 1977 only two dirt roads had reached the lip of its (middle) valley, while in its upper reaches it is perfunctorily crossed by the oblivious Lyell Highway. No one lives anywhere by its banks, there are no grazing or arable lands in its basin, no blackberries or willows have rooted in its soil.

It is a wild and wondrous thing; and 175 years after Tasmania's first European settlement, the Franklin remains much as it was before man—black or white— came to its precincts.

However in the next 25 years we may see it utterly destroyed. The Hydro-Electric Commission has advanced planning for a Lower Gordon dam which will completely flood the lower Franklin, and a Franklin dam which will flood the middle Franklin (including the Great Ravine). The Commission has also made a preliminary study of an upper Franklin dam site, immediately below the Irenabyss; a dam here will flood the upper Franklin back beyond the Lyell Highway.

Meanwhile the Forestry Commission has proposed that Crown land north of the Lyell Highway, including the upper Franklin Valley, be taken over as State Forest.

Despite such plans, no government or politician has called for the whole Franklin Valley to be protected and dedicated as a living museum of our Earth as it existed before the evolution of technological man — for governments work in the selfish way of providing only for those who vote in the present. Yet no other use of the Franklin Valley would be more gratefully applauded by our numberless progeny.

FRANKLIN RIVER: Historical Notes

The aeons	Original Tasmanians camped on the upper reaches, at least.
1824	Thomas Scott's map shows lower Franklin as Gordon tributary.
1828	James Goodwin and a fellow convict escaped from Sarah Island prison to the midlands, after crossing the river some 4 miles above its mouth (vessel — a pine log). Other escapees, notably Alexander Pierce and Matthew Greenhill in 1822, almost certainly crossed the lower Franklin. Most of them perished in their flight.
1832	W S Sharland criss-crossed the upper river in travelling from Bothwell to Sharlands Peak, in an unsuccessful attempt to climb Frenchmans Cap.
1839	Surveyor George Frankland's map notes Pyramid Island and 'rapids in this river' (the lower Franklin).
1840	Dec 24th: Alexander McKay, an ex-convict working for surveyor Calder, and his two convict assistants, viewed the Great Ravine from the Deception Range.
1840	Dec 25-26th: James Calder twice descended into this 'great ravine' and found a 'furious torrent' which 'I called the Franklin'.
1842	May: Convicts Couz and Maddox rafted across the swollen lower Franklin, leading the large party including Sir John and Lady Jane Franklin, which followed a few days later.
1887	Surveyor T B Moore crossed the river at Canyon Creek enroute to his western ascent of Frenchmans Cap.
c1900–1977	Especially pre 1950: piners cut most of the Huon Pines from the Franklin and its tributaries, approaching up-river in punts and cutting tracks from the Crotty road to the west.
1940	March: Strahan brothers Ron and Reg Morrison travelled up the Franklin to Mt Fincham in 16-18 days, hauling their 14 foot punt.
1951	John Hawkins, John Dean, Jeff Weston and Joe Scarlett canoed from Collingwood bridge to Fincham crossing.
1958	Dec 13th: Hawkins, Dean, Trevor Newland and Henry Crocker canoed from the Collingwood to Butler Island in 4-5 weeks.
1968–1970	The Franklin River Road constructed by the HEC facilitating investigations for a middle Franklin dam site.
1970–1971	Epic raft voyage down river by Fred Koolhof, David Hansen, Tim Downie and John Morley in 16 days.
1976	Jan: Don Hutton's party of 5 from Monash University canoed down river in 10 days.
	Feb 21 - March 8: Paul Smith and Bob Brown followed in inflatable dinghies.
	Mar: Stuart Graham, Neil Davidson, Mark Errey, John Davies and Helen Gee liloed down Jane River from Warnes Lookout to the Franklin.
1977-1978	Numerous parties made the downriver trip presaging an annual pilgrimage to Tasmania's last great wild river.

Snow-clad Mt Cook, giant of the Southern Alps of New Zealand.
Tasmanian Environment Centre Inc Col

The Southern Alps of New Zealand rising abruptly above Lake Matheson.
Tasmanian Environment Centre Inc Col

Milford Sound in New Zealand's Fiordland National Park.
Tasmanian Environment Centre Inc Col

World Heritage — One of A Trio

K Kiernan

The Roaring Forties beat relentlessly upon the shores of three great wild lands.

Just as they bring the characteristic sou'wester of cold crisp days, mist and sunshowers to Tasmania's South-West, so too do they provide the very conditions which both shape and enhance the harshness and beauty of New Zealand's Fiordland and the Patagonian extremity of South America.

From Tasmania they pound upon the wild western coastline of New Zealand's rugged South Island: Fiordland and the Southern Alps behind.

Undaunted, they continue their unrelenting progress uninterrupted across the huge expanse of the South Pacific to Patagonia, a vast windswept land stretching southwards from Argentina's Rio Negro to the legendary Cape Horn.

It is eastern Patagonia which is best known: the rolling steppe country of the pampas with its ranging estancias situated in the comparative shelter of the valleys cut in the plateaux. Westward lies one of the wildest of lands.

Where the spreading oceanic plate underlying the Pacific is driven in under the South American plate, there rises the longest continuous mountain chain in the world. Although the Andes here are lower than farther north, the climate is at its most severe. Here lie the great Hielos Continentales, Patagonia's two continental ice-caps. Westward, glaciers flow to the sea along the incredible fiord coast of southern Chile with its rugged islands.

Patagonia's latitudinal range extends from Tasmania to Macquarie Island, its southern mountains experiencing one of the most severe climates on earth. Midway along this range, between the heart of Patagonia and Tasmania, lies Fiordland, its glaciers, like the retreating ice-caps of Patagonia, now diminishing quite rapidly. While Tasmania bears the mark of glaciation, permanent snow has vanished from the island and it has a relatively mild maritime climate.

Together, these areas form a unique trio of wildscapes which rank among the great natural regions of the world.

The members of the trio share a common heritage, for they were probably all part of a great southern land mass which drifted apart 200 million years ago. This unity is evidenced by the

The extinct South American Borhyaenid *(prothylacinus)* resembled the Tasmanian Tiger *(thylacine)* illustrated in 2.10.
Peter Murray

fossil record which indicates a number of biological affinities. The Tertiary period saw the common occurrence of a conifer and a species of *Nothofagus*. While Tertiary borhyaenids of South America bear some resemblance to the Thylacine or Tasmanian tiger, and there are some dental similarities between the modern South American rat opossums and some Australian phalangeroids (possums), the present land vertebrate fauna of Tasmania and South America is generally dissimilar, and New Zealand is lacking in large mammals. Large flightless birds once existed in all three localities but today only Darwin's rhea survives; the Tasmanian emu and New Zealand moa are extinct.

Today, the most striking biological similarity lies in the widespread occurrence of *Nothofagus* in all three regions. As well, over thirty other plant species are common in the rainforests and montane country, while there are also some inter-tidal affinities.

In all three regions glaciation has left a legacy of swift-flowing mountain streams. They are one of the principal wild attributes of these areas yet, ironically, they also offer numerous potential damsites for the production of hydro-electricity involving the inundation of vast areas. The flooding of New Zealand's Lake Manapouri and Tasmania's Lake Pedder aroused considerable controversy. Proposals for dams on Tasmania's remaining western rivers and on Chile's Rio Baker may become equally well known around the world as conservation issues, although there is a possibility that the Baker project may be abandoned.

Other threats to the integrity of these areas have come from overgrazing by introduced species, from the exploit-

ation of their forest resources, and as result of damage caused by fire.

In both New Zealand and Patagonia overgrazing by introduced animals has proved a problem. Deer are continually culled in New Zealand, while in the Chilean pampas programmes are aimed at the restoration of damaged areas. This follows the resumption of some areas of the pampas and subsequent elimination of commercial grazing there.

The timber resources of New Zealand have been heavily utilized and there are plans for the large scale pulping of the native beech forests and the conversion of native forests to softwood plantations. Much of Tasmania's forested land, including areas of the South-West, is committed to the woodchip industry. In the Magellanes province of southern Chile over 83,000 square kilometres have been set aside as 'Reserves Forestales'. These reserves are designed to offer opportunities for multi-purpose use.

The occurrence of fire in Patagonia has been greatly reduced as a result of the drift of people to the cities and more effective enforcement methods. In New Zealand, however, areas of native forest frequently fall prey to summer wildfire. In Tasmania fires in the eucalypt forests and open sedge and heathlands affect vast areas each summer, too often the result of inadequately researched programmes of hazard reduction by deliberate firing. Massive damage is also often inflicted upon neighbouring forests by burns conducted as part of regeneration practices on clear-felled forests, while delicate alpine flora many miles distant may be set alight by burning embers carried by convection currents.

Of all the like features and factors which enable legitimate comparisons to

Photograph of Ona Indians, by A A Cameron, from *Uttermost Part of the Earth* by E Lucas Bridges, London, 1948.

Of the native peoples of all three regions, only the Maoris were able to withstand the predatory and aggressive habits of European settlers and the disease which marked their arrival in the new world. When the shrinking range of the nomadic Ona people led them to kill settlers' sheep for food in the Fuegan Isla Grande, white men were employed to hunt and kill them, and today they and the Yaghan islanders are extinct. Similarly, by 1876 the Tasmanian aboriginal race — victims of the white man's bullets and diseases alike — was extinct.

In far Patagonia A L McAulay (See p.152)

In far Patagonia swept bare and forlorn
The thundering forties are born near the Horn,
They bellow and snarl from the land of their birth,
They shriek and they howl as they rage round the earth
And they boom and they roar as they hurl on the shore
Impossible breakers, smashed wreckage and ghosts
On our thunderous grim and deserted West Coasts.

Where water and cloud and the bitter salt spray
Are mixed in a drenching torn welter of grey,
A ship, hardly noticed, slips under the sea
And sets the dim shades of its passengers free....

They merge with our West
Where deep gorges unguessed
Clothed in forest whose heart is unseen
Are twilit and secret and green
With a submarine green drowning octopus arms
Of a strange and contorted mysterious tree.

We were in the tree choked gorges where no man had ever been
Where the Horizontal writhes in a dim green gloom.
We could feel them move about us, real and firm and almost seen
And their words like whispers reached us through the surf's deep boom.

Torres del Paine in the Parque Nacional Torres del Paine, Southern Patagonia. Resumed pampas in the foreground.   *Kevin Kiernan*

be made between Patagonia, New Zealand and Tasmania, the one indisputably common denominator is the sea. Moreover, it is the influence of the sea, as much as any other single factor, which determines the character and atmosphere of these solitary places.

Here land and water not only complement one another. They are inseparable, for what affects the sea, affects the land equally.

In August, 1974, the 290,000 tonne Shell supertanker *Metula* ran aground at the eastern entrance to the Straits of Magellan—the first spillage disaster involving a fully laden supertanker. The lack of publicity was as much a product of the area's remoteness as the efforts of the company and supertanker lobby to hush the incident, but investigations have revealed massive destruction of aquatic life and sea birds and the obliteration of breeding colonies in one of the world's richest areas of marine life. No attempt was made to clean up the vast quantities of oil spilled and it is likely to remain, coating parts of the coast for 60 kilometres for up to 10 years.

The *Metula* incident emphasizes the fragile nature of the maritime frontier of wilderness and should serve to remind Tasmanians and New Zealanders not to be complacent about the oil damage to their coasts which is reported from time to time, the result of bilge pumping by passing shipping.

All three regions are increasing in popularity for walking, climbing and other recreational pursuits. The climate of the Patagonian Andes, coupled with its massive granite walls, make the other great mountain ranges of the world mere playgrounds by comparison. The great French mountaineer, Lionel Terray, first to ascend Fitz Roy, considered that the greatest mountaineering feat of all time was the ascent of one of its satellite peaks, Cerro Torre, by Maestri and Egger in 1959. Maestri's notes give an impression of the weather continually howling in across the ice-cap, for he described only 6 of his 54 days as reasonable, noting the temperature— regularly between -20° and -25°c, a humidity range of 80–90%, winds of 80–150 kph, and 18 metres of snowfall. In New Zealand, the Southern Hemisphere's principal counterpart to the European Alps, conditions are generally less severe and attract many New Zealanders and Australians. Pressure on Tasmania's milder wilderness is becoming intense.

This pressure will increase. Undoubtedly the biggest threat to the trio, once parks are established, is tourism. Dr Christian Vibe who was mainly responsible for the creation of the world's largest national park, the 700,000 square kilometre North East Greenland National Park, has suggested that once protection of an area becomes necessary, it may already be too late.

In Patagonia I was proudly shown a road being blasted up a valley draining Lago Grey at the foot of the Southern ice-cap itself. A new road is being built towards the Torres del Paine from Calafate in Argentina, and accommodation facilities have been built at Pudeto, and are planned for Lago Azul, the only remaining refuge for the puma (2 pairs) in the entire Paine park. Yet even if this is to be the fate of the foothills of Chile's most spectacular mountain parkland, large areas of the country will remain wild due to the conservation consciousness of the Chileans.

If it is easy to understand tourist development in Chile, so sorely in need of what little in foreign exchange tourism may offer, it is less easy to countenance attitudes to tourism elsewhere.

The impact of tourism and its economic value gradually gains recognition. Unrestricted tourist development is incompatible with wilderness preservation. The people of New Zealand and Tasmania need to recognise the essential conflict and to insist on adequate safeguards for the integrity of their wild lands before the opportunity is lost.

All three great southern wilderness regions are feeling the inroads of civilisation. While the governments of Chile, Argentina and New Zealand have responded to the scientific, aesthetic and recreational significance of the wild lands over which they are custodian, neither the Australian national government nor the Tasmanian state government has demonstrated real initiative.

In Chile one finds an instance of a less developed country leading the way in conservation. In the early 1970's the International Union for Conservation of Nature and Natural Resources had given its recognition to national parks in western Patagonia covering some 830 square kilometres. Today the figure is 40,000 square kilometres (more than half the size of Tasmania). Estancia country fringing the eastern Andes has been resumed and the abundant wildlife roam unhindered in their own domain. Where puma, condor and guanaco once abounded but fell to slaughter, they are now gathering their numbers.

The Chilean enthusiasm for national parks is the product of a true patriotism, for whatever the political difficulties which have beset this amazing country, its people are united by a true love for their land in a manner which gives real hope for its survival.

Neighbouring Argentina, so like Australia in many ways, has not let continuing political chaos stand in the way of its responsibility to protect its natural heritage, and 10,000 square kilometres of Argentinian Patagonia have been set aside as national parks, although it is disturbing to note that some developmental activities have occurred in one of the parks.

As long ago as 1904 the New Zealand government recognized the importance of its own south-western coastline when it established the great Fiordland National Park of over 10,000 square kilometres. Again, there has been some development within it, but generally speaking, it protects a wide and immensely valuable area. Valuable, because the demands of technological man have driven back the frontiers of the wild over so much of the world.

In early 1976 national parks covered 2,200 square kilometres of South-West Tasmania. In December 1976 this was extended to 4,283 square kilometres. The efforts of the conservationists to extend the national park area to 15,000 square kilometres continued to be met by strong resistance.

The International Biological Programme of UNESCO described the Tasmanian Government's decision to drown Lake Pedder for hydro-electric power development as 'the greatest ecological tragedy since European settlement in Tasmania'. Pedder, like the South-West in which it lay, was much more than just a Tasmanian national park. According to UNESCO, the South-West is a 'wilderness area of incomparable significance and value'. When UNESCO's 1972 convention on protection of the world's cultural and natural heritage was adopted, it had areas like the trio in mind; for these southern oceanic wildlands, like the Antarctic vastness to which they were once joined, cannot justly be claimed as the sole property of any one country.

Australia is a signatory to the World Heritage Convention which came into effect in December, 1975. It provides for the establishment of a World Heritage list of sites of universal importance and interest; and also for a list of World Heritage In Danger for those sites facing immediate threat of destruction or damage. Prior to its election to office in 1975 the Australian Government pledged to greatly expand the Southwest National Park and to nominate it as a World Heritage area. But inroads continue to scar the perimeter of a diminishing area, which is today a wilderness by Australian standards only. Ten years ago it was a true wilderness. Perhaps the relative insensitivity of Australians towards their country is simply a product of their short period of occupation of the continent. Their pioneering instincts to tame and conquer continue unsatiated, and their affinity with the land remains immature.

It is the harshness of the trio which has safeguarded them thus far, but now the South-West's comparative hospitality renders it the most vulnerable.

Chronology of Events

Jessie Luckman & Editors

1642	Abel Tasman (Dutch) first white man to sight South-West Tasmania.
1773	First recorded European landing on the south coast made by James Burney and several other crew members of Cook's ship *Adventure*. They landed at a point which appears to be Rocky Boat Harbour, east of Prion Bay.
1789	Capt. J H Cox (English) sailed around South-West Cape — and anchored in Cox Bight. The following decade found several sailing ships off the coast.
1798	Bass & Flinders circumnavigated Tasmania — naming mountains on west coast Heemskirk & Zeehan after Tasman's ships.
1815	Capt. James Kelly discovered Port Davey & Macquarie Harbour. Also noted coal at Catamaran.
1816	Dennis McCarty found coal and Huon pine in Macquarie Harbour.
1822	Penal station established at Macquarie Harbour.
1828	James Goodwin & Connolly, convicts, escaped from Macquarie Harbour and walked east to Lincoln, near Cleveland.
1829	Surveyor Frankland explored south bank of Huon River.
1830	George Augustus Robinson, in the company of an Aboriginal band, walked along the south coast to Port Davey — climbed & named Mt Hayes & the Arthur Range — and followed the west coast to Cape Grim.
1832	Surveyor W S Sharland led expedition from Bothwell towards the South-West. Climbed Frenchmans Cap almost to the summit.
1834	William Nicholls, first settler at Cygnet. Penal settlement at Macquarie Harbour abandoned. Bridle track cut from Huon River to beyond Arthur Range. Surveyors Calder & Wedge led parties south from Vale of Rasselas; named Lakes Pedder and Maria; went down Huon Plains across Cracroft River & met boat on Huon River.
1835	Surveyor Frankland led party from Lake St Clair to Serpentine River and Lake Pedder; named Mt Anne. Continued to Huon River.
1835-6	Lady Franklin bought land on Huon River to sell in instalments to free settlers who were prepared to clear it for agriculture. Now the township of Franklin.
1836	Alexander McKay & 12 convicts slashed a track from Victoria (now Huonville) along south bank of Huon River towards the Arthur Range, making possible a route for foot traffic to plains east of Port Davey and to stands of Huon pine and other timber. Soon pine-cutting began on a large scale.
1836	*Castle Forbes* put ashore sick immigrants at Hospital Bay on the Huon River. Some stayed on as settlers.
1840	Surveyor Calder staked a route from Lake St Clair, via Lachlan (or Lightning) Plains south of Frenchmans Cap, across Franklin River to Eagle Creek on the Gordon River.
1842	Sir John & Lady Franklin followed Calder's route to Gordon River, thence by boat to Macquarie Harbour and around south-west coast back to Hobart.
1845-50	Surveyor James Sprent made trigonometrical survey of much of Tasmania including the South-West where he erected a cairn on the Arthur Range.
1849	31 farmers unsuccessfully applied to rent 624,000 acres between Frenchmans Cap & Port Davey.
1850	Construction of Dawsons Road from Dunrobin Bridge on the Derwent River — extended 38 miles to Gordon Bend. Abandoned in 1856.
1855	Route marked by Thomas Walton & Joe Wilson, later surveyed by Ballantyne & approved by Calder, for a road between Hobart and Huon.
1857	Petition by inhabitants of Franklin & Victoria (Huonville) for construction of the road & a bridge over the Huon.
1859	Gould & Burgess made geological survey of the western areas. Gould later staked a route from Gordon River to a gap in the Frankland Range, thence to Hamilton. Gould & Burgess also went up the Franklin River, ascending with a boat until right under Frenchmans Cap.
1871	Artist W C Piguenit accompanied James Reid Scott on walk from Victoria (Huonville) via the Huon track to Port Davey, making such sketches as the Obelisk (Federation Peak), Hell's Gates and the 'badger boxes' (huts) of the piners.
1874	Party including Piguenit & R M Johnston (the government geologist) walked from Huon to Pedder and back.
1874	The first steam mill in the south began timber operations at Geeveston. Much felling from Huonville to Hastings.
1878	Surveyor Frodsham explored from Hamilton to Gordon Bend & the Denison Range.
1879	Parliamentary inquiry into need for better control over cutting of Huon pine and blackwood. Pine stands in Port Davey area almost cut out.
1879	T B Moore marked route from Birch Inlet, Macquarie Harbour, to Settlement Point at Port Davey.
1880	Henry Judd walked from Huonville to Mt Anne — named Lake Judd.
1881	David Jones, Francis McPartlan & others explored from Macquarie Harbour to Cracroft River for possible horse track. Party was out for 3 months & Surveyor E A Counsel was sent out to look for them.
1881	Suspension bridge constructed over Picton River.
1881	Surveyor Jones cut a track to Mt La Perouse.
1890	W Brown, Conservator of Forests, with Schnell & Eyre, went from Picton via the Old River to Port Davey.
1890	Surveyor Frodsham marked route from Tyenna River around southern end of Mueller Range and down Weld River to Huon. Schnell cut a track on the north side of Huon River to Mt Anne and the Weld.
1891	Whaler *Waterwitch* in Port Davey — valuable find of ambergris. Whaling industry all but finished.
1891	Lark MacQuarie found tin at Cox Bight.
1894	Cullen & Cawthorne marked track from near Tim Shea to the Serpentine River, through gap in the Franklands & on to west coast.

1895	Establishment of village settlement at Southport for unemployed labourers and families.
1896	E G Innes followed Cullen & Cawthorne's route from Mt Humboldt (Mt Field West) to Rookery Plains, thence north to the head of navigable waters on the Gordon — named Olga River on the way. H M Nicholls, geologist, photographed Lake Pedder on return journey. Party was out for over 12 weeks.
1898	E A Marsden cut track from Port Davey to link up with South Gordon track north of Mt Bowes.
1898	Osborne Geeves cut track from Hartz Mountains to Cracroft River.
1901	T B Moore cut track to Port Davey from Lune River via Old River, giving name 'Federation Peak' to Sprent's 'Obelisk'.
1905	Richard Geeves followed his father's 1898 route, then across South Cracroft to east side of Federation Peak, to Lake Geeves, on to connect with Moore's Old River Route.
1906	Twelvetrees made geological survey of Cox Bight.
1912	Geologist Hartwell Condor cut track from Double Cove on Macquarie Harbour to Spero River. This route was later extended to Port Davey.
1915	Scenery Preservation Act 1915.
1916	Mt Field National Park proclaimed: 10,927 ha.
1919	Hastings Caves Scenic Reserve proclaimed. Mt Field National Park extended by 4,650 ha.
1920	Forestry Act 1920.
1922	South-West Expeditionary walk to Port Davey.
1925	Town of Adamsfield founded on the osmiridium fields. (Population reached 2,000.)
1926	Tin discovered at the Ray River.
1928	Animals and Birds Protection Act 1928.
1929	Mining Act 1929.
1929	First ascent Mt Anne claimed by G T F Chapman & W Crookall.
1932	Florentine Valley Paper Industry Act 1932.
1933	Passenger ship *Zealandia* took large party of tourists to Port Davey.
1934	Discovery of payable gold at the Jane River.
1935	Bill Adams found tin at Melaleuca.
1939	Gordon River Scenic Reserve proclaimed: 4,822 ha.
1939	Lyell Highway Scenic Reserve proclaimed: 7,284 ha.
1941	Frenchmans Cap National Park proclaimed: 13,000 ha.
1941	Australian Newsprint Mills began operations at Boyer.
1941	Charles King took over the Melaleuca tin lease.
1946	Tasmanian Caverneering Club formed — surveyed and explored caves in Hastings & Lune areas.
1947	First air-drop in South-West — not recovered.
1947	Feasible route up Federation Peak found — near-successful attempt at summit by Luckman & Jackson.
1947	The commencement of an on-going programme of forestry road construction in the Southern Forests; introduction of aerial survey, photo interpretation and mapping.
1949	Summit of Federation Peak reached by members of Geelong College Exploration Society under John Bèchervaise.
1950	The National Park and Florentine Valley Act revoked western, forested section of Mt Field National Park and substituted other area. Total area reduced to 15,860 ha.
1951	Port Davey Foreshore Scenic Reserve proclaimed: 17 ha.
1951	Hartz Mountains National Park proclaimed: 9,308 ha.
1951	Frenchmans Cap National Park extension to 10,214 ha. (Recalculated 1978 — 13,000 ha.)
1952	Hartz Mountains National Park revocation of 405 ha.
1954	Forestry Act 1954.
1954	Sarah and Grummet Is. Scenic Reserve proclaimed: 6 ha. (This became an Historic Site in 1971.)
1955	Lake Pedder National Park proclaimed: 23,880 ha.
1956	HEC commenced major field work in the South-West.
1956	Denis King completed a landing strip for light aircraft at Melaleuca.
1958	Hartz Mts National Park revocation: 283 ha. revoked. (Area in 1978 — 8,620 ha.)
1958	Olegas Truchanas canoed the Gordon River from Lake Pedder to Strahan.
1962	Port Davey Foreshore & Islands Scenic Reserve proclaimed: 82 ha. added bringing total to 628 ha.
1962	South-West Committee formed (a non-government body of conservation-conscious representatives of various walking clubs and associations) — a response to growing desire for protection of all the South-West; and concern for shooting of fauna, the plight of abandoned hunting dogs, and rumours of HEC plans.
1963	Commonwealth granted $5 million for a road into the Gordon area.
1965	South-West Committee became aware of unannounced plans held by the HEC for the flooding of Lake Pedder.
1965	Inter-departmental Committee formed by Government, consisting of HEC, Forestry, Mines and Lands and Surveys Departments representatives. South-West Committee representation refused.
1965	Proposals for the flooding of Lake Pedder outlined by the Premier. Details not made available. Road works well advanced.

1966	South-West Fauna District (Conservation Area) proclaimed: 647,520 ha.
1966	Approach made to Federal Parliament for $47 million for the Gordon Scheme. The granting of this sum was not announced until the day that the middle Gordon scheme received parliamentary approval.
1966	South-West Committee's criticism of the Gordon Scheme circulated.
1967	This year ranks as one of the five major fire years on record for the Huon-Esperence region. The others were 1881, 1898, 1914 and 1934. The extensive fires stimulated concern for a policy of fire prevention and management in the South-West. The Rural Fires Board employed an officer for the South-West region in 1968.
1967	Save Lake Pedder National Park Committee formed.
1967	The middle Gordon scheme tabled in Parliament and details made public.
1967 (June)	Gordon River road opened and found to fit exactly into the only just-publicised plan for the middle Gordon scheme.
1967 (June)	Petition disapproving of scheme circulated and 8,500 signatures obtained. Petition not mentioned in Parliament.
1967 (July)	Select Committee set up by the Legislative Council to receive evidence concerning the Gordon scheme. By this time large sums of money had been spent on the scheme.
1967 (Aug)	Select Committee Report, approving the Gordon scheme, tabled.
1967	A combined survey by the Tasmanian and Queen Victoria Museums on the Lake Pedder wildlife.
1968	Lake Pedder National Park extension: 191,625 ha. (South-West National Park). The boundaries excluded some areas of the South-West, namely: (a) area at Port Davey and New River Lagoon (mining proposals) (b) area east of New River Lagoon — (forestry proposals) (c) large area of Davey River — (HEC interests).
1969	South-West National Park: revocation of 36 ha.
1970	Truchanas Nature Reserve declared: 406 ha.
1970	Dissolution of Scenery Preservation Board and Animals and Birds Protection Board.
1971	National Parks & Wildlife Service established. ('Scenic' Reserves become 'State' Reserves.)
1971	'Pedder Pilgrimage' Public meeting in Hobart organized — motion for a referendum on Lake Pedder defeated in Legislative Council by a 14–3 vote.
1971	Lake Pedder Action Committee formed.
1971	Premier Bethune bluntly refused any reconsideration of the issues at stake, despite changing environmental attitudes and failing industrial attractions.
1971	Mineral Holdings (Australia) Pty Ltd applied for a special prospector's licence for an area at Precipitous Bluff.
1971 (Nov)	Symposium on Lake Pedder at Hobart Town Hall.
1972 (March)	Public meeting at Hobart Town Hall at which the United Tasmania Group was formed to contest the election following collapse of Liberal Government. Conservation became a prominent election issue.
1972	Winter rains filled Lake Pedder, and the beach and environs were inundated during the closing months of 1972.
1972 (May)	LPAC, now a national organisation, continued its campaign to obtain an inquiry into the Gordon Scheme.
1973	Federal Committee of Inquiry, appointed in February to study Lake Pedder case, recommended a moratorium and an assessment of the feasibility of restoration of the lake. The Federal Government made an offer of $8 million to the State Government to this end, but Premier Eric Reece flatly refused to accept.
1973	National Estate Inquiry: discussion of the importance of the South-West for the National Estate.
1974	Gordon River State Reserve extension to 4,822 ha.
1974	Flooding of Lake Pedder completed forming the Huon-Serpentine Impoundment (ironically called 'Lake Pedder' by the HEC).
1974 (Nov)	Gordon dam completed.
1975	South-West Tasmania Action Committee became an active force with branches in several states.
1976	Tasmanian Government South-West Advisory Committee commenced Inquiry.
1976	Preliminary Report of the South-West Advisory Committee circulated; over 120 submissions made available.
1976	Tasmanian Wilderness Society founded.
1976	Federal grant of $75,000, for investigation of resources in the South-West, announced.
1976	Junee Cave State Reserve proclaimed: 20 ha.
1976	Major extensions to the Southwest National Park increased the protected area to 403,240 ha.
1976	Revocation of 2,150 ha. of Hartz Mts National Park passed second reading in the House of Assembly. The same Bill proposed the inclusion of Precipitous Bluff within the boundary of the enlarged South-West National Park as a condition of the revocation.
1977	Gordon storage within 10 feet of capacity.
1977	Lower Picton River bridged facilitating forestry operations westward along the south bank of the Huon River. Logging roads extended in the Weld, Picton and Huon river valleys and behind the south coast.
1977 (Nov)	Gordon Stage 1 power station operative.
1977	The total expenditure by the HEC on investigations in the King, Franklin, Lower Gordon and Davey rivers approximated 6 million dollars. The public continued to voice opposition to HEC tactics.
1978	The Franklin — Lower Gordon campaign became a prime focus of both the Australian Conservation Foundation and the Tasmanian Wilderness Society.
1978 (Sept)	The South West Advisory Committee Report was released, recommending the establishment of an independent South West Tasmania Authority.
1978 (Oct)	The Government announced that the HEC would be brought under direct ministerial control with the creation of a State Energy Advisory Council.

South-West Nomenclature

The following list of South-Western place names and their derivations is not a complete one. Of the explanations we could obtain we included the most interesting. Overall the list may give some insight into the historical sequence of discoveries in the region. It is certainly a record of man's presence in the South-West, both whiteman and aborigine.

Recent nomenclature in the areas of the Gordon and Pedder storages has been omitted. Questionable records have also been excluded.

The records of the Nomenclature Board, held in the Lands Department of Tasmania, provided a basis for the list; Jack Thwaites helped considerably with personal knowledge and informative references were found in the following publications:-

David Burn,	'The Overland Journey of Sir John and Lady Franklin to Macquarie Harbour in 1842', in G Mackanes (ed.), *Australian Historical Monographs* no.32 (1955).
R & K Gowlland	*Trampled Wilderness* (Devonport, 1975).
Harry O'May	*Wrecks in Tasmanian Waters* 3rd edn. (Hobart, 1971).
N J B Plomley	*Friendly Mission: The Tasmanian Journals and Papers of George Augustus Robinson 1829–1834* (Hobart, 1966).
Hobart Walking Club	*Tasmanian Tramp* (various issues).

ABEL PEAK
(South of the Jane River, western Tasmania)

Named by F Blake after Charles Abel, a piner of Strahan respected for his pioneering skill that took him for months at a time up many tributaries of the Gordon and Franklin rivers after stands of Huon pine.

ACACIA ROCKS
(west coast)

The 200 ton barque *Acacia* was wrecked in the vicinity about 22nd June, 1904. (See O'May, pp.126, 134.)

ACHERON RIVER
(a tributary of the Jane River)

Named by James Calder in 1840. *(achos*, alas) In Greek mythology the Acheron is one of the rivers of the Underworld. To enter the Underworld the dead had to cross Acheron on Charon's ferry-boat. Subsequently the name Acheron came to be applied to the Underworld as a whole.

ADAMSONS PEAK
(between Hartz Peak and Mt La Perouse)

Named by Captain John Hayes in 1794.

ALBINA CREEK, ALBINA ROCK
(north of Point Hibbs, west coast)

Albina was the name given to the depot on the track from Double Cove to the Spero River.

ALEC RIVULET
(flows into Mulcahy Bay, west coast)

Officially named by E A Counsel in 1919 after the Minister for Lands, the Hon. Alec Hean.

ALFHILD BIGHT, ALFHILD REEF
(north of Port Davey)

In October 1907 the 1,145 ton barque *Alfhild* reached Port Davey in bad weather. She was bound for Hobart from Rio in ballast, and was short of sail and provisions. She was driven into rocks just north of Port Davey and soon broken up by the storm. A number of hands got ashore and several days later 6 of the survivors rowed to Maatsuyker Island light station in a 14 foot punt. A search party sent back to the wreck was too late to save the men who had remained behind. (See O'May, pp.139–142.)

ALGONKIAN MOUNTAIN
(north of Prince of Wales Range)

Named by L K Ward, Assistant Govt. Geologist (1807–12), because the mountain is largely composed of Upper Precambrian (or Algonkian) sediments. **ALGONKIAN RIVULET** was named by F Blake in 1936.

ANCHORAGE COVE
(Louisa Bay, south coast)

The only safe anchorage in Louisa Bay.

ANGEL CLIFFS
(Gordon River)

Named by a piner, Archie Ware in early 1930's because of the likeness of a feature on the cliffs to an angel with outstretched wings.

MOUNT ANNE

Named in 1835 by Surveyor-General Frankland during his exploration of the country between Lake St Clair and the upper reaches of the Huon River. (See *Tasmanian Tramp* no.12, (1955) p.54.) Alternative explanation for the Anne River? :- Named by J E Calder after George Frankland's wife. Spelt on Frankland's map of 1837 'Ann'. (Records of the Nomenclature Board, Hobart.)

ARTHUR RANGES

Named by George Augustus Robinson in 1830, in honour of Governor George Arthur. According to Robinson, the country around the Arthur mountains was known as LORE.PUR.RER. LEE.VER.LER by the Aborigines, and the range was called LOIN.NE.KUM.ME.

In 1946 Ron Smith sketched the Western Arthurs from Mt Picton listing the peaks with a numerical and alphabetical system. In 1965 when the Nomenclature Board advised that such a system was unacceptable, Tim Christie, camped high in the Arthurs, conceived the idea to name the Western Arthurs after the stars, constellations and planets of the night sky.

The following passage, from an article in *Tasmanian Tramp* no.18, (1968) pp.25–29, explains the nomenclature of the lakes and peaks.

'*The eastern and western extremities of the range were called Lucifer and Hesperus after the Morning and Evening Stars. The most conspicuous peak in the range, Peak H, was called Mt Sirius after the brightest star, and Canopus, the second brightest star, gave its name to Peak K, another prominent mountain further along the range. Two of the most striking southern constellations, Orion and Scorpio, gave their names to peaks in areas where the ridge topography bore a striking resemblance to the star configuration. Peak 20, with its pointed profile and its long north ridge thrusting out into the plains, became Dorado the Swordfish. So the system developed.*

While the mountains were, in general, named after bright stars and constellations, it was decided to name the main lake systems after the planets and their satellites, and the remaining smaller lakes after the asteroids. In any interconnected lake system, therefore, the central or largest lake was called after a planet and the surrounding lakes by its satellites. Thus, for example, we have the lake Neptune, after the sea-king, flanked by its two satellites, Nereid the sea-nymph and Triton the minor sea-god, and the lake Uranus surrounded by its satellites Miranda, Titania, Ariel and Oberon. It was arranged that the lakes bear the same relative positions in the range as their planets do in the solar system, and a walker traversing from west to east would pass each "planet" from Pluto to Mercury in correct sequence.

It was decided that names should be dignified, euphonious and as much in harmony with their respective features as possible. For the rough section of Beggary Bumps harsh names were chosen like Shaula, Ganymede, Taurus and Draco (later changed to The Dragon by the Board).'

ARVE RIVER
(a tributary of the Huon River)

Named by Surveyor Frankland after a river in France and Switzerland.

BAGOTA FALLS
(east of the Franklin River)

Named by Lady Franklin in honour of George Bagot, aide-de-camp to Sir John Franklin, en route to the Franklin River in 1842. Described in David Burn's account of the overland journey, 1842

BARRON PASS
(near Frenchmans Cap)

Named after Sir H Barron or Lady Barron.

BATHURST HARBOUR

The eastern arm of Port Davey was named by James Kelly in 1815 'in honour of Lord Bathurst, Secretary of State for the colonies'. **BATHURST CHANNEL** was called MAN.WONE.ER by the Aborigines.

BAYLEE CREEK
(Macquarie Harbour)

Named after the Commandant of Sarah Island, 1831–1833.

BEWSHER SADDLE, SECOMB SCARP, RYMER CREEK

Named after Bill Bewsher and his two companions who made the first trip from Mt Wylly to Mt Bobs in 1951.

BIG CAROLINE ROCK
(outer Port Davey)

Direction Island (Scott, 1830); Sugarloaf Rock (Frankland, 1837). Called Great Caroline by whalers, according to David Burn in 1842.

BILL NEILSON CAVE
(Nicholls Range Limestone, Gordon River)

Named after the Premier of Tasmania, 1977, in that year.

BINGHAM ARCH
(Franklin River, upstream of Verandah Cliffs)

Named after the Leader of the Opposition Liberal Party, Max Bingham, in 1977.

BIRCHS INLET
(Macquarie Harbour)

Named after Thomas William Birch of Hobart Town by Captain James Kelly. Dr T W Birch financed Kelly's voyage.

MOUNT BISDEE
(Southern Ranges)

John Hutton Bisdee, (later Lieut Colonel), Tasmanian Imperial Bushmen 1869-1930. In 1900 he won a Victoria Cross in Transvaal.

MOUNT BOBS
(south of Mt Picton)

Named by T B Moore after Lord Roberts (nick-named Bobs), hero of the Boer War.

BONDS CRAIG
(Denison Range)

Named after Ernie Bond of Gordonvale, who lived in the Rasselas from the early 1930's to 1952.

BRAMBLE COVE
(Port Davey)

Named after Royal Navy ship *Bramble* used to chart Port Davey in 1851.

BRIER HOLME HEAD
(west coast)

The barque *Brier Holme* was wrecked in 1905 about 13 miles north of Port Davey. Oscar Larsen, the sole survivor, wandered around Port Davey for 3½ months, living off provisions washed ashore from the wreck. (See O'May pp.127-133.)

BRIGGS CREEK
(Macquarie Harbour)

Named after Commandant of Sarah Island, 1829-1831.

MOUNT BROCK
(Melaleuca area)

Eric Brock worked the Melaleuca tin leases from 1938-1940.

BUBS HILL
(north-west of the Raglan Range, south of Lyell Hwy.)

The name was first recorded on a map of 1908 by L K Ward, Assistant Govt Geologist. Probably named by prospectors in the area before 1900 because of its resemblance to a woman's breast.

BUCKIES BONNET
(west of The Coronets)

Named after Harry Buckie the artist, a member of the first party to land on Lake Pedder beach in 1947.

BUTLER CREEK, BUTLER ISLAND
(Macquarie Harbour, Gordon River)

'Ten miles above Expectation Reach ... the channel is divided by "Butlers Island", a small, rocky, copsy islet, called after the late Major Butler, of the 40th Regiment, Commandant at Macquarie Harbour in 1826 and other years'. (David Burn, 1842). Butler Creek named after the same person.

CALDER FERRY
(lower Franklin River)

Named after James Calder, 'road-maker, surveyor and guide' to Sir John Franklin in 1842. (David Burn, 1842.) Calder designed a pine raft to ferry the party across the Franklin River.

CALDER PASS
(near Frenchmans Cap)

Named by Sir John Franklin in tribute to James Calder who cut his track to the Gordon River through the pass which connects the Loddon Plains with Lightning Plains: '... that wild pass — a passage we now traversed in a sludge ankle-deep with slippery mud, rendered diluent with snow and rain. The ascent was effected after thirty-two minutes of toilsome exertion'. (David Burn, 1842.)

MOUNT CAWTHORN AND MOUNT CULLEN
(south of Pedder storage)

Named after Edwin Cawthorn who, with Cullen, cut tracks in the area in the 1890's.

LAKES CECILY, GERTRUDE, GWENDOLEN, NANCY AND MILLICENT
(in Frenchmans Cap National Park)

Named by Charles Whitham during the period 1896-1923 in imitation of T. B. Moore.

CHAMP CLIFF
(Gordon River)

These limestone cliffs on the Lower Gordon 'received the appellation "Champ Cliff" in honour of the Caveat Commissioner, who has done duty with his regiment (63rd) at Macquarie Harbour' (about 1829). (David Burn, 1842.)

MOUNT CHAPMAN
(South Picton Range)

G T F Chapman, a pioneer bushwalker, was one of the few to visit and appreciate the Picton Range in the 1920's and 1930's, when he and his friends were exploring the Mt Anne area and its various approaches. Also known as Abrotanella Rise.

CHINNERS LOOKOUT

Named after a forester from Victoria who inspected the Florentine Valley some years before A.N.M. began logging there.

CHRISTINA BROOK
(near Franklin River)

Named by Lady Franklin's female attendant, Stewart, in 1842.

CHRISTMAS ROCK
(Lightning Plains)

Calder and his party spent Christmas Day camping in this rock shelter in 1841. Its exact location is uncertain.

CLEAR HILL PLAIN
(between Clear Hill and the Thumbs)

Referred to as such in Twelvetrees Report of 1907-8.

CLYTEMNESTRA
(south of Frenchmans Cap)

Named by A Davern and party in 1933 after the daughter of Leda in Greek mythology.

CONDER RIVER
(tributary of Wanderer River, west coast)

Named after Hartwell Conder M A, State Mining Engineer who commenced a survey in 1912.

CONDOMINIUM CREEK
(Mt Anne)

Named in the early thirties by G T F Chapman, V C Smith and D Anderson. In naming the creek they were camped at, they were recording a political issue of the day. (Condominium — joint rule by two or more states.)

CONICAL MOUNTAIN
(east of the Spires range)

Name used by C Binks of the Launceston Walking Club in 1954.

CORONATION PEAK
(Frankland Range)

Proposed by J M Brown, Hobart Walking Club, in 1952. The name marks the coronation of Queen Elizabeth II.

MOUNT COUNSEL
(Bathurst Range)

E A Counsel was Tasmania's Surveyor-General from 1894-1924.

COX BIGHT
(south coast)

Named because Captain J H Cox anchored there in the brig *Mercury* while on his voyage of 1789. Aboriginal name KRIB.BIG.GER.RER.

CRACROFT RIVER
(a tributary of the Huon River)

Named by Surveyor-General George Frankland. The following is a quotation from a letter written by Frankland, dated 30th. May, 1836.
'...which I have named the River Cracroft in honour of Judge Cracroft of the Bengal Civil Service'.
William Cracroft arrived in Hobart Town on 4th. July, 1835 as a cabin passenger on board the *Africaine*, which had sailed from Bengal and the Isle of France. (Archives Office of Tasmania.)

CROTTY
(near Mt Jukes), west coast

James Crotty, an Irishman, was a skilled gold miner and entrepreneur. He celebrated his gold strike near Queenstown with a party which went on for 3 days. In 1891 he sold what he thought was a worthless gold mine to Bowes Kelly. The subsequent copper mine revealed one of the world's greatest deposits of that metal. (See Geoffrey Blainey's *The Peaks of Lyell*, 1967).

LAKE CURLY, MOUNT CURLY
(west of Denison Range)

Lake discovered by R Marriott, first known as Lake Amelia but approved as Lake Curly in 1953. This is the name given by W H Twelvetrees in 1908, describing the curly nature of the contorted schist.

CUTHBERTSON CREEK
(Macquarie Harbour)

Named after first Commandant of Sarah Island, 1821-22.

DALE GULCH

A gulch at the South-West Cape named after Sid Dale, a fisherman.

DAVERNS CAVERN
(near Frenchmans Cap)

Discovered by Douglas Anderson in 1932 and named after his friend Aubrey Davern with whom he was climbing Frenchmans Cap at the time. The cave sheltered them for four days of storm. This was the first ascent of the Cap after J E Philp, 1910.

DAWSONS ROAD

William Dawson surveyed a road from Repulse Station to the Florentine River, extending in the direction of the Gordon, 1850's.

DEADMANS BAY
(south coast)

'Franklin
17th. October, 1885
I come next to Dead Man's Bay which is a very small nook, taking its name from the fact of my finding on the shore a dead man, evidently starved to death and had been dead about 3 weeks. I first thought he had been some castaway from a wreck, but heard after he was one of 4 who bolted from *Briton's Queen* Whaler at Port Davey. One only succeeded in reaching 'Recherche' in a starved condition. I was weather bound in this little place for 3 weeks, and made diligent search for any other of the supposed shipwrecked crew, without success.'
(Part of a letter from Charles A Glover to C P Sprent, Deputy Surveyor-General, concerning the naming of this feature on the South Coast. See *Tasmanian Tramp* no. 15, [1961], p.26.)

DECEPTION RANGE
(south of Frenchmans Cap)

Named by Surveyor J E Calder in 1840. He made several attempts to cross the Franklin River in this region, finally avoiding what was subsequently called Deception Gorge (and changed to 'Great Ravine') by crossing the river downstream: 'I tried to lead the road across at several points, but was thwarted by the intervention of a tremendous ravine. I called these hills collectively Deception Range, from the frequency with which I was foiled, or deceived in my attempts...' See J E Calder: 'Some account of the Country between Lake St Clair and Macquarie Harbour'. (*Tasmanian Journal of Natural Science* vol. 3, no. 6., 1849.)

DENISON RIVER
(tributary of the Gordon)

Named after Lieut Governor Sir W T Denison (1847-55) probably by James Sprent.

DETENTION CORNER
(Calder Pass)

'In honest truth it was a most detestable spot; and might most appropriately have been styled, "The Nook of the Dismal Swamp"'. (David Burn, 1842.)

DE WITT ISLAND
(off south coast)

Named by Tasman after a member of the East India Company Council. Known to fishermen as the 'Big Witch'.

DOHERTYS GROUND

Doherty was cutting Huon pine at Port Davey in 1849 and for many years afterwards in the headwaters of the Davey River. The piners observed a code of honour not to cut within a certain distance of each other. A creek or flood channel was usually the centre line of each property cut over. This practice gave rise to the names, Longleys Ground and Dohertys Ground.

EAGLE CREEK

Named because of a large eagle's nest near the creek's junction with the Gordon and known as such for a long time by local piners.

EAGLE CREEK TRACK

Originally cut by the Forestry Department in 1932, it was recut in Reg Morrison in 1938. He has always referred to it as the Franklin Track whereas H.E.C. Hydrologists refer to it as the Flat Island Track.

ELEANOR FERRY

When the Franklin party was held up by the flooded Franklin River on the expedition of 1842, they built a double canoe to make a crossing. This was named 'Eleanor Isabella' after Sir John's daughter and the name was carved and fastened to the stern. Thomas Stynes, one of the convicts, built the canoe. The name 'Eleanor Ferry' was carved on a large myrtle near the spot.

ELLIOT HILL / RANGE
(near lower reaches of the Gordon River)

Named by Sir John Franklin in 1842 ... 'in compliment to the Hon. Mr Henry Elliott, His Excellency's former Aide-de-Camp'. (David Burn, 1842.)

ENDEAVOUR BAY
(south of Point Hibbs)

Name suggested by D A Smith after Commonwealth Fisheries Trawler.

EREBUS RIVER
(tributary of Jane River)

Named in 1933 from Greek mythology. Erebus is the darkness below the depths of Hades; in general, the abode of the dead.

EXPECTATION REACH

On the Gordon River, so called by Lady Franklin. The schooner *Breeze* had awaited the Franklin party there and fortunately stayed two weeks longer than arranged before transporting the party back to Hobart Town.

FARM COVE
(near mouth of the Gordon River)

Called Farm Bay by Lempriere in 1839.

FATIGUE HILL

The eastern slope of Mt Arrowsmith, up which Calder had cut his track for the Franklin expedition. This was recut in the 1870's and became known as the Linda Track.

FEDERATION PEAK

Named by Moore in 1901 in year of federation of the Australian States. First ascent by John Béchervaise and party, January, 1949. Sprent sighted Federation from Mt Wellington, also from Mt Picton, during his trigonometrical survey of Tasmania and referred to it as 'The Obelisk'.

THE FLAME
(prominent rock face in the Spires Range)

Name used by D Pinkard in 1956 following his trip from the Jane River to Gordonvale prior to that year.

MOUNT FIELD EAST / WEST

Judge Barron Field, a London barrister took up an appointment as Judge of the Supreme Court in New South Wales and visited Hobart in 1819 and 1821. Surveyor Sprent referred to the western arm of the Field massif as Field West — a name which outlasted the name 'Humboldt'.

FLAT ISLAND

An island on the Franklin River. It is used as a helicopter landing site by the H.E.C.

FLORENTINE VALLEY / RIVER

Named by Frankland in 1835 presumably after the Florentine Valley in Italy.

FLORENTINE PEAK

Originally known as 'Pimply' but later given name of the river valley which it overlooks.

THE FONT
(Spires Range)

Name proposed by J B Thwaites, 1970.

FOUSCHA CREEK

Frank Fouscha was the French seaman who cut timber in this area of the Lower Gordon and later further upstream. He and two other piners, Steadman and Peck, were drowned when their boat capsized in the Franklin in about 1896. Steadman's was the only body recovered. Charles Abel said the stream was commonly known as Foucha Creek.

FRANKLAND RANGE
(west of Pedder storage)

Surveyor-General George Frankland, 1830's.

FRANKLIN RIVER
(major tributary of the Gordon)

— after Governor Sir John Franklin. 'A large and furious torrent flows through it (the Great Ravine), which, collecting all the water that falls on a wide extent of mountainous country, emerges from the glen a large and beautiful river. I called it the Franklin.' — James Erskine Calder, 1840.
Many features of the river remain unnamed, but the following were named by Paul Smith and Bob Brown who first travelled down the river in 1976:
i) The five reaches of the Great Ravine — Inception, Serenity, Transcendence, The Sanctum, Deliverance.
ii) The four rapids separating these reaches — The Churn, Coruscades, Thunderush and the Cauldron.
iii) Two crags on the Ravine's west bank — Oriel Rock and The Belfry.
iv) Three notable features — Livingston Cut at the end of the Livingston Rivulet; and The Masterpiece and The Mousehole in Deliverance Reach.

GREAT RAVINE (the central Franklin River gorge)
Formerly known as Deception Gorge this name comes from James Calder's description in 1840: 'The great ravine, which bounds Deception Range to the westward, is very deep; I dare say 2,000 feet...' Calder was cutting the track for Governor Franklin's expedition which followed in 1842. He had sent ex-convict Alexander McKay and his two convict assistants ahead, and it was they who made the first sighting of the Ravine.

INCEPTION (REACH). The first of the major reaches of the Great Ravine.
SERENITY SOUND. The second of the major reaches — a broad stretch of water deep in the Ravine.
TRANSCENDENCE (REACH). The third and longest reach; the heart of the Ravine and a peaceful, arresting place.
THE SANCTUM. Fourth of the Great Ravine's reaches: quiet waters between the most noisome rapids.
DELIVERANCE (REACH). The fifth and last major reach; named from the relief at having negotiated the Ravine.
THE CHURN (in Great Ravine, central Franklin River). The first of four major rapids — through great boulder blocks (butter shaped).
CORUSCADES (in Great Ravine, central Franklin River). The second rapids of the Ravine (from coruscate — flash, sparkle/cascades).
THUNDERUSH (Great Ravine). The third of the major Great Ravine rapids — thunderous, between vertical rock walls; including a 3 metres falls.
THE CAULDRON (in Great Ravine). Fourth Great Ravine rapid. Here Koolhof in Dec. 1970, leapt from his raft into the raging torrent.
ORIEL ROCK. A crag that dominates Inception Reach. (Oriel — projecting upper storey window.)
THE BELFRY. Dominates the Coruscades — a crag overlooking the Great Ravine.
THE MASTERPIECE. Bronzed monolith in the Great Ravine, similar to a Henry Moore sculpture.
THE MOUSEHOLE. In the Great Ravine, where a tributary waterfall joins the Franklin via a recess in the rock wall, with a cat-like boulder set above it.
LIVINGSTON GORGE (Gorge on Livingston Rivulet). Referred to as such by John Dean and John Hawkins (1959).
LIVINGSTON CUT. A deep cut with overhanging cliffs where Livingston Gorge joins the Great Ravine.
PROPSTING GORGE. East of Mt Propsting, this is where the Franklin River flows south from the Great Ravine.
GLEN CALDER. This is the last gorge before the river opens out: '...a large and furious torrent...emerges from the glen a large and beautiful river.' (From James Calder's 1841 description.)
THE CRANKLE. The large 'hairpin' Franklin bend. Crankle means 'a bend' or 'twisting'.
PUDDING BOWL GORGE. A small gorge just above 'The Crankle' on the Franklin. Named after a large impressed rockface resembling a stirred pudding in a bowl.
IRENABYSS (Greek: eirene — peace/abyss). A spectacular chasm with 80 m. vertical walls and smooth narrow stretch of water 20 m. deep, on the middle Franklin; above Mt Fincham.
BLUSHROCK FALLS. The longest of the Franklin River's many tributary waterfalls — 100 m. It flows over pink rocks to join the river not far above the Great Ravine.
DOMINO GORGE. A small gorge; with domino-like boulders. (near Mt Fincham.)
THE SLUICE (in the Great Ravine). The last of the Thunderush Rapid.
THE DEVILS WHIRLPOOL (middle Franklin). A small but dangerous eddy, of concern to the punting piners below the Great Ravine.

FRASER CAVE
(lower Franklin)

Named in 1977 after the Australian Prime Minister of the day.

FRENCHMANS CAP

Aboriginal name — TOIN.DY, TRUL.LEN.NUER, MEBBELEK. A note in *The Voyage of the Caroline* by Rosalie Hare and Ida Lee says that it was named by Vancouver who described it from the sea when passing round Tasmania on his way to New Zealand in 1791.

FRODSHAMS GAP / PASS
(between Tim Shea and Wherrett's Lookout, Gordon road)

Thomas Frodsham, surveyor, made the first recorded attempt to find a road route across the South-West in 1878. His track stopped abruptly after crossing the Pokana River. In 1890 he explored the possibility of a road from the Florentine Valley to the Huon. (Gowlland, pp. 69–94.)

GALLAGHER PLATEAU
(south of Mt Anne)

Named after a companion of Judd and Clark who explored this area late last century. Named by V C Smith, L Giblin, A V Giblin and H Hutchison in 1921.

GARDEN POINT
(Macquarie Harbour)

Named by James Kelly in 1815. 'We cleared away about two Rods of Rich Ground, and sowed a quantity of Garden Seeds'. It was mentioned as 'the low woody land called Garden Point (which) presented its sequestered shores ...' in David Burn's account of Sir John Franklin's visit in 1842.

LAKE GEEVES / GEEVES BLUFF — The pioneering Geeves family of the Huon visited this area in the 1890's.

GIBLIN RIVER / MOUNT
(west coast) — W F Giblin was a prominent figure and Tasmanian premier in the mid-nineteenth century.

GLASSWORM TARN — This name was suggested by Dr P A Tyler of the Botany Department, University of Tasmania, for the lake above Lake Riveaux on the Picton Range. The tarn had a dense population of *Chaoborus* glassworm-larvae when sampled.

GLEICHENIA CREEK
(on the slopes of Mt Alexandria, Hastings area) — Named by R N Smith because of unique masses of fine-leaf fern growing here to a height of about 5 feet, and not seen by him anywhere else.

GLOW WORM FOREST
(near Franchmans Cap) — Named by Sir John Franklin in the course of his expedition to Macquarie Harbour in 1842. In his account, David Burn describes it as a 'dense, dank, unblest wood of live, dead and fallen myrtle and sassafras trees, their trunks and limbs strewed and inter-twisted with the most regular irregularity, forming a complication of entanglements, to which the famous Gordion Knot was simplicity itself'.

GOODWIN PEAK / GOODWINS CREEK
(near confluence of Gordon and Franklin rivers) — Named after a convict, James Goodwin, who escaped from a timber gang at Macquarie Harbour in 1828 and walked east to settled districts via Wylds Craig and the Valley of Rasselas.

GOON MOOR
(Eastern Arthurs) — Roy Goon, piloting a D H Dragonfly made the first food drop on the moor in December, 1948 for the Hobart Walking Club party's attempt to climb Federation Peak, at that date unclimbed.

GORDON RIVER — Discovered by Captain James Kelly in 1815. According to James Fenton, Kelly named it after Mr James Gordon a settler of Pittwater. Mr Gordon had lent Kelly the whaleboat in which he undertook the circumnavigation of Tasmania.

GORMANSTON
(mining town on Lyell Highway) — Named after Viscount Gormanston, Governor from 1893–1900.

GRINDSTONE CREEK — A large grindstone, lying beside the Huon Track to Cracroft, marked the spot where the track cutter, Dawson, who was carrying it, died. He put it down on the slope while he rested and it rolled down and killed him.

GROTTO CREEK
(near New River) — A grotto was found here in the 1880's containing aboriginal skeletons.

GROWLING SWALLET
(Florentine Valley) — One of the deepest caves in Australia; so named because of the rumbling noise made by the river which disappears into it.

GUELPH RIVER
(flows into Lake King William) — Florence was the centre of the struggle between the 'Guelphs' and the 'Ghibellines' in the 13th and 14th centuries (Grolier). Mentioned in Surveyor Frankland's report.

GUM RIDGE
(north-west of Prince of Wales Range) — Named by F Blake, 1936.

HANGING LAKE — An elevated lake approximately half a mile south-west of the summit of Federation Peak. Elevation approx. 1,000 m on quartz ridge.

HARRISONS OPENING
(upper Huon) — Mentioned in Parliamentary Papers by E A Counsel, 1881.

HEATHERS CREEK POINT
(Port Davey) — The Heathers were a prominent family in the timber business at Catamaran. The Heathers were probably the last family to cut Huon pine from the Davey River in Port Davey.

POINT HIBBS
(west coast) — Aboriginal names — MOON.DRIM.ER, NIB.LIN. Named after the captain of Flinder's cutter *Norfolk* by his navigator in 1798. Name appears on Charles Sprent's map, 1879.

HONEY SMITH HILL
(near South Cape Bay) — In the early part of this century one Herbert 'Honey' Smith of Recherche gained quite a reputation for his leatherwood honey, much of which was gathered from hives in the vicinity of this hill.

MOUNT HOPETOUN
(near Federation Peak) — Named by T B Moore after first Australian Governor-General (Rt.Hon. Earl of Hopetoun). (See *Tasmanian Tramp*, 1951, p.30.)

HUON RIVER — Aboriginal name — TAL.LOON.NE. Discovered and first chartered by the French Admiral d'Entrecasteaux in 1792 and named by him after Captain Huon Kermadec, his second in command. In 1794 Capt. John Hayes named the river Adamson's Harbour unaware of the Frenchman's visit.

JANE RIVER
(a tributary of the Franklin River) — Named by J E Calder in 1840 at its confluence with the Franklin, in honour of the Governor's wife, 'our indefatigable fellow-traveller, the amiable and admirable partner of our worthy Governor' (David Burn, 1842). The headwaters were called Henslow River by Sir John Franklin in 1842, undoubtedly in ignorance. The Jane appears on a sketch map of 1895 as 'Pine River South'.
Because of the magnificence and restless character of the three remote gorges of the Jane they have recently been named after characters from *The Epic of Gilgamesh*. The river and its gorges evoked thoughts of this ancient Sumerian epic for Helen Gee on a journey down river in 1976:

(GORGE OF) GILGAMESH (downstream of the Acheron River.) The middle gorge was named, because of its beauty and restlessness, after the hero of the epic. Gilgamesh lived and reigned in the ancient Sumerian town of Uruk. In search of immortality and an enduring name he set out on a journey to the 'Cedar Forest' that lay on the outer bounds of earth and reality.
ENKIDUS GORGE (upstream of the Algonkian Rivulet.) In the upper reaches, this gorge is still remote. The young river moves swiftly beneath towering cliff faces. Enkidu was reared in the wilderness, innocent of mankind. He brought the news of the mysterious 'Cedar Forest' and its monstrous guardian, and accompanied Gilgamesh on his journey.
(GORGE OF) HUMBABA (3 km upstream of the Franklin River) Named after the Anatolian god 'Humbaba', the lower gorge is as wild and foreboding as this giant. But, like Gilgamesh, the early piners of Strahan overcame Humbaba, the guardian of the forest.

JETTY LAKE
(Frenchmans Cap National Park) — Named in 1936 by J B Thwaites and party, because of the prominent jetty-like rock formations.

JOE PAGE BAY
(Bathurst Channel, Port Davey) — A piner named Joe Page had an establishment on the Spring River. He was working there when James Reid Scott visited in 1875.

MOUNT KARAMU
(South West Cape Range) — In 1925 the Union Steamship Company's S.S. *Karamu* sank near the South West Cape during a trip from Strahan to Hobart with a load of calcines. When leaving Macquarie Harbour she had struck the bar, but no great concern was felt until she began to take in water in heavy weather further down the coast. A rescue vessel was able to save all hands. (O'May, pp. 158–160.)

KELLATIE CREEK
(Port Davey) — At entrance to Davey River on eastern side of Payne Bay. Aboriginal meaning, deep water.

KELLY BASIN
(Macquarie Harbour) — Named after Bowes Kelly, a genial 16 stone giant of Mt Lyell fame.

KATHLEEN ISLAND
(Port Davey) — 'The smaller one on the north side was styled Kathleen Isle; a title given by Lady Franklin, in compliment to the wife of the writer.' (David Burn, 1842.)

KINGS TOR
(north of Bathurst Harbour) — Named after the late Charles King of Port Davey who visited the tor on a number of occasions while prospecting. His ashes were scattered on the summit of this mountain.

KING WILLIAM RANGE
(south of Lyell Highway) — 'An extensive hilly range, its points broken into bare and sharply-scarped craggy peaks, caught our eye in the southern quarter In honour of the then reigning monarch, it received the appellation of "King William's Mount".' (David Burn, 1842.)

MOUNT KING WILLIAM I — Probably Frankland's 'Princess Victoria'. The range was referred to by Jorgenson as Mt Jubilee.

KOSTKA, CRIPPS AND GROOMBRIDGE POINTS
(Pedder storage) — John Kostka, Kenneth Gilbert Cripps, Christopher Raymond Groombridge, hydrographers with the H.E.C., all drowned in the original Lake Pedder on October 2nd, 1965.

KROANNA CREEK
(tributary of the Huon) — Aboriginal: 'to climb'.

MOUNT LA PEROUSE
(south coast) — Named after the noted French explorer who disappeared in 1788. 'In September 1788 two ships, the *Recherche* and the *Esperence*, sailed under the command of d'Entrecasteaux. However, not until 1827 did a British captain, Peter Dillon, find traces of the wrecked La Perouse expedition on the reefs of Vanikoro in the Solomon Islands.' (*The Mercury* 8–4–1972.)

LARSENS ROCKS
(west coast) — Oscar Larsen, sole survivor of the *Brier Holme* wrecked in 1904, had his photograph taken here after being found. (O'May, *Wrecks in Tasmanian Waters*, 1971, pp.127–137.)

LEANING TEATREE SADDLE
(between Pindars and Precipitous Bluff) — Named by B W Davis in 1961 because of 'the ghostly effect of leaning stunted paperbarks'.

MOUNT LEE
(southern end of D'Aguilar Range) — Named after Sir Walter Lee (Premier) by the Hon. Alec Hean (Minister for Lands) in 1920. Mt Discovery is on northern end, south of Macquarie Harbour.

MOUNT LEGGE
(north of Bathurst Harbour) — Name given by T B Moore in 1901, probably after Col. W V Legge.

MOUNT LEILLATEAH
(near Recherche Bay) — Aboriginal name for Recherche Bay, (Ling Roth). Named by W H Twelvetrees in 1915.

LAKE LEO — Named in 1947 by Ron Smith after Leo Luckman on their first trip to the Eastern Arthurs.

LEWIS RIVER
(west coast)

Originally Rocky Point or Low Rocky River. First appears on 1921 state map. The Hon. Sir Neil Elliott Lewis was elected to Parliament in 1886 and later became Premier.

LIBERTY POINT
(in Macquarie Harbour)

Named by James Kelly in 1815-16. Charles Abel says Kelly named it because he liberated some swans which he had brought from Port Davey.

LIGHTNING PLAINS
(south of Frenchmans Cap)

When Calder with his party of convicts were cutting the track for the Franklin expedition during the summer of 1840, they were trapped in a rock shelter by a bushfire started by lightning. The sudden downfall of heavy rain which followed saved their lives.

LIGHTNING RIDGE
(Mt Anne area)

Given because of jagged nature of ridge crest, similar to a flash of lightning.

LINDA
(Lyell Highway)

Charles Gould, early geologist and explorer, was responsible in 1862 for the name of the river from which that of the town was derived. 'Possibly Gould had in mind the recent opera, "Linda di Chamouni" composed by the Italian, Donizetti, when he named the stream'. (Geoffrey Blainey.)

LINDSAY HILL
(Bathurst Channel)

Mr W Lindsay thoroughly explored Port Davey during thirteen visits in small craft. Ila Bay and Clytie Cove (Bathurst Channel) are named after two of his yachts.

LION ROCK
(south coast)

W H Twelvetrees, 1915. Known as 'Lion Rock' because of likeness to a lion in repose.

LIVINGSTON RIVULET

The Hobart Walking Club named this rivulet that flows off the south-east face of Frenchmans Cap in 1951 after Ray Livingston whose efforts gained the proclamation of the Frenchmans Cap National Park in 1941.

MOUNT LLOYD JONES
(eastern end of Frankland Range)

Named after the pilot who did much to gain more interest in the South-West. He was the first to land a plane on the Lake Pedder beach in 1947.

LOAPARTE COVE
(Bathurst Harbour)

'Black' — Southern Tasmanian Aboriginal word.

LODDON RIVER
(near Frenchmans Cap)

Named by J E Calder in 1840. 'I called it the Loddon from a fancied resemblance to an English stream of that name. Unlike the majority of our rivers, it is not a brawling mountain torrent ... but has all the gentleness of the course of the English stream.'

LONELY TARNS
(Gallagher Plateau)

G T F Chapman, V C Smith and D Anderson named these tarns from 'A' to 'G' in the 1930's and they have been referred to collectively as the Lonely Tarns since then.

LOORANAH CREEK

Flowing into Tomalah Creek, a tributary of the Huon. Aboriginal for 'brushwood'.

MOUNT LOT / LOTS WIFE
(Mt Anne)

Named after the Biblical character whose wife was turned into a pillar of salt, by V C Smith, L Giblin, A V Giblin and H Hutchison on a trip to the area in 1920-21.

LOUISA BAY
(south coast)

Shown on Frankland's map 1837.

LOURAH ISLAND
(Port Davey)

In 1899 the 80 ton schooner *Lourah* sailed from Hobart for Strahan with a cargo of timber. She was forced to take shelter from a heavy south-west gale in Port Davey, but the captain mistook Hannant Inlet for the entrance to Bathurst Channel. The vessel was soon wrecked on the rocks in the inlet, but the crew got ashore in the ship's boat, and were later picked up by a fishing smack. (O'May, p.122.)

LOUSY BAY
(south coast)

A poor anchorage, sometimes confused with Deadman's Bay.

LUCAS CREEK
(Macquarie Harbour)

Named after first harbourmaster and pilot at Sarah Island.

LUCKMANS LEAD
(Eastern Arthurs)

Ridge used by Leo Luckman on Federation Peak attempt, 1947.

LUNE RIVER
(Catamaran)

Aboriginal word for woman.

MOUNT PICTON

Named by Frankland, presumably after Sir Thomas Picton, famous military leader 1758-1815.

MOUNT LYNE
(Deception Range south of Frenchmans Cap)

Named by T B Moore in 1903. Presumably 'Deception Peak' as shown on Frenchmans Cap map.

MAATSUYKER ISLAND
(south coast)

Named by Tasman in 1642. Thought to mean 'mountain of sugar' because of the profusion of white tea-tree flowers, but according to *The Journal of Abel Jansz Tasman, 1642* edited by G H Keniham (Adelaide: Heritage) p. 22, the islands off the south coast were named 'after the Hon. Councillors of India'. It is shown on an old chart by John Hayes in 1794 as one of the 'Three Brothers'.

MOUNT MACKENZIE
(Bathurst Channel)

Named after Lieutenant Commander K Mackenzie of HMAS *Geranium* in 1922.

MACQUARIE HARBOUR

Aboriginal names PARRALGONGATEK, MEEB.BER.LEE (Robinson). Discovered by Captain James Kelly in December, 1815, while on his circumnavigation of Tasmania. He named it after Governor Lachlan Macquarie.

MADONNA RIDGE
(Frankland Range)

Name submitted in 1954 by the Hobart Walking Club. Mr J Wythes had suggested the likeness to a mother and child from a certain direction.

MAINWARING RIVER
(west coast)

Aboriginal name: HONE.DIM.MER (?) The name first appears on James Sprent's map 1859; possibly it was named by him, after Major Fred Mainwaring who arrived in the Colony in 1839. He was the commander of a Regiment in Launceston and popular with colonists.

McPARTLANS PLAINS / PASS
(site of present McPartlans Canal)

Francis McPartlan (1824-1888) was a postman, policeman, prospector, piner, survey assistant, track cutter and bushman extraordinaire. McPartlan's South Gordon Track of 1882 started at Fitzgerald, traversed the Plains and continued through the Pass to the Gordon River. (Gowlland, p. 81.)

McPARTLANS BLUFF

The major bluff on northern side of Mt Bobs.

LAKE MARILYN
(Frenchmans Cap National Park)

This was the name used by Jim Peterson, a geomorphologist, in his honours thesis of 1960, a gesture of appreciation for services of an assistant.

MARSDEN RANGE

Edward A Marsden, track-cutter.

MOUNTS MAUD and MARY

T B Moore (?) 1887.

MAXWELL RIVER
(tributary of Denison River)

Named by E D B Innes, 3-4-1908.

MOUNT McCUTCHEON
(Franklin River area)

This northernmost hill of the Cracroft Hills was officially named in 1968 to honour the memory of James McCutcheon, contractor of Zeehan. He pioneered access to many areas of interest to the HEC and as a bulldozer driver was involved in the construction of the Franklin River road that now passes through the high saddle of Mt McCutcheon.

McKAYS PEAK / CREEK

Suggested by A R Love in 1962 after Alexander McKay, a convict who had worked with James Calder in the area. The peak was formerly called Conical Hill.

MEWSTONE ROCK
(off south coast)

Sighted and named by Tasman in 1642, because of a supposed resemblance to a lion's head.

MILFORD CREEK
(Prion Bay, south coast)

Milford Fletcher of Glen Huon has re-cut many tracks in the South-West, including the South Coast track.

MILLIGAN FALLS

Mr Joseph Milligan was the surgeon on the Franklin expedition of 1842. The falls are on their route to the Franklin River.

MODDER RIVER
(west coast)

Recorded as having been named by T B Moore in 1900 after the battle on the river by this name near Kimberley in South Africa on 28th November, 1899.

MOINEE RIDGE
(at Cox Bight)

An aboriginal legend refers to Moinee, a spirit and creator who came down from heaven. When he died he turned to stone, allegedly at Cox Bight.

MOORES GARDEN
(Southern Ranges)

Named by B Ford, for this long, high ridge between Moores Bridge and Alexandra (Arboretum) Ridge was referred to by T B Moore as the Garden of Tasmania because of its superb display of alpine plants.

MOORES LOOKOUT
(west of the Olga River)

T B Moore, botanist, geographer, geologist and bushman, constructed or routed several tracks in the South-West, notably from Birch Inlet to Settlement Point, routed in 1879, and the Old River in 1900-01. He spent many years in the service of the Mt Lyell Company during which time he was in charge of prospecting parties.

MULCHAY RIVER

Aboriginal name TOI.ME.NIN.NE.VUTH.ER A small stream on the West Coast, named in honour of the Hon. Edward Mulchay, who was in office at the time of its traverse.

MURPHYS BLUFF
(Frankland Range)

Said to be first climbed in 1953 by K E Lancaster and Sydney climber Jack Murphy who was killed in a mountaineering accident in New Zealand two years later.

NEILSON RIVER

Neilson was one of the earliest timber workers at the Spero River and travelled the coast between Birthday Bay and the Spero.

NEW RIVER / NEW RIVER LAGOON

Aboriginal name MARAWAYLEE (A place of shadows).

NICOLES NEEDLE
(Frenchmans Cap)

Named by Mac Urquhart after a French girl who visited Frenchmans Cap with Urquhart and party.

NOMEME CREEK
(west coast)

Nomeme was a native village located in the vicintiy of Nye Bay.

MT NOROLD
(north-east of Bathurst Harbour)

Supposedly named because of its location between the North and the Old rivers. Three features on the 'Norolds' were named by Tony Moscal in 1976:
LAKE EUCRYPHIA (north-west side of Mt Norold). Named because of the rare occurrence of *Eucryphia lucida* and *Eucryphia milliganii* on the foreshore of the lake.
LOMATIA FALLS (on western slope of Mt Norold). Because of the endemic scrub below the falls, on the perimeter of the rainforest.
RICHEA PEAK (the northern peak of the 'Norolds').

NORTH COL
(above Lake Tahune, Frenchmans Cap)

Named by A R Love in 1937.

NORWAY CREEK, NORWAY RANGE
(Jane River area)

Named after 'Freddy' Edwardsen, a Norwegion prospector, by F Blake in 1936.

NYE BAY
(west coast)

NOME.ME (native village). P B Nye was a Government Geologist.

O'BOYLE'S SUGARLOAF
(between Jane and Franklin Rivers)

Named by Sir John Franklin in 1842: 'We rounded the base of a beautiful conical hill, on which the appellation, O'Boyle's Sugar Loaf was bestowed' (David Burn, 1842). O'Boyle was a writer and a member of the Franklin expedition.

OBSERVATION HILL

Named by Twelvetrees in his report of 1908–1909. He gained good views of numerous features from here.

OLGA RIVER
(a tributary of the Gordon)

Surveyor Edward George Innes named this river after his daughter. He crossed the river on 7th July, 1896 (his daughter's birthday), while on an exploratory expedition westwards.

MOUNT OSMUND

Named after Osmund Roper (Chief Draughtsman, Lands Department) by Hon. Alec Hean in 1920.

MOUNT PARRY
(Bathurst Channel)

Named after Lieut J F Parry of HMS *Dart* in 1902.

LAKE PEDDER

Named after Sir John Lewes Pedder who was Chief Justice of the Supreme Court of Van Diemen's Land at the time of the lake's discovery by J H Wedge in 1835. Pedder was born in London in 1793 and sailed to V.D.L. aboard *Hibernia* in 1824. Lake Maria near Pedder was named after his wife.

PEDRA BRANCA
(Southern Ocean)

Abel Jansz Tasman named this rock off southern Tasmania because of its similarity to the one off the coast of China. In Portuguese, PEDRA is a feminine noun meaning stone or rock and BRANCA is the feminine form of the adjective for white. The Portuguese were the first to explore the waters off China.

PERAMBULATOR RIDGE
(north of Gordon storage)

Name proposed by Fred Lakin of the Hobart Walking Club in 1959. The ridge is open and easy going.

PHILPS LEAD
(Frenchmans Cap National Park)

Named by A Davern and party in 1933 after J E Philp who cut the track from Loddon Plains to Lake Tahune in 1910.

PHILPS PEAK
(Frenchmans Cap National Park)

Named by the Hobart Walking Club in 1951, also after J E Philp.

LAKE PICONE
(Lake Shelf, Anne group)

The name was proposed by J M Wythes in memory of the late Joe Picone who was particularly attracted to the lake and died there in 1967.

PICNIC POINT
(Macquarie Harbour)

Kelly Basin residents favoured the spot for picnics.

MOUNT PICTON

Named by Surveyor Frankland, presumably after Sir Thomas Picton, a famous military leader, 1758–1815.

PIGSTY PONDS
(near Mt La Perouse)

Name in common usage for the pools that lie higgledy-piggledy on the north-east of Maxwell Ridge.

THE PIG-TROUGH
(Franklin River)

Named by J E Calder's track marking party of 1841. 'At 1 hour 19 minutes p.m. we gained the hither summit of a deep abrupt mountain dell, to which the track-clearers had given the delicate cognomen "The Pig-trough". Devil's Glen was canvassed, as well as sundry other titles; but the hollow was passed without any positive decision as to its future nomenclature'. (David Burn, 1842.)

MOUNT PIGUENIT
(a conical hill north-east of Mt Hopetoun, near Federation Peak)

Named after William Charles Piguenit, draughtsman and artist who was employed in the Lands Department in the 1850's and 60's and sketched in the South-West in the 1870's.

PINDARS PEAK
(south coast)

Named by Lieut John Hayes in 1794 after 'Peter Pindar' the nom de plume of a famous English poet and satarist of that time, John Wolcott. Wolcot took this name from an early Greek Lyrical poet, Pindar.

POPHOLE
(west coast)

A good weather anchorage used by fishermen. Possibly it is where Kelly observed Aborigines with a large quantity of crayfish.

PORT DAVEY

Aboriginal name — TOO.GE.LOW. Discovered by Captain James Kelly on December 17th 1815, and named in honour of Lieutenant Governor Davey.

PRECIPITOUS BLUFF
(south coast)

Named thus on a Mines Department map. T B Moore named it Mt Salisbury. On early maps it was Peaked Hill.

PRINCE OF WALES RANGE

Named by Sir John Franklin during his expedition to Macquarie Harbour in 1842.

PROFESSOR RANGE

The West Coast mountains Jukes, Darwin, Huxley, Owen, Lyell and Sedgwick are sometimes referred to as the Professor Range. Charles Gould, the geological surveyor, named the peaks of the West Coast Range in 1862 after famous British scientists of his day. He left England in 1859, the year in which Darwin published his revolutionary book, *The Origin of Species*, and he appears to have opposed Darwin's theory of evolution for he named three massive mountains Sedgwick, Owen and Jukes in honour of bitter opponents of Darwin's theory. In contrast he gave to three smaller mountains which lay between the giants the names of Darwin and his faithful disciples Lyell and Huxley. (Geoffrey Blainey.)

MOUNT PROPSTING / PROPSTING RANGE
(near Franklin River)

Named by T B Moore in 1903, presumably after Mr Propsting, Premier of the day.

PUNT HILL

Named by F Blake in 1936. Piners hauled their punts over this hill to avoid the difficult rapids in the second gorge upstream on the Jane River.

RAGLAN RANGE
(just south of Lyell Hwy.)

Named after Lord Raglan of the Crimean War.

MOUNT RALLINGA
(Melaleuca Range, far South-West)

Derived from aboriginal word meaning 'high windy place'.

RATTENBURY HILL
(Bathurst Channel)

Named after a family of fishermen.

RECHERCHE BAY

Aboriginal name — LEILLATEAH. Named after one of Commander d'Entrecasteaux's two exploring ships in 1792.

REDAN HILL

This small hill at the north-western end of the Collingwood Range was named after a port outside Sebastopol in the Crimea.

RIPPLE MOUNTAIN
(Norold group)

A geologist from New Zealand, A Taylor, named this mountain after the ripple marks in its rocks.

LAKE RIVEAUX, MOUNT RIVEAUX
(Mt Picton area)

Thought to have been named by J W Beattie in 1899.

RIVER PEAK NORTH, RIVER PEAK SOUTH, PEAK CREEK
(Jane River)

Named by F Blake in 1936.

LAKE RHONA
(Denison Range)

Ernie Bond named this lake after Rhona Warren, a well known bushwalking identity who frequented the area.

MOUNT ROBERT
(Hamilton Range)

Named after Robert Sticht commemorating his journey up the Gordon River in 1928. Sticht was son of the first manager of the Mt Lyell Mining Company.

ROWITTA PLAINS
(north of Bathurst Harbour)

Southern Tasmanian aboriginal word meaning wombat.

ROYLE CREEK
(western tributary of Thirkells Creek, a tributary of the Jane River)

Named by Michael Sharland during an expedition in 1938 in search of the Tasmanian Tiger. The party included a Constable Royle. (Story published in *Walkabout* 1.10.1948: 'Four men stood on the bank of a river and proceeded to "draw straws" with twigs to decide whose name the river should bear'.

SARAH ISLAND
(Macquarie Harbour)

Named by Captain James Kelly in honour of Mrs Sarah Birch, wife of Dr T W Birch who sponsored Kelly's expedition of exploration and circumnavigation of Van Dieman's Land in 1815.

MOUNT SARAH JANE
(Anne group)

On an early bushwalking trip to the Mt Anne region, V C Smith, L Giblin, A V Giblin and Hutchinson decided 'Anne should have some company' and consequently named Sarah Jane and Eliza.

SCHNELLS RIDGE
(south of Anne group)

Named after Philip Schnell, a man of German descent, who cut a track from McKay's track on the Huon River to Mt Sarah Jane in 1890.

SCHOFIELD CREEK
(Macquarie Harbour)

Named after first missionary on Sarah Island.

SCHOONER COVE
(Port Davey)

Visited in 1899 by the schooner HMS *Dart.*

SCHOONER POINT
(Payne Bay, Port Davey)

This point has a striking likeness to a ship under sail when the cliffs are viewed from Bond Bay.

SCOTCHFIRE CREEK
(tributary of the Jane River)

Named by T B Moore in 1900.

SCOTTS PEAK

In 1881 Surveyor David Jones named a peak which he could see from the Frankland Range after James Reid Scott. It is uncertain whether the hill known as Scotts Peak today is the one actually chosen by Jones. (R Gowlland, *Trampled Wilderness,* p.77.)

MOUNT SEAL
(north of the Jane River)

In 1901, L K Ward, Assistant Government Geologist, visited the area accompanied by L P Seal and two prospectors, M Donoghue and J T Riley. Ward felt that the name Mt Elliot ought to be abandoned on account of the proximity of the Elliot Range, and the change was made in 1961.

SIR JOHN FALLS
(on a tributary of the Lower Gordon River)

Named after a visit by Sir John Dodds (Chief Justice) in honour of that gentleman.

SERPENTINE RIVER
(flowed from Lake Pedder into the Gordon River)

Named by J E Calder, because of its tortuous course, on 9th March, 1837. The whole river was inundated in 1973 by the Middle Gordon Power Scheme.

SECHERON PEAK
(Frankland Range)

Named in 1954 after Frankland's home in Battery Point, Hobart.

MOUNT SHAKESPEARE
(north of Wylds Craig)

Named by Surveyor Frankland (?), 1830's.

SHARLANDS PEAK
(Frenchmans Cap National Park)

Named by the Hobart Walking Club in 1951, after Surveyor Sharland who reached the peak, from Bothwell; an unsuccessful attempt on Franchmans Cap in 1832.

SHINING MOUNTAIN
(east of Spires range)

Name used by C Binks of the Launceston Walking Club (1954) to denote 'a squarish mountain ... of gleaming white aspect, particularly along the western face.'

SMITHS TARN
(Schnell's Ridge)

From the Anne massif in the early twenties V C Smith saw a depression on Schnell's Ridge which he felt was sure to be the site of a tarn. Because of the disbelief of his friends, the nomenclature of this tarn commenced as a joke; it wasn't for some years that V C Smith confirmed the tarn's existence.

SMOKE SIGNAL HILL
(near New Harbour, south coast)

An eminence in New Harbour used for a number of years for smoke signal communication between fishermen in the harbour and miners at Cox Bight and Melaleuca Inlet.

THE SNAKE RIVER
(a tributary of the Weld River)

So named by V C Smith because Doug Anderson placed his hand on a snake in a tree near this river on an early trip to Mt Anne in the late 1920's.

SOLDIERS ISLAND
(Macquarie Harbour)

Named by Lempriere in 1839.

MOUNT SOLITARY
(now an island in the Pedder storage)

Once known as Isolated Mountain. After 1972 it became an island.

SOLLY RIVER
(a tributary of the Old River, Bathurst Harbour)

Named by T B Moore in 1901; his wife's maiden name was Solly.

LAKE SOPHIE
(Frenchmans Cap)

Named by J B Thwaites after Mrs E T Emmett.

SOUTH CAPE RIVULET

Named by W H Twelvetrees, Government Geologist.

SPENCE RIVER
(tributary of the Gordon River)

Spence was a surgeon in the first landing party at the Macquarie Harbour Penal Station on the 2nd of January, 1822.

SPERO RIVER
(west coast)

Named by T B Moore in 1901 after one of his dogs. The other was 'Spiro', after which a range west of Federation Peak was named. Previously the Spero River was known as Dobson River. It is marked Dobson on Charles Sprent's map of 1879.

THE SPIRES RANGE

'Far away south, a mighty gorge discloses its cloud-capped, shivered points, one of the south-by-east angles surmounted by three strongly-defined peaks, distinguished from their similitude to the chalky points of the Isle of Wight, by the appropriate title, "The Southern Needles". (David Burn, 1842.)

THE SPLITS
(Gordon River)

With the return of the prospectors J H Sticht, G W Harrison and C Abel from 'The Splits' in 1928 came the first reliable information regarding this section of the Gordon River. (Their detailed account may be found in The *Mercury* April 28, 1928.) It was formerly known as 'The Gorge', and for many years it was believed that the river flowed underground. The rocky slopes and sculpted cliff faces rise precipitously on either side for hundreds of feet. Olegas Truchanas visited the Splits in 1958 and subsequently did much to publicize their magnificence. Two kilometres above the Splits is another, less narrow gorge known as 'The Second Split'.

MOUNT SPRENT, SPRENT RIVER/FALLS
(a tributary of the Gordon River)

James Sprent arrived in Hobart in 1830. As a surveyor he methodically climbed every high mountain in the state, planning and supervising the construction of 206 trig stations. His son, Charles Percy Sprent, Surveyor General, was equally distinguished in the same field. Mount Sprent, Percy River and Charles Range were named in his honour.

STANNARD FLATS
(Jane River)

Stannard, a piner, was drowned in the Jane River in 1902. Charles Abel and party found his body and buried it on a small point on the Jane River just below Thirkells Creek junction.

STICHT HILLS
(north of Louisa Bay, south coast)

Named after Robert Carl Sticht, a renowned German-American metallurgist and authority on pyritic smelting, of the Mt Lyell Company.

STRAHAN

Named in honour of Sir George Strahan who was Governor of Tasmania from 1881-1886.

LAKE SURPRISE and SURPRISE CREEK
(Frankland Range)

Name proposed by Surveyor David Jones in 1881. The lake is hidden in an amphitheatre under Secheron Peak.

SURVEYOR RANGE
(north of Jane River)

T B Moore infers naming the range in 1901.

SVENOR POINT and WRECK BAY
(west coast)

Svenor, a Norwegian owned barque of 1,266 tons, was abandoned off Tasmania's west coast in 1914 after her ballast shifted. The barque eventually drifted onto a beach in what is now known as Wreck Bay. (O'May, p. 148.)

LAKE TAHUNE
(Frenchmans Cap)

Noted in an old register as Lake Winifred, named by Charles Whitham.

TANAH HILL
(north of Bathurst Harbour)

Aboriginal word for wallaby.

THIRKELLS CREEK
(a tributary of the Jane River)

Named in 1933 after Robert Thirkell the explorer.

THUREAU HILLS
(West Coast Range)

Gustave Thureau was a government geologist.

THWAITES PLATEAU
(Eastern Arthurs)

Named after Jack Thwaites, a bushwalking identity, who was among those who pioneered the route towards Federation Peak in the 1940's.

TIDDYS BEACH

Named after an Englishman who had a farm on Cape Sorell.

TOOGEE

A coastal eminence west of Kelly Basin, Bond Bay. Toogee was a native of the Port Davey tribe.

TURUA BEACH
(in Deadmans Bay, south coast)

The name of a fishing boat wrecked there.

TWELVETREES RANGE
(near the town of Strathgordon)

William H Twelvetrees was Government Geologist from 1899 until his death in 1919. During his appointment he visited the South-West on many occasions, cutting tracks and carrying out exploratory work.

TYLERS CREEK

W Tyler, with W T Harper, cut the first route along the south coast in 1906. Tyler later accompanied Twelvetrees along the route. It was not until 1915 that the route was cut into a properly formed track.

URQUHART CREEK

Named after Mac Urquhart who, with Geoff Chapman, built the cairn on Precipitous Bluff in 1930.

URQUHART RIVER

The name first appears on T B Moore's plan of tracks, 1900. Possibly named after Donald Campbell Urquhart who arrived in the colony in the late 1870's. He was a banker and a lawyer at Zeehan, elected to parliament in 1893 and became Attorney General.

VALE OF RASSELAS
(valley of the upper Gordon River)

Said to have been named by Surveyor Wedge, the name having been suggested by Dr Samuel Johnson's *Rasselas.*

VARNA BAY

The 561 ton *Varna* sailed from Greenwich on 12th August 1857 with general cargo for the colonies. B. Cuthbertson and crew found the wreck in 1972 where she lay scattered on the sea bed close inshore, about 25 miles south of Macquarie Harbour.

LAKE VERA (Frenchmans Cap National Park)	Named by J E Philp after his mother, while cutting the track to Frenchmans Cap in 1910.
MOUNT VICTORIA CROSS (Southern Ranges)	Named by T B Moore in 1901 in honour of the first Tasmanians to win the Victoria Cross. He likewise named nearby mountains after the two winners of the Cross, John Hutton Bisdee of the Tasmanian Imperial Bushmen who won the V C in Transvaal in 1900, and Guy Wylly.
WANDERER RIVER (west coast)	In March, 1858, Captain Buxton anchored the schooner *Wanderer* near Point Hibbs, intending to salvage cargo from the *Varna* (wrecked in 1857). The schooner failed to ride a storm which blew up from the south-west. Buxton and most of the crew made Port Davey in the ship's boat, and received help from the whalers anchored in the Port. (See O'May, p. 56.)
WAYENINNAH HILL (south of Federation Peak)	Aboriginal word meaning 'elbow'.
MOUNT WELD (south-east of Mt Anne)	Sir F A Weld was Governor between 1875 and 1880.
LAKE WHITHAM (Frenchman's Cap area)	Named by the Hobart Walking Club in 1951 after Charles Whitham, author of *Western Tasmania - a land of riches and beauty*. He was an enthusiastic explorer and advocate of the beauties of the region.
WHITLAM CAVE (Upstream of Shingle Island, Lower Franklin)	Named after Edward Gough Whitlam, the leader of the Federal Opposition, 1977, in that year.
WINDOW PANE BAY (south of Port Davey)	'A bay (yet to be charted) on the west... known as Window Pane Bay on account of the glistening mica schist of the hillsides'. (Clive Lord, *Papers and Proceedings of the Royal Society of Tasmania*, 1927.)
WHITE HORSE PLAINS (north of Port Davey)	Whalers had a white horse behind Bond Bay on these plains for some years.
WOMBAT GLEN (small plain beneath Mt Arrowsmith)	Called 'Wombat bottoms' by ex-convict Alexander McKay in 1840, and changed to this more seemly form by His Exellency, Sir John Franklin in 1842.
WRIGHT CREEK	Named after a Commandant of Sarah Island, 1822–1825.
WYLDS CRAIG	Known as the Peak of Teneriffe on a map of 1828 although according to surveyor Frankland (1835) it was originally named Wylds Craig.

State Reserves in South-West Tasmania Map, 1978

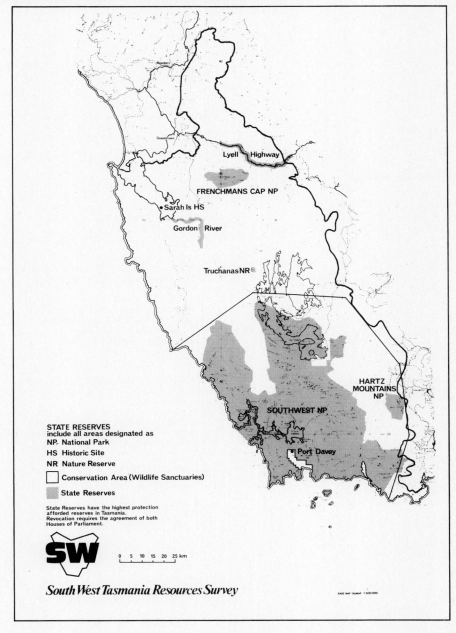

STATE RESERVES
include all areas designated as
NP. National Park
HS Historic Site
NR Nature Reserve

☐ Conservation Area (Wildlife Sanctuaries)

▨ State Reserves

State Reserves have the highest protection afforded reserves in Tasmania. Revocation requires the agreement of both Houses of Parliament.

SW

0 5 10 15 20 25 km

South West Tasmania Resources Survey

BASE MAP TASMAP 1:500 000

Directory

A concise list of organizations and institutions with a specific interest in, or responsibility for, the South-West. Unless otherwise specified they are located in Hobart, Tasmania.

VOLUNTARY ORGANIZATIONS

Australian Conservation Foundation (Administrative Office, Melbourne)
Clarence Walking Club
Climbers Club of Tasmania
Federation of Field Naturalists Club (Launceston)
Gordon River Preservation Society (Queenstown)
Hobart Walking Club
Launceston Walking Club (Launceston)
North West Walking Club (Ulverstone)
Royal Society of Tasmania
Society for Growing Australian Plants
South-West Committee
South-West Tasmania Committee (Sydney)
Scrub Club
Southern Caving Society
Tasmanian Canoe Club
Tasmanian Caverneering Club
Tasmanian Conservation Trust Inc.
Tasmanian Environment Centre Inc.
Tasmanian University Canoe Club
Tasmanian University Mountaineering Club
Tasmanian University Ski Club
Tasmanian Wilderness Society (NSW, Vic, ACT, SA, WA, Qld, Tas)

TOURIST VENTURES

Exit Cave Adventure Excursions (Hastings)
Gordon River Cruises — Morrison's Tourist Services Pty Ltd (Strahan)
Outdoor Shop
Scout Shop
Tasair Pty Ltd
Tasmanian Aviation Services Pty Ltd
Tasmanian Charters — J Brettingham-Moore
Tasventure — P C Sims (Devonport)
Wilderness Tours — Bob Geeves (Geeveston)

TASMANIAN GOVERNMENT

Department of Education
Department of Environment
Forestry Commission
Hydro-Electric Commission
Inland Fisheries Commission
Lands Department
Local Councils (Esperence, Gormanston, Hamilton, Huon, Strahan)
Mines Department
National Estate of Tasmania
National Parks and Wildlife Service. (Rangers: Mt Field, Strathgordon, Lake St Clair, Strahan)
Parliament of Tasmania — House of Assembly and Legislative Council
Rural Fires Board
State Library of Tasmania
State Rivers and Waters Supply Commission
Tasmanian Fisheries Development Authority
Tasmanian Museum and Art Gallery
Town and Country Planning Commission

AUSTRALIAN GOVERNMENT

Australian Institute of Aboriginal Studies (Canberra)
Australian National Parks and Wildlife Service (Canberra)
Bureau of Meteorology
CSIRO — Divisions of Entomology and Forest Research
Department of the Environment, Housing and Community Development (Canberra)
Department of Primary Industry. Fisheries Division (Canberra)
Heritage Commission (Canberra)
Transport Department — lighthouses (Canberra)

References

Section 1

HISTORY

Aboriginal Man
H M Gee

Australian Institute of Aboriginal Studies.	Site Card Index. Site Recording Programme (National Parks and Wildlife Service, Hobart, 1975).
J Backhouse.	*A Narrative of a Visit to the Australian Colonies* (London, 1843).
J C Beaglehole.	*The Journals of Captain James Cook*. Vol. 2. *The Voyage of the Resolution and Adventure 1772–1775* (London, 1961), p. 150.
J Burney.	*With Captain James Cook in the Antarctic and Pacific: the private journal of James Burney, second lieutenant of the Adventure on Cook's second voyage, 1772–1773*. Edited with an introduction by Beverley Hooper (Canberra: National Library of Australia, 1975), p. 36.
V R Ellis.	*Trucanini Queen or Traitor* (Hobart, 1976).
Great Britain. Parliament. Colonial Department.	*Van Diemen's Land*. Copies of all Correspondence between Lieutenant-Governor Arthur and His Majesty's Secretary of State for the Colonies, on the Subject of the Military Operations lately carried on against the Aboriginal inhabitants of Van Diemen's Land. With an historical introduction by A G L Shaw (Tasmanian Historical Research Association, Hobart, 1971).
R C Gunn.	'Remarks on the Indigenous Vegetable Productions of Tasmania available as Food for Man'. *Tasmanian Journal of Natural Science* (1842), pp. 35–52.
B Hiatt.	'The Food Quest and the Economy of the Aborigines'. *Oceania*, 38, Part 1 (1967), pp. 99–113.
R Jones.	'Fire-Stick Farming'. *Australian Natural History*, 16 (1969), pp. 224–228.
R Jones.	Rocky Cape and the Problem of the Tasmanians. Vol. III (Ph.D. thesis, University of Sydney, 1971).
R Jones.	'Tasmanian tribes'. Appendix to *Aboriginal Tribes of Australia* (A.N.U. Press. Canberra, 1974), pp. 317–354.
J Kelly.	'First Discovery of Port Davey and Macquarie Harbour'. *Royal Society of Tasmania. Papers and Proceedings* (Hobart, 1920).
F Noetling.	'The Food of the Tasmanian Aborigines', *Royal Society of Tasmania. Papers and Proceedings* (Hobart, 1910), pp. 279–305.
F Péron.	*Voyage de Decouvertes aux Terres Australes*, 2 tom (Paris, 1807).
N J B Plomley (ed.).	*Friendly Mission: The Tasmanian Journals and Papers of George Augustus Robinson 1829–1834* (Hobart, 1966).
N J B Plomley (ed.).	'French Manuscripts Referring to the Tasmanian Aborigines'. *Records of the Tasmanian Museum*, 23 (Launceston, 1966).
H Ling Roth.	*The Aborigines of Tasmania* (1st edn. London, 1890).
O W Reid.	'Additional Discoveries of Aboriginal Rock Carvings in Tasmania'. *Reprint from Royal Society of Tasmania. Papers and Proceedings* (Hobart, 1954), 88, pp. 273–278.
National Parks & Wildlife Service. Tasmania.	*Government's Southwest National Park Draft Management Plan* (Hobart, 1975).
Peter C Sims.	Letter to author 21/5/75.
Peter C Sims.	*Variations in Tasmanian Petroglyphs* (Devonport, 1974).
Tasmanian State Archives.	Records Relating to the Aborigines. C.S.O. 1/318/7578 (No. 4).

Pre-History and the Archaeology of Louisa Bay
R L Vanderwal

L R Binford.	'Post-pleistocene adaptations', in S R and L R Binford (eds.), *New Perspectives in Archaeology* (Chicago, 1968), pp. 313–341.
J B Birdsell.	'Some predictions for the pleistocene based on equilibrium systems among recent hunter-gatherers', in Lee and DeVore (eds.), *Man the Hunter* (Chicago, 1968), pp. 229–240.
S Bowdler.	'Pleistocene date for man in Tasmania'. *Nature 252 (1974), pp. 697–698*.
S Bowdler.	'Further radiocarbon dates from Cave Bay Cave, Hunter Island. North-west Tasmania', *Australian Archaeological Association Newsletter* 3 (Canberra, 1975), pp. 24–26.
R Jones.	'A speculative archaeological sequence for North-west Tasmania', in *Records of the Queen Victoria Museum* (Launceston, 1966).
R Jones.	Rocky Cape and the problem of the Tasmanians (Ph.D. thesis, University of Sydney, 1971).
R Jones.	'Tasmania: aquatic machines and off-shore islands', in Sieveking, G de G, I H Longworth and K E Wilson (eds.), *Problems in economic and social archaeology*: (London, 1976), pp. 253–256.
R Jones.	'The Tasmanian paradox', in R V S Wright (ed.). *Stone Tools as Cultural Markers* (Australian Institute of Aboriginal Studies, Canberra, 1977).
R B Lee.	'What do hunters do for a living, or, how to make out on scarce resources', in Lee and DeVore (eds.), *Man the Hunter* (Chicago, 1968), pp. 30–48.
R B Lee. & I DeVore (eds.)	*Man the Hunter* (Chicago, 1968).
H Lourandos.	Coast and Hinterland: the archaeological sites of eastern Tasmania (M A thesis, Australian National University, Canberra, 1970).
N McArthur.	'Computor simulations of small populations'. *Australian Archaeology* 4 (1976), pp. 53–57.
N J B Plomley.	*Friendly Mission: The Tasmanian Journals and Papers of George Augustus Robinson 1829–1834* (Hobart, 1966).
G Reber.	'Aboriginal carbon dates from Tasmania'. *Mankind* 6 (1965), pp. 264–268.
G Reber.	'New Aboriginal carbon dates from Tasmania'. *Mankind* 6 (1967), pp. 435–437.
W R Sigleo & E A Colhoun.	'Glacial age man in southeastern Tasmania: evidence from the Old Beach site', *Search* 6, 7 (1975), pp. 300–302.

They called it Transylvania
J S Luckman & K Davies

J Backhouse Walker.	'Early Tasmania'. *Royal Society of Tasmania. Papers and Proceedings* (Hobart, 1888).
A Bent.	Articles in *The Hobart Town Gazette* 8 June 1816, and 7 September, 1816.
K M Bowden.	*James Kelly of Hobart Town* (Melbourne, 1964).
D Burn.	'The Overland Journey of Sir John and Lady Franklin from Hobart Town to Macquarie Harbour in 1842', in G Mackanes (ed.), *Australian Historical Monographs* 32. (1955).
J Crawford, W F Ellis, G H Stancombe, (eds.).	*The Diaries of John Helder Wedge* (Royal Society of Tasmania, 1962).
W Lodewyk Crowther.	'Notes on Tasmanian Whaling', *Royal Society of Tasmania. Papers and Proceedings* (1919), pp. 130–151.
J Fenton.	*History of Tasmania* (Hobart, 1884).
Sir John Franklin.	Narrative of Some Passages in the History of Van Diemen's Land (printed for private circulation, 15 May, 1845).
R M Johnson.	*Systematic Account of the Geology of Tasmania* (Hobart, 1888).
Henry Judd.	*The Dark Lantern: or Hidden Side of Nature* (Hobart, 1896).
Will Lawson.	*Blue Gum Clippers* (Melbourne, 1949), p.71.
L H Livingston.	*News*, 3/2/1925 (Hobart, 1925).
C Lord.	'The South Coast and Port Davey, Tasmania'. *Royal Society of Tasmania. Papers and Proceedings* (Hobart, 1927).
J S Luckman & J Béchervaise.	'Federation Peak, Tasmania', *Walkabout* (Melbourne, April 1949), p. 18.
J S Luckman.	'We the Lucky Ones', *Tasmanian Tramp* 18, (1968), p. 77.
M D McRae.	'Port Davey and The South West', *Tasmanian Historical Research Association. Papers and Proceedings* 8, 3 (Hobart, 1960).
H O'May.	*Wooden Hookers of Hobart Town* (Hobart, 1957), p. 32.
W C Piguenit.	'Among the Western Highlands of Tasmania', in A Morton, F L S (ed.), Section 1 — Literature and Fine Arts, in *Report of the Fourth Meeting of the Australian Association for the Advancement of Science* (Hobart, 1892).

REFERENCES

N J B Plomley (ed.).
H Ling Roth.
Hon J R Scott M.L.C..
Tasmania. Parliament.
J West.
C Whitham.

D Burn.

C Craig.
W C Piguenit.

D Copland (ed.).

F Blake.
Ralph and Kathleen Gowlland.
D Lees.
J Luckman & P Allnutt.
A McIntosh Reid.
P B Nye.
F Peterson.
M Z Stefanski.
W H Twelvetrees.

Section 2

H G Bond. K MacKinnon & P F Noar.

Bureau of Meteorology.
E Derbyshire.

J Gentilli.
J Gentilli.
J Langford.

1. Chick & E Colhoun.
2. M K Macphail.
3. J L Davies.
4. E Colhoun & A Goede.
5. J K Davidson.
6. J A Peterson.
7. E Derbyshire. M R Banks. J L Davies & J N Jennings.

1. W C Piguenit.
2.
3. E Colhoun.
4. E Derbyshire.

5. J A Peterson.

6. M K Macphail & J A Peterson.
7. E Derbyshire.
8. M K Macphail.
9. M K Macphail.
10. M K Macphail.

11. S Bowdler.

Friendly Mission: The Tasmanian Journals and Papers of George Augustus Robinson 1829–1834 (Hobart. 1966).
The Aborigines of Tasmania (1st edn. London. 1890).
'Port Davey in 1875'. *Royal Society of Tasmania. Papers and Proceedings* (Hobart. 1875). p. 94.
Parliamentary Papers 1832–1896.
History of Tasmania (Launceston. 1852).
Western Tasmania. A Land of Riches and Beauty (2nd edn. Queenstown. 1949).

Governor Franklin's Journey, 1842

H M Gee

'The Overland Journey of Sir John and Lady Franklin to Macquarie Harbour in 1842'. in G Mackanes (ed.). *Australian Historical Monographs* 32 (1955).

Piguenit — A Tasmanian Painter

J Fenton

The Engravers of Van Diemen's Land (Tasmanian Historical Research Association. 1961).
'Among the Western Highlands of Tasmania'. in A Morton. F L S (ed.). Section 1 — Literature and Fine Arts. in *Report of the Fourth Meeting of the Australian Association for the Advancement of Science* (Hobart. 1892).

Lyndhurst Giblin visits Port Davey in Wartime

H M Gee

'On the Nation at War: Port Davey in Wartime'. in *Giblin: The Scholar and the Man* (Melbourne. 1960). pp. 121–127.

Small Mining Settlements

C D King & J Fenton

Unpublished Reports (Dept. of Mines. Hobart. 1935).
Adamsfield — The Town that Lived and Died (Devonport. 1973).
'The Count of Adamsfield'. *Tasmanian Tramp* 16 (1963). p. 66.
'Ernie Bond of Gordonvale'. *Tasmanian Tramp* 16 (1963). p. 24.
Geological Survey Typed Reports (Dept. of Mines. Hobart. 1928).
Unpublished Reports (Dept. of Mines. Hobart. 1928 & 1941).
'Adamsfield. then and now' *Tasmanian Tramp* 12 (1955). p. 4.
'Tin Deposits of the South West'. *Dept. of Mines Technical Reports*. 2 (Tasmania. 1958). p. 79.
Geological Survey Typed Reports (Dept. of Mines. Hobart. 1927).

THE NATURAL ENVIRONMENT

Climate

M Nunez

'Report on the meteorological aspects of the catastrophic bushfires in south-eastern Tasmania on 7 February 1967'. *Bureau of Meteorology Publication* (1967).
Climatic Averages. Tasmania and Miscellaneous (1975).
'A synoptic approach to the atmospheric circulation of the last glacial maximum in south-eastern Australia'. *Palaeogeography. Palaeoclimatology. Palaeoecology* 10 (1971). pp. 103–124.
Climates of Australia and New Zealand. from *World Survey of Climatology* 13. (Amsterdam. 1971).
Australian Climate Patterns (Nelson. Adelaide. 1972).
'Weather and Climate'. in J L Davies (ed.). *Atlas of Tasmania* (Dept. Lands and Surveys. Hobart. 1965) pp. 2–11.

Landforms

S H Stephens

'Quaternary Shorelines'. *Search* 3 (1972). p. 413.
The history of the vegetation and climate in Southern Tasmania since the late Pleistocene (Ph.D. thesis. University of Tasmania. 1975).
'Landforms'. in J L Davies (ed.). *Atlas of Tasmania* (Mercury. Hobart. 1965). pp. 18–25.
Quaternary Deposits of Blakes Opening (in prep.).
'Glaciation of the Mt La Perouse Area'. *Royal Society of Tasmania. Papers and Proceedings* (1970). p. 105.
'Glaciation of the Frenchmans Cap National Park'. *Royal Society of Tasmania. Papers and Proceedings* V (1966). p. 100.
'Glacial Map of Tasmania'. *Royal Society of Tasmania. Papers and Proceedings*. Special Publication 2 (1965).

Climatic Change in the Evolution of the South-West Wildscape

M Macphail

'Among the western highlands of Tasmania'. in A. Morton (ed.) *Report of the Fourth Meeting of the Australasian Association for the Advancement of Science* (Hobart. 1892). pp. 787–794.
Report of the National Estate: point 3.4. (1973).
A Quaternary climatic curve for Tasmania. (MS Presented at Australian Conference on Climate and Climatic Changes. Monash University. 1975).
'A synoptic approach to the atmospheric circulation of the last glacial maximum in south-eastern Australia'. *Palaeogeography. Palaeoclimatology. Palaeoecology* 10 (1971). pp. 103–124.
The Cirques of Southeastern Australia: Studies in morphology and distribution: history. and significance (Ph.D. thesis. Monash University. 1969).
'New deglaciation dates from Tasmania'. *Search* 6 (1975). pp. 127–130.
'Pleistocene glaciation of Tasmania: review and speculations'. *Australian Geographical Studies* 10 (1972). pp. 79–94.
'Late Pleistocene environments in Tasmania'. *Search* 6 (1975). pp. 295–300.
The History of the Vegetation and Climate in Southern Tasmania since the Late Pleistocene (Ph.D. thesis. University of Tasmania. 1975).
Post-glacial climatic change in Tasmania. Abstracts of Australian Conference on Climate and Climatic Change (Monash University. 1975). p. 43.
'Pleistocene date for man in Tasmania'. *Nature* 252 (1974). pp. 697–8.

12. W S Sigleo & E A Colhoun.   'Glacial age man in southeastern Tasmania: evidence from the Old Beach site', *Search* 6 (1975), pp. 300-302.
13. C Davis.   'Preliminary survey of the vegetation near New Harbour, South-west Tasmania', *Papers and Proceedings of the Royal Society of Tasmania* (1941), pp. 1-11.
14. W D Jackson.   'Vegetation', in J L Davies (ed.) *Atlas of Tasmania* (Department of Lands and Surveys, Hobart, 1965), pp. 30-35.
15. W D Jackson.   'Fire, air, earth and water — an elemental ecology of Tasmania', *Proceedings of the Ecology Society of Australia* 3 (1968), pp. 9-16.
16. M K MacPhail & R R Shepherd.   'Plant communities at Lake Edgar, South-West Tasmania', *Tasmanian Naturalist* 25 (1973), pp. 1-23.

Vegetation

I J Edwards

1. W D Jackson.   'Fire, air, water and earth — an elemental ecology of Tasmania', *Proceedings of the Ecological Society of Australia* 3 (1968) p. 9.
2. J M Gilbert.   'Forest succession in the Florentine Valley, Tasmania' in *Royal Society of Tasmania. Papers and Proceedings* 93 (1959), pp. 129-151.
3. R L Specht.   'Vegetation', in G W Leeper (ed.) *The Australian Environment* (4th edn, C S I R O, 1970), pp. 44-67.
4. W D Jackson.   'Conservation of Rare and Endangered Species in Tasmania', in R L Specht, E M Roe and V H Broughton (eds.) in *Conservation of major plant communities in Australia and Papua New Guinea: Australian Journal of Botany* Supplement No 7 (C S I R O Melbourne, 1974) pp. 440-448.
5. W D Jackson.   'Vegetation', in J L Davies (ed.), *Atlas of Tasmania* (Hobart, 1965), pp. 30-35.
6. L Rodway.   *The Tasmanian Flora* (Hobart, 1903).

Fire in the South-West   Fire Management in National Parks

R Tyson

1. H F Recher, D Lunney & H Posamentier.   'A grand natural experiment — the Nadgee wildfire', *Australian Natural History* 18, 5 (1975).
2. Australian Conservation Foundation.   'Bushfire Control and Conservation', *Viewpoint* Series 5 (1970).

Fire in the South-West   'Ecological Drift' An argument against the continued practice of Hazard Reduction Burning

W D Jackson

1. W D Jackson.   'Fire, air, water and earth — an elemental ecology of Tasmania', *Proceedings of the Ecological Society of Tasmania* (1968), pp. 399-416.
2. W D Jackson.   'Fire and the Tasmanian Flora', in *Tasmanian Year Book* no. 2 (Commonwealth Bureau of Census and Statistics, Govt. Printer, Hobart, 1968), pp. 50-55.
3. A B Mount.   'Eucalypt ecology as related to fire', *Proceedings Annual Tall Timbers Fire Ecology Conference* (1969), pp. 75-108.
4. C E Harwood & W D Jackson.   'Atmospheric losses of four plant nutrients during a forest fire', *Australian Forestry* 38 (1975), pp. 92-99.
5. W D Jackson.   'The Vegetation', in J L Davies (ed.), *Atlas of Tasmania*, (Mercury Press, Hobart, 1965), pp. 30-35.
6. R Jones.   'Fire stick farming', *Australian Natural History*, Sept. (1969), pp. 224-228.
7. R Jones.   'The demography of hunters and farmers in Tasmania', in D J Mulvaney & J Golson (eds.), *Aboriginal Man and Environment in Australia* (A N U, Canberra, 1971).
8. W D Jackson.   'Conservation in Tasmania', in R L Specht, E M Roe and V H Broughton (eds.), *Conservation of major plant communities in Australia and Papua New Guinea: Australian Journal of Botany* Supplement No. 7 (1974), pp. 319-448.
9. B Page & H Smith.   Wild fire hazard in the environs of Hobart (Master of Environmental Studies thesis, University of Tasmania, 1976).

Freshwater Environments and their fauna

P S Lake *et al*

1. I R Ball.   'A new genus of freshwater triclad from Tasmania with reviews of the related genera *Cura* and *Neppia* (Turbellaria, Tricladida)', *Life Sc. Contr. R. Ont. Mus.* 99 (1974).
2. J Illies.   'Notonemouridae of Australia (Plecoptera, Ins.)', *Int. Rev. Ges. Hydrobiol.* 60 (1975) pp. 221-249.
3. H B N Hynes.   'Tasmanian Antartoperlaria (Plecoptera)', *Aust. J. Zool.* 24 (1976), pp. 115-143.
4. I A E Bayly.   'The sand fauna of Lake Pedder: a unique example of colonization by the Phreatoicidea (Crustacea: Isopoda). *Aust. J. Mar. Freshwat. Res.* 24 (1973). pp. 303-306.
I A E Bayly, J A Peterson, P A Tyler & W D Williams.   'Preliminary limnological investigation of Lake Pedder, Tasmania', *Aust. Soc. Limnol. Newsl.* 5, 20 (March 1-4, 1966), pp. 30-41.
I A E Bayly, P S Lake, R Swain & P A Tyler.   'Lake Pedder. Its importance to Biological Science', in *Pedder Papers. Anatomy of a Decision.* (Australian Conservation Foundation, 1972), pp. 41-49.
R T Buckney & P A Tyler.   'Chemistry of some sedgeland waters. Lake Pedder, South West Tasmania', *Aust. J. Mar. Freshwat. Res.* 24 (1973), pp. 267-273.
R T Buckney & P A Tyler.   'Chemistry of Tasmanian Inland Waters', *Int. Revue Ges. Hydrobiol. Hydrogr.* 58 (1973), pp. 61-78.
R Frankenberg.   'Two new species of galaxiid fish from the Lake Pedder region of southern Tasmania', *Aust. Zool.* 14 (1968), pp. 268-274.
G Fryer.   'A new freshwater species of *Dolops* (Crustacea: Branihiura) parasite on galaxiid fish of Tasmania — with comments on disjunct distribution patterns in the Southern Hemisphere', *Aust. J. Zool.* 17 (1969), pp. 49-64.
V V Hickman.   'Tasmanian Temnocephalidea' *Royal Society of Tasmania. Papers and Proceedings*, 101 (1967), pp. 227-250.
B Knott & P S Lake.   'A Brief Survey of the macro-invertebrate fauna of Lake Edgar and its immediate environs (South-West Tasmania)', *Tas. Naturalist* 36 (1974), pp. 1-19.
Lake Pedder Committee of Enquiry.   *The Flooding of Lake Pedder. Final Report* (Australian Government Publishing Service, Canberra, 1974).
P S Lake & K J Newcombe.   'Observations on the ecology of the crayfish *Parastacoides tasmanicus* (Decapoda: Parastacidae) from South Western Tasmania', *Aust. Zool.* 18 (1975), pp. 197-214.
M J Littlejohn & A A Martin.   'The Amphibia of Tasmania', in W D Williams (ed.), *Biogeography and Ecology in Tasmania* (W Junk, The Hague 1974), pp. 251-289.
B J Smith.   'A new species of snail from Lake Pedder, possibly belonging to the family Valvatidae', *J. Malac. Soc. Aust.* 2 (1973), pp.429-434.
R Swain.   'The Fauna of South-Western Tasmania', *Tasmanian Year Book No. 6 1972* (Commonwealth Bureau of Census and Statistics, Tasmanian Office, Hobart, 1972), pp. 56-64.
R Swain, I S Wilson, J L Hickman & J E Ong.   '*Allanaspides helonomus* Gen. et Sp. nov. (Crustacea: Syncarida) from Tasmania', *Rec. Queen Vic. Museum* 35 (1970), pp. 1-6.
P A Tyler.   'Limnological studies', in W D Williams (ed.) *Biogeography and Ecology in Tasmania* (W Junk, The Hague, 1974), pp. 29-61.
W D Williams.   *Australian freshwater Life* (Sun Books, Melbourne 1968).
W D Williams, (ed.).   *Biogeography and Ecology in Tasmania* (W Junk, The Hague, 1974).

FURTHER READING:-
I A E Bayly & W D Williams.   *Inland waters and their Ecology.* (Longman, Australia 1973).
I A E Bayly.   'The Fate of Lake Pedder and its biota', *Aust. Soc. Limnol News.* 4, 2 (1965).

Amphibians and Reptiles

B McIntosh & P Andrews

FURTHER READING
H Cogger.   *Australian Reptiles* (Reed, Sydney, 1967).
M J Littlejohn & A A Martin.   'The Amphibia of Tasmania', in W D Williams (ed.), *Biogeography and Ecology in Tasmania* (W Junk, The Hague, 1974), pp. 251-289.

REFERENCES

Birds of the South-West   Diversity and Habitat
R W Rose

1. M G Ridpath & R E Moreau.

'The birds of Tasmania: Ecology and Evolution'. *Ibis* 108 (1966) p. 348.

2. J M Littler.

Handbook of the birds of Tasmania (Launceston. 1910).

3. H Wilson.

'The R A O U camp-out at Lake St. Clair, November 1949'. *The Emu.* 50 (1950) p. 41.

4. D G Thomas.

'The Scrub-Tit. status-ecology'. *Tasmanian Naturalist* 38 (1974) p. 1.

5. L E Wall.

'Birds'. in M R Banks (ed.) *The Lake Country of Tasmania* (Symposium published by the Royal Society of Tasmania. 1972).

6. D Johnson.

Lake Pedder. why a national park must be saved (Lake Pedder Action Committees of Vic. and Tas. and the Australian Union of Students. 1972).

7. M Sharland.

Tasmanian Birds (Sydney. 1938).

8. W Eastman.

The Life of the Kookaburra and other Kingfishers (Sydney. 1970).

9. D R Milledge.

'The Birds of Maatsuyker Island'. *The Emu.* 72 (1972) p. 167.

10. R H Green & B C Mollison.

'Birds of Port Davey and the South Coast of Tasmania'. *The Emu.* 61 (1961) p. 223.

11. D R Milledge.

'The Orange-bellied Parrot in Tasmania'. *South Australian Ornithologist.* 26 (1972) p. 56.

The February 1976 edition of the *Tasmanian Naturalist* (no. 44) is devoted to observations of birds of the West Coast of Tasmania.

Mammals
G Hocking

Anon.

'The Marsupials of Tasmania' in *Tasmanian Year Book 1971* (Hobart, 1971) pp. 70–77.

R H Green.

'The murids and small dasyurids in Tasmania'. *Records Queen Victoria Museum,* 28 (1967). Parts 1 and 2.

R H Green.

'The murids and small dasyurids in Tasmania'. *Records Queen Victoria Museum,* 32. (1968). Parts 3 and 4.

R H Green.

'The murids and small dasyurids in Tasmania'. *Records Queen Victoria Museum,* 46 (1972) Parts 5. 6 & 7.

R H Green.

The mammals of Tasmania (Launceston. 1973).

E R Guiler.

'Animals'. in J L Davies (ed.) *Atlas of Tasmania.* (Hobart, 1965). pp. 36–37.

R Swain.

'The fauna of South-Western Tasmania'. in *Tasmanian Year Book 1972* (Hobart, 1972). pp. 56–64.

Caves — A World Below
A Goede

1. N White.

'Some geochemical aspects of limestone solution', in A Goede & B Cockerill (eds.), *Proceedings 8th Biennial Conference. Australian Speleological Federation* (1972), pp. 10–17.

2. J A Harris.

'Ecosystems underground', *Australian Natural History* 18, 6 (1975), pp. 220–225.

3. A Goede.

'Underground stream capture at Ida Bay, Tasmania, and the relevance of cold climatic conditions', *Australian Geographical Studies* 7, 1 (1969). pp. 41–48.

4. P Caffyn.

'Beech forest submission', *New Zealand Speleological Bulletin* 5, 94 (1975). pp. 419, 420.

Anon.

'The Glow Worm Caves of Tasmania'. *Scientific American* (November 23, 1895).

L Gleeson.

'Exploration at Mt Ronald Cross'. *Southern Caver* 6, 1 (1974). pp. 17–19.

A Goede.

'The exploration history of Judds Cavern, Cracroft Area, Tasmania'. *Journal of the Sydney Speleological Society* 18. 9 (1974). pp. 239–247.

A Goede & P Murray.

'Pleistocene Man in South Central Tasmania: Evidence from a Florentine Valley cave site' (University of Tasmania, in prep.).

R Hawkins. K Kiernan & G Middleton.

'Reconnaissance trip to limestone areas on the Gordon and Franklin Rivers', *Journal of the Sydney Speleological Society* 18. 7 (1974). pp. 177–195.

J N Jennings.

'Karst'. *An Introduction to Systematic Geomorphology* V. 7 (A.N.U. Press. 1971). p. 252.

H Judd.

The Dark Lantern: or Hidden Side of Nature (The Mercury, Hobart, 1896). p. 35.

L Kermode.

'Glowworm Cave, Waitomo Conservation study'. *New Zealand Speleological Bulletin* 5, 91 (1974). pp. 329–344.

L Kermode.

'A philosophy of cave conservation'. *New Speleological Bulletin* 5, 92 (1974). pp. 350–353.

K Kiernan.

'Caves and karst of Junnee-Florentine, Tasmania'. *Australian Speleological Society Newsletter* 53 (1971). pp. 4–10.

K Kiernan.

'Gordon River Expedition 1974–1975'. *Southern Caver* 6, 3 (1975). pp. 2–6.

K Kiernan.

'The case for Precipitous Bluff'. *Southern Caver* 7, 2 (1975). pp. 2–29.

G Middleton & N Montgomery.

'Southern Caving Society Precipitous Bluff Expedition 1973'. *Journal of the Sydney Speleological Society* 17, 7 (1973). pp. 185–212.

G Middleton & A Sefton.

'S.S.S. Gordon-Franklin expedition 1974–1975'. Journal of *Sydney Speleological Society* 19, 11 (1975). pp. 271–291.

A Pavey, C Fisher & P Radcliffe.

'An expedition to Precipitous Bluff'. *Spar* 24 (1973). pp. 9–33.

G T Roberts & M Andric.

'Investigations into the water-tightness of the proposed Gordon-above-Olga hydro-electric storage south-west Tasmania', *Quarterly Journal of Engineering Geology* 7, 2 (1974). pp. 121–136.

D Weston.

'Weld River Trip Report', *Speleo Spiel* 41 (1969), pp. 4–5.

P Williams. (ed.).

'Report on the conservation of Waitomo Caves', *New Zealand Speleological Bulletin* 5, 93 (1975). pp. 373–395.

G Wooten.

'In search of Vanishing Falls', *Walkabout* (June—July, 1974), pp. 10–15.

Origins and Affinities of the South-West Biota
B Knott

1. J H Griffiths.

'Continental Margin Tectonics and the Evolution of South East Australia'. *The APEA Journal* 11 (1971), pp. 75–79.

2. R A Couper.

'Southern Hemisphere Mesozoic and Tertiary Podocarpaceae and Fagaceae and their Palaeogeographic Significance'. *Proc. Roy. Soc. London* 8. 152 (1960). pp. 491–500.

3. R Good.

The Geography of Flowering Plants, 4th edn (Longman. London. 1974).

4. A Keast.

'Contemporary Biotas and Separation Sequence of the Southern Continents'. in D H Tarling & S K Runcorn (eds.), *Implications of Continental Drift to the Earth Sciences* (Academic Press. London. 1973). pp. 309–343.

5. N T Burbidge.

'The Phytogeography of the Australian Region'. *Australian Journal of Botany* 8 (1960). pp. 75–211.

6. P J Darlington.

Biogeography of the Southern End of the World (Harvard University Press. Cambridge. 1965).

Further Reading:-

S Carlquist.

Island Biology (Columbia University Press. New York. 1974).

A G Smith, J C Briden & G E Drewry.

'Phanerozoic World Maps', in N F Hughs (ed.) 'Organisms and Continents Through Time', *Spec. Pap. Palaeont.* 12 (1972). pp. 1–42.

R L Specht. E M Roe & V H Broughton.

Conservation of major plant communities in Australia and Papua New Guinea; Australian Journal of Botany Supplement No. 7 (1974).

W D Williams (ed.).

Biogeography and Ecology in Tasmania. Monographiae Biologicae No. 25 (W Junk, The Hague. 1974).

Section 3

1. United States Congress.
2. Australian Conservation Foundation.

Australian Conservation Foundation.
E F Schumacher.
R C Lucas.

1. S Bardwell.
2. N.S.W. National Parks and Wildlife Service.
3. National Parks and Wildlife Service. Tasmania.

Section 4

1. T Bird. A Kile & F D Podger.
2. R L Specht. E M Roe & V H Broughton.
3. J M Gilbert.
4. J M Gilbert.
5. K W Cremer & A B Mount.

6. Australian Conservation Foundation.
7. C E Harwood & J B Kirkpatrick.

P T Unwin.
C Harwood & J Kirkpatrick.

1. M Nunez.
2. J R Ashton.
3. Hydro-Electric Commission.
4. Hydro-Electric Commission.
5. E F Schumacher.
6. Hydro-Electric Commission.
7. Hydro-Electric Commission.
8. Hydro-Electric Commission.
    P D Wilde.
9. Hydro-Electric Commission.
10. Hydro-Electric Commission.
11. Australian Bureau of Statistics.
12. Hydro-Electric Commission.
13. Hydro-Electric Commission.
14.
15. G J R Linge.
16. Hydro-Electric Commission.
17. Sir B Callaghan.
18.
19. A J T Finney.
    J D Kalma.
20. Hydro-Electric Commission.
21.
    J F Lounsbury.
22. Tasmanian State Strategy Plan.
23. Tasmanian State Strategy Plan.
24. R E Saunders.
    K Kiernan.
25. R E Saunders.
26. Hydro-Electric Commission.
27. Hydro-Electric Commission.
    R E Saunders.
28. Lake Pedder Committee of Enquiry.
    Australian Conservation Foundation.

RECREATION

What is Wilderness to Man?

P E Smith

The Wilderness Act 1964 (Public Law 88–577, 88 Congress).
Submission to The South-West Advisory Committee on the South-West National Park Draft Management Plan (Melbourne, Jan. 1976). pp. 3–4.
Wilderness Conservation, Viewpoint Series (Melbourne, 1976).
Small is Beautiful — A Study of Economics as if People Mattered (London, 1973).
'Forest Service Wilderness Research in the Rockies', in Forest Service U.S.D.A., *Western Wildlands* (U.S. Government Printing Office. 1974), 677 – 093/36, Region No. 8.

Bushwalking — Three Viewpoints   Bushwalking Today

R E Saunders

Wilderness Use in South-West Tasmania — A Pilot Study (CURRG Monograph 1, 1973).
Kosciusko National Park Plan of Management (1974).
Government's Southwest National Park Draft Management Plan (Hobart, 1975).

INDUSTRY

Forestry   The South-West and Forestry

J Kirkpatrick

'The eucalypt crown diebacks — a growing problem for forest managers'. *Australian Forestry*, 37 (1975). pp. 173–187.
Conservation of major plant communities of Australia and Papua—New Guinea: Australian Journal of Botany Supplement No. 7 (1974).
'Forest succession in the Florentine Valley, Tasmania'. *Royal Society of Tasmania. Papers and Proceedings*, 93 (1959) pp. 129–152.
'Regeneration of *Eucalyptus regnans* in the Florentine Valley. *Appita*, 13 (1960) pp. 132–135.
'Early stages of plant succession following the complete felling and burning of *Eucalyptus regnans* forest in the Florentine Valley, Tasmania.' *Australian Journal of Botany*, 13 (1965) pp. 303–322.
'Multiple use on forest land presently used for commercial wood production', *Search*, 5 (1974) pp. 438–443.
Forestry and Wilderness in the South-West (Hobart, 1978).

Forestry   The Value of a Forest   The Precipitous Bluff — Hartz Swap

C Harwood

Forest Land Use Conflicts in Tasmania (Hobart, 1976).
Forestry and Wilderness in the South-West (Hobart, 1978).

The Environment, Growth Projections and Hydro-Electricity in Tasmania's South-West

P D Wilde

This book 2.1.
Land use for power development purposes in Tasmania, Paper to eighth Australasian land Administration Conference (Hobart, 1976) p.7.
Power scheme investigations (Mimeo, 1976). pp. 3–5.
Report on Gordon River power development, stage one and thermal power station (1967). p. 18.
Small is beautiful (1974). pp. 10–18.
Report on the proposed Pieman River power development (1971).
op. cit. (1976). p. 1.
op. cit. (1967). pp. 21–24:
'Problems of planning Tasmania's electricity supply'. *Geography* 60 (1975). pp. 303–307.
Annual Reports (1955–1975).
Report for Year 1956–57 (1957).
Survey of household energy sources (1976).
Annual review 1974–1975 (1975). p. 19: Unpublished load statistics (1970–1975).
op. cit. (1967). pp. 12–13.
The Mercury, 13 July 1973. 18 April 1974, 1 June 1974, 11 January 1975, 1 October 1975, 17 January 1976, 18 September 1976.
'Secondary industry in Australia', G H Dury and M I Logan, *Studies in Australian Geography* (1968). p. 230.
op. cit. (1967). p. 18.
Inquiry into the Structure of Industry and Employment Situation in Tasmania (1977).
Australian Financial Review, 31 August 1976.
Tasmanian energy statistics 1965–1975, Working Paper No. 1, Environmental Studies, University of Tasmania (1976).
Sectoral use of energy in Australia, Technical Memorandum 76/4 CSIRO. Division of Land Use Research (1976).
op. cit. (1967). p. 10: *op. cit.* (1971). pp. 9–10.
Australian Financial Review, 23 October 1972, 14 June 1973:
'Recent developments in the aluminium industry in the U.S.', *Journal of Geography* 41 (1962), 97–104.
Draft Report. *The Mercury*, 3 August 1976.
Nature Conservation in Tasmania, Working Paper No. 19 (1976).
This book 5.1, 5.4.
This book 5.8.
op. cit.
Report for Year 1971–72 (1972). p. 22.
op. cit. (1971). pp. 23–24.
op. cit.
Report (1973): Final Report (1974):
Pedder Papers: anatomy of a Decision (Melbourne, 1972).

REFERENCES

29. Lake Pedder Committee of Enquiry.
30. I A E Bayly, P S Lake, R Swain & P A Tyler.
31. Australian Conservation Foundation.
32. Lake Pedder Committee of Enquiry.
33. Sir A Knight.
     J R Ashton.
34.
     Australian Conservation Foundation.

35.

Section 5

1. Australian Conservation Foundation.
2. F Fraser Darling.
3. R Swain.
4. H J Frith.
5. Australian Conservation Foundation.
6. Hydro-Electric Commission.
7. National Parks & Wildlife Service. Tasmania.
8. P S Lake, R Swain, A M M Richardson, P A Tyler & D J Coleman.

9. D Hooley, K McInnes, G Nodin & B Weavers.

Australian Conservation Foundation.
R Jones.

D Johnson (ed.).

National Parks & Wildlife Service. Tasmania.
1. Australian Conservation Foundation.
2. P S Lake, R Swain, A M M Richardson, P A Tyler & D J Coleman.

3. A R Costin.

4. I A E Bayly, P S Lake, R Swain & P A Tyler.

5. M F Day.
R Frankenberg.
FURTHER READING:
National Parks & Wildlife Service.

1. A Gray & J Hemsley.
2. W H Twelvetrees.
3. F Blake.
4. B Champion.
5. Tasmanian Conservation Trust and others.
6. *Mineral Holdings (Australia) Pty. Ltd.
    v. Tasmanian Conservation Trust*
7. Correspondence
8. *Stow & Ors v. Mineral Holdings (Australia) Pty. Ltd.*
    *Scenic Hudson Preservation Conference
    v. Federal Power Commission.*
9. *Citizens' Committee for Hudson Valley v. Volpe*
    Citizens to Preserve Overton Park Inc. v. Volpe.
    Environmental Law Reform Group.
P Radcliffe.
A Davey, C Fisher & R Radcliffe.
A Terauds.
K Kiernan.
K Kiernan.
K Kiernan.
K Kiernan.
K Kiernan.

op. cit. (1974), pp. 187–245, 266–276.
'Lake Pedder: its importance to biological science' Australian Conservation Foundation, *op. cit.*, (1972), pp. 41–49.
op. cit., pp. 31–39.
Final Report (1974).
speaking on This Day Tonight (ABC Television, 26 March 1976);
op. cit. (1976), p. 13.
Examiner, 3 February 1976;
'Shrug of secrecy HEC told', (press release 23 February 1976);
Australian, 24 February 1976.
The Mercury, 14 August 1976.

CONSERVATION AND THE SEVENTIES

Wilderness Conservation
R E Saunders

Wilderness Conservation, Viewpoint Series, (Melbourne, 1975) p. 5.
Wilderness and Plenty. The 1969 Reith Lectures (London, 1969).
'The Fauna of South-Western Tasmania', in *Tasmanian Year Book* 6 (Hobart, 1972), pp. 56–64.
Wildlife Conservation (Sydney, 1973), p. 362.
Habitat 3, 2 (Melbourne, 1975).
'Cross Currents' (May 1975), p. 2.
Government's Southwest National Park Draft Management Plan (Hobart, 1975).
Comments on the Draft Management Plan of the Tasmanian National Parks and Wildlife Service for the Southwest National Park (Zoology Dept. Uni. of Tasmania, 1976).
A recommendation to the Victoria Alpine Society (1975). Table 1 is adapted from this source.

The Evolving Consciousness
H M Gee

The Wonderful South-West. Special Issue Habitat Australia 3, 2 (1975).
'Lake Pedder'. A Submission to the Committee of Inquiry. Commonwealth Department of Environment and Conservation. Being a Political Interpretation and Plea for Preservation by the United Tasmanian Group (Hobart, Mar. 1973).
Lake Pedder: Why a National Park Must be Saved (Camberwell, Vic., 1972).

The Boundary Question   An Evaluation of the Tasmanian Government's 1975 Draft Management Plan for the Southwest National Park

R E Saunders

Government's Southwest National Park Draft Management Plan (Hobart, 1975).
Submission to the South West Advisory Committee on The Southwest National Park Draft Management Plan (Melbourne, Jan. 1976).
Comments on the Draft Management Plan of the Tasmanian National Parks and Wildlife Service for the South-West National Park (Zoology Dept., University of Tasmania, 1976).
'Vegetation on High Mountains in Australia in Relation to Land Use', in A Keast, R L Crocker and C Christian (eds.) *Biogeography and Ecology in Australia* (1959).
'Lake Pedder: Its importance to biological science', in *Pedder Papers. Anatomy of a decision* (Australian Conservation Foundation, Melbourne, 1972).
'The Role of National Parks and Reserves in Conservation', in A B Costin and H J Frith (eds.) *Conservation* (1971).
'Two new species of galaxiid fish from the Lake Pedder region of southern Tasmania'. *Aust. Zool.* 14 (1968), pp. 268–274.

Submission to Special Advisory Committee on South-West Tasmania (Hobart, 1976).

The Precipitous Bluff Case
P H Wessing

Report on Visit to Precipitous Bluff and New River Lagoon (Compiled for the South-West Committee, 1969).
Geological Survey Reports (Dept. of Mines, Hobart, 1927).
Geological Survey Reports (Dept. of Mines, Hobart, 1935).
'An Economic Appraisal of Limestone Quarrying at Precipitous Bluff', in *Tasmanian Conservation Trust Circular*, 68 (1974).
Warden of Mines Court, Devonport, 4th and 5th December 1972.
Tasmanian Supreme Court, Unreported judgement No. 24/1973 List 'A'.

from Professor H W R Wade, Q.C., St. John's College, Oxford, to Mrs P H Wessing (20/6/73 and 21/6/73).
Tasmanian Supreme Court (Full Bench), Unreported judgement No. 18/1975 List 'A'.
354 F.2d 608 (1965).⎫
                      ⎬ (Some of the American decisions that have
425 F.2d 97 (1970).   ⎬ challenged conservative legal principles
                      ⎪ and the legality of actions of public authorities.)
91 S. Ct. 814 (1971).⎭
The National Estate and the Public Interest: Precipitous Bluff. Environmental Rights and Mining (Hobart, 1973).
'The Precipitous Bluff Expedition'. *Sydney University Speleological Society Bulletin* (March, 1973), pp. 86, 87.
'An Expedition to Precipitous Bluff'. *Spar* 24 (Newsletter of the University of NSW Speleological Society 1973), pp. 9–33.
'Precipitous Bluff Must Not be Destroyed'. *Southern Caver* 4, 4 (1973), pp. 3–5.
'Precipitous Bluff, Tasmania' *Australian Speleological Federation Newsletter* 58, 14 (1972).
'Conservation — Precipitous Bluff & Mining'. *Southern Caver* 4,4 (1973) pp. 13–17.
'The Precipitous Bluff Snowball'. *Southern Caver* 5, 1 (1973), pp. 6–8.
'A Critical Examination of Tasmania's Cave Reserves'. *Southern Caver* 6, 2 (1974), pp. 3–25.
'The Case for Precipitous Bluff'. *Southern Caver* 7, 2 (1975).

South-West Bibliography

Compiled by Janet Fenton and Helen Gee with assistance from the staff of the State Reference Library of Tasmania, particularly Madeline Hempel.

The South-West is defined for the purposes of this bibliography as the region south and west of the Lyell Highway and the unsettled areas to the west of the Derwent and Huon Valleys. The bibliography is intended to be as comprehensive as possible to date.

Books containing only brief references to the South-West have not been included as the list is endless. We hope the most informative and the most interesting of the publically available material to mid 1978 has been included.

The bibliography is presented in subject format with the belief that this will be of widest use.

Entries are grouped as follows:-

LITERATURE:	OTHER MATERIALS:
GENERAL	MAPS
HISTORY	FILMS
PICTORIAL HISTORY	
PARLIAMENTARY PAPERS	
GOVERNMENT PUBLICATIONS	
GEOLOGY	
BIOLOGY	
CONSERVATION	
FICTION	
CHILDRENS' FICTION	
TASMANIAN TRAMP ARTICLES	

GENERAL

ADAM SMITH, P — 'Vale! Lake Pedder'. *Walkabout*, Sept. 1968, pp. 34–36.

ANGUS, M — *The World of Olegas Truchanas*, edited by N Laird. Hobart, The Olegas Truchanas Publication Committee, 1975. (The 2nd edition was published in the same year in Hobart by O.B.M., and a 4th edition in 1978.)

'Around the States: Tasmania'. *Wildlife in Australia*, v.3. no.5, Dec. 1966, p.24.

BARDWELL, S — *Wilderness use in south-west Tasmania: a pilot study*. Clayton, Vic., Combined Universities Recreation Research Group, 1973.

BENNETT, R — 'The Rugged South-West'. *Australian Photography*, v.25, Sept. 1974, pp.34–39.

BENT, P — 'Weekend in the west'. *Skyline*, no. 13, 1963, pp. 31–33.

BRAMMALL, C C D — 'Rugged Tasmania: challenge to the bushwalker'. *South-West Pacific*, no. 25, 1950, pp.59–65.

BROWN, R — 'A Tribute' (Olegas Truchanas). *Wildlife in Australia*, v.8, no.4, Dec. 1971, p.65.

CALDER, J E — 'Some account of the country between Lake St Clair and Macquarie Harbour'. *Tasmanian Journal of Natural Science*, v.3, no.6, 1849.

CHAPPELL, F R — 'S.W. Tasmania from the air'. *Tasmanian Education*, v.13, no.5, Mar. 1959, pp.138–140.

Cross Currents. (Tasmania. Hydro-Electric Commission) July 1973 and Dec. 1974.

CUTLER, C — 'Off the beaten track'. *Skyline*, no.19, 1969, pp.2–3.

DAVIES, J L (ed.) — *Atlas of Tasmania*. Hobart, Lands and Surveys Department, 1965.

EDWARDS, I J — 'Walking and awareness'. *Skyline*, no.20, 1970, pp.33–34.

ELLIOTT, D J — 'Lake Pedder'. *Southern Caver*, v.5, no.1, 1973, pp.12–13.

EMMETT, E T — 'Frenchmans Cap'. *Royal Society of Tasmania. Papers and Proceedings*, 1942, p.166.

FLEMING, K — 'Maatsuyker — south by south-west'. *Skyline*, no.22, 1976, pp.32–33.

FLEMING, P — 'Come fly with me — or how we littered the Southwest'. *Skyline*, no.17, 1967, pp.2–3.

FLEMING, P — 'The South West called the tune'. *Australian Outdoors*, June 1975, v.53, pp.10–13, 63–66.

FLEMING, P — 'The South West turned it on'. *Australian Outdoors*, v.53, July 1975, pp.27–30, 62–63.

FRAUCA, H — 'Australia's southernmost settlement'. *Walkabout*, Feb. 1959, pp.25–27.

GEE, H — 'Lilos through Gilgamesh: the Jane River'. *Skyline*, no.22, 1976, pp.14–16.

GLEESON, L — 'Exploration at Mt. Ronald Cross'. *Southern Caver*, v.6, no.1, 1974, pp.17–19.

GOEDE, A — 'Caves of Tasmania'. *Speleo Handbook*, 1967, pp.256–272.

GOEDE, A *et al* — *Caves of Tasmania*. Hobart, the Author, 1974. Limited circulation. This is a revision of the article in *Speleo Handbook*, 1967.

HALL, L — *The Canoeists Guide to Tasmania*. Ulverstone, Tasmanian Canoe Club, 1976.

HAWKINS, J as told to Frauca, H — 'Canoe saga'. *Australian Outdoors*. Part 1: July 1959, pp.27–29, 80–82; Part 2: Aug. 1959, pp.16–19, 71–73.

HIGGINS, M — 'Across a wilderness'. *Skyline*, no.22, 1976, pp.3–6.

HUTCHINSON, D — 'How the west was won'. *Skyline*, no.22, 1976, pp.28–31.

HUTCHINSON, D — 'Lyell Highway to Maydena'. *Skyline*, no.15, 1965, p.21.

JACKSON, W D — 'South-West Tasmania' (and) 'The Highlands of Tasmania'. in *Scenic Wonders of Australia*. Sydney, Readers Digest, 1976, pp.32–49.

'In the still of the bush'. *Skyline*, no.6, 1955, pp.7–8.

KIERNAN, K — 'The Descent of Khazad-Dûm'. *Southern Caver*, v.3, no.1, 1971, pp.3–5.

KIERNAN, K — 'Gordon River expedition'. *Southern Caver*, v.6, no.3, 1975, pp.2–6.

KIERNAN, K — 'Hastings Renaissance'. *Southern Caver*, v.3, no.2, 1974, pp.10–12.

KIERNAN, K — 'An historic descent'. *Southern Caver*, v.3, no.3, 1972, pp.6–8.

KIERNAN, K — 'Khazad-Dûm expedition'. *Southern Caver*, v.3, no.1, 1971, pp.6–9.

KIERNAN, K — 'The Surprise Bay area'. *Southern Caver*, v.5, no.2, 1973, pp.6–10.

LANCASTER, K — 'Algonkian'. *Skyline*, no.13, 1963, pp.56–58.

LANCASTER, K — 'Something new'. *Skyline*, no.14, 1964, pp.30–31.

LANE, H A — *I had a Quid to get: Adamsfield 1925 and Other Tasmanian Stories*. Burnie, The Author, 1976.

LYONS, G D (ed.) — 'Walks information West Coast area, south of the Lyell Highway'. *Skyline*, no.9, 1959, p.45.

McAULAY, I — 'Tasmania's wild South-West'. *Walkabout*, Aug. 1969, pp.41–46.

McGREGOR, A — 'The Island and me'. *Sunday Australian*, 30 Jan. 1972, p.19.

MAIDEN, T — 'Solid suburbia sprouts in rugged Tasmania'. *Australian Financial Review*, 6 Mar. 1970, pp.6–21.

MANNING, B — 'Back door to Mount Anne'. *Skyline*, no.12, 1962, pp.4–6.

MIDDLETON, G and MONTGOMERY, N — 'Southern Caving Society 'Precipitous Bluff Expedition'. *Sydney Speleological Society. Journal*, v.17, no.7, 1973, pp.185–212.

MIDDLETON, G and SEFTON, A	'S.S.S. Gordon — Franklin Expedition 1974-5, Tasmania'. *Sydney Speleological Society. Journal*, v.19, no.11, 1975, p.271.
MILES, T A	'Tasmania's wild West Coast'. *Walkabout*, Mar. 1955, p.29-33.
MILES, T A	'Tasmania's wild West'. *Walkabout*, Apr. 1961, p.27+.
MOSSEL, B	*Where No Road Goes*. South Australia, Enterprise Publications, 1972.
NEILSON, D	*South-West Tasmania — A Land of the Wild*. Adelaide, Rigby, 1975.
NOBLE, J A	*Australian Lighthouses*. Sydney, Nelson Doubleday, 1967.
O'BRIEN, P	'A Bit o' scoparia and a rockface'. *Skyline*, no.17, 1967, pp.13-16.
PEAKE, G	'Formidable Frenchman's Cap'. *Walkabout*, v.30, Apr. 1964, pp.30-33.
RADCLIFFE, P	'The Precipitous Bluff expedition'. *Sydney University Speleological Society Newsletter*, Mar. 1973, pp.86-87.
RAIT, N	'Huon pine is beyond man's reach'. *Australasian Post*, May 31, 1951, pp.20-21.
REID, O W	*A Hydro-Electric Town: Strathgordon*. Longman, Melbourne 1974.
REINMUTH, P	'All for Mary's wedding'. *Skyline*, no.22, 1976, pp.51-52.
SANDILANDS, B	'Federation Peak'. *Walkabout*, v.31, Dec. 1965, p.56+.
SANDILANDS, B	'Where the ice left its marks'. *Walkabout*, v.31, Mar. 1965, pp.28-31.
SKINNER, R K	'Hastings Caves'. *Speleo—Spiel*, 83, 1973, pp.5-10; 84, 1973, pp.4-5.
SKINNER, R K and SKINNER, A D	*Hastings Caves State Reserve, Tasmania: A Visitor's Guide*. Franklin, Huon News, 1976.
SMITH, P	'Duckies through Deception Gorge'. *Skyline*, no.22, 1976, pp.8-13.
SMITHIES, F	'Frenchman's Cap'. *Royal Society of Tasmania. Papers and Proceedings*, 1941, p.84.
	'South-West story'. *Wildlife in Australia*, v.5, no.2, June 1968, pp.34-38.
	Strathgordon's Button Grass Gazette. (Tasmania. Hydro-Electric Commission) 1971-1975.
THOMPSON, W I	'Traversing the Muellers'. *Skyline*, no.6, 1955, pp.30-32.
WATT, G	'Road to the Southern Frontier'. *Southern Caver*, v.3, no.1, 1971, pp.14-15.
WHITE, G	*De Witt Island Experiences*. Hobart, Cat and Fiddle Press, 1976.
WOOTEN, G	'In search of Vanishing Falls'. *Walkabout*, June/July 1974, pp.10-15.

HISTORY

ANDREW, J	'Notes in reference to "Scott's track", via Lake St. Clair to the west coast of Tasmania'. *Royal Society of Tasmania. Papers and Proceedings*, 1888, pp.49-52.
ANON	'An Historical sidelight on Judd's Cavern'. *Southern Caver*, v.3, no.1, 1971, p.30.
BEAGLEHOLE, J C	*The Journals of Captain James Cook: The Voyage of the Resolution and Adventure, 1772-1775*. London, Hakluyt Society, 1961, p.150, note 1 (from Wilby's journal).
BEATTIE, J W	Quinnat in the wild west: reprinted from the *Weekly Courier*, in 5 parts. Hobart, 1904.
BUCKIE, J	'Sir John Franklin's overland journey to Macquarie Harbour in 1842'. *Tasmanian Tramp*, no.10, 1951, pp.3-6.
BURN, D	*Narrative of the overland journey of Sir John and Lady Franklin and party from Hobart Town to Macquarie Harbour 1842*. Edited by George Mackaness. Sydney, D S Ford, 1955.
BURNEY, J	*With Captain James Cook in the Antarctic and Pacific: the Private Journal of James Burney, Second Lieutenant of the Adventure on Cook's Second Voyage, 1772-1773*. Edited by B Hooper. Canberra, National Libarary of Australia, 1975, pp.34-37.
CHAPMAN, G T F	'Looking back along the track'. *Tasmanian Tramp*, no.20, 1972, pp.92-97.
CHURCH, K	'Exploring with Frankland'. *Skyline*, no.6, 1955, pp.44-47.
COPLAND, D (ed.)	'Port Davey in Wartime'. In his *Giblin, the Scholar and the Man*. Melbourne, Cheshire, 1960, pp.121-126.
CRAWFORD, J , ELLIS, W F and STANCOMBE, G H (eds.)	*The Diaries of John Helder Wedge (1824-1835)*. Hobart, Royal Society of Tasmania, 1962.
	'Critchley Parker'. *Tasmanian Tramp*, no.6, 1945, p.5.
CROWTHER, W E L H	'Notes on Tasmanian whaling'. *Royal Society of Tasmania. Papers and Proceedings*, 1919, pp.130-151.
DAVIES, K *et al* (eds.)	'Aboriginal names in the Port Davey area'. *Tasmanian Tramp*, no.20, 1972, p.84.
	'Deadmans Bay'. *Tasmanian Tramp*, no.15, 1961, p.26.
	'83 years ago; an account of his first walk to Frenchmans Cap written by T B Moore in 1887'. *Skyline*, no.20, 1970, pp.5-9.
	'Ernie Bond of Gordonvale'. *Tasmanian Tramp*, no.16, 1963, pp.24-26.
FLINDERS, M	*Observations on the coasts of Van Diemen's Land on Bass Strait and its Islands, and on Part of the Coasts of New South Wales; intended to accompany the Charts of the Late Discoveries in those countries*. London, John Nichols, 1801.
FRANKLIN *Sir John*	*Narrative of some passages in the history of Van Diemen's Land during the last three years of Sir John Franklin's administration of its government*. Hobart, Platypus Publications, 1967. Facsimile of edition privately printed in London in 1845.
FRANKS, S M	'The First track to the West Coast'. *Tasmanian Historical Research Association. Papers and Proceedings*, Dec. 1957, pp.67-70.
FRANKS, S M	Land Exploration in Tasmania, 1824-1842, with Special Reference to the Van Diemen's Land Company. Thesis (M.A.) University of Tasmania, 1959. Part II, chapter 2, pp.127-212. (Includes maps.)
FRAUCA, H	'Death of a mining town'. *Walkabout*, June 1962, pp.26-27.
GOWLLAND, R , GOWLLAND, K and GOWLLAND, T	*Adamsfield: the town that lived and died*. Devonport, Richmond, 1973.
GOWLLAND, R and GOWLLAND, K	*Trampled Wilderness — A History of South-West Tasmania*. Devonport, Richmond, 1976.
	'The Gordon River. Exploration of "The Splits", "The Show Place of Tasmania." Sprent Falls Alone Worth the Trip'. 'Mercury' Special. Hobart, *The Mercury*, Apr. 12, 1928, p.5.
GREAT WESTERN RAILWAY AND ELECTRIC POWER CO. LTD.	West Coast of Tasmania: Some facts connected with the project known as 'The Great Western Railway'. Hobart, Mercury, 1897.
HOBART AND WEST COAST RAILWAY LEAGUE	(Report of a Subcommittee) to the Chairman and members of the Hobart and West Coast Railway League. Hobart, The League, 1897.
JUDD, H	*The Dark Lantern: or Hidden side of Nature*. Hobart, The Mercury, 1896. Held by the State Library of Tasmania.
JULEN, H	*The Penal Settlement of Macquarie Harbour*. Launceston, Mary Fisher, 1976.
KAY, J H	'Remarks to accompany Mr. Calder's paper on the country lying between Lake St. Clair and Macquarie Harbour'. *Tasmanian Journal of Natural Science, Agriculture, Statistics, etc.*, v.3, 1842, pp.389-393.
KELLY, J	'The First discovery of Port Davey and Macquarie Harbour'. *Royal Society of Tasmania. Papers and Proceedings*, 1920, pp.160-181.
LEGGE, W V	'Mr W C Piguenit: an appreciation of a Tasmanian artist'. *The Tasmanian Mail*, May 6, 1915.
LEMPRIERE, T J	'Account of Macquarie Harbour'. *Tasmanian Journal of Natural Science, Agriculture, Statistics, etc.*, v.1, 1842, pp.359-375; v.2, 1846/49, pp.17-31, 107-118, 200-208.
LORD, C E	'Notes on Captain Bligh's Visits to Tasmania in 1778 and 1792'. *Royal Society of Tasmania. Papers and Proceedings*, 1922, pp.1-21.
LORD, C E	'The South Coast and Port Davey, Tasmania'. *Royal Society of Tasmania. Papers and Proceedings*, 1927, pp.1-16 + 12 plates.
LUCKMAN, J S	'Mt Field National Park: historical notes'. *Tasmanian Tramp*, no.11, 1953, pp.30-34.
McLEAN, F K *et al*	*Report of the Solar Eclipse Expedition to Port Davey, Tasmania, May 1910*. Suffolk, R Clay, 1911.
McCRAE, M D	'Port Davey and the South-West'. *Tasmanian Historical Research Association. Papers and Proceedings*, v.8, no.3, 1960.
MONTGOMERY, H H	'A Survey of two early journeys westward — Mr W S Sharland in 1832, and Sir John Franklin in 1842'. *Royal Society of Tasmania. Papers and Proceedings*, 1899, pp.liii-lv.

MOORE-ROBINSON, J   *A Record of Tasmanian Nomenclature with Dates and Origins.* Hobart, The Mercury, 1911.

MOUNT LYELL TOURIST ASSOCIATION, Queenstown   *The Book of Mount Lyell and the Gordon: a Land of Riches and Beauty* (by C Whitham). Queenstown, The Association, 1917.

O'MAY, H   *Wooden Hookers of Hobart Town,* and *Whalers out of Van Diemen's Land.* Hobart, Govt. Printer, 1957.

O'MAY, H   'The modern fishing ketch "Derwent Hunter" — trip to the West Coast'. In his *Hobart River Craft.* Hobart, Govt. Printer, 1959, p.106.

O'MAY, H   *Wrecks in Tasmanian Waters 1797-1950.* 3rd. edn. Hobart, Govt. Printer, 1971.

PERON, F   *Voyage de decouvertes aux Terres Australes.* Paris, Imprimerie Royale, 1807-1816.

PIGUENIT, W C   *Among the Western Highlands of Tasmania.* Reprint from the Transactions of the Australasian Association for the Advancement of Science, Hobart Meeting, 1892.

PLOMLEY, N J B (ed.)   *Friendly Mission: the Tasmanian Journals and Papers of George Augustus Robinson, 1829-1834.* Hobart, Tasmanian Historical Research Association, 1966.

PRETYMAN, E R   'Pirates at Recherche Bay, or the loss of the brig "Cyprus"'. *Royal Society of Tasmania. Papers and Proceedings,* v.88, 1954, pp.119-128.

RHYS-JONES, M   *The Great Western Railway in Relation to the State and Labour.* (An address delivered to Denison No. 1 Branch, W.P.L., Hobart, July 29, 1907). Hobart, Clipper, 1907.

SCOTT, J R   'Port Davey in 1875'. *Royal Society of Tasmania. Papers and Proceedings,* 1875, pp.94-107.

SMITHIES, F   'Visit of Sir John Franklin and Lady Franklin to Macquarie Harbour in 1842'. *Royal Society of Tasmania. Papers and Proceedings,* 1943, p.245.

TASMANIA. PARLIAMENT   'Boat expeditions round Tasmania 1815-16 and 1824': reports. Parliamentary paper No.107 of 1881.

THWAITES, J B   'In the footsteps of Sir John Franklin overland from Lake St. Clair to the Gordon River'. *Royal Society of Tasmania. Papers and Proceedings,* v.89, 1954, pp.vii-ix.

WALKER, J B   *Early Tasmania. Papers read before the Royal Society of Tasmania during the Years 1888-1889.* Hobart, Govt. Printer, 1914.

WHITHAM, C   *Western Tasmania: a Land of Riches and Beauty.* Queenstown, Mount Lyell Tourist Association, 1924.

See also the Tasmanian Department of Mines' unpublished reports listed in the Geology Section.

PICTORIAL HISTORY

Although much material exists in private collections, noteworthy pictorial material of historical interest is held in several Tasmanian museums and art galleries. **The Allport Library and Museum of Fine Arts** contains prints by Charles Bruce, T J Lempriere, Joseph Lycett and J R Scott. There are also photographs by Henry Allport, Morton Allport and John Watt Beattie.

A number of photographs, some in the form of postcards by J W Beattie, and photographs by S Clifford are to be found in the **W L Crowther Library** and in the **Tasmanian Collection. The Tasmanian Museum and Art Gallery** hold a number of paintings by W C Piguenit, prints by Joseph Lycett and a small collection of lantern slides by J W Beattie. Of greatest note in the Queen Victoria Museum are two paintings, one by Haughton Forrest and one by William Duke. A number of Beattie's lantern slides are stored there also.

The Queenstown Museum, Sticht Street, contains several interesting photographs pertaining in particular to the Gordon River.

TASMANIAN PARLIAMENTARY PAPERS 1856–1950

1856:   L.C. No. 3, Gordon River Road and Dunrobin Bridge.

1856:   No. 67, Select Committee on Waste Lands Bill: Report.

1860:   No. 44, Exploration of Huon District: Report by G Innes.

1860:   No. 46, Statistics of Waste Lands of Tasmania, by J E Calder.

1860:   No. 70, Huon Exploration: Report by R Hall.

1862:   No. 26, Report on the Exploration of Macquarie Harbour, by C Gould.

1863:   No. 9, Report on the Exploration of the Western Country, by C Gould.

1863:   No. 64, Select Committee on the Waste Lands Bill: Report.

1863:   No. 71, Memorandum re Report of Select Committee on Waste Lands Bill, by J E Calder.

1867:   No. 39, Report of Surveyor Thomas on Gould's New Country.

1869:   No. 33, Report on the Waste Lands of the Colony, by R Crawford.

1870:   No. 61, Report on the Waste Lands of the Colony, by R Crawford.

1870:   No. 55, Gordon River Road: Correspondence.

1876:   No. 104, Letter from J R Scott, M.L.C. to Minister for Lands and Works, relative to Exploration of Western Country.

1877:   No. 27, Report of Crown Lands on Western Country, by C P Sprent.

1878:   No. 48, Report on Track to Macquarie Harbour from Gordon River (Gordon Bend), by T Frodsham.

1878:   No. 132, Select Committee on Preservation of Huon Pine and Blackwood.

1880:   No. 43, Report on Exploration of the Huon District, by G. Innes.

1880:   No. 112, Select Committee on the Waste Lands Bill: Report.

1880:   No. 116, Report of Select Committee on Gordon River Road Contract.

1881:   No. 121, Macquarie and Trial Harbour: Reports of C R Sprent.

1881:   No. 126, Track from Macquarie Harbour to Upper Huon: Sprent, Jones, McPartlan, Richardson and Counsel. Reports and Instructions.

1883:   No. 56, Report on Exploration of Country between Lake St. Clair and Macquarie Harbour, by T B Moore.

1886:   No. 68, Macquarie Harbour Pine Forests, West Coast: Report by G S Perrin, Conservator of Forests.

1886:   No. 128, Huon Track: Report by T B Moore.

1887:   No. 58, Expedition from Ouse to Mt. Lyell and Macquarie Harbour, E Counsel (Deputy Surveyor-General) and party.

1889:   No. 35, Huon Pine Forests, West Coast: Report by Conservator of Forests.

1890:   No. 77, Exploration of Florentine Valley: Report on Making of Track, by T Frodsham.

1890:   No. 79, Forests, Picton & Port Davey: Report by Conservator of Forests.

1891:   No. 116, Report of Select Committee on Macquarie Harbour Works Bill (Private).

1896:   No. 82, Report of Surveyors upon Country between Mt Humboldt and Mt Arrowsmith (route Rasselas—West Coast), by T Frodsham.

1897:   No. 43, Report of Route to West Coast, by H M Nicholls.

1898:   No. 48, Forests of Tasmania: Conservation and Future Management. Report by Conservator of State Forests, Victoria.

1911:   No. 39, Joint and Select Committees on the Port Davey Development Bill 1911 (Private).

1932:   No. 4, Select Joint Committees on Florentine Valley Wood Pulp and Paper Industry Bill.

1949:   No. 31, Select and Joint Committees on National Park & Florentine Valley Bill 1949 (No. 5).

1950:   No. 37, Select and Joint Committees on National Park & Florentine Valley Bill 1950.

Information about the South-West may also be found in departmental annual reports filed as parliamentary papers since 1950: those of particular relevance being Forestry Commission, Hydro-Electric Commission, National Parks and Wildlife Service and Rural Fires Board Reports.

GOVERNMENT PUBLICATIONS

AUSTRALIA. COMMITTEE OF INQUIRY INTO THE NATIONAL ESTATE   *Report of the Committee of Inquiry into the National Estate.* Canberra, Australian Government Publishing Service, 1974.

AUSTRALIA. LAKE PEDDER COMMITTEE OF ENQUIRY   *The Future of Lake Pedder: interim report, June 1973.* Canberra, A.G.P.S., 1973.

AUSTRALIA. LAKE PEDDER COMMITTEE OF ENQUIRY — *Final report, April 1974, the flooding of Lake Pedder: an analysis of the Lake Pedder controversy and its implications for the planning of major development projects and the management of natural resources in Australia.* Canberra, A.G.P.S. for the Dept. of the Environment and Conservation, 1974.

CUNNINGHAM, *Dr* T M — The Role of Tasmania's forests: a paper presented on behalf of the Tasmanian Forestry Commission at a symposium sponsored by the Tasmanian Conservation Trust, Inc. Hobart, 1974. In *The Future of Tasmania's Forests*. Hobart, Tasmanian Conservation Trust, 1974.

FORESTRY & WOOD-BASED INDUSTRIES DEVELOPMENT CONFERENCE — Canberra, 1974. *Forwood Report of Panels 3, 4, 5, 6, 7, 8.* Canberra, A.G.P.S., 1974.

SNOWY MOUNTAINS ENGINEERING CORPORATION — *Engineering review of Interim report of Lake Pedder Committee of Enquiry, June 1973 — August 1973.* Canberra, Government Printer, 1974. Parliamentary paper No. 189 of 1973.

SOUTH-WEST ADVISORY COMMITTEE, Hobart — *Preliminary Report to the Minister for National Parks and Wildlife.* Hobart, 1976. (127 submissions, containing much valuable, unpublished material, were received). *Final Report.* Hobart, 1978.

TASMANIA. FORESTRY COMMISSION — *Five year plan of operations, 1st July 1975 to 30th June 1980.* Hobart, 1975.

TASMANIA. FORESTRY COMMISSION — *Working plan for the State Forests in Southern Tasmania.* Hobart, 1974.

TASMANIA. HYDRO-ELECTRIC COMMISSION — *Annual Reports, 1955–1977.*

TASMANIA. HYDRO-ELECTRIC COMMISSION — Statement of the proposed access road to the Gordon River, S.W. Tasmania, Hobart, July 1963.

TASMANIA. HYDRO-ELECTRIC COMMISSION — *Gordon River power development, Stage one, and Thermal Power Station: (report and map).* Hobart, Govt. Printer, 1967.

TASMANIA. HYDRO-ELECTRIC COMMISSION — *Cross Currents*, July 1973 and December 1974.

TASMANIA. HYDRO-ELECTRIC COMMISSION — *Annual review*, 1974–1975.

TASMANIA. NATIONAL PARKS & WILDLIFE SERVICE — *Southwest National Park: draft management plan, 1975.* Hobart, 1975.

TASMANIA. NATIONAL PARKS & WILDLIFE SERVICE — Submission to Special Advisory Committee on South-West Tasmania, Hobart, 1976.

TASMANIA. PARLIAMENT. LEGISLATIVE COUNCIL. SELECT COMMITTEE — *Report on the Gordon River and Thermal Power Development.* Hobart, 1967. Parliamentary paper No. 25 of 1967.

See also the Tasmanian Mines Department's publications and unpublished reports in the Geology section.

TASMANIAN ACT OF PARLIAMENT — *Scenery Preservation Act, 1915* (no.15 of 1915).

TASMANIAN ACT OF PARLIAMENT — *Hydro-Electric Commission Act, 1944* (no.95 of 1944).

TASMANIAN ACT OF PARLIAMENT — *Forestry Act, 1954* (no.49 of 1954).

TASMANIAN ACT OF PARLIAMENT — *Hydro-Electric Commission (Power Development) Act, 1967* (no.30 of 1967).

TASMANIAN ACT OF PARLIAMENT — *National Parks and Wildlife Act, 1970* (no.47 of 1970).

GEOLOGY

ANON — 'The Mt Ronald Cross surveys'. *Southern Caver*, v.7, no.3, 1976, pp.4–12.

BAILLIE, P W and CLARKE, M J — Preliminary comments on the early Palaeozoic (late Ordovician — early Silurian) rocks and fossils in the Huntley Quadrangle. Hobart, Tasmania. Dept. of Mines, 1976. Unpublished report.

BAKER, W E and AHMAD, N — 'Re-examination of the fjord theory of Port Davey, Tasmania'. *Royal Society of Tasmania. Papers and Proceedings*, v.93, 1959, pp.113–115.

BANKS, M R — 'From Eddystone to Davey: The journal of a geological trek across Tasmania'. *Tasmanian Tramp*, no.18, 1968, pp.69–76.

BANKS, M R — 'Mt Field National Park: geological notes'. *Tasmanian Tramp*, no.11, 1953, pp.34–35.

BANKS, M R — 'Permian System in West Tasmania'. *Royal Society of Tasmania. Papers and Proceedings*, v.96, 1962, pp.1–18.

BANKS, M R — 'Port Davey: Geological notes on the far South West of Tasmania'. *Tasmanian Tramp*, no.15, 1961, pp.63–66.

BANKS, M R and CORBETT, K D — 'Revised terminology of the late Cambrian—Ordovician sequence of the Florentine—Denison Range area, and the significance of the "Junee Group"'. *Royal Society of Tasmania. Papers and Proceedings*, v.109, 1975, pp.121–126.

BANKS, M R and JOHNSON, J H — '*Maclurites* and *Girvanella* in the Gordon River Limestone (Ordovician) of Tasmania'. *Journal of Paleontology*, v.31, no.3, 1957, pp.632–640.

BELL, C N — 'Macquarie Harbour: its physical aspect and future prospects'. *Royal Society of Tasmania. Papers and Proceedings*, Apr. 1899, pp.xxviii–xxxiii.

BLAKE, F — The Country along route of the Craycroft track from Glen Huon to Frankland Range, Hobart, Tasmania. Dept. of Mines, 1935. Unpublished report.

BLAKE, F — Nicholls Range copper deposit. Hobart, Tasmania. Dept. of Mines, 1938. Unpublished report.

BLAKE, F — Preliminary report on Jane River gold field. Hobart, Tasmania. Dept. of Mines, 1935. Unpublished report.

BOULTER, C A — 'Structural sequence in the metamorphosed Precambrian rocks of the Frankland and Wilmot Ranges, South-Western Tasmania'. *Royal Society of Tasmania. Papers and Proceedings*, v.107, 1974, pp.105–115.

BOWEN, E A and MACLEAN, C J — 'Palaeozoic rocks of the Davey River, South-West Tasmania'. *Royal Society of Tasmania. Papers and Proceedings*, v.105, 1971, pp.21–28.

BROWN, A V, TURNER, N J and WILLIAMS, E — 'The basal beds of the Junee Group'. *Royal Society of Tasmania. Papers and Proceedings*, v.109, 1975, pp.107–109.

CHAPMAN, F — 'On the occurrence of *Tetradium* in the Gordon River limestone, Tasmania'. *Tasmania. Geological Survey. Record*, no.5, 1919.

CLARKE, M J — 'Cambrian and Ordovician fossils from the Macquarie Harbour area'. *Tasmania. Dept. of Mines. Technical Report*, no.12, 1967, pp.146–149.

COLHOUN, E and GOEDE, A — Quaternary deposits of Blakes Opening. In preparation, Hobart, April 1977.

COLLINS, P L F — Economic potential of the Gordon Limestone in the lower Gordon River area. Hobart, Tasmania. Dept. of mines, 1975. Unpublished report, no.53 of 1975.

CORBETT, K D — Sedimentology of the Upper Cambrian flyshparalic sequence (Denison Group) on the Denison Range, South-West Tasmania. Thesis (Ph.D.) University of Tasmania, 1971.

CORBETT, K D and BANKS, M R — 'Ordovician stratigraphy of the Florentine Synclinorium, South-West Tasmania'. *Royal Society of Tasmania. Papers and Proceedings*, v.107, 1974, pp.207–238.

CORBETT, K D, BANKS M R and JAGO, J B — 'Plate Tectonics and the Lower Palaeozoic of Tasmania'. *Nature Physical Science*, v.240, no.97, 1972, pp.9–11.

DAVIDSON, J K — 'Glaciation of the Mt La Perouse area'. *Royal Society of Tasmania. Papers and Proceedings*, v.105, 1971, pp.117–180.

DERBYSHIRE, E D *et al* — A Glacial Map of Tasmania. Hobart, Royal Society of Tasmania, 1965. (Includes notes and bibliography).

DUNCAN, D M — 'Reconnaissance geology of the Frenchmans Cap National Park'. *Royal Society of Tasmania. Papers and Proceedings*, v.107, 1974, pp.191–195.

FLOOD, P — 'Lower Devonian brachiopods from the Point Hibbs limestone of Western Tasmania'. *Royal Society of Tasmania. Papers and Proceedings*, v.108, 1974, pp.113–136.

FORD, R J — 'The geology of the Upper Huon-Arve River area'. *Royal Society of Tasmania. Papers and Proceedings*, v.90, 1956, pp.147–156.

GEE, R D, MOORE, W R and PIKE, G — 'The Geology of the Lower Gordon River, particularly the Devonian sequence'. Paleontology by M J Clarke. *Tasmania. Geological Survey. Record*, no.8, 1970.

GOEDE, A — 'Caves of Tasmania'. *Speleo Handbook*, 1967, pp.256–272.

GOEDE, A *et al* — Caves of Tasmania. Hobart, The Author, 1974. Limited edition. This is a revision of the article in *Speleo Handbook*, 1967.

GOEDE, A — 'Underground stream capture at Ida Bay, Tasmania and the relevance of cold climatic conditions'. *Australian Geographical Studies*, 7, 1969, pp.41–48.

GOULD, C — 'On the position of the Gordon limestones relative to other palaeozoic formations etc'. *Royal Society of Tasmania. Papers and Proceedings*, 1866, pp.27–29.

HAWKINS, R, KIERNAN, K and MIDDLETON, G — 'Reconnaissance trip to limestone areas in the Gordon and Franklin Rivers in South-West Tasmania'. *Sydney Speleological Society. Journal*, v.18, no.7, 1974, pp.177–192.

HENDERSON, Q J — Geology of country in vicinity of Old Humboldt Mine. Hobart, Tasmania. Dept. of Mines, 1939. Unpublished report.

HENDERSON Q J — Reported tin lode near Bathurst Harbour. Hobart, Tasmania. Dept. of Mines, 1938. Unpublished report.

HILLS, L — 'The Jukes-Darwin mining field'. Tasmania. Geological Survey. Bulletin, no.16, 1914.

HILLS, L — 'Geological reconnaissance of the country between Cape Sorell and Point Hibbs'. Tasmania. Geological Survey. Bulletin, no.18, 1914.

HUGHES, T D — 'Application for two gravel leases near the junction of the Huon and Picton Rivers'. Tasmania. Dept. of Mines. Technical Report, no.5, 1960, p.72.

HUGHES, T D — Copper prospects, Mt Mueller Mine. Hobart, Tasmania. Dept. of Mines, 1952. Unpublished report.

HUGHES, T D — 'Limestone in Tasmania'. Tasmania. Geological Survey. Mineral Resources, no.10, 1959.

HUGHES, T D — 'Silica deposits near Hastings'. Tasmania. Dept. of Mines. Technical Report, no.4, 1959, pp.28–34.

JAGO, J B — 'Geology of the Maydena Range'. Royal Society of Tasmania. Papers and Proceedings, v.106, 1972, pp.45–57.

JELL, J S and HILL, D — 'The Devonian coral fauna of the Point Hibbs Limestone'. Royal Society of Tasmania. Papers and Proceedings, v.104, 1970, pp.1–16.

JENNINGS, I B — 'Notes on the geology of portion of South-West Tasmania'. Tasmania. Dept. of Mines. Technical Report, no.5, 1960, pp.179–185.

JOHNSTON, R M — 'Macquarie Harbour leaf beds'. Royal Society of Tasmania. Papers and Proceedings, 1889, p.53.

JOHNSTON, R M — Systematic account of the geology of Tasmania. Hobart, Government Printer, 1888.

KEID, H G W — Geological report Port Davey. Hobart, Tasmania. Dept. of Mines, 1944. Unpublished report.

KEID, H G W — Heathorn's gold prospects, New River. Hobart, Tasmania. Dept. of Mines, 1951. Unpublished report.

KIERNAN, K — 'Caves and karst of Junee-Florentine, Tasmania'. Australian Speleological Newsletter, no.53, 1971, pp.4–10.

KIERNAN, K — 'Caves of the Hastings District'. Southern Caver, v.2, no.4, 1970, pp.3–7.

KIERNAN, K — 'Junee-Florentine'. Southern Caver, v.2, no.3, 1970, pp.13–15.

KIERNAN, K — 'The Karst area in the Weld River Valley South-Western Tasmania'. Southern Caver, v.6, no.4, 1975, pp.4–7.

KIERNAN, K — 'Revised cave list for Lower Gordon limestone area'. Sydney Speleological Society. Journal, v.18, no.7, 1974, p.193.

KNIGHTS, C J — 'Representative basin study: Sandfly Creek, south-western Tasmania'. Tasmania. Dept. of Mines. Technical Report, no.19, 1974, pp.100–105.

KOBAYASHI, T — 'Lower Ordovician fossils from Junee, Tasmania'. Royal Society of Tasmania. Papers and Proceedings, 1939, pp.61–66.

LEWIS, A N — 'A Further account of the geology of the Catamaran Coal Field'. Royal Society of Tasmania. Papers and Proceedings, 1927, pp.188–210.

LEWIS, A N — 'A Further note on the topography of Lake Fenton and district'. Royal Society of Tasmania. Papers and Proceedings, 1922, pp.32–39.

LEWIS, A N — 'Geology of the Tyenna Valley'. Royal Society of Tasmania. Papers and Proceedings, 1939 (1940), pp.33–59.

LEWIS, A N — 'Note on Pleistocene glaciation, Mt Field to Strahan'. Royal Society of Tasmania. Papers and Proceedings, 1938, pp.161–173.

LEWIS, A N — 'Notes on a geological reconnaissance of Mt Anne and the Weld River Valley, South-Western Tasmania'. Royal Society of Tasmania. Papers and Proceedings, 1923, pp.9–42.

LEWIS, A N — 'Notes on a geological reconnaissance of Mt La Perouse Range'. Royal Society of Tasmania. Papers and Proceedings, 1924, pp.9–44.

LEWIS, A N — 'A Preliminary sketch of the glacial remains preserved in the National Park of Tasmania'. Royal Society of Tasmania. Papers and Proceedings, 1921, pp.16–36 + maps and illus.

MACLEOD, W A — 'Notes on a fossil wood from Cox Bight'. Royal Society of Tasmania. Papers and Proceedings, 1898–9, pp.85–87.

MOORE, T B — 'Discovery of glaciation in the vicinity of Mt Tyndall, in Tasmania'. Royal Society of Tasmania. Papers and Proceedings, 1893, pp.147–149.

MORLEY, J — 'Limestone at Franklin River'. Southern Caver, v.3, no.1, 1974, p.10.

NICHOLLS, H W — 'Notes on the geology of La Perouse'. Royal Society of Tasmania. Papers and Proceedings, 1898–99, p.ii.

NOLDART, A J — 'Notes on antimony deposits, Joe Page Bay, Port Davey'. Tasmania. Dept. of Mines. Technical Report, no.15, 1970, pp.44–46.

NYE, P B — Antimony minerals in Tasmania. Hobart, Tasmania. Dept. of Mines, 1941. Unpublished report.

NYE, P B — Cox Bight Tin Fields. Hobart, Tasmania. Dept. of Mines, 1927. Unpublished report.

NYE, P B — Geology of the Port Davey district. Hobart, Tasmania. Dept. of Mines, 1930. Unpublished report.

NYE, P B — Gold prospects at Adamsfield. Hobart, Tasmania. Dept. of Mines, 1927. Unpublished report.

NYE, P B — Osmiridium bearing ground on Adamsfield. Hobart, Tasmania. Dept. of Mines, 1930. Unpublished report.

NYE, P B — 'The Osmiridium deposits of the Adamsfield district'. Tasmania. Geological Survey. Bulletin, no.39, 1929.

NYE, P B — Osmirdium 'lode' at head of Main Creek, Adamsfield. Hobart, Tasmania. Dept. of Mines, 1930. Unpublished report.

NYE, P B — Preliminary report, Adams River osmiridium field. Hobart, Tasmania. Dept. of Mines, 1925. Unpublished report.

NYE, P B — Preliminary report, Port Davey district. Hobart, Tasmania. Dept. of Mines, 1928. Unpublished report.

NYE, P B — Proposal to drain the Adams River flats. Hobart, Tasmania. Dept. of Mines, 1931. Unpublished report.

NYE, P B — Supposed fossiliferous rocks of upper Pre-Cambrian age from Port Davey. Hobart, Tasmania. Dept. of Mines 1930. Unpublished report.

PETERSON, J A — 'Glaciation of the Frenchmans Cap National Park'. Royal Society of Tasmania. Papers and Proceedings, v.100, 1966, pp.117–129.

POWELL, C McA — 'Polyphase folding in precambrian low-grade metamorphic rocks, middle Gordon River, South-Western Tasmania'. Royal Society of Tasmania. Papers and Proceedings, v.103, 1969, pp.47–51.

REID, A M — Adams River osmiridium field. Hobart, Tasmania. Dept. of Mines, 1925. Unpublished report.

REID, A M — Cox Bight tin field. Bore logs. Hobart, Tasmania. Dept. of Mines, 1928. Unpublished report.

REID, A M — Cox Bight tin mining (Letter to M Freney). Hobart, Tasmania. Dept. of Mines, 1928. Unpublished report.

REID, A M — 'Osmiridium in Tasmania'. Tasmania. Geological Survey. Bulletin, no.32, 1921.

ROWE, S M — 'Gordon River limestone deposits'. Tasmania. Dept. of Mines. Technical Report, no.7, 1962, pp.36–43.

SCOTT, B — 'Comments on Cainozoic history of Western Tasmania'. Queen Victoria Museum. Records, n.s. no.12, pp.1–10.

SCOTT, B — 'Lower Palaeozoic unconformities in South-West Tasmania'. Royal Society of Tasmania. Papers and Proceedings, v.94, 1960, pp.103–110.

SCOTT, T, ROBERTS, R A and HOBBS, J — Report of surveyors on coal at South Cape Bay and Adventure Bay. Hobart, Survey Office, 1826. Parliamentary paper L.C. No.16 of 1861.

SHIRLEY, B — 'Tasminex exclusive. Tin Creek boss still hopes for bonanza'. Jobson's Investment Digest, Mar. 1970, pp.3–22.

SPRY, A — 'The Precambrian rocks of Tasmania Part v. Petrology and structure of the Frenchmans Cap area'. Royal Society of Tasmania. Papers and Proceedings, v.97, 1963, pp.105–127.

SPRY, A and BAKER, W — 'The Precambrian rocks of Tasmania Part vii. Notes on the petrology of some rocks from the Port Davey, Bathurst Harbour area'. Royal Society of Tasmania. Papers and Proceedings, v.99, 1965, pp.17–26.

SPRY, A and GEE, R D — 'Some effects of Palaeozoic folding on the Precambrian rocks of the Frenchmans Cap area'. Geological Magazine, v.101, no.5, 1964, pp.885–896.

STEFANSKI, M Z — 'Denison copper prospects, western Port Davey'. Tasmania. Dept. of Mines. Technical Report, no.5, 1960, pp.60–62.

STEFANSKI, M Z — 'Geology of the Spring and Crossing rivers'. *Tasmania. Dept. of Mines. Technical Report*, no.4, 1959. pp.49–50.

STEFANSKI, M Z — 'Progress report on regional geological survey of the Port Davey — Cox Bight area'. Appendix by G Everard. *Tasmania. Dept. of Mines. Technical Report*, no.2, 1957, pp.87–106.

STEFANSKI, M Z — 'Tin deposits of the South West'. *Tasmania. Dept. of Mines. Technical Report*, no.2, 1957, pp.79–86.

STEPHENSON, J — 'An Unconformity in South-West Tasmania'. *Royal Society of Tasmania. Papers and Proceedings*, v.88, 1954. pp.151–2.

TAYLOR, A M — 'Precambrian rocks of the Old River area'. *Tasmania. Dept. of Mines. Technical Report*, no.4, 1959, pp.34–46.

TAYLOR, B L — 'Asbestos in Tasmania'. *Tasmania. Geological Survey. Mineral Resources*, no.9, 1955.

THREADER, V M — 'Reconnaissance around Strahan and Cape Sorell for stone and concrete aggregate supplies'. *Tasmania. Dept. of Mines. Technical Report*, no.10, 1965, pp.21–22.

TWELVETREES, W H — 'The Catamaran and Strathblane coalfields and coal and limestone at Ida Bay, Southern Tasmania'. *Tasmania. Geological Survey. Bulletin*, no.20, 1915.

TWELVETREES, W H — 'The Iron ore deposits of Tasmania'. *Tasmania. Geological Survey. Mineral Resources*, no.6, 1919.

TWELVETREES, W H — 'Reconnaissance of the country between Recherche Bay and New River, Southern Tasmania'. *Tasmania. Geological Survey. Bulletin*, no.24, 1915.

TWELVETREES, W H — 'Report on a journey from Tyenna to the Gordon River Crossing', in *Tasmania. Dept. of Lands and Surveys. Report*, 1908–1909. Parliamentary paper No.21 of 1909, pp.25–31.

TWELVETREES, W H — 'Report on the geological exploration of the country between Tyenna and the Gell River', in *Tasmania. Dept. of Lands and Surveys. Report*, 1907–1908. Parliamentary paper No.13 of 1908, pp.25–33.

WALLER, G A — 'Report on some discoveries of copper ore in the vicinity of Point Hibbs', in *Tasmania. Secretary for Mines. Report*, 1901–1902. Parliamentary paper No.13 of 1902, pp.92–94.

Further information can be found in the Tasmanian Department of Mines Geological Open File Reports. Company reports and reports on exploration in any part of Tasmania are filed under a quadrangle system. See Geological Open File Reports index under Quadrangles 71, 72, 73, 78, 79, 80, 81, 85, 86, 87, 91, 92, 93, 96 and 97 in the Tasmanian Department of Mines Library, Hobart.

Unpublished reports cited above are located in the Department of Mines Library, Hobart.

BIOLOGY

ANDREWS, A I — 'A Revision of the family Galaxidae (Pisces) in Tasmania'. *Australian Journal of Marine and Freshwater Research*, v.27, no.2, 1976, pp.297–349.

ANDREWS, A P — 'Some' recent mammal records from the Lake Pedder area, South-West Tasmania'. *Royal Society of Tasmania. Papers and Proceedings*, v.102, 1968, pp.17–21.

ANON — 'Birds seen at Low Rocky Cape — Birch Inlet, January 1969'. *Tasmanian Naturalist*, no.48, 1971, p.8.

AVES, K — 'Cushions and creepers in National Park'. *Tasmanian Tramp*, no.6, 1945, pp.29–31.

BAYLY, I A E — 'The Fate of Lake Pedder and its biota'. *Australian Society for Limnology. Newsletter*, v.4, no.2, 1965, pp.26–30.

BAYLY, I A E — 'The Sand fauna of Lake Pedder'. *Australian Journal of Marine and Freshwater Research*, v.24, 1973, pp.303–306.

BAYLY, I A E — 'The Scientific case for saving a lake from drowning: Pedder's death also nature's'. *The Age*, Melbourne, 12 Mar. 1972, p.9.

BAYLY, A I E *et al* — 'Lake Pedder; its importance to biological science'. In Australian Conservation Foundation. *Pedder Papers*. Parkville, Vic., The Foundation, 1972, pp.41–49.

BAYLY, I A E *et al* — 'Preliminary limnological investigation of Lake Pedder, Tasmania'. *Australian Society for Limnology. Newsletter*, v.5, no.2, 1965.

BIRD OBSERVERS CLUB OF TASMANIA — 'A Checklist of the birds of Mount Field National Park'. *Tasmanian Naturalist*, no.48, 1977, pp.6–8.

BROWN, M J, SHEPHERD, R R and JACKSON, W D — The Vegetation of Cape Sorell, EIS. for Comalco Pty. Ltd.

BUCKNEY, R T — 'Aspects of the chemical variability of some Tasmanian inland waters'. *Australian Journal of Marine and Freshwater Research*, v.27, no.3, 1976, pp.351–358.

BUCKNEY, R T and TYLER, P A — 'Chemistry of some sedgeland waters: Lake Pedder'. *Australian Journal of Marine and Freshwater Research*, v.24, 1973, pp.267–273.

CASSON, P B — 'The Forests of Western Tasmania'. *Australian Forestry. The Journal of the Institute of Foresters, Australia*, v.16, 1952, pp.17–86.

DAVIS, C — 'Preliminary survey of the vegetation near New Harbour'. *Royal Society of Tasmania. Papers and Proceedings*, 1940 (1941), pp.1–9.

DAVIS, M — 'Port Davey, South-West Tasmania'. *Victorian Naturalist*, v.72, May 1955.

FRANKENBERG, R — 'Two new species of Galaxid fishes from the Lake Pedder region'. *Australian Zoology*, v.14, 1968, pp.268–274.

GILBERT, J M — 'Forest succession in the Florentine Valley, Tasmania'. *Royal Society of Tasmania. Papers and Proceedings*, v.93, 1959, pp.129–151.

GREEN, R H and MOLLISON, B C — 'Birds of Port Davey and South Coast of Tasmania'. *Emu*, v.61, Part 3, 1961, pp.223–236.

GOEDE, A — 'New species discovered in Exit Cave'. *Speleo Spiel*, 1973, p.3.

GUILLER, E R — 'Faunal protection areas in Tasmania'. *Tasmanian Fauna Bulletin*, 3, 1966, pp.1–10.

GUILLINE, H — 'Mt Field National Park: flora and fauna notes'. *Tasmanian Tramp*, no.11, 1953, pp.36–37.

GUILLINE, H — 'The Vegetation of the Port Davey area'. *Tasmanian Tramp*, no.15, 1961, pp.67–72.

JACKSON, W D (Convenor) — 'Conservation in Tasmania'. In Specht, R L, Roe, E M and Broughton, V H, (eds.) 'Conservation of major plant communities in Australia and Papua New Guinea'. *Australian Journal of Botany*, Supplement No.7, July 1974, pp.319–448.

KIRKPATIRCK, J B (ed.) — *Proceedings of the West Coast Symposium*. Royal Society of Tasmania, 1977.

KIRKPATRICK, J B *et al* — *The Role of fire in the management of Tasmania's National Parks and the South-West area.* (Proceedings of a symposium held by the Tasmanian Conservation Trust Inc., SGAP and the South-West Committee, 1976.)

KNOTT, B and LAKE, P S — 'A Brief Survey of the macro-invertebrate fauna of Lake Edgar and its immediate environs'. *Tasmanian Naturalist*, no.36, 1974, pp.1–19.

LAKE, P S and NEWCOMBE, K J — 'Observations on the ecology of the crayfish P. tasmanicus (Decapoda: Parastacidae) from south western Tasmania'. *Australian Zoology*, v.18, 1975, pp.187–214.

LAKE, P S and TYLER, P A — Submission on conservation of Tasmanian aquatic ecosystems. Submission to the Committee of Enquiry into the National Estate, 1973.

LUCKMAN, J S and LUCKMAN, L E — 'Birds recorded in South-West Tasmania'. *Tasmanian Naturalist*, no.31, 1972, pp.3–5.

MACPHAIL, M K — The History of the Vegetation and Climate in Southern Tasmania since the late Pleistocene. Thesis (Ph.D.) University of Tasmania, 1976.

MACPHAIL, M and SHEPHERD, R R — 'Plant communities at Lake Edgar, South-West Tasmania'. *Tasmanian Naturalist*, no.34, Aug. 1973.

MILLEDGE, D — 'The Birds of Maatsuyker Island, Tasmania'. *Emu*, v.72, 1972, pp.167–170.

MILLEDGE, D — 'The Orange-bellied parrot in Tasmania'. *South Australian Ornithologist*, 26, 1972, p.56.

MILLEDGE, D — Some aspects of the natural history of Maatsuyker Island. Report to National Parks and Wildlife Service. Hobart, 1972.

RICHARDSON, A M M and COLEMAN, D J — 'Obstacles to faunal surveys and research in wilderness areas'. *Proceedings 47th ANZAAS conference*, Hobart, 1976.

RIDPATH, M G — 'The Birds of Tasmania's unique habitats'. *Wildlife Australia*, v.3, 1966, pp.125–128.

RODWAY, L — 'Botany of the Hartz and Adamson Ranges'. *Royal Society of Tasmania. Papers and Proceedings*, 1895, pp.64–67.

SHEPHERD, R R — 'Notes on a visit to the Denison River Huon Pine Reserve'. *Tasmanian Naturalist*, no.35, 1973.

SMITH, A J — A Review of literature and other information on Tasmanian wetlands. CSIRO Division of Land Use Research Tech. mem. 75/9, 1975.

SMITH, B J — 'A New species of snail from Lake Pedder, Tasmania, possibly belonging to the family Valvatidae'. *Malacological Society of Australia. Journal*, v.2, 1973, pp.429–434.

SUMNER, C E	The Taxonomy of the genus *Parastacoides* Clark. (Decapoda: Parastacoides). Thesis (B.Sc. Hons.) University of Tasmania, 1970.
SWAIN, R	'The Fauna of South-Western Tasmania'. *Tasmanian Year Book*, no.6, 1972, pp.54–64.
SWAIN, R *et al*	'*Allanaspides helonomus*. Gen. et. sp. nov. (Crustacea: Syncarida) from Tasmania'. *Queen Victoria Museum. Records*, no.35, 1970, pp.1–6 + 23 figs.
SWAIN, R, WILSON, I S and ONG, J E	'A New species of *Allanaspides* (Syncarida, Anaspididae) from South-Western Tasmania'. *Crustaceana*, 21, 1971, pp.196–202.
TASMANIAN UNIVERSITY BIOLOGICAL SOCIETY	'Port Davey report: some results of T.U.B.S. field trip to Port Davey, Bathurst Harbour and Melaleuca Inlet, 28 May — 4 June 1969'. Edited by B McIntosh. Hobart, The Society, 1969.
THOMAS, D G and WALL, L E	'Birds of Lake Pedder and the Sentinel Range, South West Tasmania'. *Tasmanian Naturalist*, no.29, no.30, 1972, pp.6–8, pp.7–8.
TYLER, W T	'Tasmania'. In Luther, H. *Project Aqua: a Source Book of Inland Waters Proposed for Conservation*. London, International Biological Programme; Oxford, Blackwell Scientific Publications, 1971, pp.218–219.
WALLIS, R L *et al*	'The prey of a native cat in South-West Tasmania'. *Tasmanian Naturalist*, no.48, 1977, pp.4–5.
WILLIAMS, W D (ed.)	*Biogeography and Ecology in Tasmania*. The Hague, W Junk, 1974.

For further information relevant to a study of the biological resources of the South-West, see references and material compiled by the South West Tasmania Resources Survey (5.5); notably, to date, the following reviews:

BOSWORTH, P, BROWN, M and WATERMAN, P	'A Review of the station of botanical information for South-West Tasmania'. Occasional Paper, no.5, South-West Tasmania Resources Survey, 1977.
KING, R	'A Review of limnological research in South-West Tasmania'. Occasional Paper, no.6, South-West Tasmania Resources Survey, 1977.
RICHARDSON, A M M	'A Review of terrestrial zoological information for South-West Tasmania'. Occasional Paper, no.4, South-West Tasmania Resources Survey, 1977.

CONSERVATION

ALLEN, R	'Pedder's last impediment'. *Ecologist*, v.3, Mar. 1973, p.83.
ANGUS, M	*The World of Olegas Truchanas*, edited by N Laird. Hobart, The Olegas Truchanas Publication Committee, 1975. (The 2nd edition was published in the same year in Hobart by O.B.M., and a 4th edition in 1978.)
	'Around the States: Lake Pedder threatened'. *Wildlife in Australia*, v.4, no.3, Sept. 1967, p.85.
AUSTRALIA. LAKE PEDDER COMMITTEE OF ENQUIRY	*Final Report, April 1974, the flooding of Lake Pedder: an analysis of the Lake Pedder controversy and its implications for the planning of major development projects and the management of natural resources in Australia*. Canberra, A.G.P.S. for the Dept. of the Environment and Conservation, 1974.
AUSTRALIA. LAKE PEDDER COMMITTEE OF ENQUIRY	The Future of Lake Pedder: interim report, June 1973. Canberra, A.G.P.S., 1973.
AUSTRALIA. LAKE PEDDER COMMITTEE OF ENQUIRY	*The future of Lake Pedder: Report of Lake Pedder Committee of Enquiry, June 1973*. Hobart, Lake Pedder Action Committee, 1973. Limited edition. (Includes proposals.)
AUSTRALIAN CONSERVATION FOUNDATION	*Pedder Papers: anatomy of a decision*. Parkville, Vic., The Foundation, 1972.
AUSTRALIAN CONSERVATION FOUNDATION	'Premier is urged to accept moratorium offer'. *Australian Conservation Foundation. Newsletter*, v.5, 1973, pp.5–6.
AUSTRALIAN CONSERVATION FOUNDATION	'The Wonderful South-West'. *Habitat Australia* v.3, no.2, 1975. This is a special issue devoted to South-West Tasmania.
AUSTRALIAN CONSERVATION FOUNDATION	'Wilderness, Will the Franklin Run Free?' *Habitat Australia* v.5, no.2, 1977.
B.G.T. ADVERTISING	'Creating the right image: the hydro campaign in Tasmania'. *Marketing and Media Weekly*, v.21, May 1971, pp.19, 61.
BANKS, C	'Lake Pedder'. *MLC News*, v.15, Aug. 1971, pp.14–15.
BAYLY, I A E	'The Destruction of Lake Pedder: getting to know the H.E.C.'.*Overland*, no.61, Winter 1975, pp.33–37.
BAYLY, I A E	'Pedder: Australia's lake beautiful'. *Operculum*, v.2, Mar./Apr. 1972, pp.44–47.
BEATTIE, J W	'Notes on the River Gordon and on the need for reservation of land along its banks'. *Royal Society of Tasmania. Papers and Proceedings*, 1908, pp.31–35.
BELSHAW, J P	'The Pilgrimage of the conservationists'. *Australian Financial Review*, 18 May 1971, pp.10–11.
BETHUNE, A	(Letter to the Editor). *Wildlife in Australia*, v.9, no.2, June 1972, p.54.
BURTON, J R and RICHARDS, B N	'Land use planning, resource management and the South-West' *Tasmanian Conservation Trust Circular*, no.90, June 1976, pp.13–19.
CATCHPOLE, M	'Wise to leave some stones unturned'. *The Mercury*, Hobart, 25 July 1974, p.12.
CHAMPION, B	'An Economic appraisal of limestone quarrying at Precipitous Bluff'. *Tasmanian Conservation Trust Circular*, no.68, June 1974, pp.5–7.
CRAWFORD, W	'Hydro sites limited in state'. *The Mercury*, Hobart, 23 Jan. 1974, p.5.
CRAWFORD, W	'State power surplus only fantasy'. *The Mercury*, Hobart, 24 Jan. 1974, p.5.
DAVIS, B W	'Preliminary report of the South-West Advisory Committee (an appraisal)'. *Tasmanian Conservation Trust Circular*, no.91, July 1976, pp.10–12; no.92, Aug. 1976 (maps).
DAVIS, B W	'Waterpower and wilderness: political and administrative aspects of the Lake Pedder controversy'. *Public Administration*, v.31, no.1, Mar. 1972, pp.21–42.
DAVIS, B W	'The Environment (Lake Pedder)' *Focus* (Sydney), v.6, Oct. 1973, pp.17–18.
ENVIRONMENTAL LAW REFORM GROUP	*The National Estate and the Public Interest : Precipitous Bluff. Environmental Rights and Mining*. Hobart, Environmental Law Reform Group, June 1973.
FRANCIS, L	'Hydro closes in on Lake Pedder'. *Sunday Review*, 16 May 1971, p.920.
GEE, H	*The Franklin, Tasmania's Last Wild River*. Hobart, Tasmanian Wilderness Society, 1978.
HARRIS, S and KIERNAN, K W	'Cave conservation and Tasmania'. *Southern Caver*, v.3, no.2, 1971, pp.13–25.
HEAN, B	'The Lake Pedder case from May, 1967'. *Origin*, v.5. Oct. 1971, pp.18–19.
HOLLIDAY, J	'Tasmania — Hydro gone mad'. *Sydney University Speleological Society Newsletter*, v.11, no.1, 1971, pp.10–11.
JOHNSON, D	'Lake Pedder: can it still be saved?'. *Wildlife in Australia*, v.9, no.4, Dec. 1972, pp.105–107.
JOHNSON, D (ed.)	*Lake Pedder: why a national park must be saved*. Camberwell, Vic., Lake Pedder Action Committees of Victoria and Tasmania and the Australian Union of Students, 1972. Published in association with The Colong Committee and the Save Our Bushlands Action Committee.
JONES, R (ed.)	*Damania. The H.E.C., the Environment and Government of Tasmania*. Hobart, Fullers, 1972. Proceedings of a symposium, Hobart, November, 1971.
JONES, R (ed.)	*The Vanishing Forests? Woodchip Production and Public Interest in Tasmania*. Hobart, Environmental Law Reform Group, 1975.
KIERNAN, K	'The Case for Precipitous Bluff'. *Southern Caver*, v.7, no.2, 1975, pp.2–29.
KIERNAN, K	'Conservation and the Gordon River'. *Australian Speleological Federation Newsletter*,no.64, 1974, pp.3–7.
KIERNAN, K	'Lake Pedder — it's not too late'. *Southern Caver*, v.3, no.1, 1971, p.31.
KIERNAN, K	'Lower Gordon River State Reserve'. *Tasmanian Conservation Trust Circular*, no.69, July 1974, pp.3–7.
KIERNAN, K	'No tragedy like too late'. *Southern Caver*, v.5, Oct. 1973, pp.19–21.
KIERNAN, K	'The Precipitous Bluff snowball'. *Southern Caver*, v.5, no.1, 1973, pp.6–8.
KIERNAN, K	'Precipitous Bluff, Tas.'. *Australian Speleological Federation Newsletter*, no.58, Dec. 1972, p.14.
KIERNAN, K	'South-West Tasmania: the significance of the Pedder campaign for the caves of the South-West'. *Australian Speleological Federation. Newsletter*, no.58, Dec. 1972, pp.3–4.

KIRKPATIRCK, J   'National Heritage in danger. The case of Precipitous Bluff'. *Tasmanian Conservation Trust Circular*, no.73. Nov. 1974, pp.3–4.

KNIGHT, *Sir* A   'Why Lake Pedder is being enlarged'. *The Mercury*, Hobart, 1 Apr. 1972, p.9.

KONIG, K   'Our vanishing wilderness'. *Australian Outdoors*, v.45, July 1971, pp.30–33,70.

LAKE, P S   'An Assessment of the voluntary movement in Tasmania 1967–1973'. (Paper presented to the National Conservation Study Conference, Canberra, 17 Nov. 1973). *Tasmanian Conservation Trust Circular*, no.63. Jan. 1974, pp.4–12.

LAKE, P S   'Geomorphology, flora and fauna of Lake Pedder could recover'. *Australian Conservation Foundation. Newsletter*, v.5, Feb. 1973, pp.3–6.

LAKE, P S   'Lake Pedder'. *Amicus*, v.11, Sept. 1972, pp.18–19.

LAKE, P S   'Lake Pedder'. *Wildlife in Australia*, v.8, Dec. 1971, pp.103–105.

LAKE, P S   'Lake Pedder: end in sight'. *Australian Flying*, v.10, Sept. 1972, pp.14–15.

LAKE PEDDER ACTION COMMITTEE   'Lake Pedder'. *Wildlife in Australia*, v.8, Dec. 1971, pp.103–105.

LAKE PEDDER ACTION COMMITTEE. Victorian Branch   *Newsletter*, no.1, Feb. 1972.

LAW COUNCIL OF AUSTRALIA   *The brief case: a souvenir of the Legal Convention in Tasmania*, edited by Mrs. R P Fagan. Hobart, Ronall Publications, 1963.

'Lobby recognised: green growth (Lake Pedder)'. *Nation Review*, 19–25 Oct. 1973, p.10.

'Long odds against Pedder'. *The Bulletin*, 21 July 1973, p.13.

LUCKMAN, J S   'The Club's role in Conservation'. *Tasmanian Tramp*, no.21, 1974, pp.4–10.

MOFFIT, I   'Canberra gets its feet wet at Pedder'. *The Australian*, 7 July, 1973, p.9.

MOFFIT, I   'Premier Reece gets Pedderized'. *The Australian*, 18 Oct. 1973, p.13.

MOSLEY, J G   Aspects of the Geography of Recreation in Tasmania. Thesis (Ph.D.) Australian National University, 1964.

MOSLEY, J G   'The Challenge of wilderness — south-west Tasmania'. *Architecture in Australia*, v.59, Aug. 1970, pp.566–578.

MOSLEY, J G   'Conserving the Southwest Tasmanian wilderness'. *Australian Natural History*, v.16, Mar. 1969, pp.145–150.

MOSLEY, J G   'The Future of nature conservation in Tasmania with particular reference to national parks'. *Tasmanian Conservation Trust Circular*, no.30, Feb. 1971, pp.11–22.

MOSLEY, J G   'Industrial man v. the wilderness: collision course in S.W. Tasmania'. *National Times*, 26 Nov. — 1 Dec. 1973, pp.40–41.

MOSLEY, J G   'Precipitous Bluff: no room for compromise'. *Habitat*, v.1, Sept. 1973, pp.4–7.

MOSLEY, J G   'Tasmania's National Parks — Policy and administrative problems'. In Cavenor, S & Whiteloch, D (eds.) *Practical Problems of National Parks; proceedings of a Seminar*. Armidale, University of New England, 1966.

'National Parks — fire and water'. *The Bulletin*, 22 July 1967, pp.22–23.

O'BRIEN, D (ed.)   'Too much power'. *The Bulletin*, 11 Mar. 1972, p.15.

OLDING, J   'A Case in point'. *Skyline*, no.13, 1963, pp.37–41.

PARR, G   'The Changing moods of Pedder'. *Australian Conservation Foundation. Newsletter*, v.5, Feb. 1973, pp.4–5.

PATTERSON, R J   'Lake Pedder' (Letter to the editor). *Institution of Engineers, Australia. Journal*, Jan/Feb. 1973, p.15.

PATTERSON, R J   'Pedder lives'. *Walkabout*, v.24, 1973, pp.36–37.

PETERSON, J A   'Rape of a wilderness lake'. *Geographical Magazine*, v.45, Feb. 1973, pp.371–376.

'Precipitous Bluff'. *Togatus*, v.44, 12 June 1973, pp.6–7.

'Proposed enlarged Southwest National Park'. *Tasmanian Conservation Trust Circular*, no.78, May 1975, p.4.

PROWSE, D   'Pedder: the price of power'. *Walkabout*, Dec. 1972, pp.32–35.

RANKIN, R   'South-west Tasmania, the last wilderness'. *Walkabout*, Aug. 1973, pp.48–54.

REECE, E E   'The river … symbol of Tasmanian progress'. *Industrial Review and Mining Year Book of Australia*, 1969, pp.264–265.

'Reece sinks to his Pedder guns'. *Nation Review*, 19–25 Jan. 1973, p.416.

RICHARDS, A M and OLLIER, C D   *Investigation and report of the ecological protection of Exit Cave near Ida Bay in Tasmania, for National Parks & Wildlife Service — Tasmania*. Sydney, University of N.S.W., 1976.

ROLLS, R, BROWN, R and THOMPSON, P   'Ride the Wild River'. *Habitat Australia* v.5, no. 2, 1977.

SAMUEL, P   'Call to drain Lake Pedder'. *The Bulletin*, 14 July 1973, pp.14–17.

SAMUEL, P   'Long odds against Pedder'. *The Bulletin*, 21 July 1973, p.13.

SANSOM, C   'The last word on Lake Pedder: it's a dreadful warning for all governments'. *National Times*, 5–10 Aug. 1974, p.47.

'Security of national parks at stake'. *The Mercury*, Hobart, 13 Aug. 1971, p.4.

SAUNDERS, R E   A critique of the Tasmanian Government's Draft Management Plan for the Southwest National Park. M.A. thesis, Monash University, 1975.

SMITH, P   'Electrical Energy, Wilderness and the Future'. *Habitat Australia* v.5, no. 2, 1977.

SOUTH WEST ADVISORY COMMITTEE, Hobart   *Report to the Minister for National Parks and Wildlife*, Hobart, August 1978. Presented by Sir George Barrington Cartland, Geoffrey James Foot and Albert George Ogilvie.

SOUTH-WEST COMMITTEE   Evidence submitted to the Select Committee of the Legislative Council. Hobart, June 1967.

SOUTH-WEST COMMITTEE   The Proposed enlarged Southwest National Park (A policy statement prepared by the South-West Committee). Hobart, June 1973.

SOUTH-WEST COMMITTEE   Submission covering conservation and development of South-West Tasmania. Hobart, 1966.

SOUTH-WEST COMMITTEE   Submission to the Minister for National Parks and Wildlife Service and the South West Advisory Committee on the Government's Draft Management Plan, 1975. Hobart, Jan. 1976.

STEPHENSON, R   'Mt Anne and the Port Davey track'. *Walkabout*, Dec. 1949, pp.29–34.

TASMANIA. INTERDEPARTMENTAL COMMITTEE   Report on the development of the South-West of Tasmania. Hobart, 1967.

TASMANIA. NATIONAL PARKS & WILDLIFE SERVICE   *Southwest National Park: draft management plan, 1975*. Hobart, 1975.

TASMANIA. NATIONAL PARKS & WILDLIFE SERVICE   Submission to Special Advisory Committee on South-West Tasmania, Hobart, 1976.

TASMANIAN CONSERVATION TRUST and AUSTRALIAN CONSERVATION FOUNDATION   South-West Management Plan (Transcript of special workshop held at the Tasmanian College of Advanced Education, Hobart, 4 Oct. 1975). Hobart, Australian Conservation Foundation, 1975.

Tasmanian Conservation Trust Circular, no.72, Oct. 1974. This edition is largely devoted to the South-West.

'Tears for drowned lake'. *The Bulletin*, Mar. 27, 1971, p.26.

'The Tasmanian Conservation Trust's Submission to the South West Advisory Committee. Summary of conclusions and recommendations', *Tasmanian Conservation Trust Circular*, no.86, Feb. 1976, pp.3–4.

TASMANIAN WILDERNESS SOCIETY   *Journal*, no's. 1–9, Hobart, The Society, 1976–8. (available from the Tasmanian Environment Centre Inc.)

TERANDO, A   'Precipitous Bluff must not be destroyed'. *Southern Caver*, v.4, no.4, 1973, pp.3–5.

TRUCHANAS, M   'A Case for wilderness'. *Tasmanian Conservation Trust Circular*, no.92; Aug. 1976, pp.6–9.

VAUGHAN, J   'Lake Pedder'. *Macquarie University Students Council. Arena*, v.6, Oct. 1973, p.8.

VINCENT, S   The Social Cost of Wilderness. Thesis, Department of Environmental Design, Tasmanian College of Advanced Education, 1974.

WALDUCK, T   'Way to better forests: management makes it possible'. *The Mercury*, Hobart, 29 Mar. 1974, p.4.

'What we have lost … an Australian tragedy'. (A tribute to Lake Pedder and Olegas Truchanas). *National Times*, supplement, 29 Mar. 1976.

WRIGHT, G   'High noon at Pedder'. *Sun*, Sydney, 9 Mar. 1972, pp.33–35.

FICTION

BUTLER, R — *The Men that God Forgot*. London, Hutchinson, 1975.
BUTLER, R — *South of Hell's Gates*. London, John Long, 1967.
CLARKE, M — *For the Term of his Natural Life*. London, Oxford University Press, 1952.
SHUTE, N — *The Rainbow and the Rose*. London, Heinemann, 1958.

CHILDREN'S FICTION

BRINSMEAD, H F — *Echo in the Wilderness*. London, Oxford University Press, 1972.
CHAUNCY, N — *Devil's Hill*. London, Oxford University Press, 1958.
CHAUNCY, N — *The Lighthouse Keeper's Son*. London, Oxford University Press, 1969.
CHAUNCY, N — *Mathinna's People*. London, Oxford University Press, 1967.
CHAUNCY, N — *The Roaring 40*. London, Oxford University Press, 1963.
CHAUNCY, N — *Tiger in the Bush*. London, Oxford University Press, 1957.
CHAUNCY, N — *World's End was Home*. London, Oxford University Press, 1952.

THE TASMANIAN TRAMP

The Tasmanian Tramp is the magazine of the Hobart Walking Club, a large and active bushwalking club founded in 1929.
The *Tramp*, printed by Richmond & Sons in Devonport, is published every 2 years, the 22nd issue appearing in 1976. *Tramp* includes articles, maps and photographs of interest to bushwalkers, as well as of historical and general interest and is a good source of information about the South-West.
The following is a selection of articles of particular interest.

ALLAN, P — 'King Williams to the Gordon Bend'. *Tramp*, no.19, 1970, pp.40–43.
ALLNUT, P — 'Notes on the walk to Frenchmans Cap'. *Tramp*, no.12, 1955, p.28.
ALLNUT, P — 'They carry the flag of adventure'. *Tramp*, no.21, 1974, pp.14–19.
ANDERSON, D — 'From Derwent to Huon'. *Tramp*, no.2, 1933, pp.33–37.
ANDERSON, D — 'Mt Picton and beyond'. *Tramp*, no.5, 1936, pp.12–16.
ANDERSON, D — 'The Lower Port Davey track'. *Tramp*, no.3, 1934, pp.15–17.
AVES, K — 'Cushions and creepers in National Park'. *Tramp*, no.6, 1945, pp.29–31.
BANKS, M R — 'From Eddystone to Davey'. *Tramp*, no.18, 1968, pp.69–76.
BANKS, M R — 'Port Davey, geological notes on the far South-West of Tasmania'. *Tramp*, no.15, 1961, pp.63–66.
BARRETT, B — 'Memory of Lake Pedder'. (a poem) *Tramp*, no.21, 1974, p.96.
BIRCH, J — 'Mt Bobs'. *Tramp*, no.22, 1976, pp.43–47.
BEWSHER, W — 'Lune to Maydena, 31 days'. *Tramp*, no.10, 1951, pp.31–36.
BROUGH, S — 'National Park and the Tarn Shelf'. *Tramp*, no.3, 1934, pp.43–46.
BROUGH, S — 'The Weld Country'. *Tramp*, no.5, 1936, pp.37–43.
BROWN, J — 'New road to the Hartz'. *Tramp*, no.14, 1959, p.18.
BROWN, J — 'Tenzing Norgay in Tasmania'. *Tramp*, no.16, 1963, pp.4–6.
BROWN, J and BROWN, U — 'Lake Pedder National Park'. *Tramp*, no.12, 1955, pp.11–14.
BROWN, R H and STEANE, D F — 'The Snowy Range'. *Tramp*, no.8, 1948, pp.7–12.
BUCKIE, J — 'Breathing space: memories of Frenchmans Cap'. *Tramp*, no.14, 1959, p.68.
BUCKIE, J — 'Sir John Franklin's overland journey, 1842'. *Tramp*, no.10, 1951, pp.3–6.
CANE, H — 'Judds Cavern'. *Tramp*, no.22, 1976, pp.40–43.
CHAPMAN, G T F — 'Looking back along the track'. *Tramp*, no.20, 1972, pp.92–96.
CHAPMAN, G T F — 'Mount Anne'. *Tramp*, no.2, 1933, pp.22–26.
CHRISTIE, T — 'The Federation Box'. *Tramp*, no.17, 1966, pp.15–23.
CHRISTIE, T — 'From the Crags of Andromeda to the Evening Star — A nomenclature of the Western Arthurs'. *Tramp*, no.18, 1968, pp.25–29.
CLOSS, L — 'Lake Pedder: masterpiece of time' (a poem). *Tramp*, no.20, 1972, p.15.
COLE, B — 'The Huon Track'. *Tramp*, no.18, 1968, pp.30–42.
COLE, B — 'Ski facilities at Mt Mawson'. *Tramp*, no.16, 1963, pp.27–33.
COX, J — 'To the Denison Range and Adamsfield'. *Tramp*, no.5, 1936, pp.31–36.
— 'Critchley Parker'. *Tramp*, no.6, 1945, p.5.
CROSS, A — 'Federation weekend'. *Tramp*, no.17, 1966, pp.64–66.
DAMGAARD, A — 'The South-West Committee'. *Tramp*, no.17, 1966, pp.50–52.
DAMGAARD, A — 'Moods of the South-West'. *Tramp*, no.20, 1972, pp.82–83.
DANIELS, W — 'Federation Peak in a day'. *Tramp*, no.21, 1974, pp.21–24.
DAVERN, A — 'The Discovery of "Davern's Cavern"; (from a letter to a friend, 1953)'. *Tramp*, no.12, 1955, pp.26–27.
DAVIES, K — 'Aboriginal names in the Port Davey area'. *Tramp*, no.20, 1972, p.84.
DAVIES, R — 'High Camp Memorial Hut'. *Tramp*, no.21, 1974, pp.68–70.
DAVIS, B W — 'Lake Pedder' (a poem). *Tramp*, no.12, 1955, p.15.
DAVIS, B W — 'The Dial search'. *Tramp*, no.13, 1957, pp.33–36.
DAVIS, B W — 'Federation Peak'. *Tramp*, no.14, 1959, pp.23–38.
DAVIS, B W — 'P.B.'. *Tramp*, no.15, 1961, pp.17–25.
DAVIS, B W — 'The Western Arthurs traverse'. *Tramp*, no.16, 1963, pp.15–23.
DAVIS, B W — 'The Franklands traverse'. *Tramp*, no.20, 1972, pp.73–81.
DAVIS, B W and DAVIS, R J — 'For those going South-West'. *Tramp*, no.13, 1957, pp.17–22.
DAVIS, R J — 'The Spires'. *Tramp*, no.16, 1963, pp.68–71.
— 'Deadman's Bay'. *Tramp*, no.15, 1961, p.26.
— 'Denison River Huon Pine Reserve'. *Tramp*, no.20, 1972, pp.53–55.
DREAPER, R — 'The Anne Circuit'. *Tramp*, no.15, 1961, pp.49–54,
EMMETT, E T — 'Longfellow at National Park'. *Tramp*, no.2, 1933, pp.20–22.
ENGLAND, J — 'Supply dropping'. *Tramp*, no.21, 1974, pp.86–89.
— 'Ernie Bond of Gordonvale'. *Tramp*, no.16, 1963, pp.24–26.
GIBSON, M G — 'Ray Livingston'. *Tramp*, no.6, 1945, pp.42–43.
GILBERT, J M — 'Mt Gell and Upper Franklin Valley'. *Tramp*, no.8, 1948, pp.45–49.
— 'Gordonvale'. *Tramp*, no.11, 1953, p.3.
GULLINE, H — 'The vegetation of the Port Davey area'. *Tramp*, no.15, 1961, pp.67–72.
GULLINE, H and WILSON, D — 'Wylds Craig'. *Tramp*, no.9, 1949, pp.34–39.
HAWES, C — 'Sufferation weekend'. *Tramp*, no.21, 1974, pp.66–67.
HEAN, B — 'The tragedy of Lake Pedder'. *Tramp*, no.20, 1972, pp.10–14.
HEWITT, M — 'Rain on Wylds Craig'. *Tramp*, no.19, 1970, pp.88–89.
HODGSON, W — 'Sir Edmund Hillary's camp, 1960'. *Tramp*, no.15, 1961, pp.44–45.

HOLLOWAY, G — 'A wet trip'. *Tramp*, no.20, 1972, pp.42–44.
HUDSPETH, K — 'Precipitous Bluff'. *Tramp*, no.7, 1946, pp.15–17.
JOHNSON, K — 'Report from an American sojourner'. *Tramp*, no.21, 1974, pp.38–41.
KING, D — 'The Weld River caves'. *Tramp*, no.17, 1966, pp.13–14.
KNIGHT, A C E and DREAPER, R — 'Lune to Dover — the hard way'. *Tramp*, no.13, 1957, pp.23–30.
KOOLHOF, F — 'Rafting down the Franklin'. *Tramp*, no.21, 1974, pp.97–107.
LEES, D — 'The Count of Adamsfield'. *Tramp*, no.16, 1963, p.66.
'The Legend of Solitary'. *Tramp*, no.15, 1961, pp.34–36.
LIVINGSTON, L — 'The South-West Expeditionary Club'. *Tramp*, no.11, 1953, pp.20–22.
LOVE, A R — 'The Denison Lakes'. *Tramp*, no.8, 1948, pp.38–41.
LUCKMAN, J S — 'The Club's role in conservation'. *Tramp*, no.21, 1974, pp.4–10.
LUCKMAN, J S — 'Early history of Mount Anne'. *Tramp*, no.12, 1955, pp.54–55.
LUCKMAN, J S. — 'Federation Peak'. *Tramp*, no.8, 1948, pp.16–23.
LUCKMAN, J S — 'Ladies first'. *Tramp*, no.10, 1951, pp.27–29.
LUCKMAN, J S — 'Skiing and winter sports notes'. *Tramp*, no.11, 1953, pp.40–42.
LUCKMAN, J S — 'We, the lucky ones'. *Tramp*, no.18, 1968, pp.77–79.
LUCKMAN, L — 'South West Cape'. *Tramp*, no.11, 1953, 14–17.
MARTIN, D — 'The Snowy Mountains'. *Tramp*, no.6, 1945, pp.18–21.
MOSCAL, A — 'Reflections on the Crossing River'. *Tramp*, no.21, 1974, pp.44–48.
MOSLEY, J G — 'The Tasmanian National Parks system'. *Tramp*, no.17, 1966, pp.37–49.
NEWHAM, D — 'Charles King Memorial Hut'. *Tramp*, no.15, 1961, pp.60–61.
PEATE, J — 'A new approach to Federation Peak'. *Tramp*, no.19, 1970, pp.79–81.
PETERSON, F — 'Adamsfield, then and now'. *Tramp*, no.12, 1955, pp.4–10.
RATHBONE, C — 'Diamond Peak from the Jane River track'. *Tramp*, no.21, 1974, pp.33–37.
ROLLS, E. — 'Sou'west by sou'west'. *Tramp*, no.21, 1974, pp.77–81.
SHARP, L M — 'Storm on Mt Field West'. *Tramp*, no.13, 1957, pp.4–8.
SHAW, N E — 'Towards the Arthurs'. *Tramp*, no.7, 1946, pp.43–45.
SHAW, N E — 'Highlights and shadows'. *Tramp*, no.8, 1948, pp.13–14.
SHAW, N E and LUCKMAN, J S — 'La Perouse — Pindars peak'. *Tramp*, no.7, 1946, pp.12–14.
SKLENICA, A — 'Pedder to the Gordon'. *Tramp*, no.16, 1963, pp.40–56.
SMITH, R — 'Finding the northern gateway to the south-west'. *Tramp*, no.7, 1946, pp.41–42.
SPARGO, D — 'The Mountain shrimp, (*Anaspides tasmanae*)'. *Tramp*, no.3, 1934, pp.39–42.
STEPHENSON, R — 'The New River country, S.W. Tasmania'. *Tramp*, no.6, 1945, pp.7–11.
'Tasmanian nomenclature'. *Tramp*, no.11, 1953, p.43.
THWAITES, J B — 'Overland from Port Davey'. *Tramp*, no.2, 1933, pp.26–32.
THWAITES, J B — 'Federation Peak'. *Tramp*, no.9, 1950, pp.16–20.
THWAITES, J B — 'Philp's track to Frenchmans Cap'. *Tramp*, no.12, 1955, pp.18–22.
THWAITES, J B — 'Port Davey'. *Tramp*, no.14, 1959, pp.39–55.
THWAITES, J B — 'Sir Edmund Hillary in the South-West'. *Tramp*, no.15, 1961, pp.37–43.
THWAITES, J B — 'King of the South-West'. *Tramp*, no.19, 1970, pp.72–78.
TRUCHANAS, O — 'The Gordon Splits'. *Tramp*, no.20, 1972, pp.67–71.
WALKDON-BROWN, T — 'Where angels fear to tread'. *Tramp*, no.18, 1968, pp.5–7.
WARREN, R — 'Diary of two wretched females on a trip to Frenchmans Cap'. *Tramp*, no.5, 1936, pp.44–48.
WAYATT, G — 'Li-lo on the Gordon'. *Tramp*, no.17, 1965, pp.34–35.
WHITHAM, L — 'Hartz to Adamsons'. *Tramp*, no.6, 1945, pp.13–17.
WILKINS, B — 'Are you going to Frenchmans?'. *Tramp*, no.14, 1959, pp.64–67.
WILLIAMS, R — 'The Prince of Wales Range'. *Tramp*, no.18, 1968, pp.9–16.
WILLIAMS, R — 'Federation — a review'. *Tramp*, no.21, 1974, pp.11–13.
WILLIAMS, U — 'W S Sharland's expedition westwards'. *Tramp*, no.11, 1953, pp.4–11.
WILSON, D W — 'An early air-drop'. *Tramp*, no.15, 1961, pp.32–33.
WOODWARD, T — 'Overland from Macquarie Harbour to Port Davey, 1952–1953'. *Tramp*, no.11, 1953, pp.48–56.

MAPS

HISTORICAL MAPS — Much of historical interest is contained in early maps of Van Diemen's Land and Tasmania. These are described in R V Tooley's bibliography:- *Printed Maps of Tasmania 1642–1900*. London, F Edwards, 1975.

Western Tasmania: (maps: Northern and Southern Sections). Compiled from official surveys and from explorations and sketch surveys by H Hellyer, C Gould, J R Scott, C P Sprent; drawn by W C Piguenit. Hobart, 1876. Held in the Archives Office of Tasmania.

NAUTICAL MAPS — Bathurst Channel (map). Admiralty Sheet 1, BA 3410, London, 1931. Scale: 1:12,500.

Bathurst Channel (map). Admiralty Sheet 2, BA 3411, London, 1928. Scale: 1:12,500. 1:7,500 (The Narrows), 1:25,000 (Barhurst Harbour).

Low Rocky Point to Hobart (map). R.A.N. Hydrographic Service, AUS 354, Sydney, 1969. Scale 1:300,000.

Macquarie Harbour (Pilot Bay to Strahan) (map). Admiralty, London, 1933. Scale: 1:79,500.

HOBART WALKING CLUB SKETCH MAPS — Cox Bight — Ironbound (map). R N Smith, Hobart Walking Club, 1956. Scale: 1:126,720.

Federation Peak Area (map). J E Young, M.U.M.C., for Hobart Walking Club, 1958. Scale: 1:253,440.

Field West — Cox Bight (map). R N Smith, Hobart Walking Club, 1956. Scale: 1:126,720.

Huon Track (map). R N Smith, Hobart Walking Club, 1948. Scale: 1:253,440.

Lake Pedder National Park (map). Hobart Walking Club, 1956. Scale: 1:63,360.

Picton — La Perouse Sketch Map. R N Smith, Hobart Walking Club, 1957. Scale: 1:126,720.

Rasselas Valley (map). A C E Knight, Hobart Walking Club, 1953. Scale: 1:63,360.

Spring River (map). R N Smith, Hobart Walking Club, 1956. Scale: 1:126,720.

HYDRO-ELECTRIC POWER DEVELOPMENT — Gordon River Power Development Stage 1 (map). The Hydro-Electric Commission and Lands and Surveys Dept., Hobart, 1967. Scale: 1:126,720.

Power Developments (map). The Hydro-Electric Commission, Hobart, 1960. 1961. Scale: 1:126,720.

South West Tasmania; feature map showing hydro-electric power development and Gordon River road. Hobart, Mercury Press, 1967. Scale: 1:200,000.

South West Tasmania. 3rd. edn. Hobart, P Broughton, 1970. Scale: 1:200,000.

FORESTRY COMMISSION — Adamson (map). Forestry Commission no. 93/3–16, Hobart, 1949. Scale: 20 chains: 1 inch.

Adamson (map). Forestry Commission 93 B, D, Hobart, 1949–50. Scale: 40 chains: 1 inch.

King William (maps). Forestry Commission no. 7, 8, 11, 12, 15, 16 (1963); 66–3, 4 (1968). Scale: 20 chains: 1 inch.

Ouse (map). Forestry Commission no. 67–1, 5 (1965), 13 (1963). Scale: 20 chains: 1 inch.

Picton (map). Forestry Commission no. 87/1–16, Hobart, 1947–49. Scale: 20 chains: 1 inch.

Picton (maps). Forestry Commission no. 87 A—D, Hobart, 1948–50. Scale: 40 chains: 1 inch.

Styx (map). Forestry Commission, no. 81/1–16, Hobart, 1952–1960. Scale: 20 chains: 1 inch.

South Cape (map). Forestry Commission no. 97B, Hobart, 1961. Scale: 40 chains: 1 inch.

Styx (map). Forestry Commission no. 81–A, D (1961), B (1963), C (19   ). Scale: 40 chains: 1 inch.

South Cape (maps). Forestry Commission no. 97/3, 4, 7, 8, Hobart, 1954. Scale: 20 chains: 1 inch.

Tasmanian Forest Classification (map). Forestry Commission Sheets 2–8, Hobart, 1973. Scale: 1:250,000. Produced for Forwood Conference.

Tasmanian Forest Concessions and Reserves (map). Forestry Commission, Hobart, 1976. Scale: 1:500,000.

LANDS DEPARTMENT (Lands and Surveys Department prior to 1970)

Franklin (map). Lands and Surveys Dept., Sheet 8013, Hobart, 1953. Scale: 1:63,360.

Franklin (map). Lands Dept., Sheet 8013, Hobart, 1971. Scale: 1:100,000.

Frenchmans Cap National Park (map). Lands and Surveys Dept., Hobart, 1961. Scale: 1:63,360.

Geeveston Topographical (map). Lands and Surveys Dept., Sheet 8211–1–S, Hobart, 1966. Scale: 1:31,680.

Glen Huon Topographical (map). Lands and Surveys Dept., Sheet 8211–1–N, Hobart, 1966. Scale: 1:31,680.

Huon (map). Lands Dept., Sheet 8211, Hobart, 1971. Scale: 1:100,000.

Lyell C Topographical (map). Lands and Surveys Dept., Sheet 58C, Hobart, 1958. Scale: 1:31,680.

Lyell D Topographical (map). Lands and Surveys Dept., Sheet 58D, Hobart, 1958. Scale: 1:31,680.

Mt Field National Park (map). Lands and Surveys Dept., Hobart, 1967. Scale: 1:63,360.

Nive (map). Lands Dept., Sheet 8113, Hobart, 1972. Scale: 1:100,000.

Old River (map). Lands Dept., Sheet 8111, Hobart, 1971. Scale: 1:100,000.

Olga (map). Lands and Surveys Dept., Sheet 8012, Hobart, 1958. Scale: 1:63,360.

Olga (map). Lands Dept., Sheet 8012, Hobart, 1972. Scale: 1:100,000.

Pillinger A Topographical (map). Lands and Surveys Dept., Sheet 65A, Hobart, 1959. Scale: 1:31,680.

Port Davey. Lands and Surveys Dept., State Map, Sheet 7, SK/55–7, Hobart, 1961. Scale: 1:250,000.

Port Davey (map). Lands Dept., Sheet 8011, Hobart 1971. Scale: 1:100,000.

Queenstown. Lands and Surveys Dept., State Map, Sheet 5, SK/55–5, Hobart, 1961. Scale: 1:250,000.

South East Cape (map). Lands Dept., Sheet 8210, Hobart, 1971. Scale: 1:100,000.

South West Cape (map). Lands Dept., Sheet 8110, Hobart, 1972. Scale: 1:100,000.

Southport Topographical (map). Lands and Surveys Dept., Sheet 8211–11–S, Hobart, 1966. Scale: 1:31,680.

Wedge (map). Lands and Surveys Dept., Sheet 8112, Hobart, 1956. Scale: 1:63,360.

Wedge (map). Lands Dept., Sheet 8112, Hobart, 1970. Scale: 1:100,000.

MINES DEPARTMENT

Hobart (map). (Geological Survey of Tasmania). Dept. of Mines, Sheet SK55/8, Hobart, 1975. Scale: 1:250,000.

Oatlands (map). (Geological Survey of Tasmania). Dept., of Mines, Sheet SK55/6, Hobart, 1975. Scale: 1:250,000.

Port Davey (map). (Geological Survey of Tasmania). Dept. of Mines, Sheet SK55/7, Hobart, 1977. Scale: 1:250,000.

Queenstown (map). (Geological Survey of Tasmania). Dept. of Mines, Sheet SK55–5, Hobart, 1974, 1975. Scale: 1:250,000.

South West Sketch Map. Dept. of Mines, Hobart, 1938. Scale: 1:158,400.

West Coast of Tasmania Sketch Map. Dept. of Mines, Hobart, 1938. Scale: 1:158,400.

FILMS—16 mm

Adventure Camp. Tasmanian State Film Unit, 1967, colour, 11 minutes.

Climbing Frenchman's Cap. Tasmanian State Film Unit, 1969, colour, 6 minutes.

Five, South West. Island Films (Tasmania), 1960, colour, 18 minutes.

Flowing Through Tasmania. Tasmanian State Film Unit, in association with Leo Burnett for Hydro-Electric Commission, 1972, colour, 13 minutes.

For the Term of His Natural Life. Australasian Films Ltd., 1927, B & W, 66 minutes, (24 fps) 99 minutes (16 fps).

Forest Regrowth. Tasmanian State Film Unit, 1968, colour, 9 minutes.

Foresters Island. Tasmanian State Film Unit for the Directorate of Industrial Development and Trade, 1973, colour, 18 minutes.

Fortune in the Forest. Tasmanian State Film Unit for Tasmanian Forestry Commission, 1964, colour, 9 minutes.

Hillary Ventures South. Island Films (Tasmania), 1961, colour, 13 minutes.

Industrial Journey. Tasmanian State Film Unit, 1963, colour, 10 minutes.

Keepers of the Light. A.B.C. 'A Big Country', 1975, colour, 32 minutes.

Kings of Melaleuca. A.B.C. 'A Big Country', 1971, B & W, 29 minutes.

Lake Pedder, Tasmania, February 1971. Tasmanian State Film Unit, 1971, colour, 21 minutes.

The Last Wild River. Paul Smith, 1978, colour, 28 minutes.

Look to the Wild Side. Tasmanian State Film Unit, 1968, colour, 22 minutes.

A Matter of Survival. Tasmanian State Film Unit, 1971, colour, 11 minutes.

Mountain Sanctuary. Tasmanian State Film Unit, 1962, colour, 18 minutes.

Mountain Valley. Tasmanian State Film Unit, 1964, colour, 9½ minutes.

One hundred years or more (The Huon pine industry in Tasmania). A.B.C. 'A Big Country', 1976, colour, 29½ minutes.

Safety in the Bush. Tasmanian State Film Unit, 1968, colour, 10 minutes.

The Splendour of the Peaks. Film Australia, 1963, colour, 10 minutes.

Strathgordon: Birth of a Township. Banks Advertising (Tasmania) for C.H.I., 1970, colour, 21 minutes.

The Struggle for Pedder. Peter Dodds and Ross Matthews (Australia), 1974, colour, 31 minutes.

Summertime. Tasmanian State Film Unit, 1971, colour, 10 minutes.

Tasmanian Tiger. Tasmanian State Film Unit, 1963, colour, 18 minutes.

Tasmanian Wilderness. Peter C. Sims (Tasmania), 1973, colour, 102 minutes (Parts 1 and 2).

Tasmanian Wildlife. Tasmanian State Film Unit, 1974, colour, 26 minutes.

Walk into Wilderness. Impala Films (Tasmania), 1973, colour, 24 minutes.

Water is the Key. Tasmanian State Film Unit for Directorate of Industrial Development and Trade, 1974, colour, 14 minutes.

All the above films are available from the State Library of Tasmania.

Additional Bibliography
(Third Impression)

A great number of papers and reports as well as several books have been published since 1978, reflecting the increasing scientific and political interest in the South-West. A bibliography covering these would be extensive indeed.

Some of the most important publications dealing with the South-West which have been published over the past five years are:

BROWN, R and DOMBROVSKIS, P.   **Wild Rivers.** Hobart, Peter Dombrovskis, 1983.

HARWOOD, C. and HARTLEY, M.   **An Energy Efficient Future for Tasmania.** Hobart, Tasmanian Conservation Trust, 1980.

KIERNAN, K, JONES, R and RANSON, D   'New evidence from Fraser Cave for glacial age man in south-west Tasmania'. **Nature** v. 301, no. 5895, 1983.

KIRKPATRICK, J B (ed.)   **Fire and Forest Management in Tasmania.** Hobart, Tasmanian Conservation Trust, 1981.

KIRKPATRICK, J B   **Hydro-electric development and wilderness in Tasmania.** Hobart, Dept of Environment, 1979.

McQUEEN, J   **Not Just a River.** Melbourne, Penguin, 1983.

SHARP-PAUL, A (ed.)   **Lower Gordon River Scientific Survey.** 24 vols., Hobart, Hydro-Electric Commission, Tasmania, 1978-9.

TASMANIA. HYDRO-ELECTRIC COMMISSION.   **Report on the Gordon River Power Development Stage 2.** Hobart, Govt Printer, 1979.

TASMANIA. LEGISLATIVE COUNCIL SELECT COMMITTEE   **Report of the Co-ordination Committee on Future Power Development.** (The Evers Committee). Hobart, Govt Printer, 1980.

TASMANIA. LEGISLATIVE COUNCIL SELECT COMMITTEE   **Future Power Development, Final Report.** Hobart, Govt Printer, 1981.

TASMANIA. NATIONAL PARKS AND WILDLIFE SERVICE   **Proposal for a Wild Rivers National Park.** Hobart, 1979.

THOMPSON, P   **Power in Tasmania.** Melbourne. Australian Conservation Foundation, 1981.

WATERMAN, P (ed.)   **South West Project Report. South West Tasmania Resources Survey.** Hobart, National Parks and Wildlife Service, 1981.

Index

Page numbers in *italics* refer to pictures.

Page numbers in *italics* refer to pictures.